STAGES OF CONFLICT

STAGES OF CONFLICT

A Critical Anthology of Latin American Theater and Performance

Edited by Diana Taylor and Sarah J. Townsend

Translation coordinator, Margaret Carson

THE UNIVERSITY OF MICHIGAN PRESS   Ann Arbor

2011   2010   2009   2008   4   3   2   1

A CIP catalog record for this book is available from the
British Library.

Library of Congress Cataloging-in-Publication Data

Stages of conflict : a critical anthology of Latin American
        theater and performance / edited by Diana Taylor
        and Sarah J. Townsend ; translation coordinator,
        Margaret Carson.
            p.   cm.
        Includes bibliographical references (p. [238]–253).
        ISBN-13: 978-0-472-07027-5 (cloth : alk. paper)
        ISBN-10: 0-472-07027-4 (cloth : alk. paper)
        ISBN-13: 978-0-472-05027-7 (pbk. : alk. paper)
        ISBN-10: 0-472-05027-3 (pbk. : alk. paper)
        1. Latin American drama—20th century—Translations
into English.   I. Carson, Margaret.   II. Taylor, Diana,
1950–   III. Townsend, Sarah J.
    PQ7087.E5S77 2008
    862'.608—dc22   2008011484

To Latin American theater artists,
who have long shown us how to
live and work in troubled times.

Acknowledgments

First and foremost, we would like to thank the writers and theater artists whose works are included or discussed in this collection. Our work depends on their work, and we recognize that for many of them, that work has entailed great costs.

As always, we would like to express our gratitude to the wonderful scholars and students who have helped to build this field. It is a measure of their success that they are too many to list. That said, particular appreciation is due to the many scholars and colleagues who have contributed time, suggestions, materials, and ideas to this book: Diego Benegas, Alissa Cardone, Michael C. Cohen, Kahlil Chaar, Marie Rutkoski, Enrique del Risco, Santiago Deymonnaz, Ana Puga, Doris Difarnecio, Vivian Martínez Tabares, Miguel Gandert, Julio Ortega, and Carolyn Dean. For their generous advice and support, Margaret Carson gives many thanks to Marcela Fuentes, Lisa Jarnot, Isaías Lerner, Luis Millones, Mercedes Roffé, Ekaterina Sukhanova, and Mark Weiss.

The editors, Diana Taylor and Sarah J. Townsend, would in turn like to extend a special recognition to Margaret Carson, who has gone above and beyond the call of duty in her role as translation coordinator. Not only is Margaret a gifted translator, she has also been remarkably level-headed and patient during the many years that it took us to complete this project.

Finally, we would all like to thank the many editorial assistants at the University of Michigan Press who have worked on this project, including Rebecca Mostov, Anna Szymanski, and Catherine Cassel. Marcia La Brenz was particularly instrumental in the final stages of the project. Most especially, we owe thanks to our editor, LeAnn Fields. LeAnn has believed in this project from the beginning, and it is quite possible that without her it would not have come to fruition.

Contents

Preface

Stages of Conflict is the first English-language collection to provide an overview of both theater and performance practices in Latin America dating back to the Conquest. This project and its accompanying Web site (available through www.hemisphericinstitute.org) introduces readers to a variety of theatrical pieces from a very expansive and rich archive of performance practices generated in Latin America. It also poses several questions that we address throughout the essays and introductory notes to each play. First, what is the difference between *theater* and *performance?* In general we might say that theater—a representational art form whose genealogy is usually traced back to ancient Greece—is but one form of performance, a much broader set of practices that encompasses dance, music, ritual, and formalized behaviors and conventions. But why is the distinction useful or necessary? What does the concept of performance allow us to include that a focus on theater alone might leave out? Second, if *performance* is taken to include conventional (though often nonscripted) forms of social behavior and cultural practices, how can we incorporate them in a book made up of texts? How can we know about past performances, enacted and transmitted by living bodies, if those bodies are now gone? What counts as evidence? Can we glean information about live practices from textual and visual sources and communicate it through the same venues?

Other problems are of a more practical nature, yet they, too, have ethical and aesthetic implications. How do we go about selecting fewer than twenty plays that span five centuries and supposedly represent twenty-six countries? From the outset, it is important to acknowledge that no volume, or even dozens of volumes, could do justice to the richness and diversity of theater and performance in the many nations, not to mention the many regional, ethnic, and linguistic communities, that make up Latin America.[1] Yet, even as we admit the impossibility of ever producing an all-inclusive and representative volume, it is nonetheless surprising to realize that no single panoramic compilation of Latin American plays exists in English.[2] Although one could argue that it is equally impossible to offer a volume that does justice to "American drama," numerous volumes have in fact been published, and some of them are very successful in offering a coherent (if always partial) overview. This volume offers readers a substantive collection of plays that have participated in shaping and contesting collective identities in Latin America. In doing so, it attempts to demonstrate that Latin America, like theater and performance, is not a static category but one whose contours are continually shifting. Two of the plays in this anthology were written within what are now the geographical boundaries of the United States, while many of the performance practices we discuss are making themselves felt in the United States and are becoming part of debates about national and binational identity through the activities of

Latin American immigrants as well as Chicano/Chicana and Latino/Latina playwrights.[3] In addition to expanding the range of what English-language readers and theater practitioners know about Latin American theater and performance, we also hope that this book will prompt people to take a new look at "American drama" and think about where its own limits lie.

Stages of Conflict brings together different traditions—indigenous theater, plays that are more influenced by European styles, popular performances—to suggest some of the ways in which these practices take part in struggles involving wide disparities in power. Our selection of materials reflects one way of mapping an enormous body of work. There are other ways of approaching the corpus, and hopefully other collections will be forthcoming. While we have made some attempt at representation—to include different kinds of plays from diverse parts of Latin America—our focus is not on tracing the development of every "national" tradition; indeed, at various moments we look at the ways in which national canons can create their own sets of exclusions and hierarchies.[4] Our aim has been to bring together works that reflect multiple kinds of performance practices, different ideas about the social function that theater and performance should play, and multiple ways in which performances have in fact functioned within their sociopolitical contexts.

Because Latin American theater and performance is understudied, we want to encourage scholars and students from other fields to use the materials in this volume. The introduction provides a general overview of Latin American theater from the sixteenth century through the present, indicating the ways in which the performance texts included in this anthology figure in relation to the broader picture while also highlighting connections among individual plays and larger trends. Because it was impossible to include all of the genres, countries, regions, communities, and playwrights that merit attention, we also make reference to other resources and plays that would be useful supplements to the texts in this book. Additional translations, as well as sources such as films and Web sites, are indicated in notes. Each of the plays is accompanied by an introductory essay and selected bibliography, which help to contextualize the work and point the way toward more in-depth study. Whenever possible, we have provided references to sources in English, though in many cases the most pertinent critical sources are only available in Spanish and Portuguese. All translations of quoted material, unless otherwise indicated, are our own. Because *Stages of Conflict* is envisioned not as a comprehensive collection but as one that facilitates further research and debate, we have created a special *Stages of Conflict* Web "cuaderno" that will be periodically updated with materials such as additional plays, videos, bibliographies, interviews, and articles. This *Stages of Conflict* Web page can be accessed from the Hemispheric Institute of Performance and Politics Web site: www.hemisphericinstitute.org.

A NOTE ON TRANSLATION

This volume includes plays that were originally written or performed in Spanish, Portuguese, Quiché, Nahuatl, and Quechua. Many of the translations were newly commissioned for this reader and appear for the first time in English. Others had been previously translated and are reprinted here with new introductory essays. Some plays were translated primarily to be read, while others were translated with more of an eye toward performance. The various texts reflect these different origins, translators, and methods of translation.

NOTES

1. *Latin America* is a nineteenth-century term that usually refers to the twenty-six countries that make up Mexico, the Caribbean, and Central and South America in which Spanish and Portuguese are the main colonial languages. Other European languages (Dutch, English, and French) are also spoken in some of these countries, as are numerous native languages. This collection includes only plays written in areas colonized by the Spanish and Portuguese.

2. There is no general reader of Latin American theater and performance available in English. There are several short collections of Latin American plays in translation, but these usually limit themselves to four or five plays. In the 1960s and 1970s several such collections appeared; William Oliver, ed., *Voices of Change in the Spanish American Theater* (Austin: University of Texas Press, 1971) and George Woodyard, ed., *The Modern Stage in Latin America: 6 Plays* (New York: Dutton, 1971) are the best known. There is a small collection of one-acts, including Francesca Colecchia and Julio Matas, eds., *Selected Latin American One-Act Plays* (Pittsburgh: University of Pittsburgh Press, 1973). Several plays by novelists are featured in Sebastian Doggart and Octavio Paz, eds., *Latin American Plays: New Drama from Argentina, Cuba, Mexico, and Peru* (London: Nick Hern, 1996). Recently, Diana Taylor and Roselyn Costantino edited *Holy Terrors: Latin American Women Perform* (Durham: Duke University Press, 2004). How-

ever, there is no work that brings together a broad range of materials or that traces the ways in which performances negotiate ethnic, linguistic, and political tensions over time.

3. Because of the necessarily limited scope of this book, we have not included work by contemporary U.S.-based Latino artists. There are, however, several readers already available, including Caridad Svich and Maria Teresa Marrero, eds., *Out of the Fringe: Contemporary Latina/Latino Theatre and Performance* (New York: Theatre Communications Group, 2000); and Alberto Sandoval-Sánchez and Nancy Saporta Sternbach, eds., *Puro teatro: A Latina Anthology* (Tucson: University of Arizona Press, 2000).

4. For a country-by-country look at Latin American theater, see Eladio Cortés and Mirta Barrea-Marlys, eds., *The Encyclopedia of Latin American Theater* (Westport, Conn.: Greenwood, 2003); for theater written prior to the 1960s, see William Knapp Jones, *Behind Spanish American Footlights* (Austin: University of Texas Press, 1966). Several overview essays and extensive bibliographies are available in the three-volume *Cambridge History of Latin American Literature,* edited by Roberto González Echevarría and Enrique Pupo-Walker (Cambridge: Cambridge University Press, 1996). For biographies and bibliographies of individual playwrights, see Adam Versényi, *Latin American Dramatists* (Detroit: Thomson Gale, 2005). For essays on Latin American and Latino performance artists, see Coco Fusco, ed., *Corpus Delecti: Performance Art of the Americas* (London: Routledge, 2000).

Introduction

Diana Taylor and Sarah J. Townsend

Stages of Conflict. Like countless other titles of books dealing with theater or performance, this one revolves around a play on words. Stage: "the platform on which actors perform in a theater"; "a particular phase, period, position, etc. in a process or series"; "the scene of any action." This multifaceted definition, which links a particular artistic practice to a notion of temporal change *and* a sense of place, captures many of the complexities that shape this critical anthology. Rather than taking *Latin American theater and performance* as a self-evident category, we approach it as a historical, cultural, and political problem. This involves addressing several questions at the outset: What is the purpose of bringing such a broad spectrum of cultural practices together, if not only the practices themselves but also the experiential frameworks through which they are understood vary so widely across time and space? If our intention is to gain insight into the way in which embodied cultural practices participate in past and present conflicts, how do we deal with the fact that the "body of evidence" available to us has itself been shaped by unequal relations of power? How can we use terms like *Latin America, theater,* and *performance* productively while recognizing that they, too, have a history?

Take *Latin America,* for instance. Today, the term is widely used to refer to the regions of the Americas where Spanish and Portuguese (sometimes French is included) are the dominant languages. Yet it is a relatively recent invention, and its origin is hardly innocent: some trace it back to Napoleon III, who installed his nephew Maximilian as emperor of Mexico in 1863. In one sense, then, it is anachronistic to apply the term to the cultural practices of the colonial period and potentially misleading to use it in reference to indigenous practices. At the same time, "Latin America" does correspond to certain geopolitical realities in our own era, and it allows us to trace commonalities and historical connections across a broad geographical area and over a long period of time. When treated as a historically constructed category, it can also be used to call comfortable definitions and borders into question. For instance, should we consider the cultural practices of Spanish and Portuguese speakers living in the United States as "Latin American"? What about traditions that originated in places like Texas, New Mexico, and California—parts of what are now the United States that were once under Spanish rule?

The question of how to define *theater* is no less vexing. In our attempt to take cultural differences into account, we might say that theater is a European cultural form that was originally developed by the Greeks and brought over to the Americas at the time of the Conquest. But what do we mean by "theater"? If it is true that the word itself has existed since the time of Aeschylus, it is also true that what Aeschylus called theater is quite different from what Harold Pinter, say, meant when he used the same word. To complicate matters, we have to keep in mind that embodied cultural practices and concepts about representation were undergoing dramatic shifts in Europe at the time of the Conquest. Classical texts, including Aristotle's *Poetics* and the great Greek tragedies, were being "rediscovered" and reinterpreted; perspectival representation was being developed; and the truth value of rituals was changing under pressures from the Reformation and the backlash of the Inquisition. In the midst of all this, "theater" acquired a new institutional identity. As Melveena McKendrick states in her book on Spanish theater, it is only in the sixteenth century that we can see the emergence of theater "as we would still recognize it today—the theater understood as performances by professional players before a public audience in a secular setting."[1]

Although it falls outside the purview of this book, it is important to recognize that these changes did not occur in isolation but through encounters with non-European peoples. This is particularly true of Spain and Portugal. In France and England, medieval religious drama provides precedents for the emergence of theater in our more modern sense, even if its social function was radically different. This tradition existed on the Iberian Peninsula, but it appears to have been more fragmentary, perhaps in part because the Christian population lived side by side with large numbers of Jews and Muslims until 1492—the year of Columbus's so-called discovery of the Americas but also the year of the Reconquista (Reconquest), when the Jews and Muslims were expelled from the Iberian Peninsula. By the beginning of the seventeenth century, however, theater had come to play an immensely powerful role in Spanish society.

Partly because theater was so closely associated with the emergence of a Spanish and Portuguese imperial identity, it seems problematic to use the word in relation to Amerindian and Afro-American cultures. Alongside theater, then, we use the term *performance,* a broader concept that includes practices such as ritual and dance that do not presume the notion of a "stage." Performance has the advantage of being a relative newcomer without some of the baggage that theater carries in tow; the word was not used by the Spanish or Portuguese conquerors, and it only recently gained currency in English. It also implies a sense of agency that has historically been denied to those who got the short end of the stick in their "encounter" with the Europeans. Yet it is not without its own difficulties. Today, the word performance is invoked by business people as often as it is by academics. And if we are not careful, the concept's very flexibility and amplitude can lead us to overlook important differences among practices that fall under its wide umbrella, conflating terms as distinct as *olin,* a Nahuatl term meaning movement but also the motor behind everything that happens in life, and *areito,* a kind of song-dance that derives from the Arawack word *aririn.* Our use of the word is also complicated by the fact that in the case of pre-colonial practices, much of our evidence comes from accounts by the Spanish and Portuguese, who often *did* apply theatrical categories to what they saw.

Perhaps the best way of illustrating some of these complexities is by way of a concrete example. In his *Historia natural y moral de las Indias,* published in 1590 and translated soon after into several European languages, the Spanish missionary José de Acosta wrote that a temple for the worship of Quetzal-coatl, one of the principal Aztec deities,

> had a courtyard of middling size, where on the god's feast day great dances and celebrations were performed as well as very amusing theatrical performances. For this purpose there was a small theater about thirty feet square in the middle of the courtyard, thoroughly whitewashed, which they embowered and adorned for that day with all possible care. . . . The actors came out and performed short comic pieces, pretending to be deaf, afflicted with colds, halt, blind, and missing an arm, all coming to the idol to ask for health. The deaf ones would give foolish answers and those with colds coughed. The halt, limping about described their miseries and complaints, and made the people laugh heartily. . . . After this was over they performed a *mitote,* or dance, with all these actors, and the festival ended; they usually did this at the most important festivals.[2]

Like the many other European conquerors and missionaries who wrote and published extensive descriptions of native rituals and customs, José de Acosta establishes equivalences between the practices he encounters and those with which he is familiar.[3] He describes the space as a *pequeño teatro*—a small theater; he uses the Nahuatl word *mitote* but immediately translates it as *baile,* or dance; and what has been rendered into English as "amusing theatrical performances" and "short comic pieces" he actually calls *entremeses*—a specific genre in Spain that usually dealt with popular characters and was performed during the interlude of a longer play. The word "actors" is, in Spanish, *representantes* (or representors), which implies a notion of the performer's function that is probably quite different from the one the performer himself possessed, especially in the context of a religious festival. The Spaniard also states that the activities *se hacían* (were made, or done), implying a "put on" quality that does not necessarily capture the fact that these native performances seem to have been both a representation *of* and a presentation *to* the gods. Finally, *se hacían* is translated into English as "performed"—interestingly, Spanish does not have an exact equivalent for "to perform." The fact that this excerpt is a translation entails yet another layer of meaning, yet another act of transmission.

Keeping all of these factors in mind, what can we say about "performance" practices in what is now known as "Latin America" before the Spanish and Portuguese arrived? Our knowledge of the many migratory and small-scale societies is relatively limited; yet we do know that spectacular events organized social life in the times of the Aztecs, Mayans, and Incas. Performances that included rituals, recitations, dialogues, dance, music, acrobatics, and perhaps even forms that we might now call theater were an integral part of everyday life.[4]

Large public spectacles were key to the functioning of these societies, making visible political hierarchies, religious beliefs, and social mores. High priests, trained as advanced astronomers, were reported to have astounded populations with their power to block out the sun and moon in ritual ceremonies (orchestrated, of course, to coincide with eclipses). Aztec schools and specialized academies trained warriors and young men and women in dance. Important figures, from the ruler on down, danced in public. Ordinary men and women performed in the many celebrations, commonly choreographed as two parallel rows of dancers moving in straight lines, turning around, and dancing in the opposite direction[5] or in concentric circles.[6] The dances were massive, at times involving thousands of people. One was described as a war dance "in which 800 Indians, or more or less, dance with small flags in a great war measure, among all of them not one being out of time."[7] Musicians played on two-toned and turtle shell drums, trumpets, gourds, notched bone, shells, flutes, and rattle boards.[8] Men, moreover, often dressed as women and mimed gender practices (such as weaving) associated with those roles. Some festivities, like the one just described, accentuated comic and at times even licentious elements. Usually, the performances took place outdoors, sometimes in very public spaces such as temples and courtyards, sometimes in the semisecluded space of a private patio.

Aztec musicians, as represented by native artists in Bernardino de Sahagún's sixteenth-century *General History of the Things of New Spain: Florentine Codex,* book 4.

Performance was fundamental to indigenous and European colonial epistemologies—a primary means through which both cultures maintained or contested social authority. The essays that accompany the first plays in this collection signal the ways in which native audiences attempted to negotiate their rapidly changing world after the arrival of the Europeans. While all these plays are in some sense products of the "encounter," some are clearly far more indigenous in form and content while others reflect strong European roots. Yet they all reveal numerous strategies for negotiating the relationship with the "other."

The first text in this book deals with the native ritual that Europeans usually found most alien: human sacrifice. The sacrifice of women, children, and war captives had evident political power in the expanding Aztec, Mayan, and Incan empires; at the same time, it also served a sacred function. Mesoamerican creation myths told of how the gods had sacrificed themselves for human beings, and they in turn required similar sacrifices in order to continually re-create the universe anew. The Mayans, for example, referred to certain forms of sacrifice as *ahil,* acts of creation.[9] Although the text of the Mayan dance-drama *Rabinal Achi* that appears in this anthology dates from the nineteenth century and was divided into theatrical scenes by its French transcriber, it deals with fourteenth and fifteenth-century events and is believed to have been performed since that time. The dance-drama, which deals with the capture and eventual sacrifice of the Queché Warrior by his enemies, is not simply a mimetic "representation" for its practitioners. As with many other indigenous rituals throughout the Americas, actors normally take a vow to participate for a certain number of years; the enactment is preceded by rites of bodily purification and takes place in the context of a series of sacred acts. *In a sense,* it is itself a form of sacrifice, a debt rendered to the gods—yet it is clearly *not* an actual human sacrifice. It is neither a theatrical representation nor a performance (in the sense of "completing" or "carrying out thoroughly") of the events it invokes; rather, it is something else, which does not quite correspond to our own vocabulary.

With the Conquest, "theater"—with an emphasis on the self-consciously mimetic and representational—became an instrument of colonization and evangelization. Impressed by the highly developed visual culture of the Americas, and finding the linguistic obstacles almost insurmountable, missionaries claimed that the native inhabitants "only learned through their eyes." To facilitate the conversion process, they introduced evangelical theater, drawing on their knowledge of medieval Spanish drama. The so-called New World became the site for new versions of European mystery plays, Corpus Christi celebrations, and *pastorelas,* or shepherd's plays, which portrayed the Three Wise Men's battles against evil en route to visit the infant Jesus. Included in the present collection is *Final Judgment,* a sixteenth-century morality play that features the allegorical characters of the Holy Church, Death, and Penitence. Originally written in Nahuatl, the language of the Mexica (Aztecs), it is an example of European traditions brought over to the Americas and performed in indigenous languages, with indigenous actors, traditions, and props, adapted to reflect contemporary concerns. This type of church-sponsored missionary theater, which was introduced by the Franciscans, died out by the end of the sixteenth century—along with the estimated ninety percent of the indigenous population that died of violence and disease. Nevertheless, elements of it can still be found in popular religious processions today.

Although theater, as the scholar María Sten argues, was as central to the Conquest as horses and gunpowder, native actors, designers, and participants also found ways of using it to their own benefit.[10] Traditions were strategically altered and employed by various social groups to achieve specific ends. For the native populations, the sensuous performance modes provided by Catholic rituals and sumptuous colonial ceremonies offered ways to transmit some of their own practices. The *cofradías* (religious confraternities) introduced by the Europeans also enabled Amerindians and Africans to insert their cultural repertoires—mainly music and dance—into colonial structures, finding in them ways of preserving some of their own values and performance modes. So, while the Europeans controlled the theater—as in texts and theatrical spaces—Amerindian and African populations had extensive performance traditions that adapted and survived through popular fiestas and festivities. The ways in which one performance practice can exist and renew itself within another, even hostile one goes some distance in illuminating the differences in cultural repertoires today between peoples colonized by Catholics and those colonized by Protestants, who were often suspicious of images and elaborate ceremonies. This volume attempts to convey a sense of the often parallel tracks—the erudite and the popular—of theater and performance in Latin America. While practitioners of popular performance may not appear as "authors" in many collections, the traditions they developed make themselves felt not only in the early colonial dramas but often into the present.

The mock battles known as *moros y cristianos,* which originated in Spain, are an excellent example of a performance practice of European origin that has undergone profound changes over the course of many centuries and across several continents.[11] As mentioned above, Christopher Columbus's "discovery" of the Americas in 1492 coincided with the expulsion of Muslims and Jews from the Iberian Peninsula, and Spaniards transposed the "Reconquest" of Spain onto their own conquest of overseas territories. The fight for the Holy Land that dated back to the Crusades took on new life in the Americas, where pageants such as the *Destruction of Jerusalem* and *The Conquest of Rhodes* were performed by indigenous actors at the behest of friars, who often baptized the "heathens" en masse after the Moors' symbolic defeat.[12] In some instances, however, native performers seem to have been successful in staging their own, alternative visions of the Conquest—one intriguing reference to a performance of the *Destruction of Jerusalem* in 1539, for example, indicates that the Turkish sultan was made to resemble the conqueror of Mexico, Hernán Cortés.[13] The defeat of the Turks, then, was turned into a symbolic defeat of the Spanish. *Los Comanches,* which appears in this reader, is a variation on this tradition that reenacts a late-eighteenth-century struggle between Spanish/Mexican settlers and Comanche Indians. Although the play is believed to have been written by a soldier, it was performed in mestizo communities throughout New Mexico in the nineteenth and early twentieth centuries in the midst of ethnic struggles around the newly redrawn border between the United States and Mexico. Like the moros y cristianos pageants, which are still performed in places such as Zacatecas, Mexico and Sevilla, Spain, *Los Comanches* is staged every year in the town of Alcalde, New Mexico.

The memory of another historic defeat has been passed on through the generations in the Andean dance-dramas that reenact the capture and execution of Atau Wallpa (also spelled Atahualpa), the Incan ruler at the time of the Spaniards' arrival. Different versions of this conquest drama are performed in villages throughout Peru and Bolivia today, usually in a mix of Spanish and Quechua, and as part of a festival dedicated to the town's patron saint.[14] Unlike *Los Comanches,* which appears to have originated as a written text and later entered into circuits of oral transmission, *The End of Atau Wallpa* in the version we have included here clearly postdates the origin of the performance tradition; the transcriber (some say author), Jesús Lara, even labels it a "tragedy," a European genre. The essay on this play traces the way in which the cultural and political battles waged in the dance-drama itself are replayed in debates surrounding the text's "authenticity."

During the long colonial period, new hybrid forms of theater developed in the Americas that drew from both European and indigenous roots, despite countless efforts by the Catholic Church to ban and/or regularize all forms of native performance. Many of these performances persisted, enacted year after year in front of the church (*atrio*) and in accordance with a Christian calendar. A local community leader, and often an entire barrio, became the guardian of the tradition, committing the words, dances, and music to memory and preserving the masks and instruments in secure, hidden locations. Traces of these performances may be gleaned from current practices, although we have no scripts for these early works. The scripts we do have are (as in the case of *Rabinal Achi* and, perhaps, *The End of Atau Wallpa*) based on more recent performances of the work dating from the eighteenth or nineteenth centuries. We also have numerous references to the performances that tempt us to speculate that some survived—transformed, of course, yet more or less uninterrupted for hundreds of years. The endless series of edicts prohibiting certain performance practices (such as indigenous peoples wearing masks, and men wearing skirts during celebrations) attest to the ongoing nature of these traditions.[15] Chroniclers also witnessed and wrote about recurring fiestas and performances. The African presence, however, is far less visible in such documents in part, perhaps, because blacks were not "natives" and therefore constituted less of an object of ethnographic interest for Europeans.[16]

One of the many versions of the Atau Wallpa (Atahualpa) dance-drama, in a 1984 performance in the town of Carhuamayo, Peru. The tradition was introduced to Carhuamayo in the 1930s by a local resident who had seen a play about the death of Atau Wallpa performed by a theater company from Cuzco. It is now an important event in the annual Fiesta de Santa Rosa. Photo by Luis Millones.

The mixing of native, European, and African influences (also referred to as mestizaje, hybridity, and creolization, among other terms) is one of the most salient features of colonialism, even though (and because) colonialism depends on creating and policing hierarchies of privilege through discriminatory laws, codes, and practices.[17] *El Güegüence,* a seventeenth-century play from Nicaragua (available on the Web site that accompanies this volume) is a wonderful example of attempts by mixed communities to debunk colonial power. The work depicts a rogue merchant anxious to marry his son to the governor's daughter. The name of the colonial figurehead, Governor Tastuanes (from *tlatoani,* Nahuatl for "authority figure"), points to the multiple systems that have come together to create this new social order. He, too, is a mestizo, racially and culturally mixed, but he is complicit with imperial norms, acting as a henchman in a corrupt and capricious system. Race becomes a subject of scorn and an insult as Güegüence calls his son "you bad breed" (*mala casta*). The mock marriage at the end signals how "whitening" serves as a strategy of social mobility and empowerment.[18] The masks, meanwhile, brilliantly reflect the content as style. The masks of the governor and mayor show white faces, blue eyes, and blond wavy hair tucked under fancy silk hats, while those for Güegüence and his sons are clearly mestizo—brown skin, dark eyes, black moustaches, and dark hair covered by large straw hats. The nineteenth-century translator, Daniel Brinton, notes that the play circulated among the indigenous and mestizo populations and that, unlike plays introduced by the Spanish, in *El Güegüence* "there is absolutely no moral purpose nor religious tone; so much, indeed, of the reverse, that we cannot conceive of its introduction by a priest."[19]

Scripted, single-authored plays also appeared in the sixteenth century, with Juan Pérez Ramírez (Mexico) and Cristóbal de Llerna (Dominican Republic) vying for the title of first playwright of the Americas.[20] The Jesuits, who arrived in the Americas in 1572, introduced theater in their schools for young Spanish and Creole boys throughout the continent; a school for indigenous boys was founded in Mexico in 1586. Women had no access to education and thus no access to participation in theater. The Jesuits started a tradition of school (and later university) theater that still persists. The classical and humanistic character of these works influenced the formation of national theaters.[21] In Mexico, then part of New Spain, a special space was set aside for the *corral* (theater) in 1573. A hospital in Lima became the site of the first stable theater there in 1604.[22] In Brazil, the Jesuit missionary José de Anchieta (1534–97) wrote trilingual missionary plays in Portuguese, Spanish, and Tupi to educate natives and colonizers in indigenous languages.[23]

In most of the Spanish- and Portuguese-speaking Americas, the clergy retained control of theatrical activity throughout the sixteenth, seventeenth, and early eighteenth centuries. Allegorical *autos sacramentales* by Portugal's Gil de Vicente and Spain's Calderón de la Barca were performed, sometimes translated into native languages. However, secular material became increasingly popular. Spanish playwrights such as Lope de Vega and the Mexican Creole luminary Juan Ruiz de Alarcón (1581–1639) wrote brilliant *comedias* that delighted audiences in Europe and the Americas. Huge religious celebrations paid for by the city council, both religious and courtly in nature, presented all sorts of performances. The births, weddings, and coronations of royalty back in Europe were cause for celebration, as were special sacred festivals such as Corpus Christi. These massive celebrations helped perpetuate native memories of conquest and allowed for the insertion of Amerindian and African traditions.

One fiesta held in Mexico in 1610 to celebrate the beatification of "Padre Ignacio" (Loyola) involved some thirty thousand people, drawing on many cofradías to organize displays. The fiesta illustrates the numerous elements drawn from native and African traditions—the cartloads of flowers, *cohetes* (firecrackers or noisemakers), drums, *cajas* (wooden boxes used as drums), and *castillos* (elaborate fireworks structures). Alongside these, vignettes and tableaux derived from the Spanish medieval tradition were staged on moving wagons. One notable cofradía, made up of "*morenos criollos*" (American-born Africans), staged an elaborate show of fireworks and "such curious dances that it delighted the procession."[24] So too, "*morenos*," born in Ethiopia, presented the most extravagant and exoticized version of themselves as envisioned by their Mexican audience—a make-believe king riding an elephant (which moved on wheels and turned out to be hollow) "of marvelous size and grace. It was frightening to see his figure and form so naturally represented. . . . On top of this animal sat a Moreno in the form of a king, with a scepter in his hand and a crown on his head, vividly representing the King of Ethiopia. It was a wonderful thing."[25] Performances staged in churchyards, such as the "Danza o

Corpus Christi Procession: Parish of San Cristóbal, ca. 1674–80. Cuzco, Museo de Arte Religioso. Artist unknown. This painting is one of a series of sixteen canvases depicting the feast of Corpus Christi in Cuzco. Each indigenous parish was represented by a cacique, or elite member of the community descended from the Inca dynasty (standing to the left, below the parrot). As "evidence" of past performances, such paintings are valuable but cannot necessarily be taken at face value—art historian Carolyn Dean has pointed out that accounts of the processions in Cuzco at this time do not mention *carros,* or mobile carts, like the one seen here. She suggests that native artists carefully copied the images of the carros from prints of ones used in Spain in order to represent the spectacular potential of the Cuzco fiestas. In place of the statues that adorned the Spanish carros, they inserted images of local saints. Photo courtesy of Carolyn Dean.

Coloquio de la Conquista," presented in 1788, staged the conflict between Cortés and Moctezuma. In this version, each leader and his army occupied a *tablado,* or platform, while the other characters and groups danced between them.[26]

We also find information regarding popular performances in the highly erudite texts that characterize the seventeenth-century Mexican baroque, suggesting perhaps that the schism between scripted theater and nonscripted performance is more pronounced in hindsight than it was in lived experience. Sor Juana Inés de la Cruz (1651–95), Mexico's legendary and enigmatic nun/writer/scientist, praised as the tenth muse and the "phoenix of the Americas," wrote *autos, comedias, villancicos,* and poetry that, according to one of Mexico's major playwrights of the twentieth century, Rodolfo Usigli, "blend with the lilting dialects of Indians and Negros."[27] Her introductory psalm, or *loa,* for the *Auto Sacramental of The Divine Narcissus,* which is included in this volume, depicts the encounter between the indigenous woman "America" and the European woman "Religion" by introducing representations of the indigenous songs and dances that had never seen the colonial stage. The *Loa,* while ostensibly meant to educate the "pagan" natives about important similarities between their religious system and Catholicism, is in fact addressed to Spanish

and Creole viewers, educating the "real" spectators in the courts of Mexico and
Spain. Sor Juana's writing bridged deep divides between sacred and courtly
writings, erudite and popular traditions, and Spanish and Creole aesthetics
while calling attention to the gender inequalities and diminished opportunities
and expectations for women in the rigidly hierarchical male worlds of church
and state.

In the late eighteenth century, civil officials began to highlight the importance of theater in the formation of an orderly, civic character. While the
Church throughout the Americas became nervous about the popularity and
growing secularism of theater, the municipal authorities defended it as "one of
the best schools for manners, language and urbanity, and thus useful in a city
that lacks other healthy diversions."[28] The theater space itself, they recognized, could also be used to dramatize the preeminence of civil authority. The
first stable theater in Argentina, Teatro de la Ranchería (1783), boasted a special section, or *palco,* reserved for the viceroy. The luxurious balcony, with the
official insignia surrounded by velvet and gold, reaffirmed the supremacy of
state power. The play could not begin until the viceroy occupied his exalted
place and was properly saluted by the actors.[29]

The plays staged in these theaters were devotional, historical, imported
from Europe, or—increasingly—nationalist in character. As discontent between *criollos* (American-born people of European descent) and the colonial
power structure began to grow, the theater became a contested space in the formation of social memory and opinion. In Argentina, Viceroy Vértiz y Salcedo
defended theater's didactic civil potential but agreed that it had to be kept in
line. His 1783 decree mandated that dramatic texts be censored, that actors'
body language be controlled, that actors be prohibited from "executing any
movement or action . . . that might cause the slightest scandal," and that audiences be segregated by sex and social class.[30] Regardless of what took place onstage, the event itself was a performance of social norms and values. White
men sat in the front rows, men of color (mulattoes, mestizos, and blacks) stood
at the back of the room, and working-class women were confined to *la cazuela*
(the pot), a balcony with standing room only reserved for women of all races.[31]
Breast-feeding was prohibited. The restriction and physical arrangement of
bodies highlighted the regulatory function that civil authority sought to confirm in and through theater. The performances reaffirmed, and at times indirectly called into question, the norms that positioned the white, upper-class
male as the privileged spectator and physically pushed women and men of
color to the sidelines. Yet, even though the civil authorities occupying the pal-
cos and the white men in the front rows were the principal spectators, minority men and women of all races had access to the performance and could interpret what they saw. Moreover, the professional theater allowed women to
gain visibility onstage. Not only could they act, interact with men, and earn
wages (all previously forbidden), but the newly arrived European plays—
whose plots were rife with disguises, role switching, and gender confusion—
permitted some play with regard to gender and race. In Brazil prior to the
nineteenth century most actors were mulattoes who performed in whiteface.
In some places, women of color and slaves were allowed to act and coexist on-

stage and in theater companies before society was ready to sanction any such interactions. Yet many stipulations remained. Women were frequently not allowed to dress as men from the waist down or show their ankles or feet (a wooden board blocked the audience's line of vision). Thus, there was a complicated play of restrictions and transgressions going on as women and people of color strove for more options in late-eighteenth-century society. In Mexico, even as spectators grumbled that the cazuela segregated "decent" women from their husbands and sons, this system of exclusions gave way in the early nineteenth century to performances of excess. One astounded commentator notes that the first time he saw an elegant, upper-class woman smoking was in the theater in 1832.[32]

Toward the beginning of the nineteenth century, which was marked by wars of independence throughout most of the Americas, theater began rehearsing a sense of national or continental (rather than ethnic or colonial) identity. José Joaquín Fernández Lizardi (1776–1827), the journalist and novelist known as "The Mexican Thinker," wrote several plays and two *unipersonales*, dramatized political monologues that were instrumental in circulating liberal, pro-independence ideas. Operas, ballets, and entire theater companies were imported from Europe, as were plays that reaffirmed the emerging elite's sense of self-importance. By the end of the century there was also a move to build massive national theaters rivaling those to be found in Europe. Local playwrights who aspired to literary greatness adopted the neoclassical style in vogue in Europe, though they occasionally looked closer to home for their subject matter. Luis Ambrosio Morante (1755–1837), an actor and playwright who was active in Buenos Aires and Chile, wrote *El 25 de mayo* in 1812 to commemorate the second anniversary of the initial revolt against Spanish rule, and his 1821 tragedy *Túpac Amaru* centered on a 1780 rebellion against the Spanish led by a descendant of the Incan royalty. Like many works from this turbulent time period, however, some of his scripts were lost or destroyed. Plays like the great Peruvian work *Ollantay* strategically looked to the past, using pre-Hispanic themes as a way of depicting "national" histories as grand continua. Romanticism, closely associated with the ideology of national sovereignty, was particularly significant in Brazil, which became an independent empire in 1822, as well as in Cuba and Puerto Rico, which remained under Spanish rule until 1898. Although most of the works performed during the nineteenth century came from Europe, the traffic in theatrical production occasionally moved in the other direction. The Cuban Gertrudis Gómez de Avellaneda (1814–73) wrote historical dramas that were among the most popular of their day in Spain, where the author lived for much of her adult life. The Puerto Rican Alejandro Tapia, meanwhile, used Cuba as the setting for his three-act melodrama *La cuarterona* (The Quadroon) about the doomed love between a young man from the white elite and a beautiful, self-abnegating woman who, despite her pale complexion, is the illegitimate daughter of a mulatta slave and her master.

Few of the "serious" cultural productions of this era are performed or studied today. Of more enduring influence were the *comedias de costumbres* (regional comedies of manners) by writers such as Luis Vargas Tejada (Colombia, 1802–29), Manuel Ascensio Segura (Peru, 1805–71), and Daniel Barros

Grez (Chile, 1834–1904), which focus on the local scene and its typical customs and characters to encourage populations to look for identity at home rather than overseas. In Brazil, the related genre of the *comédias de costumes* was popularized in the 1830s by Luís Carlos Martins Pena, whose play *The Jealous Officer, or The Fearsome Slave Catcher* is included in this collection. Martins Pena's immensely popular works offer insight into a period in which local elites were seeking to carefully control theatrical images of the new nation, banning actors of color from the stage and privileging national variations on European-style high art. *The Jealous Officer* is a clever parody of *Othello*—not the original, but a Brazilian version of a melodramatic French adaptation in which the title character was a white man. Martins Pena transforms Shakespeare's jealous Moor once again, this time into a police officer who moonlights as a slave catcher and guards his wife and daughter under lock and key. In addition to drawing explicit parallels between the plight of women and black slaves, the play calls up the whitewashing of Brazilian theater when one of the characters uses a blackface disguise to fool the imperious officer. It also reflects the playwright's well-publicized dislike of the police, who patrolled the theaters and enforced censorship decrees; not surprisingly, his play, too, was censored.

Martins Pena was not the only playwright who explored the performative nature of racial identities; in Cuba, a popular genre of blackface parodic theater known as *teatro bufo* made the growing influence of blacks in the national arena visible, yet it also ridiculed what it depicted as their efforts to assimilate into white, Creole society.[33] Pastorelas continued to be popular throughout this period and were often transformed into a venue for political lampooning. Burlesques imported from Europe also provided venues for critique and reimaginings; operettas, known as *zarzuelas,* were common, as were *revistas,* musical "reviews." Populations left out of the high cultural sphere of elegant theaters, playwrights, and published scripts also produced their own performance forms that circulated in the "live" circuits of non-print culture. Yet the boundaries between print culture and performance during this period were more fluid than is often acknowledged. Beginning in 1884, for example, the *circo criollo* (creole circus) in Argentina and Uruguay presented the pantomime *Juan Moreira,* about a gaucho who does not fit the new "national" project. Originally the protagonist of a novel published in installments in a daily newspaper, Moreira gained lasting fame as the star of the circus troupe's later spoken version (included in this collection), and he went on to inspire a whole range of plays and performances that ran the gamut from the scandalous to the respectable. His migrations between distinct cultural spheres are a reminder that what we commonly designate as "theater" is itself an aesthetic construct that creates exclusions and often writes its own popular antecedents out of history.

At the beginning of the twentieth century, some of the most active sites of performance were workers' halls and small theaters where urban and agrarian laborers gathered to participate in and applaud music recitals, political speeches, and plays. *Teatro obrero* (workers' theater) is rarely studied, in part because there are few extant texts but also because academic definitions of

¿A qué espectáculo van ustedes?

A la Opera.

A la Comedia.

Al drama criollo.

Al «Café-chantant».

A la zarzuela chica.

Al Teatro Chinesco.

Dib. de Giménez.

An illustration from the April 27, 1901 edition of *Caras y caretas,* a weekly magazine published in Buenos Aires. The heading asks, "To which show do you go?" Below are caricatures of different social "types" and the genre of theater each presumably attends, in order of decreasing prestige: opera; comedy; the *drama criollo,* dealing with national themes (such as *Juan Moreira*); "café-chantant," which was similar to cabaret; *zarzuela chica,* a genre of musical comedy originally brought over from Spain; and the "Chinese theater" of working-class immigrants.

theater tend to exclude works that do not shy away from political "propaganda." Yet these plays ask us to interrogate the institution of "art" and how it circumscribes what can be said or done and by whom. The Puerto Rican feminist and anarchist Luisa Capetillo led strikes, wore pants, got arrested, and traveled throughout the Caribbean and the United States meeting other workers and activists. She was also one of many women writers that got their start in the labor movement. Although scholars are just beginning to study this facet of Capetillo's work, we have included her short play *After Death,* an amusing but pointed parody of romantic drama that undermines idealized, class-based notions of femininity. Like more self-consciously "literary" plays such as *The Eternal Feminine* (1975), an experimental farce by the Mexican writer Rosario Castellanos, it uses humor to highlight the link between the oppression of real-life women and the perpetuation of cultural myths.[34]

In many countries, the upsurge of labor militancy during this time period was fueled by large numbers of immigrant workers arriving from Europe. This was particularly true in Argentina, where millions of foreigners, predominantly Italian, arrived between 1880 and 1930. The *Juan Moreira* circus pantomime portrayed an Italian immigrant as the arch-enemy of the valiant gaucho, though, as our essay on the play indicates, this character was quickly transformed into the comic hybrid Cocoliche, an unstable figure whose early-twentieth-century permutations embody the struggle over how to define a changing national identity. Cocoliche made his appearances in the annual carnival processions, but immigration was also the subject of theatrical works such as the 1904 melodrama *La gringa* by the Uruguayan-born Florencio Sánchez, one of Latin America's first internationally known playwrights.[35] Among immigrant audiences, the most popular genre was the *sainete criollo,* a Spanish-derived, one-act farce frequently punctuated by tango music. The later *grotesco criollo* was a darker, more critical version of the sainete criollo that pushed beyond the bounds of realism into the absurd. Italian influence marked both the style and content of this most Argentine of genres: Armando Discépolo, whose 1923 play *Mateo* is regarded as the original grotesco criollo, drew on the Italian grotesque and Pirandello's metatheatrics in depicting the economic and psychological degradation of working-class immigrants who speak in a Spanish-Italian pidgin.

One of the most dramatic conflicts of the early twentieth century was the Mexican Revolution, which began in 1910 as a series of regional struggles over divergent and at times conflicting aims. Like the state-funded muralist movement led by Diego Rivera, performance was an integral part of the postrevolutionary government's plan to remake the Mexican nation. A sixty-thousand-seat stadium in Mexico City inaugurated in 1924 played host to sporting events, official ceremonies, theatrical spectacles, and innovative "mass ballets" involving over a thousand participants.[36] Theater was also used as an educational tool by teachers sent to rural communities as part of the government's ambitious Cultural Mission Program. In areas where the indigenous population did not speak Spanish, didactic skits were the means by which teachers conveyed the dangers of alcoholism or the advancements achieved by the Revolution. As the scholar Adam Versényi has pointed out, these modern, secular missions were modeled on the practices of the colonial Spanish clergy, though instead of Christianity they preached the gospel of cultural mestizaje that was to create a new "cosmic race."[37] Despite their frequent use of Aztec themes, the colossal stadium shows also harked back to the early evangelical plays (such as *Final Judgment*) that had culminated in mass baptisms. Performance was a means of physically and symbolically incorporating audiences into the national framework, a process that often entailed mythologizing the Revolution as a single, monolithic struggle and papering over the fact that the victorious faction was hardly the most "revolutionary" of those who had fought. In his own quest to create a national theater, the playwright Rodolfo Usigli both exposed and emulated the theatrical nature of populist politics; his classic *El gesticulador* (1938, translated as *The Impostor*) is a three-act "play for demagogues" in which a humble history professor gains fame by passing himself off as a revolutionary hero long believed to be dead.[38] Even today the Revolution's ghosts continue to haunt Mexican playwrights: Sabina Berman's *Between Pancho Villa and a Naked Woman* (1993), for example, is a comic take on sexual politics in the neoliberal 1990s that features surrealistic guest appearances by the notorious war hero.[39]

The 1920s and 1930s were a high point for comedy in many Latin American countries. Cabaret was popular in urban centers and gave rise to legendary performers such as the Afro-Brazilian drag artist João Francisco dos Santos, better known as Madame Satã.[40] In Mexico, itinerant *carpa* (tent) performers moved from town to town, setting up camp in public plazas where they presented informal routines combining comedy, songs, and short skits; this was where Cantinflas, the film star known as the Mexican Charlie Chaplin, got his start. According to some, it was also the heyday (others called it the decline) of the *teatro de revista*. In Brazil, these musical revues often afforded professional opportunities to nonwhite actors that were off-limits in "legitimate" theaters, though they also frequently capitalized on racial and gender stereotypes. There were even a few mulatto and all-black revista companies, one of which was a stepping stone for Grande Otelo, the undisputed comic genius of Brazilian cinema.[41] The second act of Oswald de Andrade's 1934 play *The Candle King* (included in this anthology) is a spoof on these risqué spectacles, though it adds some extra zing to their satire by presenting the ugly underside of imperialism and the Brazilian class structure.

The Candle King's ambivalence toward market-driven forms of entertainment is characteristic of the avant-garde, known in Spanish America as the *vanguardia* and as *modernismo* in Brazil. If Europe had its dadaists, futurists, and surrealists (the list goes on and on), there were *estridentistas* and *contemporáneos* in Mexico, Chilean *creacionistas*, Puerto Rican *noístas*, and numerous other groups that proclaimed manifestos and performed the occasional act of public provocation. In Latin America, poetry was initially the favored form for vanguardist experimentation. Performances were usually intimate affairs, like the unusual *Pascanas nocturnas* (Nocturnal Interludes) held in the late 1920s by the Grupo Orkopata in Puno, Peru, in which participants dressed in indigenous garb, chewed coca leaves, read poetry, and performed songs in Quechua and Aymara. Although some vanguardists cultivated a formalist, art for art's sake aesthetic, many set out to reconcile cosmpolitanism with an exploration of local cultures. Alejo Carpentier's *Miracle of Anaquillé,* an "Afro-Cuban ballet,"[42] and Joaquín Pasos and José Coronel Urtecho's *Chinfonía burguesa* (Bourgeois Chymphony), a hyperbolic exercise in wordplay performed by the Nicaraguan Anti-Academy in 1936, are two examples of what Vicky Unruh has called "performance manifestos"—multigeneric texts that simultaneously illustrate and act out conflicting aesthetic stances while rehearsing a more reciprocal relationship with untraditional theater audiences.[43]

The vanguardists' turn to theater in the 1930s was largely driven by political imperatives: in many countries authoritarian governments rose to power, and there was growing resistance to U.S. hegemony in the region. Writers such as Oswald de Andrade and the Chilean Vicente Huidobro, both of whom joined the Communist Party, saw theater as an effective means of mobilizing the masses. However, efforts to produce their works were stymied by censorship and unfavorable policies established by growing state bureaucracies that were often willing to tolerate (and even patronize) progressive poetry and prose but were more wary of live art forms like theater, which had the potential to bring different publics into direct contact. Like *The Candle King,* many plays written during this period were published and read but not staged until the 1960s when they made their mark on the formation of a new avant-garde. One of the few exceptions was in Argentina, where the Teatro del Pueblo and the journalist and novelist turned playwright Roberto Arlt laid the groundwork for an independent theater movement with plays that focused on the frustrated dreams of the marginalized classes while denouncing the theatrical politics of fascism. Venezuela's José Ignacio Cabrujas is one of many later playwrights who would draw inspiration from this era; his play *El día que me quieras* (The Day You Love Me, 1979) takes its title from a tango song by the Argentine film star Carlos Gardel and is set during his visit to Caracas in 1935 during a period of extreme ideological polarization under the dictatorship of Juan Vicente Gómez and the rise of Stalinism in the Soviet Union.

A recurring motif among the vanguardists was the need to create a "modern" theater. They were not the first to raise this cry, nor would they be the last. Throughout the twentieth century, theater artists have worried that theirs is an antiquated art in danger of being supplanted by the newer media of mass culture, particularly film. Yet in Latin America this debate has unique implications due to the region's subordinate position in the world economy and theater's own status as a marker of European culture. Often companies have not had the resources necessary to introduce expensive technological changes in staging. Furthermore, because modernity has historically been identified as a Western phenomenon and defined in opposition to the non-white, "backward," "underdeveloped" areas of the world it poses a representational challenge in (post)colonial regions. Virgilio Piñera's *Electra Garrigó* (1948), which is included in this volume, plays on the double paradox embedded in the idea of a modern Latin American theater by turning the Greek myth of Electra on its head and transplanting it to contemporary Cuba. The illustrious patriarch Agamemnon turns into a slovenly, corrupt dictator, the chorus becomes a group of *guajiros* (peasants) who sing to the tune of "Guantanamera," and black servants take the place of the silent slaves of the original. European high art is removed from its pedestal and placed side by side with local traditions in a humorously critical performance of Cuba's own, distinctly heterodox modernity.

Piñera is one of many playwrights who have invoked the plight of Greek heroines to condemn undemocratic societies; Luis Rafael Sánchez's *La pasión según Antígona Pérez* (1968, Puerto Rico), José Triana's *Medea in the Mirror* (1962, Cuba),[44] Griselda Gambaro's *Antígona furiosa* (1986, Argentina),[45] Ricardo Monti's *The Obscurity of Reason* (1994, Argentina),[46] and *Antígona*, performed by Peru's Grupo Cultural Yuyachkani (2000), are just a few. Others have appropriated the classical model to explore private passions and invent new myths. The *tragédias cariocas* of Nelson Rodrigues, whose 1945 play *The Wedding Gown* is credited with inaugurating modern Brazilian theater, provoked outrage by depicting the respectable citizens of Rio engaging in incest, adultery, and homosexuality—all the old "sins" of the ancients.[47] These parodies and adaptations of Greek tragedy raise a series of questions: Are the archetypes and techniques of Western drama truly universal and timeless? In what ways does a mulatta Medea or an Argentine Antigone shed new light on old myths? Or do playwrights simply turn to them as Trojan horses—sneaking their political critiques past their censors?[48] Is theater (like the concept of modernity) always slightly "out of place" in Latin America and, if so, can this lend it a critical and creative edge?

Regionalism and neocostumbrismo, which have resurfaced at various points throughout the twentieth century, might appear to represent the flip side of the search for the "modern." Like the comedias de costumbres of the nineteenth century, plays influenced by these trends highlight local customs; their characters often speak in a regional dialect, use colloquial expressions, and evoke familiar social "types." Yet, as often as not, what these plays register is not just tradition but also change. This is the case with *The Oxcart* (1952) by René Marqués, Puerto Rico's most famous playwright, which follows the fortunes of a rural family that leaves the land and moves to San Juan before immigrating to New York (where the play had its debut).[49] The regionalist trend that came out of the northeast of Brazil presents a similar dynamic. Alfredo Dias Gomes's 1960 tragedy *O Pagador de Promessas* (*Payment as Pledged*) portrays a poor white farmer who undertakes a pilgrimage to the city in fulfillment of a vow made to the gods of the Afro-Brazilian religion known as *candomblé*.[50] Ariano Suassuna's *Auto da Compadecida* (translated as *The Rogue's Trial*), on the other hand, is a hilarious take on the morality plays that were introduced in the area by colonial missionaries; its complex plot involves a funeral for a dog, a cat that excretes gold coins, one of the region's legendary bandits, and a final judgment scene featuring a black Christ. First staged in 1957, it continues to be one of the most popular Brazilian plays of all time, and a film version in 2000 set a record as the country's highest-grossing national production.[51] This kind of intimate relationship between the presumably competitive arts of theater and film is not uncommon. The playwright Emilio Carballido (1925–2008), for instance, was a towering figure on the Mexican theater scene for over fifty years; his many classics include *I, Too, Speak of the Rose* (1965), in which the central character, the Medium, draws on oral traditions and fore-grounds processes of interpretation that are often overlooked in the media blitz of mass societies. At the same time, Carballido was also a screenwriter who worked on over fifty films, including several adaptations of his own plays.[52]

At times, playwrights (and writers generally) have enjoyed positions of public trust and authority in countries where politicians lack both, and in turn they have been highly scrutinized and censored by those in power. Virgilio Piñera's apparent endorsement of patricide in *Electra Garrigó* was lauded as prophetic after the triumph of the Cuban Revolution in 1959, an event that profoundly altered Cuban life and inspired a wave of cultural and political activity throughout Latin America. Four hundred and fifty years of imperialism could not be undone simply by overthrowing one corrupt, oppressive regime, and the new Cuban government sought to revolutionize an entire culture that had perpetuated a system of extreme social inequality and injustice. Ordinary Cubans were given the opportunity to study acting, music, and dance; playwrights such as Eugenio Hernández Espinosa and the choreographer Ramiro Guerra sought inspiration in Afro-Cuban rituals; and unprecedented numbers of people (sometimes over twenty thousand) lined up to see new plays within weeks of their debut.[53] As the U.S. Central Intelligence Agency (CIA) began to undertake hostile actions against the island, however, Cuba aligned itself with the Soviet Union and clamped down on political debate, a move that contributed to quelling the initial burst of artistic innovation. Like Piñera, José Triana was at first celebrated by the new cultural establishment but later marginalized when his revolutionary credentials were called into question. In the polarized political climate of the cold war, plays such as his *Night of the Assassins,* which highlighted ambiguities and disrupted clear-cut distinctions, posed unsettling problems of interpretation for a regime that was in the process of instituting its own rituals.

The 1960s and 1970s were an extremely turbulent period in a Latin America caught between the euphoria and contradictions of revolutionary independence and the violence of authoritarian backlash. One after another, several countries suffered brutal military coups (Brazil, 1964; Panama, 1968; Chile, 1973; Uruguay, 1973; Argentina 1976) while others lived under perpetual dictatorships (Guatemala, El Salvador, Haiti, Honduras, Paraguay) that were often supported by the U.S. government. Colombia experienced a seemingly interminable period of civil conflict that came to be known simply as *la violencia,* "the violence." Enrique Buenaventura's *Documents from Hell* (parts of which are included in this volume), like Triana's *Night of the Assassins* and the early works of Griselda Gambaro (such as *The Walls, Siamese Twins,* and *The Camp* [the last of which is included in this volume]),[54] are examples of what Diana Taylor has called "theater of crisis." Written between 1965 and 1970, when the ideological fervor inspired by the Cuban Revolution was waning and antidemocratic forces were gathering strength in many countries, these plays register the breakdown of interpretive frameworks and the dissolution of personal and collective identities. Taylor states that "the theater of crisis mirrors the *effects* of sociopolitical crisis—the objective, systemic rifts in combination with the subjective experience of decomposition—without yet evolving *beyond* crisis toward reconstruction."[55] These plays are generally anti-Aristotelian and lack a clear resolution; scholars based in the United States and Europe often compared them to absurdist dramas, though Brecht and Artaud were also identified as important influences. Nonetheless, these works offer prophetic insights into the limitations and dangers of the particular sociopolitical contexts in which they were written. They explore what happens when there is no "outside" from which to analyze or critique a situation—no outside the Revolution, as in Triana's play, no outside colonialism, as Buenaventura takes us farther into the depths of "hell," no escaping the onslaught of criminal politics that Gambaro foresaw in her early works on disappearances and concentration camps such as *The Camp* (1967).

The work of Enrique Buenaventura was instrumental in fomenting the collective theater movement that arose in the 1960s and 1970s. In 1962, Buenaventura formed the Teatro Experimental de Cali (TEC) as a rejection of the consumer-oriented commercial theater that dominated the artistic scene. Like the Brazilian director Augusto Boal, whose "theater of the oppressed" has circulated worldwide, TEC traveled across the continent, offering performances and workshops for amateur actors, factory workers, and campesinos. Similar collectives sprang up in nearly every country during this time period: the famous Candelaria, based in Bogotá; Tiempoovillo, founded by architecture students in Paraguay; Ollantay in Ecuador; Nixtayolero from rural Nicaragua; Cuba's Escambray; Venezuela's Rajatabla; Brazil's Galpão. What links these groups is not an aesthetic but rather a politics of theatrical practice. Inspired by Marxist and anti-imperialist ideals, these groups developed a form that came to be called *nuevo teatro popular* (new popular theater) with a *by the people, for the people* approach to dramaturgy and social change. Plays were often written collectively, and the individually authored ones evolved during rehearsals with input from the actors. Because the groups tended to be mobile, performing in remote rural areas as well as at international and Latin American theater festivals, the works relied on improvisation and technical simplicity, though they were often stunningly beautiful. Buenaventura quipped that Latin American artists, like the Polish director Jerzy Grotowski, practiced "poor theater"—the only difference was that theirs had no money.[56] Performances, followed by forums in which the artists discussed the show with audience members, offered everyone a chance to participate in imagining a new social order. While many groups started out with a Brechtian approach, they often came to work with local repertoires and performance practices that they learned from their audiences. Peru's Grupo Cultural Yuyachkani, which came together over thirty-five years ago to support striking miners, is one such group. Their piece *Adiós Ayacucho* (1990), adapted from Julio Ortega's novella of the same name, is an outstanding example of more recent collective work that is included in this collection.

Theater collectives and individual artists had to struggle to survive after the wave of military coups in South America and counterinsurgency campaigns in Central America began to come to a head in the 1960s. The death camps prophesied in Gambaro's *The Camp* became a reality during Argentina's "Dirty War" from 1976 to 1983, when thirty thousand people were murdered by government forces. In Guatemala, over two hundred thousand were killed, the vast majority of them Mayan Indians massacred by the army and right-wing death squads. All of these U.S.-backed regimes used strikingly similar tactics—murdering and torturing leftists, student activists, trade unionists, and indigenous people while handing over control of industries and natural resources to foreign corporations.

In El Salvador and Guatemala, displaced communities were unable to hold their usual festivals, and the national and university companies collapsed. In some countries artists, such as the Brazilian Augusto Boal and his compatriot José Celso, who directed the controversial staging of *The Candle King* in 1967, were arrested and tortured; many more went into exile, an experience that is represented in this volume by Diana Raznovich's *Personal Belongings* (1974, Argentina). Yet, after an initial period of repression, independent theaters in most South American countries managed to regroup and adapt. Playwrights such as Carlos Manuel Varela (Uruguay), Marco Antonio de la Parra (Chile),[57] and Eduardo Pavlovsky (Argentina)[58] employed allegory and abstraction to bypass the censors. Some, including Roberto Cossa (Argentina), cloaked their critique in the guise of tradition by turning to older genres such as the sainete and grotesco.

The phrase "stages of conflict" was more than just a metaphor during this period. In 1975, Guatemala's burgeoning theater scene suffered a setback after one of the major theaters was damaged in a suspicious fire and an actor was shot while entering the building. A 1968 performance of Chico Buarque's *Roda Viva* in São Paulo was interrupted by right-wing paramilitaries who attacked actors and musicians, ransacked the theater, and later kidnapped the leading actor and actress. In one of the most notorious cases of retaliation against opposition artists, Teatro Abierto (1981), a festival of twenty-one plays by blacklisted Argentine theater practitioners was temporarily derailed when the theater was burned to the ground; determined that the show would go on, the artists moved to another location and attracted twenty-five thousand spectators during a two-month run. At times, prisons served as makeshift stages. The Uruguayan playwright Mauricio Rosencof became the leader of the Tupamaros guerrilla resistance and continued to write plays during his thirteen years in prison, often without access to paper and pencils. Inmates at a concentration camp in Puchuncaví, Chile, wrote and performed several allegorical religious works about unjust power.[59]

The dictatorships broke down the boundaries between politics and performance—not in the manner envisioned by postmodernist fantasies, or in the progressive sense that popular theater collectives sought, but in the most brutal way imaginable. State-sponsored violence was carefully orchestrated to terrify not only its victims but also those who witnessed it. People were literally "disappeared" in broad daylight, taken away by death squads and security forces to be tortured and killed in secret detention centers, their bodies buried in mass graves or tossed out of airplanes into the sea. Consequently, live, embodied acts took on a special urgency for people attempting to force local and international publics to take responsibility for what they had learned not to see. One of the best-known examples is the Mothers of the Plaza de Mayo, a group of women whose grown children had been abducted by the Argentine military. Every week, they marched around the main square in Buenos Aires, carrying banners and photos of their missing sons and daughters while wearing white head scarves in a conscious performance of conventional motherhood. CADA, a group of writers and visual artists who remained in Chile after the coup, performed "art actions" such as tracing giant crosses on the streets and dropping leaflets from airplanes, while members Raúl Zurita and Diamela Eltit resorted to public acts of self-scarification to viscerally foreground bodily pain and attack the traditional gender roles enforced by Augusto Pinochet's "modernizing" dictatorship.[60] Performance can be a valuable conceptual tool with which to trace the ways aesthetic interventions into the political sphere share and/or contest the underlying assumptions and strategies of more explicitly political practices that rely on public spectacle. Yet it is an unstable concept, just as performance itself is a mutable practice. The challenge is to use it critically rather than replicating the logic underlying the dictatorships' own violation of boundaries and bodies.

This is no straightforward matter. Indeed, artists themselves often disagree about what constitutes effective resistance. During and after the dictatorships, one of the most sensitive issues was the staging of violence and torture. Is it ethical to create aesthetic representations of violence that may end up evoking a certain sense of pleasure? If so, how should the audience position itself in relation to what it sees? What kinds of cases should be taken as representative? Two monologues in this anthology offer contrasting perspectives on another contentious issue: humor. Juan Radrigán has criticized fellow playwrights who turn tragedy into an occasion for laughter, and his piece *Isabel Banished in Isabel* is a bitter portrait of the despair suffered by countless Chileans who were impoverished and marginalized by Pinochet's economic reforms. Raznovich's *Personal Belongings,* on the other hand, uses morbid humor to defy an oppressive system that operates by instilling fear.

As civilian rule was restored, actors and playwrights returned from exile eager to stage works they had written abroad along with new ones written for the tentative transition to democracy. Under the dictatorships, spectators had come to rely on theater as an arena in which to confront hidden political practices and social realities; in a cruel inversion, theater suddenly seemed less necessary in the postdictatorship moment. Countries that suffered economic collapse after the demise of the costly authoritarian regimes began to experience a different kind of disappearance: there was no money, nothing to buy, and groceries and canned goods vanished from the shelves. *Teatro callejero* (street theater) became a way of reclaiming public space and rebuilding the public sphere, a process that often entailed revising national myths and archetypes in light of the recent bloodshed. In Argentina, for example, a street theater group that formed in 1983 created an updated version of *Juan Moreira* for its first show.

It is impossible to draw hard-and-fast distinctions between the dictatorships and what has followed. Very few of those responsible for the atrocities have been tried; in most countries the accused were granted amnesty, though in some cases those laws are now being overturned. The HIJOS, a group of young Argentine activists whose parents were disappeared, continue to organize *escraches,* theatricalized protests that expose perpetrators by leading crowds to their houses and following them to public places. Many theatrical works have taken the form of frustrated rituals, funeral rites that cannot be completed because there is no body to bury or personal traumas that cannot be overcome because political conditions have not sufficiently changed. Ariel Dorfman's internationally renowned *Death and the Maiden* (1991) is the most famous example, though many productions have fixated on the protagonist's obsession with interrogating her torturer/rapist at the expense of exploring her commentary on the activities of the Chilean Truth Commission.[61] A very different process of transmitting the memory of trauma takes place in the performance piece *Adiós Ayacucho,* which Yuyachkani first staged in 1990, when the Peruvian military was still murdering tens of thousands of innocent people in its war against the Maoist Shining Path rebels. As in Buenaventura's *The Schoolteacher* (one of the vignettes from *Documents from Hell*) the protagonist speaks to us from the dead, though in this case a masked dancer from popular Andean festivals channels the victim's spirit in an act of embodiment meant to remind us that the past is not over.

Throughout Latin America, the 1980s and 1990s were a period of political and financial instability as "free" markets and the reduction of social spending widened the gap between rich and poor and led to massive emigration. In Mexico, the gradual downfall of the Institutional Revolutionary Party, which was voted out of office in 2000 after seven decades in power, motivated playwrights to look back on their history to reveal how old scenarios are repeated in the present. The plays of Sabina Berman and Víctor Hugo Rascón Banda, for instance, deal with everything from the role of women in the Conquest to corruption in the banking industry.[62] On the other hand, some young playwrights, many of whom are also actors and directors, have rejected "political" theater, preferring to focus on explorations of language, time, imagery, and scenic space. Yet this refusal to be read within an existing political framework is, at least for some, a meaningful gesture. The four Argentine plays that were recently staged in New York as part of the Buenos Aires in Translation festival, for example, were all pointedly devoid of any concrete historical or geographical references; on the face of it, they could have easily been written by a New York-based artist for a home audience. Yet their apparent legibility was misleading. The physicality and underlying agression that was emphasized in the production of Daniel Veronese's *Women Dreamt Horses* hinted at the magnitude of what lay unspoken behind the play's enigmatic references to past violence and children whose parents had mysteriously disappeared. Rafael Spregelburd's *Panic,* meanwhile, rushed ahead at breakneck speed as it followed the antics of a family attempting to find a missing key to a safe-deposit box before the bank collapses. Many critics were impressed by the dialogue, but others complained: sure, the play was a clever take on the low-budget aesthetics of the horror film genre, but what else? The "what else" was nothing less than the panic produced by the political and economic collapse of Argentina in December 2001, when people's savings had indeed vanished and several protestors were killed by police, raising the specter of the country's not-so-distant history of state violence. *Panic,* like *Women Dreamt Horses,* pointed to the failure of political and artistic representation in a way that was lost on audience members who were unfamiliar with the events that the plays intentionally failed to represent.[63]

Alberto Pedro Torriente's comedy *Manteca* (1993), which appears in this volume, deals with some overlapping issues but from a quite different vantage point. The play was written during the "special period" following the collapse of the Soviet Union when Cuba was experiencing severe shortages of everything, including food. Like José Triana's *Night of the Assassins,* it deals with three siblings who are stuck in one room debating whether or not to commit an act of violence; this time, however, they are trapped between their hunger and their apprehension in the face of global capitalism. The characters—a communist, a gay writer, and a homemaker—are representative "types" in the *costumbrista* tradition, yet the play's philosophical bent and its cultivated air of mystery subtly complicate the politics of representation by showing that there is more to identity than meets the eye.

In light of this, it is interesting to note that in the United States Pedro Torriente would most likely be known as a black playwright, as would Triana, who is mulatto. Yet Cuban critics seldom mention their race, even when referring to their plays that deal explicitly with this issue. The relationship among race, art, and self-representation is not universal, and as with all of the plays in this book it is crucial to keep in mind that concepts about identity that are often taken for granted here (though they have not gone uncontested) do not necessarily hold sway in all Latin American countries. Taking plays out of their original context can create interpretive challenges, as it did in the case of the aforementioned Argentine plays performed in New York; yet de- and re-contextualization can also provide new repertoires that make old problems more visible. Abdias do Nascimento, for instance, decided to form Brazil's Experimental Black Theater in 1944 after taking offense at a performance in Lima of Eugene O'Neill's *The Emperor Jones* in which the protagonist was performed by a white actor in blackface.[64] *Manteca,* on the other hand, is deeply concerned with the rise of xenophobia that has accompanied globalization, but it can also be seen as an implicit challenge to the paradigm of identity politics that has recently predominated in the United States.

Other artists have developed performatic trans-genres that parody, contest, or simply fly in the face of commonplace notions about Latin American "identity." The "essential theater" of the Brazilian solo artist Denise Stoklos combines everything from vaudeville, pantomime, and Brechtian epic theater to Greek tragedy, relying on corporeal expression to bend the limits of intercultural communication. Stoklos performs in Portuguese, Spanish, English, Ukranian, and Russian, and, although her work deals with political and historical themes, her minimalist stage sets are deliberately unplaceable. In this volume we have included her 1987 performance piece *Mary Stuart,* which reimagines the events surrounding Elizabeth I's execution of Mary Stuart as a way of exploring the transhistorical and transcultural reality of state power. Stoklos's mordant and hilarious commentary on the shared experience of violence across time and space enacts the difficulty of breaking through the political and linguistic barriers signified by the "isolated" language of her country. The Mexican performance artist and playwright Jesusa Rodríguez and her partner, Argentine composer and singer Liliana Felipe, create satires that jumble together opera, carpa, teatro de revista, German-style cabaret, and indigenous drama. One of their most recent works, *Pastorela Terrorista* (2003), is a parodic critique of the war on Iraq that subverts the conventions of the *pastorela* or shepherd's play; rather than a Christian battle between good and evil, it is a battle between bad and worse whose protagonists include George W. Bush, Tony Blair, Ariel Sharon, and the head honchos of transnational corporations. The cabaret-style bar and theater in Mexico City that Rodríguez and Felipe managed for fifteen years (they recently passed it on to a group of younger women) hosts concerts, political discussions, and appearances by well-known artists such as the Mexican-Mayan-Lebanese show woman Astrid Hadad and Tito Vasconcelos, who has revitalized the time-honored tradition of drag.[65]

Astrid Hadad in a modern-day homage to the Aztec goddess Coatlicue. From Hadad's performance piece *Heavy Nopal.* Photo by Cheryl Bellows.

Professional artists are not the only ones who are putting old performance practices to new uses. In January 2000, tens of thousands of indigenous Ecuadorians converged on Quito demanding an end to economic policies imposed by the International Monetary Fund. Over the next few days they camped out in parks and plazas, where people of different cultural groups performed music and danced for each other and the city's urban residents. On January 21, they occupied the National Congress, forced the unpopular president to resign, and conducted a ritual *limpieza,* or "cleansing," before inaugurating a short-lived People's Parliament. Many of the events were televised, and participants made it clear that their intended audience was larger than local—it included other native peoples throughout the Americas and the millions of Ecuadorian immigrants living abroad, as well as the international business community.

Some of the most interesting developments in Latin America today, in terms of both politics and performance, are taking place in the context of indigenous movements. In Bolivia, the inauguration of the country's first indigenous president in January 2006 was accompanied by celebrations that included traditional dances and songs, as well as skits and puppet shows. In Mexico, the Zapatistas have gained international attention with their armed struggle for economic justice and their use of video and the Internet to articulate a very different vision of indigenous identity, one that denies the legitimacy of the state. The final piece in this book—*The Demon's Nun,* written by Petrona de la Cruz Cruz and Isabel Juárez Espinosa—might seem like a more regional effort. But while Cruz Cruz and Juárez Espinosa work primarily in their native Chiapas, where their women's theater cooperative also runs literacy and job-training programs, their plays have been performed all over the Americas, and they connect local realities to international phenomena such as tourism, migration, and religious evangelization.

In the plays, performance pieces, and introductory essays that follow, we hope to illustrate the many interconnected ways in which theater and performance practices function as meaning-making systems for their audiences. These works, stages of conflict, reveal the fraught histories and perspectives that form cultural memories and political identities in Latin America. Theater and performance practices cover the spectrum—from a theater of colonization to a theater of the oppressed that counters colonization, from performances of repression to performances of resistance. They are unstable practices, but they are vital ones because they not only reveal but also help constitute the ways societies think about themselves. *Stages of Conflict* includes works that illuminate how traditions, genres, and themes pass on through generations, worked and reworked to convey current concerns and envision new resolutions. While a five-hundred-year scope cannot begin to do justice to the diversity and complexity of these traditions, it does enable readers to appreciate the ways in which performance practices seldom disappear; rather, they undergo transformations of function and form. These continuities, which are also indexes of change, are what allow us to think of *Latin American theater and performance* as a coherent topic, even though regional, linguistic, and ethnic variations are so distinct. This volume, the first of its kind in English, will hopefully open the way for more discussion, more publications, and more scholarship in this important field.

NOTES

1. Melveena McKendrick, *Theatre in Spain: 1490–1700* (Cambridge: Cambridge University Press, 1989), 6.

2. José de Acosta, *Natural and Moral History of the Indies,* trans. Frances López-Morillas (Durham: Duke University Press, 2002), book 5, chap. 30, 326–27.

3. Other examples, in addition to those cited in this essay, include Fray Diego Durán, *Book of the Gods and Rites, and The Ancient Calendar,* trans. and ed. Fernando Horcasitas and Doris Heyden (Norman: University of Oklahoma Press, 1971) and Durán's *History of the Indies of New Spain,* trans. Doris Heyden (Norman and London: University of Oklahoma Press, 1994); Hernán Cortés, "Third Letter," in *Letters from Mexico,* trans. Anthony Pagden (New Haven: Yale University Press, 1986); and Bernabe Cobo, *Inca Religion & Customs,* trans. Roland Hamilton (Austin: University of Texas Press, 1990).

4. For a more extended treatment of this topic, see Diana Taylor, "Scenes of Cognition: Performance and Conquest," *Theatre Journal* 56 (October 2004): 353–72.

5. See Francisco Javier Clavijero's eighteenth-century work, *Historia Antigua de México,* book 2, chap. 43 (Mexico City: Porrúa, 1945), 300.

6. Women, according to the Franciscan missionary Bernardino de Sahagún, commonly "bailaban en corro" (danced in a circle). Quoted in Alfredo López Austin, *La educación de los antiguos nahuas,* vol. 2 (Mexico City: Secretaría de Educación Pública, 1985), 37.

7. Spanish friar Diego de Landa, *Yucatan Before and After the Conquest,* trans. William Gates (Mexico City: Editorial San Fernando, 1993), 58–59.

8. See Bernardino de Sahagún, *General History of the Things of New Spain: Florentine Codex* (Santa Fe: School of American Research, 1950–1982), especially books 8 and 9.

9. David Stuart, "La ideología del sacrificio entre los Mayas," *Arqueología Mexicana* 11, no. 63 (2003): 28.

10. María Sten, *Vida y muerte del teatro Náhautl* (Veracruz: Biblioteca Universidad Veracruzana, 1982), 14.

11. The earliest known reference to a "dance of Moors and Christians" is from 1150. Some scholars claim that the tradition has popular roots, though Max Harris traces it to royal tournaments and court festivities and believes that it did not become a regular practice until the fifteenth century. See Harris's *Aztecs, Moors, and Christians: Festivals of Reconquest in Mexico and Spain* (Austin: University of Texas Press, 2000).

12. For a version of *The Destruction of Jerusalem,* as well as several other texts of Nahuatl religious drama, see Marilyn Ekdahl Ravicz, ed., *Early Colonial Religious Drama in Mexico: From Tzompantli to Golgotha* (Washington, D.C.: Catholic University Press, 1970). Recent translations of several Nahuatl plays have also been published in Barry D. Sell and Louise M. Burkhart, eds., *Nahuatl Theater: Death and Life in Colonial Nahua Mexico* and *Nahuatl Theater: Our Lady of Guadalupe* (Norman: University of Oklahoma Press, 2004), the first two of a projected four-volume series.

13. The Spanish spectator was Fray Toribio Motolinía, and the performance is described in his *History of the Indians of New Spain.* Cited in Harris, *Aztecs, Moors, and Christians,* 137.

14. Rather than dying out, the tradition of the Atahualpa dance-drama seems to be spreading; in several towns, it was introduced only recently by individuals who witnessed performances in other villages or by professional theater companies. For a description and analysis of several recent performances, see Luis Millones, *Actores de altura: Ensayos sobre el teatro popular andino* (Lima: Editorial Horizonte, 1992).

15. Maya Ramos Smith, ed., *Censura y teatro novohispano (1539–1822)* (Mexico City: CONACULTA, INBA, CITRU, 1998).

16. In his book *Africans in Colonial Mexico: Absolutism, Christianity, and Afro-Creole Consciousness, 1570–1640* (Bloomington: Indiana University Press, 2003), Hermann L. Bennett shows how the Church's decision to classify Africans as "Old World" residents led to divergent experiences for the colonized. It meant that Africans, unlike the indigenous, could be tried under the Inquisition, and they accounted for nearly 50 percent of all cases in New Spain. He claims that Spanish mastery of blacks in spectacles of the Inquisition and as objects of "conspicuous consumption" served as cultural capital that underwrote the conquest of the indigenous: "Like writing, walled cities, wheat, olives, and wine, Spaniards relied on the servile African population to signify their cultural identity as the civilized" (20).

17. For a discussion of the differences among these terms, see Diana Taylor, "Cultural Memory and Identity: Mestizaje, Hybridity, and Transculturation," in *The Archive and The Repertoire* (Durham: Duke University Press, 2003).

18. See José Daniel Prego, "Y otra vez El Güegüence." *Tramoya* 33 (October–December 1992): 42–52.

19. Daniel G. Brinton, *El Güegüence: A Comedy Ballet in the Nahuatl-Spanish Dialect of Nicaragua* (1883 edition), xlii.

20. See Armando de María y Campos, *Guía de representaciones teatrales en la Nueva España, siglos XVI–XVIII* (Mexico: B. Costa-Amic, 1959), 49–50.

21. Ibid., 53.

22. Ricardo Silva-Santisteban, ed., *Antología general del teatro peruano,* vol. 2, *Teatro Colonial* (Lima: Pontificia Universidad Católica del Peru, 2000), xv.

23. See Lorena B. Ellis's study of Anchieta on the Hemispheric Institute's Web site: http://hemi.nyu.edu/course-nyu/perfconq04/sites/lorenasite/index.htm

24. Andrés Pérez de Ribas, *Corónica y historia religiosa de la Compañía de Jesús de México en Nueva España* (Mexico City: Imprenta del Sagrado Corazón de Jesús, 1896), vol. 1, book 5, chap. 4, 250. Thanks are due to Maya Ramos for identifying this work.

25. The original reads, "de maravillosa grandeza y gracia. Espantó ver su figura y forma tan al natural retratada. . . . En lo alto de este animal estaba sentado un Moreno en forma de rey, con su cetro en la mano y corona en la cabeza, representando muy al vivo al de Etiopia. Era cosa maravillosa" (ibid., 250).

26. María y Campos, in *Guía de representaciones teatrales,* describes the play and observes the following about popular performances in general: "As is typical with this type of representations, which are transmitted orally from generation to generation . . . the text, which the oldest actors preserve in their memory, is so altered, the words so disfigured, that in many cases the phrases do not even make sense, and undoubtedly even the actors do not know what they are reciting from memory. Only the spectator who is familiar with the episodes of our history will succeed in divining the course of the plot" (33).

27. Rodolfo Usigli, *Mexico in the Theater,* trans. Wilder P. Scott (University, Ms.: Romance Monographs, 1976), 56.

28. This is how the Argentine theater historian Adolfo Casablanca summed up the position of the viceroy, Don Juan José de Vértiz y Salcedo. The quote is from his *El teatro en la historia argentina* (Buenos Aires: Edición del Honorable Consejo Deliberante de la cuidad de Buenos Aires, 1994), 18.

29. Teodoro Klein, *El actor en el Río de la Plata,* vol. 1 (Buenos Aires: Ediciones Asociación Argentina de Actores, 1984), 12.

30. Viceroy Juan José de Vértiz y Salcedo, "Ynstrucción que deverá observarse para la representación de comedias en esta ciudad" (1783), quoted in Luis Ordaz, *Historia del teatro argentino* (Buenos Aires: Centro Editor de América Latina, 1982), 316.

31. Casablanca, *El teatro en la historia argentina,* 19.

Raúl Castagnino suggests that women of all classes and races shared the balcony in his *El teatro en Buenos Aires durante la época de Rosas,* vol. 1 (Buenos Aires: Academia Argentina de Letras, 1989), 57.

32. María y Campos, *Guía de representaciones teatrales,* 60.

33. See Jill Lane, *Blackface Cuba, 1840–1895* (Philadelphia: University of Pennsylvania Press, 2005). See, too, Rine Leal's prologue to the anthology *Teatro bufo, siglo XIX: Antología* (Havana: Editorial Arte y Literatura, 1975).

34. Rosario Castellanos, *The Eternal Feminine,* trans. Diane E. Marting and Betty Tyree, in *A Rosario Castellanos Reader: An Anthology of Her Poetry, Short Fiction, Essays, and Drama,* ed. Maureen Ahern (Austin: University of Texas Press, 1988), 273–367.

35. *La gringa* is translated as *The Foreign Girl* in Florencio Sánchez, *Representative Plays,* trans. William Knapp Jones (Washington, D.C.: Pan American Union, 1961). Although the play's aged, domesticated gaucho loses his land and ends up impoverished due to the actions of an industrious Italian immigrant, all turns out well when the son and daughter of the two antagonists fall in love. Other plays by Sánchez are not so optimistic; *Barranca abajo* (Down the Gully, 1905) ends with the impoverished gaucho committing suicide.

36. For information about the stadium and performances, along with photos, see Rubén Gallo, *Mexican Modernity: The Avant-Garde and the Technological Revolution* (Cambridge: MIT Press, 2005).

37. Adam Versényi, *Theatre in Latin America: Religion, Politics, and Culture from Cortés to the 1980s* (Cambridge: Cambridge University Press, 1993).

38. Rodolfo Usigli, *The Impostor,* trans. Ramón Layera in collaboration with Don Rosenberg (Pittsburgh: Latin American Literary Review Press, 2005).

39. Sabina Berman, *Between Pancho Villa and a Naked Woman,* trans. Shelley Tepperman. *Theatre Forum* 14 (1999): 91–108.

40. The 2002 film *Madame Satã,* directed by Karim Ainouz, is available in many U.S. libraries. It includes several scenes of the title character performing in the Blue Danube Club in Rio's bohemian Lapa district.

41. For more on race, the development of mass culture, and teatro de revista in Brazil, see Tiago de Melo Gomes, *Um Espelho no Palco: Identidades Sociais e Massificação da Cultura no Teatro de Revista dos Anos 1920* (Campinas: Editora UNICAMP, 2004).

42. Alejo Carpentier, *The Miracle of Anaquillé,* trans. Kathleen Ross, *Latin American Literary Review* 8 (spring–summer 1980): 55–62. It was not staged until 1960, after the Cuban Revolution. For another "Afro-Cuban ballet" by Carpentier, see *La Rebambaramba,* trans. Jill A. Nechinsky, *Latin American Literary Review* 15 (July–December 1987): 68–77.

43. See Vicky Unruh, *Latin American Vanguards: The Art of Contentious Encounters* (Berkeley: University of California Press, 1994).

44. José Triana, *Medea in the Mirror,* trans. Gwynne Edwards, in *The Methuen Book of Contemporary Latin American Plays* (London: Methuen Drama, 2004).

45. Griselda Gambaro, *Antígona furiosa,* in *Information for Foreigners: Three Plays by Griselda Gambaro,* trans. and ed. Marguerite Feitlowitz (Evanston: Northwestern University Press, 1992).

46. Ricardo Monti, *The Obscurity of Reason,* in *Reason Obscured: Nine Plays,* trans. and ed. Jean Graham-Jones (Lewisburg, Pa.: Bucknell University Press, 2004).

47. Nelson Rodrigues, *The Wedding Dress,* trans. Fred M. Clark (Valencia: Albatros, 1980). Many of Rodrigues's plays have been adapted for film; the most popular is Arnaldo Jabor's 1973 *Toda Nudez Será Castigada* (All Nudity Shall Be Punished).

48. There was a time in the 1970s when classical Greek plays were banned by the dictatorship in Greece while Latin American plays were staged, whereas ancient drama was passed over by Latin American censors who banned works from their own regions.

49. René Marqués, *The Oxcart,* trans. Charles Pilditch (New York: Scribner, 1969).

50. Alfredo Dias Gomes, *Payment as Pledged,* trans. Oscar Fernández, in *The Modern Stage in Latin America: Six Plays,* ed. George W. Woodyard (New York: Dutton, 1971). The play was made into a 1962 film that became the only Brazilian film ever to win the Palme d'Or prize at the Cannes Film Festival.

51. Ariano Suassuna, *The Rogue's Trial,* trans. Dillwyn F. Ratcliff (Berkeley: University of California Press, 1963). The English title of the film version, distributed by Columbia Tristar, is *A Dog's Will.*

52. See Emilio Carballido, *I, Too, Speak of the Rose,* trans. William Oliver, in *The Modern Stage in Latin America: Six Plays.* For a collection of translations of Carballido's work, see *The Golden Thread, and Other Plays,* trans. Margaret Sayers Peden (Austin: University of Texas Press, 1970).

53. See Randy Martin, *Socialist Ensembles: Theater and State in Cuba and Nicaragua* (Minneapolis: University of Minnesota Press, 1994).

54. For plays by Gambaro in English, see Feitlowitz, *Information for Foreigners.*

55. Diana Taylor, *Theatre of Crisis: Drama and Politics in Latin America* (Lexington: University Press of Kentucky, 1991), 7.

56. Enrique Buenaventura, "Theatre and Culture," trans. Joanne Pottlitzer, *TDR: The Drama Review* 14 (winter 1970): 156.

57. See Marco Antonio de la Parra, *The Theatre of Marco Antonio de la Parra: Translations and Commentary,* trans. Charles Philip Thomas (New York: P. Lang, 1995).

58. See Eduardo A. Pavlovksy, *Three Plays,* trans. Paul Verdier (Hollywood: Stages Theatre Press, 1994).

59. For the text of *San Pablo Dirigente,* which was staged during Holy Week of 1976 in the prison's dining hall, see Sonia Gutiérrez, ed., *Teatro popular y cambio social en América Latina* (San José: Editorial Universitaria Centroamericana, 1979), 424–51.

60. More on Eltit, including translations of excerpts from her novel *Lumpérica,* can be found in Diana Taylor and Roselyn Costantino, eds., *Holy Terrors: Latin American Women Perform* (Durham: Duke University Press, 2003). For a multimedia look at CADA and the Escena Avanzada, a related movement, see Antonia Thompson's "Repasos: Art and Life in Chile under Pinochet," on the Hemispheric Institute's Web site: http://hemi .nyu.edu/cuaderno/repasos/index.html#

61. Ariel Dorfman, *Death and the Maiden* (New York: Penguin, 1992). Roman Polanski's 1995 film version, starring Sigourney Weaver, was also very successful.

62. See Sabina Berman, *The Theatre of Sabina Berman: The Agony and the Ecstasy and Other Plays,* trans. Adam Versényi (Carbondale: Southern Illinois University Press, 2003). Rascón Banda's *Murder with Malice* appears in Carlos Morton, ed., *The Fickle Finger of Lady Death and Other Plays* (New York: Peter Lang, 1996).

63. See *BaiT: Buenos Aires in Translation,* trans. and ed. Jean Graham-Jones (New York: Martin E. Segal Theatre Center, 2008). In addition to Veronese's *Women Dreamt Horses* and Spregelburd's *Panic,* this collection also includes Lola Arias's *A Kingdom, a Country or a Wasteland, in the Snow* and Federico León's *Ex-Antwone,* both of which were also performed as part of the festival at Performance Space 122 in New York during November 2006.

64. See his 1959 play in Abdias do Nascimento, *Sortilege* (Black Mystery), trans. Peter Lownds (Chicago: Third World Press, 1978). See, too, his 1979 play *Sortilege II: Zumbi Returns,* in *Crosswinds: An Anthology of Black Dramatists in the Diaspora,* ed. William B. Branch (Bloomington: Indiana University Press, 1993).

65. For translations of pieces by Denise Stoklos, Jesusa Rodríguez, and Astrid Hadad, and for critical essays on their work, see Taylor and Costantino, *Holy Terrors.* On Tito Vasconcelos, see Antonio Prieto, "Camp, Carpa, and Cross-Dressing in the Theater of Tito Vasconcelos," in *Corpus Delecti: Performance Art of the Americas,* ed. Coco Fusco (London: Routledge, 2000).

GUATEMALA

Rabinal Achi

Rabinal Achi (Man of Rabinal in English), also
known as *Quiché Vinak* (Lord of Quiché) and
Xajoj Tun (Dance of the Trumpets), provides an
invaluable glimpse at the highly ritualized nature of ancient Amerindian performance. The
two warriors, the Rabinal warrior and the
Queché, are locked in a stylized battle that
ends with the death by sacrifice of the latter.
The plot is straightforward: the Queché warrior
attacks the neighboring people of Rabinal and
is caught by their warrior, the king's son. Codes
of honor govern the ways in which the captors
treat their illustrious captive. While it is clear to
all from the onset that the Queché warrior must
die, he will be shown every honor until the
final moment.

The play consists of verbal and physical
dueling as the two characters literally go
around and around—dancing, fighting, and
challenging each other. The action moves from
the present of captivity into the past as we discover the acts and ancient animosities that provoked the current crisis. The plotline, then, is
almost circular. The end brings us up to the
present moment and moves on to the foresee-
able end—the death of the Queché warrior on
the sacrificial stone.

Woodcut illustration of the Rabinal Warrior and the
Queché Warrior from the Mayan dance-drama *Rabinal
Achi*. Artist unknown. (Reproduced in Francisco
Monterde, ed., *Teatro indígena prehispánico (Rabinal Achi)*.
Mexico City: Universidad Nacional Autónoma de México,
1979.)

The circularity is reinforced by the repetitive nature of the dialogue as
each actor sums up what the other has said before adding his own words. In
part, the repetition is an integral characteristic of the oral tradition. Peoples
without writing need a repetitive, codified mnemonic structure in order to
remember. Pragmatics rather than aesthetics originally dictated these stylistic
choices. Still, what we know is inseparable from how we know it. In other
words, the Maya-Quiché worldview of cosmic order and balance is intri-
cately embedded in the circularity of expression. This circularity underlines
what French scholar Georges Raynaud in 1928 identified as pre-Conquest
notions of equilibrium and parallelism—pairs, balanced images, matching
dialogues, mirrored movements, and so forth.[1] Nonetheless, the stark oppo-
sitionality at the heart of the work, reflected concretely by the two warriors
confronting each other in the circle of seemingly endless motion, also points
to the Mesoamerican sense of conflict at the very center of the cosmos. The

universe, for the Mesoamericans, was both perpetually in circular motion and at risk of ending abruptly due to warring elements that need to be confronted and vanquished daily.

Rabinal Achi belongs to a tradition that Angel María Garibay, in *Historia de la literatura náhuatl,* calls the "baile de los cautivos" (dance of captives). Garibay makes a connection between this work and the pre-Conquest practice of highly ritualized human sacrifices, which involved elaborate costumes and codified acts.[2] Some scholars believe the work dates to pre-Conquest times untouched by European influences. Raynaud claimed in the 1920s "that this is the only work of ancient Amerindian theatre that has reached us in which we cannot discover a trace—either in form, in content, in words, ideas, or events—of European origin."[3] Others couch such claims. The U.S. scholar Dennis Tedlock, for example, argues that it is a "direct descendant" of "one of the most popular plays to emerge during the early colonial period" and that it "had an all-Mayan cast of characters speaking all-Mayan dialogue, featured Mayan music played on long wooden trumpets, and dramatized the capture and sacrifice of a prisoner of war."[4] He notes European influences in the text but stresses that Mayans did not simply adopt European performance modes wholesale. According to Tedlock, the work centers on events that took place during the reign of Quicab, the most famous Quiché king, who led an expansionist campaign in the late fourteenth and early fifteenth centuries. A revolt initiated by Quicab's son (the possible model for Cawek, the Queché Warrior in the play) was responsible for the unauthorized invasion of the neighboring regions of Rabinal and Cakchiquel. However, Tedlock states that "as a representation of Mayan culture, and the culture of Mayan royalty in particular, it reaches much deeper into the past"—at least to the classical period, which lasted from the fourth through the tenth centuries.[5]

In one version or another—not necessarily the one we have inherited—*Rabinal Achi* is likely a song-dance (*mitote*) from the fifteenth century. References to *danzas del tun* (dance of the trumpets) can be found in sixteenth-century documents prepared by the Inquisition that prohibit them.[6] In 1702, Fray Francisco Ximénez referred to a song-dance that "the Quiché Indians continue to celebrate in their dances, for they do not dance others in their fiestas except this one, that they call Quiché-Vinac, that means Lord of the Quiché."[7] *Rabinal Achi* has been performed periodically for the past three hundred years during the *fiestas patronales* (patron saint's day festivals) held in January in the town of Rabinal, Guatemala. An elder, Bartolo Zis, the *holpop* (singer/performance specialist) who performed the play, wrote down his memory of it as "Baile del Tun" in 1850.[8] In 1855 he dictated a version of the play to a French priest, Charles Etienne Brasseur, who saw the danced performance. Brasseur transcribed it in Quiché and translated it from Quiché into French in 1862 with the help of three native specialists. Years later Raynaud complained that Brasseur's translation indirectly introduced a "nefarious European influence"—that is, the fact that religion plays almost no role in the work and that the number of warriors (thirteen, a number sacred to the Mesoamericans) was changed to twelve, which had particular significance for the Europeans.[9] This should be kept in mind when reading the translation included in this volume, which is based on Brasseur's version.

The textual basis and "authenticity" of indigenous performance practices have long been debated and contested in the Americas. Original documents disappear, copies and transcriptions lead to errors, and translations vary in their faithfulness to the spirit and language of the original. To further complicate matters, it is important to remember that "originals" are based on actual performance practices that undergo change. While performance specialists guarded the script (and continue to do so in many native performance traditions), actors never memorized the lines exactly. The relationship between the script and the performed event has always been a fluid one. So which is the "authentic" cultural manifestation? This is not simply a problem that plagues historical scholarship in this field. New versions, such as Dennis Tedlock's recent translation, are often influenced by the specific performances in which the translators participated. The live, changing relationship between the performed and scripted works is a characteristic of indigenous performance practice both past and present.

As important as examining the text, then, is an understanding of the context of the performance. *Rabinal Achi,* like many quasi-religious dance-dramas, requires ritual preparation by participants. For the 1955 celebration of this work, according to one observer, "a series of rites were performed in the twenty days preceding the performance, and sexual continence was required of everyone connected with the performance for thirty days before and thirty days after the performance."[10] These mandates were accompanied by others: salutation and offerings to the surrounding hills, prayer, the drinking of *aguardiente* (cane alcohol), and the preparation and blessing of the costumes, masks, and musical instruments before the performance.[11] And, like almost all indigenous performances, this one is staged outdoors either in the plaza or in front of the church. Tedlock, who saw the dance in 1998, describes "a theater of four sides and four corners, like the four sides and corners of the Mayan world."[12] The Costa Rican performance specialist Alejandro Tosatti, who witnessed the same performance, mentions that the best position from which to view the play is from the church, as the performance is staged for the holy image inside rather than the people standing around outside. The coexistence of pre- and post-Conquest elements is not surprising. Many traditional Amerindian performances are multilayered and double or triple coded as pre-Conquest elements hide behind contemporary forms, adapting in order to stay vital. While they may retain elements that predate the arrival of the Europeans, their current enactment is often linked to events in the Christian calendar. *Rabinal Achi* now celebrates the feast days of Saint Sebastian (January 20) and Saint Paul (January 25), the patron saint of Rabinal. As these performances were frequently targeted by the Inquisition and government edicts, they often underwent change in order to placate the authorities. Originally, as Tedlock notes, the dance-dramas were sung and danced not recited. But since the Conquest indigenous "dramatists" seeking to keep "the memory of Mayan court drama" alive and avoid censorship have "separated the words from the music and removed all but the outlines of the original

religious content from public view. To this day, the dialogue is spoken by actors rather than sung by a chorus, and the dance music is purely instrumental."[13] As time passes, the performances outlast social memory. They become
a way of both remembering and forgetting what came before. That is, while
the adaptations in form and calendar were responses to specific kinds of social pressure, the people who enact them may very well have forgotten that
the pressures brought about the change in the first place. For some dancers
today, the performance is offered up to the holy image in the Catholic
Church, and it is not certain that they recall that the change in venue was an
adaptive one initially forced by the conquering Christian powers.

Now, as before, the fiestas involve many events and performances taking
place at the same time. The performance is only part of a much larger celebration that includes worship, feasting, drinking, socializing, and other activities. Dancers in the *Rabinal Achi* wear elaborate costumes and masks. They
dance and recite, though their words are often incomprehensible—at times
because the words are archaic, at times because the masks muffle the voices.[14]
Both men and women perform. The musical instruments seem much the
same as those mentioned in documents four hundred years ago: two trumpets, a *tun* (sacred drum), wood and clay instruments, and flutes. Maracas
made of gourds and gourds with metal wires are also used, as are marimbas.

Nowadays, dancers perform this ancient work only sporadically. For one
thing, its presentation involves a major commitment of economic and human
resources; dancers have to commit to dance seven years in a row, memorize
long speeches, and make their masks and costumes. Interestingly, sometimes
outsiders will underwrite the costs for specific reasons. The 1998 performance was paid for by the International Red Cross to underline the concept
of treating one's enemies honorably in an area devastated by decades of civil
war. Yet the aim of the sponsors might have little to do with the intentions of
the performers. And, although the dance-drama is not regularly staged, it receives only passing attention from spectators. The performance event has no
clear beginning or end. At times it starts up and peters out only to start up
again later. Rabinal and other traditional indigenous communities have no
tradition of watching a play as if it were Western-style theater. Spectators
come and go. There is no such thing as a "director." The keeper of the script,
rather, coaches the actors with their lines and checks for orthodoxy. Performers seem to address religious forces rather than the immediate audience; they
conceal their identities—they are, as Alejandro Tosatti calls them, *danzantes
de fe* (dancers of faith) who see their participation as a form of religious and
social debt payment—not entertainment. There is little dramatic action, and
the movement is slow and repetitive. Nonetheless, an important drama is
staged every time the performance takes place—the drama of communal
memory itself: interrupted, sporadic, often ignored, yet always vital to the
way the community thinks about itself.

—Diana Taylor

NOTES

1. See the appendix by Georges Raynaud (1928) in *Teatro indígena prehispánico (Rabinal Achí)*, ed. Francisco Monterde (Mexico City: Universidad Nacional Autónoma de México, Biblioteca de Estudiante Universitario, 1979), 133.

2. Garibay refers to the "procession and exhibition and skirmishes of those who don the skins of the sacrificial victims" and the "mock battle" that typically preceded sacrifice, as well as the incredible adornments—eagles, jaguars, and so on—which are "of great theatricality, because with astounding agility, they come and go, they join hands, they bow down until they touch the earth, as though lying down, they rise up violently, they look to one side and then the other, they simulate battles, they leap" (334).

3. Raynaud, appendix, 123. José Juan Arrom writes that the work "seems to be the legacy (*supervivencia*) of an authentic indigenous representation, not contaminated with later contact with Spanish forms." Arrom, *Teatro hispanoamericano colonial* (Havana: Anuario Bibliográfico Cubano, 1956), 13.

4. Tedlock, *Rabinal Achi: A Mayan Drama of War and Sacrifice* (Oxford: Oxford University Press, 2003), 2.

5. Ibid., 1.

6. Anita Padial Guerchoux and Manuel Vázquez-Bigi, *Quiché Vinak, tragedia* (Mexico City: Fondo de Cultura Económica, 1991), 43.

7. Ibid., 18.

8. He wrote that on "October 28, 1850, I transcribed the original of this Baile del Tun, property of our city of San Pablo de Rabinal, in order to leave my descendants a memory, which will endure forever with them.—Let it be thus. —Bartolo Zis." Quoted in Monterde, *Teatro indígena prehispánico,* xiii–xiv.

9. Raynaud, appendix, 136.

10. Richard E. Leinaweaver, "Rabinal Achi: Commentary," *Latin American Theatre Review* 1 (spring 1968): 11

11. Ibid., 13

12. Tedlock, *Rabinal Achi,* 246.

13. Ibid., 2.

14. Dennis Tedlock and Alejandro Tosatti, two scholars present at the 1998 performance, tell slightly different versions. Tedlock says that actors can be heard through the gills in the masks, though both Tedlock and Tosatti agree that what they say is often unintelligible. According to Tedlock, the language includes "the sounds of ancient words whose meaning is no longer clear and the names of places whose locations have been forgotten" (*Rabinal Achi,* 11). Tosatti refers to the "inaudible and incomprehensible verbal duel that reconstructs the vicissitudes of war." (Personal communication to Diana Taylor, San Juan, Costa Rica, 2002.)

SELECTED REFERENCES

Acuña, René. *Introducción al estudio del Rabinal Achí.* Mexico City: Universidad Nacional Autónoma de México, 1975.

Arrom, José Juan. *Teatro hispanoamericano colonial.* Havana: Anuario Bibliográfico Cubano, 1956.

Breton, Alain. Introduction to *Rabinal Achi, un drama dinástico maya del siglo XV.* Mexico and Guatemala: Centro Francés de Estudios Mexicanos y Centroamericanos, 1999.

Mace, Carroll E. *Two Spanish-Quiché Dance-Dramas of Rabinal.* New Orleans: Tulane Studies in Romance Languages and Literature 3. Tulane University, 1970.

Monterde, Francisco, ed. *Teatro indígena prehispánico (Rabinal Achí).* Mexico City: UNAM and Biblioteca de Estudiante Universitario, 1979.

Muñoz Castillo, Fernando. *Teatro maya peninsular: Precolombino y evangelizador.* Mérida: Capital Americana de la Cultura, 2000.

Padial Guerchoux, Anita, and Manuel Vázquez-Bigi. *Quiché Vinak, tragedia.* Mexico City: Fondo de Cultura Económica, 1991.

Schele, Linda, and Mary Ellen Miller. *The Blood of Kings: Dynasty and Ritual in Maya Art.* New York and Fort Worth: George Braziller and the Kimbell Art Museum, 1986.

Sodi M., Demetrio. *La literatura de los maya.* Mexico City: Editorial Joaquín Mortiz, 1964.

Tedlock, Dennis. *Rabinal Achi: A Mayan Drama of War and Sacrifice.* Oxford: Oxford University Press, 2003.

Westlake, E. J. *Our Land Is Made of Courage and Glory: Nationalist Performance of Nicaragua and Guatemala.* Carbondale: Southern Illinois University Press, 2005.

Rabinal Achi

Translated by Richard E. Leinaweaver

CHARACTERS:

CHIEF FIVE-RAIN, Governor of the town of Rabinal
RABINAL WARRIOR, highest dignitary among the warriors; son of Five-Rain
QUECHÉ WARRIOR, Governor of the Grand Council of Cunen and Chahul, son of the
    Wizard of the Warriors, Wizard of the Woven Bundle, Governor of the Queché men
The WIFE of Chief Five-Rain
PRECIOUS EMERALD, Mother of the Green Feathers, Mother of the Green Birds,
    promised bride of the Rabinal Warrior
IXOK-MUN, servant
A SERVANT of the Rabinal Warrior
Twelve YELLOW EAGLES, twelve YELLOW JAGUARS, young warriors of the town of
    Rabinal[1]
Numerous WARRIORS, numerous SERVANTS

The action takes place in Cakyug-Zilic-Cakocaonic-Tepecanic.[2]

SCENE ONE

In front of the fortress
(The RABINAL WARRIOR and his people dance in a circle. The QUECHÉ WARRIOR suddenly arises and begins to dance in the middle of the circle moving his short spear as if he intends to wound the RABINAL WARRIOR in the head. With each revolution the movement of the circle becomes more rapid.)

QUECHÉ WARRIOR: Come here, odious chief, despicable chief! Will you be the first whose very root, whose trunk, I cannot cut; that chief of the Chacach, of the Zaman, the Caük of Rabinal![3] This I swear to do before heaven and earth; and for this reason I need say no more. Heaven and earth be with thee, oh most remarkable of the stalwarts—Warrior of Rabinal.

RABINAL WARRIOR: *(As he starts to dance he twirls a lasso with which he threatens to subdue his enemy.)* Aha! Courageous warrior. Chief of the Cavek Queché. Thus you spoke before heaven and earth: "Come near, odious chief, despicable chief. Will you be the only one whose very root, whose trunk I cannot cut. I, chief of the Chacach, of the Zaman, the Caük of Rabinal." Did you not say that? Yes, by all means! Heaven and earth bear witness! Surrender to the son of my arrow, to the son of my shield, to my mace, to my stranger's axe, my net, my accoutrements, to my

sacrificial earth,[4] to my magic herbs, to my vigor, to my courage. Be it thus or no, before heaven and earth will I bind you with my strong lasso. Heaven and earth be with thee, courageous warrior, my prisoner and my captive!

(He snares him with the lasso, which he pulls in order to bring his prisoner towards him. The music stops and the dance is interrupted. There is a prolonged silence during which both men, feigning anger, face each other, without musical accompaniment or dancing.)

Now, valiant warrior, my prisoner and my captive. Already your heaven and earth wither! Truly the heaven and earth have delivered you to the son of my arrow, to the son of my shield, to my stranger's mace, to my net, to my accoutrements, to my sacrificial earth, to my magic herbs. Speak now. Reveal the location of your mountains and of your valleys; and if you were born on the side of a mountain, at the back of a valley.[5] Are you not a son of the clouds, a son of the mist? Have you not come flying before spears, before war? Thus speaks my voice before heaven and earth. For this reason I will speak briefly. Heaven and earth be with thee, prisoner and captive!

QUECHÉ WARRIOR: Ah, heaven and earth hear me! Is it true that you said that, that you threw such absurd words at heaven, at the earth, to my lips and my

---

face?[6] That I am a courageous man, a stalwart man? Thus spoke your voice. Come, come! Would I be courageous? Come, come! Would I be a stalwart man and would I have come hurled by spears, by war? But here you also said: "Speak. Reveal the location of your mountains, your valleys." Thus you spoke. Come, come! Would I be courageous? Come, come! Would I be stalwart and at the same time would I tell, would I reveal the description of my mountains, the description of my valleys? Is it not clear as day that I was born on the side of a mountain, on the side of a valley, that I am the son of the clouds, the son of the mist? Come, come! Would I reveal, would I make known my mountains, my valleys? Rather that the skies and the earth disappear. For this reason I speak briefly, remarkable among the stalwarts, Warrior of Rabinal. Heaven and earth be with thee!

(The dance is renewed—the music starts to play.)

RABINAL WARRIOR: Wait! Valiant warrior! My prisoner, my captive. Does your voice speak thus to the face of heaven, to the face of the earth? "Come, come, would I be courageous? Come, come, would I be a stalwart one, by revealing my mountains, my valleys. Is it not clear as day that I was born on the side of a mountain, on the side of a valley—I, the son of the clouds, the son of the mists?" Did not your voice speak thus? Very well, if you will not reveal the description of your mountains, the description of your valleys—heaven and earth witness that I will make you go, dead or in chains, before my governor, before my ruler, to my vast walls, in my vast fortress. Thus do I speak before heaven and earth. Heaven and earth be with thee, my prisoner and my captive.

QUECHÉ WARRIOR: Ah, heaven and earth hear me! Your voice spoke thus before heaven and earth: "You can change and destroy the voices, the words which I speak to you before heaven, before earth. Now I have something to compel the birth of these words, something to compel their departure, something to force you to reveal the description of your mountains, the description of your valleys. If you do not tell them—if you do not reveal them, witness the heavens and the earth that I will make you go, dead or in chains, before my governor, my ruler." Thus spoke your voice before heaven and earth. Ah, heaven! Ah, earth! Whom should I tell, to whom reveal the description of my mountains, the description of my valleys? To you, oh birds, who sing like nightingales, to you, eagles? I, the courageous one, I, the stalwart man, chief of the Grand Council of Cunen, of the Grand Council of Chahul! I, the Wizard Chief of the Stalwart Ones, Wizard of the Woven Bundle, ten times have I come down the road from the clouds, from the mist, from my mountains, from my valleys to go to war. How to cause the words to descend, to cause the words to rise; the things that I

would speak to you before heaven, before earth? Heaven and earth be with you, remarkable among the warriors of Rabinal.

RABINAL WARRIOR: Courageous warrior of the Cavek Queché, are you my favorite? Are you my elder? Are you my younger brother? Wonderful! And how then could my heart have forgotten having seen you there in the vast walls, in the vast fortress! No doubt you were the one who imitated the bark of the coyote, the one who imitated the cry of the fox, the scream of the squirrel, of the jaguar outside those immense walls, in the vast fortress, in order to bring us, the white children, the white son, to you; in order to take us from the vast walls, before the vast fortress; in order to feed us with wild yellow honey, which our governor drinks, our ruler, our grandfather, Five-Rain.[7]

Therefore, why must you boast, as you have done, and provoke my determination, my bravery? Was it not those calls which provoked us, which brought us out, the twelve chiefs, each one chief of his rampart, of his fortress? Truly, did you not tell us: "Come here, young men, you twelve valiant young men, you twelve heroes; come and hear that which you must do, because all your food, all your drink are dissolved, consumed, destroyed, transformed into pumice stone.[8] Only the crickets, male and female, still make their song heard on the walls, in the fortress of those white children, of those white sons; for now almost nothing remains, only nine or ten of their houses and fortresses. There we have ceased feeding on the white children, on the white sons, because now we eat the fried dish, the great bean, the plate of crabs, the plate of parrots, the mixed plates."[9] Was this not the advice that you gave to the chiefs, to the warriors? Was there not something in this which went beyond the desires of your bravery and boldness? And at Beleh Mokoh, Beleh Chumay,[10] with that bravery, that boldness, had they not become accustomed to defeat, become accustomed to burial by our warriors, by our chiefs, in the places called Qotom and Tikiram?[11] Behold you must atone for this calamity under heaven, above the earth.

Thus, you have said your last good-bye to your mountains, to your valleys; because here we will sever your root, your trunk, under heaven, above earth. Nevermore will you be able to descend either by day or by night to your mountains, to your valleys. Now you must die here, here you will disappear,[12] between the sky and the earth. That is why I will announce you to my governor, to my ruler in the vast walls, in the vast fortress. Thus speaks my voice to the face of the sky and of the earth. For this reason I speak briefly. Heaven and earth be with thee, man of the Cavek Queché!

QUECHÉ WARRIOR: Eh! Valiant warrior, most remarkable among the stalwarts, Warrior of Rabinal! Is it thus your voice spoke before heaven and earth? "Why boast of my courage, of my daring?" Thus you spoke. It was they who first called, first provoked my governor, my ruler. This was the only reason for my coming, for my departure from my mountains, from my valleys. From here came the summoning message, between the heavens and the earth, in front of the ramparts of the commander of Cakyug-Zilic-Cakocaonic-Tepecanic, the names of the mouth and the eye of this fortress and of this castle. Was it not here that the ten loads of cacao were held, the five loads of perfect cacao[13] destined for my governor, my ruler, Wizard chief of the Warriors, Wizard of the Jaguar; names of the mouth and the eye of my fortress and my castle.

Since that message was presented, the chief, Wizard chief, Wizard of the Jaguar, for that reason desired the death of the Chacachs, of the Zaman, of the Caük of Rabinal, before the Uxab, before the Pokomames.[14] Let them say that you wish to see the courage, the daring, of the chief of the Queché mountains and valleys; to come and take possession of my beautiful mountains, of my beautiful valleys. Come, then, my brother and my elder. Come and take possession here between the sky and the earth, of these beautiful mountains, of these smiling valleys. Come and sow your seeds, build your lairs, there where the sprouts of our cucumbers grow among our fine pumpkins and the sprouts of our bean plants. By this he confirmed your defiance, your cry of summons, before my governor, my ruler. In this way the defiance, the war cry of my governor, my ruler, was offered: "Ah! My courageous one! My warrior, go sound the alarm and return immediately because a message of summons has arrived, one which arrived beneath the heavens, above the earth. Raise your vigor, your bravery, son of my arrow, son of my shield; return as soon as possible to the mountainsides, to the valley's slope." Thus came the challenge—the war cry of my governor, of my ruler.

I quickly departed. I put the landmarks there where the sun sets, where the night begins, where the cold tortures, where the ice tortures, in the place called Pan-Tzahaxak. Then I brandished the son of my arrow, the son of my shield. I came back to the side of the mountain, to the side of the valley. There, for the first time, I hurled my challenge, my war cry, before Cholochic-Huyu,[15] Cholochic-Chah[16] called thus. I went from there and in the same manner I hurled my challenge, my war cry, for the second time, to Nimché Paraveno,[17] to Cabrakan,[18] called thus. I went from there and hurled my challenge, my war cry, for the third time at a place named Panchalib.[19] I went from there. I was going to hurl for the fourth time my challenge, my war cry, to Xol-Chacach, called thus. It was there I found the twelve yellow eagles, the twelve

yellow jaguars, sounding the great drum of blood, the small drum of blood. The heavens shook, the earth trembled with the great noise, the great excitement of the twelve yellow eagles, the twelve yellow jaguars, reunited with the servants of the great warriors. My song began there to the face of the sky, to the face of the earth. "Come, come, odious and despicable chief!! Will you be the first whose root, whose trunk I will never sever; this chief of the Chacach, of the Zaman, the Caük of Rabinal?" Thus did I speak. What would you do, oh chief, since I have not been able to annihilate or destroy you; since I have only been able to voice my thoughts, to sing before heaven, before earth, remarkable among the stalwarts, Warrior of Rabinal? Speak now in your turn. Heaven and earth be with thee, remarkable among stalwarts, Warrior of Rabinal!

RABINAL WARRIOR: Ah! Valiant warrior; man of the Cavek Queché. Is it thus your voice spoke before heaven and earth? Are these words you have spoken truthful and without variance? "A message of summons truly departed from here; truly we were called to the Queché mountains, to the Queché valleys." But certainly it was no crime that we sent to hear him, the Wizard chief, the Jaguar Wizard, when he desired the death, the disappearance, of the chief of the Chacach, of the Zaman, of the Caük of Rabinal, by the Uxab, by the Pokomames, here under heaven, above earth. "Let us proceed so that the chief of the Queché mountains, of the Queché valleys, may come with his courage, with his daring. May he come and take possession of the beautiful mountains, of these rich valleys. May he come to plant, come to make his home." Well and good! Let us plant, let us make our homes, there where the sprouts of our fine cucumbers crowd among the sprouts of our good pumpkins and our good bean plants. Thus spoke our voice to the face of the sky, to the face of the earth.

That is why you provoked us needlessly, why you threatened us in vain, between the heavens and the earth. Thank heaven, thank earth, you have come to present yourself before our walls, our fortress. That is why we will accept the challenge: we will accept the strife; we will fight the Uxab and the Pokomames. Consequently I will instruct you as to the mission of the summons. Go. Run hard by the Royal Road where the bird drinks in the water; to the place called Cholochic-Zakchun.[20] But do not give in to those who would take you to the chiefs of the Uxab and the Pokomames. Do not allow them to return to their mountains, their valleys. Annihilate them! Destroy them! Here, between the heavens and the earth!

Thus spoke my voice. But in truth it was not necessary that you should see, that you should look at the Uxab, at the Pokomames, because they were transformed into flies, into butterflies, into an army of ants, large and small; and only their columns and files, showing brightly, ascended the slopes of the mountain called Equempek Ganahal.[21] Then I directed my eyes and my gaze toward the heavens and toward the earth; and in the very moment that I saw the Uxab, the Pokomames, my heart sank, my soul was hurt seeing you, observing that you had agreed to that which the Uxab, that which the Pokomames desired. Then I hurled my war cry, my challenge against you: Eh! Eh! valiant warrior, man of the Cavek Queché. Why do you move so easily among the Uxab and the Pokomames in their mountains, in their valleys? Heaven and earth hear me! Certainly they expected in our mountains, in our valleys, that you would hurl your challenge, your war cry, against the Uxab, against the Pokomames, those who had hurled back your challenge, your war cry? Ah! Ah! Let them return quickly, those chiefs of the Uxab, those chiefs of the Pokomames, to listen to my commands here between heaven and earth.

Thus spoke your voice. Then the chiefs of the Uxab, the chiefs of the Pokomames, answered you: "Eh, valiant warrior, man of the Cavek Queché, abandon this struggle in our mountains, in our valleys. Were we not born here, with our children, our sons, where the black clouds, the white clouds, come down, where the cold tortures, where the ice tortures, where there is nothing to envy? Far away, with my children, my sons, are found the branches, the green branches, the yellow cacao for the market, the fine yellow cacao, the gold, the silver, the embroideries, the golden jewelry. Here are my children; here are my sons; there, if they want to work, suffering does not exist for them, real or relative; even while you stand there, a load of cacao is arriving to be purchased, a load of fine cacao.[22] For they are embroiderers, sculptors, and goldsmiths and it will be so forever. But consider your children, look at the sons of the most remarkable one among the stalwarts, of the Warrior of Rabinal. With great pain, with great suffering they can barely subsist, and it will be thus forever. One of their legs is in front, another leg behind; there are only cripples and the one-armed;[23] the nephews, the grandsons of the most remarkable among the stalwarts, of the Warrior of Rabinal, from dawn to dusk, forever." Thus he answered to the challenge, the war cry, of the Uxab, of the Pokomames, because of the fury which devoured their hearts. And you replied to them: "Eh, eh! chiefs of the Uxab. Ah, chiefs of the Pokomames! Did your voices speak thus before heaven, before earth? In that which concerns those children, those sons of the Warrior of Rabinal, they do not blush over the means of their existence, their subsistence and their living is under the wide sky, at the four corners of the earth, from the peaks of the earth, to the sides of the

mountains; because they are vigorous, because they are brave and valorous. Your children, your sons, on the contrary, are lost, dispersed; they come and they go; they move in long lines, returning to their mountains, to their valleys. Perhaps from there only one or two may return to their walls, to their fortress, because they are annihilated, they are pursued while they search for their food, their source of living. Among the children, the sons of the valiant one, of the most remarkable warrior among the stalwarts, of the great Warrior of Rabinal, if one or two go away, then one or two come back to your walls, to your fortress." Thus spoke your voice to the chiefs of the Uxab and the Pokomames.

But this is what my voice said: Eh, eh! Courageous warrior, man of the Cavek Queché. The challenge, the war cry hurled by the Uxab, by the Pokomames, has been heard. Heaven and earth hear me! It was certain that they would be enraged on account of having to abandon their places between the heaven and the earth to our children, our sons. It was certain that they could not take possession of those beautiful mountains, of those smiling valleys. It is a miracle that you have come to end so many days and so many nights under heaven, above earth; that you have come to shatter the point of your arrow, the hardness of your shield; that you have come to break the force of your arms, the instrument of your power. You have obtained nothing and it is certain that you have taken possession of nothing under heaven, above earth. You know where the limits of your land are which form a junction at the sides of the mountains, at the start of the plains. It is also certain that *I* am the valiant one, the great warrior, remarkable among the stalwarts, the Warrior of Rabinal, who reigns constantly here with my children, with my sons, here between heaven and earth. Thus speaks my voice to the face of the sky, to the face of the earth. Heaven and earth be with you, valiant warrior, man of the Cavek Queché!

QUECHÉ WARRIOR: Ah! Ah! Hear me, heaven and earth! It is certain that I have not managed to take possession here, under heaven, above earth, of these beautiful mountains, of these smiling valleys. Was it useless, in vain, that I came here to conclude so many days, so many nights, under heaven, above earth? My courage, my bravery, therefore, have they served me naught? Heaven and earth hear me! Now let us go there, to my mountains, to my valleys. Thus speaks my voice before heaven, before earth. I walked along the sides of the mountain, at the start of the plain; there, on the point which is called Camba,[24] I placed my landmarks and here my voice spoke to the face of the sky, to the face of the earth. Could I not call the chief of Camba to come out, in order to crush him under my sandals, to place my sandals on the heads

of the children, the heads of the sons of the most remarkable among the stalwarts, of the great Warrior of
Rabinal?[25] Thus my heart speaks its lament. But even
if heaven and earth punished me, my voice would
still say: I will go away from here again to place my
landmarks at the peak of the mountain and at the
plain of Zaktihel;[26] and I will hurl my challenge, my
war cry. Ah, hear me, heaven and earth! Is it true that
I have taken possession of nothing here under
heaven, above earth? From there I came down immediately to the mouth of the river, and then I saw and
considered the freshly sown lands; the lands of the
yellow corn, of the yellow beans, of the white beans,
of the birds with talons. My voice then said this, before heaven, before earth: Can I not carry away a little
of this freshly sown earth, with the help of the son of
my arrow, the son of my shield? Then I took possession by imprinting my sandals there in the freshly
sown earth. From there I went immediately to plant
my markers over the Xtincurun point, in front of
Ximbalha, called thus.[27] I went from there, too: I
went to plant my markers at the point called Quezen-
tun; there I sang out because of the anguish in my
heart, during thirteen-times-twenty days, thirteen-
times-twenty nights,[28] because I had not succeeded
in taking possession of these beautiful mountains, of
these smiling valleys. Thus spoke my voice before
heaven and earth: Alas, heaven and earth! Hear me! Is
it true that I have succeeded in taking possession of
nothing here under heaven, above earth; that I came
uselessly, in vain, to waste many days, many nights?
Thus spoke my voice before heaven and earth. I
came, consequently, to the end of my strength, the
end of my energy; my valor, my daring, no longer
served me. My voice said this to the face of the sky, to
the face of the earth. I headed for our mountains, our
valleys. My heart now told me to run from mountainside to mountainside, to the side of the valleys; thus
spoke my voice. Heaven and earth be with thee, most
remarkable among stalwarts, Warrior of Rabinal!

RABINAL WARRIOR: Ah! Valiant one, warrior, man of
the Cavek Queché. My children! Why did you carry
off my children, my sons? You had nothing to do with
them. Leave them in their mountains, in their valleys.
If you do not leave them alone I will upset and overturn the earth and the sky. Thus said my challenge.
For I had gone away; I was occupied with placing the
landmarks of the earth there at the point called Mu-
cutzuum[29] when you kidnapped the white children,
my noble sons, at the point of your arrow, by the
force of your shield, without your heart caring to hear
my challenge, my war cry. Then I ran from mountainside to mountainside, to the sides of the valleys and
put my markers on the place called Panahachel.[30]
There I hurled my challenge, my war cry against you.
Only then and there did you release these beautiful

children, the white sons, there at the Great Woods of
Cabrakan Paraveno, called thus, at just a short distance from the Queché mountains, from the Queché
valleys. From there they returned, they ran from
mountainside to mountainside, to the sides of the valleys; with empty bellies, with hollow stomachs, they
returned. Nevertheless, they did not return to their
walls, to their fortresses, but they settled near the
place called Panamaka. Then you encountered my
governor, my ruler, there at the fountain called the
Bath of Tohil.[31] Was I not absent, was I not on the
point of placing the landmarks in the earth, there in
Tzamha, before the place called Qulavach-Abah?
Then once more I turned my eyes, my contemplation,
toward the heavens and the earth. Great was the horizon over which the clouds ran, the horizon where the
mists roll, before the high walls of the vast fortress.
There I hurled my challenge, my war cry, to the face
of the sky, to the face of the earth.

My voice spoke thusly: Eh, eh, valiant one, stalwart, man of the Cavek Queché! Why did you come
inside the vast walls, inside the vast fortress, to kidnap my governor, my father? You had nothing to do
with him. Permit him, then, to return inside his vast
walls, inside his palace! Thus spoke my voice; but
your heart was not touched by hearing my challenge, my war cry. My voice also said: If you do not
release my governor, my ruler, may heaven permit,
may the earth permit, that I overturn and upset the
earth and the sky. May the heavens run over, may the
earth run over. Thus spoke my voice. But your heart
was not disturbed hearing my challenge, my war cry.
Then I climbed up and down the slopes of the
mountains, to the flat plains, and I went to place my
landmarks among the vast walls, within the vast
fortress. But I saw only the horizon where the clouds
moved, the horizon where the mists rolled by constantly rising to the vision of the vast walls of the
palace. The cicada and the cricket alone sang; they
alone interrupted the silence of those vast walls, of
those abandoned buildings. But my soul grew desolate, my heart grew faint, and I ran anew along the
sides of the mountains and the sides of the valleys
until I arrived at the mountains and valleys of the
Queché; until I succeeded in finding my governor,
my ruler, walled up behind and in front with stone
and lime. I hurled myself at it with the son of my
arrow, and the strength of my shield, my stranger's
mace, my stranger's axe, my valor, my daring. It was
thus, alone, that I saw my governor again, my ruler,
imprisoned completely alone in the stone and lime. I
carried him away from there in my arms by the son
of my arrow, by the strength of my shield. For truly,
if I had not been there, you would have severed the
root, the trunk of my governor, my ruler, among the
mountains and valleys of the Queché. That is how I

came to see him again, with the help of the point of my arrow, by the force of my shield, and I led my governor, my ruler, inside the walls of the palace. Did you not destroy two, three towns: the cities with narrow streets of Balamvac whose sandy soil resounds with footsteps; of Chi-Calcaraxah of Chi-Cunu, of Chi-Gozibal-Tagah-Tulul called thus? When will your heart cease this mad drive toward valor and daring? But you will pay for it, under heaven, above earth. I will announce the news of your presence inside the high walls of the vast fortress, to my governor, to my ruler. That is why you have said your last good-bye to your mountains, to your valleys, because here your root and your trunk will be severed, here between the heavens and the earth. It will truly be thus. For this reason I will not speak abundant words. Heaven and earth be with thee, man of the Cavek Queché!

QUECHÉ WARRIOR: Eh, valiant one, stalwart, Warrior of Rabinal! Is it thus that your voice speaks to the face of the sky, to the face of the earth? I will not change the words you have spoken to the face of the sky, to the face of the earth, before my mouth and before my face. Without doubt it is I who have transgressed in obeying the orders of our governor, our ruler. "They provoked us, they challenged us," had said the voice of our governor, of our ruler, the chief of Teken-Toh, the chief of Teken-Tihax, Gumar-machi, and Taktazib, Taktazimah, Cuxuma-Ah, of Cuxuma-Cho, of Cuxuma-Zivan, of Cuxuma-Cab, of Cuxuma-Tziquin. These are the names, the lips, the eyes of our governor, of our ruler! "Come then, you others. The twelve bold ones, the warriors; come to listen to the orders." This was the voice which spoke to them at the beginning, and later to you. In truth this is the cause of the misery, the destruction, the disorder which existed in the rooms of the great fortress. Now on the vast walls, in the vast fortress, there are only nine or ten white sons inside the vast walls of the fortress. This was the voice which spoke to them and to you. It is because I was unable to conquer anything here; because of the envy which raged in my heart, I forced the white children to come back, I forced the white sons to return while they were distracted in Iximché looking for the beehives of yellow honey, of green honey. When I saw them, my voice said before heaven, before earth: Would I not be able to kidnap those white children, those white sons, in order to place them within my mountains, my valleys? My voice said: I will conduct them before my governor, my ruler, to the Quiché mountains, to the Quiché valley. And my voice replied: Here then is something of these freshly plowed lands which have already born fruit of the white open ears, of the yellow beans, of the white beans.

From there I returned toward the place called Pan-Cakil because my heart went out to the white children, to the white sons. For this reason, then, you hurled your challenge, your war cry. Then my heart, my heart groaned at hearing your challenge, your war cry. It was for this that you came to Panahachel, to hurl your cry. But immediately I let them go free, there in the Great Wood, in the place called Cabrakan Pan-Araveno. The white children, the white sons, had only a short way to go before they arrived at my mountains, at my valleys, at the Queché mountains, at the Queché valleys. Thus returned the white children, the white sons, with dry and swollen stomachs. They continued the march by the sides of the mountains, by the sides of the valleys. Nevertheless, they did not get as far as their walls, their fortress; they approached, instead, the place called Panamaka. Truly it was I who transgressed when I kidnapped your governor, your ruler, there in the place of the Baths of Tohil; for while he was bathing himself I kidnapped him, by the strength of my arrow and of my shield. I brought him to my mountains, to my valleys, to the Queché mountains, Queché valleys, because of the envy that raged in my heart, because I had not been able to take possession of anything between the heavens and the earth. Thus did I confine him, then, in the walls of lime and stone; I buried him behind the lime, the stone. Without doubt it is I who transgressed; in your owns words you said: "You destroyed two or three towns; the deeply ravined cities of Balamvac, where the sandy soil resounds with footsteps; of Chi-Calcaraxah, of Chi-Cunu, of Chi-Gozibal-Tagah-Tulul, called thus." Certainly I transgressed then because of the envy that consumed my heart, and here I will pay for it now under heaven, above earth. There are no other words in my mouth, in my heart. Only the squirrel, only the bird, here before my eyes, will perhaps have something to sing, mighty chief! Did not your voice also say: "I will announce the news of your presence to the face of my governor, my ruler, within the high walls of the vast fortress? You have said your last good-bye to your mountains, to your valleys, because here we will sever your root, your trunk, here beneath the heavens, above the earth?" Thus spoke your voice.

But could we not proceed agreeably and honestly as brothers? I would adorn you; I would decorate you with my gold, with my silver, with the son of my arrow, with the strength of my shield, with my stranger's mace, with my stranger's axe, with all that I possess, even with my sandals. I would work here, I would serve you and your children as your son, here beneath the heavens, above earth, as supreme sign that you will let me return to my mountains, to my valleys. Thus speaks my voice before heaven and earth. Heaven and earth be with thee, valiant warrior, remarkable among the stalwarts, great Warrior of Rabinal!

RABINAL WARRIOR: Ah, valiant warrior, man of the Cavek Queché! Did not your voice say before heaven, before earth: "Could I not adorn you, and decorate you, with my gold, with my silver, with the son of my arrow, with the son of my shield, with all that I possess, even with my sandals, to work here, to serve, under heaven, above earth?" Thus spoke your voice. But what then would I go to say to the face of my governor, of my ruler? That a valiant warrior had fought us behind the vast walls, the vast fortress, for thirteen-times-twenty days, thirteen-times-twenty nights; so that our sleep was without rest or repose. And then, suddenly, I am adorned, I am decorated, by his gold, with his silver, with his stranger's mace, with his stranger's axe, with all that he possessed, even his sandals. And I would say to the face of my governor, of my ruler, that I had then allowed this warrior, following this battle, to return to his mountains, to his valleys! Could I say this to the face of my governor, to the face of my ruler? I am already well provided for; I am heaped with gifts from my governor, my ruler; I already have gold and silver; I have the son of my arrow, the son of my shield, my stranger's mace, my stranger's axe; I am well provided for, I am already heaped with gifts from my governor, the ruler of those vast walls, of the vast fortress. For this reason I will announce the news of your presence inside the walls of his vast fortress, to the face of my governor, of my ruler.

If my governor, my ruler, tells me to let you depart to your mountains, to your valleys, yes, if my governor says it, then I will allow you to go to your mountains, to your valleys; I will permit you to leave. But if my governor, my ruler, says: "Bring him before my lips, before my eyes, in order that I may see that his face is that of a valiant one, of a warrior"; if my governor, my ruler, says that, I will take you to appear before him. Thus speaks my voice before heaven and earth. Heaven and earth be with thee, valiant one, stalwart, man of the Cavek Queché!

QUECHÉ WARRIOR: Very well, so be it, valiant one, stalwart, great Warrior of Rabinal! If you announce the news of my presence to the face of your governor inside the vast walls of his vast fortress, announce me now. Heaven and earth be with thee, most remarkable among the stalwart ones, Warrior of Rabinal!

SCENE TWO

Within the fortress
(Before CHIEF FIVE-RAIN, who occupies a low seat, the back of which is adorned with ancient carving. Near him is his WIFE, and they are surrounded by SLAVES, SERVANTS, WARRIORS, EAGLES, and JAGUARS.)

RABINAL WARRIOR: I salute you, oh Chief. I salute you, oh Lady. I give thanks to heaven, I give thanks to earth, that you are here, spreading the shadow of your protection, your shelter, under the awning of green feathers, within the vast walls of this vast fortress. Since I am a valiant one, a stalwart, and since I have come before your lips and before your face, inside the great buildings of the fortress; in the same manner I have captured another valiant one, a stalwart, who confronted us for thirteen-times-twenty days, for thirteen-times-twenty nights, behind the high walls of the fortress, where our sleep was without rest or repose. Heaven has delivered him to me, earth delivered him bound to me, cast down by the son of my arrow, by the force of my shield. I have tied him, I have bound him, with my strong cord, with my strong rope, with my stranger's mace, with my stranger's axe, with my net, with my manacles of chiseled bone, with my magic herbs. Likewise, I forced him to declare himself without murmur or protest. Soon this valiant warrior spoke the names of his mountains, of his valleys, to my face, to me, the valiant hero.

It was this valiant one, this warrior, who imitated the cry of the coyote, who imitated the cry of the fox, who imitated the cry of the weasel, behind the vast walls of the fortress, in order to bring forth, in order to provoke, the white children, the white sons. It was this valiant one, this stalwart, who destroyed nine or ten white children, white sons. It was also this valiant one who kidnapped you in the baths. It was this valiant warrior who laid waste two or three towns; the deeply ravined city called Balamvac, where the sandy soil resounds with footsteps. Does not your heart desire to put an end to this bravery, to this audacity? Have we not received messages from our governors, our rulers, each one the governor of his own walls, of his own fortress, saying that he must pay for his misdeeds: the chief of Teken-Toh, the chief of Teken-Tihax, Gumarmachi, Taktazib, Taktazimah, Cuxuma-Ah, Cuxuma-Cho, Cuxuma-Zivan, Cuxuma-Cab, Cuxuma-Tziquin? These are their names, their lips, their faces. Now he comes to pay the penalty beneath the heavens, above the earth. Here we will sever his roots, his trunk; here between the heavens and the earth, oh, my governor, Chief Five-Rain.

CHIEF FIVE-RAIN: My valiant one, my stalwart! Thanks be to heaven, thanks be to earth, that you have arrived at the walls of the vast fortress, before my lips, before my face, before me, your governor, I, Chief Five-Rain. I give thanks to the heaven, thanks to earth, for what heaven has given you; that the earth has delivered to you this valiant one, this stalwart; that he was hurled onto the son of your arrow,

before the force of your shield; that you have conquered him; that you have bound up this valiant one,
this stalwart. Now let him be brought before my lips
and my face that I may see just how brave, how
heroic, are his lips, his face. But let him make no outcry, and let him make no commotion when he arrives
at the entrance to the great fortress; that way he will
be esteemed, he will be admired within the vast walls
of the fortress.[32] For there will be found his twelve
brothers, his twelve kinsmen, guardians of the treasures, guardians of the precious stones. Their lips,
their faces, are not complete; something is missing.
Perhaps he has come to complete their number in the
vast walls, in the vast fortress. Here also there are
twelve strong eagles and jaguars; their number, too, is
not complete; perhaps this valiant one, perhaps this
stalwart, has come to complete them. Here there are
great benches of precious metals and silver thrones;
there are some where one may be seated; there are
others where one may not be seated; perhaps this
valiant one, this stalwart, has come to seat himself in
those. Here there are twelve drinks, twelve intoxicating liqueurs called Waiting-Hummingbird—sweet
drinks, refreshing, lighthearted, pleasing, attractive,
appealing; of which one drinks before sleeping, here
in the vast walls of the fortress, the Chief's liqueurs;
perhaps this valiant one came to drink them. Here
there are very fine and well-woven materials, brilliant, splendid, the work of my mother, of my wife;
for this splendid work of my mother, of my wife, perhaps this valiant one, this stalwart, intends to be the
first wearer of its delicacy. Also here is Mother of the
Feathers—Precious Emerald, brought from Tzam-
Gam-Carchag; perhaps this valiant one, perhaps this
stalwart, intends to be the first to see her lips, her
face; perhaps he came to dance with her, within the
vast walls of this vast fortress. Perhaps this valiant
one came in order to become the clan's son-in-law,
brother-in-law of the clan, in the vast walls in the vast
fortress. Let us see then if he is obedient, if he is modest, if he humbles himself, if he bows his face on entering. Thus says my voice before heaven, before
earth! Heaven and earth be with thee, remarkable
among the stalwarts.

RABINAL WARRIOR: Chief Five-Rain, give me your
blessing, before heaven, before earth. Here is my
strength, my bravery, that you have given me, that you
have affirmed to my lips, to my face. I will leave here
my arrow, my shield. Keep them, then; guard them in
your covered house, in your arsenal; let them rest
there; I, too, will rest because when we should have
been sleeping, there was no rest for us because of him.
Consequently, I leave them with you, inside the walls
of this vast fortress. Thus speaks my voice before
heaven, before earth. Heaven and earth be with thee,
my governor, my ruler, Chief Five-Rain!

CHIEF FIVE-RAIN: My valiant one, my warrior, did
not your voice say before heaven, before earth, "Here
is my strength, here is my daring; here is my arrow,
here is my shield, that you have given me, that you
had affirmed before my lips, to my face. I deliver
them unto you, then, in order that you may keep
them; in order that you may guard those in the vast
walls, in the vast fortress, in your covered house, in
your arsenal"? Is this not what your voice said? But
how will I keep them, how will I guard those in the
covered house, in the arsenal? What weapons will
you have, then, to protect us against those who
might come and be seen at the head of the lands, at
the feet of our lands?[33] What weapons, then, would
you have to protect our children, our sons, when
they go out from these lands to seek their nourishment in the four corners, in the four directions?
Here, once again and one last time, you must take
your valor, your daring, your arrow, your shield, that
I here give to you, my valiant one, my stalwart, remarkable among warriors, great Warrior of Rabinal.
Heaven and earth be with thee.

RABINAL WARRIOR: Very well! Here, then, I will take
back my vigor, my bravery, that you have given me;
that you have entrusted to me before my lips, to my
face. Thus I will take them once again and one last
time. Thus speaks my voice to the face of the sky, to
the face of the earth. And now I will leave you for a
moment inside the high walls of your palace. Heaven
and earth be with thee, my governor, my ruler, Chief
Five-Rain.

CHIEF FIVE-RAIN: It is well, my valiant one, my stalwart! Be careful: do not fall into some trap or be
wounded, my valiant one, my stalwart, remarkable
among the warriors, great Warrior of Rabinal!
Heaven and earth be with thee!

SCENE THREE

In front of the fortress

RABINAL WARRIOR: (*He frees the QUECHÉ WARRIOR
of the ties that fastened him to the tree.*) Greetings!
Valiant warrior, man of the Cavek Queché. I have returned from having announced you within the walls
of the vast fortress, before the face of my governor,
my ruler.

My governor, my ruler, ordered me, brave warrior,
to say to you:

"Let him make no uproar and let him cause no
commotion when he arrives at the entrance of the
vast walls, of the vast fortress, here beneath heaven,
above earth; but let him humble himself, let him
bow his head; that way he will be esteemed, he will
be admired within the walls of the vast fortress; for
the interior of the vast walls, of the vast fortress, will

already be crowded. Already there are twelve of his brothers, twelve of his kinsmen, guardians of the treasures, guardians of the precious stones. Their lips and their faces are not complete; perhaps that stalwart comes to complete this group. There are also twelve strong eagles and jaguars. Their number, too, is not complete; perhaps that valiant one, that stalwart, comes to complete one or the other. Also there are benches of precious metals and silver thrones; perhaps that valiant one, that stalwart, comes to sit on them. Here, also, is the Mother of the Feathers, Precious Emerald, who comes from Tzam-Gam-Carchag. Her lips are inviolate; her face has not been touched; perhaps this valiant one, perhaps this stalwart, comes in order to take the first taste of her lips, her face. There are also twelve kinds of intoxicating liqueurs, twelve delicious poisons, cool and sparkling, drinks of the chieftain who rules within the walls of the vast fortress; perhaps this valiant one, perhaps this stalwart, comes to drink them. There are also very fine and well-woven materials, brilliant, resplendent, the work of my mother, of my wife; perhaps this valiant one, perhaps this stalwart, comes to use them first. Will he not also come as my people's son-in-law, brother-in-law of my people, here within the high building of the vast fortress?" Thus said the voice of my governor, my ruler.

I come, then, to warn you against making an uproar, from causing a commotion when you arrive at the entrance of the high walls, of the great palace; I come to warn you that you should bow down, that you should kneel, when you enter the presence of my governor, my ruler, the grandfather, the Chief Five-Rain. Thus speaks my voice before heaven, before earth. Our conversation need continue no further. Heaven and earth be with thee, man of the Cavek Queché!

QUECHÉ WARRIOR: Eh! Valiant one, stalwart, great Warrior of Rabinal! Does not your voice speak thusly before heaven and earth? "I have conveyed the news of your presence to my governor, before my ruler, in the vast walls of the vast fortress. For this reason I come to warn you, valiant one, stalwart." Did not your Chief say: "Bring him so that he may appear before my lips, before my face, on the vast walls, in the vast fortress; so that I can see in his lips, so that I can see on his face, if he is brave, if he is a valiant warrior. Go to warn him to make no uproar, to cause no commotion, when he comes before my lips, before my face; let him humble himself, let him bow his head; because if he is a valiant one, a stalwart, he should be submissive and humble. For here he will be esteemed and honored, here within the walls of the great fortress." Thus spoke your governor, your ruler.

Come, come! Would I be a hero, would I be a stalwart, if I were to humble myself, if I bowed my head? Here, you see how I will humble myself: here, with my arrow; here, with my shield; here, with my stranger's mace; here, with my stranger's axe; that is how I will be humble, how I will bow when I enter the gates of the fortress, of the great palace. If heaven and earth permit I will demolish the grandeur and the majesty of your governor, your ruler. If heaven and earth permit, I will strike with my fist those lips and that mouth, within the great fortress and the great palace, and you, take some of those injuries first, you valiant warrior!

(*On saying these words he approaches and menaces the WARRIOR OF RABINAL.*)

IXOK-MUN: (*Interposing himself between them*) Stop, valiant warrior, man of the Cavek Queché, do not kill my valiant one, my stalwart, the most remarkable among the warriors, the great Warrior of Rabinal!

SCENE FOUR

Within the fortress

QUECHÉ WARRIOR: (*Advancing before CHIEF FIVE-RAIN*) I salute you, warrior! I am he who has just arrived at the entrance of the great fortress, at the entrance of the great palace, where you extend your shade and your majesty over all. I am he whose coming was announced to your lips, to your face. I am the valiant warrior, the stalwart, to whom your valiant warrior, your stalwart, the great Warrior of Rabinal, came to hurl his challenge, his war cry, to my lips, to my face.

He said: "I have announced the news of your coming to the face of my governor, to my father, within the vast walls of the vast fortress. The voice of my governor, of my ruler, spoke thusly: Bring this valiant one, this stalwart, before my lips, before my face, in order that I may see on his lips, in order that I may see in his face, how valiant he is, how great a warrior he is. Advise this valiant one, this stalwart, that he must make no uproar, that he must not raise a commotion, that he should humble himself, that he should bow his head when he enters the great fortress, when he enters the great palace." This your great warrior said to my mouth, to my face.

Well then! I am the valiant one, I am the warrior, and if I must humble myself, bow my head and bend my knee, then this is what I will humble myself with: here is my arrow, here is my shield, with which I will destroy your splendor and your glory; with which I will strike your mouth and your lips; that is how you will be tested, mighty chief!

(*Brandishing his weapon toward FIVE-RAIN*)

IXOK-MUN: Valiant warrior, man of the Cavek Queché, do not attempt to kill my governor, my ruler, Chief

Five-Rain, within the vast walls of his great fortress wherein we stand!

QUECHÉ WARRIOR: Command, then, that they prepare my seat, my throne, because thus it was in my mountains, in my valleys, that my destiny was celebrated, that the day of my birth was celebrated. There I have my bench, there have my seat. It is not I who will be exposed to the wind; it is not I who will be exposed to the cold. Thus speaks my voice to the face of the sky, to the face of the earth. Heaven and earth be with thee, Chief Five-Rain!

CHIEF FIVE-RAIN: Valiant one, stalwart, man of the Cavek Queché: I thank heaven and earth that you have come to the vast walls of the vast fortress where I extend forth my shade and my majesty, I, the grandfather, the Chief Five-Rain. Speak then. Reveal why you imitated the cry of the coyote, the cry of the fox, the cry of the weasel beyond the vast walls, beyond the vast fortress, in order to provoke, in order to bring forth my white children, my white sons, in order to bring them outside the vast walls, the vast fortress, in Iximché; in order to try to find, to discover, the yellow honey, the green honey of the bees, the nourishment that was mine, the grandfather, the Chief Five-Rain, on the vast walls, in the vast fortress?

You were also the one who kidnapped the nine or ten noble children, the white sons, who were about to be taken to the Queché mountains, to the Queché valleys, if my boldness, my bravery, had not been found vigilant; because there you would have severed the root, the trunk of these noble children, of these white sons.

You came also to kidnap me there at the Baths of Tohil. There I was seized by the son of your arrow, the strength of your shield. You shut me up among the stone and lime walls, among the Queché mountains, among the Queché valleys; there you would have ended by severing my root, my trunk, in the Queché mountains and valleys. But, my valiant one, my stalwart, the most remarkable among the stalwarts, the great Warrior of Rabinal, freed me from there, pulled me out of there, by the strength in his arrow and in his shield. Had it not been for my valiant one, my stalwart, you would have certainly severed my root, my trunk. Thus he again brought me to the vast walls, to the vast fortress.

You also laid waste two or three towns: the deeply ravined cities of Balamvac, where the sandy soil resounds under the footsteps, of Calcaraxah, Cunu, Gozibal-Tagah-Tulul, called thus.

When will the unrestrained desire of your heart, your determination, your boldness, cease to dominate you? When will you allow them to act, when will you allow them to move? Did not this determination, this daring, remain buried, concealed, in Qotom, in Tikiram, in Beleh Mokoh, in Beleh Chu-

may? Was not this determination, this daring, buried, concealed, by us, the governors, by us, the rulers, in each of the walls of the fortress? But you will pay for these misdeeds here between heaven and earth. You have said your last good-bye to your mountains, to your valleys, because here you will die, you will perish, under heaven, above earth. Heaven and earth be with thee, man of the Cavek Queché!

QUECHÉ WARRIOR: Chief Five-Rain, with your permission before heaven, before earth. True are the words, the opinions, that you have expressed before heaven, before earth; for truly it is I who have transgressed. Your voice also said: "Have you not called to and provoked the white children, the white sons, in order to bring them out to seek, to discover, the yellow honey, the green honey, of the bees, nourishment for my table, the grandfather, Chief Five-Rain, inside the walls of the vast fortress?" Thus spoke your voice. Certainly it is I who am the transgressor because of the envy that eats at my heart, because I had not been able to obtain possession of these beautiful mountains, of these beautiful valleys, here between the heaven and the earth. Your voice has also said: "It was you who came to kidnap me; who seized me in the baths of Tohil." Again, in truth, it is I who am the transgressor, because of the envy which rends my heart. Your voice also said: "You laid waste two or three towns: the deeply ravined cities of Balamvac, where the sandy soil resounds with footsteps, of Calcaraxah, of Cunu, of Gozibal-Tagah-Tulul." Thus said your voice. Certainly it is I who am the transgressor, because of the envy that consumes my heart, because I have not been able to conquer the beautiful mountains, the smiling valleys, here between heaven, above earth. Your voice also said: "Say a last good-bye to your mountains, to your valleys; let your voice speak, because here you will die, here your life will end; here we will sever your root, your trunk; here between the sky and the earth." Thus said your voice. Certainly, I disobeyed your laws, your commands, because of the envy that devours my heart.

If it is necessary that I end my life here, that I meet death here, then this is what I say to your lips, to your face: Now that you are well provisioned, that you are so rich, here in the high walls of the great palace, I will borrow from you some of your table, the Chief's drinks called Ixtatzunun; the twelve liqueurs that intoxicate, the twelve poisons so sweet, so refreshing, so lighthearted, that are drunk before going to bed, within the vast walls of this vast fortress; I will borrow from you the marvels of your mother, of your wife. I will taste them immediately, as supreme symbol of my death, of my end, here between the sky and the land. Heaven and earth be with thee, Chief Five-Rain!

CHIEF FIVE-RAIN: Valiant warrior, man of the Cavek Queché! Thus spoke your voice before heaven, before earth: "Grant me your food, your drinks. I will borrow them and taste of them now, as the supreme sign of my death, of my end." Then I give them to you. Then I grant them to you. Slaves, serving women, let my food, my drinks, be brought. Let them be given to this valiant one, this stalwart, man of the Cavek Queché, as the supreme sign of his death, of his end, between the sky and the earth.

A SERVANT: It is well, my governor, my ruler. I will give them to this valiant one, to this stalwart, man of the Cavek Queché.

(The SERVANTS bring a table loaded with food and drinks.)

QUECHÉ WARRIOR: (Eats and drinks with disdain. Then he goes to dance before the court. Afterwards he returns and says:) Oh, Chief Five-Rain. Is this your nourishment, is this your drink? There is little to be said; there is nothing in any of them that tempts my lips or my eyes. If you could taste for an instant in my mountains and valleys the excellence of the beverages, the sweet, refreshing drinks that I taste in my mountains, in my valleys! My voice says this to the face of the sky, to the face of the earth! Is this your table and your foods?

But here is the goblet from which you drink. It is the skull of my ancestor, the skull of my father,[34] which I see, which I observe! Can you not do the same with *my* bones, with *my* skull; to engrave and paint my mouth and my face? In this way, when my children, my sons, leave my mountains, my valleys, to barter five loads of cacao, five loads of fine cacao from my mountains, my children, my sons, can say: "Here is the head of our ancestor, of our father." This will my children, my sons, repeat in my memory as long as the sun is in the sky.

Here is also the bone of my arm; let it be the handle of the gourd of precious metals that will resound, that will produce noise on the vast walls, in the vast fortress. Here is also the bone of my leg; let it be the drumstick of the great drum, of the little drum, that will make heaven and earth throb on the vast walls, in the vast fortress.

Here is that which my voice also says: I will borrow from you the splendid gold brocade, well-designed, the work of my mother, of my wife, in order that I may adorn myself within the vast walls of the vast fortress, to the four corners, to the four extremities, as the supreme sign of my death, of my end, here beneath the heavens, above the earth.

CHIEF FIVE-RAIN: Valiant stalwart, man of the Cavek Queché! What do you wish, then; what is it that you ask? No matter what, I will give it to you as the supreme sign of your death, of your end, here beneath the heavens, above the earth. Slaves, serving women, bring the golden brocade, the work that you have done in the vast walls, in the vast fortress; let it be given to this valiant one, to this stalwart, as a supreme sign of his death, of his end, here under the heavens, above the earth.

A SERVANT: Very well, my governor, my ruler. I will give this valiant one, this stalwart, that which he asks. Valiant one, stalwart, here is the gold brocade you desire, which you asked for. I give it to you, but do not harm it. Do not mistreat it.

(The SERVANT gives the QUECHÉ WARRIOR a mantle in which he wraps himself.)

QUECHÉ WARRIOR: You, musicians and drummers, play now a song on my flute, on my drum. Let them play, then, the great melody, the brief melody. Let my stranger's flute, my stranger's drum, my Queché flute, my Queché drum, play the prisoner's dance, the captive's dance of my mountains, of my valleys, in order that it make the sky shake, in order that it make the earth tremble. May our foreheads, our heads, be bowed when the beating of our feet echoes off the sun, when we dance, keeping time to the music, beating the ground, with the slaves, with the serving women, here under heaven, above earth. Heaven and earth be with you, oh musicians, oh drummers!

(He dances in a circle before the court and goes to each corner to hurl his war cry.)

Oh, Chief Five-Rain. With your permission before heaven, before earth. Here you have that which you had lent me, that which you had given to me. I come to return it, to leave it at the entrance of the great fortress, of the vast palace; keep it, guard it in your shaded arch, within the vast walls of the vast palace.

You agreed to my petition, to my desires, before heaven, before earth; and I have worn and shown it in the vast walls, the vast fortress, in the four corners, at the four extremities, as the supreme sign of my death, of my end, here between heaven and earth. But if it is true that you are rich and wealthy, now grant that I borrow the Mother of the Feathers, the Mother of the Little Green Birds, Precious Emerald, brought from Tzam-Gam-Carchag, whose lips are as yet untasted, whose eyes have not yet been touched, in order that I might first taste her mouth, that I might first touch her face, that I might dance with her, that I might exhibit her in the vast walls, in the vast fortress, in the four corners, at the four sides, as the supreme symbol of my death, of my end, here under heaven, above earth. Heaven and earth be with thee, Chief Five-Rain.

CHIEF FIVE-RAIN: Valiant one, stalwart, man of the Cavek Queché! What do you wish, then; what is it that you seek? No matter what, I grant you that which you wish; here is the Mother of the Feathers, the Mother of the Little Green Birds, Precious Emerald, brought from Tzam-Gam-Carchag, whose lips are as yet untasted, whose eyes have not been touched; and I grant her to you, valiant warrior, as the supreme symbol of your death, of your end, here, under the sky, above the earth. Slaves, bring forth the Mother of the Feathers, the Mother of the Little Green Birds; give this valiant one, give this warrior, that which he desires, that which he entreats, as a supreme symbol of his death, of his end, under the sky, above the earth.

IXOK-MUN: Very well, my governor, my ruler. I will give her to this valiant one, to this hero.

(PRECIOUS EMERALD *is brought to the* QUECHÉ WARRIOR.)

Here she is, valiant warrior, man of the Cavek Queché. I give you that which you desire, that which you request; but do not offend, do not harm the Mother of the Feathers, the Mother of the Little Green Birds, Precious Emerald. Content yourself only to dance with her within the walls of the vast fortress.

(The QUECHÉ WARRIOR *salutes* PRECIOUS EMERALD, *who keeps herself separated from him while they dance, always turning her face toward him. He follows her in the same way, undulating before her, while rippling and flaring the mantle. In this way they do turns around the court, to the music of the trumpets, and afterwards they return to a place near* CHIEF FIVE-RAIN.)

QUECHÉ WARRIOR: Chief Five-Rain, with your permission before heaven, before earth. Here I return her whom you lent me, whom you granted me as a companion. Now I have exhibited her. I have danced with her face to face to the four corners, to the four extremities, within the buildings of the great palace. Now take her back, guard her, enclose her within the vast walls of the vast fortress.

My voice also says: Grant that I borrow the twelve yellow eagles and jaguars whom I met by day, by night, with their weapons, their arrows in hand. Lend them to me that I may amuse myself with them, at the point of my arrow, with the strength of my shield, in the four corners, at the four sides, within the vast walls, in the vast fortress, as a supreme symbol of my death, of my end, here between heaven and earth. Heaven and earth be with thee, Chief Five-Rain!

CHIEF FIVE-RAIN: Valiant warrior, man of the Cavek Queché! Your voice spoke thus before heaven, before earth!: "Grant that I borrow the twelve yellow eagles and jaguars." Thus says your voice. Very well, I grant you the twelve yellow eagles, the twelve yellow jaguars which you desire, which you request to my lips, to my face. Go then, oh my eagles, my jaguars! Proceed so that this valiant one, this stalwart, may amuse himself and his warrior's prowess with the point of his arrow, the strength of his shield, in the four corners, at the four sides.

QUECHÉ WARRIOR: (Comes forth with the EAGLES and the JAGUARS, and performs with them a war dance around the court. Afterwards he returns to the royal platform where CHIEF FIVE-RAIN is seated with his family.) Chief Five-Rain, with your permission before heaven, before earth. You have granted me that which I wished, that which I requested: the yellow eagles, the yellow jaguars. I have exercised with them the art of war with the son of my arrow, with the son of my shield. Are these, then, your eagles? Are these, then, your jaguars? They are almost nothing to speak of before my lips, before my face, because some of them can see; some of them do not see; they have neither the eagle's beak nor the jaguar's claws. If you could but see for a moment those of *my* mountains, of *my* valleys! What a magnificent sight is theirs, and they fight magnificently with teeth and claws.

CHIEF FIVE-RAIN: Valiant warrior, man of the Cavek Queché! We know well the teeth of the eagles, of the jaguars, that are in your mountains. What is, then, *your* image, *your* picture, of the eagles and jaguars who are in your mountains, in your valleys?

QUECHÉ WARRIOR: Chief Five-Rain, with your permission before heaven, before earth. Thus speaks my voice one more time to your lips, to your face: Grant me, if you can, thirteen-times-twenty days, thirteen-times-twenty nights to say one last good-bye to the face of my mountains, to the face of my valleys, where I used to live, to the four corners, to the four directions, to see again my place of hunting, my place of rest and nourishment.

(No one answers the QUECHÉ WARRIOR *who dances and disappears for a minute. Afterwards, without returning to the royal platform where* CHIEF FIVE-RAIN *is sitting, he approaches the* EAGLES *and the* JAGUARS *who are arranged in the middle of the court around an altar.)*

And you eagles! You jaguars! "He has departed," you no doubt said. I had not departed; I went only to say good-bye to the vision of my mountains, to the image of my valleys, where I used to hunt something to nourish me, for my favorite game in the four corners, at the four extremities.

Ah, heaven and earth hear me! My courage, my daring, have served me nothing. I searched for my way under heaven, I searched for my road over the earth, crossing the grass, crossing the thistles. My determination, my daring, have served me nothing.

Ah, heaven and earth hear me! Must I really die, must it end here between the earth and the sky? And you now, my gold and my silver! You son of my arrow, son of my shield! My stranger's mace, my stranger's axe, my wreaths, my sandals—all will return to my mountains, to my valleys! Carry the news of me to my governor, my ruler, because the voice of my governor, my ruler, said this: "It has already been too long that my determination, my bravery, have been on the hunt." Thus said the voice of my governor, my ruler; let him no longer say it since I await only my death, my end, my destruction, here between the earth and the sky! Heaven be my aid! Earth hear me! If it is true that I must die, that I meet death, here under heaven, above earth, why can I not change places with that happy squirrel, that bird, who dies on the limb of the tree, on the branch of the tree, on which he lived, on which he ate, under heaven, above earth?

And you eagles! You jaguars! Come now! Do what must be done! But let your teeth, your claws, kill me quickly, because I am a great warrior who comes from my mountains, my valleys. Heaven and earth be with all of you! Oh eagles! Oh jaguars!
(The EAGLES and the JAGUARS encircle the QUECHÉ WARRIOR, stretching him out on the sacrificial stone in order to open his breast. After his death all the actors dance in a circle.)

THE END

NOTES

Richard E. Leinaweaver includes 106 footnotes in his translation of *Rabinal Achi*. As he notes in the Preface, his English language translation is based on Charles Brasseur's text in Queché and his translation into French, with "generous reference" to Francisco Monterde's translation into Spanish. In his footnotes, Leinaweaver credits information derived from Charles Brasseur de Bourbong, Georges Raynaud, and Francisco Monterde. All the footnotes here are taken from Leinaweaver with the exception of those drawn from Dennis Tedlock's *Rabinal Achi,* which are duly noted.

1. Rabinal is a small town in Guatemala, founded in 1537. "Rabinal," according to Leinaweaver, "probably means 'family' (or line, house) of *rab.*"

2. "As there is no known legend or myth which refers to this town, the translation 'Red healing wounds, irritated and aggravated' suggests that it is exceedingly fanciful." Dennis Tedlock, in his version of a contemporary performance of the play, writes: "The scene is a plaza or courtyard in a town surrounded by mountains."

3. Leinaweaver notes that the terms in the original, Vorom ahau, cakon ahau, "have obscene meanings which Brasseur and Monterde decline to translate. Brasseur says they deal with sodomy and substitutes *infâme* (infamous) and *odieux* (odious). Monterde uses *violentador* (irrascible) and *deshonesto* (dishonorable)."

4. "Zahcab: The white earth, with which the victim was rubbed before the sacrifice. After sacrifice it was a symbol and a magic means of victory."

5. "To 'reveal your mountains, your valleys, etc.,'" according to Leinaweaver not only gives someone's enemies power over him, but it "was also a species of dishonor for a vanquished warrior (and for his people) to make this kind of revelation. 'Mountains and valleys' means the entire country."

6. "To my lips, to my face," Leinaweaver notes, is a Quiché expression that can be translated simply as "to me."

7. "One imitates the screams of the animals in order to cause the hunters to leave the walls of the fortress and come outside" and "white (or good) children, white (or good) sons indicate the vassals, subordinates of the tribe, and also the warriors, subordinate to the great chiefs or to the supreme chief." Tedlock translates the "white" children as "the sons of light" (36) and "the children of light" (3).

8. Pumice: "Disappeared, as a liquid in a porous stone."

9. "This listing of dishes could signify: 'We no longer kill, we no longer eat your warriors in the sacrificial meals partly because now there are no more; for another reason because our victory has left us rich and permits us other foods.'"

10. "Beleh Mokoh, 'Nine hillocks.' Beleh Chumay: 'Nine Cubits—the place of an important Queché defeat'."

11. "Qotom: 'sculptured, engraved' or 'regulated, ordered.' Tikiram: A chain of mountains to the north of the prairie of Rabinal. Cakyug, where Rabinal Achí took place, would be situated above one of the narrow passes."

12. "Death is not a complete destruction, however immediate, but a kind of disappearance, as is indicated in the feeling of: 'Place of vanishment, of the disappearance' of the name Xibalbá, subterranean place beyond the tomb, illuminated during the night by the sun and by the moon in the day."

13. Tribute.

14. "The Uxab and the Pokomames pertain to the Maya group."

15. "Row of Hills."

16. "Row of Pines."

17. Nimché: "great forest."

18. Cabrakan: "'great giant of the earth,' serves to designate the earthquakes or the gods who cause them," according to Leinaweaver.

19. Panachalib: "In the river bend," of the river of the mountain.

20. "Prepared white line."

21. "Beneath the cavern of the dry yellow earth."

22. "*My* administrators, *my* subjects, have a life so

much easier and happier, containing so much that the country gives them (plants and minerals), they must add up the great commercial profits of their artistic industries; fortune comes when they sleep."

23. *"Your* officials, *your* subjects, have no industry, they are very poor; they are always ready to leave, to migrate, no matter where, to escape their misery."

24. Camba: "Neighboring place to the prairie of Rabinal."

25. "To conquer, to force to surrender, to subdue to vassalage, to receive tribute."

26. Zaktihel: "Limestone." Near the plain of Rabinal.

27. Neighboring localities near the plain of Rabinal.

28. "The ritual period of the moveable feast. Although the text does not give the reason the activity lasted this long, it is an interesting fact: it shows the intimate relationship of religion and magic with war."

29. "Buried 'hummingbirds or hidden spears.' Further off from the city of Salamá."

30. "It is still actually called the town of Panahachel, in the matazanas (possibly 'place of magic'); it is near the lake of the same name, also called Lake Atitlán (more precisely *Atitlán* 'place of the magic ancestral grandmother.')."

31. "Tohil, principal tribal god of the Quichés. There are thermal fountains, six leagues to the southwest of Cubulco."

32. "The dignified and heroic attitude of a captive who was to be sacrificed was much admired."

33. "At the limits of the land."

34. "As with other peoples, the Quechés had goblets made of the skulls of famous defeated enemies. The more noble the warrior had been, the more adorned and highly esteemed was the goblet. It was, then, a sign of glory for a captive to know that his skull would be a goblet, and it is this that Queché Warrior ardently *demands.* He petitions that the bones of his arms be made the handle of the instruments of religious and military music formed of a gourd; he demands that the bones of his legs serve as drumsticks to play the war drum. In order to support his high pretensions, he refers to an antecedent or hereditary right, seeming to recognize the skulls of his forefathers in the goblets that are presented to him."

A representation of the Final Judgment from Friar Juan de la Cruz's *Doctrina christiana en lengua guasteca* (1571). (Reproduced in Fernando Horcasitas, *El teatro náhuatl.* Mexico City: Universidad Nacional Autónoma de México, 1974)

Final Judgment
(Attributed to Andrés de Olmos)

In this way certain vices were represented and censured in this play. Hell had a secret door by which those inside went out, and when they got out the place was set on fire and burned so terribly that it seemed as if no one had escaped and that devils and damned were all burning up. The devils and the souls of the damned cried out and shrieked, which produced a feeling of horror and fear even in those who knew that no one was really being burned.

—Fray Toribio Motolinía,
History of the Indians of New Spain[1]

Although Fray Toribio Motolinía, one of twelve Franciscan friars who arrived in Mexico in 1524, was not referring to *Final Judgment* (*Ejemplo llamado Juicio Final*) in the epigraph to this essay, he might as well have been. Other chroniclers describe the "marvel" and "amazement" that the representation "of the destruction of the world" provoked in native viewers both in Tlatelolco in 1533 and in Mexico City around 1539.[2] In a play they refer to as *Juicio Final,* Christ called the living and the dead to judgment. Those who had turned to this new Christian god were forgiven, while those who ignored the call—like the poor Lucía—were engulfed by the flames of hell. Allegorical figures such as Holy Church, Death, Penitence, and others exhort the neophytes to repent their sins before it is too late. Lucía is made into an example for having ignored the seventh sacrament and refused marriage.

The staging of this "example," like the medieval morality plays that inspired it, was wondrous and terrifying. The friars blended Mexica performance practices—usually monumental in scope and richly populated with people, costumes, color, symbolism, flowers, and landscapes—with their own. The Mesoamerican habit of fully integrating the environment into their cosmic stagings is put to use for Christian purposes: the split-level scenery now literally depicted heaven-earth-hell. Fire, drums, and gunfire rendered destruction immanent. Trapdoors allowed the sinful to fall into hell, while ropes and ladders linked heaven and earth. These morality plays were performed and designed by Amerindians, who recited the lines in Nahuatl. The later production, according to Fray Bartolomé de las Casas, involved eight hundred indigenous actors: "Never have men seen such an admirable thing made by men," he claims. "If this had been done in Rome, the whole world would know about it."[3]

Final Judgment, in the version included here, is attributed to the Franciscan friar Andrés de Olmos. Although the play is considered the first staged in the Americas, the date of the text itself remains uncertain. It is usually dated 1531 or 1533 based on descriptions of the performances in various chronicles. Othón Arróniz argues that it dates from the sixteenth century because the theme of marriage and monogamy, so urgent then, lost valence in the seventeenth century with the drastic decline of native populations. He also points out that evangelical theater died out as the indigenous population started learning Spanish.[4] Barry D. Sell has recently made a case for dating the text later, toward the end of the seventeenth century.[5] As a staged performance, however, *Final Judgment* is one of eleven plays that we know date back to the sixteenth-century Franciscan missionary theater in New Spain.[6] Franciscans recognized the passion that Amerindians had for spectacles of all kinds, including dance, acrobatics, and mime, and decided to exploit this to further their missionary ends. Performances were easier to follow than sermons. Native peoples liked participating and would congregate at plays even as they shied away from more traditional Christian services. Under the watchful eyes of the friars, they organized rehearsals, learned their lines, designed the sets, performed the roles, and flocked to the churchyard to take part in or watch the performance. The friars, at least initially, considered these massive spectacles effective in transmitting Christian ideology. While many of the stagings continued indigenous performance and linguistic patterns, the content reflected a radically diverse worldview. The hope, of course, was that Mesoamericans would absorb the ideology as they engaged in the practice.

Final Judgment is an excellent example not simply of what happens to sinners who disregard Christ but of how different belief systems come together in performance. Arróniz calls the play a "sermon dialogue," but this is clearly not the only way to think about hybrid forms.[7] The staging and themes allow plenty of room for maneuver, for including elements that mean something in one system and something quite different in the other. The following observations point to some stylistic continuities with pre-Conquest Mesoamerican forms and some interesting tensions between Christian and Mexica beliefs and practices made visible in this play.

As in *Rabinal Achi,* though far less so, we note here the rendition of what westerners would consider a single concept. Instead of saying that neophytes are deaf and blind, Penitence bemoans, "They will die in their sins! They are deaf; they are hard of hearing; they are blind; they are sightless! It may properly be said that through their sins their eyes have been destroyed." This accumulation of accusations works on at least two registers simultaneously. On one hand, it reflects the Nahuatl style of finding terms for a range of equivalences that are not reducible to one thing. On the other, it captures the vehemence of religious sermons that admonish, cajole, and persuade presumed sinners to change their ways. The senses, important sources of knowledge and pleasure for the Mexica, come under direct attack by Catholicism, whose suspicion and hostility toward them is made evident in the writings of theologians such as Saint Augustine and Saint Thomas Aquinas.

The repetition, however, also resonates deeply in the Mexica worldview. When St. Michael begins the play by announcing that God will end the world, the repetition-as-style echoes the repetition-as-belief system: "He our beloved God and Father will end, will destroy the world and all He has made. Everything He has created will perish, will come to an end. All the birds and animals, and you too will be annihilated!" For the Mexica, this is not the first time the world has been extinguished. The four previous suns died, wreaking devastation. Yet life and death were not considered radical opposites but rather complementary stages of an ongoing cycle. Repetition, for the Mexica, emphasized the circular nature of time; there is no absolute "end" but constant (at times catastrophic) transformation. Every fifty-two years, in the New Fire ceremony, the Mexica rehearsed the destruction of the world.[8] Ceremonies, for the Mexica, were meant to be repeated. Writings from the period warn that indigenous peoples should marry—but only once—implying that some thought it necessary to repeat the ceremony.[9] To this day, there are areas in Mexico where festive events and rituals are repeated; the Day of the Dead is celebrated twice in Tepoztlán, Morelos, once on November 1 and again a week later. The celebration for the Virgin of Guadalupe takes place on December 12 and again on January 12. For many native communities, once is (quite literally) never enough.

The apocalyptic prophesy in *Final Judgment* seems familiar and perhaps even expected—one more destruction. In fact, however, the word *final* ushers in a profoundly different understanding of temporality. Time, a character in the play, is presented as absolute, universal, and linear. Death, the "officer of the Law," introduces a new sense of finality. Christ, the destroyer of Time, brings about the end of the world and an entire cosmology. Time also heralds a new organizational order. Before daily routines were organized around Mexica domestic and social practices—sweeping, gathering wood, cooking, and so forth. The Conquest, with its imposition of churches in the center of towns, reorganized space. The church bells, which still peel on the quarter hour in towns throughout Mexico, reorganized and centralized time. As Time insists, "I am he who continues ever-questioning the people. Our Lord God sent and established me to keep them, care for them, warn them, remind them day and night. Never do I stop speaking!" The changes in the soundscape and landscape deeply affected the Mexica sense of lived experience.

So, while the transformation at the end of the play, in which God judges the "quick and the dead," might resemble the new life that surges from devastation in the Mexica worldview, this is a different world—one in which life is separated from death, minds from bodies, and salvation is deemed individual rather than communal. The fate of the collectivity rehearsed in the New Fire ceremony, for example, gives way to individual responsibility in Catholicism: "They must take their own defense in the presence of God as they are individually called." Christ asks St. Michael to summon the living and the dead for resurrection: "Wake up, you living. . . . Take your bodies (your flesh) with you!" then, "Arise, oh dead! Come forth from the nether regions where you are. Bring your bodies." Following this, the stage directions indicate that "The Dead come forth with their bodies."

Nonetheless, indigenous beliefs and practices continued, modified but apparent, through these performances intended to supplant them. The two belief systems, apparently theoretically antithetical, are deeply entwined. The final image of Lucía, "Flames are her adornment. A serpent is her necklace, and with one (a serpent) they bind her," makes this evident. The snake, the symbol of the devil in Catholicism, is a regenerative and powerful deity for the Mexica. Quetzalcoatl, the plumed serpent, will always return, always negotiate the underworld and the heavens, the past and the future. The play's last image—as opposed to the last word—is that the "final" may not be so final, though the friars were slow to pick up that meaning. As Friar Bernardino de Sahagún lamented, "[T]hrough [our] lack of knowledge of this, they perform many idolatrous things in our presence without our understanding it."[10] The final cautionary note, "Be awakened! Be advised!," may have resonated for both the conquered and the conquerors. The "example" both groups witnessed was not only one of suppression but also of transformation and regeneration.

—Diana Taylor

NOTES

1. Fray Toribio Motolinía is summarizing a description by Fray Antonio de Ciudad Rodrigo. Toribio Motolinía, *History of the Indians of New Spain,* trans. and ed. Elizabeth Andros Foster (Berkeley: Cortes Society, 1950), 119.

2. This description of *Juicio Final* was written in 1602, by Francisco San Antón Chimalpahín, "on the destruction of the world, which caused the Mexicans great wonder and astonishment" (19). Contemporaries referred to it as *tlamauizolli* (something marvelous), and "miraculous" (20). See Fernando Horcasitas, *El teatro náhuatl* (Mexico City: Universidad Nacional Autónoma de México, 1974), 561ff.

3. Quoted in Othón Arróniz, *Teatro de evangelización en Nueva España* (Mexico City: Universidad Nacional Autónoma de México, 1979), 40.

4. Ibid., 28.

5. Barry D. Sell, "Nahuatl Plays in Context," in *Nahuatl Theater* (Norman: Oklahoma University Press, 2004). For another discussion about dating this play, see Horcasitas, *El teatro náhuatl,* 561ff.

6. Like much theater from this period, the original manuscripts are lost. A copy dating from 1678, entitled *Ejemplo llamado Juicio Final,* in Nahuatl and Spanish, is housed in the Manuscript Division, Library of Congress, *Nexcuitilmachiotl Motenhua Juicio Final* (AC.1139, III–48–C, 4), in Washington, D.C.

7. Arróniz, *Teatro de evangelización,* 28.

8. See Enrique Florescano, "The Nahua Concept of Space and Time," in *Memory, Myth, and Time in Mexico: From Aztecs to Independence,* trans. Albert G. Bork (Austin: University of Texas Press, 1994).

9. It is interesting to note that the sixteenth-century friar Diego de Landa's edicts prohibit neophytes from being baptized or married more than once; *indígenas* were accustomed to repeating special events.

10. Bernardino de Sahagún, *Florentine Codex,* ed. and trans. Arthur J. O. Anderson and Charles E. Dibble (Santa Fe: School of American Research and the University of Utah, 1982), prologue, book 1, 45.

SELECTED REFERENCES

Arróniz, Othón. *Teatro de evangelización en Nueva España.* Mexico City: Universidad Nacional Autónoma de México, 1979.

Burkhart, Louise M., and Barry D. Sell, eds. *Nahuatl Theater. Volume I: Death and Life in Colonial Nahua Mexico.* Norman: University of Oklahoma Press, 2004.

Clavijero, Francisco Javier. *Historia Antigua de México.* Vol. 2. Mexico City: Porrúa, 1945.

González Dávila, Gil. *Teatro eclesiástico de la primitiva iglesia de las Indias occidentales, vida de sus arzobispos y obispos, cosas memorables de sus sedes, en lo que pertenece al reino del Perú.* 2 vols. León, Spain: Junta de Castilla y León, 2001.

Horcasitas, Fernando. *El teatro náhuatl: Épocas novohispana y moderna.* Mexico City: Universidad Nacional Autónoma de México, 1974.

Ravicz, Marilyn Ekdahl. *Early Colonial Religious Drama in Mexico: From Tzompantli to Golgotha.* Washington, D.C.: Catholic University of America Press, 1970.

Rivera, Octavio. "Texto y representación en el teatro misionero: *El sacrificio de Isaac* y el *Juicio Final.*" *Literatura Mexicana* 4, no. 2 (1993): 313–25.

Sell, Barry D. "Nahuatl Plays in Context." In *Nahuatl Theater, Volume I: Death and Life in Colonial Nahua Mexico,* ed. Louise M. Burkhart and Barry D. Sell, 3–28. Norman: University of Oklahoma Press, 2004.

Sten, María, ed. *El teatro franciscano en la Nueva España.* Mexico City: Universidad Nacional Autónoma de México, 2000.

Final Judgment (Attributed to Fray Andrés de Olmos)

Translated from Nahuatl by John J. Cornyn and Byron McAfee[1]

[handwritten margin note: • all characters in the play performed by natives]

CHARACTERS:

ST. MICHAEL
CHRIST
LUCIFER
SATAN
ANTICHRIST
LUCÍA
THREE DEVILS
THE LIVING
THE DEAD
FIRST ANGEL
SECOND ANGEL
PRIEST
HOLY CHURCH
PENITENCE
DEATH
TIME
CONFESSION
ANGELS OF THE COURT OF HEAVEN
DEVILS OF THE HOSTS OF LUCIFER[2]

[handwritten margin note: played literally by the dead — corpses of native Americans on the stage]

FINAL JUDGMENT[3]

(There is a sound of trumpets.[4] The Heavens open, and ST. MICHAEL descends.)

ST. MICHAEL: Oh creatures of God, know—but then you already know—that, according to the sacred Commandments of the Lord Almighty, He our beloved God and Father will end, will destroy the world and all He has made. Everything He has created will perish, will come to an end. All the birds and animals, and you too will be annihilated! Yet you may be sure that the dead will come to life; that God, the upright and just Judge, will take the righteous who served Him to His heavenly mansion the place of everlasting bliss, Paradise, abode of the blessed and of the saints. But the wicked who did not serve the Lord our God may be sure that they will receive the torments of hell! Weep because of this! Remember this: be in fear. Be in deadly fear! For the day of judgment will descend upon you, fearful, dreadful, frightful, paralyzing! Take warning and lead a proper life. The day of judgment is at hand. It is here now! It is upon you at this very moment!

(There is a sound of trumpets. ST. MICHAEL ascends. Enter PENITENCE, TIME, HOLY CHURCH, CONFESSION, and DEATH.)

PENITENCE: From now on it will not be possible to speak or to talk about all the follies of the people of the world. As for them, they are beaten down with many sins. What have they done? What are they doing? They can no longer quit their deadly sins, their hardness of heart, their blindness! Oh a thousand times unfortunate that they are![5] Ah! They will die in their sins! They are deaf; they are hard of hearing; they are blind; they are sightless! It may properly be said that through their sins their eyes have been destroyed. They have found sin pleasant to the taste and sweet-scented. They have received Sensuous Pleasure into their homes and clothed her. They looked upon her as their drink and food.[6] They forgot their Lord God! Oh a thousand times unfortunate that they are! Their life on earth is now ended!

TIME: I am Time. I am he who continues ever-questioning the people. Our Lord God sent and established me to keep them, care for them, warn them, remind them day and night. Never do I stop speaking! I am continually shouting in their ears so that they may remember their Creator, their Maker, the Lord God. I take care that they cry out to Him; that they bless Him; that they serve Him; that they do as the Lord our God wishes. I urge them to go to His house and to praise Him; to ask for His Divine Grace. But as for them, they waste my life and my work. And so I say: "I leave them. I have done my duty to them. I am not to be blamed on their account. They must make their own defense in the presence of God as they are individually called and questioned. They know how they are going to purge their sins. As for me, I am going to render my account to God the Father. He has invested all His Power in me. The people will not be able to excuse themselves because of me. They are going to be called to be judged right away!"

HOLY CHURCH: I am the ever-merciful mother. My beloved Son Jesus Christ has established me here for the people of the earth. I am always weeping for them, especially when some of them die. For when I shed tears, I pray to my beloved Mother, the sacred fountain of joy, to have pity on her creatures and to give light to them. May the seventh Sacrament not be neglected! I am keeping it for them in case they may sometime wish it. The hungry I shall feed, and I shall give drink to the thirsty. Now I am waiting for them. Would that they might come and live proper lives! My heart is sad for them. Would that they might pray to be pardoned; that they might weep and repent of their shortcomings and sins!

PENITENCE: Oh mother of complete faith, all that you say is quite true! The people do not remember this. They do not want to. Their only desire is to sin. Do I not use all of my efforts? I am ever crying out to them! Daily I advise them to repent, to keep watch, to rise up early in the morning and do penance, to grow cool—that is, to spiritually purify their hearts and souls, to fast, to refrain from eating that they may be shown pity and pardoned. Otherwise they cannot enter the princely mansion of the Lord our God. They will certainly be lost if they do not first do penance. But if they are deserving, I shall take them to me; I shall bestow favors upon them, for to them belongs the celestial ladder which leads to heaven, the time is not far off when they will be called into the presence of the Lord our God that each may give an accounting to him of how they lived on earth. May they not offer resistance to us in the presence of God. . . .[7]

DEATH: I am the officer of the law, the appointed one, the messenger empowered by heaven. Here on earth the power spreads forth to the uttermost limits as the rays of the sun shining forth in the heavens, and over the whole earth. Let the people of the earth remember that soon the beloved Son of God will come down to judge the quick and the dead. The good He will take to His celestial mansion in the heavens; and the wicked—those who did not serve Him here on earth—He will hurl into the nethermost hell. May the people of the earth remember that the day of judgment will descend upon them! This fearful thing must happen to them. Let them rectify their lives, for the time and hour of judgment is at hand when they shall answer as to how they served the Lord our God.

HOLY CHURCH: What you have just said, just expressed, is quite true. For you are the servants, the workers, of the only Son of my consolation, my beloved spiritual Spouse, Jesus Christ. He gave you your being in order that you might warn and call out to the sinners of the world whom He died to save. With great sin they have covered and besmirched their hearts and souls. Let us go now and cry out to them to come and prepare themselves spiritually with weeping and tears. I am waiting to purify them, to bathe them spiritually; to cleanse them through the seventh Sacrament, marriage, which I am reserving for them.

TIME: I am going right now to cry out to them; to remind them what they must do in order not to ill-use or waste the span of life which our Lord God has given me (for them).

(TIME alone exits.)

HOLY CHURCH: I am the divine light of the only faith. I enlighten and give spiritual vision to all Christians that they may come so that I may cleanse them; for they are dizzy and stupid with sin. If they weep and are sad, then my beloved Youth, Jesus Christ, will pardon them and give them the kingdom of heaven.

(HOLY CHURCH alone exits.)

DEATH: The people of the earth are deserving of great pity. They are blind. They do not remember that they will at some time be brought to justice. Sensuality soils their souls with sin. The people of the world are blind, sightless. They have blackened themselves with great sins,[8] but their hearts and souls are not distressed because of this. Let them wash themselves. Let them bathe themselves in the divine light of goodness. Perhaps when the day of judgment dawns upon them they will remember, and they will weep. But then they may be sure that there will no longer be any pity for them. Oh, a thousand times unfortunate are the people of this world! Soon the day of judgment will visit them! Now the day is at hand! The time and place is now!

(There is a sound of trumpets. Both DEATH and PENITENCE exit.[9] Enter LUCÍA, who is greatly troubled.)

LUCÍA: Oh You, my God! Oh my Lord Jesus Christ! Oh, unfortunate that I am! What is happening to me now! My soul is terribly afflicted as if I were entering a cloud. What shall I do now? I shall go and confess! Perhaps that will ease my soul a little. I'll go now and look for my confessor for I am really suffering.

(LUCÍA goes and knocks on the door. Enter the PRIEST.)

LUCÍA: May our Lord God be with you, dear father!

(The PRIEST comes forward and speaks.)

PRIEST: May the Lord our God lead you here, my dear daughter! You are welcome here. What is it that you wish?

LUCÍA: You must know why I have come, dear father. May I not make you angry, honored sir!

PRIEST: What do you want, dear daughter? Tell me! For the Lord our God has instituted us that we may receive the confessions of the people of the world.

LUCÍA: Dear father! I want to confess before our Lord God and you, dear father.

PRIEST: My dear daughter, you make me very happy. I am listening to what is troubling you and afflicting you—that is, your sins. Let us go to the house of the Lord our God.

(LUCÍA confesses and, while she is confessing, the PRIEST suddenly springs up very frightened.)

PRIEST: Lord! Lord! What is this you are saying? What have you done? Are you not a Christian? Do you not know that this thing which you have done is a cardinal sin? It is all over with you! Oh unfortunate that you are! Would that you had found salvation for your soul! Would that you had cleansed it! Why have you not received spiritual things? All you have done is to follow the devil! Why have you not accepted the seventh Sacrament, holy matrimony? It is all over! Oh a thousand times unfortunate you are! Up until now you have never wanted to be married here on earth. But you may be sure that you are going to be married down there in the nethermost hell. You deserve the torments of the infernal regions. And now what kind of account are you going to give to your Lord God? You cannot help yourself in any way; for the time is up, and God's judgment day has arrived! Now you will meet the blessed Son of our Lord God when He comes to judge the quick and the dead. Each must give an account to Him, his Maker. And you too must appear before the true Judge, Jesus Christ, the beloved Son of God!

(Exit the PRIEST, LUCÍA remains.)

LUCÍA: Alas! Oh God! It is all over! Oh, I have been greatly unfortunate here upon earth! What have I heard? What has the beloved Son of God said to me? What fear it brings when God's Beloved speaks thus! Would that I had believed in God and listened to what my father, mother and relatives advised me to do. But all I did was to become angry and curse the sacred Sacrament of Holy Matrimony. It is all over now! Oh, a thousand times unfortunate that I am! Accursed be my pride! What have I done? How has

pride benefited me? Accursed be both earth and time! Now the world is coming to an end; it is about to terminate! All is finished! I am a thousand times unfortunate, great sinner that I am!

(Sound of trumpets is heard. Enter THE LIVING. They sit down on the ground. LUCÍA is also seated. They cover their faces. Enter the ANTICHRIST. He wears the cloak of the wicked and with it only a gown. He lifts the finger of his left hand. There are fireworks as he comes out.)

ANTICHRIST: My dear children, do you not recognize me? I am He who suffered for you on earth! For you I have gone through torment. And now you may be sure that I shall bring to an end and shall destroy the world. Have faith in me, my creatures, and I shall pardon your sins and your transgressions. Believe in me! Behold my dear blood, my dear flesh!

FIRST LIVE PERSON: You are not the one we are waiting for! Our dear Lord God is coming. It is He who suffered for us, and who died on the cross. There they stretched out His arms because of our countless sins.

LUCÍA: You are surely He for whom we are waiting! Our Lord and our God! Pardon our sins!

ANTICHRIST: Yes I am. I shall help you. Do you not know all my power that is in the world?

(They all begin to sing CHRISTUS FACTUSES.[10] The heavens open. CHRIST appears. ST. MICHAEL goes ahead carrying the scales of justice while CHRIST bears the cross. He stops at the edge of heaven as the ANTICHRIST goes out quickly. There are fireworks.)

CHRIST: Come, my war leader, St. Michael, here into heaven. For now I am going to end and destroy time. This is called the day of judgment—the day of reckoning—as I have announced in my sacred law. I shall assuredly cleanse both heaven and earth.[11] For the people of the earth, both the living and the dead, have defiled things through their evil lives. Now wake up the living and the dead, the good and the bad. To the good I shall give heaven: the life of flowery bliss, the celestial jewel, Paradise, the heavenly palm! But the wicked may be sure that their reward will be the house of hell,[12] the sufferings of hell! For they have not kept my sacred commandments.

(CHRIST descends. ST. MICHAEL salutes CHRIST.)

CHRIST: I have told you what you are to do, my war leader.

ST. MICHAEL: Yes, you certainly have, my dear Master. The dead are to be revived, and the living awakened. They are to gather together their bones and to assemble them in their places. They are to resume their dust and ashes [bodies] that You may give them their resurrection, as well as their holy spirit and their souls that they may answer to You; that they may declare what good they have done and what evil they have committed—that is, their deeds.

CHRIST: It is true that through my power they shall

arise from the dead, and that they will live again. Just as I myself rose on the third day, so also may my creatures rise!

(There is a sound of trumpets. Exit CHRIST through another door. He does not rise again to heaven.)

(ST. MICHAEL blows his trumpet.)

FIRST ANGEL: Wake up, you living, at the command of God! Take your bodies [your flesh] with you!

(ST. MICHAEL again blows his trumpet. He calls out to THE DEAD where they are.)

SECOND ANGEL: Surgite mortui! Venite a judicio![13] Arise, oh dead! Come forth from the nether regions where you are. Bring your bodies for it is the command of our Lord God.

(THE DEAD come forth with their bodies. ST. MICHAEL again blows his trumpet.)

ST. MICHAEL: Now that you have arisen from the dead, come all of you together to give an account of what you have done to the upright Dispenser of Justice, the Judge! Don't any of you be excited now! Wait for your God and your Creator!

(There is a sound of trumpets. Exit ST. MICHAEL. Enter the ANTICHRIST who comes to deceive THE LIVING and THE DEAD. [Enter CHRIST somewhat later.])

ANTICHRIST: I have come in order to have you carry out my precious word.

(They chant the TE DEUM LAUDAMUS.[14] The ANTICHRIST exits in haste. There are fireworks. Enter the CHRIST. The FIRST and SECOND ANGELS come forward. ST. MICHAEL is leading them.)

CHRIST: Come here, oh pearl of heaven, St. Michael the Archangel! Call the living and dead to assemble here before me that I may ask them to account for how they lived here on earth.

ST. MICHAEL: So be it, my dear master. I shall call them.

(ST. MICHAEL blows his trumpet, and one by one they go before CHRIST and sit down. An ANGEL weighs their sins on the scales. The FIRST DEAD kneels down.)

CHRIST: Come hither, you. Have you kept my commandments while you lived on earth and moved about? Speak! Answer me! Speak now just as you were in the habit of speaking on earth.

FIRST DEAD: My Lord! My God! I kept and observed, I fulfilled your divine commandments. I have done your will. Ask my guardian angel, my dear Master.

CHRIST: You have served me well. In heaven you will have eternal glory and bliss. Your happiness will never end!

(CHRIST blesses him. ST. MICHAEL puts him on the right hand of CHRIST.)

CHRIST: Come hither, you living. Whom did you honor and whom did you love on earth?

FIRST LIVING: You, oh my God and Lord!

CHRIST: If I am really your God and your Lord, have you kept my sacred commandments? Have you fulfilled them?

FIRST LIVING: I have not done so, my God. Pardon me, oh sinner that I am.

CHRIST: There is no more forgiveness now! Go!

(ST. MICHAEL places him on the other side, and the SECOND DEAD kneels before CHRIST.)

CHRIST: Come hither, you who were dead! What did you do while you were living on earth? Did you do my work? Did you serve me while on earth? Answer me!

SECOND DEAD: Not in any way. Forgive me, my Lord, my Master, my God!

CHRIST: There is no forgiveness on the day of judgment! Go!

(ST. MICHAEL shoves THE DEAD away. The DEVILS drag him off to one side. LUCÍA, the SECOND LIVING, kneels.)

CHRIST: Come hither, you living. Have you kept my sacred commandments, the ten? Have you loved your neighbors and your father and mother?

SECOND LIVING: [LUCÍA] Certainly! First of all, I loved You! And after You, My God, my father and my mother.

CHRIST: If I am really your God and you loved me first of all, and after me your father and your mother, have you kept my commandments and those of my dear and honored Mother concerning the seventh Sacrament, Holy Matrimony? Have you remained pure while on earth? What have you done for a living?

LUCÍA: No, Lord I have not served You! Nor have I recognized your dear Mother. Forgive me, my God, my Lord!

CHRIST: Never up until now—never while on earth has your heart honestly addressed itself to us. You served only your own lasciviousness. Go away! You are condemned never to forget and to be the slave of your evil life. Well you know that you may expect nothing from heaven, oh unfortunate that you are! You never wanted to be married while on earth. You have won for yourself a dwelling place in the nethermost hell. Go to those whom you have served, for I do not know you!

(He pushes her toward THE DEVILS.)

CHRIST: Come here you living who are yet on earth. What was occupying your attentions? Was it, by chance, my Divine Word? Were you constantly calling out to me when sleeping and awake?

THIRD LIVING: I never forgot You, in my eating or drinking, asleep or awake, my dear Master!

CHRIST: You have served me well, my creature. And as I have always remembered you, I am saving for you a flowery garland.

(ST. MICHAEL sends him over with the Righteous.)

CHRIST: Come, oh dwellers in hell! Take away your servants to the nethermost regions. Put this wicked woman into a bath of fire and torture her there.[15]

SECOND DEVIL: Our Lord, You have done us a favor. We knew about and were only awaiting your coming! We are happy that You have graciously granted that we may secure your creatures. Go quickly and bring the fiery chain and the fiery rod with which we shall beat them. And tell our lord Lucifer that we are taking his servants down there; and to send the iron fire seat in haste to where we are taking his servants.

(Exit SATAN who goes to bring the iron fire seat.)[16]

SATAN: Here I bring along everything with which we may chain [bind] them so that they cannot escape from our hands.

(The Condemned speak:)

THE CONDEMNED: Now we have what is coming to us [our water and our food, e.g., the ration idea] here in the nethermost hell.[17]

(SATAN speaks:)

SATAN: We have all used our power so that they might fall into our hands, these servants of ours!

(They all shout: Oh Lord Help Us!)

CHRIST: You have nothing more to hope for. You may be sure of that. You will be ceaselessly tormented down there in the nethermost hell!

(Again they all shout: Oh Lord, Save Us Sinners That We Are! Then they all run out. There are fireworks. They [the Damned] go out shouting. To the Righteous they give garlands of flowers and palms. CHRIST ascends to heaven. Halfway up the stairs He speaks.)

CHRIST: Oh my servants, climb up here that you might get what I am keeping for you: happiness, everlasting and without end.

(There is a sound of trumpets. ANGELS, CHRIST, and the Righteous climb up. LUCÍA is brought out. Flames are her adornment.[18] A serpent is her necklace, and with one [A Serpent] they bind her. She comes out shouting and the DEVILS answer her.)

FIRST DEVIL: March, oh wicked woman! Do you not remember what you did on earth? Now we are going to reward you down here in the nethermost hell. March! Get along!

LUCÍA: It is all over! Oh a thousand times unfortunate that I am! I am a great sinner deserving of hell.

SATAN: So you have just been shouting, wicked woman! Now we shall give you pleasure in the nethermost hell. Down there we shall marry you in our palace, since you were never married on earth. March! Get along! For your lord Lucifer is awaiting you.

LUCÍA: Oh! Oh! It is all over, unfortunate sinner that I am! I deserve and have won the sufferings of hell. Would that I had not been born on earth! Oh! Oh! Accursed be the earth and the time when I was born! Accursed be the mother who bore me! A curse on the milk that nourished me and all that I ate and drank on earth. Oh! Accursed be the land I trod upon, and all the clothes I wore there. Everything has turned to fire and is burning me fearfully. Flames are all about my ears. They symbolize the ornaments with which I used to beautify myself. And wound around my neck is a fearsome fire-snake which symbolizes the necklaces I used to wear. What I have wound around my waist, a horrible fire-snake—the heart of the house of hell—is that which symbolizes the pleasures with which I enjoyed myself on earth. Oh! Oh! Would that I had become married! Oh! It is all over. Oh unfortunate that I am!

SECOND DEVIL: Now you are going to suffer and to pay for all the inattention you gave to the [advice] of your relatives while on earth.

(They scourge her.)

SATAN: Get along, you wicked woman! So now you remember that you should have been married? How is it that you did not remember this while you were still living on earth? Well, you are going to pay for all your wickedness now! March! Get along!

(They scourge her as they drive her out. There are fireworks. The DEVILS go along blowing horns. The PRIEST enters.)

PRIEST: My dear children! Christians, children of God! Now you have seen this fearful miracle! It is true for it is written in the Holy Book. Be awakened! Be advised! See yourselves [as you are] so that what befalls your neighbors may not befall you. This is a symbol, an example which our Lord God gives you. The day of judgment is coming soon [tomorrow or the day after]. Pray to our Lord Jesus Christ and to the Virgin Mary, that she may entreat her beloved Son Jesus Christ that you might merit and deserve the joy of Heaven—that is eternal glory! Amen. Ave Maria!

THE END

NOTES

All notes to the play are by the editors of this volume.

1. This translation, completed in 1932 and published by Marilyn Ekdahl Ravicz in *Early Colonial Religious Drama in Mexico: From Tzompantli to Golgotha* (Washington, D.C.: Catholic University of America Press, 1970), is a "draft" into English from the Nahuatl copy found in the Library of Congress according to Fernando Horcasitas (*El teatro náhuatl: Épocas novohispana y moderna* [Mexico City: Universidad Nacional Autónoma de México, 1974], 567). John J. Cornyn, one of the translators, praised the Nahuatl version as being "metrically perfect when it has not been altered by the copyist" and deeply "influenced by courtly Aztec literary style" (566). Horcasitas bases his translation into Spanish on the Nahuatl version, though he refers to the Cornyn and McAfee English translation when in doubt.

Horcasitas's *El teatro Náhuatl* presents the works bilingually, in Nahuatl and Spanish, though in his efforts to clean up the original text he has in fact altered it significantly. See Barry D. Sell, "Nahuatl Plays in Context," in *Nahuatl Theater*, ed. Louise M. Burkhart and Barry D. Sell, 3–28 (Norman: University of Oklahoma Press, 2004). We also had access to the recent translation (2004) by Louise M. Burkhart and Barry D. Sell in manuscript form, before it was published as part of *Nahuatl Theater*. When there are discrepancies among the various translations, we will merely point them out.

2. There is no list of characters in the Nahuatl and Spanish versions. Horcasitas added "JESUS" at the top of the text in Spanish. The Nahuatl text has a cross, as if the actor were literally standing in the heavens looking down on the performance. Horcasitas added the *cuadros* (scenes) in Spanish.

3. This second title does not appear in the Nahuatl and Spanish versions. Burkhart and Sell title their translation "Exemplary Model Called Final Judgment." The title in Nahuatl is "Nexcuitilmachiotl motenehua Juicio Final."

4. This is translated as "flutes" rather than "trumpets" by Horcasitas and as "wind instruments" by Burkhart and Sell.

5. The expression in Nahuatl is "four hundred times," which, as Burkhart explains, means "a whole lot, a zillion" (personal communication, June 2, 2004).

6. This version feminizes sin ("They have received Sensuous Pleasure into their homes and clothed her"). The Spanish reads, "Se han adiestrado en el pecado como si se edificaran una casa, como si se cubrieran de un manto" ("They have trained in sin, as if they were building a house, as if they were covering themselves with a cloak"). Burkhart and Sell have, "They have considered sin to be quite sweet, they have considered it to be pleasing to the nose. It is as if they housed themselves and dressed themselves with lustful living."

7. The Nahuatl version has a speech here by a character named Tlachpanaliztli, which Horcasitas translates as "Confesión" (Confession) and Burkhart and Sell translate as "Sweeping." Their translation reads as follows:

You are his mother [Jesus] of perfect and complete faith. It is all correct, what you say. They do not remember what they do not desire; they just want to go on sinning. Do I not exert all my effort? I always cry out to them, every day. I induce them to sweep things, to keep vigil, to arise in the morning, to do penance, to suffer cold, that is, in a sacred way to sweep their spirits, their souls, to fast, to abstain from food so that they will receive compassion and be pardoned. And if not, there is no way at all that they will be able to enter the royal home of our lord God. They will not be able to be pardoned if they do not first do penance. I bring the instrument of penance. It does them a favor, for it is considered the ladder of heaven, by which they will be able to enter into heaven. For it will not be long until they are called before our lord God so that each of them will give him an accounting of how they lived on earth. May they not use us to defend themselves before God. (*Nahuatl Theater*, Vol. 1, 193).

8. Burkhart and Sell's translation is more graphic: "[T]hey have really masturbated themselves black in the face." They note that the Nahuatl verb *matoca* literally means "to masturbate" (195).

9. Burkhart and Sell translate this as "Death and Sweeping exit" (195).

10. Burkhart and Sell write, "*Christus Factus est:* short for *Christus factus est pro nobis obediens usque ad mortem* (Christ became for us obedient even unto death)." The rest of the verse is: "*mortem autem cruces. / Propter quod et Deus / exaltavit illum / et dedit illi nomen / quod est super omne nomen*" (201).

11. In Horcasitas and Burkhart and Sell, Christ announces that he will "sweep" the things made dirty by humans.

12. The Horcasitas and Burkhart and Sell versions use "the place (*casa*) of the dead" instead of the Christian "hell."

13. This is in Latin in the original. It translates as "Arise, oh dead, and come to judgment."

14. Te deum laudamus translates as "We praise you as God."

15. Horcasitas and Burkhart and Sell have Lucía thrown into a *temazcal*, or sweat bath of fire, following the native use of sweat houses.

16. This would appear to be a mistake in the translation, since Satan should be entering rather than exiting. Burkhart and Sell's translation reads, "(Satan enters. He goes along grasping the fiery metal warping frame.)" (205).

17. This character does not appear in the list. Burkhart and Sell attribute this line to Satan.

18. Both the Horcasitas and Burkhart and Sell versions have Lucía wearing "fire butterflies" as earrings.

The End of Atau Wallpa, a Tragedy (Version of Jesús Lara)

The End of Atau Wallpa takes debates about the authenticity of "texts" of native and mestizo popular performances to new levels. As in the case of *Rabinal Achi*, this one has been enacted more or less regularly throughout the Andes since shortly after the Conquest. It belongs to the genre that one scholar has termed *dramas de conquista* (Conquest dramas) and another *danzas de la conquista* (dances of the Conquest).[1] This genre, related to *Rabinal Achi*, is a *danza dialogada* (spoken dance), or *taki* (Quechua for "sung dance"), as well as a variation of the *moros y cristianos* tradition.[2]

Several sixteenth- and early-seventeenth-century versions tell of the fateful confrontation between the Inca Atahualpa, who had recently become leader of the Incas after brutally defeating his brother Huáscar, and Francisco Pizarro, the Spanish conquistador who conquered Peru in 1532. Felipe Guaman Poma de Ayala, in his *Nueva Corónica* (ca. 1615), describes the meeting between Atahualpa and Pizarro, translated by the indigenous interpreter Felipillo and attended by the conqueror Diego de Almagro and the Friar Vicente de Valverde.

The Inca Atahualpa confronted by Pizarro and Fray Vicente Valverde. (From Felipe Guaman Poma de Ayala's *Nueva Corónica y Buen Gobierno*, ca. 1615.)

Pizarro, Almagro and Friar Vicente de Valverde waited for Atahuallpa, who was carried from the baths to the town of Caxamarca on the *usno,* a golden throne with steps which was mounted on his open litter. He arrived in great state surrounded by his officers and about 100,000 Indians, many of whom were crammed into the public square around him.

Then Francisco Pizarro, speaking for himself and Almagro, explained through the Indian interpreter Felipe that he was the messenger and ambassador of a great ruler who desired friendship with the Inca and that this was the only object of his mission to Peru. Atahuallpa listened with close attention to the words spoken by Pizarro and then by the interpreter. He answered with great dignity that he had no reason to doubt the fact of the Spaniards' long journey or their mission from an important ruler. However, he had no need to make any pact of friendship with them because he too was a great ruler in his own country.

After this reply Friar Vicente joined in the conversation. He came forward holding a crucifix in his right hand and a breviary in his left and introduced himself as another envoy of the Spanish ruler, who according to his account was a friend of God, and who often worshipped before the cross and believed in the Gospel. Friar Vicente called upon the Inca to renounce all other gods as being a mockery of the truth.

Atahuallpa's reply was that he could not change his belief in the Sun, who was immortal, and in the other Inca divinities. He asked Friar Vicente what authority he had for his own belief and the friar told him it was all written in the book which he held. The Inca then said: "Give me the book so that it can speak to me." The book was handed up to him and he began to eye it carefully and listen to it page by page. At last he asked: "Why doesn't the book say anything to me?" Still sitting on his throne, he threw it on to the ground with a haughty and petulant gesture.[3]

This version includes one particularly interesting detail that is absent in other contemporary versions of the Conquest: Atahualpa takes the Bible that the Dominican friar Vicente Valverde hands him, listens to it, shakes it, and claims disparagingly that the book does not speak to him. He then throws it on the ground. This gesture, seen as a blasphemous rejection of Christianity, prompts the devastating massacre of the Incas by a small Spanish force. Other chroniclers offer variations of this incident. Francisco de Jerez, Pizarro's scribe, claims in his *Verdadera relación de la conquista del Perú* (1534) that Atahualpa flung the book and struck Fray Valverde's hand. Juan de Santa Cruz Pachacuti, in his early-seventeenth-century *Relación de Antigüedades deste Reyno del Pirú,* recounts that twelve thousand Incas were killed during the massacre. Although he does not recount the Bible incident, he does say that the attack started after Atahualpa's conversation with Friar Vicente de Valverde.[4] Titu Cusi Yupanqui, a nephew of Atahualpa, also recounts the Spanish slaughter of unarmed Incas, who were trapped in the square like "sheep," defenseless and unable to move. He states that Atahualpa flung the Bible in retaliation for an offence against an Incan sacred object by the Spaniards the day before.[5] The Inca Garcilaso de la Vega says that Valverde dropped it.[6] Regardless of the facts, the book seems central to most versions of the actual event—though the irony is that Francisco Pizarro, the conqueror, could not read or write.

The first written reference to a performance about the death of the Inca Atahualpa dates from 1555 during a spectacular festivity in the Andean mining area of Potosí.[7] The Incas, like the Mesoamericans, had important performance practices at the time of the Conquest.[8] As in other places, the colonizers took advantage of these traditions to forward their own evangelical project. Plays such as *El hijo pródigo* and *Yauri Tito Inca: El pobre más rico,* performed in Quechua, combined indigenous and European elements. As in Mexico, official edicts prohibiting certain native practices appeared soon after the Conquest in an attempt to extinguish pre-Conquest beliefs and values. Some edicts explicitly prohibited "public functions that Indians use to remember their old Incas."[9]

While several of the chroniclers mentioned earlier witnessed many indigenous fiestas and performances, it is impossible to assess the relation of these to the play we include in this volume. Most versions lament the loss of the Incan empire. Popular enactments in various parts of Peru and Bolivia emphasize the spirit and nobility of the Incas. Lara's version, like many popular performances, is thoroughly revisionist. He praises the altruism of Atahualpa, who (Huáscar's murder notwithstanding) he claims "never provoked war between brothers." Pizarro, in defiance of historical fact, dies at the feet of the king of Spain after having been condemned for his barbaric treatment of Atahualpa. Even the violence of the Spanish Conquest is mitigated at the end. The king (called Spain in the play) is compassionate and recognizes Atahualpa as an equal. Only cruel individuals such as Pizarro could do something as barbarous as execute the Inca. Other existing scripts bear little resemblance to the Lara text. The 1784 manuscript *Atahualpa* by D. Cristoval María Cortés, which was written to be performed at the Spanish court in Madrid, praises the Spanish for putting an end to vile idolatry.[10] Before engaging the debates regarding "authenticity," we should turn to *The End of Atau Wallpa*.

Jesús Lara's text reads like a long lament, characterized by the repetitions that we have come to expect of works transmitted through oral performance. The elaborate salutations, foreshadowings, and dream interpretations recall a rich history of transmission through embodied and ritual practices. The Incas' networks are based on kinship; daughters, sons, and cousins gather to reassure the great Inca, who is seen as passive, free from sin—a saint or martyr. Women speak, though their words are limited to lamentation. This text does not include the famous scene in which Atahualpa supposedly flings the Bible. Nonetheless, the topic of writing, textuality, and understanding signs is central. The Incas were trained in one system of beliefs and protocols. Atahualpa turns to omens and dreams to decipher the foreboding he feels. A sacred figure appeared to him and in "my dreams has shown me / an incredible scene, / hard to understand, / impossible to describe." Atahualpa understood too late that the Spanish conquerors were working within a radically different system of signs. Atahualpa and his followers receive a written message, a *chala*, described by those who see the marks as resembling a "swarm of ants," "the tracks a bird leaves, / on a muddy riverbank," "a llama / with its head down." All who see it agree that the markings are impossible to comprehend: "[T]he *chala* you have brought / tells me nothing." Toward the end of the play, Valverde gives the Bible to the Inca, offering words that resonate with Guaman Poma's description: "Then accept the Bible as you listen. / It is far better than me and will speak / to you more clearly." But the meaning shifts with the positioning of the incident. The Inca Atahualpa has already been captured by the conquerors and condemned to death. He needed to accept the domination of the Spaniards, and their written language, whether he wanted to or not. Here, then, the scene with the Bible functions less as a sign of the incommensurability and indecipherability of two systems than as a sign of Spanish power.

Indecipherability in this play is effectively conveyed through speech. The Europeans move their lips, but no sound comes out. They require an interpreter, the infamous figure of Felipillo, accused of betraying native interests to the conquerors. This brilliant staging strategy captures, and reverses the traditional stereotypes of the mute "Indian." During most of the play, the Incas speak. This play centers on their relationships, their trauma, and their fate in the face of the Spaniards. Yet the topic of speechlessness and misunderstanding weaves throughout the work. At the end, when Pizarro returns to Spain with the Inca's head as a trophy, the king (Spain) says: "What are you telling me, Pizarro! / You leave me speechless! / How did you come to do that? / That face which you bring to me / is the equal of my face. / When did I order you / to put this Inca to death? / You will now be brought to justice."

While all orally transmitted, popular performances have a vexed relationship to scripted versions of them, this relationship is especially problematic in the case of *The End of Atau Wallpa.* Why? And why does it matter? We know that *Rabinal Achi,* performed for centuries, was written down various times and that each script reflects only one version of the performed event. No text can claim stability just as the performance practice changes over the years. Neither the script nor the performance is any less legitimate or important because popular practices change. Yet the stakes seem higher in the case of this play. Lara claims to have transcribed his version from a manuscript in Quechua found in Chayanta, Bolivia, dated 1871. This manuscript, like the others we have seen, would have presumably been based on a performance. However, the linguist César Itier claims that Lara's translation is a falsification intended to trick people into thinking it was a sixteenth-century piece. According to Itier, the play "was entirely written by Lara himself as he wished to prove that the Incas developed a great literature and that the heritage of this literature survived in Bolivia."[11] So are we looking at a performance with roots in the sixteenth century or at a single-authored manuscript dating from the mid–twentieth century?[12]

While we may never be able to entirely resolve this debate about the authenticity of Lara's text, this play points to a performance tradition that has continued to keep the past alive for many indigenous and mestizo rural communities in the Americas. While it is impossible to say how long these traditions have been practiced, and what changes they have experienced along the way, what the play does illuminate is how each generation brings the past alive for itself, emphasizing the issues valued *now.* In other words, each performance event is an updating, a re-presentation, based on characters and conflicts drawn from the past. There is no authentic native performance that has endured since the Conquest. So the question of whether a performance is authentic is the wrong one to ask of performed material; embodied practice, drawn from repertoires of cultural memory, does not work like that. The question might be, rather: was Lara's version based on performed material? Does it indeed record a practice or is it a single-authored text in which literary values such as authenticity apply? We have chosen to include the play toward the beginning of this volume as a reflection of this important Andean performance tradition and as an occasion to touch on questions about authenticity in performed and literary practices.

—Diana Taylor

NOTES

1. *Dramas de conquista* is the term preferred by Fernando Horcasitas in *El teatro náhuatl: Épocas novohispana moderna* (Mexico City: Universidad Nacional Autónoma de México, 1974). Luis Millones uses *danzas de la conquista* in his *Actores de altura: Ensayos sobre el teatro popular andino* (Lima: Editorial Horizonte, 1992).

2. Millones, *Actores de altura,* 26.

3. Guaman Poma, *Nueva Corónica,* trans. and ed. by Christopher Dilke as *Letter to a King: A Peruvian Chief's Account of Life under the Incas and under Spanish Rule* (New York: Dutton, 1978), 109.

4. Juan de Santa Cruz Pachacuti, *Relación de Antigüedades deste Reyno del Pirú* (Lima: l'Institut Français d'Études Andines, 1993), 165.

5. The quote is from "Relación de Titu Cusi Yupanqui," in Miguel León-Portilla, *El reverso de la conquista* (Mexico City: Editorial Joaquín Mortiz, 1964), 161. Titu Cusi's reference to the Bible is cited in Patricia Seed, "'Failing to Marvel': Atahualpa's Encounter with the Word," *Latin American Research Review* 26, no. 1 (1991): 20.

6. See Seed, "Failing to Marvel," 25.

7. The event is mentioned in José Juan Arrom, *Historia del teatro hispanoamericano (época colonial)* (Mexico City: Ediciones de Andrea, 1967), 127.

8. Jesús Lara claimed that "several sources provide evidence that the Incas knew theater in two perfectly differentiated genres: the *wanka* and the *aránway.* The first was eminently historical and was responsible for the commemoration of the lives and deeds of the monarchs and the great leaders of the empire. . . . The aránway enjoyed a wider thematic range and could take on any kind of episode related to daily life" (*Tragedia del fin de Atawallpa, Cochabamba* [Cochabamba: Impresa Universitaria, 1957], 15–16).

9. The original reads: "funciones públicas, de las que suelen usar los indios para memoria de sus dichos antiguos Incas" (José Antonio Areche, quoted in Millones, *Actores de altura,* 15).

10. This manuscript was discovered by Luis Millones in the Biblioteca Nacional de Chile. The text, along with a wealth of information about more popular versions (videos, scripts, essays, and bibliographies of four recent performances), can be found in the *web cuaderno* created by Luis Millones and Ulla Berg on the Hemispheric Institute Web site: http://www.hemisphericinstitute.org/cuaderno/atahualpa.

11. César Itier, "¿Visión de los vencidos o falsificación? Datación y autoría de la *Tragedia de la muerte de Atahuallpa.*" *Bulletin de l'Institut Français d'Études Andines* 30, no. 1 (2001): 103–4.

12. Several scholars have intervened in the debate. Arrom, in *Historia del teatro hispanoamericano,* states that he believes Lara's vision is legitimate. So, too, does Nathan Wachtel in his *The Vision of the Vanquished* (Sussex: Harvester Press, 1977). Itier asserts that these scholars legitimate Lara's text.

SELECTED REFERENCES

Acosta, José de. *Natural and Moral History of the Indies* (1590). Ed. Jane E. Mangan. Trans. Frances López-Morillas. Durham: Duke University Press, 2002.

Arrom, José Juan. *Historia del teatro hispanoamericano (época colonial).* Mexico City: Ediciones de Andrea, 1967.

Cánepa Koch, Gisela. "Los *ch'unchu* y las *palla* de Cajamarca en el ciclo de la representación de la *muerte del Inca.*" In *Música, danzas y máscaras en los Andes,* ed. Raúl R. Romero, 139–78. Lima: Pontificia Universidad Católica del Perú, 1993.

Castro-Klarén, Sara. "Dancing and the Sacred in the Andes: From the Taqui-Oncoy to Rasu-Ñiti." In *New World Encounters,* ed. Stephen Greenblatt, 159–76. Berkeley: University of California Press, 1993.

Cobo, Father Bernabe. *Inca Religion and Customs.* Trans. Roland Hamilton. Austin: University of Texas Press, 1990.

Guaman Poma de Ayala, Felipe. *Letter to a King: A Peruvian Chief's Account of Life under the Incas and under Spanish Rule.* Trans. Christopher Dilke. New York: Dutton, 1978.

Itier, César. "¿Visión de los vencidos o falsificación? Datación y autoría de la *Tragedia de la muerte de Atahuallpa.*" *Bulletin de l'Institut Français d'Études Andines* 30, no. 1 (2001): 103–21.

León-Portilla, Miguel, ed. *El reverso de la conquista.* Mexico City: Editorial Joaquín Mortiz, 1964.

Millones, Luis. *Actores de altura: Ensayos sobre el teatro popular andino.* Lima: Editorial Horizonte, 1992.

Seed, Patricia. "'Failing to Marvel': Atahualpa's Encounter with the Word." *Latin American Research Review* 26, no. 1 (1991): 7–32.

Vega, Garcilaso de la (El Inca). *Royal Commentaries of the Incas and General History of Peru.* Trans. Harold V. Livermore. Austin: University of Texas Press, [1612] 1994.

Wachtel, Nathan. *The Vision of the Vanquished: The Spanish Conquest of Peru through Indian Eyes (1530–70).* Sussex: Harvester, 1977.

The End of Atau Wallpa, a Tragedy

Translated by Margaret Carson from the Spanish version by Jesús Lara

CHARACTERS:

THE INCAS
    INCA ATAU WALLPA, the King
    INCA WAYLLA WISA, a high priest and sorcerer
    INCA SAIRI TÚPAJ
    INCA CHALLKUCHIMA
    INCA KHISHKIS
    INCAJ CHURIN, son of Atau Wallpa
    WARMA, a messenger
    ÑUST'AKUNA, the two princesses:
        QHORA CHINPU
        QÚYLLUR T'IKA
THE BEARDED ENEMIES
    PIZARRO
    SPAIN
    ALMAGRO
    FATHER VALVERDE
    FELIPILLO, the translator

ATAU WALLPA
  My beloved and gentle princesses,
  my heart is heavy with grief.
  A strange anxiety devours me
  and all reason has fled.
  I wake up in torment.
  Why for the past two nights
  has the same ill-fated dream
  come to disturb me?
  Both times I saw the Sun,
  our purifying Father,
  hidden in thick black smoke.
  I saw the wide open sky
  and all the mountains
  burning as red as the chest
  of a *pillku*[1] bird.
  Maybe death is hovering near.
  Maybe the Sun and Moon,
  our purifying Parents,
  will lead us from death's presence.
  O my adored
  Qhora Chinpu,
  O my beloved
  Qúyllur T'ika,
  my gentle princesses,
  sorrow drowns us.

  We awaken in anguish.
  Thus has our life been changed.
QHORA CHINPU
  My beloved and only lord,
  Atau Wallpa, my Inca,
  tell us, then, if in this dream
  repeated for two nights
  you saw something else.
ATAU WALLPA
  O my adored
  Qhora Chinpu,
  O my beloved
  Qúyllur T'ika,
  my gentle princesses,
  a *wak'a*[2] has given me a dark omen.
  Twice he has enchanted me
  and in my dreams has shown me
  an incredible scene,
  hard to understand,
  impossible to describe.
  Perhaps it means
  that men dressed in warlike iron
  will come to our land
  to demolish our homes
  and seize my domain,
  Qhora Chinpu, my princess.

Tragedia del fin de Atau Wallpa. Quechua and Spanish version of Jesús Lara, Bolivia, sixteenth century/1957. Translated from Spanish by Margaret Carson.

QHORA CHINPU
  My beloved and only lord,
  Atau Wallpa, my Inca
  if your dream were really true,
  what fate, then,
  what fate would await us,
  your children?
  Summon the high priest,
  your first cousin,
  he who sleeps and sees the future,
  so that his dreams will clarify
  what you have dreamed.
  If the portent is confirmed,
  assemble all your sons and first cousins.
  Have them and all
  your vassals convene.
  And then our warriors, with their
  mighty slings, will drive out
  the impudent ones
  giving up no ground.
  This I tell you, my only lord,
  my Inca Atau Wallpa.
  How beautiful it would be
  if the Sun, our Father,
  who purifies and illuminates the world,
  wished it. Then it would be so.
ATAU WALLPA
  Much beloved Inca Waylla Wisa,
  he who sleeps wisely, where
  are my two golden serpents,
  where is my golden axe?
  My Inca Waylla Wisa, where is
  my docile and fearsome *anutara*,[3]
  where is my golden sling
  of invincible might?
  Waylla Wisa, where are
  my vassals, why haven't
  they come asking for their Inca?
WAYLLA WISA
  Venerable lord and
  mighty Atau Wallpa,
  my Inca.
  May the exalted Sun, our Father,
  who illuminates the world,
  keep you safe.
ATAU WALLPA
  May he protect you as well,
  high priest who prophesies
  while sleeping,
  my first cousin.
WAYLLA WISA
  Here are your two golden serpents.
  Here is your golden axe
  and your golden sling
  of invincible might.

And here is your docile
and fearsome *anutara*.
ATAU WALLPA
  Waylla Wisa, Inca who divines
  while sleeping,
  my first cousin.
  Long ago you lived
  in the mountains, alone,
  close to the Sun, our Father,
  who cleanses us.
  You know
  what those mountains say.
  You heard
  from the jagged mouth of the *chullpas*[4]
  what no one else has heard.
  Come closer and hear me.
  For two straight nights
  I've seen nothing favorable
  in my dreams.
  When I wake up, a restless turmoil,
  a horrible anxiety invades me.
  In these two dreams
  countless men covered in angry iron
  sprang out as if from
  the bowels of the earth,
  destroyed our houses and
  greedily sacked our temples of gold
  and all our gods.
  The sky and the mountains
  burned in flames as red as the chest
  of the *pillku* bird.
  Go, Inca Waylla Wisa,
  Go and sleep
  in your golden dwelling.
  Perhaps if you sleep
  my dream will come to you.
  Go, then, Inca Waylla Wisa,
  my first cousin.
WAYLLA WISA
  Very well, my mighty lord,
  Very well, my Inca who commands me,
  I will carry out your order.
  Perhaps if I sleep
  your dream will come to me.
  I'll go with the courage of the *waychu* bird,
  mighty lord, my Inca.
ATAU WALLPA
  The eternal Father of us all,
  merciful Qhápaj Manko,[5]
  son of the purifying Sun,
  was honorable and venerated.
  From him descended
  the mighty Inca *Wiraqucha*.[6]
  It was he who by misfortune
  saw enemies wearing metal vestments

and thus he knew, back in those days,
that they would come to our land.
And I am Atau Wallpa,
son of the Inca Wayna Qhápaj.[7]
With my mighty power
I'll spill a thousand lakes of blood.
Why do they come to trample my land,
my dominion, these men
dressed in warlike iron?
There's reason to think
they've come for me,
these red-bearded enemies,
who know only of victory.
Maybe they intend to seize our land
after putting us to death.
We shall see, and we shall know
if our Father,
the Sun who purifies
and gives light to the world,
will leave and abandon us
or do the opposite,
and without mercy
turn into ashes those who have come
lusting after our gold and silver.

WAYLLA WISA
Venerable ancestors
never-forgotten Incas,
my heart is wounded.
In truth, I don't know what I've divined,
I fear our lord's dream
will become true.
I'll go to the house of my only lord
and will advise him . . .
O my beloved and mighty sovereign
a shadow has been cast over my heart.
A grave danger
hovers over us.
We may see your dream
become real.

ATAU WALLPA
O Waylla Wisa, venerable sorcerer,
he who sleeps and prophesies,
my first cousin,
what sad language you use.
Tell me what you have seen.

WAYLLA WISA
O my beloved and mighty sovereign
I've seen ominous things.
None are pleasing.
Men with long beards, all red, came
by sea in iron ships.

ATAU WALLPA
O Inca Waylla Wisa,
my first cousin,
what a sad thing you've seen,
what a cruel prophecy you bring!
Go, go back, and see
if they will truly invade
our home, our land.
Go, take an *anutara*
and while riding on its back
look from one side to the other.
Look all around these parts.
See if it is true
that the bearded enemies are coming.

WAYLLA WISA
Very well, my lord, you who command me,
I'll carry out your order,
I'll return, I'll go, I'll investigate
with firm resolve.
My dear *anutara,*
my *anutarita,* you know how
to follow me
from the tops of the mountains.
You whose vision spans the distance,
may your eyes see far.
Why do I think
that unknown enemies are
heading near,
singing songs never heard before
beating great big drums
and playing iron flutes.
But I look this way
and see nothing.
I look that way
and see nothing.
I look over there
and see nothing.
I look in every direction,
and there is nothing to be seen;
neither the cold, nor the wind.
Nothing is headed this way.
I must go to sleep again.
Maybe then I'll see something.

ÑUST'AKUNA (THE PRINCESSES)
Enemies have arrived,
my Inca,
by sea,
my Inca.
Why has misfortune,
my Inca,
come to darken our days,
my Inca.
O my beloved Waylla Wisa,
my Inca,
how long will you sleep,
my Inca.
My beloved Sairi Túpaj,
my Inca,
wake him up, make him rise,
my Inca.

SAIRI TÚPAJ
Woe is me, my beloved
Waylla Wisa, wise sorcerer,
you have slept too long.
Wake up, then, and listen to me,
and tell me what you were able
to see in your dreams.
You cannot stay asleep
when danger is approaching us.

WAYLLA WISA
What is it, what is happening, where?
I'm certain that bearded and warlike men
are coming by sea.
They come in red swarms.
I must go to sleep once again
in order to see more clearly.

ÑUST'AKUNA (THE PRINCESSES)
O my beloved Waylla Wisa,
my Inca,
how long will you sleep,
my Inca.
What cloud of sorrow is that,
my Inca,
a darkening approaches us,
my Inca,
what fatal misfortune,
my Inca,
is brought in its mist,
my Inca,
My dearly loved Challkuchima,
my Inca,
a red downpour inundates our doorway,
my Inca,
Come, maybe you,
my Inca,
can awaken this priest,
my Inca.

CHALLKUCHIMA
Waylla Wisa, wise sorcerer,
how long do you intend to sleep?
Open your eyes now
and move your lips
and tell us at once
what you saw
in your dream.
Wake up, then, rise.
Much beloved Inca Khishkis,
my first cousin
sleeps so deeply
he can't hear me.
Come as close as you can,
maybe you can awaken him.

KHISHKIS
I'll approach him, then,
to see if I can
startle him from his sleep.

Woe is me, my beloved
Waylla Wisa, lord who sleeps,
my dear Inca,
how tightly his dream has fastened him.
Our heart has become clouded
adversity is upon us.
Wake up, then, arise,
tell us what you have seen
in your dreams.

WAYLLA WISA
What is happening, what is this, where am I?
It is clear that bearded, warlike men
are coming by sea
in great iron ships.
They come in red swarms.
They carry three sharp horns
just like *tarukas*[8]
and white flour dusts their hair.
Their jaws have beards, all of them red,
like long skeins of wool,
and in their hands they carry
extraordinary iron slings,
with a hidden power.
Instead of launching stones,
they vomit flames.
And on their feet they wear
strange iron stars
that sparkle.
Woe is me! I'll go this way.
Woe is me! I'll go the other way.
My body is clumsy.
My feet trip me up and
my tongue is tied.
I'll fly, I must tell my only lord,
my Inca, my beloved sovereign.
Though I've seen nothing
an inner voice tells me
that the bearded and fierce men
are headed this way,
those who came over the waters
in great ships . . .
My beloved and only lord,
Atau Wallpa, my Inca,
I saw
bearded and warlike men arrive.
They spread out in a red swarms.
They carried three sharp horns
just like the *taruka*.
Their hair was powdered,
their beards were skeins of red wool,
iron slings were in their hands,
and at the far end of their slings,
there were fiery flames,
and on their feet, bright iron stars.

ATAU WALLPA
Woe is me, Waylla Wisa,

clever sorcerer, my first cousin,
what bitterness you bring me,
what adversity you announce!
But don't grieve.
We will take measures.
Go and meet those
bearded enemies,
ask them why they have come, and
what leads them to search for me.

WAYLLA WISA
  Very well, my only lord, my Inca,
  very well, my leader,
  I'll carry out your order.
  I'll go and meet
  those bearded enemies,
  I'll discover the reason
  they've come searching for you
  and what it is they want . . .
  Red men, bearded enemies,
  what brings you to this land,
  why are you searching for my lord,
  my Inca?

(ALMAGRO moves his lips.)

FELIPILLO
  Waylla Wisa, he who sleeps,
  the lord with the light hair says,
  "We have been sent
  by the most powerful lord on earth.
  All men owe him blind obedience."
  Messenger, tell me,
  who is the Inca who governs you?

WAYLLA WISA
  Don't you know
  that it is Atau Wallpa, the only lord,
  the mighty lord?
  Don't you know
  that only he can stand with
  the Sun and the Moon?
  Don't you know
  that the mountains and the trees
  and all living things
  submit to his will?
  Don't you know
  that only he can make his docile
  and fearsome *anutara*
  devour multitudes?
  With his invincible golden sling
  he can wound the stars, even.

(ALMAGRO moves his lips.)

FELIPILLO
  This foreigner says to you:
  "Don't speak more than you should
  and don't say stupid things.
  Understand this well:
  We don't know fear."

WAYLLA WISA
  Bearded enemy, red man,
  what dark windstorm
  has brought you
  to our country, to our land!

(ALMAGRO moves his lips.)

FELIPILLO
  This mighty lord says:
  "We have come
  in search of gold and silver."

(FATHER VALVERDE shouts.)

FELIPILLO
  This priest says:
  "No. We have come
  to make you see
  the true God."

WAYLLA WISA
  The Sun, our Father,
  is made of brilliant gold,
  and the Moon, our Mother,
  of radiant silver
  and they are both in Qurikancha.[9]
  To approach them
  you must first kiss the earth.

(FATHER VALVERDE moves his lips.)

FELIPILLO
  This wise priest says:
  "We kneel only
  in the presence of
  our Lord Jesus Christ
  the Virgin Mary, our Mother,
  and the saints."

WAYLLA WISA
  Get lost, red man who burns like fire.
  Go back to your land
  before I unleash my golden sling.

(ALMAGRO moves his lips.)

FELIPILLO
  This mighty lord tells you:
  "Don't provoke
  a fight with us.
  It's better to deliver
  this message to your lord."

WAYLLA WISA
  Bearded enemy, red man,
  what kind of white *chala*[10] is this?
  Wait here a moment,
  I'll go to my lord's dwelling place
  and I'll show him the *chala*
  you have brought . . .
  Beloved and only lord,
  Atau Wallpa, my Inca,
  this *chala* was given to me
  by those bearded and warlike men.

ATAU WALLPA
  Waylla Wisa, he who dreams,

the *chala* you have brought
tells me nothing.
WAYLLA WISA
    Give it to me,
    my much loved and only lord, my Inca,
    so that I can examine it.
    Who knows what this *chala* will say.
    Maybe I'll never know.
    Seen on this side
    it's a swarm of ants.
    On the other
    it reminds me of
    the tracks a bird leaves
    on a muddy riverbank.
    Seen like this, it's like a *taruka*
    turned upside down.
    If we look at it the other way
    it's like a llama
    with its head down
    wearing *taruka* horns.
    Who can understand this?
    No, no;
    it's impossible for me
    to understand.
ATAU WALLPA
    My brother, Waylla Wisa,
    you must go like the wind.
    Hand this *chala*
    to the Inca Sairi Túpaj,
    our first cousin.
    Ask him, maybe he knows
    what this *chala* advises.
WAYLLA WISA
    Very well, my lord,
    my Inca who commands me,
    I must take it then,
    and go like the wind
    to the Inca Sairi Túpaj,
    my cousin.
    May the Sun who purifies
    and gives light to the world
    keep you safe.
SAIRI TÚPAJ
    The same to you, Waylla Wisa,
    highest priest,
    my father, my father.
WAYLLA WISA
    Our lord sends you this *chala*.
    which the bearded warriors gave to him,
    to see if you can unravel
    its meaning.
SAIRI TÚPAJ
    Waylla Wisa, he who sleeps,
    what white *chala* is this?
    Give it to me, perhaps I will
    understand its warning.

No; I don't understand
what it means.
It cannot be anything good.
In my dreams I've seen Túkuy Jallp'a[11]
and heard from her lips that she wants
those bearded enemies.
Take this *chala*
to our Inca Challkuchima:
maybe he can decipher it.
WAYLLA WISA
    I'll take it
    to our Inca Challkuchima . . .
    My beloved Inca Challkuchima,
    may the Sun, our Father, who cleanses
    and brightens the world,
    bestow light on you.
CHALLKUCHIMA
    And may he give his light to you,
    Waylla Wisa, my Inca.
WAYLLA WISA
    The Inca Sairi Túpaj
    sends you this *chala*.
    He cannot understand
    this handiwork of the enemies.
CHALLKUCHIMA
    Give it to me, then.
    But what kind of white *chala*
    are you giving me?
    And what kind of black etchings
    is it covered with?
    I'm unable to decipher it.
    Take it, then, to the Inca Khishkis,
    our first cousin.
    Maybe he'll understand what it says.
WAYLLA WISA
    I'll take it, then, to
    our Inca Khishkis . . .
    My well-beloved Inca Khishkis,
    may the Sun, our Father,
    who purifies and gives light to the world,
    grant his light to you.
KHISHKIS
    May he give you his light in return,
    Waylla Wisa, he who sleeps,
    my father, my father.
WAYLLA WISA
    Our Inca Challkuchima says:
    "Let him decipher the *chala*
    that the bearded enemy
    has sent to our lord."
KHISHKIS
    Waylla Wisa, sorcerer,
    how can we interpret something
    that seems unintelligible.
    But if our Mother Moon
    enlightens me, perhaps I'll understand

what is locked
inside this *chala*.
I already knew
that the enemies would come.
More than four months ago,
in my dreams, our Mother Moon
told me three times
that our lord's existence
was nearing its end,
that all would soon be over.
There's no need for me
to see this *chala*.
My whole being is shaken,
my heart is destroyed.
Sorrow falls upon us,
the day of misfortune has arrived.
My Inca, my father,
he who sleeps wisely,
take this *chala*
to the son of our Inca.
Maybe he can interpret it.

WAYLLA WISA
I'll take it, then,
and give it to the son of our Inca.
Much-beloved son of our Inca,
may the Sun who cleanses, our Father,
the light of the world,
give his light to you.

INKAJ CHURIN (SON OF THE INCA)
May he give his light to you in return,
Waylla Wisa, he who sleeps.
Why do you walk
one way then the other?
Tell me now.
Maybe I'll understand you.

WAYLLA WISA
Our Inca Khishkis believes
that you may be able
to decipher this white *chala*
sent by our enemies
to our Inca, our only lord.

INKAJ CHURIN
Waylla Wisa, sorcerer,
give it to me, then.
Maybe I can untangle it.
Oh! What is this, where is it from,
what are these black marks
scratched and scattered upon it?
Who is capable of understanding it?
Go, give it back
to our Inca, our only lord,
and tell him that among our Incas
no one can understand
this *chala*.

WAYLLA WISA
I'll take it once more

to our Inca, our only lord . . .
But first I want to take it
to my Inca Sairi Túpaj.
Much-beloved Sairi Túpaj,
my first cousin,
the Incas have not been able
to decipher this *chala*.

SAIRI TÚPAJ
Waylla Wisa, high priest,
you must return it
to our Inca, our only lord.

WAYLLA WISA
Sairi Túpaj, my Inca, help me return it.

SAIRI TÚPAJ
Very well, Waylla Wisa, high priest,
so be it. Walk, then . . .
My dearly loved and only lord,
son of our Father Sun,
Túkay Jallp'a, your mother, visited me
the night before last in my dreams,
and she told me:
"I want Pizarro,
my enemy with the red beard."
Maybe his word
is on the *chala,*
but he doesn't want
to make himself clear to us.
Command Waylla Wisa,
he who sleeps, our *amauta,*[12]
to reveal what misfortune
will befall us.

ATAU WALLPA
Waylla Wisa, high priest,
my first cousin,
I command you to tell us
what will happen.

WAYLLA WISA
My dearly loved and only lord,
Atau Wallpa, my Inca,
that dream of yours will become
a clear and certain event.
What misfortune is this,
what will become of us,
all the Incas,
your children
and our grandchildren?
Thus will our end arrive.

ATAU WALLPA
Waylla Wisa, he who sleeps,
perhaps it won't happen that way.
You must go to sleep again,
perhaps you can clarify
what will happen.

WAYLLA WISA
Very well, my Inca, he who orders me,
I'll follow your command . . .

ATAU WALLPA
  Waylla Wisa, high priest,
  how long will you sleep?
  Dear Sairi Túpaj,
  my Inca, my first cousin,
  wake up this mortal,
  the one who sleeps.
SAIRI TÚPAJ
  Waylla Wisa, high priest,
  wake up, wake up,
  look at us, we're all waiting for
  your serene word.
  Waylla Wisa,
  how long will you sleep?
ATAU WALLPA
  My much-beloved Challkuchima,
  captain of captains,
  you've been asked
  to make this sorcerer wake up.
CHALLKUCHIMA
  Waylla Wisa, high priest,
  what kind of heart do you sleep with?
  Don't you see that our Father,
  the Sun, who purifies,
  is wrapped in clouds of sadness?
  Waylla Wisa,
  how long will you sleep?
ATAU WALLPA
  Beloved Inca Khishkis,
  peerless in battle,
  come closer, maybe
  this priest will awaken
  if you call.
KHISHKIS
  Beloved lord who sleeps,
  Inca Waylla Wisa, high priest,
  why do you sleep so much?
  Wake up, wake up,
  we are waiting for your word.
  Don't you see? Misfortune
  is showering ashes upon us.
  Waylla Wisa,
  how long will you sleep?
ATAU WALLPA
  My life's tender shoot,
  my beloved son,
  draw near, who knows if
  you can make this sleeping
  sorcerer awaken?
INKAJ CHURIN (SON OF THE INCA)
  Beloved lord who sleeps,
  my father, my father,
  why have you let sleep
  overcome you thus?
  How long must we
  wait for your true word?

  Don't you hear
  the sorrowful wind sighing on the roofs
  and in the branches of the trees?
  Waylla Wisa, my father,
  how long will you sleep?
ATAU WALLPA
  Much beloved Waylla Wisa,
  my first cousin,
  walk a little, then,
  come a little closer,
  and listen to my command.
WAYLLA WISA
  My dearly loved and only lord,
  Atau Wallpa, my Inca,
  here you have me, here I come,
  I am at your command.
ATAU WALLPA
  Go, then, fly to Sairi Túpaj's house,
  our first cousin,
  tell him that I command him,
  as a messenger, to meet the bearded enemy,
  to speak to them respectfully,
  and to ask them
  what it is they want in our land.
WAYLLA WISA
  Very well, my lord who commands me,
  I will carry out your orders,
  I will fly.
  I will fly to call on
  our first cousin,
  Inca Sairi Túpaj . . .
  My beloved Inca Sairi Túpaj,
  my first cousin,
  our Inca sends me
  and orders you to come before him.
SAIRI TÚPAJ
  Waylla Wisa, he who sleeps,
  my father, my father,
  I beg you, tell me
  the reason he calls me.
WAYLLA WISA
  Our only lord the Inca
  orders, "He, as our messenger, shall go and
  speak in proper language
  to the bearded enemies."
SAIRI TÚPAJ
  I will go, then, I will fly,
  I will go to his palace . . .
  My revered and only lord,
  Atau Wallpa, my Inca, our Father,
  may the Sun that purifies
  and gives light to the world
  keep you safe.
ATAU WALLPA
  And keep you safe in return,
  Inca Sairi Túpaj,

my first cousin.
Here is your golden mace
and your golden serpents.
Here is your golden sling
of invincible might
and your ferocious and obedient *anutara*.
It is you who must meet
the bearded enemy,
as the strongest of the strong;
go, then, and see what they are doing
in our land,
go, then, and ask them
why they are searching for me.

SAIRI TÚPAJ
Very well, my lord, he who commands me,
I'll carry out your noble order.
I'll go, I'll walk with no rest
until I find the bearded enemy . . .
Where, where are you,
coarse red men?
Where, where are you,
bearded enemy?
Where, where are you, you who
are looking for my only lord?

(PIZARRO moves his lips.)
Bearded enemy, red man,
Why have you been searching
for my lord, my Inca?
Don't you know that Atau Wallpa
is our Inca, our only lord?
Maybe you don't know
that he is the master of this golden mace?
Maybe you don't know
that these two golden serpents
are his property?
Before I raise
this golden mace, before these two
golden serpents devour you,
go, go back to your land,
bearded enemy, red man.

(PIZARRO moves his lips.)
Red man who burns like fire,
whose jaw has thick wool,
it's impossible for me to understand
your strange language.
I don't know what you're saying,
there's no way I can understand it.
Before my only lord, my Inca,
becomes enraged,
go, leave this place.

(PIZARRO moves his lips.)
FELIPILLO
Sairi Túpaj, Inca who commands,
the lord with light hair says:
"What foolish things have you come
to tell me, poor savage?

It's impossible for me to understand
your dark language.
But I'm asking you
where I can find your lord Inca.
I've come searching for him
and intend to capture him;
if not, I'll take his head or
his royal insignia for the mighty lord,
the king of Spain, to see."
That's what this warrior says,
Sairi Túpaj, Inca who commands.

SAIRI TÚPAJ
Bearded enemy, red man,
I can't understand your language either.
Come to the place where my lord dwells,
maybe he can understand you.
Meet him and speak to him.
He holds greater sway.

(FELIPILLO chatters with PIZARRO.)
O my much beloved
Atau Wallpa, my Inca!
I cannot decipher
the enemy's language.
The blazing light of his iron sling
fills me with fear.
It's up to you, my Inca, my only lord,
as powerful as you are,
to meet him and speak as equals.
Maybe you can decipher
their thunderous language;
I can't understand a word.
Here is your golden mace,
your two serpents,
your fierce *anutara,*
and your golden sling
of invincible might.

ATAU WALLPA
Nothing can be done then.
My well-beloved Incas,
fight, one and all,
with sling or mace;
make them return to their land;
make them go back
the same way they came.
Don't let the bearded enemies
defeat you.

WAYLLA WISA
My well-beloved Incas,
gather quickly.
We'll fight the bearded enemies
as one.
We'll defeat them
and throw them back
to their land.

WARMA
The one lord whom we fear,

who defeats and rules over all,
Atau Wallpa, my Inca,
bearded warlike men
who stain the path red
are headed this way.

ATAU WALLPA

Bearded enemy, red man,
where have you wandered from, lost?
Why have you come,
what winds have brought you here,
what do you want
in my house, here in my land?
On the route you followed
weren't you burned by the fiery sun?
Didn't the cold pierce you?
The mountain, which drew back
as you advanced—didn't it crush you
beneath its peaks?
And as the earth opened under your feet,
didn't it bury you?
And the ocean,
didn't it engulf you,
make you disappear?
By what means did you come
and what do you want from me?
Go, return to your country
before I lift my golden mace
and put an end to you.
Bearded enemy, I tell you:
Go back to your land.

(PIZARRO shouts, making furious gestures.)

FELIPILLO

Lord Inca Atau Wallpa,
this commander says to you:
"It's useless for you to talk
or unleash a torrent of words
I can't understand you.
I'm a stubborn man
and all humble themselves before me.
I'll allow you a minute
to get ready
to say farewell
to those around you.
Prepare yourself. You must leave
with me for a city named Barcelona.
In the same way that you humiliated
your brother, Inca Huáscar,[13] when
he was in your hands,
you will likewise bend before me."

SAIRI TÚPAJ

Bearded enemy, why
are you tying
the hands of the Inca, my only lord,
so roughly?
He was born free and unbound,
the same as the *taruka;*

he is as strong as the puma.
A man as noble and generous
as our Inca, doesn't exist.

(PIZARRO moves his lips.)

FELIPILLO

Sairi Túpaj, Inca who commands,
the lord with light hair says:
"I already told you why I came to this land:
I must lead this lord
into the presence of my all-powerful majesty.
I will not say it again."

ATAU WALLPA

Woe is me! My well-beloved lord,
you who seem like Wiraqucha,
I'm in your hands.
Why do you still lose your temper?
Maybe you feel tired;
rest awhile;
maybe the sun has overcome you;
sit in the shade under
my golden tree.
I am doubled over
at your feet, under your control.

ÑUST'AKUNA (THE PRINCESSES)

My only lord, Atau Wallpa,
my Inca,
the bearded enemy has chained you,
my Inca,
to put an end to your existence,
my Inca,
to seize your lands,
my Inca.
The heart of the bearded enemy,
my Inca,
is impatient for gold and silver,
my Inca.
If he demands gold and silver,
my Inca,
we will hand it over now,
my Inca.

(PIZARRO moves his lips.)

FELIPILLO

Atau Wallpa, the only Inca,
this mighty lord says:
"Today you will go
wherever I tell you."

ATAU WALLPA

O lord Wiraqucha,
don't behave this way.
If you want gold and silver,
I'll spread it out at once
and cover all the land
within the range of my slingshot.

(PIZARRO moves his lips.)

FELIPILLO

Inca Atau Wallpa, the only lord,

this mighty lord says:
"I want you to cover
this field with gold and silver."
SAIRI TÚPAJ
My well-loved and only lord,
Atau Wallpa, my Inca,
we'll walk, we'll fly
just like the *waychu*[14] bird
and we'll bring gold and silver
to these bearded enemies
until we cover this field.
(PIZARRO *moves his lips.*)
FELIPILLO
My only lord, Atau Wallpa,
this mighty lord says to you:
"I've come for the sole purpose
of taking your head
or at least your royal insignia
so that my sovereign can see it."
ATAU WALLPA
O bearded enemy, Wiraqucha,
when we met yesterday
you could see me among
my countless vassals,
honored, carried aloft
on a majestic golden litter.
And now you see me
at your feet,
humiliated, and
you speak to me with arrogance.
Have you forgotten
that everything depends on my will,
that the gold and silver
are under my command?
Ask me for whatever
you want, and
I'll hand it over to you.
Here is my golden *llaut'u;*[15]
here is my golden mace.
Take my golden sling.
I give this all to you.
But don't end my existence,
mighty lord.
ÑUST'AKUNA (THE PRINCESSES)
Our luck has run out,
misfortune is with us,
our days have been darkened,
there is nothing but tears in our eyes.
From now on, in our hearts
only sadness will prevail
and in the midst of a desert
our existence will languish.
Mighty enemy, don't take
the life of our Inca;
if it's gold and silver you need,
we'll give it to you now.

(PIZARRO *moves his lips.*)
FELIPILLO
Lord Inca Atau Wallpa,
this mighty lord says:
"I haven't come because you are powerful,
or to look for gold and silver,
but to lead you away;
if you resist leaving with me,
everything will end
and I'll take your head
or your royal insignia
to my majesty."
ATAU WALLPA
Woe is me! In that case,
my Wiraqucha, my lord,
wait a moment for me.
I must lament my tragedy
and then you can lead me
wherever you want.
Bearded men, enemies,
from now on you will suffer greatly;
whatever gold and silver there is,
let it be hidden deep in the rocks
and if some is left over
let it turn to ash.
Opulence, hide yourself,
poverty, come forth.
He who covets gold,
let him work to find it
sweating like a slave.
(PIZARRO *moves his lips.*)
FELIPILLO
My only Inca, Atau Wallpa,
this mighty lord says:
"I'll wait a moment
so that you can say farewell
to your friends."
ATAU WALLPA
O my beloved and gentle princess,
these bearded enemies
truly wish to take my life.
And what remembrance will I leave you?
I'll leave you my golden *llaut'u.*
You must tell it
all your sorrows. It will protect
you at all times.
ÑUST'AKUNA (THE PRINCESSES)
In what spirit do I receive
this, your golden *llaut'u*?
How can we forget
your tender affection?
ATAU WALLPA
Ah, you, my other princess,
you, my heart's favorite,
the delight of my eyes,
What will I leave you,

my princess?
I'll leave you my golden sling.
If you find yourself in any trouble
you only need to confide in it.
At any moment, it will help you
in my stead.

ÑUST'AKUNA (THE PRINCESSES)

In what spirit do I receive
this, your golden sling?
How can I ever forget
your worthy rule?

ATAU WALLPA

My much-beloved Sairi Túpaj,
my first cousin,
now, to you,
what can I leave?
It will be this golden mace.
Let it know everything
and it will help you
in my stead.

SAIRI TÚPAJ

O my beloved
Atau Wallpa, my Inca,
in what spirit do I receive
this your golden mace?
How could I ever forget you,
Inca, my only lord.
Now I will seek refuge
in the bosom of the mountain
accompanied by your golden mace.

ATAU WALLPA

My beloved Inca Khishkis,
my first cousin,
what shall I leave you?
I'll leave you these
two golden serpents of mine.
Care for them gently
and always remember that they were tamed
by your Inca and lord.
You must tell them all that happens to you
and in my place
they will help you in every way.

KHISHKIS

O much-beloved lord
who rules us all,
Atau Wallpa, my Inca,
what will become of us,
the Incas, your children,
when your life is extinguished,
when your rule is ended, when we find
ourselves in the hands of the bearded enemies,
when we see that they rule
our land and our home?
Thus the end
of your existence is near.

We will heed
your warnings, and leave.
We'll go to the far reaches
of our lands, leading all our subjects,
and there will guard the memory
of your rule and of how you met your end.
We'll remember the words we heard you say
at the moment of your death.

CHALLKUCHIMA

My much-beloved and only lord,
Atau Wallpa, my Inca, may the Sun
that purifies and gives light to the world,
our Father, keep you safe.

ATAU WALLPA

May he protect you as well
my much-beloved Challkuchima,
first among my vassals,
who will never be conquered,
who will never humble himself,
who will always achieve victory.
It was because of your strength,
because of your invincible power,
that I was able to move my dominion
from one territory to another.
Acknowledging all this, Inca,
what can I possibly leave you?
It will be this, my golden shield.
Tell it the sorrow that you feel, and it will
keep watch over all you do.
When you find yourself overcome
with sorrow, turn your eyes to it
and say, "This is the golden shield
that the Inca, my only lord,
gave me when his death approached."

CHALLKUCHIMA

My beloved and only lord,
Atau Wallpa, my Inca,
how sorrowful
to be given your golden shield.
My hands, in anguish, receive it.
Will it come to pass
that the bearded enemy
will take your life?
How can we live
without you, our father?
Must I seek refuge in
the bosom of the mountain,
protecting your golden shield,
remembering that it was
for my Inca and father, Atau Wallpa,
that I was raised?

ATAU WALLPA

My much-beloved and gentle Inca,
son I raised with all my love,
where are you? Where do you go?
Come, come near me.

INKAJ CHURIN (SON OF THE INCA)
> My much-beloved and only lord,
> my father, Atau Wallpa, may the
> Sun who purifies, the light of the world,
> our Father, keep you safe.

ATAU WALLPA
> May he protect you as well,
> my adored and only son.
> In what kind of trance are we:
> is it real or is it a dream?
> Our Father Sun has abandoned us
> and allowed all our subjects
> to fall into ruin.
> Now my life is almost over.
> I'm finished, without a chance;
> my being has been shattered,
> my heart is crushed.
> I'll disappear forever,
> abandoning my land,
> and I'll scatter my children, the Incas,
> in sorrow.
> Only the bearded enemies
> will remain in my land
> subjugating my children.
> But my children to come
> will remember that this was
> the land of Atau Wallpa, their Inca,
> their father, their only lord,
> and they will throw out
> all the bearded enemies who have come
> lusting after our gold and silver
> and force them to return
> to their land.

INKAJ CHURIN (SON OF THE INCA)
> My father, Inca, my Inca,
> what are you saying?
> How forsaken we will be
> lacking your shadow.
> Where must I go then,
> whom should I approach,
> who will accompany my life,
> who will guide me as I walk?
> As a fatherless child,
> I will go from place to place
> with no direction and no destination.
> O my father, you who command me,
> thus shall we Incas
> meet our end, for eternity.
> If it were not so, we would
> die together with you
> in order to dwell with the Sun,
> our Father,
> like the ancient Incas.
> O my father, my father!

ATAU WALLPA
> O my son! And what

will I leave you?
> I will leave you this bright
> and shining diamond.
> Take it with you.
> Leave this place
> and seek refuge in Willkapanpa[16]
> accompanied by the Incas,
> your first cousins
> and all your subjects,
> without letting the bearded enemy
> get near your home.
> He will be the one
> to end your existence.

INKAJ CHURIN (SON OF THE INCA)
> My beloved father,
> my only lord, my Inca,
> in what spirit do I receive
> this your diamond,
> so beautiful and luminous?
> How can I ever forget,
> my only Inca Atau Wallpa.
> I will go from here
> and head towards Willkapanpa,
> and the Incas, your children,
> my first cousins,
> and all your vassals,
> will go with me.
> Thus we will wander
> until the end of our days.
> O lord, my Inca,
> my father, my father.

ATAU WALLPA
> My much-beloved Waylla Wisa,
> my adored first cousin,
> what shall I leave you?
> I will leave you our Father Sun
> and our Mother Moon.
> In the midst of sorrow
> you will turn to them.
> When your existence has ended,
> you will descend into
> the bosom of the sea
> together with them.

WAYLLA WISA
> My much-beloved and only lord,
> Atau Wallpa, my Inca,
> how could I forget you, sturdy tree,
> after you have fallen?
> To whom do I turn,
> whom do I seek,
> what door do I approach,
> to whom do I tell my sorrows?
> I'm still alive,
> but I must seek refuge
> in the bosom of the sea

together with our Father Sun
and our Mother Moon.
(PIZARRO *moves his lips.*)
FELIPILLO
    Inca Atau Wallpa, our only lord,
    this mighty lord says to you:
    "My ears are tired
    of listening to all
    this Inca has been saying.
    I can no longer
    listen to him."
ATAU WALLPA
    Bearded enemy, Wiraqucha,
    I haven't gone anywhere,
    I'm not used to divining
    anyone's misfortunes.
    On this memorable day
    you will take my life;
    but I will live in your thoughts;
    you will carry
    the stain of my blood
    eternally.
    My subjects will never
    look you in the eye.
    And do you think
    my children will be pleased
    by what you've done?
    Even the bird that has no feeling
    will augur misfortune wherever you go.
    You will walk without rest,
    and fierce enemies will
    destroy you with their hands.
    You will curse
    my unshakeable power for all eternity.
(PIZARRO *moves his lips.*)
FELIPILLO
    Powerful Inca Atau Wallpa,
    this mighty lord says:
    "Talking to this fool
    is a waste of time.
    Perhaps he wants to put me to sleep
    and trick me into falling captive.
    I don't want to listen
    to one more word."
(PADRE VALVERDE *moves his lips.*)
    My one lord, Inca Atau Wallpa,
    this wise priest says:
    "Inca of all mortals,
    a new light awaits you.
    Renounce your idols
    and believe in our Father.
    Adore God the all-powerful;
    and be blessed with holy
    and redeeming baptismal water
    lest you suffer
    for all eternity

in the burning flames of hell.
    Inca of all mortals,
    confess your sins.
    It's not good to die
    without washing them away.
    Through my intercessor,
    our Lord Jesus Christ,
    our merciful Father,
    I forgive your sins
    and he himself will raise
    you to eternal glory.
    Inca of all mortals,
    you don't seem to understand
    the words I say.
    Then accept the Bible as you listen.
    It is far better than me and will speak
    to you more clearly."
ATAU WALLPA
    It says absolutely nothing to me.
(PADRE VALVERDE *moves his lips.*)
FELIPILLO
    This prudent priest says:
    "Children of the Almighty,
    come and help me!
    This foolish man has uttered a blasphemy!
    Punish him! His sin
    must not go unpunished!"
(PIZARRO *moves his lips.*)
    This mighty lord says:
    "My Father, my Father,
    sprinkle on his body
    a final absolution, at least."
(PADRE VALVERDE *moves his lips.*)
    This wise priest says:
    "Thus have your sins been forgiven
    through the intercession of baptism."
(PIZARRO *moves his lips.*)
    This powerful lord says:
    "O august Mary,
    my Immaculate Mother, my Queen,
    give me the courage to
    cut off this man's head.
    Dark savage, at this very moment
    I will put you to death
    with this iron sword."
ÑUST'AKUNA (THE PRINCESSES)
    My Inca, my only lord,
    what misfortune rains down,
    my Inca, my only lord.
    The great tree has fallen,
    my Inca, my only lord.
    We lived in your shadow,
    my Inca, my only lord,
    you were our day,
    my Inca, my only lord.
    This your beautiful golden *llaut'u,*

my Inca, my only lord,
was stolen by the enemies,
my Inca, my only lord.
Seeing your golden *llaut'u*,
my Inca, my only lord,
your majesty and your power,
my Inca, my only lord,
came to our minds,
my Inca, my only lord.
We don't have the heart to forget you,
my Inca, my only lord,
our revered Inca,
my Inca, my only lord.
We find ourselves in anguish,
my Inca, my only lord,
how will our hearts live,
my Inca, my only lord,
without the protection of your shadow,
my Inca, my only lord,
prodigious tree, now fallen,
my Inca, my only lord.
We will never again see,
my Inca, my only lord,
that beautiful *llaut'u* of gold,
my Inca, my only lord,
as resplendent as the Sun,
my Inca, my only lord.
All, all is darkening,
my Inca, my only lord,
like a storm cloud,
my Inca, my only lord.
A whirlwind has been unleashed,
my Inca, my only lord,
the mountains are falling,
my Inca, my only lord,
blood flows in the river,
my Inca, my only lord,
the diaphanous sky,
my Inca, my only lord,
is dressed in mourning,
my Inca, my only lord.
What hand is there,
my Inca, my only lord,
to hold your royal scepter of gold,
my Inca, my only lord.
Your noble and manly voice,
my Inca, my only lord,
made the world tremble,
my Inca, my only lord,
your unequaled might,
my Inca, my only lord,
made the mountains speak,
my Inca, my only lord.
Since you have abandoned us,
my Inca, my only lord,
to whom should we lift,
my Inca, my only lord

our tear-filled eyes,
my Inca, my only lord.
KHISHKIS
    Tarukas of the plains,
    condors high above,
    rivers and rocky places,
    come and weep with us.
    Our father and lord the Inca
    has left us alone,
    lost in profound grief.
    What shadow do we search for
    and to whom shall we turn?
    What martyrdom will we suffer,
    what tears will drown us?
    Atau Wallpa, my Inca,
    perhaps we should seek refuge
    in the bowels of the earth.
    My father, Inkaj Churin,
    walk, come closer,
    help lead us to
    our Inca and only lord,
    don't look at us with indifference.
    The gold and silver is lost.
    The splendor of our Inca,
    our only lord, has ended.
    Our mighty Inca has died at the hands
    of the bearded enemy.
ÑUST'AKUNA (THE PRINCESSES)
    Bearded enemies,
    you have put my lord to death
    with your iron swords.
    Thus you too shall die.
    You have annihilated our father
    with the burning fire of those irons.
    Yet with that same fire
    you too shall burn.
    My Inca, your illustrious power
    ruled the world;
    it exists no longer,
    for the cloud has darkened.
INKAJ CHURIN (SON OF THE INCA)
    My Inca, my only lord,
    in what hands do you leave me,
    a boy with no experience?
    Which way do I walk?
    What anxieties will I face?
    In what caves will I stumble,
    in whose shadow will I find refuge?
    What is my life's purpose?
    O my Inca, my father,
    how can I forget you,
    my Inca, my only lord?
    Your precious words
    have been extinguished,
    your sovereign power has vanished.
    Venerable and everlasting Sun
    purifying light of the world,

my Father, my Father,
Why did you let them
take his life?
Didn't he strive
to carry out your will?
Didn't he keep
your sacred precepts?
Woe is me! My father
no longer hears me!
His eyes are darkened; he no
longer needs me.
Woe is me! My much-beloved
first cousins,
to whom shall we turn?
Look upon our Inca.
He no longer sees us;
his breath is extinguished.
And the Sun that purifies, our Father,
is leaving us.
How will we survive
without the Inca, our lord?
Is it real or only a dream
that the great tree has fallen?
You, Pizarro, Wiraqucha,
greedy for gold and silver,
who struck down our Inca,
you will die a pitiless death!
May your powerful might
vanish forever.
Bearded enemy, Wiraqucha,
you will be a prisoner
of your remorse.
What will we do now
without the all-powerful Inca?
All is darkening
like a storm cloud.

PIZARRO
Venerable lord of Spain,
I come having fulfilled
your royal will.
I bring you the head and
the *llaut'u* of that Inca.

SPAIN
What are you saying, Pizarro?

PIZARRO
My powerful and only lord,
your just and royal mandate
has been carried out and executed.
Here is the head and here is the *llaut'u*
of that ignorant Inca.

SPAIN
What are you telling me, Pizarro!
You leave me speechless!
How did you come to do that?
That face that you bring me
is the equal of my face.

When did I order you
to put this Inca to death?
You will now be brought to justice.

PIZARRO
Woe is me! woe is me, Jehovah!
Woe is me! woe is me, Lord of Israel,
I've committed an offense.
I've mocked the heavens
and I've mocked you as well!
On my own feet I traveled
and plotted subtle intrigues
to lead that brave and noble Inca
to his death.
With this my cursed sword
I spilled the blood
of that Inca whose conscience
was clean. Accursed was the day
that was so ill-fated to me.

SPAIN
O my exalted Mother,
what stands before my eyes!
Religion, justice, happiness—
don't they already exist?
O uncontrolled sinner,
man poisoned by gold,
here is your downfall! O Pizarro,
Pizarro, what a base traitor you are!
Your heart was born
for plunder! Why did you
cut off the head of the Inca?
Did you not see him govern
countless subjects in the midst
of good fortune and happiness
and in unshakeable harmony,
always with a kind word?
Did you not hear him speak
in a serene voice?
It was like a joyful song.
Did you not see
his palace adorned with gold?
There the dawn broke for the Inca,
in the midst of flowering trees,
lulled by singing birds.
He sat on his golden throne,
venerated by his vassals.
He never provoked war
between brothers, he gave
his favor to those who earned it,
and he punished the guilty.
Where are my guards?

ALMAGRO
My noble and only lord,
here I am, at your feet.

SPAIN
Look at this vassal, then.
He seems dead already.

ALMAGRO
    My noble and only lord,
    he is surely dead.
SPAIN
    If that's true, take him away.
    Go, put him on the fire.

May he perish and with him, all his descendants,
and destroy his house.
Nothing shall remain of this infamous soldier.
Those are my orders.

NOTES

All notes to this play are by the translator.
1. A brightly colored bird.
2. A term applied to all sacred objects or places.
3. A bear.
4. Conical tumulus; funerary towers constructed by the Indians for burial.
5. According to legends, he was the first Inca.
6. One of the three most important Inca gods according to the Spanish chroniclers.
7. The father of Atau Wallpa.
8. A kind of deer.
9. A sacred precinct or Temple of the Sun.
10. A corn husk.
11. The mother of Atau Wallpa.
12. A philosopher.
13. Inca Huáscar was the first-born of Wayna Qhápaj and the brother of Atau Wallpa. He was defeated and killed by Atau Wallpa's army in a war of succession.
14. A bird with a brown breast and white tail.
15. A red string wrapped around the forehead that indicated royal status.
16. The last of the Incan cities and the hiding place of the last Inca king, Manco Inca.

MEXICO

The Loa for the Auto Sacramental of The Divine Narcissus (Sor Juana Inés de la Cruz)

There was nothing ordinary about her person or her life. She was exceptionally beautiful, and poor. She was the favorite of a Vicereine and lived at court, courted by many; she was loved, and perchance she loved. Abruptly she gives up worldly life and enters a convent—yet, far from renouncing the world entirely, she converts her cell into a study filled with books, works of art, and scientific instruments and transforms the convent locutory into a literary and intellectual salon. She writes love poems, verses for songs and dance tunes, profane comedies, sacred poems, an essay in theology, and an autobiographical defense of the right of women to study and to cultivate their minds. She becomes famous, sees her plays performed, her poems published, and her genius applauded in all the Spanish dominions, half the Western world. Then suddenly she gives up everything, surrenders her library and collections, renounces literature, and finally, during an epidemic, after ministering to stricken sisters in the convent, dies at the age of forty-six.

—Octavio Paz, *Sor Juana, or the Traps of Faith*

Sor Juana Inés de la Cruz. Portrait attributed to Juan de Miranda. (From the Dirección General del Patrimonio, Universidad Nacional Autónoma de México, Mexico City.)

Even in her own time, Sor Juana Inés de la Cruz, born Juana de Asbaje y Ramírez de Santillana, possibly between 1648 and 1651, in the town of San Miguel de Nepantla near Mexico City, was considered to be an extraordinarily brilliant and creative thinker. Most of her learning was self-taught. Minimal instruction was available to girls, and women were not allowed to attend university. She wrote, "[When I] discovered that in the City of Mexico there was a university with schools where different branches of learning could be studied . . . I deluged my mother with urgent and insistent pleas to change my manner of dress and send me to stay with relatives in the City of Mexico so that I might study and take courses."[1] As cross-dressing was apparently not an option, she taught herself. Her approach to Latin offers an example of her style of self-instruction: "I used to cut four or five fingers' width from [my hair] . . . making it my rule that if by the time it grew back to that point, I did not know such-and-such a thing which I had set out to learn as it grew, I would cut it again as a penalty for my dullness . . . for I did not consider it right that a head so bare of knowledge should be dressed with hair."[2] Her mother allowed her to go to Mexico City to live with relatives when she was about ten years old, and her remarkable intelligence and beauty brought her to the attention of the court, where she was made a lady-in-waiting to the vicereine, the marquise de Mancera, with whom she formed a close bond. It is not clear why she left this position to enter a convent, first in 1666 and then permanently when she entered the San Jerónimo Convent in 1669, although, given her poor economic circumstances and her self-proclaimed "total disinclination to marriage,"[3] it was probably her best option to continue her life of study. Called the "tenth muse" and the "Mexican Phoenix," she attracted visitors from throughout the viceroyalty of New Spain and Europe who would attend her regular *tertulias* (gatherings) in the convent to discuss her work and ideas. David Pasto, in the introduction to his translation of her comic cloak-and-dagger play *The House of Trials,* states that "the Viceroy and the Vicereine, as well as other members of the court, visited the convent frequently to attend vespers, hear the musical and dramatic presentations, and chat in the locutory."[4] Later Sor Juana became even closer with the subsequent viceroy, the marquis de la Laguna and his wife, María Luisa, the countess of Paredes, with whom scholars suggest she had a close, perhaps even passionate relationship.[5] María Luisa saw to the publication of a collection of Sor Juana's poetry, *Inundación Castálida,* in Madrid in 1689, and Sor Juana dedicated the volume to her. She also wrote work at the request of the vicereine, including *The Divine Narcissus,* whose *loa* (introductory praise poem) is included here. In spite of the protection the court authorities offered her, Sor Juana infuriated strict theologians who attacked her for her love of learning and public profile.[6] After the return of the viceroy and vicereine to Spain in 1688, Sor Juana was far more vulnerable to the demands and restrictions imposed on her by highly censorious religious leaders. She was forced to give up her books and her scientific and musical instruments and sign a document, in her own blood, stating that she renounced "Humane Studies." A few months before dying, she asked her "beloved sisters the nuns . . . to commend me to God, for I have been and am the worst among them." The document is signed, "I, worst of all the world, Juana Inés de la Cruz."[7]

The social values and organization made visible in this brief outline of Sor Juana's life—the strict, male hierarchy, the tension between Church and civil powers, the strict policing of ideas and religious orthodoxy, the exclusion or control of women—also played out in the broader social spectacles of the period. The theatricality of the massive seventeenth-century displays of religious and state power, at times rivaling each other, reminded everyone of their place in the scheme of things. The displays served as a form of public pedagogy that extended the sixteenth-century notion that semiliterate or illiterate populations learned through the eyes. These demonstrations made power visible. Church authorities promoted festivals such as Corpus Christi (the celebration of the Holy Eucharist and the triumph of Catholicism), which consisted of elaborate processions that included ecclesiastical and political figures, triumphal arches covered with thousands of flowers, and various types of performances.[8] Traditions from medieval Spain mingled with native elements to create spectacles such as medieval mystery plays on *carros* (wheeled carts), Nahuatl versions of biblical stories, tableaux vivants, and mock battles between Moors and Christians. Far grimmer examples of Church power were performed through the autos-da-fé of the Spanish Inquisition, the public processions and burnings of "heretics" either in the flesh or in effigy. Representatives of the Spanish crown rivaled the Church for public attention with stunning celebrations to commemorate royal marriages, births, deaths, and ascensions to the throne.

In addition to the intense theatrics that accompanied the emergence of New Spain, a lively theater scene sprang up in Mexico in the late sixteenth century. The first theater, or *casa de farsas,* was built in 1587 followed by the *corral* of the Hospital Real de Indios, a permanent theater that contributed to the financial support of the hospital. After the first university of the Americas was founded in Mexico in 1551, university theater became popular, and by the seventeenth century plays were regularly staged there. Finally, starting in the mid–seventeenth century, the court became another site for theatrical performances. Certain conditions were imposed by civil and Church authorities: while women were allowed to act, they had to behave in an "honest" manner, and cross-dressing was not allowed. Men and women occupied separate spaces in the audience. All texts had to be approved by the archbishop, and representatives of the law were to attend all performances.[9] It is important to keep in mind, though, for the understanding of Sor Juana's *Loa,* that two kinds of performances were prohibited by the Holy Inquisition during this period: masked dances and festivities by the native populations outside the realm of the Catholic Church, and performances in the convents (and their churches).[10] This means that the native dances performed in Sor Juana's *Loa* would not have been permitted and that she, as a nun who never left her convent, would have enjoyed few opportunities to either stage or see her plays performed, although she did teach theater to young girls as part of her duties as a nun at San Jerónimo.

The Divine Narcissus is an *auto sacramental,* a long one-act play in honor of the Holy Eucharist that was usually performed during the feast of Corpus Christi. The *Auto,* which is not included here, can, as one commentator puts it, be summed up quite clearly: "[I]f one gives up the pleasures and pains of this life (love, sex, honor, rivalry) in favor of the duties of the Church (commandments, sacraments, responsibilities), one will be rewarded with tranquility of a society marked by law and order, and in the next life one will achieve ecstatic union with God."[11] On one level this is true, though the play, like Narcissus, who fell in love with his own reflection, is all about mirroring and refraction; there is nothing clear or straightforward about it. Like all of Sor Juana's writings, it is rife with double and triple meanings, meaningful silences, and elegant shifts and evasions that allow her to say what she wants to say without saying it too directly. "I want no trouble with the Holy Office," she wrote.[12] She was well aware that many audiences were paying attention to her work, some more admiring than others.

The *Loa,* which preceded the full-length play during Corpus Christi, is an allegory that stages the confrontation between America (a native woman) and her consort, Occident (a "gallant-looking" native man), and Religion (a "Spanish lady") and her consort, Zeal (a captain "in armor"). In the opening, pre-Conquest scene, the actors do the unspeakable—that is, they verbalize the "heretical" and therefore prohibited tenets of Mexica faith and dance the steps that natives were forbidden to dance. Moreover, the scene depicts the natives as beautiful and gracious. The play then introduces the Spaniards in Scene Two. The sight of the indigenous celebration offends Religion, who incites Zeal to arms. Only after he sets off to "take revenge" does Religion decide to show mercy and try to redeem her victims through evangelization and argumentation. What follows is a brilliant reflection on the colonial predicament. Force can vanquish the unarmed America, but it cannot change the hearts and minds of people. In Scene Three, Occident responds to Religion: "I must bow to your aggression / but not before your arguments." America vows resistance: "A weeping captive, I may mourn / for liberty, yet my will grows / beyond these bonds; my heart is free / and I will worship my own gods!" Occident reminds us that conquest's "cruel might / has limits." Coercion, Sor Juana knew well from her own experience, was not the best path to faith. Determined not to let America die as Zeal suggests ("la necesito viva" or "her life is of some worth to us"), Religion needs to win the hearts of her captives. Scene Four, then, is about convincing the conquered that what they perceive as "coercion" is really "affection" by finding a system of equivalences that shows that both religions in fact share basic similarities.

This strategy of finding equivalencies rather than categorical and fixed certainties is of course remarkable for various reasons. For one thing, this strategy characterizes native cosmologies, as suggested in the introduction to this collection. Thus, Sor Juana is turning to the Mexica worldview, rather than the European, to find a solution to the impasse. Second, Catholics were reluctant to accept the possibility of any similarity between their religion and what they claimed was pagan devil worship. Friar Diego Durán, who wrote *History of the Indies of New Spain* around 1581, explains the similarities by stating that the Mexica were descended from the Hebrews, thus explaining the resemblance of their creation stories to chapters 1 and 2 of Genesis.[13] Friar Bernardino Sahagún denies the similarities and states that the devil (the Antichrist we see in *Final Judgment*), the master of deception, brought imitations of Christianity to the native populations, which learned them. Sor Juana offers a radically different version. Religion asks America and Occident about their beliefs. Although she, too, rejects their response as the work of the "false, sly, and deceitful snake," she does so in an "aside" and continues the dialogue until they find points of commonality. The Christian God is not "new" but rather "unknown" to them; He is boundless and invisible but can paradoxically be touched and served by humble and unworthy priests—both Christian and native. The ritual cannibalism (*teoqualo,* or "eating of the god") that the Spaniards considered an abomination is compared to communion, and America is happy to learn that the new God is "lovingly / transformed for me into a meal." Both identify similar practices around religious observance—such as bathing and baptism. And finally, of course, Christ is presented by Religion as a victim of sacrifice. But America and Occident, like all native people according to the colonists, learn less from argumentation than from demonstration; they need to see to believe.

Yet the final scene, which deals with the planning of the auto that will satisfy America and Occident's need to see to believe, is all about staging the auto in Spain. If we follow the logic used in the *Loa,* then they—the Spanish—are the ones who need to see to believe. And what they see, if Religion succeeds in "loading the whole Indies on / a stage to transport to Madrid," would be a highly refined image of America and Occident. They also see a notable shift in Religion from the figure who initially prods Zeal into violence to another Sor Juana—a writer motivated by "obedience," not "arrogance," who becomes almost indistinguishable from her seeming coauthor, America, who apologizes for these "awkward lines." While part of this transformation has to do with the loa form itself, it cannot have escaped the notice of Sor Juana's critics that the *Loa* ends as it began. In an ironic inversion, America and Occident have converted Religion and Zeal, who leave the stage, all praising the "great God of Seeds." No wonder so many clerics distrusted her. No wonder so many scholars, artists, and feminist commentators have found her such a model of resilience and inspiration.

—Diana Taylor

NOTES

1. Sor Juana, *Reply to Sor Philothea,* in *A Sor Juana Anthology,* ed. Alan S. Trueblood (Cambridge: Harvard University Press, 1988), 211.

2. Ibid., 211–12.

3. Ibid., 212.

4. David Pasto, introduction to Sor Juana Inés de la Cruz, *The House of Trials* (*Los empeños de una casa*), trans. David Pasto (New York: Peter Lang, 2002), 4.

5. Octavio Paz notes, "Most of Sor Juana's biographers, while aware of her relationship with María Luisa Manrique de Lara, have preferred to skirt the issue." Octavio Paz, *Sor Juana, or, The Traps of Faith,* trans. Margaret Sayers Peden (Cambridge, Mass.: Belknap, 1988), 197. Paz states that much of Sor Juana's writing is typical of her time, though he notes that when *Inundación Castálida* was published in 1689 a "Warning" preceded the poems to the countess of Paredes, addressing the poet's "love utterly pure and ardent for her Excellency" (199). Paz himself puts the passion down to "sublimation of sexuality," a position that has been parodied by artists such as the Mexican performer, director, and writer Jesusa Rodríguez, in her full-blown lesbian rendition of the relationship in *Sor Juana in Jail* (See Diana Taylor and Roselyn Costantino, *Holy Terrors: Latin American Women Perform* (Durham: Duke University Press, 2004).

6. In *Reply to Sor Philothea,* Sor Juana mentions that she was prohibited by a "very holy and very ingenious prelate" from studying, which she obeyed in the literal sense for three months—though not in the broadest sense of the word, writing, "I saw nothing without reflecting on it; I heard nothing without wondering at it" (224). There is so much to be learned from simple, everyday things such as cooking, she writes with humor, that "if Aristotle had been a cook, he would have written much more" (226).

7. Paz, *Sor Juana,* 464–65. A 1990 film by the Argentine filmmaker María Luisa Bemberg focusing on the life of Sor Juana is called *Yo, la peor de todas* (I, The Worst of All).

8. See Dalmacio Rodríguez Hernández, "La relación de fiestas como género histórico literario," in *Texto y fiesta en la literatura novohispana, 1650–1700* (Mexico City: Universidad Nacional Autónoma de México, 1998).

9. See *Teatro y censura en el Mexico Virreinal,* a multimedia Web *cuaderno* edited by Martha Toriz, on the Hemispheric Institute Web site: http://hemi.nyu.edu/cuaderno/censura/index.htm.

10. As of 1660, theater performances were prohibited in the chapels of convents, such as Sor Juana's San Jerónimo. See Hildburg Schilling, *Teatro profano en la Nueva España* (Mexico City: Imprenta Universitaria, 1958), 12.

11. Matthew D. Stroud, "The Desiring Subject and the Promise of Salvation: A Lacanian Study of Sor Juana's El divino Narciso," *Hispania* 76 (May 1993): 204.

12. Sor Juana, *Reply to Sor Philothea,* 209

13. See Fray Diego Durán, *History of the Indies of New Spain,* trans. Doris Heyden (Norman and London: University of Oklahoma Press, 1994), 9.

SELECTED REFERENCES

Arróniz, Othón. *Teatro de evangelización en Nueva España.* Mexico City: Universidad Nacional Autónoma de México, 1979.

Arróniz, Othón. *Teatros y escenarios del siglo de oro.* Madrid: Editorial Gredos, 1977.

Bénassy-Berling, Marie-Cécile. "Sor Juana y los indios." In *Humanismo y religión en Sor Juana Inés de la Cruz,* 307–24. Mexico City: Universidad Nacional Autónoma de México, 1983.

Checa, Jorge. "El divino Narciso y la redención del lenguaje." *Nueva revista de filología hispánica* 38 (1990): 197–217.

Glantz, Margo. "Las finezas de Sor Juana: Loa para *El divino Narciso."* In *Borrones y borradores.* Mexico City: Ediciones del Equilibrista, 1992.

Lorenzano, Sandra, ed. *Aproximaciones a Sor Juana.* Mexico City: Universidad del Claustro de Sor Juana and Fondo de Cultura Económica, 2005.

McKendrick, Melveena. *Theatre in Spain, 1490–1700.* Cambridge: Cambridge University Press, 1989.

Paz, Octavio. *Sor Juana, or, The Traps of Faith.* Trans. Margaret Sayers Peden. Cambridge, Mass.: Belknap, 1988.

Poot Herrera, Sara, ed. *Sor Juana y su mundo, una mirada actual.* Mexico City: Universidad del Claustro de Sor Juana and Fondo de Cultura Económica, 1995.

Rodríguez Hernández, Dalmacio. *Texto y fiesta en la literatura novohispana, 1650–1700.* Mexico City: Universidad Nacional Autónoma de México, 1998.

Schilling, Hildburg. *Teatro profano en la Nueva España.* Mexico City: Imprenta Universitaria, 1958.

Sor Juana Inés de la Cruz. *The House of Trials (Los empeños de una casa).* Trans. David Pasto. New York: Peter Lang, 2002.

Sor Juana Inés de la Cruz. *A Sor Juana Anthology.* Ed. Alan S. Trueblood. Cambridge: Harvard University Press, 1988.

Stroud, Matthew D. "The Desiring Subject and the Promise of Salvation: A Lacanian Study of Sor Juana's El divino Narciso." *Hispania* 76 (May 1993): 204–12.

The Loa for the Auto Sacramental of The Divine Narcissus

(Sor Juana Inés de la Cruz)

Translated by Patricia A. Peters and Renée Domeier

CHARACTERS:

OCCIDENT
AMERICA
ZEAL
RELIGION
MUSIC
SOLDIERS
AZTECS

SCENE 1

(Enter OCCIDENT, a gallant-looking Aztec, wearing a crown. By his side is AMERICA, an Aztec woman of poised self-possession. They are dressed in the mantas[1] *and huipiles[2] worn for singing a* tocotín.[3] *They seat themselves on two chairs. On each side, Aztec men and women dance with feathers and rattles in their hands, as is customary for those doing this dance. While they dance, MUSIC sings.)*

MUSIC

O, Noble Mexicans,
whose ancient ancestry
comes forth from the clear light
and brilliance of the Sun,
since this, of all the year,
is your most happy feast
in which you venerate
your greatest deity,
come and adorn yourselves
with vestments of your rank;
let your holy fervor be
made one with jubilation;
and celebrate in festive pomp
the great God of the Seeds!

MUSIC

Since the abundance of
our native fields and farms
is owed to him alone
who gives fertility,
then offer him your thanks,
for it is right and just
to give from what has grown,

the first of the new fruits.
From your own veins, draw out
and give, without reserve,
the best blood, mixed with seed,
so that his cult be served,
and celebrate in festive pomp,
the great God of the Seeds!

(OCCIDENT and AMERICA sit, and MUSIC ceases.)

OCCIDENT

Of all the deities to whom
our rites demand I bend my knee—
among two thousand gods or more
who dwell within this royal city
and who require the sacrifice
of human victims still entreating
for life until their blood is drawn
and gushes forth from hearts still beating
and bowels still pulsing—I declare,
among all these, (it bears repeating),
whose ceremonies we observe,
the greatest is, surpassing all
this pantheon's immensity
the great God of the Seeds.

AMERICA

And you are right, since he alone
daily sustains our monarchy
because our lives depend on his
providing crops abundantly;
and since he gives us graciously
the gift from which all gifts proceed,
our fields rich with golden maize,
the source of life through daily bread,

Sor Juana Inés de la Cruz, Mexico, ca. 1688. Translated from Spanish by Patricia A. Peters and Renée Domeier. Originally published in Sor Juana Inés de la Cruz, *The Divine Narcissus/El divino Narciso,* trans. Patricia A. Peters and Renée Domeier (Albuquerque: University of New Mexico Press, 1998). Copyright © University of New Mexico Press.

we render him our highest praise.
Then how will it improve our lives
if rich America abounds
in gold from mines whose smoke deprives
the fields of their fertility
and with their clouds of filthy soot
will not allow the crops to grow
which blossom now so fruitfully
from seeded earth? Moreover, his
protection of our people far
exceeds our daily food and drink,
the body's sustenance. Indeed,
he feeds us with his very flesh
(first purified of every stain).
We eat his body, drink his blood,
and by this sacred meal are freed
and cleansed from all that is profane,
and thus, he purifies our soul.
And now, attentive to his rites,
together let us all proclaim:
They [OCCIDENT, AMERICA, Dancers] and MUSIC
we celebrate in festive pomp,
the great God of the Seeds!

SCENE 2

(They exit dancing. Enter Christian RELIGION as a Spanish lady, ZEAL as a Captain General in armor, and Spanish SOLDIERS.)
RELIGION
How, being Zeal, can you suppress
the flames of righteous Christian wrath
when here before your very eyes
idolatry, so blind with pride,
adores, with superstitious rites
an idol, leaving your own bride,
the holy faith of Christ disgraced?
ZEAL
Religion, trouble not your mind
or grieve my failure to attack,
complaining that my love is slack,
for now the sword I wear is bared,
its hilt in hand, clasped ready and
my arm raised high to take revenge.
Please stand aside and deign to wait
till I requite your grievances.
(Enter OCCIDENT and AMERICA dancing, and accompanied by MUSIC, who enters from the other side.)
MUSIC
And celebrate in festive pomp,
the great God of the Seeds!
ZEAL
Here they come! I will confront them.
RELIGION
And I, in peace, will also go
(before your fury lays them low)

for justice must with mercy kiss;
I shall invite them to arise
from superstitious depths to faith.
ZEAL
Let us approach while they are still
absorbed in their lewd rituals.
MUSIC
And celebrate in festive pomp,
the great God of the Seeds!
(ZEAL and RELIGION cross the stage.)
RELIGION
Great Occident, most powerful;
America, so beautiful
and rich; you live in poverty
amid the treasures of your land.
Abandon this irreverent cult
with which the demon has waylaid you.
Open your eyes! Follow the path
that leads straightforwardly to truth,
to which my love yearns to persuade you.
OCCIDENT
Who are these unknown people, so
intrusive in my sight, who dare
to stop us in our ecstasy?
Heaven forbid such infamy!
AMERICA
Who are these nations, never seen,
that wish, by force, to pit themselves
against my ancient power supreme?
OCCIDENT
Oh, you alien beauty fair;
oh, pilgrim woman from afar,
who comes to interrupt my prayer,
please speak and tell me who you are.
RELIGION
Christian Religion is my name,
and I intend that all this realm
will make obeisance unto me.
OCCIDENT
An impossible concession!
AMERICA
Yours is but a mad obsession!
OCCIDENT
You will meet with swift repression.
AMERICA
Pay no attention; she is mad!
Let us go on with our procession.
MUSIC and all [AZTECS onstage]
And celebrate in festive pomp,
the great God of the Seeds!
ZEAL
How is this, barbarous Occident?
Can it be, sightless Idolatry,
that you insult Religion,
the spouse I cherish tenderly?
Abomination fills your cup

and overruns the brim, but see
that God will not permit you to
continue drinking down delight,
and I am sent to deal your doom.

OCCIDENT
And who are you who frightens all
who only look upon your face?

ZEAL
I am Zeal. Does that surprise you?
Take heed! for when your excesses
bring disgrace to fair Religion,
then will Zeal arise to vengeance;
for insolence I will chastise you.
I am the minister of God,
Who growing weary with the sight
of overreaching tyrannies
so sinful that they reach the height
of error, practiced many years,
has sent me forth to penalize you.
And thus, these military hosts
with flashing thunderbolts of steel,
the ministers of His great wrath
are sent, His anger to reveal.

OCCIDENT
What god? What sin? What tyranny?
What punishment do you foresee?
Your reasons make no sense to me,
nor can I make the slightest guess
who you might be with your insistence
on tolerating no resistance,
impeding us with rash persistence
from lawful worship as we sing.

MUSIC
And celebrate with festive pomp,
the great God of the Seeds!

AMERICA
Madman, blind, and barbarous,
with mystifying messages
you try to mar our calm and peace,
destroying the tranquility
that we enjoy. Your plots must cease,
unless, of course, you wish to be
reduced to ashes, whose existence
even the winds will never sense.

(to OCCIDENT)
And you, my spouse, and your cohort,
close off your hearing and your sight
to all their words; refuse to heed
their fantasies of zealous might;
proceed to carry out your rite.
Do not concede to insolence
from foreigners intent to dull
our ritual's magnificence.

MUSIC
And celebrate with festive pomp,
the great God of the Seeds!

ZEAL
Since our initial offering
of peaceful terms, you held so cheap,
the dire alternative of war,
I guarantee you'll count more dear.
Take up your arms! To war! To war!

(Drums and trumpets sound.)

OCCIDENT
What miscarriages of justice
has heaven sent against me?
What are these weapons, blazing fire,
before my unbelieving eyes?
Get ready, guards! Aim well, my troops,
Your arrows at this enemy!

AMERICA
What lightning bolts does heaven send
to lay me low? What molten balls
of burning lead so fiercely rain?
What centaurs crush with monstrous force
and cause my people such great pain?

(Within)
To arms! To arms! War! War!

([Drums and trumpets] sound.)
Long life to Spain! Long live her king!

(The battle begins. Indians enter through one door and flee
through another with the Spanish pursuing at their heels.
From backstage, OCCIDENT backs away from RELIGION
and AMERICA retreats before ZEAL's onslaught.)

SCENE 3

RELIGION
Give up, arrogant Occident!

OCCIDENT
I must bow to your aggression,
but not before your arguments.

ZEAL
Die, impudent America!

RELIGION
Desist! Do not give her to Death;
her life is of some worth to us.

ZEAL
How can you now defend this maid
who has so much offended you?

RELIGION
America has been subdued
because your valor won the strife,
but now my mercy intervenes
in order to preserve her life.
It was your part to conquer her
by force with military might;
mine is to gently make her yield,
persuading her by reason's light.

ZEAL
But you have seen the stubbornness

with which these blind ones still abhor
your creed; is it not better far
that they all die?

RELIGION

Good Zeal, restrain
your justice and do not kill them.
My gentle disposition deigns
to forbear vengeance and forgive.
I want them to convert and live.

AMERICA

If your petition for my life
and show of Christian charity
are motivated by the hope
that you, at last, will conquer me,
defeating my integrity
with verbal steel where bullets failed,
then you are sadly self-deceived.
A weeping captive, I may mourn
for liberty, yet my will grows
beyond these bonds; my heart is free,
and I will worship my own gods!

OCCIDENT

Forced to surrender to your power,
I have admitted my defeat,
but still it must be clearly said
that violence cannot devour
my will, nor force constrain its right.
Although in grief, I now lament,
a prisoner, your cruel might
has limits. You cannot prevent
my saying here within my heart
I worship the great God of Seeds!

SCENE 4

RELIGION

Wait! What you perceive as force
is not coercion, but affection.
What god is this that you adore?

OCCIDENT

The great God of the Seeds
who causes fields to bring forth fruit.
To him the lofty heavens bow;
to him the rains obedience give;
and when, at last, he cleanses us
from stains of sin, then he invites
us to the meal that he prepares.
Consider whether you could find
a god more generous and good
who blesses more abundantly
than he whom I describe to you.

RELIGION

(Aside)

O God, help me! What images,
what dark designs, what shadowings

of truths most sacred to our Faith
do these lies seek to imitate?
O false, sly, and deceitful snake!
O asp, with sting so venomous!
O hydra, that from seven mouths
pours noxious poisons, every one
a passage to oblivion!
To what extent, with this facade
do you intend maliciously
to mock the mysteries of God?
Mock on! for with your own deceit,
if God empowers my mind and tongue,
I'll argue and impose defeat.

AMERICA

Why do you find yourself perplexed?
Do you not see there is no god
other than ours who verifies
with countless blessings his great works?

RELIGION

In doctrinal disputes, I hold
with the apostle Paul, for when
he preached to the Athenians
and found they had a harsh decree
imposing death on anyone
who tried to introduce new gods,
since he had noticed they were free
to worship at a certain shrine,
an altar to "the Unknown God,"
he said to them, "This Lord of mine
is no new god, but one unknown
that you have worshipped in this place,
and it is He, my voice proclaims."
And thus I—

(OCCIDENT and AMERICA whisper to each other.)

Listen, Occident!
and hear me, blind Idolatry!
for all your happiness depends
on listening attentively.

These miracles that you recount,
these prodigies that you suggest,
these apparitions and these rays
of light in superstition dressed
are glimpsed but darkly through a veil.
These portents you exaggerate,
attributing to your false gods
effects that you insinuate,
but wrongly so, for all these works
proceed from our true God alone,
and of His Wisdom come to birth.
Then if the soil richly yields,
and if the fields bud and bloom,
if fruits increase and multiply,
if seeds mature in earth's dark womb,
if rains pour forth from leaden sky,
all is the work of His right hand;
for neither the arm that tills the soil

nor rains that fertilize the land
nor warmth that calls life from the tomb
of winter's death can make plants grow;
for they lack reproductive power
if Providence does not concur,
by breathing into each of them
a vegetative soul.

AMERICA
    That might be so;
then tell me, is this God so kind—
this deity whom you describe—
that I might touch Him with my hands,
these very hands that carefully
create the idol, here before you,
an image made from seeds of earth
and innocent, pure human blood
shed only for this sacred rite?

RELIGION
Although the Essence of Divinity
is boundless and invisible,
because already It has been
eternally united with
our nature, He resembles us
so much in our humanity
that He permits unworthy priests
to take Him in their humble hands.

AMERICA
In this, at least, we are agreed,
for to my god no human hands
are so unstained that they deserve
to touch him; nonetheless, he gives
this honor graciously to those
who serve him with their priestly lives.
No others dare to touch the god,
nor in the sanctuary stand.

ZEAL
A reverence most worthily
directed to the one true God!

OCCIDENT
Whatever else you claim, now tell
me this: Is yours a God composed
of human blood, an offering
of sacrifice, and in Himself
does He combine with bloody death
the life-sustaining seeds of earth?

RELIGION
As I have said, His boundless
Majesty is insubstantial,
but in the Holy Sacrifice
of Mass, His blessed humanity
is placed unbloody under the
appearances of bread, which comes
from seeds of wheat and is transformed
into His Body and His Blood;
and this most holy Blood of Christ,
contained within a sacred cup,

is verily the offering
most innocent, unstained, and pure
that on the altar of the cross
was the redemption of the world.

AMERICA
Such miracles, unknown to us,
make me desire to believe;
but would the God that you reveal
offer Himself so lovingly
transformed for me into a meal
as does the god that I adore?

RELIGION
In truth, He does. For this alone
His Wisdom came upon the earth
to dwell among all humankind.

AMERICA
And so that I can be convinced,
may I not see this Deity?

OCCIDENT
And so that I can be made free
of old beliefs that shackle me?

RELIGION
Yes, you will see when you are bathed
in crystal waters from the font
of baptism.

OCCIDENT
    And well I know,
in preparation to attend
a banquet, I must bathe, or else
our ancient custom I offend.

ZEAL
Your vain ablutions will not do
the cleansing that your stains require.

OCCIDENT
Then what?

RELIGION
    There is a sacrament
of living waters, which can cleanse
and purify you of your sins.

AMERICA
Because you deluge my poor mind
with concepts of theology,
I've just begun to understand;
there is much more I want to see,
and my desire to know is now
by holy inspiration led.

OCCIDENT
And I desire more keenly still
to know about the life and death
of the God you say is in the bread.

RELIGION
Then come along with me, and I
shall make for you a metaphor,
a concept clothed in rhetoric
so colorful that what I show
to you, your eyes will clearly see;

for now I know that you require
objects of sight instead of words,
by which faith whispers in your ears
too deaf to hear; I understand,
for you necessity demands
that through the eyes, faith find her way
to her reception in your hearts.

OCCIDENT

Exactly so. I do prefer
to see the things you would impart.

SCENE 5

RELIGION

Then come.

ZEAL

Religion, answer me:
what metaphor will you employ
to represent these mysteries?

RELIGION

An *auto* will make visible
through allegory images
of what America must learn
and Occident implores to know
about the questions that now burn
within him so.

ZEAL

What will you call
this play in allegory cast?

RELIGION

Divine Narcissus, let it be,
because if that unhappy maid
adored an idol which disguised
in such strange symbols the attempt
the demon made to counterfeit
the great and lofty mystery
of the most Blessed Eucharist,
then there were also, I surmise,
among more ancient pagans hints
of such high marvels symbolized.

ZEAL

Where will your drama be performed?

RELIGION

In the crown city of Madrid,
which is the center of the Faith,
the seat of Catholic majesty,
to whom the Indies owe their best
beneficence, the blessed gift
of Holy Writ, the Gospel light
illuminating all the West.

ZEAL

That you should write in Mexico
for royal patrons don't you see
to be an impropriety?

RELIGION

Is it beyond imagination
that something made in one location
can in another be of use?
Furthermore, my writing it
comes, not of whimsical caprice,
but from my vowed obedience
to do what seems beyond my reach.
Well, then, this work, however rough
and little polished it might be,
results from my obedience,
and not from any arrogance.

ZEAL

Then answer me, Religion, how
(before you leave the matter now),
will you respond when you are chid
for loading the whole Indies on
a stage to transport to Madrid?

RELIGION

The purpose of my play can be
none other than to glorify
the Eucharistic Mystery;
and since the cast of characters
are no more than abstractions which
depict the theme with clarity,
then surely no one should object
if they are taken to Madrid;
distance can never hinder thought
with persons of intelligence,
nor seas impede exchange of sense.

ZEAL

Then, prostrate at his royal feet,
beneath whose strength two worlds are joined
we beg for pardon of the King;

RELIGION

and from her eminence, the Queen;

AMERICA

whose sovereign and anointed feet
the humble Indies bow to kiss;

ZEAL

and from the Royal High Council;

RELIGION

and from the ladies, who bring light
into their hemisphere;

AMERICA

and from
their poets, I most humbly beg
forgiveness for my crude attempt,
desiring with these awkward lines
to represent the Mystery.

OCCIDENT

Let's go, for anxiously I long to see
exactly how this God of yours
will give Himself as food to me.
(*AMERICA, OCCIDENT, and ZEAL sing:*)

The Indies know
and do concede
who is the true
God of the Seeds.
In loving tears
which joy prolongs
we gladly sing
our happy songs.

ALL
  Blest be the day
  when I could see
  and worship the
  great God of Seeds.
(They all exit, dancing and singing.)

NOTES

All notes to the play are by the editors of this volume.

1. A manta is either a blanket or, as in this case, a poncho.

2. A huipil is a kind of loose blouse traditionally worn by many native women in Mexico and Central America. It is often colorfully embroidered with designs that are representative of the wearer's village and/ or family history.

3. A tocotín was a form of popular Nahuatl poetry and an accompanying dance.

A recent performance of *Los Comanches* in the town of Alcalde, New Mexico. (Photo by Miguel Gandert.)

Los Comanches

Los Comanches, a play that reenacts a historic struggle between Comanche Indians and Spanish/(New) Mexican settlers, illustrates some of the difficulties involved in pinning down the meanings of conquest dramas in the Americas. Does every repetition of the old scenario of victory and defeat simply reinforce the play of power it represents? To what extent can participants appropriate performance traditions originally used as tools of domination in order to stage acts of resistance? And what happens when the combatants can no longer be so easily separated into two opposing camps?

The Spanish conquest of the area that is now New Mexico began in 1598 with an expedition led by explorer Don Juan de Oñate. In his notes from the trip, Oñate mentions that one of his captains commemorated the occasion by writing a drama that was performed following a mass for an audience of both Europeans and indigenous inhabitants; its purpose, Oñate claims, was "to show us the tremendous welcome with which all of New Mexico greeted the arrival of the Church."[1] Slowly, in the face of considerable opposition from the native Pueblo Indians, the number of Spanish/Mexican settlers increased, and by the beginning of the eighteenth century nomadic Comanches from the north had begun arriving in the region to trade with the newcomers. The intercultural zone known as the Comanchería grew out of these networks of economic exchange, as well as the abduction of thousands of women and children on both sides who were incorporated into Spanish and Comanche communities depopulated by war and epidemics. In September 1774, as part of a punitive campaign that abandoned earlier policies of limited diplomacy in favor of outright extermination, the notorious Indian fighter Don Carlos Fernández launched a surprise attack on a Comanche camp east of Galisteo that ended with more than four hundred of the roughly five hundred Comanches either dead or captured. Five years later, in August 1779, the newly appointed governor, Don Juan Bautista de Anza, decimated a large settlement southwest of what is now Colorado Springs. Among the dead were the legendary Comanche leader Tabivo Naritgant (known to the Spanish as Cuerno Verde or Green Horn), Naritgant's son, and all his chiefs.

Los Comanches appears to present a conflation of these two historic battles since the Spanish commander is identified as Don Carlos Fernández but the play ends in Cuerno Verde's death. The translation included here is based on the Spanish text published in 1907 by Aurelio Espinosa, who states that the manuscript (not the original) most likely dates from 1840–50 and that the play's author was reported to be one Don Pedro Pino of Santa Fe. Most recent scholars agree that it was probably composed at the end of the eighteenth century by Pedro Bautista Pino, a New Mexican militiaman who had participated in campaigns against the Comanches.[2] How and when it entered the realm of oral culture is unknown, although it is believed to have been performed throughout the nineteenth century in many small communities in northern New Mexico.[3] Espinosa's version was the first published manuscript, and in the 1920s and 1930s, as the area around Taos was inundated by Anglo artists, it became an object of folkloric interest.[4] Shortly thereafter the tradition died out, evidently because of migration during the Depression era and the loss of many young men in World War II. In the late 1950s, however, residents of the town of Alcalde compiled a new manuscript based on their memories of performances from twenty years before and reinstated the pageant as part of their Christmas season celebrations.[5]

Written in the octosyllabic verse form typical of Spanish popular poetry, *Los Comanches* reflects the opposition between conqueror and soon to be conquered in its very structure. It begins with Cuerno Verde's stately boast of his superior military prowess, followed by an equally ostentatious rebuttal by Don Carlos Fernández. The rest of the dialogue, interrupted by frequent skirmishes, alternates between the Spanish characters' threats to annihilate the "savage barbarians" and the Comanches' denunciations of the "arrogant Christians." The drama is clearly a variation on the *moros y cristianos* tradition that originally developed in Spain to commemorate the Christians' defeat of their Muslim enemies and was later brought over to the Americas, where the indigenous were cast as Moors and often baptized en masse following their symbolic defeat. Like these plays, *Los Comanches* is staged outdoors as an elaborate spectacle that includes songs, dances, and mock battles between warriors on horseback. The moros y cristianos pageants revolve around the defense of a castle, but the "fortress of faith" in the New Mexican version is a wagon, which protects two Spanish children who have been recaptured by their relatives after being kidnapped and raised by Comanches. At various points, Don Carlos and his captains invoke the Virgin Mary and Santiago, whose name was the battle cry for Christian crusaders. Yet, whereas moros y cristianos plays typically end with the infidels renouncing their idols and accepting the "true faith," the conquerors in *Los Comanches* seem utterly uninterested in converting their opponents. In this sense, the play remains true to historical fact: what these Spaniards want are not Christian Indians but dead ones. Critics have pointed out that the play's final word is given to the farcical Barriga Duce (whose name is a corruption of the Spanish for "sweet belly"), a Spanish camp follower and spectator of the battle who sticks around only to claim the spoils of the dead Comanches. Sandra Dahlberg, for instance, argues that Barriga Duce's speech "destabiliz(es) the foundational rhetoric presented earlier in the drama" by revealing that the Spanish are not motivated by religious zeal or even patriotic fervor but by a more material glory that is in fact greed.[6]

As always, it is in the act of performance where the cut-and-dried drama of conquest is most likely to be complicated if not turned on its head. One description from 1938 relates that before the pageant began, while Indians from nearby pueblos joined local villagers at mass, the actors dressed as Comanches pilfered small items from the churchgoers' automobiles and wagons and took onlookers hostage, insisting that their "captives" pay a ransom (a quart of wine at the local bar) that served as the performers' payment.[7] Were these gleefully unrepentant "heathens" simply reinforcing stereotypes of the Indians inside the church or did their sanctioned assault on the social order express a certain ambivalence, perhaps even opposition, to the hierarchies established by history? In his analysis of early-twentieth-century performances of the play, Curtis Marez explains that the elite Anglo minority that began consolidating its power in New Mexico at the end of the nineteenth century adopted many of the accoutrements of Spanish culture, such as music and colonial architecture, as a means of naturalizing its own dominance. In this context, he concludes, the act of imitating Comanches may have allowed lower-class mestizo and Pueblo Indian participants to "ritually reproduce antipathies to the territorial rulers in 'Spanish' drag."[8] Marez views the play as a performative re-creation of the Comanchería and suggests that "with their repeated references to Indian/Nuevo Mexicano exchange and transculturation, performances of 'The Comanches' recalled histories of contact, conflict, and copying that were at odds with Anglo expansion."[9]

While the distance imposed by time obviously lends a speculative quality to critics' interpretations of performances in the past, even those who have observed recent performances in Alcalde disagree on the significance of what they have seen. Dahlberg, for example, notes that the subversive Barriga Duce character has no part in this version and that the actors playing Comanches speak a grammatically incorrect, heavily accented Spanish. She concludes that the Alcalde tradition is a solemn celebration of Spanish heritage that reinforces cultural differences. Enrique Lamadrid, on the other hand, sees the same performances as an example of "cultural mestizaje" and emphasizes that all of the characters are embodied by actors who are racially mixed descendants of Spanish and Indians. He argues that the Alcalde version downplays the rhetoric of conquest and points out that the Spanish commander Don Carlos delivers some lines that in earlier versions were spoken by Cuerno Verde. This is evidence, he says, that "the old differences and oppositions dissolve into a new synthesis in the edifying spectacle" in which a "new cultural sign is forged for the battles of the twentieth century."[10]

The performance history of *Los Comanches* indicates that regardless of what the text may seem to suggest, the conquest represented in the play is not a one-act drama; it is a battle that, like the play itself, has to be fought again and again. The actors change, the precise meaning of the conflict varies, and it is always possible that next time the ending will be different.

—Sarah J. Townsend

NOTES

1. Capitán Gaspar Pérez de Villagrá, *Historia de la Nueva México* (Mexico City: Imprenta del Museo Nacional, 1900). Quoted in Reed Anderson, "Early Secu-

lar Theater in New Mexico," in *Pasó por Aquí: Critical Essays on the New Mexican Literary Tradition,* ed. Erlinda Gonzales-Berry (Albuquerque: University of New Mexico Press, 1989), 102.

2. This conclusion is based on Espinosa's informa-

tion and Pino's own *Exposición sucinta y sencilla de la provincia del Nuevo Mexico,* which he presented to the Spanish Cortes in 1812 while serving as the New Mexican representative. Pino's report praises many aspects of Comanche culture and criticizes military campaigns against them because of the sacrifices they required of New Mexican settlers. See H. Bailey Carroll and J. Villasana Haggard, eds., *Three New Mexico Chronicles* (Albuquerque: Quivira Society, 1942).

3. The only account of a performance of *Los Comanches* prior to the twentieth century located in research for this essay is in Rafael Chacón, *Legacy of Honor: The Life of Rafael Chacón, a Nineteenth-Century New Mexican,* ed. Jaqueline Dorgan Meketa (Albuquerque: University of New Mexico Press, 1986), 76. Chacón gives a very schematic description of performances in the 1840s that resemble the plot of the Campa and Espinosa manuscripts. Interestingly, he refers to the play as a comedy.

4. There are several manuscripts of *Los Comanches.* Aside from Espinosa's, the one most frequently cited is the one published by Arthur L. Campa in 1942. According to Campa, his version is based primarily on an 1864 manuscript written down by one Miguel Sandoval, although Campa references other manuscripts and integrates parts of them into his own. Most of the dialogue in Espinosa's and Campa's manuscripts is nearly identical, but Campa's is longer; it includes additional dialogue by Spanish/New Mexican characters at the beginning, before Cuerno Verde arrives, and at the end. Campa admits that the shorter version published by Espinosa was the one most frequently performed in New Mexico in the 1930s and 1940s.

5. The effort to compile the new manuscript was led by Alberto Vialpando, an Alcalde resident and college professor. Many of the speeches in the Alcalde version are exactly the same as in the two published manuscripts, although the Alcalde version is much shorter.

6. Sandra L. Dahlberg, "Having the Last Word: Recording the Cost of Conquest in *Los Comanches,*" in *Recovering the U.S. Hispanic Literary Heritage,* vol. 2, ed. Erlinda Gonzales-Berry and Chuck Tatum (Houston: Arte Público Press, 1996), 140.

7. See Lorin W. Brown, *Hispano Folklife of New Mexico: The Lorin W. Brown Federal Writers' Project Manuscripts* (Albuquerque: University of New Mexico Press, 1978), 40–43.

8. Curtis Marez, "The Rough Ride through Empire: 'Los Comanches' after 1898," in *Recovering the U.S. Hispanic Literary Heritage,* vol. 4, ed. Silvio Torres-Saillant. (Houston: Arte Público Press, 2002), 33.

9. Ibid., 43.

10. Enrique Lamadrid, "The Comanches: Text, Performance, and Transculturation in an Eighteenth-Century New Mexican Folk Drama," in *Recovering the U.S. Hispanic Literary Heritage,* vol. 3, ed. María Herrera-Sobek and Virginia Sánchez Korrol (Houston: Arte Público Press, 2000), 183.

SELECTED REFERENCES

Anderson, Reed. "Early Secular Theater in New Mexico." In *Pasó por Aquí: Critical Essays on the New Mexican Literary Tradition,* ed. Erlinda Gonzales-Berry, 101–27. Albuquerque: University of New Mexico Press, 1989.

Campa, Arthur L., ed. *Los Comanches: A New Mexico Folk Drama.* Albuquerque: University of New Mexico Press, 1942.

Dahlberg, Sandra L. "Having the Last Word: Recording the Cost of Conquest in *Los Comanches.*" In *Recovering the U.S. Hispanic Literary Heritage,* vol. 2, ed. Erlinda Gonzales-Berry and Chuck Tatum, 133–47. Houston: Arte Público Press, 1996.

Dahlberg, Sandra L. "'Los Comanches' at Alcalde: Two Centuries of Tradition." In *Multilingual America: Transnationalism, Ethnicity, and the Languages of American Literature,* ed. Werner Sollors, 81–90. New York: New York University Press, 1998.

Espinosa, Aurelio M., ed. *Los Comanches: A Spanish Heroic Play of the Year Seventeen Hundred and Eighty.* Albuquerque: University of New Mexico Press, 1907.

Harris, Max. *Aztecs, Moors, and Christians: Festivals of Reconquest in Mexico and Spain.* Austin: University of Texas Press, 2000.

Lamadrid, Enrique. "The Comanches: Text, Performance, and Transculturation in an Eighteenth-Century New Mexican Folk Drama." In *Recovering the U.S. Hispanic Literary Heritage,* vol. 3, ed. María Herrera-Sobek and Virginia Sánchez Korrol, 173–88. Houston: Arte Público Press, 2000.

Lamadrid, Enrique, with photographs by Miguel A. Gandert and accompanying compact disc. *Hermanitos Comanchitos: Indo-Hispano Rituals of Captivity and Redemption.* Albuquerque: University of New Mexico Press, 2003.

Marez, Curtis. "The Rough Ride through Empire: 'Los Comanches' after 1898." In *Recovering the U.S. Hispanic Literary Heritage,* vol. 4, ed. Silvio Torres-Saillant, 31–49. Houston: Arte Público Press, 2002.

Marez, Curtis. "Signifying Spain, Becoming Comanche, Making Mexicans: Indian Captivity and the History of Chicana/o Popular Performance." *American Quarterly* 53 (June 2001): 267–307.

Los Comanches

Translated by Gilberto Espinosa

CHARACTERS:

CUERNO VERDE (Green Horn), Chief of Comanches
DON CARLOS FERNÁNDEZ, Spanish General-in-Chief
DON JOSÉ DE LA PEÑA, a Spanish Captain
EL TENIENTE (The Lieutenant), a Spanish officer, name not given
DON SALVADOR RIVERA, a Spanish Captain
OSO PARDO (Grey Bear), a Comanche chieftain
CABEZA NEGRA (Black Head), a Comanche chieftain
LOBO BLANCO (White Wolf), a Comanche chieftain
ZAPATO CUENTA (Beaded Moccasin), a Comanche chieftain
TABACO, a Comanche chieftain
DON TORIBIO ORTIZ, a Spanish General
BARRIGA DUCE, a Spanish camp follower

Scene—on the staked plains of New Mexico.
Time—in the year 1777.

CUERNO VERDE, *Chief of all the Comanches, speaks:*

From the sunrise to the sunset,
From the South to frigid North
Is seen the glitter of my arms
And my trumpet blares go forth,
And alike among all nations
Boldly I make my camp and rest.
Such is the valor, such the bravery
That reigns within my breast.
And my banners are unfurled
To the breeze where none else do
For the most enraged I humble
And the haughtiest I subdue.
Unrestrained and without fetter,
Knowing none who master me,
Like the savage bear and tiger
Wandering unopposed and free,
For there's not a hill or mountain,
Not a stone and not a tree,
But that will not be a witness,
Of the praise they tell of me.
Those who have opposed my progress
Have had reason to regret,
And this proud and haughty Castle
Will also feel my vengeance yet.
Today's sun will see its downfall,
See in ruin its haughty walls,
Though its strength be great and mighty

I'll assault it till it falls.
Well I know they are preparing
To receive my warriors bold.
I have watched their preparations,
And much more I have been told.
Let them ask the many nations
Who have felt my conquering heel,
Let them ask my might and prestige,
Learn the misery they now feel.
Today they find themselves abandoned,
And their homes in ruin see.
Let them ask the Caslana nation,
What it is to war with me.
Today their star is dimmed forever,
For from such prestige they fell,
That . . . but why should I repeat,
Facts which everyone knows well.
Everyone except these Christians
And without number though they be,
Today for certain blood will flow—
Blood that means revenge for me.
This recalls to my memory
One of these, though brave and bold,
He left his blood to stain the flowers
On a battlefield of old.
Those I've slain are without number
They have slipped my memory now
Without counting all the captives,

Southwest United States, late eighteenth century/1840-50. Translated from Spanish by Gilberto Espinosa. Originally published in *The New Mexico Quarterly* 1 (May 1931).

Men and women and children. Now
My brave men, valiant Redmen,
Let this order go with care,
I, your general, give this edict,
Let everyone his arms prepare.
Prepare we must, and meet them ready,
What general would seek to rest,
With the enemy before him.
Prepare to do your best.
I will never be contented
With a victory half complete.
Don your war paint, sound the war drums,
We must bring them to our feet.
I shall go and seek this general,
This foolhardy, impious man.
Let him meet me in this battle
And survive me if he can.
Who is he, what do they call him,
Whomsoever he may be.
I, Cuerno Verde, challenge him
To come and combat me.

DON CARLOS FERNÁNDEZ, *the Spanish general, answers the Comanche:*
Bide your time, Oh bloody heathen,
I will come without your call.
Your challenge is not needed—
I will meet you one and all.
But first, tell me, who are you,
And whence those idle boasts?
Hearken to these words I utter,
You and your savage host.

CUERNO VERDE, *the Comanche, speaks:*
I am that mighty captain
At whose name men shake with fear.
I am the brave, the bold, the terrible,
This horn which you can see
Green and golden, see it glisten,
All its fame it takes from me.
Today I claim the homage of
Not alone these warriors at my side
But all men proclaim me master,
Through this nation far and wide.
From the sunrise to the sunset,
From the South to frigid North,
Caiguas, Quituchis, Indios, Caumpes,
All follow me when I go forth.
Many others without number,
There's no need to name them all,
Yield to me their blind allegiance,
And are ready at my call.

DON CARLOS FERNÁNDEZ, *the Spanish general, answers Cuerno Verde:*
Bide your time, oh bloody heathen,
I will be your master yet.
You will find your spirit broken,
When the Spaniard you have met.

In the land across the waters,
There reigns a prince of right
Who rules the world from pole to pole
Through his power and his might.
Throughout this entire world you see
His power reigns supreme.
Germans, Englishmen, and Turks,
All peoples whomsoever they be
When they hear the name of Spaniard,
Bend and tremble at the knee.
You have never met a worthy foe
Nor do you know the might
Of Catholic arms in battle—
You will learn this in this fight.
This is why your idle vauntings,
This is why your spirit bold.
I shall meet you in this battle,
I shall leave you dead and cold.
And if you wish to know who I am,
I shall state that you may know.
This is not my first encounter,
This battle you offer, and so,
Here you find me in your own land
And though I am advanced in years,
Know and note, oh impious stranger,
Carlos Fernández has no fears.
Your lands I've always invaded,
When it suited me that way.
And now, oh boastful captain,
Go prepare you for the fray.

CUERNO VERDE, *the Comanche chieftain, replies:*
You have said it, without fail,
We shall see who shall prevail.

DON CARLOS FERNÁNDEZ, *the Spanish general, addresses his men:*
This war again presents to us
An opportunity to show
The valor of your Catholic arms
That all the world may know,
That Spanish arms in battle,
Never yet have left the field
Without honor to their country.
A Spaniard will never yield.
You have heard how this Comanche,
This untutored savage beast
Comes before us with such boasting,
'Tis high time that this should cease.
He addressed me with such vauntings,
Applauded by his savage bands,
Asking who could be this general
Who had dared invade his lands.
Told us of the hosts he'd murdered,
Of the lands he'd filled with fear,
And I answered with equal frankness
That his equal he'd find here.
Told him that the Spanish soldier

Knows no rival, knows no peer.
Told him of that mighty nation
At whose name men shake with fear.
But 'tis time to cease this vaunting,
We must hasten to the fray,
You, my captains, speak your counsel,
How we best can win the day.
Let Tomás Madril come forward,
José de la Peña too,
And Don Salvador Rivera.
Bring your sergeants all with you.
We must all consult together
And decide what we must do.

DON JOSÉ DE LA PEÑA, *a Spanish captain, speaks:*
Oh, my brave and worthy general
Of whose valor we well know,
Plan your battle, give your orders,
We shall follow where you go.
A more worthy, a more just
War than this was never seen.
Let us haste and give them battle,
And exterminate this spleen.
For my heart cries loud for action,
And the issue holds no fear.
With the aid of Virgin Mother,
I see victory is near.
Through her Immaculate Conception,
Born of woman, without sin,
Full of grace and full of mercy,
She will surely help us win.
And besides to help us conquer,
Is that celestial martial band,
With the blessed angel Michael
Who will surely be on hand.
He, the patron of my brave men,
Who are ready for the fray.
Give your orders, we are ready,
This is all I have to say.

EL TENIENTE, *the Lieutenant, speaks:*
The worthy José de la Peña
Has spoken what I would say.
Only one word I have to offer,
Then I am ready for the fray.
Listen, Oh worthy Don Carlos,
My obedience to you I yield.
'Tis a special honor to serve you,
Proof I'll give you on this field.
My will is made, I am ready,
To go forth to battle this day,
To fight for your honor and glory,
Or to perish in the affray.
Well I know I am not worthy,
To serve in such an honored task.
In truth the honored post I have,
Is more than I would ask.
Don Carlos, I shall not fail you.
This is all I have to say.

I am ready for the battle.
I shall follow Don José.

DON SALVADOR RIVERA, *a Spanish captain, speaks:*
Señor Don Carlos Fernández
I have hearkened to what you say.
I am ready with the lieutenant,
With the lieutenant and Don José.
With powder and ball we'll assail them.
We shall make them repent their sins,
And forget their idle boastings.
Faith and valor is what wins.

CUERNO VERDE, *the Comanche chieftain, addresses his war captains:*
Hear, ye lions, all my captains
You, the bravest in the fray.
All prepare your arms of battle
We are out to win the day.
Up and at them with a fury
Let them know whom they assail,
And remember that united
You can never, never fail.
Bear in mind what you have pledged me.
Fight with valor, fight with might.
With the valor of your forebears,
You are battling for the right.
I shall be there with a vengeance.
This is not an idle boast.
You well know me and my mettle.
We shall crush this savage host.

OSO PARDO (Grey Bear), *a Comanche chieftain, speaks:*
I also rise to speak a word.
It is both meet and right,
That the promises given Cuerno Verde,
We should ever keep in sight.
Remember, you are the chosen ones,
Whom your captains called to war.
Yon Spaniards, answer me today
Or be silent forevermore.
What captain from amongst you
Will match this savage bear?
This bear who tames the savage beasts.
Who will assault him in his lair?
The fiercest lion of the wilds
Flees to the forest deep,
When this Grey Bear presents himself,
Now who will dare to leap
And with this Grey Bear match his arms
This day in single battle?
Whence is your courage, whence your might
Come forth and prove your mettle.

DON JOSÉ DE LA PEÑA, *the Spanish captain, speaks:*
This Grey Bear shall be my quarry,
This rock shall prove his end.
Rock of valor, rock of prowess,
Tame this savage that he may send
No more idle threats and boastings.
Idle glutton, boastful one,

I shall prove your false feigned courage
On this field e'er we are done.
And the high sun of your glory
Soon will set, your day is o'er,
When we meet in mortal combat
That sun for you will rise no more.
Not long ago I met your warriors,
In numbers great they came to fight.
With but a handful of my brave men
I met and put them all to flight.
Valor such will merit boasting
Deeds like these, in days gone by,
Rolando and his twelve immortals
Performed beneath the Spanish sky.
But, you know not whence I speak,
Of whom I speak or what I say.
Did you know, and having met us,
You would think them here today.

CABEZA NEGRA (Black Head), *another Comanche chieftain, speaks:*
Why this chatter, why this waiting?
Worthier tasks we have to do.
See this sharp and glistening lance point?
It shall pierce their general through.
Pierce that proud and haughty Christian,
Leader of these hosts they say.
Cease this talk and reminiscing,
I have come to kill and slay.
Be there brave men from amongst you,
In your haughty warrior band,
Who would meet Cabeza Negra,
In single combat, hand to hand?

LOBO BLANCO (White Wolf), *another Comanche chieftain, speaks.*
First he addresses Cabeza Negra:
Worthy sir, hold back a while yet,
Soon we'll have them in our foils.
I must be the first to meet them,
For my blood within me boils.
Let me first show them my prowess.
Their fury is not new to me.
We have met before in battle,
And I've nothing new to see.
And because we've met in battle,
And I thirst for vengeance too,
Let me be the first to smite them,
With a vengeance they shall rue.
It is time this battle started,
Time we struck them with our might.
We are fighting for our hearth fires,
For our honor and our rights.

ZAPATO CUENTA (Beaded Moccasin), *another Comanche chieftain, addresses CUERNO VERDE and his warriors:*
Valiant Redmen, bend your war bows,
With a true unerring eye, that
With each arrow from your bowstrings,

We may see a Spaniard die.
Don your paint and gaudy feathers,
Sound the war drums, take your stand.
Sing of joy and sing of battle,
For the hour is at hand.
I, your captain, will support you,
You will find me at your side.
Zapato Cuenta is your chieftain
And in him you can confide.

TABACO, *a Comanche chieftain and an ambassador seeking peace, speaks:*
Noble Redmen, you have ordered,
That your men be ready all.
And these Christians who seek battle,
Soon will hear your martial call.
Tabaco is also a mighty captain,
With many warriors at his command,
And we recognize no master,
In this broad and mighty land.
Alone, unarmed, and fearing no one,
To Taos I went, among these men,
On a peaceful mission went I,
And we signed a treaty then.
I can say this of the Spaniard,
He respects a worthy foe.
Without fear I went amongst them,
Mingled freely, and you may know,
This is why I cannot join you.
I cannot join this strife today.
I cannot prove a traitor
To the peace I've made to stay.
I go forth to seek the Spaniard,
Urge him to leave and save his life,
For if he persist most surely,
He will perish in this strife.
I shall tell him Cuerno Verde,
With his numerous warrior band,
Has come to meet the Spaniard,
And drive him from this land.
That I come from the Napeiste,
Bringing him these tidings true,
That Oso Pardo and Cabeza Negra,
Are here to give him battle too.
If you choose, go forth to battle,
This is what I have to say.
I will keep the pledge I've made.
I and mine will leave today.

DON TORIBIO ORTIZ, *a Spanish general, speaks:*
I am Don Toribio Ortiz,
And a general's rank I hold.
In the service of my king,
I have grown gray and old.
But my right arm still is potent,
And my step is firm and steady.
Come, a champion from your ranks,
Don Toribio Ortiz is ready.
Cuerno Verde I have heard it,

That you are a valiant foe.
Come you hither, give me battle,
I would let your warriors know,
That to me your strength and valor,
Means but little, when we meet,
I shall smite you with this sharp sword,
And will lay you at my feet.
All my troops, stand at attention,
Let no one seek the fray,
Till I give the word to battle,
We must conquer these today.
Let each lance thrust claim a victim,
Every one of them must yield.
Either crown yourself with glory,
Or leave your bodies on the field.
Our Immaculate Mother Mary,
She shall be our strength and guide,
Send a message of your prowess,
Through this nation far and wide.

DON CARLOS, *the Spanish general, again speaks:*
Your assurances make me happy,
For I know you all are true.
And on many fields of battle,
You've been tested through and through.
Since we all are of one spirit,
And all are eager for the fray,
Form your men in line of battle,
Unleash your war dogs and away,
Sound the trumpets, Santiago!
Holy Virgin! Lend your aid!
Cross through yonder willow thicket,
That is where their camp is made.

CUERNO VERDE, *the Comanche chieftain, speaks to his*
warriors:
They advance! They seek the issue,
Meet them with your battle cry.
In their midst I see their general,
Either he or I must die.
Hear their shouts, oh valiant Redmen,
Of the brave Comanche race,
You who've never met your equal,
Here or any other place.
You alone of all the Redmen,
Still defy the Spanish might.
We have clashed with them in battle
And we've put them to the flight.
Wave aloft my lofty banners,
Which have never known defeat.

Up and at them with a fury,
That will sweep them off their feet.

BARRIGA DUCE, *a Spanish camp follower, speaks as he*
views the battle from afar:
Let them die, the more the better,
There will be more spoils for me.
Soft tanned skins of elk and beaver,
What a comfort they will be.
Meat of buffalo in abundance,
Everything that one might need,
I will fill my larder plenty,
I have many mouths to feed.
My good wife shall want for nothing,
She shall cook a gorgeous meal.
Oh my comrades, give them plenty,
What a happiness I feel.

(The Comanches abandon their camp and BARRIGA
DUCE enters.)

BARRIGA DUCE, *a Spanish camp follower:*
Ah, at last I've reached their treasure,
There is plenty here indeed.
Sugars, fruits, and meats, and jellies,
What a life these heathens lead.
Everything to tempt the palate,
What a feast, fit for a king.
I shall eat and then I'll gather,
I'll not leave a single thing.
Let them fill themselves with glory,
While I eat with joy and mirth.
With their arms they prove their valor,
My glory is measured by my girth.
And if anyone should doubt this,
Let him measure side by me.
Not with words and idle boasting,
But with proof that all may see.
Give no quarter, comrades, smite them,
Do your duty, have no fear,
Strike them, smite them, without mercy,
I'll attend to what is here.
Santiago! You are with us.
How the battle rages fierce!
See our brave and valiant comrades,
How they cut and thrust and pierce.
Like the autumn leaves they scatter,
It is o'er. They all have fled.
While upon the field of battle
Lies Cuerno Verde, with his dead.

THE END

The Jealous Officer, or The Fearsome Slave Catcher
(Luís Carlos Martins Pena)

If we were to lose all the laws, documents, and memoirs of Brazilian history from the first fifty years of the nineteenth century, which is coming to an end, and we were left with only Martins Pena's comedies, it would be possible to reconstruct from them the moral physiognomy of that entire era.

—Sílvio Romero, *História da Literatura Brasileira*

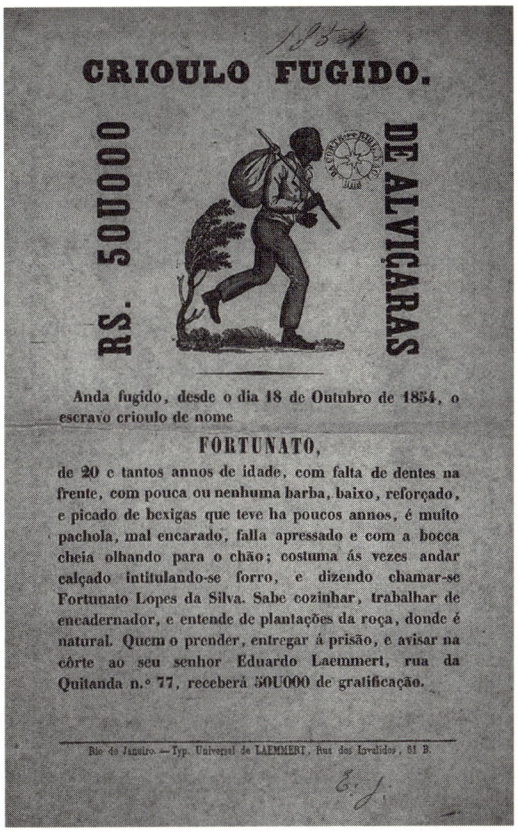

Announcement of a reward offered in exchange for the return of a slave named Fortunato who escaped on October 18, 1854. It reads, in part, "[T]wenty or so years old, missing his front teeth, with little or no beard, short, strong . . . he speaks quickly, mumbling and looking down at the ground." (From *Almanak Laemmert*. Rio de Janeiro, Fundação da Biblioteca Nacional.)

Since it first appeared in his five-volume history of Brazilian literature, Romero's pithy assessment of Luís Carlos Martins Pena (1815–48) has become an almost obligatory quotation when referring to the father of Brazilian comedy. It neatly sums up the opinion of those who defend Martins Pena's historical significance against critics who dismiss his brief, one-act farces as humorous but trivial fare, lacking both the dignity and artistry necessary to be accorded a place in the national canon.[1] Indeed, Martins Pena's champions rarely deny that his plots are predictable or that his characters lack psychological depth; rather, most contend that despite—or even because of—their apparent superficiality, his immensely popular plays abound in "sociological value" and bring to light those characteristics that are most authentically "Brazilian." Sábato Magaldi, a well-known drama historian, credits the playwright with launching the "real roots of our democratic spirit" and argues that "Martins Pena transports the language of the people to the stage, and because of that the Brazilian sees in him, with good reason, his own image."[2]

The society that Martins Pena brought to the stage, however, was hardly a picture-perfect democracy. In 1808, the Portuguese court relocated to Rio de Janeiro after being driven out of Portugal by Napoleon, and when the king finally returned to Portugal thirteen years later his son Dom Pedro stayed behind to govern in his name. In 1822, under pressure from separatists, Pedro declared Brazil a sovereign state and adopted the title of emperor. Many people remained suspicious of Pedro's ties to the country of his birth, and in 1831 he abdicated and returned to Portugal, leaving the country under the control of regents for the next ten years until his young son and successor, Pedro II, was old enough to assume control. Much of the real power, however, lay in the hands of provincial slaveholding elites until 1888, when slavery was abolished and the first Brazilian republic was established.

The social upheaval during this period had a profound effect on the theater, where audience members from opposing factions traded barbs and frequently came to blows.[3] The arrival of the Portuguese royalty spurred an enormous increase in theatrical activity, along with a campaign to clean up the disreputable stage. Throughout the eighteenth century, many actors had been mulattoes who performed in whiteface, but as high society attempted to transform the theater into a place where it went to see and be seen by the "impressionable" lower classes, nonwhites were increasingly swept off the stage or relegated to minor roles. Political independence fueled the movement to develop an autonomous theatrical tradition, one that would cultivate native talent and generate homegrown high art so that Brazilians could hold their own among the many Portuguese, French, and Italian companies that passed through Rio. The first Brazilian drama company was founded in 1833 by the legendary actor João Caetano dos Santos. For over three decades Caetano dominated the national stage, producing and starring in grandiose epic sagas and romantic tragedies by French authors such as Alexandre Dumas.

The year 1838 saw the debut of two plays that continue to serve as competing milestones in the annals of theater history. The first was Gonçalves de Magalhães's *Antônio José ou O poeta e a Inquisição* (Antônio José, or The Poet and the Inquisition), a romantic tragedy commonly held to be the first drama written by a Brazilian playwright on a national theme. It was staged by João Caetano's company, as was Martins Pena's first play, *O Juiz de Paz na Roça* (The Country Judge), which debuted less than seven months later. *O Juiz,* a good-natured satire that pokes fun at provincial manners and government corruption, received none of the fanfare that had accompanied the opening of Magalhães's weighty drama. It was not the evening's main attraction but an unpretentious curtain closer presented after a lengthier romantic tragedy in accordance with a common practice during the period that was meant to lighten the mood before sending the audience home. Yet the play was an unprecedented success, and Martins Pena, a low-level government clerk, quickly gained fame among a public that was clamoring to see itself onstage. Over the next ten years, until his death from tuberculosis at the age of thirty-three, he wrote a total of twenty-two comedies that are perennial favorites even today.[4] He is regarded as the creator of the Brazilian *comédia de costumes,* or "comedy of manners," a genre that was the most popular form of theater in Brazil through the early twentieth century.[5]

Like most English and French comedies of manners, Martins Pena's plays join witty dialogue with clever plots that revolve around stock situations and characters.[6] Most are set in Rio and lampoon the superficiality of middle-class society, while those that take place in the country parody absurd attempts to imitate the courtly fashions of the capital. The plot typically features a romantic intrigue between a young man and woman who, after a series of mishaps caused by parental interference or mistaken identity, are rewarded for their perseverance and allowed to wed. Meddling foreigners speaking mangled Portuguese are frequent objects of ridicule and are inevitably sent packing at the end, as in *Os Dous, ou o Inglês Maquinista* (The Two of Them, or The Engineering Englishman), a family romance in which the obstacles to true love include a materialistic mother, a scheming English entrepreneur, and a Brazilian slave trader. Martins Pena's characters discuss run-of-the-mill, everyday events, and many of his plays are capped off with a song and dance in celebration of a popular religious festival. Although nearly all have blissfully happy endings, many of the finales are so implausible and sudden as to arouse suspicion; rather than a lack of artistry, their inverisimilitude could be seen as an ironic reflection on a society in which appearances count for more than the truth.

Written in 1845 and first performed the following year, *The Jealous Officer* (*Os Ciúmes de um Pedestre*) was the only one of Martins Pena's plays to be censored by the Brazilian Dramatic Conservatory, of which he was a founding member.[7] The censors' main objection was that certain elements of the plot had been inspired by two recent scandals that had put a stain on the stately image of Brazil's royal city. The first involved a Portuguese citizen who was deported after being caught climbing into the attic of a respected family whose daughter he planned to carry off and marry; evidently, the police had come under fire from the public for overreacting and damaging the family's good name. The other had to do with a white man accused of hiding the body of a dead slave in a sack, which he later ordered another slave to toss into the sea. The conservatory finally granted permission to perform the play after the author agreed to make some minor alterations to the text and change the original title to *O Terrível Capitão do Mato* (*The Fearsome Slave Catcher*), a way of blunting the play's numerous jabs at the police who were in charge of enforcing censorship decrees and patrolling the raucous theaters.[8]

It seems unlikely that the omission of a few phrases about rooftops, cracks, and holes would have prevented audiences from recognizing the allusions to contemporary events, especially given that the playwright skillfully employs the art of stagecraft to imply that there is always more to appearances than meets the eye.[9] The plot centers on a police officer who locks his wife and daughter up at night while he leaves to track down runaway slaves. When the play begins, it is dark, and the audience sees a shadowy figure descending a ladder into the living room of a modest home. We soon learn that it is Paulino, a neighbor, who has been flirting with the Officer's wife, Anacleta, and has climbed in through the attic for a rendezvous. Frightened by the noise, the Officer's daughter, Balbina, comes to the opening of her bedroom door and calls out to her stepmother on the opposite side of the stage. The two women decry the injustice of being held like material possessions; Anacleta accuses the Officer of driving his first wife to the grave and scoffs that her husband "thinks you can guard a woman by keeping her under seven locks and keys! Simpleton! He doesn't know that when women don't guard themselves, all the locks and doors in the world can't hold them back." Meanwhile, Balbina's suitor, Alexandre, uses an ingenious strategy to gain entrance to the house: disguised as a runaway slave, he camps out near the door so that the gullible Officer will capture him and bring him inside. Once the entire crew is under the same roof, the farce begins in earnest. The Officer happens on various clues that point to his wife and daughter's deception and begins muttering about the need to invent a "lock with no keyhole." Several offstage "murders" occur and madcap confusion ensues before the action is interrupted by the unlikely arrival of Anacleta's long-lost father, who abandoned her as a child but has returned after many years in Africa and India (what he was doing there remains mysteriously unsaid). There is no need to spoil the grand finale, but suffice it to say the Officer receives his comeuppance and Alexandre and Balbina end up in each other's arms.

The unsavory plot elements that mimicked reality a bit too closely for comfort were not the only reason *The Jealous Officer* faced resistance from the conservatory's quality control team. Some censors also took issue with the fact that the play was clearly an over-the-top parody of *Othello,* which João Caetano—the pride and joy of Brazilian theater—was starring in at the time. Caetano was known for staging adaptations of Shakespearean dramas, usually derived from French versions that transformed the originals into sensationalist, sentimental melodramas. One of the most popular was *Othello,* based on a translation of a French adaptation by Ducis. This version, in which Shakespeare's famous Moor became the white owner of a dry goods store, was Caetano's signature piece for more than twenty years.[10] *The Jealous Officer* plays on the popularity of these tearjerkers by upping the ante, raising the level of hyperbole to ludicrous heights and stretching the bounds of credibility to the breaking point. The Officer boasts of his ability to outdo his Old World counterpart, but his overblown histrionics make his passion more laughable than tragic: "I'd be a tiger, a lion, an elephant! I'd kill her, I'd bury her, I'd skin her alive! Oh, already I tremble with fury! I saw *Othello* many times in the theater, when I went there on duty. Othello's crime is a crumb, a bauble, a trinket compared to mine." More than a parody of one particular play, *The Jealous Officer* is a burlesque of the entire Western theatrical tradition, with the playwright overusing and abusing every stage convention in the book—including many that he himself was known to employ. Plot twists occur when characters discover letters not intended for their eyes; others, like Hamlet, are convinced they see "ghosts," though the figures that appear before them are really just flesh and blood. And, to top it all off, a deus ex machina (Anacleta's father) drops out of the sky to deliver a happy ending.

As is usually the case in Martins Pena's plays, however, these metatheatrical antics also reveal something about local realities. *The Jealous Officer* exposes the paradoxes of a power structure that requires rigidly patrolling both the external and internal boundaries of the nation—those constructed around categories of race, gender, and class. Alexandre's use of blackface and black dialect to gain access to the Officer's daughter is particularly striking because it conjures up anxieties about miscegenation and suggests the fallibility of categories based on physiognomy. It points to the whitewashing of the original Othello and evokes the unsettling memory of the mulatto actors who were banished from the stage when it acquired the task of representing the new nation. The jealous husband, meanwhile, is a lower-class white man who unsuccessfully attempts to become Man of the House by enforcing the rules of a patriarchal and racist society in which human beings are property.

For all its humor, *The Jealous Officer* is haunted by ghosts, though they aren't the ones the protagonist imagines he sees. Rather, they are the ones he has to shut out in order to protect his own illusion of control: his first wife, the one who wasn't saved in the nick of time by an unexpected plot twist; the anonymous slave found dead in a sack who inspired his story; and the dark-skinned actors behind white masks who are the spectral inversion of the blackfaced Alexandre. Written and performed at a time when Brazilian patriots were struggling over who would determine the face of the nation, *The Jealous Officer* offers a far from superficial glimpse of something that most laws, documents, and memoirs from the period do their best to deny. It reveals the absurdity and self-deception involved in trying to create a lock with no key, in basing one's authority and sense of self on keeping certain people out while locking others in.

—Sarah J. Townsend

NOTES

1. Until recently, many histories of Brazilian theater did not include Martins Pena or mentioned him only in passing. This is changing as more critics are coming to acknowledge the importance of the comedic tradition.

2. Sábato Magaldi, *Panorama do Teatro Brasileiro* (São Paulo: Global Editora, 1997), 62.

3. In her book *As Noites do Ginásio: Teatro e Tensões Culturais na Corte, 1832–1868* (Campinas: Editora da UNICAMP, 2002), Silvia Crístina Martins de Souza describes a deadly riot that took place in September 1831 in the Teatro Constitucional Fluminense. It supposedly began when one spectator shouted "Long live the Republic!" and another called out "Long live Dom Pedro II!" The verbal dueling led to physical violence, and when soldiers entered the theater shots were fired and the furious crowd rushed upon them. It ended with three people dead and many more injured, and the theater was closed for several months.

4. Martins Pena also wrote six dramas, although critics agree they are better off forgotten. Most of his dramas are set in Europe, although he did write one with an Indianist theme called *Itaminda, ou o Guerreiro de Tupã* (Itaminda, or The Warrior of Tupã).

5. Later writers who cultivated this genre include Joaquim José da França Jr. (1838–90) and Artur Azevedo (1855–1908).

6. An interesting comparison from the same era would be the American Anna Cora Ogden Mowatt's 1845 classic *Fashion; or, Life in New York.* Mowatt's play utilizes many of the same plot conventions, and it also depicts Americans' attempts to imitate foreign customs while dealing with questions of race and gender.

7. The Brazilian Dramatic Conservatory was founded in 1843 and given the task of granting licenses for theatrical productions and evaluating all new works according to standards of artistic quality and propriety. As Souza attests in *As noites do Ginásio,* however, there was considerable tension between the conservatory and the police over who had the authority to make the final call on censoring plays.

8. Martins Pena's dislike of the police who patrolled the theaters was well known since he wrote many newspaper chronicles that include anecdotes about conflicts between the police and audience members. According to him, officers were trained to arrest on the slightest suspicion and treated theatergoers as if they were criminals. He accused them of provoking many of the scuffles and riots for which the theaters were notorious. As with *The Jealous Officer* itself, these comments are ambiguous; one could read an element of class prejudice in them since the officers were generally lower class.

9. The translation included here is the uncensored version. The differences are very slight. Most of the phrases that directly mention "roofs" and "rooftops" were cut, and in Scene VIII, Anacleta's repetition of the phrases the Officer reads from the letter were eliminated (although it is not clear why). Details can be found in Raymundo Magalhães, *Martins Pena e a Sua Época* (São Paulo: Livros Irradiantes, 1971); and Souza,

As Noites do Ginásio. Perhaps because of the controversy, it was not published until 1956, when it was included in the collection of Martins Pena's works published by the Instituto Nacional do Livro.

10. For information on João Caetano's version, as well as other parodies of *Othello,* see Eugenio Gomes, *Shakespeare no Brasil* (Rio de Janeiro: Ministério de Educação e Cultura, 1961).

SELECTED REFERENCES

Albuquerque, Severino João. "The Brazilian Theater up to 1900." In *Cambridge History of Latin American Literature,* vol. 3, ed. Roberto González Echevarría and Enrique Pupo-Walker, 105–25. Cambridge: Cambridge University Press, 1996.

Arêas, Vilma Sant'Anna. *Na Tapera de Santa Cruz: Uma Leitura de Martins Pena.* São Paulo: Martins Fontes, 1987.

Gomes, Eugênio. *Shakespeare no Brasil.* Rio de Janeiro: Ministério de Educação e Cultura, 1961.

Lyday, Leon F. "Satire in the Comedies of Martins Pena." *Luso-Brazilian Review* 5 (December 1968): 63–70.

Magaldi, Sábato. *Panorama do Teatro Brasileiro.* São Paulo: Global Editora, 1997.

Magalhães, Raymundo. *Martins Pena e Sua Época.* São Paulo: Livros Irradiantes, 1972.

Pierson, Colin M. "Martins Pena: A View of Character Types." *Latin American Theatre Review* 11 (spring 1978): 41–48.

Romero, Sílvio. *História da Literatura Brasileira.* Rio de Janeiro: J. Olympio, 1943.

Souza, Silvia Cristina Martins de. *As Noites do Ginásio: Teatro e Tensões Culturais na Corte, 1832–1868.* Campinas: Editora da UNICAMP, 2002.

The Jealous Officer, or The Fearsome Slave Catcher

(Luís Carlos Martins Pena)

Translated by Sarah J. Townsend

CHARACTERS:

ANDRÉ JOÃO CAMARÃO, a low-ranking police OFFICER[1]
BALBINA, his daughter
ANACLETA, his wife
ALEXANDRE, Balbina's lover
PAULINO, Anacleta's lover
ROBERTO, Anacleta's father
The PATROL CHIEF
PATROLMEN

An ordinary room. Doors at the rear and on either side. Center right, an armoire, and center left, a ladder that the audience is to assume leads to a window in the roof. Each of the side doors has a large hole cut into its upper half. A table, on top of which is an unlit candle. It is nighttime.

SCENE I

(When the curtain rises, the stage is dark and deserted. A bell striking midnight can be heard in the distance. As soon as the last ring has ceased, PAULINO appears at the top of the ladder and cautiously begins to climb down it.)

PAULINO: *(Still at the top of the ladder)* Midnight. Time to descend . . . *(Begins to climb down)* He's gone . . . Out and about in search of runaway slaves . . . How silent it is! Is my beloved still awake? The risks I take for her! I slipped on the roof and nearly fell to the street. I thought I was a goner! But, as it happens, rooftops are footpaths for both cats and lovers on the prowl. Just take heed how it all turns out! *(He is now on the bottom rungs of the ladder.)* I hear a noise . . .

SCENE II

(BALBINA, at left, sticks her head out through the hole in the door.)

BALBINA: *(Calling out)* Stepmother? Stepmother?
PAULINO: *(Aside)* Drat! The daughter is awake.
BALBINA: *(Same)* Dona Anacleta? Dona Anacleta?
ANACLETA: *(At right, sticking her head out through the hole in the door)* What do you want, Balbina?
PAULINO: *(Aside)* It's her . . .
BALBINA: It's midnight . . .

ANACLETA: And you called me only to tell me that? Go to sleep, I'm in no mood for a chat at this hour and from this perch. Good night.
BALBINA: For heaven's sake, wait!
ANACLETA: Why?
BALBINA: I'm frightened . . .
ANACLETA: Come, don't be a child. Go to sleep.
BALBINA: I can't! I was sewing, and I went to snuff the candle and . . . I was left in the dark. Just then it struck midnight. My hair stood on end . . . I got up and was about to jump into bed dressed just as I was, when I heard the floor in the garret creak as if someone were walking across it . . .
PAULINO: *(Aside)* And right she was . . .
ANACLETA: That's nothing but your fear talking.
BALBINA: No, it wasn't fear, I heard it . . . It gave me such a fright that I didn't dare so much as breathe. Finally, I gathered up the courage to come this far and call to you.
ANACLETA: Who could be walking around up in the garret at this hour?
PAULINO: *(Aside)* Me . . .
BALBINA: I don't know.
ANACLETA: You were mistaken. The floor planks creak at night from the heat.
BALBINA: Maybe so; but I'm afraid. I can't stay all alone in the dark, I'll die of fright for sure. If I could go over there . . .
ANACLETA: You know very well that's impossible.

Os Ciúmes de um Pedestre, ou O Terrível Capitão do Mato, Luís Carlos Martins Pena, Brazil, 1845. Translated from Portuguese by Sarah J. Townsend.

Both these doors are locked and your father took the keys with him.

BALBINA: Good grief! But then stay there awhile and talk to me till my father comes home.

ANACLETA: You mean to say that you want us to stay here till dawn, when he's due to return?

PAULINO: (Aside) Very good, right I was!

BALBINA: Dear me, oh dear, why must my father be so distrustful and leave us locked up like this, each in her own room? If he at least locked us in together!

ANACLETA: He says that a woman on her own is capable of deceiving the devil, and that two of them together would deceive the whole of hell.

PAULINO: (Aside) Well isn't that officer something? And what's more is that he doesn't have it all wrong . . .

BALBINA: So that's why he separates us and locks us up when he leaves to see to his affairs. Well, look here: If my father continues to give me a hard time, I'll give him a good . . .

ANACLETA: As will I.

PAULINO: (Aside) Bravo, I'd like nothing better . . .

BALBINA: I've never given him any cause to treat me this way.

ANACLETA: And I, what cause have I given him? The only remedy is to have patience. Good night.

BALBINA: No, no, wait!

ANACLETA: Listen. Go over to the table in the left-hand corner, take out the little box of matches that I placed in the drawer this morning and light your candle.

BALBINA: Very well, but don't move while I'm looking for the match.

ANACLETA: Chickenheart! Go then, I'll stay here and wait.

BALBINA: For heaven's sake, don't leave! (Disappears into the bedroom)

SCENE III

(BALBINA, PAULINO, and ANACLETA at the opening in the door)

PAULINO: (Aside) Getting closer, old pal . . . (Walks cautiously toward the sound of ANACLETA's voice)

ANACLETA: My husband thinks you can guard a woman by keeping her under seven locks and keys! Simpleton! He doesn't know that when women don't guard themselves, all the locks and doors in the world can't hold them back. Sometimes being distrustful is the worst thing a man can do.

PAULINO: (Aside, walking) No doubt about it, being distrustful is the worst thing a man can do . . .

ANACLETA: A husband's unfounded jealousy can lead his wife to think of things that would never have gone through her head, had her husband only been more trusting.

PAULINO: (Aside) Poor husbands! I'm going to venture a word with her . . .

ANACLETA: If mine hadn't tormented me with his jealousy, I would've paid no mind to my neighbor, to be sure . . .

PAULINO: (Aside) Oh, she's talking about yours truly!

ANACLETA: But because my husband doesn't trust me, I'll have to dally with Paulino, even if it's only to avenge myself . . .

PAULINO: (Aloud) Yes, yes, my love, avenge yourself! I'm here so that we can avenge ourselves together!

ANACLETA: Ay, ay, thieves! (Steps back from the hole in the door and continues shouting from inside the bedroom)

PAULINO: (Startled, knocking on the door) There now, darling! I startled you! It's me, it's me! It's the neighbor . . . I'm not a thief, don't shout . . . Look, it's me! (ANACLETA continues to shout from inside the room.) Worse! This isn't going as planned . . . (Knocking on the door) It's me, your beloved neighbor . . . Take this little letter . . .under the door . . . (As he says this, he slides a letter under the door. BALBINA appears at the hole in the other door.)

BALBINA: What is going on? What is all this shouting?

PAULINO: (Aside) This is going badly. Better make ourselves scarce, old pal, there's one more of them here than we bargained for. (Begins to leave)

BALBINA: Stepmother? (PAULINO falls against a chair.) Who's there?

PAULINO: (Losing his head) No one . . .

BALBINA: (Steps back from the hole and begins to scream) Thieves, thieves!

PAULINO: (Alone and startled) And now this! I'd best make myself scarce . . . Listen to her scream! What a set of pipes! If the Officer arrives, I'll be a goner! Rooftop love affairs always end up like this . . . Where the deuce is the ladder? (Bumping into the armoire) It's an armoire . . . I've lost my bearings . . . They've gone silent. The ladder should be on this side . . . I hear footsteps! Good grief, could it be him?

OFFICER: (Inside) Walk straight ahead . . .

PAULINO: Oh, hang it all, it's him! If he catches me here, he'll kill me . . . Or at least haul me off to jail. (Anxiously searches for the ladder) Ah, at last! (He hurriedly begins to climb up, but the ladder breaks and he tumbles across the stage.) Ay, ay! (Quickly getting up) Confounded romance! What should I do? The ladder broke! The door is opening! Egad! (Searches for the armoire) Ah! (Hides inside the armoire)

SCENE IV

(Door at rear opens and the OFFICER enters, carrying a dark lantern in his left hand. With his right hand he drags ALEXANDRE, who is disguised in blackface, by the collar.)

OFFICER: Enter, boy . . .

ALEXANDRE: Yes Massa . . .

(After entering, the OFFICER locks the door from inside.)

OFFICER: You're on the run . . .

ALEXANDRE: No Massa . . .

(The OFFICER lights a candle on top of the table and puts out the lamp.)

OFFICER: *(While lighting the candle)* Who is your master?

ALEXANDRE: My massa is Massa Majó who live in Tijuca.

OFFICER: Ah! And what were you doing on the street at midnight, here in the city?

ALEXANDRE: I was takin' some air, Massa.

OFFICER: Taking some air! What a scoundrel you are . . . You were running away.

ALEXANDRE: No Massa.

OFFICER: Never mind, I shall show you. I'll tie you up and deliver you to your master. *(Aside)* But I shall do it four days from now, so the reward will be bigger. *(To ALEXANDRE)* Come here. *(Heads with ALEXANDRE toward the second door at left and tries to open it)* Ah yes, it's locked . . . And the key is in Balbina's room. *(To ALEXANDRE)* Wait right there. If you take one step, I'll shoot you.

ALEXANDRE: Eee!

OFFICER: Eee, eh? Watch out! *(Heads toward the door of BALBINA's room, takes a key out of his pocket and opens the door. BALBINA, hearing the door open, begins to scream.)*

BALBINA: *(Inside her room)* Ay, ay! Who will save me? Who will save me?

OFFICER: What is going on in there? Balbina, why are you screaming? It's me. *(Opens the door and enters the room)* What the deuce!

SCENE V

(ALEXANDRE, PAULINO peeking out from the armoire door, and ANACLETA peeking out of the hole in the door)

ALEXANDRE: *(Speaking in his normal manner)* I'm all alone . . . I took on this disguise, the only one that would gain me entrance to this house, so that I might speak to my beloved Balbina . . . Her father guards her so vigilantly! Who knows how I'll come out of all this . . . Who knows . . . Very badly, perhaps; the Officer is vicious . . . Courage, none of this weakness now . . .

PAULINO: *(Aside, from inside the armoire)* I'm done for! How can I escape?

ANACLETA: *(Appearing at the hole in the door)* A black man! My husband is home . . . And the neighbor? The letter was from him . . . Did he leave?

PAULINO: *(Seeing ANACLETA at the opening in the door)* It's her! Psss . . .

ALEXANDRE: *(Turning around)* Who's there? *(PAUL-*

INO *and* ANACLETA, *seeing the black man turn around, disappear.)* There's someone here . . . This is no good, I'm not enjoying this anymore . . . *(Looking around, frightened)*

SCENE VI

(Enter the OFFICER and BALBINA)

OFFICER: Why were you shouting?

BALBINA: I thought you were a thief. I heard a commotion in the room . . .

ALEXANDRE: *(Aside)* How my heart beats! Caution . . . *(Begins to signal to BALBINA)*

OFFICER: It was I who entered, earlier than usual. I found this scamp sleeping on the sidewalk, right here in front of the door. He was taking some air . . . Thieves, you say? Thieves in an officer's house? They wouldn't be so foolish. There's nothing here to steal, and they'd be walking straight into the lion's den where they'd be caught red-handed, wouldn't they?

BALBINA: *(Recognizing ALEXANDRE)* Good grief!

OFFICER: Hmm?

BALBINA: *(Dissembling)* Nothing, no sir. *(Aside)* What madness! *(ALEXANDRE now has in his hand a letter, which he reveals to BALBINA.)*

OFFICER: Go along, run to bed, you're dreaming. And you . . . *(Turns around toward ALEXANDRE and catches him showing the letter to BALBINA)* Ah! *(Lunges at him and tears the letter away from him)*

BALBINA: *(Aside)* Good grief!

OFFICER: Ah, scoundrel, so you come bearing letters! *(Turning around toward his daughter)* And you receive them . . . Jezebel!

BALBINA: *(Backing away)* Father!

OFFICER: Let us first see who has written to you; then I'll punish you. *(Opens the letter and reads)* "My love . . . *(Speaking)* Oh, so he's already your love? *(Continues to read)* Despite all your father's precautions, a ruse will lead me to you. *(Speaking)* Ah, a ruse! *(Looks around apprehensively)* . . . and, after I tear you away from his cruel grip, you shall be my wife." *(Speaking)* It's not signed . . . *(He ponders.)*

BALBINA: *(Aside)* Oh, how I tremble!

ALEXANDRE: *(Aside)* What will he do? This is some scrape I got myself into!

OFFICER: *(Walks toward ALEXANDRE without saying a word and smacks him)* I will begin with you . . . *(ALEXANDRE, forgetting the character he is playing, wants to throw himself at the OFFICER. But seeing BALBINA, who with her hands clasped as if in prayer begs him to restrain himself, he holds back. The OFFICER, grabbing ALEXANDRE by the collar)* Who sent this letter?

ALEXANDRE: *(Aside)* Am I ever lucky he's never met me . . .

OFFICER: Who sent this letter? Speak, or I'll . . .

ALEXANDRE: I's dunno, Massa; it was a white man gave me it.

OFFICER: What white man?

ALEXANDRE: I's dunno, Massa.

OFFICER: Ah, so you don't know? (*Moving to pull out his sword*)

BALBINA: Father!

OFFICER: You just wait, it'll be your turn to talk soon. (*To ALEXANDRE*) Well then? Who is the white man?

ALEXANDRE: I gwine to tell everything. A white man says to me: José, want to earn ten tostões? When it strike midnight, go to Alley o' the Afflicted an' play like a run'way slave . . . An' when de Officer who live right there on Alley o' the Afflicted leave, let 'im catch you an' take you to his house . . . An' deliver this letter to the Missus Balbina . . . This one . . . But I's dunno who's de white man . . . It was jus' to earn ten tostões . . .

OFFICER: Hmm, is that so? What a scheme! Come here, my dear little *negrinho,* you scamp you . . . To-morrow, eh? Jail, a shaven head and . . . (*Makes the motion of striking ALEXANDRE*) But until then, eh? My little negro, I must give you a resoundingly righteous bludgeoning. Come now, my little negro man . . .

ALEXANDRE: (*Trying to resist*) But Massa . . .

OFFICER: Come here, come over here . . . (*Takes him to the second room on the left and puts the key in the lock*)

BALBINA: (*Aside, while the OFFICER is opening the door*) Poor Alexandre, the risks he takes for me! But he's mad, disguising himself that way!

PAULINO: (*Aside, spying from the armoire*) This is starting off very badly . . . And it's going to end up even worse!

OFFICER: (*Pushing ALEXANDRE into the bedroom*) Enter! (*Closes the door and removes the key*)

BALBINA: (*Aside, trembling from fright*) Woe is me! Kill me, dear Lord! (*The OFFICER makes his way toward BALBINA and, reaching her side, observes her for a few minutes, silent.*)

(*BALBINA trembles from fright, while her father observes her. The OFFICER, without saying a word, turns around and, opening the table drawer, takes out a caning stick.*)

BALBINA: (*Seeing him*) Ah!

OFFICER: (*Moving toward her*) Put out your hand!

BALBINA: Father!

OFFICER: Put out your hand!

BALBINA: Oh! (*Backing away*)

OFFICER: (*Following her*) Put out your hand!

BALBINA: (*Hiding her hands behind her back*) I'm not a child that you can strike with the cane!

OFFICER: You aren't a child . . . But you *are* a coquette, and it's my job to teach coquettes lessons with the cane. The holy remedy! Come!

BALBINA: Father, Father, for the love of God!

OFFICER: So the girl has suitors, she receives letters and wants to marry against my will! We'll see about that . . . Come and get it while it's hot . . . Come!

BALBINA: (*Falling to her knees*) Have mercy!

OFFICER: Four dozen, only four dozen . . .

BALBINA: Oh no, no, Father! (*Throwing her arms around his legs*) My father, what have I done to you? What fault is it of mine, if someone writes to me? Can I keep someone from writing to me?

OFFICER: You can, you can! Don't entice them! Come!

BALBINA: But this is an injustice! I don't know anyone, I don't see anyone, I live here locked away . . .

OFFICER: (*Aside*) All the more so if she wasn't alive . . .

BALBINA: What fault is it of mine, if someone takes it into his head to write to me? I have no power to stop them . . . Some stranger writes to me, sends me a letter by way of a black man . . . and I'm the one who pays the price, I, who am blameless! Father, pardon me! Find the man who wrote to me and punish him . . . But me? Oh, forgive me, my dear kind *paizinho!*

OFFICER: Stand up. Look, I'll spare you the rod this time, but stop trying to pull the wool over my eyes. I want to know who this character is that thinks he can plan a ruse to outwit me. Outwit me! Me, who is an old hand in the business! . . . I'd like to see if he manages to set one foot in this house or if he can get you to take a single step outside. So, you say you don't know who he is?

BALBINA: I already told you no, Father.

OFFICER: Fine, call your stepmother. Take the key. She will tell me. (*BALBINA goes to open the door and exits through it.*)

SCENE VII

(*OFFICER, and PAULINO in the armoire. The OFFICER paces, thoughtful, from one side of the room to the other.*)

PAULINO: (*In the armoire. Aside*) What the deuce is he thinking about!

OFFICER: A ruse! What could the ruse be? It's necessary to take the utmost precaution . . . By Jove, isn't that the way of it! These women are locked up, bolted in and still they manage to find a tiny little chink in the armor so they can get us right in the eye. Ah, but leave them to me . . . Only those who are unfamiliar with their ways can be outwitted. The door'll be kept locked—and as for the crafty ravens hovering outside the cage . . .

PAULINO: (*Aside*) But I'm no longer outside . . .

ALEXANDRE: (*Aside, looking out the hole in the door*) I'm already inside!

OFFICER: We'll see who is capable of outwitting me . . . Outwit André Camarão! As for the girl, I'll take the cane. Holy panacea for dalliances! And my wife . . . Oh, if the idea of deceiving me, of letting herself be seduced, so much as crosses her mind, if it gets as close as the ends of her hair . . . Ah, don't even mention it, don't even think it! I'd be a tiger, a lion, an elephant! I'd kill her, I'd bury her, I'd skin her alive! Oh, already I tremble with fury! I saw *Othello* many times in the theater, when I went there on duty. Othello's crime is a crumb, a bauble, a trinket compared with mine! . . . Deceive me? Deceive me, her?!? Ah, I don't even know what I might be capable of! She and her lover all tied up . . . I'd send them to the devil as a gift; they'd end up on the end of this sword, in the claws of these hands, under the heels of these boots! I don't even want to say what I might do!

PAULINO: *(Aside, in the armoire)* God take pity on me!

OFFICER: Oh, I'd kill the human race, if the human race seduced my wife!

PAULINO: *(Aside)* Who will pray for my soul?

OFFICER: She's coming . . . And I don't trust her . . .

SCENE VIII

(The same characters, plus ANACLETA and BALBINA)

ANACLETA: You called for me?

OFFICER: Yes, wait. And you *(to BALBINA)* go warm up a cup of coffee, I'm feeling very hotheaded. *(Exit BALBINA)*

PAULINO: *(Aside)* Look out . . .

OFFICER: *(To ANACLETA)* Come here. *(Sits down)*

ANACLETA: *(Approaching him)* Here you have me.

OFFICER: Who visits this house when I am away?

PAULINO: *(Aside)* No one . . .

ANACLETA: Are you having a laugh at me? *(Looking around)* He's gone . . .

OFFICER: Answer my question. Who visits this house?

ANACLETA: When you leave, do you not lock all the doors, and do you not leave us imprisoned, each one of us on her own side? How do you suppose someone could come visiting?

OFFICER: *(Standing up)* Locked doors! What good are locked doors? Do locks not have holes?

ANACLETA: *(Aside)* What sort of a man did I marry!?!

OFFICER: *(Aside)* I must see if I can find some locks without holes . . . *(Aloud)* Anacleta, listen well to what I am going to tell you. You know me, and you know I am capable of doing everything I say—and more. Whenever I leave I lock the house, doors and windows, and whenever I'm here I keep on the lookout. And despite all these precautions, Balbina deceived me.

ANACLETA: She deceived you?

OFFICER: She has a lover, she receives letters and she is involved in a ruse to outwit me. *(Looks around)* But we shall see about that . . . Where the deuce did she meet that character? When, how? That's what vexes me, what defeats my officer's expertise and turns my head. So many precautions, and finally outwitted! Ah, women! Demons! Come now, you must know who he

is? What is his name? Where did Balbina meet him? In what place? Through what hole? Through what crack?

ANACLETA: I don't know a thing.

OFFICER: *(Taking her by the arm, furious)* You don't know a thing?

ANACLETA: No!

OFFICER: Wife!

ANACLETA: Go ahead and kill me, so that my suffering might end!

OFFICER: Kill you! I will save that for when you do something to deserve it . . . For now, it's enough for me to be more cautious. All the doors, all the windows of this house are going to be nailed shut . . . A small passage in that door—just big enough for my body—is all I need so that I can leave . . . And the opening will be closed with a wooden cover and a bolt—none of these locks with keyholes! The light will come in through the roof . . . No, no, roofs too are very dangerous . . . There will be a lighted candle here day and night. I'd like to see if they can outwit me then.

ANACLETA: *(Very calmly)* Now that I have heard you out, you hear me out. Go ahead and lock all these doors, nail them shut, caulk them, surround me with sentinels and precautions, and still I will find a way to escape!

OFFICER: You? Oh!

ANACLETA: Yes, me! And I will go straight back to the convent, and then to the authorities.

OFFICER: Do you really have it in you to escape?

ANACLETA: I do!

OFFICER: Good heavens, what must I do to lock up these demons, these fiendish women?

ANACLETA: My mother—God forgive her!—cast me into the turning box at the foundling hospital. In the Holy House I was raised and educated . . .

OFFICER: A fine education!

ANACLETA: Deprived of maternal affection, poor and abandoned as I was, I found Christian relief and protection in that house of compassion; there I grew up, and there I learned to pray to the Lord for my benefactors and for my mother, who had abandoned me, my mother, of whom I possess not a thing in the world but this cross that has accompanied me from the cradle . . . *(Upon saying this, she kisses a small cross hanging from her neck.)*

OFFICER: I've heard this story many times before, and it puts me to sleep . . .

ANACLETA: Then sleep.

OFFICER: As if I were so foolish . . . He who marries, doesn't sleep, or . . . I know well what I say.

ANACLETA: Well then keep listening. As a lay sister, I had a dowry of four hundred thousand réis . . . And you married me on account of those four hundred thousand réis, and only for them.

OFFICER: Right now I'd give them away to the first person that agreed to free me from the burden of maintaining you.

ANACLETA: And so I left a house of peace for this inferno in which I live. Oh, but I'm resolved, I shall make a vow. I shall flee from this house, where I live like a miserable slave; I shall go to my benefactors, I shall tell them what I have suffered since I left them. I shall demand justice, for myself and for your first victim . . . Oh, remember, André, that your first wife, Balbina's unfortunate mother, died, crushed by her sorrow, and that your insane jealousy was what dug her grave . . .

OFFICER: She died for the benefit of my peace of mind; I don't have to keep watch over her any longer . . .

ANACLETA: Oh, what a monster!

OFFICER: Anacleta! Anacleta! You really want to cut me to the quick! I've never heard you speak in such a way, and if you are doing it now, it is because you feel guilty . . .

ANACLETA: No, I feel tired; I can't take this life anymore; I don't want to die like her.

OFFICER: Up till now I've been nothing but a gentleman, you've lacked nothing, if not your freedom . . .

ANACLETA: (Aside) It's what is necessary.

OFFICER: I trusted you . . . because I always locked the door. But my daughter deceived me, in spite of locked doors, and you too will deceive me . . .

ANACLETA: Oh!

OFFICER: (With a piercing voice) If you haven't already deceived me!

ANACLETA: This is too much!

OFFICER: (Taking her by the arm) Wife, if I had the slightest suspicion, the least indication that . . . you know what I'm saying . . . I . . . I . . . I would kill you!

ANACLETA: (Backing away, horrified) Ah!

OFFICER: (Walking toward her) Yes, I would bathe the affront to my honor in your blood, and my . . . (In her bodice he sees the tip of the letter that PAULINO slid under the door, and he quickly snatches it.)

ANACLETA: Ah! (Aside) I'm lost!

OFFICER: (With the letter in his hand) A letter! The second one today! It's raining letters in my house, despite the locked doors! One for her too! (Going toward ANACLETA) Who is this letter from? I fear to read it!

ANACLETA: This letter?

OFFICER: Yes!

ANACLETA: I don't know . . .

OFFICER: Oh! (Opening the letter angrily and then crumpling it in his hands) There it is! (Shoving it away from his eyes, shaking)

ANACLETA: (Suppliant) André!

OFFICER: Proof of my dishonor! (Taking her by the arm, he leads her to the candle on the table.)

ANACLETA: Let go of me! What do you want from me?

OFFICER: (Presenting her with the letter by the light of the candle) Read!

ANACLETA: André, have pity! (Terrified)

OFFICER: Read along with me! (Reading) "My fair Anacleta . . .

ANACLETA: (Repeating) My fair Anacleta . . .

OFFICER: (Reading) . . . Your husband is an animal . . .

ANACLETA: (Repeating) . . . Your husband is an animal . . .

OFFICER: (Same) . . . and you are an angel.

ANACLETA: (Same) . . . and you are an angel.

OFFICER: (Same) Tonight I will come to see you . . .

ANACLETA: (Same) Tonight I will come to see you . . .

OFFICER: (Same) . . . and if I do not have the good fortune to find you . . .

ANACLETA: (Same) . . . and if I do not have the good fortune to find you . . .

OFFICER: (Same) . . . I will leave you this letter . . .

ANACLETA: (Same) . . . I will leave you this letter . . .

OFFICER: (Same) . . . so that you will know how much I love you . . .

ANACLETA: (Same) . . . so that you will know how much I love you . . .

OFFICER: (Same) . . . and how much I despise your ass of a husband."

ANACLETA: (Same) . . . and how much I despise your ass of a husband.

OFFICER: (Pulling her to the front of the stage, crossing his arms very calmly) What do you have to say?

ANACLETA: Everything is closing in on me . . .

OFFICER: And incriminating you. (Changing his tone of voice) Look at me! Do you recognize me?

ANACLETA: Oh, why oh why did I leave the convent to follow this man?

OFFICER: Have you said your prayers?

ANACLETA: What are you saying?

OFFICER: Commend your soul to God, I can wait a minute. (Paces)

ANACLETA: Oh, André, André, have mercy! Listen to me! (Enter BALBINA with a cup of coffee)

BALBINA: Here is the coffee, Father. (The OFFICER strikes the cup with a blow of his hand and sends it flying into the air.) Ah!

OFFICER: (Turning to ANACLETA, unsheathing his sword) Are you ready?

ANACLETA: (Grabbing onto BALBINA) Balbina! Balbina!

BALBINA: Ay, ay!

OFFICER: (He pulls ANACLETA by the arm, and she drags BALBINA with her.) Die, you faithless woman, you traitoress!

ANACLETA: (Screaming) Who will save me, who will save me?

BALBINA: (At the same time) Father, Father!

OFFICER: No one will tear you from my hands now! I shall be avenged! Die!

ALEXANDRE: *(From the hole in the door)* Hold it right there!

OFFICER: *(Upon hearing this voice, he turns around and lets go of ANACLETA's arm.)* Ah, the negro, drat!

ANACLETA: *(Seeing that she is free, runs inside)* Help!

OFFICER: *(Realizing that it was the black man who spoke, he follows ANACLETA, furious.)* Wait, wait! *(Exeunt both)*

BALBINA: Father, Father!

ALEXANDRE: Psss! Psss! Balbina, come here!

PAULINO: *(From the armoire)* What will become of me? Mercy, what carnage!

BALBINA: *(Running to ALEXANDRE)* Flee, flee! If you don't, he'll kill me too!

ALEXANDRE: Open the door, we'll flee together. I don't want to stay here a minute longer.

BALBINA: He took the key!

PAULINO: *(Inside the armoire)* Zounds, the black man wants to run away with the girl! What have I gotten myself into?

ALEXANDRE: Balbina, Balbina, what will become of us? What possessed me to come here? But I love you so!

PAULINO: *(From the armoire)* This is the story, now I see: he disguised himself, painted himself black in order to get into the house. What a chap! If I weren't frightened out of my wits, I'd have a good chuckle at the prank he pulled on the Officer. *(Screams and commotion are heard from backstage, as from a person rolling down the stairs.)*

BALBINA: Good grief, he killed her!

ALEXANDRE: *(From the hole in the door)* It's not possible!

PAULINO: *(In the armoire, closing the door)* I'm feeling faint . . . Who will come to my rescue?

ALEXANDRE: Powers of mercy, powers of mercy, I can't stay here any longer . . . My legs are shaking . . . *(Disappears from the hole)*

SCENE IX

(Enter the OFFICER with the sword still in his hand and looking very pale and frightened)

BALBINA: Father, Father, what's wrong? You're so pale! Answer me! And my stepmother?

OFFICER: *(Pointing to the bedroom, trembling all over)* Dead!

BALBINA: Dead! Good grief! *(She runs into the bedroom.)*

PAULINO: *(In the armoire, to himself)* A murder! And I'm the cause, oh!

OFFICER: *(Terrified)* She was deceiving me . . . She's dead! Dead! And now? She will be buried . . . and I will rest in peace. Yes, in peace, calm. Tomorrow they will ask after her and I will . . . Oh, perhaps I did wrong . . . wrong? If she was innocent . . . Inno-

cent? . . . Oh! *(Tenderly)* Anacleta, Anacleta! But she betrayed me, I did right . . . A man must avenge himself . . . *(Tenderly)* Anacleta! Someone is coming . . .

BALBINA: *(Entering)* Father, Father, there may still be time to save her! She rolled down the steps and is fallen there, cold and senseless . . . Go to her!

OFFICER: No. She betrayed me; she forgot my name, my love, my trust.

BALBINA: Come, or go call a doctor!

OFFICER: *(In a fearsome voice)* No!

BALBINA: Dear Lord, take pity on us! *(Exit)*

OFFICER: Dead, dead, dead! Perhaps she wasn't guilty; perhaps, who knows? What an abyss! Innocent! But the letter? The letter? "Your husband is an animal . . ." Animal! Oh, if I had that shameful seducer beneath my feet, if I saw him trembling, stuck on this sword, ah! How happy I'd be! Faithless woman! Insulted, dishonored! Oh, I'd like to swim in blood! Faithless woman! *(Nervously walks about the room)* The ladder is broken . . . Did he come down through here? Did he enter through the roof? Ah, *(seeing the cap)* a cap! A cap in my house! A cap! Could it be any clearer? But a cap on its own is innocent, a cap is worthless . . . The head that it covered is everything. Let's look for the head. *(Begins to search the room, furious)* He must not escape me. *(Goes to the armoire and opens it)* Aha, here he is!

PAULINO: Who will come to my rescue? Who will save me?

OFFICER: *(Yanking him out of the armoire and pushing him toward the front of the stage)* Oh, so it's you? Executioner of my honor, of my tranquility!

PAULINO: *(Trembling with fright)* Not I, sir, not I!

OFFICER: *(Putting the cap on his head)* This cap is yours . . . and your head is mine!

PAULINO: Ay, ay, ay!

OFFICER: *(Furious)* Ah, so you thought you would enter the conjugal sanctuary through the roof, and rob the husband of his precious goods! Ah, so you were counting upon my weakness! You are to die in the evening tide!

PAULINO: Ay, ay, who will come to my rescue?

OFFICER: Scream all you like. I have every right to kill you. I'm going to tear out that heart of yours . . . Scream . . . and die!

PAULINO: *(With a rapid movement he frees himself from the OFFICER's hands and runs around the room, screaming.)* Ay, ay, who will come to my rescue? He wants to kill me!

OFFICER: *(Following closely behind PAULINO)* You shall not escape me; you must die! *(Lunges at PAULINO with his sword, from behind)* Die!

PAULINO: *(Letting himself fall facedown on the ground, with his arms outstretched)* Ay, I'm dead!

OFFICER: *(Stopping suddenly)* Dead! He too! I killed him! *(Dropping his sword, trembling, he goes to sit down* next to the table and remains there for a few minutes, silent. As he is walking toward the table, and during the time he remains seated, PAULINO raises his head and watches him. The OFFICER continues, after a few moments of silence.) I did what I had to do.

PAULINO: (Aside) So did I.

OFFICER: (Standing up, pensive) A man is born, peaceful and innocent, only to bring about two deaths . . . Two deaths! The fate and destiny of humankind! (Walks over to PAULINO, who remains motionless) Vile seducer, abhorrent corpse! (Shoves PAULINO with his foot and PAULINO rolls over) Rise up from the dead, I want to kill you all over again, to gorge myself on your blood, tear out your bowels! Oh, rise up from the dead!

PAULINO: (Aside) As if I were so foolish!

OFFICER: My vengeance is complete; I will sleep in peace . . . In peace? And the gallows? The gallows! Oh, I forgot all about the gallows! Oh, why did justice raise that horrid phantasm between man and his legitimate revenge? Clearly whoever invented the Code of Laws and the gallows was never betrayed by a woman . . . What will I do? How can I conceal these two deaths, how can I hide these two bodies, what will I do? Ah! (As if struck by a sudden idea, he runs to the room where ALEXANDRE is and exits.)

PAULINO: (Cautiously lifting his head and spying) He left . . . What was he going to do? If the key were in the door, I'd skedaddle out of here . . . But that archfiend took it . . . It's best to continue playing dead. But what the deuce does he want to do with my body? Well now, this will teach me not to get in over my head, jump across rooftops and monkey around with other men's wives. If I escape from this mess, all those with wives can sleep with the door wide open, I renounce all of it, abrenuntio . . . Here he comes . . . I'm dead.

SCENE X

(Enter the OFFICER, leading ALEXANDRE with one hand and carrying a sack in the other)

OFFICER: (To ALEXANDRE) Not a word, and do as I tell you; if not, I will kill you just as I killed him . . . (Pointing)

ALEXANDRE: (Frightened, seeing PAULINO) Ah!

OFFICER: Well then?

ALEXANDRE: (Aside) It's the middle of the night, and I'm here all alone with this heartless man in his house . . .

OFFICER: Make up your mind!

ALEXANDRE: Yes Massa. (Aside) It's best to obey and see if I can slip away . . .

OFFICER: Come here. I have to put him in this sack, help me. (Both begin to place PAULINO in the sack.

During this operation, PAULINO maintains the appearance of a dead body.) Hurry up, don't tremble. He's still warm . . . Scoundrel! You are to carry him on your back like this, in the sack, and throw him into the sea. (Taking a cord out of his pocket) Let's tie the sack closed. (They tie it closed.) I will accompany you to the beach; afterward I will grant you your freedom . . . Good, it's tied. Now wait a moment while I check to see if there's a patrol nearby, or if anyone is passing by in the street. (Exits through the back and locks the door from the other side)

SCENE XI

(ALEXANDRE, and PAULINO inside the sack)

ALEXANDRE: He locked the door . . . and left me alone with a dead man! But who is this man? Why did he kill him? Oh, my hair is standing on end . . . Alone with a corpse! Why did I come here? What a dreadful night! And Balbina? She's with her stepmother, who is also dead . . . Oh, that fearsome officer! What will I do, what will I do?

PAULINO: (Inside the sack, sitting up) We'll escape . . .

ALEXANDRE: (Backing away, terrified) Ah!

PAULINO: Don't be frightened, I'm alive . . .

ALEXANDRE: Alive!

PAULINO: Yes, yes. Do you not hear me speaking?

ALEXANDRE: (Approaching) Ah!

PAULINO: He left . . . And I hope you won't toss this sack into the sea with me inside. Go on, get me out of here. I know quite well why you're here; I heard everything. You came for one, I came for the other. Go on, get me out of here and we'll escape . . . Hurry up, uf! (ALEXANDRE, who appears to be thinking as PAULINO speaks, exclaims Balbina, Balbina! and exits through the door at right, running.)

SCENE XII

(PAULINO, alone, inside the sack)

PAULINO: Well then? Sir? He left . . . Now this! (Stands up) And he left me all alone, inside the sack . . . If only I could tear it! (Makes an effort) It's no use! I'm practically dead and buried, I mean, look at me, I'm already bagged. And my friend? (Takes several steps, gets tangled up in the sack and falls) Ouch, I bumped my head. What ever possessed me to come here? (Sitting up) Mister Paulino, Mister Paulino, who could have guessed that one day you'd find yourself in a situation like this . . . (Kneeling) Our Lady of Refuge, give me refuge in my time of need, and I will promise you a sack of coffee, a sack of beans and a sack of flour! (Standing up) But in the meantime, while I'm hoping that our Lady of Refuge will remember me, it wouldn't be a bad idea to try to escape on my own. The door should be on this side; there'll be the devil to pay if I run into my killer . . . Let's risk it, old pal, we'll hop like a toad; otherwise, you're a gone goose. (*Begins to cross the stage, jumping with his feet together*)

SCENE XIII

(*Enter ALEXANDRE and BALBINA*)

ALEXANDRE: (*Entering*) It's the only way to save ourselves!

PAULINO: (*Stopping*) I hear voices . . .

ALEXANDRE: Your stepmother has already come round; she was just in a daze after falling down the stairs as she was fleeing from your father. She's resting in bed. She's safe; now let's save ourselves too . . . The way I described to you is our only choice. And once we're out of here, I have my own plan . . .

BALBINA: I place myself in your hands. (*ALEXANDRE kisses her hand.*)

ALEXANDRE: (*To PAULINO, who is motionless*) Um, sir?

PAULINO: (*Hearing someone speaking to him, he jumps quickly, running away.*) Let me be, let me be, don't kill me, Officer!

ALEXANDRE: (*Running after him and assuring him*) Don't be frightened, it's me . . .

PAULINO: Oh, it's you?

ALEXANDRE: Yes, it's me. Do you want out of this sack?

PAULINO: (*Promptly*) Yes, sir!

ALEXANDRE: Do you want out of this house?

PAULINO: Yes, sir!

ALEXANDRE: In the free and clear?

PAULINO: Yes, sir!

ALEXANDRE: Do you swear to do as I tell you?

PAULINO: I swear, yes sir!

ALEXANDRE: On your word of honor?

PAULINO: On my word of honor!

ALEXANDRE: Very well. (*Unties the sack*)

PAULINO: (*Sticking his head out of the sack*) Ah, at last!

ALEXANDRE: I have your word . . .

PAULINO: You can count on it. (*Having gotten out of the sack*)

ALEXANDRE: (*To BALBINA*) Balbina, come, don't be frightened. As I told you, this is the only way for us to get out of here. (*ALEXANDRE places the open sack on the ground and BALBINA, standing on top of it, allows ALEXANDRE to enclose her in it.*)

PAULINO: What the deuce is all this about? In this house they bag people like they do flour . . . And how am I to get out of here?

ALEXANDRE: (*Tying the sack shut*) Do you want to go back in the sack?

PAULINO: Not in the slightest, I want to know how I'm to get out of this den of assassins.

ALEXANDRE: By sneaking out behind me when I leave with the Officer, carrying this sack on my back.

PAULINO: Bravo, I understand perfectly! It's better than being thrown into the sea. (*The sound of a key in the lock is heard.*)

ALEXANDRE: He's coming . . . (*PAULINO quickly runs and hides in the armoire, and ALEXANDRE places BALBINA, inside the sack, over his shoulder.*)

SCENE XIV

(*Enter the OFFICER*)

OFFICER: Everything is silent, no one is passing by . . . I went to the corner and didn't see a living soul. Let's go, carefully; I will return for the other body later on. Let's put out the light. (*Puts out the candle and exits followed by ALEXANDRE, who carries BALBINA on his back. After exiting, he locks the door from the other side.*)

SCENE XV

(*As soon as the OFFICER and ALEXANDRE exit, PAULINO opens the armoire door and cautiously emerges.*)

PAULINO: I think he locked the door . . . Drat! And he left me in the dark. (*Goes over to the door and tests it to see if it is locked*) It's locked! Locked! Oh, the devil take it, I'm still a prisoner and in his power! Good grief, when will I get out of this accursed house? Alone, in the dark with a dead woman . . . She's in there, dead, and I'm the cause of her death! It won't be long before her soul comes out here and takes me to task . . . My hair is already standing on end! I escaped dying at the end of a sword and dying by drowning, but I'll end up dying of fright for sure. What a night, what a night! (*In the distance, a clock strikes one.*) One o'clock! The hour when otherworldly spirits come out . . . And I'm locked up all alone with a dead woman! (*A cat jumps onto the stage through the hole in the first door on the left; upon hearing the noise, PAULINO gives a start and falls to his knees, frightened.*) Ay, have mercy, mercy! Our Father, who art in heaven, hallowed be thy name . . . hallowed . . . thy kingdom come . . . who art in heaven . . . thy name . . . hallowed . . . our daily bread . . . hallowed . . . as it is in heaven . . . be thy name . . . thy debts . . . I think it went away. I don't hear anything. (*Stands up*) It's the poor woman's spirit, it's grieving . . . Unfortunate woman, may the Lord take pity on you and keep you by his side for a long time, far from me . . . Why, isn't it a wonder! The way my love for this woman vanished after she died . . . I suspect the fright I've had tonight is what changed things. Ay, ay, ay, I would trade the love of every woman, single, married, widowed and etcetera, just to be out of here . . . (*Door on the right opens*) Ay, here she comes! It's a white shadow . . . as high as the ceiling . . . Ay, ay! (*Falls to his knees*)

SCENE XVI

(*Enter ANACLETA from the right*)

ANACLETA: (*Entering*) They left me all alone . . . everyone fled . . . What a barbarous man! How dark it is! I'm alone, alone and abandoned. I'm so shaken from the horrible fall I took . . . Perhaps Balbina is in her room; let's see. She wouldn't have the heart to forsake me, weak as I am.

PAULINO: (*While ANACLETA delivers this short monologue, he quietly prays.*) Hail Mary, who art in heaven . . . in this valley of tears . . . pardon our daily bread . . . as are we in eternal life . . . amen Jesus . . . (*Etc. ANACLETA, heading left toward BALBINA's room, bumps into PAULINO, who is on his knees, and both are startled.*)

ANACLETA: (*Startled and backing away*) Ah!

PAULINO: (*Falling face down*) Have mercy! Have mercy!

ANACLETA: (*Aside*) Who could it be?

PAULINO: (*Face down*) Lady, otherworldly soul, take pity on me! It was your husband who killed you . . . Lay hold of him and carry him off to hell . . . But me, your lady?

ANACLETA: Oh, it's the neighbor, he's still here and he thinks I'm dead. (*To PAULINO*) Sir . . .

PAULINO: (*Aside*) Sir!?! This is a very polite spirit . . .

ANACLETA: It's me, don't be startled, don't be frightened . . .

PAULINO: (*Aside*) She seems like such a good person, the poor dear!

ANACLETA: How is it that you're still here? Answer!

PAULINO: As if I were so foolish!

ANACLETA: My husband believes me to be dead.

PAULINO: (*Getting up little by little*) He believes you to be dead?

ANACLETA: Only because, while fleeing from his fury, I rolled down the stairs and fell senseless.

PAULINO: (*Seated*) So you're not dead? Then I'm not speaking to your spirit?

ANACLETA: Me, dead! Perhaps they all think I'm dead, and that's why they abandoned me. But thanks be to God, I'm still alive.

PAULINO: (*Standing up*) She's still alive! And I too am still alive . . . I too was dead. We're both alive and locked inside this house together. And he's the one who locked us in here . . . He himself, the husband . . . Oh, what a stupid officer!

ANACLETA: Sir!

PAULINO: Have no fear . . . An hour ago I would have given everything I own to be as I am, all alone with you. But things have changed; this hour alone has

aged me more than fifty years. I jumped out of my window, I climbed onto your roof, I slipped three times, I came down your ladder, I broke it, I witnessed your husband's fury, I cried over your death, I was murdered, stuck in a sack, good grief! And all that in an hour! Would I not be better off lying in my bed, snoring away beneath the sheets?

ANACLETA: You are the one who bears the blame for all that, just as you are the one who caused all my suffering.

PAULINO: I accept the blame for everything, I'll shoulder all of that too—today I'm ready to take on anything. But even so I'll have you know that, if you had closed your window in my face when I was wooing you from mine, none of this would have happened.

ANACLETA: I never misled you; I knew my duties. If I paid you notice at times, it was only to distract myself from the boredom in which I live.

PAULINO: (*Furious*) To distract yourself!?! Distract yourself!?! And everything I risked! Oh, you huge blockhead, you ass! Stupid, dunderhead, you risked everything for a woman who was playing with you! I'm going to explode!

ANACLETA: Don't shout so loudly, he could come . . .

PAULINO: The Officer! Oh, now my death is certain . . . And what kind of death? And for whom? Out of the way, woman, out of the way! Right now I'd rather be with your spirit . . .Yes, with your spirit, because I have yet to see a husband who is jealous of his wife's spirit . . .

ANACLETA: Sir!

PAULINO: Oh, I might have to kill you just to be left alone with your spirit!

ANACLETA: Good grief!

PAULINO: It's all over, all of it! Tomorrow I'll be dead! Oh sun that shone upon me, tomorrow you will see my funeral procession climbing the slope of Santo Antonio . . . I won't escape, I can't escape . . . Found here, alone with her, I will die at his hands. Oh!

ANACLETA: Let's run away, let's run away!

PAULINO: Run away with you!?! I would run away *from* you, if the door were unlocked. Run away with a woman! Oh, may the devil take all women and anyone who believes them and . . .

ANACLETA: (*Very frightened*) He's coming! (*Heads right and exits*)

PAULINO: (*Frightened*) He's coming! (*Heads left, enters the room and closes the door*)

SCENE XVII

(*Enter the OFFICER, very frightened*)

OFFICER: I'm lost! I'd best escape while there's still time . . . I'll need to take some things along. (*Heads to the table and, opening the drawer, takes out a small box of matches and lights a candle)* On turning the second corner, we ran straight into a patrol . . . The negro took to his heels with the sack on his back, and so did I. Catch them, catch them! the patrol shouted, and I shouted in the same way, Catch him, catch him! so that they wouldn't suspect me. But at the first corner I doubled back and headed for home as quickly as I could . . . Ah, but I can't escape! The negro will be arrested with a dead body on his back; he'll talk . . . They'll come here, and the other corpse . . . It's all over, I was born to hang on account of women, who have caused me so much trouble . . . I'm going to round up the little money I have and hightail it . . . Whoever wishes to can bury her . . . Oh, the devil, I left the door open! *(Goes to close the rear door)*

SCENE XVIII

(The OFFICER, upon arriving at the door, backs away as ROBERTO appears.)

ROBERTO: *(From the door)* May I?

OFFICER: *(Backing away)* Ah! *(Aside)* I'm lost!

ROBERTO: *(Entering)* Pardon me, at this time of night . . .

OFFICER: *(Aside)* Anytime is a good time to arrest and hang a man . . .

ROBERTO: Only a very compelling motive would oblige me to trouble you at such an unseemly hour . . .

OFFICER: Ah, the man isn't who I thought . . . He's not here to arrest me . . . No doubt he wants me to find some runaway slave or another. *(Aloud)* How can I serve you, Your Lordship?

ROBERTO: Sir, not twelve hours ago I disembarked upon arriving from India . . .

OFFICER: Ah, and he already escaped . . . Upon disembarking, no doubt . . .

ROBERTO: Who might "he" be?

OFFICER: Your slave.

ROBERTO: I have not come to discuss any slave of mine.

OFFICER: Ah! *(Aside)* What the deuce could it be? *(Aloud)* Then do me the favor of telling me at once why you have come. You understand that at this hour . . . *(ANACLETA now spies through the hole in the door and remains there as the scene continues).*

ROBERTO: I will tell you why I have come, and I beg you to excuse me. Eighteen years ago a motive, which it would be pointless to mention now, obliged me to leave Rio de Janeiro, my homeland. I departed for the coast of Africa; but before leaving, cruel and compelling necessity forced me to cast my beloved little daughter into the turning box for foundlings. I left this land with a broken heart, mourning the lover who had been stolen from me by the grave and the daughter whom I had delivered unto the charity of others. Eighteen years of exile . . . Ah, but by dint of hardship and toil I amassed a princely fortune. *(The OFFICER removes his cap, which was still on his head.)* A colossal fortune to offer my daughter, who had spent her youth in abandonment . . . This morning I entered the harbor; three ships bearing riches followed in my wake . . . And those three ships belong to me.

OFFICER: Three ships!

ROBERTO: Upon setting foot on land, I quickly headed to the Santa Casa da Misericórdia to discover if my daughter was still alive. How anxious and trepidant I felt! Arriving there, I asked after that innocent girl who for eighteen long years had given me the strength to suffer and the courage to toil . . . I provided the necessary signs—a cross of polished gold, edged in blue . . .

OFFICER: *(Stunned)* A gold cross!

ANACLETA: *(From the door. Aside)* A gold cross!

ROBERTO: I was told that this girl, having been left unclaimed, was given a dowry by the convent and married off. I asked to whom; they informed me that it was to a man who later became a police officer.

ANACLETA: *(From the door. Aside)* Good grief!

OFFICER: *(Shocked, at the same time)* It's her! Oh! *(PAULINO now begins to spy through the hole in the door on the left; cautiously, however, so as not to be seen.)*

ROBERTO: A police officer! I exclaimed. It matters not. If that man has made her happy, if in the poverty to which his occupation condemns him he has eased her fate with the blessings of his soul, if in domestic life he has made her forget the abandonment of her youth, that man will be my son-in-law. Tomorrow he will have a magnificent palace, countless servants, sumptuous furnishings . . .

OFFICER: *(Aside)* Oh, and I killed her!

ROBERTO: . . . gold with which he may indulge himself, gold in abundance to satisfy his every whim.

OFFICER: *(Aside)* And I killed her!

ROBERTO: Tomorrow he will tread upon the haughtiest with his immense wealth and he will crush the wealthiest with his splendid ostentation.

OFFICER: *(Aside)* Oh, and I killed her!

ANACLETA: *(At the door. Aside)* Good grief, is this possible?

ROBERTO: The men who were listening to me first allowed this torrent of exaltation to subside, and then told me the way to my son-in-law's home. I got into a carriage and headed to your home. And now, Sir, you who are her husband, pray tell me: my daughter?

OFFICER: *(As if hallucinating)* Your daughter?

ROBERTO: Does she live happily? Does she curse her father?

OFFICER: *(Same)* Her father!

ROBERTO: Where is she? I wish to embrace her.

OFFICER: *(Same)* Embrace her! Embrace her!

ROBERTO: Yes, to hold her against my breast, to make her happy . . . And you as well, you who have provided for her. Oh, lead me, lead me to her!

OFFICER: (With his face contorted and taking ROBERTO by the arm) Your daughter . . . is dead!

ROBERTO: Dead!

OFFICER: Yes, and it was I, I myself who killed her!

ROBERTO: Oh, great God, what is this I hear? (During this time ANACLETA disappears into the bedroom.)

OFFICER: (Crazed) She betrayed me . . . her lover . . . I killed them, and I was right to do so! Locked doors . . . served for nothing . . . She deceived me . . . I killed her . . . She's dead! Palaces, furnishings, gold, lots of gold, she caused me to lose it all . . . Because of her I'll live in misery!

ROBERTO: (As though destroyed) Good grief!

OFFICER: Oh, if only she hadn't let me kill her, right now I'd have three ships, three! Demons that tempted me! I would have been rich, rich, really rich . . . Oh, wife, what you made me lose!

ROBERTO: (Energetically) Ah, so you are her killer? My daughter's killer? Ah, you shall not escape from my hands!

OFFICER: (Paying no attention to ROBERTO) Wife who bested me in life and in death, wife who did me injury in life and then ruined me in death, wife who pursues me even when dead, may the demons take you!

ROBERTO: Ah, I will call for justice, I will clamor for vengeance!

OFFICER: (As if confidentially) Listen, listen . . . in secret . . . so no one hears us . . .

ROBERTO: Assassin!

OFFICER: (Same) Listen . . . I'll give you one of my three ships if you'll bring her back to life and that way I can keep the other two . . . Come, she's over there . . .

ROBERTO: Over there!

OFFICER: Yes, yes, she's dead . . . But you'll bring her back to life for a ship . . . come . . . silence . . . I'll give you one of the ships she made me lose . . .

ROBERTO: (Allowing himself to be led by the OFFICER) Oh!

PAULINO: (From the hole. Aside) Look out, here it comes. (When the OFFICER and ROBERTO are two steps away from the door, it opens suddenly. ANACLETA comes through it and embraces ROBERTO.)

ANACLETA: (Embracing ROBERTO) Father! Father!

ROBERTO: (Surprised) Ah!

OFFICER: (Seeing ANACLETA, he backs away in terror to the extreme left and comes to find himself at the door, where PAULINO is peering out from the hole.) A ghost! A ghost!

ANACLETA: (In ROBERTO's arms) It is I, my father, I am your daughter, here is the cross . . . (Showing the cross to her father)

ROBERTO: (Embracing her) Yes, yes, it is my daughter! Daughter, beloved daughter! Good grief!

ANACLETA: (At the same time) My father, my father! (As ROBERTO embraces his daughter and they continue in a mute scene of recognition and effusiveness, the OFFICER is terrified and leans against the door, trembling.)

OFFICER: It's her, it's her spirit! Let me be, let me be!

PAULINO: (From the door. To the OFFICER) Hey, don't be scared . . . Stop shaking . . .

OFFICER: (Hearing someone speak above his head, he looks and, seeing PAULINO's face, says in extreme terror) Oh, the other ghost too! (Rushes toward the rear door to escape)

PAULINO: Wait . . .

(The mute scene between ROBERTO and ANACLETA continues. The OFFICER heads toward the rear of the stage, and as he is going to leave, he runs into ALEXANDRE who, still carrying BALBINA on his back inside the sack, arrives in police custody. At this unexpected visit, the OFFICER shouts and retreats to the extreme right of the stage, where, falling to his knees, he trembles in fright.)

CHIEF: (Entering accompanied by two PATROLMEN and ALEXANDRE) Who is the owner of this house?

PAULINO: Bravo, we're all reunited!

ROBERTO: Soldiers! What is this about?

CHIEF: Who is the owner of this house?

ANACLETA: (To the CHIEF, pointing to the OFFICER) He's right there. But, Mr. Official . . .

CHIEF: (Going over to the OFFICER) Sir, stand up. (The OFFICER stands up.) That negro was found in the street with a sack on his back, and inside it is a corpse . . .

ROBERTO: A corpse!

ANACLETA: (At the same time) A corpse!

CHIEF: Yes, a corpse that came from this house. And I have brought it back here in like manner in order to proceed to the corpus delicti.

ROBERTO: A corpse!

OFFICER: (Getting up) Yes, a corpse . . . (Pointing to PAULINO, who is still looking out of the hole in the door) . . . and there is his spirit!

PAULINO: Hah, hah, hah!

ALL: His spirit!

OFFICER: It was I who killed him! Open it and you'll see . . . It was I who killed him, just as I killed this woman . . .

ANACLETA: I'm alive, thanks be to God!

PAULINO: As am I.

ALEXANDRE: (Who by this time has stood the sack on the ground and untied it to reveal BALBINA's face) As is this one . . .

CHIEF: Oh!

ROBERTO: (At the same time) Oh!

ANACLETA: Balbina!

OFFICER: Alive! All of them alive! They were resurrected! Oh! (Heading towards his wife) Wife!

ANACLETA: (Taking cover behind ROBERTO) Father, save me!

ROBERTO: (To the OFFICER) Stand back!

OFFICER: Wife, I killed you . . . I killed him too . . . *(Pointing to PAULINO)* And you and he remained alive in this house, together, locked in . . . and locked in by me, by me! Oh, what was the use of barring the doors and causing two deaths? *(Speaking to BALBINA)* And you let yourself be carried off by a negro that I myself led out of the house . . . Oh, of what use were the locks, the precautions, the jealousy, the caning stick? Oh, I've been undeceived! *(Speaking to ROBERTO)* Sir, take your daughter, she no longer belongs to me . . . I killed her, I'm a widower . . . Give her all your ships and riches; go live with her in a palace, but I, no . . . In a palace! Oh, in a palace, where there are so many doors and windows! This house has only one door, and even so . . . No, no, take her . . . I can't keep watch over women, I've been undeceived, I'm going to be a monk!

ANACLETA: André!

OFFICER: Away with you!

ROBERTO: Daughter! *(Holding her back)*

OFFICER: *(To BALBINA)* And you, who so shamefully deceived me, go ahead and marry that negro, and I'll be avenged!

ALEXANDRE: I accept your blessing. *(Runs his hand across his face and, wiping it clean, looks at the OFFICER)*

OFFICER: Oh, that was the final straw! My vow is taken . . . *(To the CHIEF)* Sir, arrest me and take me to the monastery; I want to be a prisoner. *(Saying these words, he grabs onto the collar of one of the PATROLMEN and the collar of the CHIEF.)* I'm under arrest!

PAULINO: Hah, hah, hah!

CHIEF: Let me go, let me go!

OFFICER: Don't let me escape . . .

ANACLETA: André!

BALBINA: *(At the same time)* Father!

OFFICER: *(To both of them)* Let me be, I've been arrested by the police and am being taken away to be a monk! *(To the CHIEF)* Don't let me escape . . . Goodbye, world, goodbye, women! Let's go! *(Goes to the rear, taking the CHIEF and the PATROLMAN with him)*

CHIEF: *(Dragged by force)* Wait, wait!

ANACLETA: Father!

ROBERTO: *(At the same time)* Daughter!

BALBINA: *(At the same time)* Alexandre!

ALEXANDRE: *(At the same time)* You will be mine!

OFFICER: *(Exiting at the rear)* I'm going to be a monk!

PAULINO: And I'm going to sleep, it's past one o'clock . . . *(ALEXANDRE kneels at BALBINA's feet; ROBERTO embraces ANACLETA. The curtain falls, but the OFFICER's voice can still be heard.)*

OFFICER: *(From behind the curtain)* I want to be a monk, I want to be a monk!

THE END

NOTE

1. The Officer's last name (Camarão) translates as "shrimp."

Nineteenth-century illustration of a circus performance of *Juan Moreira*. Artist unknown. (Courtesy of the Museo Nacional del Teatro, Buenos Aires.)

Juan Moreira (Eduardo Gutiérrez and José Podestá)

For a fictional character who is fated to die, Juan Moreira has had a remarkably long and varied life in the cultural imaginary of the Río de la Plata region. A rugged outlaw who has ridden roughshod through circus shows, avant-garde literature, and the silver screen, the legendary gaucho dons a different disguise in every adaptation. He has been a gay gaucho, a woman warrior, a macho patriarch, and a victim of torture; he is both the standard-bearer of nationalism and the champion of those it excludes.

The "real" Juan Moreira who bequeathed his name to this long line of diverse progeny was one of the last of the nomadic horsemen and cowherds who rode the vast pampas of Argentina and Uruguay from the mid-eighteenth to the mid–nineteenth century. Key players in the series of civil wars that kept the region in turmoil for over half a century after its independence from Spain in 1816, gauchos were denounced as "barbarians" and "white-skinned savages" by those who saw the triumph of urban civilization as the only path to modernity.[1] As the railroad was extended into the interior and the lands on which livestock grazed were partitioned by barbed wire, the gauchos lost their livelihood and were forced to become peons on the newly enclosed estates or migrate to the city. The historical Moreira managed to avoid such a fate by serving as a hired gun for the Autonomist leader Adolfo Alsina until he switched sides and went over to the Nationalist Bartolomé Mitre in 1872.[2] His luck finally ran out on April 30, 1874, when he was killed in a gun battle with the police of the province of Buenos Aires in Lobos, Argentina.

Five years later the writer and journalist Eduardo Gutiérrez granted him a second life by making him the protagonist of a *novela de folletín* (serial novel). Unlike the gaucho hero of José Hernández's famous epic poem *Martín Fierro*, Moreira emerged in the distinctly commercial milieu of a Buenos Aires newspaper and found his followers among middle- and lower-class readers, some of whom were themselves recent migrants from the pampas. Furthermore, at least according to Gutiérrez, his story was the plain, unvarnished truth. The author portrays Moreira as a respectable family man unjustly thrust into the life of an outlaw after killing the Italian saloon owner Sardetti, who has taken his money and defamed his reputation. Although such acts of revenge were defensible within the gaucho's traditional code of honor, the local mayor, who covets Moreira's wife, invokes the rule of law and dispatches the army to capture the freedom-loving horseman so he can be sent off to the perilous frontier to fight Indians.

The novel was such a success that Gutiérrez went on to create a pantomime version, which was staged for the first time in 1884 by the renowned circus performer José Podestá. According to Podestá's memoirs, the performance took place on an assembled stage and in the circus ring; the only spoken parts were a mournful tune sung by the protagonist during the rural fiesta and the accompaniment of two black musicians. What observers called the extreme "realism" of the drama struck an immediate chord with the audience, and one show after another drew a packed crowd. One of the few reporters who commented on the phenomenon stated, "They laughed at the novel *Juan Moreira*, they continue to laugh at the pantomime *Juan Moreira*. They call it 'a thing for the rabble', but the novel has turned the newspaper into a success . . . and the pantomime attracts an unending chain of spectators." High society's opinion notwithstanding, he predicted that "the national theater has been born . . . since the first night in which a national production was accepted by a large majority of the public."[3]

Two years later, on April 10, 1886, in the town of Chivilcoy near Buenos Aires, the Podestá-Scotti circus troupe premiered the first spoken version of the play. Much of its self-consciously colloquial dialogue came straight from Gutiérrez's novel. The play's unprecedented success was largely responsible for ushering in the period from around 1890 to 1916 known as the golden age of the *circo criollo* (creole circus), a distinctly regional tradition of traveling circuses that featured two-part shows, the first half consisting of the usual acrobatics and animals and the second of a theatrical performance, most often a gaucho drama. But the stage on which Moreira cut his teeth bore little resemblance to the elegant theaters of Buenos Aires and Montevideo, which featured mostly European dramas for the small upper class. The circus ambience fostered improvisation and an unusually fluid distinction between performance and offstage action.

> The patrons are invited to enter the circus ring to act as patrons; the spectators are moved by their hero's adventures to the point of being unable to distinguish between fiction and reality: some of them jump up on stage, knife in hand, to defend their hero in a fight where he's at a disadvantage, others leave the circus emboldened and challenge the first group of police officers that crosses their path to a duel.[4]

As the quote suggests, the reciprocity that characterized the relationship between spectacle and spectators was not only imaginary but also physical. The historian Angel Rama has pointed out that *Moreira*'s origin as a pantomime indelibly impacted its subsequent development since the play is composed of what he calls a "a plural language within which words are only one of the ingredients, sometimes the least decisive."[5] Moreira is a man of action, and Rama attributes a large part of the play's success in creating a public to its assembly of a regional repertoire of physical gestures and poses. He states that "just as the Río de la Plata has generated a particular form of Spanish . . . and an intonation characteristic of the speaker, one might well suspect that it has produced a corresponding form of corporeal expression."[6] The circus performers, he says, picked up on the physical idiosyncracies of their compatriots in far-flung locales and incorporated stylized versions of them in their traveling shows. A drama of tragic resistance to the modern state's centralizing authority, the roving *Moreira* paradoxically propelled the integration of the dispersed and divided nation.

His journey took him not only outward across the pampas but also up the social ladder. In 1891, the Podestá-Scotti company debuted the "national drama" *Juan Moreira* at the Teatro Politeama Argentino, one of the most distinguished theaters in Buenos Aires. Although some members of the literary elite were appalled and there was a debate in the press over whether such an event signaled a disastrous decline in artistic standards, the play was a hit among high society; it had a run of fifty performances, and the president of the Republic attended several times.[7] In his new guise as a respectable rebel, Moreira was lauded as the essence of *argentinidad*, a virile representative of the (implicitly white) "race." His success inspired an entire genre of gaucho dramas such as Martiniano Leguizamón's *Calandria,* many of which downplayed the gaucho's oppositional politics in favor of a more folkloric representation of rural culture.

Yet these domesticated icons of creole masculinity had to compete with other incarnations of Moreira that continued to proliferate onstage, at the circus, and in the street. As early as 1893, for example, newspapers reported performances of the play by all-female casts, and in 1934 *Doña Juana Moreira* made her debut.[8] Moreira became a popular character in the annual Carnival parades, where he was accompanied by Cocoliche, the most memorable of the many comic characters that came to life during improvisatory moments in the *Moreira* circus spectacles. The parodic figure of an Italian immigrant dressed in an exaggerated gaucho getup who proclaims his creole pride in a pidgin language that is more Italian than Spanish, Cocoliche was such a hit that he soon became a stock character in popular dramas. Like Moreira himself, he was an ambiguous sort whose political and cultural affiliations were forged in the act of performance. Although he arose as a way of ridiculing the Italian immigrants who were arriving in huge numbers at the time, his hybrid, feminized persona was soon adopted by Italian carnivalgoers themselves. Micol Seigel describes Cocoliche as a burlesque clown who mocks the categories upheld by advocates of exclusionary nationalism because he is "both immigrant and native, both male and female, both senile and infantile, both same and Other, both marginal and entirely central." She concludes that "if the gaucho was indeed an 'ideological weapon' for Argentina's modernizing elite, the weapon slipped from elite hands when immigrants transformed the gaucho into the cocoliche."[9]

While the text may seem strangely reticent in light of its protagonist's checkered past, it is still possible to glean a sense of *Moreira's* multiple sites of performance. A true *drama criollo,* it pays no regard to the Aristotelian principles of unity of time and space; on the contrary, it is a national drama that is literally all over the map. Like the authority of the modern state, the action ranges across the wide-open plains and traverses distinct social spheres, including the mayor's office, a *pulpería* (local tavern), a gaucho campsite, a courthouse, and the domestic space of Moreira's home, which is invaded by representatives of the Law. The State chases the protagonist across the countryside and into a small, enclosed patio from which there is no escape.

This final, wordless scene lays bare what is at the heart of the play: violence. Despite the singing and dancing that provide moments of relief, it is the conflict between different ethics of violence that propels the dramatic action of the play and identifies the social groups to which individual characters belong. Nowhere is this so clear as when Moreira finally comes face-to-face with his rival Don Francisco. Whereas Moreira arrives with dagger in hand, ready for an up close and personal struggle, the mayor reaches for his revolver, the modern weapon of choice. "That's the way you people kill," Moreira says to him with scorn, "from a distance and with no risk." The gaucho's bravery wins him the admiration of all, including that of the soldier Navarro who is sent to arrest him, but in the end he pays a high price. Neither the hero nor his nameless killer is given the chance to speak, to tell the audience what his death means. Does it uphold the legitimacy of the state by showing the ultimate futility of resistance? Or does it galvanize and grant moral justification to the marginalized?

Moreira's compatriots have debated this subject for the past 125 years, and a final answer is nowhere in sight. Indeed, what is most remarkable about Moreira is that he dies a different death every time he goes onstage. The critic Josefina Ludmer, rather than trying to ascribe to him a single meaning, traces a genealogy of Moreiras from the novel through his latest role as a cybernetic business traveler at odds with indigenous groups. She suggests that "if we read Moreira at a certain juncture, we can clearly see the violences of that moment . . . [for] each time the Moreiras appear, they allow us to see the violence of the state, political violence, and popular violence." Precisely because Moreira marks the place where these opposing paradigms of violence come head to head, she says, he "tells 'Argentine stories,' and his violent body announces a politics of visibility, technology, language, and death."[10]

This capacity to unveil violence explains why Moreira was reclaimed by opponents of the state in the aftermath of the "Dirty War" that lasted from 1976 to 1983. The authoritarian government had disappeared tens of thousands of people, and Moreira made the victims of its brutality visible. In December 1983, the director Enrique Dacal formed the Teatro de la Libertad, a small collective that was part of a movement of *teatro callejero* (street theater) that arose during the transition to democracy. The group's first show was an adaptation of *Juan Moreira* written by Dacal. Although this new version retained the original's colloquial language and even incorporated many comic elements of the circus, it interspersed the gaucho's tragic story with scenes depicting torture and other indications of contemporary events. Dacal explains,

> I tried to make the text reflect not the history of a social bandit (as the official versions insist on classifying this type of character), but of a bandit society that generates these emergent beings in order to then cripple them and continue to justify its own appalling existence.[11]

Following his first performance on the streets of the San Telmo neighborhood in Buenos Aires, the Teatro de la Libertad's Moreira retraced his predecessor's journey, giving hundreds of performances in parks, in jails, for human rights organizations, and in public plazas all across the country.

As you read the skeletal, schematic text, you may want to keep these multiple Moreiras before the mind's eye. For those who claim him as their hero, both Moreira's power and his vulnerability lie in this very multiplicity, this ability to embody the unifying drama of the nation and, at the same time, to reveal its most violent fissures. Because he fights on the messy frontlines of national-popular culture, the significance of his sad, lonely death is always uncertain until the moment of truth arrives. The basic scenario may remain the same, but the significance of his words can be altered by a gesture, a look, the intervention of a single spectator, or unforeseen events far beyond the scope of the performance. And no matter which way he swings, the whole thing takes place onstage, for all the world to see.

—Sarah J. Townsend

NOTES

1. The long civil wars pitted Federalists (who argued for a loose federation) against Unitarians (who argued that the provinces should be united under a strong central government located in Buenos Aires).

2. The Nationalist Bartolomé Mitre, president of Argentina from 1862 to 1868, supported centralization and the subordination of the provincial governments under the mandate of the national government. His opponent, Adolfo Alsina, was governor of the province of Buenos Aires from 1862 to 1868 and vice president of Argentina from 1868 to 1874. As leader of the Autonomists, he defended the autonomy of the province of Buenos Aires against the authority of the national government.

3. The critic was Carlos Olivera in a column he wrote for the newspaper *El Diario* later published in his *En la brecha* (Buenos Aires, 1887). Quoted in Beatriz Seibel, *Historia del circo* (Buenos Aires: Ediciones del Sol, 1993), 58.

4. Horacio Legrás, "Palimpsesto, cultura popular, y modernidad política en el Juan Moreira teatral," *Latin American Theatre Review* 36 (spring 2003): 27.

5. Angel Rama, *Los gauchipolíticos rioplatenses: Literatura y sociedad* (Buenos Aires: Calicanto Editorial SRL, 1976), 34.

6. Ibid., 135.

7. Seibel, *Historia del circo,* 64.

8. Mentioned in ibid., 74.

9. Micol Seigel, "Cocoliche's Romp: Fun with Nationalism in Argentina's Carnival," *TDR: The Drama Review* 44 (summer 2000): 64. Seigel also notes, however, that Cocoliches were often accompanied in Carnival processions by immigrants lampooning indigenous and Afro-Argentines, and she suggests that Cocoliche was complicit in the formation of a "hybrid whiteness" that became the racial basis for Argentine nationalism.

10. Josefina Ludmer, "The Moreiras," in *The Corpus Delicti: A Manual of Argentine Fictions,* trans. Glen S. Close (Pittsburgh: University of Pittsburgh Press, 2004), 84. Ludmer mentions that in 1994 Gerardo Pensavalle staged a production in which Moreira's wife Vicenta is killed and his son Juancito is disappeared.

11. Enrique Dacal, "Una concepción estética y un espacio escénico que nos representen," *Conjunto* 66 (October–December 1985): 95. Dacal states that the group's aesthetic was shaped by *radioteatro* (radio theater), a popular genre from the 1940s and 1950s that was itself heavily influenced by the circo criollo. Many of the radio actors were originally circus performers and also gave weekend performances for live audiences. *Juan Moreira* was a favorite radio play. In 2003, the Teatro del Pueblo, one of the oldest independent theater groups in Latin America, began a series titled "Teatro como en la radio," which incorporated aspects of radio theater into staged plays. The first play of the cycle was *Juan Moreira.*

SELECTED REFERENCES

Dacal, Enrique. *Teatro de la Libertad: teatro 'callejero' en la Argentina desde el movimiento grupal de los '80.* Buenos Aires: Ediciones Madres de Plaza de Mayo, 2006.

Foster, David William. "The Theatrical Vision of Juan Moreira: Dramatic Structure and Audience Competence." *Romance Notes* 20 (1979): 182–89.

Gutiérrez, Eduardo. *Juan Moreira*. Buenos Aires: Editorial Universitaria de Buenos Aires, 1961.

Legrás, Horacio. "Palimpsesto, cultura popular y modernidad política en el Juan Moreira teatral." *Latin American Theatre Review* 36 (spring 2003): 21–39.

Ludmer, Josefina. "The Moreiras." Chapter 3 in *The Corpus Delicti: A Manual of Argentine Fictions*. Trans. Glen S. Close. Pittsburgh: University of Pittsburgh Press, 2004.

Podestá, José. *Medio siglo de farándula: Memorias*. Buenos Aires: Galerna, Instituto Nacional del Teatro, 2003.

Rama, Angel. "La creación de un teatro nacional." Chapter 6 in *Los gauchipolíticos rioplatenses: Literatura y sociedad*. Buenos Aires: Calicanto Editorial SRL, 1976.

Revista del Instituto Nacional de Estudios de Teatro 5, no. 13 (1986). Special issue in commemoration of the hundredth anniversary of the spoken version of *Juan Moreira*.

Seibel, Beatriz. *Historia del circo*. Buenos Aires: Ediciones del Sol, 1993.

Siegel, Micol. "Cocoliche's Romp: Fun with Nationalism in Argentina's Carnival." *TDR: The Drama Review* 44 (summer 2000): 56–83.

Juan Moreira: A Drama in Two Acts

(Eduardo Gutiérrez and José J. Podestá)

Translated by Margaret Carson

CHARACTERS:

JUAN MOREIRA
DON FRANCISCO, the MAYOR
SARDETTI
GRANDPA
JULIÁN
MARAÑÓN
GIMÉNEZ
NAVARRO
BARKEEPER
JUANCITO, Moreira's son
VICENTA, Moreira's wife
SOLDIERS
GAUCHOS
MEN FROM THE PAMPAS
NEIGHBOR
BANDITS
AGAPITO
WOMEN

ACT ONE

SCENE I

A courtroom on the pampas.

DON FRANCISCO, the MAYOR: Sardetti, you've been called here because Moreira claims you owe him ten thousand pesos.

SARDETTI: It's not true—I don't owe him a single peso.

DON FRANCISCO: Moreira, why are you telling lies? Why did you come here to demand money that's not yours?

MOREIRA: I'm here to collect the money I lent him, and it's because I need it. This man's stealing from me if he says he doesn't owe me anything. That's why I'm here, Your Honor, to seek justice.

DON FRANCISCO: The only justice I'll give you is putting you in the stocks, you thief, for coming here with lies.

MOREIRA: You say you don't owe me anything?

SARDETTI: Not one peso.

MOREIRA: And you won't make him pay?

DON FRANCISCO: Of course not, since he doesn't owe you anything. You're playing dirty.

MOREIRA: Okay, my friend. You say you don't owe me the money I gave you plenty of time to pay back. Now my knife will draw blood for every thousand pesos you took. And you, Don Francisco, you're treating me this way out of spite—watch out. This may end up being my downfall, but I've had enough of your justice.

DON FRANCISCO: (*Addressing the SOLDIERS*) Put him in the stocks for defiance of authority. (*MOREIRA is put in the stocks and punished. Afterwards, the MAYOR orders his release, telling him:*)

DON FRANCISCO: One more time and I'll ship you to the frontier in leg irons.

MOREIRA: 'Til we meet again, Don Francisco.

(*MOREIRA mounts his horse and rides away. Once he is gone, the MAYOR nods to SARDETTI, who leaves.*)

SCENE II

The pampas. A tavern where several gauchos play cards and sing milongas.[1]

FIRST GAUCHO: Don Mariano, quit strummin' your guitar and sing us a milonga.

Eduardo Gutiérrez, Argentina and José Podestá, Uruguay, 1886. Translated from Spanish by Margaret Carson.

FIRST MAN: Now listen, friends:
  like straw blown by the wind
  let's sing for the moment.
  Stop playing cards
  and sing a milonga
  as good friends do.
  He who drops out first
  will pay for drinks.
  So if you want to begin
  don't be shy—
  there's a crowd of people here
  and now's the time;
  don't miss the chance
  to raise the ante
  and have some fun.

SECOND MAN: I'll see your bet and raise you.
  If I'm not scared of the devil,
  why should I be scared of you?
  Let me tell you, I'm a born singer.
  You're challenging
  a master improviser.

FIRST MAN: That's what I want,
  a rival to spur me on,
  someone who's good
  at contrapunto and milonga,
  a philosopher who sings
  night and day,
  booming like thunder.

SECOND MAN: Like thunder? Who, me?
  If fun is what you want
  let me warn you:
  don't laugh at me
  'cause I'm the best
  and you sound
  like a fool.

FIRST MAN: You say I'm a fool?
  You don't mean it.
  I'll forgive you now,
  but if it happens again,
  watch out.
  What happened to Don Mateo
  will happen to you:
  for givin' advice
  his ugly face was smashed in.

SECOND MAN: You say I'm ugly?
  Well, you're uglier still.
  But if you want to see
  the ugliest of all,
  everyone, look at Sardetti.

FIRST MAN: Things are going bad for Sardetti.
  If Juan Moreira catches him
  he'll get skinned.
  'Scuse me, Señor Sardetti,
  for what I just said;
  but from what I understand,
  you treated him wrong.

SECOND GAUCHO: Speaking of Moreira, did you see, everyone, what the Mayor did to him?

THIRD GAUCHO: Yes, but Moreira's a good man. Before long he'll come here seeking revenge for all their dirty lies. Sardetti, pour me another drink before he gives you a good whipping.

(*MOREIRA enters.*)

FIRST GAUCHO: (*Shakes MOREIRA's hand*) May God protect you, Moreira, my friend.

ANOTHER GAUCHO: What winds bring you here?

MOREIRA: Disgrace, maybe.

ANOTHER GAUCHO: Moreira, how goes it? We were talking about what happened with that sonofabitch Mayor. Is it true what they say, that your head was put in the stocks, that they beat you to a pulp?

MOREIRA: They think I'm a cow they can milk without tying up, but wait 'til I gore them! They thought I was gentle—but now they're gonna pay for it. Hey, barkeeper, more drinks! Friends, I'll get this round. My patience isn't made of gold and now there's no stopping me. Last night I was the Mayor's target and he put me in the stocks. But today the cow's turned into a bull. *Paisanos,* you know I lent this man ten thousand pesos. I had to go to court for my money because he wouldn't pay me back. Do you know what he said? He said I was lying, that he didn't owe me a peso.

SARDETTI: It's true, Moreira. I said that 'cause I don't have any money. If I confessed they would've sold my business. I know what I owe and I'll pay you one day.

MOREIRA: They put my head in the stocks, like a common thief. They beat me when they knew I couldn't defend myself. Finally they threatened me with a hot branding iron, telling me they'd send me to the frontier.

FIRST GAUCHO: Yeah, you're right to be angry, but a dog like Sardetti isn't worth what you'll lose by seeking revenge. What's more, you have a son, and he'll suffer the consequences. If not because of what I say, then do it for the sake of your little one. Let's have one more drink and leave.

MOREIRA: I'm not leaving 'til I carry out my word and finish what I came here to do. And I won't drink because then tomorrow they'll say I didn't have the guts to do it sober.

FIRST GAUCHO: Moreira, don't do it. Remember, you have a family.

MOREIRA: Leave me alone, my brother. I have to get even. Sardetti, let's agree, you're late. I'm here to make you give me ten thousand pesos, or I'll carry out my word.

SARDETTI: I don't have the money, Moreira. Wait a few days and I swear to God I'll pay you to the last peso.

MOREIRA: I can't wait any longer. Let me see my ten thousand pesos, or else I'll carve ten thousand mouths into your body so you can say that Juan Moreira keeps his word, the devil take him. (*He pulls out a knife.*) Pay now, or I'll open you like an armadillo.

SARDETTI: I don't have the money . . .

FIRST GAUCHO: Moreira, don't throw yourself away. This man isn't worth it. You'll have to flee the province.

MOREIRA: (*Shoves the GAUCHO aside and heads towards SARDETTI to kill him. Then he stops.*) What is it, why don't you defend yourself? Do you want me to skin you like an armadillo?

SARDETTI: I don't have a weapon. But even if I did, this is murder.

FIRST GAUCHO: Stop. (*SARDETTI picks up the knife that MOREIRA throws to him.*)

MOREIRA: That's what I was waiting for, you liar. (*They fight until SARDETTI wounds him in the chest.*) I have no pity for you. (*He knocks SARDETTI down and kills him.*) Now may my destiny unfold.

THIRD GAUCHO: Did you see what happened to Sardetti for lying?

SCENE III

MOREIRA's house.

VICENTA: Grandpa, I'm worried about Juan. Ever since they put him in the stocks and beat him, he's been acting strange. I'm scared because he's not home yet.

GRANDPA: Don't worry, my child. He'll be back before long. You see, a man of his character shouldn't have things like that done to him. When the cards get shuffled too much, they begin to wear thin. One of these days, my Juan will do something so brave it'll astound us.

VICENTA: Go search for him, Grandpa. I have a feeling Juan went to kill Don Francisco. He's gone after him.

GRANDPA: Whatever Juan sets out to do, he'll get done, even if the devil gets called in. When he goes off like that, he's already made up his mind, and if I plead with him he might get angrier. Leave him be. He'll return soon.

VICENTA: And if they kill him?

GRANDPA: There's no one who can take Juan down. They'd need a battalion at least.

VICENTA: God willing, he'll be back soon. (*A horse neighs.*)

GRANDPA: Here he comes. (*VICENTA goes outside to meet him and they enter together.*)

VICENTA: Where've you been, Juan? What took you so long?

MOREIRA: I was with my friends. Why are you asking me? Were you scared because I wasn't here?

VICENTA: Yes, Juan.

MOREIRA: Go, Vicenta, and brew us some *mates*.[2] (*She*

leaves. *MOREIRA takes the old man's hands.*) I'm done for, old man. I've killed someone.

GRANDPA: Did you kill him for a good reason?

MOREIRA: Look. (*He shows his chest wound.*)

GRANDPA: And? What do you think you'll do now?

MOREIRA: I'm leaving the province for a few days, 'til all the excitement dies down. Don Francisco wasn't at home, so Sardetti was the only one I killed. But his time will come. Right now, take care of Vicenta and Juancito for me, old man—they're your loved ones, too. God knows when I'll be back and it's not right that they should suffer on account of me. I'll leave now, and then at dawn, before I hit the trail, I'll see my friend Giménez and tell him what happened. If I'm not back soon, don't worry about me.

VICENTA: (*Enters*) What? You're leaving now?

MOREIRA: Yes, Vicenta, I've got to go, but I'll be back. Don't worry, I'm going to my friend's. Good-bye.

VICENTA: Good-bye.

(*MOREIRA says good-bye to the old man, kisses his son in the cradle and leaves. DON FRANCISCO the Mayor arrives with two soldiers; they knock on the door. VICENTA opens it.*)

How can I help you, sir?

DON FRANCISCO: We've come looking for Moreira.

VICENTA: Moreira isn't here, sir.

DON FRANCISCO: Tell me where he is or else you're going to jail.

VICENTA: But what if we don't know!?

DON FRANCISCO: Very well! (*Turns to the old man*) Old man, don't you know where Moreira is?

GRANDPA: I don't know, sir.

DON FRANCISCO: I see, you don't want to talk. All right. (*To the SOLDIERS*) Take this man and search him for weapons. And you, señora, you're coming with me.

VICENTA: No! Not Grandpa! Help!

SCENE IV

The pampas. MOREIRA enters on horseback and dismounts.

MOREIRA: Here's where I'll wait for my friend Julián. He's searching for news of my family and to see what happened after Sardetti's death. Ah! Sardetti's death is the beginning and Don Francisco's will be the end. Soon his turn will come. And my son? What will become of my son and Vicenta? Grandpa is sick, and if they put him in the stocks to make him confess where I am, it's liable to kill him. Ah! Don Francisco, you don't have enough lives in you to pay me back for how much you've wronged me! (*A horse neighs.*) Julián has finally arrived. Out of the saddle, man, and start talking.

JULIÁN: Be brave, Moreira. You won't like everything

you hear. Before things go well, the devil's got to get his own first.

MOREIRA: Tell me everything, Julián, my friend. Let it out. I'm man enough to hear the news. Don't take pity on me and hold it back, no matter how bad it is.

JULIÁN: I'll take it slow, my friend, and start at the beginning so it makes sense. As I traveled around the province, the only thing people talked about was what you did to Sardetti and about the search party that left with orders to kill you on sight, and then say you'd resisted arrest.

MOREIRA: Kill me? If they can, and it'll take them plenty of work. Keep talking.

JULIÁN: Your friend Giménez did everything he could to free Vicenta from jail, but they didn't want to let her go. They say that as long as she's a prisoner, you'll come back to the province. That's why Don Francisco has moved into your house with two soldiers from the regiment, and there they are, having a good time.

MOREIRA: They won't have to wait long for me.

JULIÁN: What are you going to do?

MOREIRA: I'm going to get even with Don Francisco. He's already at my house, so I don't want to keep him waiting.

JULIÁN: I won't let you go there alone.

MOREIRA: No, my friend, this is my job! Understand?

JULIÁN: But Moreira, if you can't count on a friend at times like these, then he's not worth the butt end of a rifle. But there's one more thing I need to tell you. Brave men like you, Moreira, are used to pain. Now listen to some bad news. Damn! A drop more or a drop less, it's all the same poison, and just as bitter! One of my first stops was at the jail, to visit Vicenta, but it wasn't easy to talk to her. They thought I was your messenger, but I allayed their suspicions. I gave her the latest news and told her not to cry, telling her you have many friends and everything would work out. But Vicenta kept crying and said these words, which pierced me like a dagger: "Tell my Juan not to worry about me and not to go home, because they'll kill him like they killed my father, who they said fell off a horse. Tell Juan to run far away. As long as he's my husband, he'll be hunted and chased to the frontier. That's what Don Francisco said last night, when he told me the only way he'd leave Juan in peace would be if I went with him to a post in Navarro."

MOREIRA: Not even the devil could save him from the point of my dagger now.

JULIÁN: Be careful, Moreira, the cards are stacked against you.

MOREIRA: It doesn't matter, my friend. We'll see if God is on my side. Good-bye, Julián, 'til I return. You're sure to hear about me.

JULIÁN: Good-bye, my friend! (*Aside*) I can't let him go alone. He's seething with anger and liable to kill for no reason. What are friends for, dammit? In the end, he doesn't have a good head for this kind of business. Moreira's horse is fast, and mine is a little lame. Still, he won't get that far before I catch up with him. I want to give him a hand in case he needs it.

SCENE V

Inside Moreira's house. DON FRANCISCO, two NEIGHBORS and two SOLDIERS.

DON FRANCISCO: As soon as Moreira falls into my hands, the game's up.

NEIGHBOR: But sir! Moreira's a fine man and you would've done the same thing. When a man like him gets in trouble, he needs help. It's hard being on the run.

DON FRANCISCO: I have to hunt him 'til I find him, and when I find him, I'm going to kill him like a dog. But before I kill him, I'm going to make him suffer by carrying off his wife, because he stole her from me years ago when I wanted to marry her. I'll make her my woman. (*MOREIRA kicks the door open. When he enters, everyone freezes.*)

MOREIRA: The only one who's going to kill, and kill like a man, is me, Don Francisco. I'm here to fight and have the pleasure of twisting you on the point of my dagger, like a dog. (*DON FRANCISCO takes out his revolver and fires a shot.*) That's the way you people kill, from a distance and with no risk.

(*DON FRANCISCO fires another shot and tells the SOLDIERS:*)

DON FRANCISCO: What are you doing! Why don't you kill this man?

(*With their sabers in hand, the two SOLDIERS fight MOREIRA, first one and then the other. MOREIRA kills both of them. On seeing this, DON FRANCISCO takes out his sword. MOREIRA says to him:*)

MOREIRA: Let's see what your guts look like, and how you handle that rusty piece of tin.

(*They fight until MOREIRA disarms him. DON FRANCISCO, in retreat, says:*)

DON FRANCISCO: Help! In the name of justice!

MOREIRA: Don't cry so loud, Don Francisco. I didn't disarm you to kill you, but to say a few words before you die. You chased me for no reason, reducing me to my present state. You hit me while I was in the stocks because you couldn't fight me one-on-one. Not satisfied with that, you said you killed me so that you could take my wife as yours, when you're not worthy to be her servant. I'm going to kill you, not because I'm scared of you, but so that Vicenta doesn't have to hear more of your shameless propositions while I'm away.

(*MOREIRA throws him a sword and says:*)

Defend yourself—this time it's for real. (*They fight and MOREIRA wounds him.*)

DON FRANCISCO: Help! Murder! I've been killed!

MOREIRA: You lie, you villain, I killed you for a good reason, and here are my witnesses.

(*MOREIRA leaves, and on the way out meets JULIÁN, who shakes his hand and says in amazement:*)

JULIÁN: You've got more courage than a bull, Moreira. Too bad for the law, because you'll take down all the soldiers in the province.

(*They exit. The curtain falls.*)

ACT TWO

SCENE I

A field covered with water hemlock plants. A moonlit night. Five men in ponchos enter and hide amid the plants. MARAÑÓN, a young, well-dressed man, enters and crosses the field, but the five men immediately accost him, daggers in hand. The young man pulls out his revolver and tries to stop them.

BANDIT: We're here to kill you. No use resisting—your hour has come.

(*MARAÑÓN turns to look at the path behind him, and sees a man coming towards him whom he recognizes as JUAN MOREIRA, carrying a dagger in his hand. The young man hesitates. MOREIRA leaps forward, grabs him by the waist and throws him to the ground. He fights the BANDITS and kills one of them.*)

MOREIRA: Surrender to Juan Moreira, you cowards!

(*The BANDITS flee and MOREIRA laughs loudly. He walks towards MARAÑÓN, who in the meantime has stood up.*)

MARAÑÓN: How did you get here at just the right moment? (*He extends his hand to MOREIRA.*)

MOREIRA: I knew those cowards were going to kill you (*still laughing*) and I hid myself, to give you a hand, so it wouldn't be so uneven. (*MOREIRA approaches the man lying on the ground and realizes he's dead. He tells MARAÑÓN:*) Let's go. I'll escort you home, even though I doubt these cowards are man enough to come back. They're afraid I'm following them and are still running.

SCENE II

MARAÑÓN's house. Nighttime.

MARAÑÓN: What is it that guides you, Moreira? What made you act so nobly?

MOREIRA: I went there to save you, first because I like you, and second, because I can't let five men gang up on one. You're an important man in these parts, and your enemies wanted to get rid of you because you cast too big a shadow. They paid those bandits fifteen thousand pesos to kill you, but their plans were foiled. Someone else is dead in your place.

MARAÑÓN: And how did you know they were going to kill me?

MOREIRA: Because they first proposed the job to someone who was man enough to tell me and send those cowards to hell.

MARAÑÓN: I'm grateful for what you've done, Moreira. If I can help you in any way someday, just ask. From this day on I'm your friend.

MOREIRA: Don't thank me for anything, sir. Anyone would have done what I did. I care for you because I've got to care for someone, and to me you're like family, like a son or a brother. I'm a cursed man who was born to suffer and be always on the run from mankind, which has brought me to my ruin. By helping you I can breathe more easily. It's a sweet feeling. But if you order me to surrender, I'll give myself up in an instant.

MARAÑÓN: Why do you wander from place to place and do things in defiance of the law? Why don't you go back to your old life and give up this lawless existence?

MOREIRA: (*Very sad*) The sorrow in my heart could make me cry for a year. I was happy at the side of my wife and son, and never wronged any man. But I was born under an unlucky star, and fortune has turned its back on me. Now, all of a sudden, I'm being hunted down, and I have to fight to save my skin. You must have heard about everything that's happened to me, sir.

MARAÑÓN: (*Clapping MOREIRA on the shoulder*) Yes, but why don't you leave the province of Buenos Aires? I'll help you find work in Santa Fe or Córdoba, where you can still live in peace and happiness. I've got plenty of friends there and I'll give you letters of introduction. After a few years you can return. Your crimes will have been forgotten, and you can go back to your old life again.

MOREIRA: I can't leave the province because I don't want to be separated from my wife and son—without me, the law will strike them down and make them pay for my mistakes.

MARAÑÓN: I'll give them whatever they need to join you. You can stay there forever, watching your son grow at your side, being loved by your wife.

MOREIRA: You're talking to my soul. I was right to give you my affection, but though I'm flattered by your offer, I can't accept it 'til I find out what's happened to those two treasures of mine. I may need to take revenge. Us poor stink like the dead, and we get kicked around 'til the smell goes away. God knows what's happened to those wretched beings, whose only fault is to be my wife and son. God willing, nothing's happened, and they haven't had to suffer for a minute. I'm not a bad man, sir, but I know that if anyone touches a hair on their heads, or a thread of their clothes, I'm capable of a sacrilege not even the Indians could— . . . Well, I've taken enough of your time. Until we meet again.

MARAÑÓN: Good-bye, Moreira. Think about what I told you. Whether or not you accept, remember that you can count on me, whatever your plight.

MOREIRA: Yes, sir. Good-bye.

MARAÑÓN: Thank you, Moreira. (*He extends his hand.*) Today I've been born again; I owe my life to this man. He was put here to do good, but fate took him down the wrong path and pushed him over the brink.

SCENE III

Change of scene. VICENTA, GIMÉNEZ, and MOREIRA's son. A shabby room. To the right is a bed, to the left a table with a bottle holding the stub of a candle. As the curtain rises, barking dogs are heard. GIMÉNEZ gets out of bed and dresses in a hurry. VICENTA wakes up, surprised, but GIMÉNEZ puts his hand over her mouth, warning her to be quiet. He goes over to the window, ready to escape as soon as the door opens. When he hears it open, he jumps out the window and unties his horse. MOREIRA's voice is heard, saying:

MOREIRA: Hang it! He's escaping—there goes my revenge! (*On hearing MOREIRA's voice, VICENTA lets out a piercing scream and says:*)

VICENTA: Blessed spirits, it's the soul of my Juan who can find no rest! (*She embraces her son and kneels to pray. MOREIRA enters, dagger in hand, and throws it to the floor.*)

MOREIRA: I finally killed those mangy dogs! But while I was fending them off, I couldn't avenge myself against Giménez. I put all my trust in him, and the ingrate paid me back by living with my wife.

(*He begins to cry. On hearing his sobs, VICENTA gets out of bed and lights a match. She sees MOREIRA and is horror-struck. MOREIRA strikes a match and then lights the candle on the table. He looks at the bed and runs over to take his son in his arms. He covers him with kisses. He carries him over to the candle and gazes at him, then kisses him again. JUANCITO takes his father's hand and says:*)

JUANCITO: Papa, why haven't you taken me out on my pony?

MOREIRA: I couldn't come, Juancito, I've had a lot to do. (*He carries the child to bed, kisses him, and looks sadly at VICENTA.*) Vicenta, come here, come closer, I'm not here to hurt you. I forgive you for everything you've done.

VICENTA: How is it possible? Is it you? You mean you didn't die? Why did they lie to me? (*She covers her face with her hands. MOREIRA looks for the dagger on the floor. When she sees him do this, VICENTA says:*) Kill me, Juan!

MOREIRA: God won't allow it. (*He puts the dagger away.*) You're not to blame. Our son needs you; I can't take him with me. Who will take care of him if I bloody my hands killing you? Good-bye, Vicenta. We'll never see each other again. Now I'm sure to be killed. This earth holds nothing for me but sorrow and bitterness . . .

(*He moves to the bed and kisses the child. He puts his hands over his face and begins to take his leave.*)

VICENTA: Don't go, dear Juan—kill me before you go. (*She clings to his chiripá.*)[3] I've wronged you, so kill me like a dog—but first, forgive me, it wasn't my fault. They lied to me, they told me you were dead. Whatever I did, it was to keep our son from dying of hunger. Forgive me, then I'll die in peace.

MOREIRA: I could never kill you! Then who would take care of him? (*He points to JUANCITO, who stretches his arms out.*) Enough! I must go now. Good-bye.

VICENTA: I don't want you to leave.

(*She tightens her grip on MOREIRA's chiripá.*) Juancito, call him, don't let him go. (*MOREIRA frees himself from his wife, blows a kiss to his son and runs out. JUANCITO gets out of bed.*)

JUANCITO: Papa. . .papa. . . papa. (*He hugs his mother.*)

SCENE IV

A courthouse. MOREIRA rides up and pounds on the door with the handle of his whip.

SOLDIER: Who the hell is pounding on the door? What do they think this is, a Basque tavern?

MOREIRA: It's Juan Moreira, who wants to die an honorable death. Soldiers, come out, this is your chance.

SOLDIER: If you're Juan Moreira, then I'm the President of the Republic. Get out of here, you idiot, before I break your face.

MOREIRA: I want you to come out, or else I'll set fire to the courthouse.

SOLDIER: Come back tomorrow, my friend. The judge left us orders not to open the door for anyone.

MOREIRA: Go to hell, you scrawny bastard. The first chance I get, I'll tan your hide. (*Aside*) That's the way it is with these cowards: when there's only a few of them, they crawl into a hole, and when there's a lot of them, they begin shooting like frightened sheep.

(*After a moment, a SOLDIER steps out with a rifle but immediately retreats, terrified.*)

SCENE V

An open-air camp on the pampas. GAUCHOS arrive on horseback, in wagons and on foot, with guitars and accordions. They play jacks, prepare mate for brewing, make fried cakes, dance typical dances. MOREIRA enters. The GAUCHOS surround him and ask about his life.

MOREIRA: I spend my life wandering from place to place because there's nowhere I can rest. I spend life fighting soldiers and killing as many as I can, because the law's responsible for all that's gone bad in my life—that's why I'm being hunted like a wild animal wherever I go. What can we do with all our sorrows? Let's drown them out. Whoever wants to join me, I'll pay this round. Barkeeper, start pouring. Drinks are on me.

ALL: Long live Moreira! (*A GAUCHO enters and is startled to see MOREIRA.*)

GAUCHO: Moreira, how is it that you're traveling in these parts?

MOREIRA: Why do you ask?

GAUCHO: The cavalry rode off this morning looking for you, with an order to search the entire province. They've got orders to kill you on sight, then say later that you were armed and resisted arrest.

MOREIRA: And they'll run away the same way they came! I can beat them with my left hand, with the handle of my whip!

GAUCHO: Look, my friend, according to what I heard, this time the search party is led by Don Goyo Navarro, their top sergeant. They say he's a mean bastard who's ready to take you hog-tied to be shot by a firing squad.

MOREIRA: Don't listen to that. There's no one who can take me prisoner, because luck is on my side. Let's drink to Goyo—he's in for a big surprise.

GAUCHO: Give me a drink.

MOREIRA: If you want, tell him I'm here waiting for him. You'll see what I do to those cowards. They don't even deserve to be slapped!

ALL: Good luck, Moreira!

A MAN: Let's dance a *gato.*[4]

ALL: Let's dance! (*They dance a gato; as they dance a black man, AGAPITO, says:*)

AGAPITO: Moreira, my friend, let me dance with that lovely girl.

MOREIRA: It's just like you to ask—okay, come here. (*Addresses the woman*) My darling, a man who dances better than me wants to accompany you; he's a little burned by the sun, but that doesn't mean he'll be a bad partner.

(*They dance. When the dance ends, everyone asks MOREIRA to sing. He takes a guitar and sings a décima.*[5] *When he's done, the GAUCHO who spoke earlier enters.*)

GAUCHO: (*Very nervously*) Moreira, you'd better leave. There's a battalion coming with at least four hundred soldiers.

MOREIRA: Let them come, if that's what they want. I won't run away, even if they've come to slit my throat. Today I feel like fighting. I won't let that swaggering officer leave without seeing me. I'll bet he doesn't even know what I look like. (*He mounts his horse. SERGEANT NAVARRO and other officers enter on horseback.*)

NAVARRO: (*Addressing MOREIRA*) Are you Juan Moreira?

MOREIRA: Here I am, at your service. What is it?

NAVARRO: Pardon me, but I have a judicial order for your arrest. (*He takes the reins of MOREIRA's horse.*) Kindly follow me.

MOREIRA: Let's go slow, my friend. I'm not an old nag you can stop with one hand, or a light you can snuff out so easily.

NAVARRO: There's no use resisting; I have an order to arrest you and I must carry it out. Give yourself up.

MOREIRA: It's not that easy, dammit! Not even my father would talk to me like that. (*MOREIRA takes out a pair of guns.*)

NAVARRO: (*To the SOLDIERS*) Get him! (*He takes out his saber.*) Careful, don't kill him. I have to bring this coward back alive. (*MOREIRA opens fire and a SOLDIER falls.*)

NAVARRO: Don't let him escape!

(*He charges at MOREIRA, who wounds him in the right arm. NAVARRO switches the saber to his left hand.*)

MOREIRA: Ah! You bastard! That's how I like tyrants!

(*He takes the saber from NAVARRO's hand and the SERGEANT falls to the floor. MOREIRA asks the BARKEEPER for a stretcher and tells the others to carry it. When NAVARRO has been lifted onto the stretcher, MOREIRA examines him, ties a handkerchief around his forehead, and gives him some brandy to drink.*)

MOREIRA: How are you, how do you feel?

NAVARRO: Thank you, *paisano.* You're a real gentleman. I'm not surprised by the stories of all your great deeds.

MOREIRA: Sergeant, I'm leaving, but before I go, let's have a drink. We may never see each other again. I don't have the stomach for this kind of business—something's bound to happen.

NAVARRO: If I can't capture you, no one will, unless they catch you asleep or someone betrays you.

MOREIRA: May God hear you. I hope you recover soon. (*He mounts his horse after paying what he owes to the barkeeper.*) Friends, the party was spoiled by an interruption. Maybe some other time. Barkeeper, take good care of this man so he'll be able to tell this story. Good-bye.

ALL: Good-bye, Moreira.

BARKEEPER: (*To NAVARRO*) Count yourself lucky that bandit didn't slit your throat. He's got the courage of a bull and nothing will stop him from using his dagger.

NAVARRO: Anyone who says he's a bandit is a pig and I'll skin his hide.

BARKEEPER: Very well, my friend. (*They all exit.*)

SCENE VI

A dance hall. Several GAUCHOS are dancing. MOREIRA and JULIÁN enter and ask two WOMEN to dance. MOREIRA leaves to go to sleep, as does JULIÁN. The POLICE enter, looking for MOREIRA. Everyone exits.

NOTES

All notes to this play are by the translator.

1. *milonga:* An often improvised song accompanied by the guitar that can also be danced to.

2. *mate:* A tealike beverage made from the leaves of the South American mate tree.

3. *chiripá:* An item of clothing worn by gauchos, typ-

CHANGE OF SCENERY

A patio with a well on one side. To the rear is a tall fence. To the left are the rooms where MOREIRA and JULIÁN are sleeping. The POLICE enter and take formation. The death of MOREIRA.

ically consisting of a rectangular flannel cloth, usually beige, that was passed between the legs and tucked into the waist at four points or kept in place with a wide sash. A loose, baggy garment, it allowed the gaucho to move about and perform his work with great freedom.

4. *gato:* A typical Argentine folk dance.

5. *décima:* A poem with ten lines, each of which is eight syllables long.

Luisa Capetillo in Havana on July 24, 1915, shortly before being arrested for wearing men's clothing. (Photo originally published in the Havana newspaper *El Día*.)

After Death (Luisa Capetillo)

The Puerto Rican writer and labor agitator Luisa Capetillo (1879–1922) is more famous for her offstage activities than her dramatic works. Most likely, this would not have disappointed her. A radical feminist and anarchist, Capetillo believed in the power of words to change people's ideas, but she also believed that true change only happens when people put ideas into action. She was a proponent of free love who denounced marriage as legalized prostitution, and she had her three children out of wedlock. She wrote propaganda arguing that workers should have the right to determine the conditions of their labor, and then she followed it up by organizing farmhands in the fields and leading strikes. She thought dresses were unhygienic and impractical, so she became the first woman in Puerto Rico to wear pants in public.

Capetillo's life exemplifies the global circulation of people and ideas that fostered the emergence of working-class movements at the turn of the century. Born in the town of Arecibo, she was the daughter of a French (possibly French Caribbean) laundress and a Spanish immigrant who worked a variety of odd jobs. Both of her parents were well versed in the radical ideas of their day, and although Capetillo completed no more than two years of formal schooling, she received a broad education at home. One of her first jobs was as a *lectora* (reader) in a tobacco factory. At the time, workers throughout the Caribbean and United States commonly pooled their resources and hired someone to read aloud as they rolled cigars; consequently, even though many were unable to read or write, cigar workers often knew the ins and outs of novels by writers such as Zola, Dostoyevsky, and the Colombian anarchist José María Vargas Vilar and engaged the ideas of political philosophers in debates.[1] They were also among the most militant workers, and it was here that Capetillo got her start in the labor movement. Her debut as an organizer came in 1905 during a farmworkers' strike, and she soon became a prominent leader of the Federación Libre de Trabajadores (Free Federation of Workers), traveling all over the island giving speeches and selling the union newspaper along with a publication of her own called *La mujer*

(Woman). In the face of considerable resistance, she pushed the union to prioritize women's workplace issues and challenged male workers to embrace the fight for gender equality as central to their own struggle.

Capetillo's travels were not limited to the country of her birth. In 1912, she made the first of many trips to New York City, where she wrote articles for the local Spanish press and established a guesthouse. Later she lived and worked as a reader at a tobacco factory in the Cuban/Italian/African American community of Ybor City, Florida. And it was in Havana, in 1915, that she was arrested for dressing as a man—a provocative, highly theatrical act that landed her a picture in the newspaper and a public platform at the trial.[2]

What we might now identify as "performance" was an important part of the vibrant working-class culture that arose throughout Latin America during this time period. Effective public orators such as Capetillo were praised for their ability to mobilize people to action, strikers improvised songs and chants on the picket line, and mass demonstrations incorporated music, comedy, and occasional skits. Given the high level of illiteracy and the focus on collective action, it is no surprise that theater also played an important role. Workers commonly contributed a portion of their salaries to cultural societies that sponsored festivals and evenings of entertainment combining instrumental and choral music, politico-philosophical dialogues, speeches, poetry (usually recited by children), theatrical pieces (in which women were particularly active), and, frequently, a final dance. The early works of Florencio Sánchez, who later went on to become one of Latin America's foremost playwrights, were written to be performed in anarchist cultural centers in Uruguay. Workers in the salt mines of northern Chile formed a collective called Arte y Revolución that presented plays such as Luis Emilio Recabarren's *Desdicha obrera* (Workers' Misfortune) and the *First of May* by Pietro Gori, the notorious Italian anarchist who lived for several years in Argentina and the United States.[3] In São Paulo, Brazil, where nearly a third of the city's population was made up of Italian immigrants, a 1902 performance of Gori's drama was interrupted by police, who made several unwarranted arrests and harassed the audience of men, women, and children.[4]

The culture that took shape on these stages was in many ways more "international" than the elite theater of its day. In countries where immigrants made up a large percentage of laborers, an evening's program frequently brought together multiple languages and divergent intellectual and performative traditions. No single style prevailed, though there were heated debates about the proper nature of "proletarian art"—anarchists in Cuba and Argentina, for example, condemned traditions such as Carnival for perpetuating unequal power relations and providing another opportunity for the bourgeois to make money off the masses.[5] Yet in many cases what are now accepted as self-evident distinctions between "high" and "low" were routinely ignored and "education" and "entertainment" were not viewed as mutually exclusive. In Puerto Rico, the few surviving programs from these sorts of events list *zarzuelas* (operettas), *milongas* (Argentine music related to the tango), dialogues by the Mexican revolutionary Ricardo Flores Magón, arias from Verdi operas, rousing choral renditions of the "La Marseillaise," and the ever-popular allegorical drama *La emancipación del obrero* (The Emancipation of the Worker), written by the Puerto Rican typesetter Ramón Romero Rosa.

Although there is no direct evidence that Capetillo's works were performed—the physical archive of these theaters is slim—her widespread fame presumably would have made them obvious choices. In many of her plays, however, she also has another audience in mind: middle- and upper-class feminist readers. Capetillo never joined forces with suffragists like the writer and educator Ana Roqué, who founded the Puerto Rican Feminist League in 1917; most suffragists took issue with Capetillo's belief in free love and the general strike, and she saw little reason to support a movement that was fighting for voting rights on behalf of "educated," "literate" women. Yet through her own writings Capetillo engaged with their ideas, arguing that women's liberation and workers' freedom were inextricably linked.[6] In 1911, she published *My Opinion about Woman's Liberties, Rights, and Duties,* now commonly cited as the first feminist treatise by a Puerto Rican author. In this heterodox collection of texts, she defends women's right to experience sexual pleasure, explains her unusual interest in spiritism, and reiterates her call for solidarity across all cultures, races, and borders. Such resolute internationalism was a bone of contention in Puerto Rico, where nationalist ideology was gaining strength as a defense against the United States, which had taken over from Spain as the imperial power in 1898. Capetillo pulled no punches in responding to those who dismissed her ideas as utopian: "[T]hey call themselves patriots and fathers of the homeland. What idea of the homeland can they have? One that is egotistical, which begins and ends with them."[7]

Capetillo's fictional work appears in *The Influence of Modern Ideas* (1916), most of which was written during her time in New York and Florida. A multi-generic book of short fiction, letters, first-person narratives, informal "notes," and drama, it invokes various literary paradigms while remaining on the margins of the "literary." The author critiques Schopenhauer, quotes Diderot, and waxes poetic on the beauty of nature and the "agony of love"; yet she also discusses breast-feeding and the importance of physical exercise, a reflection of her belief that the body is an integral part of the person and worthy of respect. Her writing highlights the class-based assumptions underlying Romantic and modernist aesthetics, and it tests the universality of humanism's ideals of love and liberation by holding them to the letter of their own law and showing where they fall short in the context of women's daily lives. Capetillo does not dismiss literature, nor is her writing a straightforward parody; rather, in keeping with anarchist discourse, she insists that "true art," like free love, can lead to political change.

Nowhere is this more evident than in her theatrical pieces. The title play in *The Influence of Modern Ideas* is a three-act drama about an upper-class woman who, through her readings of Tolstoy and her romantic relationship with a young proletarian, comes to support the striking workers in her father's factory. Most of the other pieces are brief, no more than a few pages long. A group of sketches called *The Corruption of the Rich and the Poor,* for example, draws attention to the ways in which women, regardless of class, become objects of exchange. In *How Rich Women Are Prostituted,* an affluent woman escapes being married off to a Spanish nobleman by stealing her inheritance and running away with her lover; its companion piece, *How Poor Women Are Prostituted,* has no such happy ending since the protagonist's only alternative to literal prostitution is to go work in an unsanitary factory for a starving wage. Very few of the plays give any indication of their geographical location; although Capetillo's language is informal, she avoids colloquial terms or references that would place the characters or setting. Rather, her plays seem as though they were written to be transported, easily adapted, and understood by any Spanish-speaking audience.

After Death (*Después de muerta*), written in Florida in 1913, is unusual in that it specifies that the action takes place "in the tropics, in a Caribbean city." A young woman named Lelia stands at the graveside of her friend, reciting poetry filled with hackneyed images, such as pearls, diamonds, and roses, that link aesthetic beauty to cultivated gardens and material wealth. She is interrupted by the arrival of Mauly, an aristocratic man absurdly overdressed for the heat, who has come to pour out his undying love for this absent, idealized image of femininity. But an obstacle stands in the way of his self-serving act of contrition: the living woman, Lelia, who tells him bluntly, "[Y]ou should have said all of that to her when she was alive." Mauly defends himself by insisting that the woman "betrayed" him with another man—never mind his own extended absences and trips to the brothels—and it is not exactly a surprise when the supposed villain Fabio shows up to pay his respects. The two men argue over who bears the blame until Lelia steps in and recites a poem that she claims was written by the dead woman. The aesthetic object, the passive object of male desire, thus turns the tables on her eulogizers; yet the poem's lyric subject is not an "authentic," authorial voice but rather a nameless, theatricalized one that comes to life in the voice of another. The recitation is followed by a moment of violence, an anticlimactic spoof on the Romantic tradition of the duel, and then the men go their separate ways, leaving Lelia—as well as the play's readers and spectators—to contemplate their own fate.

The language of the translation might come across as excessively quaint; if anything, it is even more so in the original. But this "real-life comedy" cleverly plays on generic conventions to provoke intriguing questions that the ending leaves unresolved. For instance, what exactly was the nature of the relationship between the dead woman and Lelia? To whom is the poem—titled simply "To You"—addressed, and which man is "that one"—the one she has forgiven? Is it her brief but passionate fling, Fabio, as Mauly clearly assumes? Or is it Mauly himself, who betrayed the genuine love of a real-life woman because she failed to live up to his false ideal?

In *How Poor Women Are Prostituted,* when a client enjoins the protagonist to take a job as a wage slave rather than ruin her virtue, she asks him, "If they buried two girls of the same size and age, one an immaculate virgin, the other corrupted by poverty and vice, would the earth respect one more than the other? Would the virgin be saved from the worms?" Capetillo had seen women's bodies destroyed by hard labor and consumed by diseases contracted in overcrowded factories; she, too, would die of tuberculosis at the age of forty-two. *After Death* is a reminder that none of us will be saved from the worms and that it is here, in *this* life, that we must act.

—Sarah J. Townsend

NOTES

1. See Julio Ramos's introduction to Luisa Capetillo, *Amor y anarquía: Los escritos de Luisa Capetillo* (Río Piedras: Ediciones Huracán, 1992). As Ramos points out, many working-class intellectuals were cigar makers. Owners repeatedly tried to ban readers from factories; by the 1930s, radio had taken their place.

2. For more on Capetillo's life, see Norma Valle Ferrer's 1991 biography, recently published in translation as *Luisa Capetillo, Pioneer Puerto Rican Feminist,* trans. Gloria Waldman-Schwartz with students from Graduate Program in Translation, University of Puerto Rico (New York: Peter Lang, 2006).

3. The texts of these plays and others are reprinted in Pedro Bravo Elizondo, *Cultura y teatro obreros en Chile, 1900–1930* (Madrid: Ediciones Michay, 1986).

4. A report of the event, originally published in *O Amigo do Povo* (June 6, 1902), is quoted in Maria Thereza Vargas and Mariângela Alves de Lima, *Teatro operário na cidade de São Paulo* (São Paulo: Secretaria Municipal de Cultura, 1980), 17. Gori's drama was extremely popular throughout Latin America; almost all sources consulted mention performances of the play.

5. See Kirwin R. Shaffer, *Anarchism and Countercultural Politics in Early Twentieth-Century Cuba* (Gainesville: University Press of Florida, 2005), 204–6; see also Juan Suriano, "Tiempo libre, fiestas y teatro," in *Anarquistas: Cultura y política libertaria en Buenos Aires, 1890–1910* (Buenos Aires: Manantial, 2001), 153–56.

6. Capetillo frequently wrote for the proletarian press, but her fame also allowed her access to more established venues and her ideas were well known among more affluent feminists. Félix V. Matos Rodríguez notes that Capetillo and Roqué exchanged ideas and that in the second edition of *Mi opinión* (1913) Capetillo dedicated a new section to Roqué's epistolary novel *Luz y sombra.* See Matos Rodríguez's introduction to Luisa Capetillo, *A Nation of Women: An Early Feminist Speaks Out,* trans. Alan West, ed. Félix V. Matos Rodríguez (Houston: Arte Público Press, 2004), xix, xlviii (40n).

7. Capetillo, *A Nation of Women,* 4.

SELECTED REFERENCES

Bravo Elizondo, Pedro. *Cultura y teatro obreros en Chile, 1900–1930.* Madrid: Ediciones Michay, 1986.

Capetillo, Luisa. *A Nation of Women: An Early Feminist Speaks Out (Mi opinión sobre las libertades, derechos y deberes de la mujer).* Trans. Alan West, ed. Félix V. Matos Rodríguez. Houston: Arte Público Press, 2004.

Dávila Santiago, Rubén, ed. *Teatro obrero en Puerto Rico, 1900–1920: Antología.* Río Piedras: Editorial Edil, 1985.

Echevarría, Ana M. "Performing Subversion: A Comparative Study of Caribbean Women Playwrights." PhD diss., Cornell University, 2000.

Fiet, Lowell. *El teatro puertorriqueño reimaginado: Notas críticas sobre la creación dramática y el performance.* San Juan: Ediciones Callejón, 2004.

Ramos, Julio. "Introducción." In Luisa Capetillo, *Amor y anarquía: Los escritos de Luisa Capetillo.* Ed. Julio Ramos. Río Piedras: Ediciones Huracán, 1992.

Sánchez González, Lisa. "Luisa Capetillo: An Anarcho-Feminist *Pionera* in the Mainland Puerto Rican Narrative/Political Tradition." In *Recovering the U.S. Hispanic Literary Tradition,* vol. 2, ed. Erlinda Gonzales-Berry and Chuck Tatum, 148–67. Houston: Arte Público Press, 1996.

Shaffer, Kirwin R. *Anarchism and Countercultural Politics in Early Twentieth-Century Cuba.* Gainesville: University Press of Florida, 2005.

Suriano, Juan. "Tiempo libre, fiestas y teatro." In *Anarquistas: Cultura y política libertaria en Buenos Aires, 1890–1910,* 145–78. Buenos Aires: Manantial, 2001.

Unruh, Vicky. *Performing Women and Modern Literary Culture in Latin America: Intervening Acts.* Austin: University of Texas Press, 2006.

Vargas, Maria Thereza, and Mariângela Alves de Lima. *Teatro operário na cidade de São Paulo.* São Paulo: Secretaria Municipal de Cultura, 1980.

After Death: A Real-Life Comedy in Verse and Prose
(Luisa Capetillo)

Translated by Sarah J. Townsend

CHARACTERS:

LELIA, a twenty-six-year-old young lady
MAULY, a thirty-eight-year-old gentleman
FABIO, a thirty-four-year-old gentleman

The play takes place in the tropics, in a Caribbean city.
A splendid tropical forest, a wrought-iron gate that simulates the entrance to a garden, trees, gar-
lands, colored lights, a grave marked by a marble tombstone surrounded by flowers; a lamp
strung up between the trees hangs above the grave.
The grave should be on the right side of the stage near the curtain.

(LELIA enters calmly and with a meditative air, wearing an elegant white dress. Goes over to the grave, picks up a flower that has fallen on the white stone, contemplates it)

LELIA: She was a flower that generously yielded her fragrance, she was a pearl hidden in the rough human sea! What good fortune it would have been to find her, and treasure her, like a diamond!

Poor little blossom, withered
By the sun's first beams,
Humble purple violet hidden
Beneath lifeless leaves.

Brilliant pearl, for but a minute
She glimmered unpretentiously!
She was a perfume that drifted
In pursuit of another home,
She was a pearl that sparkled—
In simple elegance she shone.
As a flower she was divine,
As a pearl, beyond compare,
A rose so gentle and fine
As ever bloomed anywhere.

(Speaking slowly, with delight, like someone savoring a delicious nectar in a gentle, delicate, expressive manner)

The flower was cruelly snipped
One early sunless dawn;
The pearl was untimely ripped
From the youthful clasp of love.
One by one, the days went by
Sadly observing from above,
As the blushing flower of joy
Faded away from unrequited love.

(Kissing the flower, which falls apart in her hands)

You flew away, lovely psyche
To the mansion of light;
Go, with your rich ambrosia
To grace the cerulean heights.

(Properly dressed, in top hat and tails, gloves, cane and cape, MAULY opens the gate. The stage is in semidarkness, with flashes of lightning and thunder, as if it were storming in the mountains. Upon opening the gate and entering, he looks around at the scene, frowning, and exclaims:)

MAULY: Everything is somber, like myself. It appears that nature wishes to accompany me in my grief, in my indescribable anguish . . .

(Reaching into a pocket inside his tailcoat, he pulls out a wallet, opens it and says:)

Today is the twenty-fifth of December . . .

(He writes something down, puts his wallet back, and continues until he arrives at the grave, where he meets LELIA. Startled by this encounter, he offers her a gallant greeting, and stands, pensive.)

LELIA: I never imagined I would see you here, Mauly . . .

MAULY: This is a memorable date for me, and I hardly expected to find you here either . . .

LELIA: My home is nearby and I come every day to care for the flowers, she entrusted it to me . . .

MAULY: A day, just like today, I saw her for the first time, at her home—angelic! divine!—in a simple flowered dress, violet-rose, that gave her a suggestive appearance; we were introduced by a lawyer, a mutual friend, who is also now dead.

As soon as I entered the room, it seemed as though the doors of the unknown had opened before me, offering me a world of inexplicable delights! Standing beside her, I trembled. That young girl

---

Después de muerta, Luisa Capetillo, Puerto Rico, 1913. Translated from Spanish by Sarah J. Townsend.

had taken power over me, she shattered my tranquility, drove me wild . . .

LELIA: How long ago was all this, Mauly?

MAULY: Eighteen years ago! But listen. When, as a courtesy, they offered me a beer, I couldn't contain myself, and I said to her: I will kneel at your feet if you do not take the first sip . . . She moistened her heavenly lips . . . and I drank down to the bottom of that fine glass, as though wanting to absorb her breath. I took one of her hands and kissed it enthusiastically. That little girl who was right on the cusp of life drove me mad, those strange eyes of hers captured my soul . . .

LELIA: There's no reason to recall all of that now, you should have said all of that to her when she was alive, now what's the poi . . .

MAULY: Let me speak, allow me to unburden myself here, before her grave. It weighs heavily upon me . . . After only a few days we pledged our love, and every day she wrote me letters, endless ones, very affectionate, she copied poems and sent them to me, her love bordered on frenzy.

   Several years passed, and her fidelity was so great, her persistence so idolatrous, that I eventually grew careless, so that between my travels and absences, two years went by.

LELIA: But what were you doing? It took you till now to recognize that you behaved badly? It's a little late.

MAULY: Ignorance, my dear friend, listen; she who was patience and sweetness personified, with a love that came close to madness—filling me with satisfaction and pride and leading me to neglect my duty—she was awoken from her innocence of life. The slave that once was love rebelled. Patience fled in punishment of my carelessness. The loving enthusiasm she had conveyed by writing to me, sending me poems by famous authors and feverish letters calling for me . . . all that began to grow faint as I ran away . . . away from that fire, believing that it would consume itself on its own . . . (wiping away his sweat).

LELIA: But were you indifferent to her displays of affection? Did they have no effect on you? Why did you act that way?

MAULY: My dear, previous excesses led me to maintain a certain reserve that I could not explain to her, nor could she understand. So, after returning from my trip to Paris, I rarely went to see her, certain pleasures I had enjoyed while abroad lured me away from her home, and to the parlor houses, where I sought to replicate them . . .

LELIA: So vices and bad habits are stronger than love! What have we come to! How disgusting! And shameful! So much for social morality!

MAULY: Don't interrupt me so often, my dear, listen in silence. And besides, in addition to those reasons, I was ill . . . A few months later I received news that made my blood run cold and caused me

to go red with shame, thinking of the offense I had given her, the neglect for which I was now paying with the loss of my most prized affections and hopes; another man was calling her attention to the fact that I was not fulfilling my duty, that her luxurious surroundings were no nourishment for a woman in love . . . And she was truly in love with me! . . . The man was a friend . . . but at that moment he seemed to me a hellish phantasm! . . . one that threw in my face my poor conduct, my abandonment of the one woman I adored, in whom all my first memories of love were condensed, the woman I was saving for the future, for my sad and desolate old age. I wanted to reserve that embodiment of purity so that I might later delight in it, and instead he aroused her passion.

LELIA: But sir, how selfish you were. You wanted to deform her nature, to mold her according to your whims, how cruel.

MAULY: Let me finish and don't reproach me, my grief is more than enough to bear. So then, when that naive woman, with unequaled honesty, confessed her transgression, describing the situation . . . how guilty that man appeared! If he had awoken certain sensations in his function as doctor, he should have notified me, summoned me, so that I could avoid my disgrace. Was he not my friend? But oh! Such disappointment! When I heard that detailed confession, desperation took hold of me, the horizon of all my hopes grew dark, my eyes shed burning tears and (energetically) at that moment I would have torn the man to shreds! I would have crushed him, as one crushes a reptile that awaits the opportune moment to inject his treacherous poison! What led that girl-woman to succumb to him? Her solitude, my neglect? Even so, I don't blame her! No! A thousand times, no! That man is a criminal, I told myself, and in a fit of madness I confronted him, I would have smacked him right there in the middle of the plaza if our friends hadn't intervened, because that man, for a single moment of pleasure, destroyed my happiness and stole my love from its cradle of illusions . . . Idiot! Fool! And all the times he called upon my friendship! Treacherous wretch! Traitor! Cynic!

LELIA: You shouldn't blame others for your mistakes, you received your just desserts.

MAULY: But for years she assured me that she hadn't loved him, that her thoughts and soul belonged to me alone.

LELIA: Then why didn't you forgive her? And go back to her?

MAULY: Because social conventions obliged me to express something I didn't feel.

LELIA: How cowardly, you allowed her to suffer knowing that she loved you. You were heartless, leaving her with those children who've been deprived of your affection and care.

MAULY: In truth, you are not mistaken, and I have suffered.

LELIA: You could have prevented everything that happened. Why weren't you by her side?

MAULY: My ignorance of human passions was to blame, but now, allow me to beseech her *(drawing near her grave)*. Forgive me, azure vision of my unrealized dreams! You escaped to other regions, while I vegetate here in pain, the pain of having made you suffer! Forgive me . . . *(He stands, silent, with his head bowed.)*

LELIA observes him with a compassionate look, and neither of them notice when a man enters, his identity hidden behind his upturned collar, protected by darkness. The man approaches the grave and kneels. LELIA, upon seeing him, says: A man!

MAULY: *(Surprised, he stands up, saying)* A man! What are you doing here? *(Aiming his revolver at the man)*

FABIO: Fulfilling a duty! Who might you be, asking me for explanations?

MAULY: *(Drawing near the lamplight)* Look!

FABIO: Good heavens! What are you doing here?

MAULY: You are asking me!?! Sarcasm! I am here, yes, here, where I should be and where I have every right to be, at the grave of the woman I loved, as one cannot love twice.

FABIO: You make me laugh. This love of yours must have flowered after she died, because when she was alive, you abandoned her. Have you come to guard her mortal remains?

MAULY: It's no concern of yours whether or not I abandoned her, you have some gall, showing up at this time and in this place.

FABIO: Oh, so this grave belongs to you? And you have some special right to keep me from it? Or is it that you've suddenly discovered the virility you lacked when she was alive?

MAULY: Insolent brute! You have no respect, even for her grave. Defend yourself, or I'll give you the death you deserve *(pointing the revolver at him)*.

FABIO: Shoot me, that's bravery for you *(sticking out his chest)*.

LELIA: *(Who has remained silent, runs and stands between them)* What are you doing, my friends! Is this any way to honor her memory? After death what does she gain from these arguments? Allow me to recite a composition written by our dear departed friend.

TO YOU

Who is it that calls to me
In my solitary bed,
Murmuring a quiet prayer,
A desperate, tender bid?
Who is the mournful shadow
That meditates so silently,
Cloaked in nocturnal mystery,
Thinking of me, lying down below?

Now listen closely to what I say:

He who, indifferent to my fate,
Along my journey of sorrows
Crossed through my peaceful gate,
Robbing me of my precious morrows;
That brazen man who sought
To extinguish my proud star
And my youthful bliss did mar
By ruffling my tranquil thoughts;
The man who, rash and bold
Profaned my inner soul,
Penetrating my sacred hold,
And my happiness thus stole;
That one! . . . that man I do absolve.
Henceforth, may no one judge him
And let none other begrudge him
Nor punish him . . . except God!

MAULY: She forgives him! . . .

(In his surprise, he drops the revolver and it fires, injuring FABIO, who totters and falls.)

LELIA: *(After finishing the poem she walks away, but hearing the sound of the revolver, she comes running and, seeing FABIO on the ground, asks MAULY:)* What have you done?

MAULY: It wasn't my fault, it fell and the trigger fired on its own. *(They both go to FABIO's side and try to lift him.)*

LELIA: How can we stop the bleeding?

FABIO: Take a little grass and press it over the wound . . .

(LELIA does this, and between the two of them they manage to lift FABIO onto his feet.)

FABIO: *(To MAULY)* Are you satisfied? Do you forgive me now? I'm not the only one to blame, she wanted to take revenge on you for your indifference and distance! I knew that what she felt for me wasn't love, but I was tempted because she was an alluring woman and I was too weak to resist the strange influence she exerted, in that solitude in which I always found her!

MAULY: Did she proposition you?

FABIO: It wasn't premeditated. It was weakness on my part, an excess of life on hers, the crushing solitude that made her desperate and desirous of love, of affection . . . she threw herself into my arms . . . Forgive me!

MAULY: Did you force yourself upon her?

FABIO: Never! I was always a gentleman. You're the one to blame for abandoning her.

MAULY: If you were such a proper gentleman, why didn't you warn me so I could fulfill my duties?

FABIO: So I needed to warn you in order for you to fulfill your duties? *(With irony)*

MAULY: I'm not satisfied. You took liberties that were not yours to take; and as for her wanting to take revenge on me, did she express that to you?

FABIO: No, but I surmised it, because the woman was crazy about you, as soon as I arrived she would ask me if I had seen you, if I knew where you were.

MAULY: What did you tell her? Why didn't you notify me?

FABIO: I told her that I had seen you in the casino or the café, and I didn't notify you because a myriad of circumstances kept me from it.

MAULY: That's it? You didn't set her against me?

FABIO: There was no need to, she had sufficient reasons to be upset with you . . .

MAULY: Well, regardless of all that, I still believe you are to blame, and I cannot be your friend. Your presence mortifies me, it wounds me, it drives me to kill you!

FABIO: Kill me and have done with it, then! (*Standing before MAULY*)

MAULY: No, go away! . . . No one will learn of this unexpected encounter; since I've been away, no one will know. I'll depart once more and that'll be the end of it.

LELIA: (*To FABIO*) Are you in pain?

FABIO: A little, accompany me to the gate. (*LELIA takes him by the arm and leads him to the gate.*) Thank you, I appreciate it. Farewell!

(*MAULY remains pensive as the other man leaves.*)

LELIA: Farewell. (*She returns and goes to MAULY's side.*) What are you thinking about?

MAULY: About this woman, who suffered so much and found it in herself to forgive. I won't be the one to punish him. Did you really believe I would have harmed him?

LELIA: It was a natural assumption, since you'd threatened him. Afterward I realized it was unintentional.

MAULY: My dear, I'm leaving. I'm going to take advantage of the darkness and steal away like a criminal. As you can see, that's what the circumstances call for. Farewell and don't forget me, pray for me, and for her. Farewell!

LELIA: Farewell. Take a flower from her grave. (*Plucking a flower and giving it to him.*) Farewell. (*She stands there, somewhat sad, and recites*)

You flew away, lovely psyche
To the mansion of light;
Send your rich ambrosia
To grace this starless night.

The Candle King
(Oswald de Andrade)

Theater, as we have argued throughout this book, is not simply a mirror for that grand off-stage drama that goes by the name of "reality"; it is an active agent that participates in the creation of myths, identities, and repertoires of everyday behavior. On the flip side, it can also be an act of destruction—or, as the author of *The Candle King* might say, a ritual of consumption.

Oswald de Andrade (1890–1954), the enfant terrible of twentieth-century Brazilian letters, was one of the principal figures of *modernismo*, the Brazilian counterpart to the Spanish American *vanguardias* of the 1920s and 1930s. Closely linked to European avant-gardes including Dada and surrealism, modernismo coupled a self-consciously cosmopolitan outlook with a reevaluation of Brazilian history and a redefinition of the project of nation building. Many nineteenth-century writers, such as José de Alencar, had sought to create an authentic national culture out of a mythic past populated by an idealized Indian akin to Rousseau's "noble savage." Oswald de Andrade and some of his fellow *modernistas* went the way of the "bad Indian": cannibalism. Invoking the practices of certain indigenous groups in Brazil

Toto Passion Fruit and Mrs. Cesarina exchange words in the second act of *The Candle King*, directed by José Celso, Teatro Oficina, 1967. (Photo courtesy of Vivian Martínez Tabares.)

Modernismo

Vanguardias

who disposed of their enemies by eating them, they argued that the only way to escape the trap of cultural dependency was by devouring the colonizer's culture—not swallowing it whole but chewing it up and absorbing its strength. "I am only concerned with what is not mine. Law of man. Law of the cannibal," Oswald wrote in his "Cannibalist Manifesto," dated "the 374th Year of the Swallowing of the Bishop Sardinha," a characteristically campy reference to a Portuguese bishop cannibalized in 1556 by Indians who took unkindly to his evangelizing. In the pages of his infamous *Revista da Antropofagia* (*Anthropophagist Review*) he turned the tables on Eurocentrism, insisting that the French first learned about the rights of man from the egalitarian indigenous societies of Brazil and that capitalism was not progress but simply a debased form of cannibalism.

Although modernistas often invoked Brazilian performance traditions such as Carnival in their work, theater played a limited role in the movement.[1] Oswald de Andrade was already well known for his poetry, prose, and polemics when he turned to playwriting in the 1930s, shortly after entering into a fraught relationship with the Communist Party.[2] His political radicalization was spurred by the Revolution of 1930, which had installed the populist leader Getúlio Vargas in the presidency. Although Vargas's government gave women the right to vote and initially appeased workers' demands by passing some of the country's first labor legislation (the spurious "social laws" referred to in *The Candle King*), his authoritarian tendencies were evident long before he imposed the Estado Novo (New State) dictatorship in 1937. Vargas's "modernizing" regime eagerly fomented the movement of cultural rejuvenation, yet it also enforced censorship and sought to make the arts dependent on state patronage.[3] Oswald's first play was *O Homen e o Cavalo* (Man and the Horse), a bizarre "Spectacle in Nine Tableaux" whose characters include Cleopatra, Fu Man Chu, the Voice of Eisenstein, St. Peter, and Napoleon's White Horse; an allegory of the defeat of fascism by a worldwide communist revolution, it was written in 1933 for an experimental theater company that was shut down before the play's debut by dozens of police officers who unexpectedly showed up to see a ritualistic performance piece that included profanity and a primarily black cast. It is little surprise, then, that despite (or rather because of) Oswald's desire to mobilize the masses none of his plays was performed during his lifetime.

O Rei da Vela (The Candle King) was written in 1933 and published in 1937 along with *A Morta* (The Dead Woman).[4] If *Man and the Horse* prophesied a global future, *The Candle King* ferociously attacked the nation's present. It illustrates the author's thesis that until the Brazilian working class destroys the mechanisms of economic imperialism any so-called revolution will (like Vargas's movement) only bring more of the same exploitation and injustice. The play wastes no opportunity to offend bourgeois morality, thumb its nose at verisimilitude, and violate the conventions of patriotic drama. It is a work of performative cannibalism, a Brazilian spin on *Ubu Roi*, the celebrated farce by Alfred Jarry that is itself an absurdist remake of Shakespeare's *Macbeth*. As if one victim weren't enough, Oswald calls his protagonists Abelard and Heloise, after the twelfth-century French couple whose names are bywords for romantic love—a notion that *The Candle King* tears from limb to limb.[5] Heloise of Lesbos comes from São Paulo's landed aristocracy, though her family has fallen on hard times due to the international crisis of 1929, which caused the collapse of the Brazilian coffee economy. Her fiancé is Abelard I, a representative of the new bourgeoisie who made his fortune selling the candles traditionally used to mourn the dead. Behind the scenes, he is also a moneylender who takes advantage of others' misfortunes, keeping clients in a cage under the supervision of his assistant, Abelard II, a socialist who dresses as a lion tamer and carries a whip. Theirs is a marriage of convenience between old and new money, and Abelard I willingly shares his claim to Heloise's charms with Mr. Jones, the American banker who is his partner in crime.

The Candle King's unabashed theatricality bears the stamp of an amalgam of influences, from the saucy Brazilian *revistas* (musical revues) parodied in the second act to the constructivist theater of Vsevelod Meyerhold, the Russian director whose work also influenced Bertolt Brecht.[6] Like these two avant-garde artists, Oswald employs antimimetic strategies to distance the audience from the action and force it to take a critical perspective on the art of illusion making. Abelard I openly acknowledges the play's debt to the more "modern" medium of cinema when his rival telephones his office in the third act to determine whether or not he is dead and the Candle King calls it a "trick from the cinema. In the theater we don't have any of our own, so he's using this one." The protagonist compares his own plans for marriage and a respectable family life to the plot of a nineteenth-century drama and tells Somersault, the Intellectual, that what is needed to keep the populace submissive is "A stupefying literature. . . . Transferring solutions out of existence and into the book or the theater."

But Oswald, like Brecht, believed that drama should provoke its spectators to enact real, offstage revolutions rather than represent fictitious onstage resolutions. His play, therefore, performs a kind of self-cannibalization that continually threatens to destroy its own theatrical image. Its ritualistic repast is consummated in the third act when the moribund Abelard I, who shoots himself after being swindled by his alter ego, Abelard II, fires the prompter and looks out into the audience to ask, "Are you there? If you want to witness a stylish agony just wait!" He then dissolves as a character right before our eyes and his role is slowly usurped by his double. On one level, then, the play would seem to confirm Peter Bürger's oft-cited thesis that the goal of the historical avant-garde was the destruction of art as a social institution, that is, the "liquidation of art as an activity that is split off from the praxis of life."[7] And yet, when *The Candle King* was written, theater in Brazil was clearly not the well-established, relatively "autonomous" institution that it could lay some claim to being in countries such as France or Germany. Despite the emergence of several important playwrights in the nineteenth century, most of the plays performed in "legitimate" theaters still came from Europe and the audiences represented a minute proportion of the population. Oswald's play, then, turns on a tension between its impulse toward destruction (of the imperialist "Other," the capitalist order, and bourgeois art itself) and its push to construct a viable theater that can thwart the legacy of cultural colonialism.

His dramatic dissection of the "gangrenous corpse of Brazil" remained nothing but a curiosity piece until it was exhumed in the 1960s by the director José Celso and the Teatro Oficina, a group that would later go on to collaborate with the Living Theatre.[8] After the 1964 military coup that overthrew President João Goulart, leftist artists and intellectuals went through a period of intense self-reflection. Many began to critique the national-popular paradigm of political art upheld by theater practitioners such as the Teatro Arena and its director, Augusto Boal, who operated under the premise that artists should align themselves with "the people." If this were really effective, their critics asked, why had Brazilians responded so passively to the coup, despite the artistic mobilization of the early 1960s? Some began to suggest that, rather than rejecting the rapidly developing industries of mass culture, artists should subvert them from within, appropriating their technologies to spread the message of progressive politics.

The September 29, 1967 premiere of *The Candle King* is now recognized as one of the milestones in this debate. Celso dedicated the production to the recently released *Terra em Transe* (*Land in Anguish*), a groundbreaking film by the Cinema Novo director Glauber Rocha that combined Brechtian methods with the sacred rhythms of the Afro-Brazilian *candomblé* religion to create an allegory of the coup and the failure of the leftist artist-intellectual.[9] *The Candle King* was billed as a "spectacle-manifesto" that, like Rocha's film, created a "revolution in form and content to express a non-revolution."[10] The play shocked the public, stunned the critics, and had to be modified several times to placate the censors before its controversial director was imprisoned and then forced into exile in 1974.

In the meantime, however, Teatro Oficina's production left a permanent mark on Brazilian stagecraft with its hodgepodge of Brazilian popular culture, avant-garde stylistics, and mass media pop bound together by an aesthetic of intentionally bad taste. Each act was designed to parody a different genre: the first, building on Abelard II's lion tamer outfit, was turned into a mock circus show; the second, which features a large ensemble cast romping on one of Rio's postcard-pretty beaches, became a spoof on the Brazilian film musicals called *chanchadas;* and the melodramatic final act took on the trappings of tragic opera. The actors' histrionic performances and unusual costumes also emphasized their characters' fragmentary and artificial nature. Heloise's mother, Dona Cesarina, who secretly makes eyes at her future son-in-law, was dressed from the waist up as a respectable São Paulo matron and from the waist down as a showgirl. Several of the characters in the final act wore monkey masks (a play on primitivism and the idea of Brazilian culture as imitative), while Mr. Jones was dressed as the Lone Ranger. The musical accompaniment was no less of a stylistic mishmash: it ranged from selections by Vivaldi and the Brazilian opera composer Carlos Gomes to John Philip Sousa and "Yes, We Have No Bananas," the song made famous by Hollywood's favorite Brazilian, Carmen Miranda. Most of the action took place on a revolving stage, although it often spilled over into the aisles, and at times the spectators in the front row became the object of the characters' aggression.

What caused the biggest stir was the barrage of phallic symbols and obscenities. The text is full of such off-color humor, from the symbolic candle to the sexual eccentricities of Heloise of Lesbos and her siblings, which show up the hypocrisy of their class's discourse on propriety. Teatro Oficina's staging, however, cranked Oswald's politically incorrect parody of patriarchy up another notch. Many of the male characters, along with Heloise in the second act, wore a codpiece on the outside of their pants. Some appeared on stage nude, and Abelard I spent the entire three acts thrusting his pelvis. In front of the stage stood a fifteen-foot puppet whose most salient feature was the "cannon" between its legs that illuminated and became erect whenever Abelard I executed one of his clients. Even more disturbing was the manner in which Abelard I died: after shooting himself, as he does in the text, he was sodomized with a candle by Abelard II.

The play's vulgar desecration of Brazilian nationalism was part of a calculated assault on the audience's senses, a strategy similar to the theater of cruelty advocated by Antonin Artaud. It was meant to offend its spectators, to shake them out of their lethargy and force them to see the underlying ugliness of middle-class Brazilian life that had paved the way for the dictatorship's program of "conservative modernization." Describing his "theater of aggression," Celso explained that "if we take this public as a whole, the only way of forcing it to undergo a real political process lies in the destruction of all its defence mechanisms. . . . We have to put him [the spectator] in his place, to reduce him to zero."[11]

Many of those in the audience, however, appeared to enjoy the abuse, and the play was one of the biggest commercial successes in the history of Brazilian theater. Teatro Oficina was invited to perform the play at international festivals in Florence and Nancy, and the show premiered in Paris on May 10, 1968— the very evening of the legendary Night of the Barricades, a violent battle between student strikers and police that mobilized the Parisian public and led to a real would-be revolution. *The Candle King* phenomenon soon became associated with the emergence of Tropicália, an urban counterculture movement led by pop musicians Caetano Veloso and Gilberto Gil that was heralded as the fulfillment of the modernista project. The *tropicalistas* updated the practice of anthropophagy by mixing samba and rock and roll, using pop icons and catchy tunes to talk about underdevelopment and anticolonial struggles in a playful, parodic style that made an art form out of kitsch. Along with *The Candle King* and the Cinema Novo movement in film, they achieved what the original modernistas had not: a "popular" avant-garde art.

But not everyone applauded. In an oft-cited essay written in 1969, shortly after the implementation of the AI–5 (Institutional Act 5), which initiated a wave of violent repression, the critic Roberto Schwarz underlined some of Tropicália's disturbing ambiguities. In discussing the Teatro Oficina's staging of *The Candle King,* he noted that, while it was effective in illustrating the brutality and crass commercialism of contemporary society, it also turned the theatrical experience into a "trial of strength." Spectators who objected to being insulted by the actors and left the theater were ridiculed; those who stayed reveled in their fortitude and ended up identifying with the "collective aggressor" rather than rejecting what they saw. Such a performance is a double-edged sword, Schwarz claimed, since "by its content, this action is extremely demoralizing; but since we are in the theatre, it is also an image, and that is where its critical power derives from."[12] Schwarz saw this paradox as typical of art at a time when, "against the ambiguous background of modernization, the line between sensibility and opportunism, or between criticism and social integration, is blurred."[13]

Schwarz's analysis rests on a distinction between form and content that is at odds with the performative ethos of Teatro Oficina's production. Like all theoretical frameworks, his has certain limitations, but his diagnosis proved to be perceptive: since it was popularized in the late 1960s, Brazilian cannibalism has been thoroughly canonized. In the year 2000, the Companhia de Atores in Rio attempted to revive *The Candle King* for the twenty-first century by updating it with references to recent cases of political corruption and video projections. Yet despite positive reviews by critics who affirmed that Oswald's play was as relevant as ever, it sparked little debate. What happened? some critics asked, speculating that the problem was a public that had lost faith in the possibility of social transformation. Perhaps, but surely "the public" does not bear all of the blame. For one thing, the play is no longer a novelty, and jumbling high and low culture is now old hat. The aesthetic of shock that was so innovative in Oswald's day has been monopolized by the mass media, and as often as not its effect is to immobilize, rather than mobilize, its audiences. One has to wonder, too, what kind of repercussion the play's parody of bourgeois decadence was expected to have given that the production's corporate sponsor was the Bank of Brazil. In an age when globalization and transnational capital are the watchwords of the new candle kings, it is difficult to know what "eating the Other" means.

At the end of *The Candle King,* it is Abelard II—the "first socialist to appear in Brazilian Theater"—who morphs into Abelard I and walks down the aisle with Heloise. No surprise, then, that now that the man-eating Indian has replaced the noble savage as the icon of the cultural establishment, he seems to have lost a bit of his bite. If both capitalist savagery and its critics gain their strength by eating the Other, how can avant-garde performance keep the profane rituals of anthropophagy from losing their transformative power? Is there a secret to consuming the enemy without being swallowed up by the culture of commodification?

—Sarah J. Townsend

NOTES

1. The other main figure of modernismo, Mário de Andrade, researched indigenous and Afro-Brazilian performance traditions, many of which appear in his famous novel, or "rhapsody," *Macunaíma* (1928). He also wrote an operetta entitled *O Café* (Coffee, 1934), which was never staged, and several unpublished musical dramas based on his ethnographic work.

2. Oswald broke with the Communist Party in 1945 and prior to this time had publicly criticized Stalinism. Oswald's poetry includes *Pau Brasil* (Brazilwood Poetry, 1925); his novels include *Memórias Sentimentais de João Miramar* (Sentimental Memoirs of John Seaborne, 1924) and *Serafim Ponte Grande* (*Seraphim Grosse Pointe,* 1933). In addition to his plays from the 1930s, he wrote two early theatrical pieces in French called *Mon coeur balance* and *Leur âme* (1916).

3. Many modernistas were given positions within the Ministry of Education, though Oswald stayed clear of the Vargas regime. See Daryle Williams, *Culture Wars in Brazil: The First Vargas Regime, 1930–1945* (Durham: Duke University Press, 2001).

4. *A Morta* was first performed in 1992 by the Companhia de Atores in Rio. *O Homem e o Cavalo* has never been staged, though José Celso's Teatro Oficina has performed public readings of the play.

5. Peter Abelard was a controversial French philosopher. Heloise, renowned as one of the most beautiful and well-educated women of the era, was his pupil. Heloise became pregnant and the couple secretly married, but Heloise's uncle sent people to attack and castrate her lover. Both Heloise and Abelard subsequently took religious orders and exchanged passionate letters that were discovered in the thirteenth century.

6. Meyerhold is mentioned several times in Oswald's "Do Teatro, que é Bom . . . ," in *Ponta de Lança* (Rio de Janeiro: Civilização Brasileira, 1972). Written in 1943, it is a dialogue between two speakers who give their opinions on dramaturges, philosophers, and musicians all the way from Shakespeare and Calderón de la Barca to Nietzsche, Henrik Ibsen, Jean Cocteau, Eugene O'Neill, and Dmitry Shostakovich. A constant theme is the argument for the role of a "theater of shock" and a "stadium theater" in educating the masses.

7. Peter Bürger, *Theory of the Avant-Garde,* trans. Michael Shaw. Theory and History of Literature, no. 4 (Minneapolis: University of Minnesota Press, 1984), 56.

8. This image comes from a line in *A Morta* and was often cited by Teatro Oficina members and critics.

9. The Cinema Novo movement existed from about 1960 to 1972. It was characterized by leftist, anticolonialist politics; personal, poetic style; and formal innovation. Cannibalism was a common theme in the later period. See Randal Johnson and Robert Stam, *Brazilian Cinema* (New York: Columbia University Press, 1995).

10. José Celso Martinez Corrêa, "*O Rei da Vela:* Manifesto da Oficina," in Oswald de Andrade, *O Rei da Vela* (São Paulo: Difusão Européia do Livro, 1967), 46.

11. From an interview translated in *Partisans* 47 (1968). Quoted in Roberto Schwarz, "Culture and Politics in Brazil, 1964–1969," in *Misplaced Ideas: Essays on Brazilian Culture,* ed. John Gledson (London: Verso, 1992), 158 (fn10).

12. Schwarz, "Culture and Politics," 153.

13. Ibid., 141. For several other more recent essays on the Tropicália movement, and for a number of manifestos by its participants (including a different version of the Oficina manifesto), see Carlos Basualdo, ed., *Tropicália: A Revolution in Brazilian Culture* (1967–1972) São Paulo: Cosac Naify, 2005).

SELECTED REFERENCES

Andrade, Oswald de. "Cannibalist Manifesto." Trans. Leslie Bary. *Latin American Literary Review* 19 (July–December 1991): 35–47. In Portuguese: "Manifesto Antropófago." *Revista de Antropofagia* 1, no. 1 (May 1928).

Andrade, Oswald de. "Do Teatro, que é Bom." In *Ponta de Lança,* 85–92. Rio de Janeiro: Civilização Brasileira, 1972.

Basualdo, Carlos, ed. *Tropicália: A Revolution in Brazilian Culture (1967–1972).* São Paulo: Cosac Naify, 2005.

Celso Martinez Corrêa, José. "*O Rei da Vela:* Manifesto da Oficina." In Oswald de Andrade, *O Rei da Vela,* 45–52. São Paulo: Difusão Européia do Livro, 1967.

Dunn, Christopher. *Brutality Garden: Tropicália and the Emergence of a Brazilian Counterculture.* Chapel Hill: University of North Carolina Press, 2001.

George, David Sanderson. *The Modern Brazilian Stage.* Austin: University of Texas Press, 1992.

Lara, Cecília de. *De Pirandello a Piolim: Alcântara Machado e o Teatro no Modernismo.* Rio de Janeiro: Instituto Nacional de Artes Cénicas, 1987.

Magaldi, Sábato. *Teatro da ruptura: Oswald de Andrade.* São Paulo: Global Editora, 2004.

Schwarz, Roberto. "Culture and Politics in Brazil, 1964–1969." In *Misplaced Ideas: Essays on Brazilian Culture,* ed. John Gledson, 126–59. London: Verso, 1992.

Silva, Armando Sérgio da. *Oficina: Do Teatro ao Te-ato.* São Paulo: Editora Perspectiva, 1981.

Unruh, Vicky. *Latin American Vanguards: The Art of Contentious Encounters.* Berkeley: University of California Press, 1994.

The Candle King (Oswald de Andrade)

Translated by Ana Bernstein and Sarah J. Townsend

CHARACTERS:

ABELARD I
ABELARD II
HELOISE OF LESBOS
JOAN, also known as JOHN OF THE DIVANS
TOTO PASSION FRUIT
COLONEL BELARMINO
MRS. CESARINA
MISS POLOCA
SPITTLE
The AMERICAN
The CUSTOMER
SOMERSAULT THE INTELLECTUAL
The SECRETARY
MALE DEBTORS, FEMALE DEBTORS
The PROMPTER

ACT ONE

São Paulo. Usury office of Abelard & Abelard. A portrait of the Mona Lisa. Piles of boxes stacked on top of one another. A futurist divan. A Louis XV secretary. A brass candlestick. A telephone. Alarm buzzer. A showcase with candles in all sizes and colors. To the right, a massive iron door that rolls horizontally on a track, revealing the bars of a cage inside. File cabinet, with drawers displaying the following labels: SCOUNDRELS—DELINQUENTS—FLAT-BROKES—REPOSSESSIONS—In another section: LIENS—LIQUI-DATIONS—SUICIDES—STRIPPED-NAKEDS.

Through a large open window the clamor of morning in the city enters and the clack of typewriters from the front room exits.

(ABELARD I, ABELARD II, and the CUSTOMER)

ABELARD I: *(Seated, talking to the CUSTOMER. He presses a button and a buzzer is heard.)* Let's see . . .

ABELARD II: *(He wears boots and a lion tamer's outfit. His hair is pomaded and he has a huge handlebar moustache. Monocle. A revolver in his belt.)* Yes, Mr. Abelard.

ABELARD I: Bring me this man's file.

ABELARD II: Certainly! Your name?

CUSTOMER: *(Ashamed, hat in hand, a tie made of rope around his thin neck)* Manoel Pitanga de Moraes.

ABELARD II: Occupation?

CUSTOMER: I was a property owner the first time I came here. After that I was an employee of the Soro-cabana Railroad for two years. The loan, the first one, I believe that was for the birth. When the girl was born . . .

ABELARD II: I remember. It's in DELINQUENTS. *(Hands over the requested file and leaves)*

ABELARD I: *(Examines the file)* Look at this! This is not businesslike, Mr. Pitanga! You took out the first loan at the end of '29. You paid it off in May of 1931. You took out another one in June of '31, now we're in March of '33. You keep rolling it over. Two months ago you stopped paying the interest . . . This is not businesslike . . .

CUSTOMER: Exactly. The second time I came to you it was because the Railroad delayed payment of salaries, with the Revolution of 1930 . . . The first time was for the birth. The kid was already two years old. And the Revolution of 1930 . . . It was a terrible success that complicated everything . . .[1]

ABELARD I: You know, our company's policy is to roll over debt. But we can't work with people who don't pay interest . . . This is our livelihood . . . You've committed the gravest of crimes against the company system and the security of our business . . .

CUSTOMER: It's only been two months since I stopped paying interest.

ABELARD I: Two months. And you think that's nothing?

O Rei da Vela, Oswald de Andrade, Brazil, 1933. Translated from Portuguese by Ana Bernstein and Sarah J. Townsend.

CUSTOMER: That's why I want to settle the loan. Make a deal. So I'm not repossessed. What the hell! You've helped so many people . . . You're everyone's friend . . . Why can't you cut me a deal?

ABELARD I: There are no deals here, my friend. Here, it's all about payment!

CUSTOMER: But I'm in a sad situation. I can't pay everything, Mr. Abelard. Maybe I can get an advance so that I can settle . . .

ABELARD I: Despite your failure to pay on time, we will take a look at your proposal . . .

CUSTOMER: But I was on time for two and a half years. I paid for as long as I could! My debt was one conto de réis. In interest alone I've already brought you more than two and a half contos. And up till now I haven't invoked the law against usury.

ABELARD I: (*Interrupting him, brutal*) Ah! My friend! Go ahead and invoke that immoral and iniquitous thing . . . Once the usury law comes up, negotiations are over . . . Get out!

CUSTOMER: Come on, Mr. Abelard. You know me. I wouldn't do that!

ABELARD I: Don't even mention that monstrosity to me because I'll have you repossessed today. I'll take the shirt off your back, you hear me? The very shirt you're wearing.

CUSTOMER: I won't take advantage, Mr. Abelard. I want to pay you. But I want to propose a deal. My situation is sad . . . It's not my fault I was laid off. I got another job. They got rid of me to cut costs. I don't send my daughter to school because I can't buy her shoes. I shouldn't have to starve to death too. Sometimes we don't have anything to eat at home. Now my wife's fallen sick. Even so, I'm a skilled man. I've looked for a job everywhere, with no luck. The only thing I get is a big fat no. As big as the sky! Now I've learned bookkeeping, I'm doing some accounting. Odd jobs. I'll get there . . . I'm going to see if they'll give me an advance so I can pay you back.

ABELARD I: So, getting to the point, what is it you're proposing?

CUSTOMER: A small reduction of the principal.

ABELARD I: Of the principal! Are you crazy?! Reduce the principal? Never!

CUSTOMER: But I've already paid you more than twice the amount I borrowed . . .

ABELARD I: Tell me something, Mr. Pitanga. Was it I who went looking for you to sign this IOU? Was it my car that stopped in front of your hovel to ask you to accept my money? By what right do you propose that I reduce the capital I loaned you?

CUSTOMER: (*Disoriented*) I've already paid two times over . . .

ABELARD I: Out of my sight! (*Stands up*) Get out or I'll call the police. It's just a matter of pressing the anticrime button on this device. The police still exist . . .

CUSTOMER: To defend the capitalists! And their crimes!

ABELARD I: To defend my money. You'll be repossessed this very day. (*Presses the buzzer*) Abelard! Give orders to repossess this man! Out! Let's go. Shoot him . . . It's the company system.

CUSTOMER: I'm a coward! (*Leaves, crying*) You're taking advantage of a weakling, a coward!

(*Same characters minus the CUSTOMER*)

ABELARD I: Don't let anyone else in today, Abelard.

ABELARD II: The cage is full . . . Mr. Abelard!

ABELARD I: But this scene is enough to identify us to the audience. I don't need to speak to any of my other customers. They're all the same. Above all, do not bring me any fathers who can't buy shoes for their kids . . .

ABELARD II: That one has no reason to gripe. He doesn't have much of a brood. Only one daughter . . . A small family!

ABELARD I: Don't confuse things, Abelard! Family is something distinguished. Broods are the result of pro-liferation, which is done by pro-letarians. Family requires property and vice versa. Those who don't have property should procreate. When it comes to working, children are the poor man's fortune . . .

ABELARD II: But nobody buys that anymore . . .

ABELARD I: It's social disorder, unemployment, it's Russia! That man owned a little house. He had the right to have a family. He lost the house. He should have had a bigger brood! Mr. Abelard, family and property are two girls who frequent the same *garçonnière*, the same bacchanal . . . when there's plenty of bread to go around. But when bread is scarce, one goes out the door and the other flies out the window . . .

ABELARD II: The family is the ideal of all mankind! Property too. And Miss Heloise is an angel.

ABELARD I: You know there's no other kind on the market. I wasn't about to marry the younger sister who's known all around as the Crisis Girl and as John of the Divans. Or the younger brother that everybody calls Toto Passion Fruit!

ABELARD II: A degenerate . . .

ABELARD I: Things we understand and excuse in an old family! Heloise, despite the vices they pin on her . . . You know, everybody knows. Heloise of Lesbos! People made jokes when I bought an island in Rio for us to get married on. They said it was in Greece. But for all that, she's still the most decent flower of that old Bandeirante tree.[2] One of the founding families of the Empire.[3]

ABELARD II: The old man is broke. He lost everything to his creditors.

ABELARD I: Who cares? For us, advanced men who only know the cold value of money, buying the remnants of a coat of arms is still good business, it makes an impression in a medieval country like ours! Do you know that São Paulo only has ten families?

ABELARD II: And the rest of the population?

ABELARD I: They're one big brood. What I'm doing, what you want to do, is to leave the brood and become family, to buy an ancient coat of arms. That might sound like nineteenth-century theater. But in Brazil it's still new.

ABELARD II: So it is! The bourgeoisie only produced a theater of class. The performance of class. Today we've evolved. We've arrived at the ridiculous.

ABELARD I: All right. Let's take a look at the *bordereau* . . . Did the bank send much back?

ABELARD II: Uh! An avalanche! We're in a pickle, Mr. Abelard!

ABELARD I: Go on . . .

ABELARD II: (*Reading*) Five contos seven hundred and seventy. Dr. Carlos Magalhães de Moraes Benevides Fonseca. Single loan . . . Do we roll it over? He hasn't paid interest in two months.

ABELARD I: Roll it over.

ABELARD II: Antunes & Lapa . . . three contos . . . I already executed it. Mangioni . . . Luiz . . . The bookie . . . Dr. João Carlos de Menezes Rocha . . . two contos . . .

ABELARD I: Repossession.

ABELARD II: Baron Gama Lima, five hundred thousand réis . . .

ABELARD I: Repossession!

ABELARD II: Moura Melo . . . seven hundred thousand réis.

ABELARD I: Repossession.

ABELARD II: Abraão Calimério . . . ten contos.

ABELARD I: Repossession!

ABELARD II: Carlos Peres . . . This one already bit the dust yesterday . . .

ABELARD I: He didn't ask to roll it over?

ABELARD II: No.

ABELARD I: Why not?

ABELARD II: He drank two glasses of lemonade laced with iodine. It's right here in the newspaper. (*Searches*) It says he's in a coma, at Santa Casa Hospital . . .

ABELARD I: Send Benvindo to foreclose. Fast. Before he dies and the store shuts down . . .

ABELARD II: All right. This one is . . . that government clerk, Mr. Pass-the-Hat . . . And his hat is empty! He sent his daughter here.

ABELARD I: Pretty?

ABELARD II: A bombshell! Eighteen years old . . . Each bazonga this big.

ABELARD I: He sent his daughter? Last month it was the wife.

ABELARD II: I saw her. A real looker . . . But too chatty. She wanted to know where you lived, talked about you buying the island in Rio where you're getting married. Went on about you taking a bunch of people there from São Paulo by plane.

ABELARD I: (*Kicking a big cardboard box*) What's this?

ABELARD II: Blocks for making hats. (*Points to the brass candlestick*) The take from the lien on Madame Lanale. It was only this and the candelabrum. There was barely enough to pay off the cops who helped us.

ABELARD I: And the furniture . . .

ABELARD II: We left it in the street, all busted up. There were just two old pieces made of iron. It caused a scandal. The staff had to get rough. The people wanted to intervene. It drew a crowd . . .

ABELARD I: What staff?

ABELARD II: The court officials . . .

ABELARD I: But it set an example!

ABELARD II: And it'll bear fruit.

ABELARD I: The whole street knows that I repossessed them just because they owed me a lousy two hundred thousand réis. The whole city knows. Maybe I took it too far. . . . What does it matter? *Dura lex*, that's what I learned at law school!

ABELARD II: I wish you'd seen the outcry! The widow was bawling at the window:—*Gli orfani! Gli orfani! Non abiamo piu lavoro!*

ABELARD I: What?

ABELARD II: She was saying that the orphans had nothing left to eat. We took away the tools of their trade.

ABELARD I: Crafty woman . . .

ABELARD II: Prosperity only comes at the cost of great misfortune. A lot of misfortune indeed . . .

ABELARD I: If it wasn't that way, how could I guarantee payment to my depositors? If I didn't take it from the other side? I offer interest rates the banks don't offer. Rates that only a few of them paid even when times were good. Four and five percent a year!

ABELARD II: And the money's flowing our way! . . . The banking section downstairs is packed!

ABELARD I: I offer good security. And I also demand good security when I make loans . . .

ABELARD II: At five and ten percent a month . . . Philanthropy! (*The telephone*) It's your brother.

ABELARD I: My lawyer.

ABELARD II: (*On the phone*) Yes, sir. He's here. (*To ABELARD*) He says he's at the courthouse with three executives. He wants to talk to you . . .

ABELARD I: (*On the phone*) What? It's me . . . Abelard. Theodore? He wants to press charges under the usury law? That asshole! And he wants me to roll his loan over! Lynch the guy. Spray him with DDT and strike a match! (*Hangs up forcefully*) To hell with that bandit! Law against usury! Scoundrels! Bolsheviks! That's why this country is going to the dogs. And there's a bastard who wants to avail himself of that iniquity.

ABELARD II: Social laws . . .

ABELARD I: A gang of crooks. Messing around with interest. Restricting my sacred right to lend my money at the rates I choose! And that everyone accepts. And not just that! They come here begging for it! Is it me who goes chasing after them asking them to sign my IOUs? Or is it they who come and crowd my waiting room every day? Open the cage!

(ABELARD II obeys with whip in hand. The iron door rolls open heavily.)

(More CUSTOMERS.

The CUSTOMERS appear at the bars, trampling over one another. It is a collection of crises, motley, expectant. The men and women remain quiet under the threat of ABELARD II's enormous whip.)

ABELARD I: Out! Not one more transaction! I'm going to close this mess down.

VOICES: *(From the cage)* For the love of God! For pity's sake! I can't pay my rent! Roll my debt over! I'm going bankrupt!

ABELARD I: Out! Who can work anymore in a country like this! With such monstrous laws!

VOICES: I have to close down the factory! I won't be able to pay my two hundred workers and they'll be left with no bread! Have mercy! Add the interest on to the capital! We have excellent collateral!

ABELARD I: *(To ABELARD II)* Close that door! I won't see anyone else!

(ABELARD II cracks his lion tamer's whip.)

VOICES: We'll fool the government! Save me! Save me!

ABELARD I: Out! Bastards! I know what you all say about me on the outside!

(ABELARD II makes them back away from the bars, brandishing the whip and threatening them with the gun.)

A WOMAN'S VOICE: Oh, Jesus! We have nothing to eat! I'm not leaving! I'll wait all night! I'm ruined!

ANGRY VOICES: *(ABELARD II tries to close the iron door.)* Bastard! Scumbag! You bled us dry! Thief! We're not leaving!

An ITALIAN: Pamarona! Momanjo isto capitalista!

A FRENCH WOMAN: Sale cochon! Si c'est possible! Con!

A WHITE RUSSIAN: Svoloch!

A TURK: George pay depth! No ixecuti George . . .

VOICES: *(In chorus)* Murderer!

ABELARD I: Close it! Open fire!

(ABELARD II shoots into the air. The CUSTOMERS step back screaming. He closes the door noisily.)

VOICES: *(Muffled)* Dog! Candle King! Skinflint!

A WOMAN'S VOICE: *(Yelling from the other side of the door)* My husband drank strychnine!

ANOTHER WOMAN: My mother drank Drano!

ANOTHER ONE: My father jumped off a bridge!

ABELARD I: Drano! Strychnine! Bridges! That's what you need, bastards!

(Minus the CUSTOMERS.

Telephone)

ABELARD II: *(Answering)* Hello! It's the priest! About the interview! He's here, Father! He's coming . . .

ABELARD I: But did you make an appointment?

ABELARD II: I didn't make any appointment.

ABELARD I: *(Taking the phone)* Good morning, Father! It's me. Abelard . . . Ah! I'm very honored . . . I'll await your Reverence. How about four o'clock? So . . . undoubtedly . . . I kiss your hands! I'm at your service. *(Puts the phone down)* That priest is a funny one . . . He won't leave me alone . . . But I'm not on the electoral board . . . He doesn't want money . . .

ABELARD II: He wants your soul . . .

ABELARD I: That would be a first. A man worrying over me without thinking about cash . . . How much?

ABELARD II: He'd rather go straight for your will.

ABELARD I: Useless. I'll die an atheist, and married.

ABELARD II: That's exactly what he wants. Your widow will want to take good care of your soul, which will have departed . . . for purgatory . . .

ABELARD I: Tell me something, Mr. Abelard, are you a socialist?

ABELARD II: I'm the first socialist to appear in Brazilian Theater.

ABELARD I: And what is it you want?

ABELARD II: To take your place at that table.

ABELARD I: From what I've seen, socialism always starts off like this in backward countries . . . Entering into an agreement with property at the first opportunity . . .

ABELARD II: Indeed. We're in a semicolonial country . . .

ABELARD I: Where we can have ideas, but we're not made of steel . . .

ABELARD II: Yes. Without breaking tradition.

ABELARD I: If need be the priest will take your soul too . . . All right. Let's examine the proposals. *(Sits down and reads)* Carmo Belatine . . .

ABELARD II: That's the one from the sausage factory . . . The cold storage plant . . . Who bought the piece of land in Lapa.

ABELARD I: Age?

ABELARD II: Thirty-nine.

ABELARD I: Social status?

ABELARD II: Still low. He uses a soup bowl to shave, with soap and a secondhand razor . . .

ABELARD I: Does he speak Portuguese yet?

ABELARD II: He still gets mixed up.

ABELARD I: Does he spend less than what he extracts from the workers?

ABELARD II: Much less!

ABELARD I: Grown children?

ABELARD II: Still little.

ABELARD I: In good schools?

ABELARD II: Yes. Oiseaux, Sion, São Bento.

ABELARD I: Well then. Write this down. We'll lend

him money while the kids are still in school. When the daughters start their military "service" at the *garçonnières* and the youngest has wheels, when the missus has learned how to dress, then we'll make a loan, preferably to her dressmaker. By then the old man's social status will have changed. He'll own an automobile, a house in Jardim America. We'll cut his credit little by little. Not one more IOU! He'll come here bringing the contracts of the businessmen he deals with as collateral. And then one day I'll repossess everything. I'll take the factory, the long-term bonds, and the junkyard.

ABELARD II: And the wife will say it was the workers who ruined them.

ABELARD I: And they will have, as a matter of fact. I consider the workers' demands to be an essential factor in these things. Minimum wage. Paid vacations. What the hell. The so-called social laws shouldn't only be against capital . . .

ABELARD II: No, no, they aren't. You can rest easy. I understand socialism. Look. The vacation law has only produced one result. There are no more weekly or monthly salaries. It's all done by the workday or by contract. If you add them all up, the Sundays, holidays, and sick days used to cost more than paid vacations cost today.

ABELARD I: Fine. Keep this application with the SOLIDS. Close the deal. The standard rate. The company system. Call Secretary #3. I have a letter to dictate.

(ABELARD II leaves.)

(ABELARD I and SECRETARY #3)

SECRETARY: *(A young woman, tall, with glasses and enormous blonde braids. She is modestly dressed. She has a pencil and a writing pad in her hands.)* Is it to be typed, Mr. Abelard?

ABELARD I: No. Shorthand. Not even. You know how to compose. Better than I do. Write a letter. Sit there. *(They sit close to each other.)* Miss Aida . . . Blonde Aida . . . Wagner's Aida. And so? Don't you need a Radames?

SECRETARY: I need a raise. The cost of living in Brazil has gone up thirty percent.

ABELARD I: I'm very interested in the cost of your life . . . But you know . . . Life is difficult for all of us these days . . . It's not like the old times . . . Those braids! . . . I'll end up hanging myself with those braids! . . . May I? *(Tries to touch her hair)*

SECRETARY: Behave yourself, Mr. Abelard!

ABELARD I: No? . . . Heartless girl!

SECRETARY: Never. I'm a romantic. I don't sell my love!

ABELARD I: Let's have a picnic . . . *(He points to the divan under the Mona Lisa.)* . . . beneath that mango tree?

SECRETARY: I'm engaged.

ABELARD I: So am I.

SECRETARY: But I'm faithful . . .

ABELARD I: Fine! Then don't come asking me for advances later, huh! I also know how to be faithful to the company system. Go on. Write! No. Take notes. Listen. It's a confidential letter. To one Cristiano de Bensaúde. An industrialist in Rio. He pretends to be a writer. Draft a letter in flawless Portuguese. The man was a literary critic and a progressive, when he was penniless . . . He wrote to me proposing a united front against the workers. Answer in the hypothetical *(the SECRETARY takes notes)*, insinuate that it's better for him to be a flat-out cop. To maintain rigorous surveillance of the factories. Ward off communist propaganda. Denounce and pursue the agitators. Make arrests. That business of writing sociology books about angels is counterproductive. Nobody believes it anymore. As advanced industrialists, it makes us look ridiculous. In the eyes of the Americans and the English. Listen, say this. That the bourgeoisie dies without God. Refuses extreme unction. Cite the example of the Vatican itself. Concrete things. The Church giving its political backing in exchange for one billion seven hundred thousand liras, religious education, and the law against divorce. Give-and-take. Doesn't he see that a mountain climber like Pius XI sets angels up in business?[4] Go draft it and bring it back right away. To be sent today . . . Let's see if this man will stop getting in the way. A feudal subject. Victim of his own system. He pays a medieval salary, twenty thousand réis every two weeks.

SECRETARY: *(Turning around at the door)* A-ni-mal!

(She leaves, bumping into HELOISE OF LESBOS who, dressed as a man, enters like the morning outside.

Minus the SECRETARY, plus HELOISE)

ABELARD I: *(Laughing)* You! My love! During business hours!

HELOISE: Our marriage is a business deal . . .

ABELARD I: Is that why you came dressed as Marlene Dietrich?

HELOISE: A business deal, but not like the deals you make with that band of desperate people that just left here shouting . . . There's still a bunch of them downstairs. Elderly women, young women, Turks, Italians, Russian peddlers, it's like the fauna you'd find at an asylum.

ABELARD I: Ingrates! I satisfied their hunger! I fed them illusions!

HELOISE: And now you treat them like this!

ABELARD I: To give you an island. An island for you alone!

(Plus ABELARD II)

ABELARD II: *(Entering)* There's a guy out there who doesn't want to leave. He's resisting. A new customer.

ABELARD I: Who is he?

ABELARD II: An intellectual. He says he won't leave

without seeing you. He wants to write your biography. Illustrated. With photographs. He says it'll make a good book. Thick!

ABELARD I: Send him in. Him I want to see.

(Plus SOMERSAULT THE INTELLECTUAL)

SOMERSAULT: *(Enters carrying a poet's hat in his hand. A lyrical tie. Smiling. Bowing. He uses an enormous wooden knife as a cane.)* Good morning, master.

HELOISE: *(Lets out a piercing scream)* Ah! The knife!

ABELARD I: Disarm that man! The very idea! *(ABELARD II throws himself on top of the INTELLECTUAL and grabs the symbolic knife from him.)* Letting armed people come in here!

SOMERSAULT: *(Apologizing humbly)* It's harmless . . . made of wood!

ABELARD I: Confess that you planned an attack! Confess!

SOMERSAULT: Absolutely not! Who do you take me for? It's an occupational knife, harmless, it doesn't kill . . .

ABELARD I: *(Examining it)* It's covered in blood . . . coagulated blood . . .

SOMERSAULT: Just a few little slices . . . to eat . . .

(In response to a gesture from ABELARD I, he sits down. ABELARD II remains in the background, holding the knife horizontally with both hands, like an ancient servant.)

It's the crisis that obliges me to . . . But I'm no gangster, no. I'm a biographer. I live by my pen. I'm too old to write novels, or poetry . . . The national theater turned into a theater of ideas. And I confess my ignorance, I don't understand politics. Nor do I want to understand . . .

ABELARD I: Are you a rebel?

SOMERSAULT: Absolutely not! I was when I was in school. Today I'm practically a conservative! What I lack is conviction.

ABELARD I: Do you have any social inclinations . . . Bolshevik, I mean?

SOMERSAULT: No sir! Poor people make my stomach turn . . . working people . . . Not my sort of thing!

ABELARD I: Very good!

SOMERSAULT: People who stink . . .

HELOISE: No one gives them soap so they can wash themselves.

ABELARD II: They don't get bread, let alone soap . . .

ABELARD I: *(Reassuring SOMERSAULT, who turned around at the last sentence)* Don't worry. He's a socialist. But a moderate one, and with a knife, too. *(They both smile.)* So then, what literary genre do you cultivate, my friend?

SOMERSAULT: The great men! I intend to be like Ludwig.[5] To write about the great lives! There is no nobler mission on the planet! The heroes of our age.

ABELARD I: It can also be extremely dangerous. If you exalt popular heroes and enemies of society in your

biographies. Imagine if you wrote about the sailors' revolt and featured João Cândido[6] . . . or some communist killed in a rally!

SOMERSAULT: There's no danger. The police would come after me.

ABELARD I: So you're a self-policing intellectual . . .

SOMERSAULT: I take pride in maintaining a moderate and distinguished stance!

ABELARD I: Have you published anything?

SOMERSAULT: Yes. A little book! The life of Estácio de Sá.[7] It didn't turn out so well. But I'm writing another one . . . This one will turn out better . . .

ABELARD I: The life of Charlemagne? . . .

SOMERSAULT: No. Of Paschoal Carlos Magno[8] . . . Something inoffensive . . .

HELOISE: Then your books can be read by young ladies . . .

SOMERSAULT: Certainly! I'd like to be a social Delly![9] Do you understand?

ABELARD I: Perfectly! A stupefying literature. Giving the poor girls illusions about life. Transferring solutions out of existence and into the book or the theater. Freud . . .

SOMERSAULT: Oh! Freud is subversive . . .

ABELARD I: A wee bit. But you see, if it wasn't for him, we'd all be much more unmasked. He's clueless about the class struggle! Or pretends to be clueless. It's marvelous!

HELOISE: It's all very amusing when you're emancipated. *(Takes out a cigarette and smokes)*

SOMERSAULT: I prefer biographies!

ABELARD I: You don't write fiction?

SOMERSAULT: In Brazil fiction doesn't pay!

ABELARD I: True, it's friction that's profitable. It has to be that way, my friend. Imagine if you, the people who write, were independent! There'd be a deluge! Total subversion. Money is only useful in the hands of the untalented. You writers, artists, you need to be kept by society in the harshest and most permanent misery! Serving as good lackeys, obedient and helpful. That's your social function!

HELOISE: Do you write verse?

SOMERSAULT: When necessary . . . Little quatrains . . . acrostics . . . sonnets . . . ads.

HELOISE: Futuristic?

SOMERSAULT: No, ma'am! I was a futurist once. I even believed in independence . . . But it was a tragedy! People started treating me like a crackpot. Looking at me sideways. Not receiving me anymore. At home the children were constantly crying. I've got three children. The newspaper wasn't paying either, due to the crisis. I had to live off odd jobs. Ah! I renounced everything. Got myself that tool *(points to the knife)* and became old-fashioned.

ABELARD I: But what political stripes do you wear in these agitated days of social debate?

SOMERSAULT: I stick to an intermediary position, neutral . . . I don't get involved.

ABELARD I: Neutral! It's incomprehensible! It's inadmissible! No one is neutral in today's world. You either serve the lower class . . .

SOMERSAULT: And be left shirtless?

ABELARD I: Then don't be shy about serving those on top. But not just with neutral biographies . . . We need lackeys . . .

SOMERSAULT: You're right! But they say the Social Revolution is on its way. All around the world. If things take a turn?

ABELARD I: You'll be executed with all due honors. It's better to die as an enemy than as a convert.

SOMERSAULT: And my family . . . The three kids?

ABELARD I: (Getting up angrily) Get out! Villain! Opportunist! You won't get so much as 10,000 réis, believe me! My class needs lackeys. The bourgeoisie demands clear positions! Lackeys, yes! Ones who wear uniforms. Out!

(ABELARD II gives the knife to the INTELLECTUAL, who leaves grimly. Then he exits.

Minus SOMERSAULT THE INTELLECTUAL and ABELARD II)

HELOISE: Poor fellow!

ABELARD I: He'll be back! In a yellow, blue or green shirt.[10] And with a pike. And he'll stand guard at my door! And he'll defend me with his own life from the red tide that threatens to rise up and take over the world! Intellectuals must be treated that way. The kids crying at home, the weepy, weak, hungry wives are our weapons! Only when they're destitute will they serve us with unconditional loyalty and dedication! And we'll have accolades, applause and guaranties. They'll defend my positions and your island, my love!

HELOISE: A Brazilian island! . . . I almost don't want it.

ABELARD I: A pier . . . Where you've moored . . . After alighting in many lands . . . seeing many landscapes . . .

HELOISE: My safe harbor . . .

ABELARD I: A sanitized harbor . . . with warehouses . . . cranes . . . and a throng of workers to sweat for us . . .

HELOISE: In exchange for my freedom. We've settled on marriage . . . Which you used to claim was the most immoral of all human institutions.

ABELARD I: And the most useful to our class . . . The one that defends our inheritance . . .

HELOISE: Well . . . here I am . . . bought and sold. Like valuable merchandise . . . I don't deny it . . . Badly educated in millionaire boarding schools in Switzerland and carpeted salons in São Paulo . . . going from hangovers to indolence to romantic intrigues . . . I couldn't endure more than two years on the destitution circuit. (Silence) And the admiration you aroused in me, with your cold and calculated look and your appalling victory amid the general collapse . . . The knowledge I gained of your cynicism and your indifference to human suffering . . .

ABELARD I: I know only one thing—reality. And because of that I subjugate you who are pure dream . . .

HELOISE: (Pointing to the Mona Lisa) Why do you have that painting . . .

ABELARD I: The Mona Lisa. A chunk of beauty. The first bourgeois smile . . .

HELOISE: You're a realist. And because of that you magically became rich. While my people, after one hundred years of working the land, became poor in two . . .

ABELARD I: For ninety-eight years they worked and made thousands of people work, for me . . . (Withdrawn silence)

HELOISE: They say so many things about you, Abelard . . .

ABELARD I: I know . . . The steps of crime . . . that I courageously descended. With the paid silence of the newspapers and the blindness of my class's justice! The ghosts of the past . . . The men I betrayed and murdered. The women I abandoned. The suicides . . . The contraband and the pillage . . . The whole arsenal of our grandparents' moralist theater. None of that impresses me, and it doesn't impress the audience anymore either . . . The miraculous key of fortune, a Yale key . . . I play with it!

HELOISE: The panic . . .

ABELARD I: Why not? The panic of the coffee crisis. I used English money to buy coffee at the doors of desperate plantations. I used inside knowledge of government secrets to play hardball with coffee stocks! I piled up ruins on one side and gold on the other! But there's also the constructive work, industry . . . I calculated in view of the partial regression that the crisis provoked . . . I discovered and stimulated the regression, the return to the candle . . . under the sign of American capital.

HELOISE: You became the Candle King.

ABELARD I: With great honor! The King of the miserable candle of the moribund. The king of the tallow candle. Of the feudal candle that lulls us to sleep when we're children, thinking about the stories told to us by our old black mammies . . . The petit bourgeois candle of oratories and writing at home . . . The crisis put the electric companies out of business . . . No one could afford the price of electricity anymore . . . The candle went back on the market under my provident hand. See how I produce candles of all sizes and shapes. (Gestures toward the showcase) Candles for the month of the Virgin Mary in backwoods towns, for groceries in the interior where they do business and gamble at night, for children's study time, for smugglers out at sea . . . But the greatest candle is the candle of death, that little tallow candle that I spread throughout all of Brazil . . . In a medieval country such as ours, who would dare to cross the threshold of eternity without a candle in his hand? I inherit a penny from each of the nation's dead!

HELOISE: *(Musing)* My father was Colonel Belarmino, who owned seven plantations, that sumptuous house in Higienópolis . . . stocks, automobiles . . . Two addicted daughters, two morally degenerate sons . . . He ended up living in our little house in Penha and going to Mass to ask God for the solution the Government didn't provide . . .

ABELARD I: That it didn't provide to people who can't live without loans.

HELOISE: My parents . . . my uncles . . . my cousins . . .

ABELARD I: The old lords of the land who had to make way for the new lords of the land!

HELOISE: Yet they say that the era of lords and large landed estates is over . . .

ABELARD I: You know that my case proves the opposite to be true. I don't yet have the number of plantations your father had, but I've already cultivated an area bigger than anything he had in his heyday.

HELOISE: Ten years ago . . . A bag of coffee was at two hundred thousand réis!

ABELARD I: We have, in fact, come to a critical point at which small farms may predominate in both appearance and number. But never as a financial power. Within capitalism, small property will meet the same fate as the single stock has in corporations. The owner of one is an economic myth. My dear fiancée, the concentration of capital is a phenomenon I can feel with my own two hands. Under the law of competition, the strong will forever eat the weak. The large landed estates of São Paulo are being reconfigured right now under new ownership.

HELOISE: That's some swell work you do!

ABELARD I: Don't be ironic about your own happiness! We both know that thousands of workers toil from dawn till dusk so that we can carouse and live in comfort. With a hoe in their calloused and dirty hands. But I bear as much guilt for that as a well-placed slot machine does for filling up with coins everyday. That's just the way our society is. The capitalist regime protected by God . . .

HELOISE: And you fear nothing?

ABELARD I: The English and the Americans fear for us. We're tied to their destiny. We owe everything, what we have and what we don't have. We've mortgaged palm trees . . . waterfalls. Our cardinals!

HELOISE: I read in a newspaper that we owe three hundred million pounds to England alone, but that only thirty million actually ever made it over here . . .

ABELARD I: It's not unlikely! But a commitment is a commitment! Inferior countries must work for superior countries just as the poor must work for the rich. Do you think New York would have those liv-

ing Babels of skyscrapers and the twenty thousand prettiest legs on the planet if everyone from Ribeirão Preto to Singapore and from Manaus to Liberia didn't work for Wall Street? I know I'm just a simple overseer of foreign capital. A lackey, if you will! But I don't complain. That's the reason I have a motorboat, an island, and you . . .

(Plus ABELARD II)

ABELARD II: *(Entering)* Pardon me! The American is here! . . . *(Exits)*

(Minus ABELARD II)

ABELARD I: *(To HELOISE)* It's time for you to go, my darling!

HELOISE: Why?

ABELARD I: I owe the man . . .

HELOISE: Good-bye!

ABELARD I: You can go through this door! It won't hurt for him to see you leaving . . . *(Evasive gesture from HELOISE)* On the contrary. You look lovely . . .

HELOISE: Okay, good-bye!

ABELARD I: He'll ask me who you are . . . *(HELOISE exits. Alone, in the middle of the stage, ABELARD bows down to the ground before the open door.)* Please be so kind as to come in, Mr. Jones. Welcome back!

CURTAIN

ACT TWO

A tropical island in Guanabara Bay, Rio de Janeiro. Throughout the act, birds sing exotically in the brutal trees. Sounds of a motor. The sea. On one side of the beach, a plane at rest. Tent. Beach umbrellas. A flag pole flying an American flag. Palm trees. The stage represents a terrace. Stairs at the rear lead to the sand. A steel-blue railing with green and brightly colored cacti in black vases. Mechanical furniture. Drinks and ice. A hammock from the Amazon. A radio. The characters are dressed to reflect the most ardently equatorial bourgeois fantasy. Half-naked brunettes. Sportive men. Hermaphrodites, menopausals.

With the curtain still closed, the live sound of a bugle is heard. The stage remains empty for a moment as the curtain rises. The sound of an approaching motorboat is heard.

By the stairs at the rear, in openly sexual comaraderie, enter HELOISE and the AMERICAN. They exit stage right. After them, TOTO PASSION FRUIT, glum. He exits. Immediately following him, MISS POLOCA and JOHN OF THE DIVANS. They exit. After them, the old COLONEL BELARMINO, smoking a hand-rolled coffin nail and rigorously dressed as a golfer. He exits. Following him, a couple bursting with life: MRS. CESARINA, fanning herself with an enormous feathered fan and wearing a Copacabana bathing suit, and ABELARD I in egg-yolk-colored trousers and an athletic shirt. They remain onstage.

(ABELARD I and MRS. CESARINA)

ABELARD I: Here we are! We've arrived. (*Deposits her in the hammock*) A motorboat is approaching. It must be Spittle, your son. In Europe they do it that way. They sound a bugle every time a motorboat arrives! The American flag is an homage. It indicates that an Admiral is on board! Our guest, the American . . .

MRS. CESARINA: So it is. I told Belarmino. Never in my life have I eaten ice cream like that! Delicious! Only a rich and distinguished future son-in-law such as yourself could offer me such ice cream. What do you call it?

ABELARD I: Banana Royale!

MRS. CESARINA: Toto was licking it up! Poor thing! He's so upset . . .

ABELARD I: It's true! Toto is heartbroken! But he'll straighten himself out, eating Banana Royale!

MRS. CESARINA: Just think. Ending a three-year friendship. They were like brothers . . . He and Godofredo lived in the same room. It's because of such things that I don't like to delude myself. Your gallantries . . .

ABELARD I: My gallantries are sincere . . . my dear future mother-in-law . . . Who told you to dress like that, in that slithery bathing suit! Not even a saint could resist! See, my gallantries are serious, all too serious!

MRS. CESARINA: You want to make me even angrier . . . Even sadder than yesterday. Are you going to continue to misbehave?

ABELARD I: But Mrs. Cesarina! Believe me! Please!

MRS. CESARINA: Liar!

ABELARD I: Is it my fault that I'm weak? That I have feelings?

MRS. CESARINA: That's not it . . .

ABELARD I: But then what is it . . .

MRS. CESARINA: I have a sense of foreboding . . . A fear of being misunderstood!

ABELARD I: But what's wrong? Why don't you smile anymore and emit that fragrance of withered roses? Pretend to be a cemetery amongst cypresses!

MRS. CESARINA: That's where I'll end up because of you . . .

ABELARD I: I give unto Caesar what is Caesar's. Or better yet, unto Cesarina what is Cesarina's.

MRS. CESARINA: You're just putting on a show! Tell me one thing. Why do you lie so much, hmm? And tempt me so!

ABELARD I: I swear!

MRS. CESARINA: You know I can't drink champagne. The other night, when we danced that foxtrot, you got me soused, and then you started with all that tomfoolery and immorality. Don't you know that God doesn't like us to say things we don't mean? That it's a mortal sin to covet thy neighbor's wife? You're headed straight for hell . . .

ABELARD I: No. I already know I'm going to purgatory . . .

MRS. CESARINA: We should never say things we don't mean. It's horrible to be deceived!

ABELARD I: And if it were true? If my heart were aflame with the contagion of your luminous summer?

MRS. CESARINA: Well now, only I know exactly how old I am!

ABELARD I: My Vesuvius!

MRS. CESARINA: (*Laughing and threatening him*) Watch out, I'm still smoldering . . .

(*Plus TOTO*)

TOTO PASSION FRUIT: (*Appears stage right, with a fishing rod and a bag of bonbons in his hand, rapt and sorrowful*) I'm a failure!

MRS. CESARINA: Come here, my little boy. My heart's little love!

TOTO: I don't want to. (*Stamping his foot*) I don't want to. Leave me alone!

MRS. CESARINA: But come here, Toto. Come talk to your mummy! When was the last time you gave me a kiss?

TOTO: I won't, I won't, I won't!

MRS. CESARINA: What are you going to do?

TOTO: Can't you see? Go fishing on the cliff. It's my destiny!

ABELARD I: Be careful on this beach! It's got the darnedest catfish!

TOTO: May God hear you! (*Approaches and fawns over ABELARD I*) My future brother-in-law. What a lovely complexion! How old are you, eh? Do you know about the latest fashion in gloves? I'm off now to feed bonbons to the catfish. Want some?

ABELARD I: Eh! No thanks, my friend. I don't like those fish. Or bonbons either! What a family!

MRS. CESARINA: Give me a little kiss, Toto!

TOTO: (*Exiting by the stairs in the rear*) No, I won't! I won't! I won't!

(*Minus TOTO*)

MRS. CESARINA: Oh! Poor dear! Ever since he and Godofredo argued he's like a different person . . . Thin. Fussy.

ABELARD I: I understand. Breakups are painful . . . (*Picking up the fan from the table*) What a beautiful fan . . .

MRS. CESARINA: (*Silence. Takes the fan from him. Mute scene*) Give me the fan that guards those fervent words of yours from the dance party . . . like a safe . . .

ABELARD I: That guards the most terrible and secret of all confessions . . .

MRS. CESARINA: Tell me something, Mr. Abelard, aren't you jealous?

ABELARD I: (*Surprised*) Say what!

MRS. CESARINA: That German!

ABELARD I: German? American. An American, and a banker!

MRS. CESARINA: He's been playing quite rough with Heloise!

ABELARD I: Ah! The boxing. She's learning to box. Every once in a while he shows her a few wrestling moves . . . He's a champion of that kind of stuff on Wall Street!

MRS. CESARINA: Well now, listen, Mr. Abelard. It would tear me to pieces if someone I loved took such liberties with a stranger.

ABELARD I: But Mrs. Cesarina! I pride myself on being a man of my time! You want me to waste my time with jealousy? (*Dramatically imitates a couple fighting*) Tell me, Heloise! Who was that man?—I only went to deliver a message.—You went there! You confess! You went to that house, that den of vice! You betrayed me, you've perjured yourself!—Oh! My love, such distrust, what an injustice! An ugly man like that! I only went there on account of the message!—Accursed woman! Bang! Bang! (*He laughs.*) Oh! Oh! Ah! Is that it? That nonsense that entertained and stained generations of idiots with blood. That's it . . . Jealousy!

MRS. CESARINA: Well, you might not have any shame, Mr. Abelard, but I do! Look at this fan! This fan can still do a lot of damage! (*Gets out of the hammock*)

ABELARD I: I understand! It's Lady Windermere's fan!

MRS. CESARINA: Mr. Abelard, don't look at me that way! I'm bound by the sweetest of all sacraments to the most dignified of all spouses. No! Never! The life of a wife must be one of renunciation, sacrifice, purification! As painful as it may be . . .

(*Plus MISS POLOCA*)[11]

MISS POLOCA: (*Appearing at the top of the stairs*) Over there, hmm? What a lovely pair . . .

MRS. CESARINA: Excuse me. I'm going to go tell them to serve the *rabigalos*—the rooster tails.

ABELARD I: *Rabigalos?*

MRS. CESARINA: It's the official Portuguese translation of "cocktail," coined by the Academy of Letters![12] (*She exits.*)

(*Minus MRS. CESARINA*)

MISS POLOCA: (*She draws near.*) Flirting with your mother-in-law!

ABELARD I: What's this, Miss Poloca? Are you playing special police now?

MISS POLOCA: I heard every word!

ABELARD I: Well you heard wrong. I was very respectfully explaining to my mother-to-be that we belong to two different generations. She is a character of the witty Oscar Wilde. I'm a Freudian character!

MISS POLOCA: What?

ABELARD I: Aren't you familiar with Freud? The last great novelist of the bourgeoisie?

MISS POLOCA: Would you lend me his novels? Are they innocent?

ABELARD I: Oh! Yes. Haven't you heard of the *Oedipus Complex?* That's my case!

MISS POLOCA: What about me, Mr. Abelard? Of which writer am I a character?

ABELARD I: You, ma'am, are a collaborative creation . . . of Castilho and Lamartine Babo![13] (*Humming*) Heh! You think I don't know?

MISS POLOCA: (*Indignant*) Well *you* are that gentleman from *The Bells of Corneville!*[14]

ABELARD I: Correct! Why do you have to be so nice when we're alone? And so vile when we're with other people?

MISS POLOCA: But how do you expect me to behave in society?

ABELARD I: I want you to behave like a human being.

MISS POLOCA: And since when is humanity a piece of marmalade, Mr. Abelard? Do I defend my convictions regarding family and tradition? Intransigently. I'm your best friend (*affectionately*) in secret. But I can't be friendly in public with a nouveau riche, a social climber, a Candle King!

ABELARD I: And if I made you Queen of the Candlestick?

MISS POLOCA: I prefer being the granddaughter of the Baroness Pau-Ferro. The poor and invalid granddaughter who has always lived off her brothers' bread and whose family was saved by . . . by an intruder!

ABELARD I: By an intruder . . .

MISS POLOCA: Who rescued us from ruin but who must remain aware of the social distinctions that separate us. I'm sixty-two years old. I saw the few families that are still left from the Empire degrade themselves with inferior alliances. Like my brother who married that hussy! I know it's the fate of my people. Still, I resist and stand firmly opposed to the facile and equivocal relationships of modern society.

ABELARD I: Tell me something, Miss Poloca, if it weren't for that profligacy . . . Pardon the expression . . . It's like something out of Flaubert!

MISS POLOCA: Say "decadence." It sounds better!

ABELARD I: Fine! If it weren't for that "decadence." It really is, it's softer. But how would you, if you'll allow me the expression, eat . . .

MISS POLOCA: Mr. Abelard, one doesn't live on food alone!

ABELARD I: On that point I profoundly disagree with Your Majesty! We shall never see eye to eye. You live on air . . . And I on steak.

MISS POLOCA: You're bourgeois! I'm a noblewoman who had the great fortune of kissing Her Royal Highness Princess Isabel's hands, do you hear me?[15]

ABELARD I: But tell me just one thing, Miss Polaquinha, pardon me, Miss Poloquinha.[16] In your entire life, a life so full of nobility, did you never once love a commoner?

MISS POLOCA: (*Daintily*) In secret. But never in public

like that pleasure-loving woman that God gave me for a sister-in-law!

(Plus HELOISE and JOHN [JOAN])

HELOISE: Another flirtation! Yesterday it was Mum! Today Aunt Poloca. How many times an hour do you make a cuckold of me, Abelard?

ABELARD I: It's all in the family. *(They sit, laughing.)* It doesn't count!

HELOISE: Just so long as you don't betray me with Toto!

JOHN: Toto is my difference. He's already hitting on the American! All I have to do is make a move on someone, and he comes running! I'm a failure!

ABELARD I: The poor guy! Give him a break . . . He's heartbroken!

JOHN: That other time too, in São Paulo, after he argued with Godofredo. He was ill with sorrow! And even so he stole Big Miguel away from me! The bandit!

ABELARD I: But the American, from what I've seen, has a thing for Heloise's masculine type. Mister Jones is a lesbian!

JOHN: The American has eyes for the chauffeur. Luckily! Look who's coming . . . The Colonel.

HELOISE: Daddy!

JOHN: He looks like Clark Gable!

MISS POLOCA: That Carnival outfit is restoring my brother's youth!

(Plus BELARMINO)

BELARMINO: I continue to take delight in the landscape that this enchanted island unveils. A truly paradisiacal island. Moreover, Rio de Janeiro may be the most beautiful city in the world! It must be! What a bay. The most beautiful bay in the world! Not even Constantinople, not even Naples, not even Lisbon can compare!

ABELARD I: Indeed, Colonel.

BELARMINO: Over there, up top, the Corcovado mountain with its open-armed Christ. It comforts me to see Rio de Janeiro at the foot of the cross! Brazil is truly a blessed land. We even have a Cardinal. All we're missing is a Mortgage Bank!

ABELARD I: Albeit, in my opinion, Christ should be a bit closer to us. To exercise control. To hear our complaints. He's a long way away . . . up there . . .

HELOISE: Where then, Abelard?

JOHN: Where?

ABELARD I: In a picturesque spot, down here. Close. At Saco de São Francisco, for instance . . .

BELARMINO: A very good thought! At the Saco de São Francisco inlet. And alongside it a Mortgage Bank.

ABELARD I: What for? We don't have anything else to mortgage . . .

BELARMINO: It's true that we're already in a great deal of debt.

ABELARD I: Stripped naked . . . Colonel. As in the era of the Discovery . . .

BELARMINO: But tell me something, Mr. Abelard, why can't we pay our debts with coffee? We have debts. And we burn coffee.[17] It's a mystery! Wouldn't you agree?

ABELARD I: Indeed, my future father-in-law! Coffee is gold. Black gold! We're in debt and we burn gold! I'll ask Mr. Jones . . . We're at the end of our rope. Headed for the grave.

BELARMINO: A Mortgage Bank, my future son-in-law, would solve the crisis. But it would have to be a strong bank . . .

ABELARD I: An American bank . . . or an English one.

BELARMINO: Exactly. After the Empire fell apart in the inept hands of the people from Itú,[18] we needed foreign capital. Loans . . .

ABELARD I: And paper currency . . .

BELARMINO: Paper currency too. I'm not against issuing paper currency, Mr. Abelard! But you know what the people need. Peace and calm, so they can work. Obviously. Give them peace and calm and a Mortgage Bank and you'll see the results . . .

ABELARD I: Our own national banks could transform themselves . . . The mortgage portfolio of any one of them!

BELARMINO: They're ruined, my friend! Ruined! Can't support the old clients. An upstanding man can't get so much as a nickel out of them! If it wasn't for your uncommon nobility, pulling me out of the predicament I was in, with that loan . . . granted on the basis of purely moral collateral! *(He pulls out an enormous red handkerchief and wipes his eyes and his beard.)*

HELOISE: Oh Daddy!

ABELARD I: Really, there's no need . . . *(Consternation)*

HELOISE: Daddy . . .

BELARMINO: My daughter, when you get married, I want you to pray. And to be the mother of the poor, the protectress of the unfortunate . . .

HELOISE: I promise, Daddy! Where are you going now?

BELARMINO: Wandering, my daughter!

MISS POLOCA: Wandering, life on board is but wandering! That's a verse by Dom Pedro II![19]

ABELARD I: Yes, yes! We're all on board.

BELARMINO: *(Declaiming as he leaves)* What are the young men doing? What are the young men doing?

(Minus BELARMINO)

MISS POLOCA: The young men are all like you . . . atheists! Freemasons, do you hear me? And that Englishman . . . with the chauffeur!

ABELARD I: What became of the American?

JOHN: He probably fell into a glass of whiskey!

ABELARD I: I'll go save him. So long! *(Exits to the right)*

(Minus ABELARD I)

HELOISE: Aunt Poloca sure is full of talk today!

MISS POLOCA: I won't say anything more, because I live off other people's bread. But in my day, we were more discriminating. We didn't marry adventurers just because they were rich and had been to the United States.

JOHN: That's why you're still a virgin!

HELOISE: At the age of sixty-three!

JOHN: She already turned sixty-nine!

MISS POLOCA: Young lady! I'll call your father! Go do something innocent, go on! Go watch the sunset! Go leaf through the family photo album that I brought! Maybe the portraits of your grandparents will teach you some shame! Go see if Spittle has arrived all dressed up in his soldier's outfit. Magnificent!

JOHN: That indecent fascist!

MISS POLOCA: He's the only one of the family who's worth anything!

HELOISE: Don't pester Auntie. Go on! You little beast!

JOHN: Is it my fault she's hardheaded?

MISS POLOCA: In my time, girls were proper. They went to novenas. They recited the rosary. Today the devil rules!

JOHN: The devil is the most enchanting man in the world. The Candle Man . . . Heloise's Candle Man.

HELOISE: The Candle King. Give me a cigarette, Auntie.

JOHN: Either way. It's his candle that saved us.

MISS POLOCA: *(Smokes with HELOISE)* I don't like that man one bit. He doesn't fear God. I can even see him refusing to get married in the Church. But Spittle will make him do it. That nephew of mine is worth something! He taught me how to inhale.

HELOISE: He'll do it! He's changing. He told me today that he'll marry me in the Church too. The Cardinal will come out to the island . . . It's an honor! An event!

MISS POLOCA: Fine. But he doesn't have family.

JOHN: And we have too much. I'd be out of luck, if it wasn't for him . . . After Toto stole Big Miguel from me!

MISS POLOCA: That indecent Turk!

JOHN: A very good catch. A palace on Paulista Avenue! A car! Big bucks!

MISS POLOCA: But he's an assassin!

HELOISE: He is, John! He stabbed his brother eighteen times . . .

JOHN: But the jury acquitted him. Temporary loss of sanity.

HELOISE: And of intelligence.

JOHN: That's his normal state. But if Toto hadn't showed up he would've fallen for me. He would've given me such a life! Toto is a bandit! He stole the Turk from me!

HELOISE: Those amphibians!

JOHN: They're all bastards! If it weren't for your king I'd still be squandering my preparatory school French in apartments and hotels. Cruising around in cars, trying to outhustle the *midinettes* . . . A bunch of tramps . . . harlots . . .

HELOISE: I ran into Mag on the Avenue, in a dazzling getup. Who would've thought? That little milliner from Boa Vista Street. A hot pink dress! Crazy!

MISS POLOCA: Did Mrs. Etelvina write?

HELOISE: She sent a telegram. She's coming tomorrow with the guests. Bringing her cold feet! A romantic, that one. What can I say, Abelard wants people with a pedigree . . .

MISS POLOCA: My social connections have always been better than yours . . .

JOHN: Another virgin! She's the one who takes x-rays of her intestines along when she travels, looking for medical celebrities to consult!

HELOISE: It's true.

JOHN: *(Gnawing on her thumbnail)* Mademoiselle Tubing!

HELOISE: Mrs. Lea is also coming tomorrow . . . Madame La Baroness de Machadô!

MISS POLOCA: That *polaca*, here! A prostitute! The shame!

JOHN: Not po-LACA, Auntie Poloca, she's Po-LISH. And very distinguished! Décio was a victim of his own ignorance of geography. He married her by mistake.

HELOISE: What do you mean, John?

JOHN: At that time, ladies of pleasure were all French. He married her thinking she was a French woman from Paris. But she'd never even been to Marseilles!

HELOISE: Migdal has other ports! But the important thing is that today she's a pillar of society. A philanthropist. She goes to Mass every day . . .

JOHN: She's got ducats! *(Begins furiously gnawing on her thumbnail)*

HELOISE: She's part of the Women's Electoral Convention . . . She may even be elected a representative of the Catholic party . . .

MISS POLOCA: John, stop irritating me with that nail. *(Takes JOHN by the arm)*

JOHN: Leave me alone! Ouch!

(Plus ABELARD I and the AMERICAN)[20]

ABELARD I: What kind of Roman wrestling match is this?

JOHN: *(Struggling)* It's that pigheaded auntie of mine, who doesn't want to allow me a single vice . . .

MISS POLOCA: Shut your mouth! In my time, girls only spoke after the age of eighteen!

JOHN: My eye. I'm John of the Divans. Isn't that right, Mister John? John and John! A new brand of whiskey.

AMERICAN: Yes, darling! Glorious day!

ABELARD I: Do you really enjoy biting your nail?

JOHN: *(Skipping around, fascinated)* Mmm! It's marvelous! *(She continues chewing.)*

MISS POLOCA: She even lets the nail grow, just so she can spend hours biting it . . .

ABELARD I: I knew a woman who started off that way and ended up chewing on a balustrade!

JOHN: (*Hysterical*) It must be divine! Must taste like a nail! I'm going to try it!

HELOISE: (*Caressing the AMERICAN's arm*) So, Jones. How are Abelard's businesses doing?

AMERICAN: Finances dominate world. Abelard has good nose . . . He will jump . . .

ABELARD I: Into the abyss . . .

HELOISE: Of my arms! Tell me something, Jones, why doesn't Brazil pay its debts with all the coffee it's burning?

AMERICAN: Brazil need airplanes . . . Machine guns . . . Lots . . .

HELOISE: But what for?

AMERICAN: Trade for coffee . . . Oh! Good Business! Shut up!

ABELARD I: It's true! War! We need to arm ourselves for war . . .

HELOISE: But against whom?

ABELARD I: Against anyone! Any war! External or internal. We need to give the unemployed something to do. Distract the people. And trade coffee for the arms that are overstocked abroad. The leftovers from the arms race. Don't you see? Or against Russia! Russia is pestering the whole world!

JOHN: (*She turns on the radio. A waltz by Strauss softens the ambience.*) What a drag! It's always Strauss! Well! (*Turns to another station. The radio squeaks. ABELARD intervenes.*)

ABELARD I: No. Let Strauss play! It's adultery! The purest voice of adultery . . . Listen! (*Turns the dial*)

HELOISE: The Great War ended with all those refugees . . .

JOHN: I'd prefer a foxtrot . . .

AMERICAN: A fox dance. Waltz is sad!

JOHN: Hullo, Jones! (*She changes the station and exits to the sound of a foxtrot, glued to the AMERICAN's arm.*) So long for now! I'm off to see the peaks of Itatiaia.[21]

AMERICAN: (*Laughing*) Everest! Everest!

(*Minus the AMERICAN and JOHN*)

MISS POLOCA: (*Scandalized*) The little trollop! Crisis Girl! (*Silence*) I'm going to change into my bathing suit. Cool myself off from these hot flashes! Are you coming, Heloise? (*Exits*)

HELOISE: In a minute, Auntie . . .

(*Minus MISS POLOCA.*

Screams are heard coming from back stage. TOTO PASSION FRUIT appears on the stairs. He doesn't have anything in his hands.

Plus TOTO)

ABELARD I: What happened?

HELOISE: Toto . . . What happened?

TOTO: A huge fish. He took the fishing rod and the bonbons from me. He took everything . . . It must've been a shark.

ABELARD I: No. It was most definitely a swordfish. How excited you got! Such palpitations . . .

TOTO: Most definitely!

ABELARD I: I thought you were used to these fishing expeditions . . .

HELOISE: Wait. I'll be right back. (*Exits to the left*) I'm going to change.

(*Minus HELOISE*)

TOTO: (*Throwing himself into a chair*) I've been fishing incessantly for three days. Sorrow, Mr. Abelard!

ABELARD I: A broken heart . . .

TOTO: Just imagine! Godofredo! Balling me up!

ABELARD I: That's part of life. You'll feel better, you'll forget!

TOTO: Never! I can't forget.

ABELARD I: Now now, time is the best remedy . . .

TOTO: It's no use. It was a very serious affair. After all my devotion! Three years! It was very serious!

ABELARD I: Quite serious! But everything passes. *Tout passe, tout casse* . . .

TOTO: If it wasn't for that little detail! Imagine, I told Godofredo: You can betray me with any woman. Any, huh? But that one I won't allow! And it was with that exact one! I have proof!

ABELARD I: Very well. But nature is full of imperatives . . .

TOTO: And what about good breeding, Mr. Abelard? What about conventions, social prejudices, differences of origin and class . . . Everything that makes the world delicious. (*He moans.*) To betray me with a whore from the Red Light District!

ABELARD I: From the Red Light District?

TOTO: From the Red Light District, yes. It was a cataclysm. I'm a failure! (*Stands up*) The fish assault me, the ocean unnerves me, the landscape incapacitates me. I'm going to my room . . . okay? (*Exits*)

(*Minus TOTO*)

ABELARD I: Run along . . . Ophelia . . . Get thee to a nunnery! (*Turns the radio off*) Next it'll be the other one, the one who arrived in the motorboat. The boozer. He's coming to ask for money. More money! I spent my whole life extracting the flesh, blood, and bones of half the world just to end up being exploited . . . by a colonial fascist!

(*ABELARD I and SPITTLE.[22]*

SPITTLE enters, clicks his heels and gives a cabalistic military salute. ABELARD sits without responding.)

SPITTLE: Glory!

ABELARD I: What do you want from me?

SPITTLE: (*Straddles the chair as if it were a horse. Takes out a cigarette. Offers it. Smokes*) I want to make a business proposition . . .

ABELARD I: Another one? Can't you go knock on someone else's door?

SPITTLE: It's a transaction that will interest you . . .

(*Silence*)

ABELARD I: You're a lush!

SPITTLE: Who are you to call me that?

ABELARD I: A man who fed your starving family! Before I've even become a part of it!

SPITTLE: Cur!

ABELARD I: You're insulting me?

SPITTLE: That's how I do things! On the plantation I still use the whip . . .

ABELARD I: Not with me, you don't. Insult and mistreat those who work . . . Those who gave you the beautiful clothes you wear while you're losing rivers of money at the Jockey Club or the Automobile Club . . . Happily that's all over, my friend . . .

SPITTLE: *(Cynical)* I don't gamble anymore!

ABELARD I: Because you have no money. Now you drink. I know that the plantation was a complete mess for an entire week! Because you, who are supposed to be overseeing it in your father's name, were going on twenty-four-hour benders with the administrator at the Big House. You were found half dead in a pool of vomit. You know, one day the plantation workers will erect a statue made of vomit in your honor. Right after they hang you . . .

SPITTLE: *(Calm)* And then they'll go to the towns and capital cities . . . to erect identical statues to usurers.

ABELARD I: Wretch!

SPITTLE: Thief!

ABELARD I: Tell me what you want!

(Silence)

SPITTLE: I've noticed a growing sense of dissatisfaction among the workers on the plantation and on some of the neighboring properties. They're getting hard to please.

ABELARD I: Naturally . . . They've always been hard to please . . .

SPITTLE: They're becoming insolent, rude, even. And there's only one remedy. We need to punish them and spread fear. I have old friends, almost all of them unemployed . . . People who are willing . . . who know how to fight . . .

ABELARD I: I see! The noctambulating scum of São Paulo, the winos at the bars, the cardsharks from the casinos, the gigolos in the brothels . . .

SPITTLE: They all come from excellent families . . .

ABELARD I: Like you!

SPITTLE: I have a project. To give them employment. Put them to use.

ABELARD I: What use can that riffraff have?

SPITTLE: A brown shirt is all they need! Guns, ammunition, and . . .

ABELARD I: Money!

SPITTLE: All joking aside. The situation demands it. Let's organize a patriotic militia. What do you think? We'll set ourselves up temporarily at the Big House. We'll join forces with the other plantation owners. We'll enlist people, the thugs are always ready . . . It'll be our headquarters. And if the workers make so much as a peep . . .

ABELARD I: It'll be a massacre . . . Familiar tactics!

SPITTLE: Of course. The buzzards will get fat! And peace will reign once again on the old plantation!

ABELARD I: *(After a silence)* How much do you want?

SPITTLE: Ten contos!

ABELARD I: I know you're going to gamble that money away. Make one last bet. Parasite! *(He thinks.)* Still, your idea isn't bad. It must not be yours. As a matter of fact, it's a copy of what's being done in the capitalist countries in despair! *(Writes out a check)* Here! If the militia isn't organized within a week, I'll have you thrown in jail!

SPITTLE: For being a friend?

ABELARD I: No, for forging my signature on a check for thirteen contos that was cashed by Pereira & Brothers. Embarrassing me with that absurd amount! But I've already taken measures.

SPITTLE: You knew about that too?

ABELARD I: Would you like me to give you more details about your life?

SPITTLE: *(Referring to the check, to which he points as he leaves)* No! This is enough for today.

(Minus SPITTLE)

ABELARD I: Reprobates! Scum! First there's Toto Passion Fruit! Then this dangerous drunkard! Now he's turned fascist. My sister-in-law came to sit on my lap wearing a bathing suit so I could scratch her rear end . . . with checks, naturally. The fallen mother-in-law . . . The other hag . . . And it's me who should feel honored . . . by being allowed to become part of such a dignified and exceptional family.

(Plus HELOISE)

HELOISE: *(Enters in a bathing suit)* Aren't you going to the beach? They're all ready.

ABELARD I: I'm not going! I've got a bit of a headache. I'd rather rest. Take that blasted American . . . My dear, I'm starting to realize that I busted my rump for ten years, just to have a bunch of pirates play yo-yo with my money!

HELOISE: You're having misgivings? Don't I bring you social advantages? Physical advantages? Political . . . and business . . . advantages . . .

ABELARD I: It's just that sometimes, all of a sudden, I lose confidence. It's as if the ground went from under me. I know you have good connections. Tomorrow we'll have a dinner where we'll fraternize under the stars of the Yankee pavilion. Even the most degenerate of your siblings will be useful to me.

HELOISE: The Little Fruit?

ABELARD I: The other one, for the time being. The drunk. He's going to found the first fascist rural militia of São Paulo. You know who'll be thrilled about this, it's that Cristiano Bensaúde . . . the writer . . . you know. He's coming tomorrow.

HELOISE: The guy you called an angelic sociologist,

the one you were going to have a new samba written for—*The Fasting Pirate* samba?

ABELARD I: (*Laughing*) Yep. Difficult times force a person to make concessions. Besides, the American wants unity—of religious beliefs, political parties . . . We need to justify, before the distrustful eyes of the people, the idleness of an entire class. Nothing better than Christian doctrine for that . . .

HELOISE: What? So that's what you've come to?

ABELARD I: Catholicism declares that this life is but a passage. Which means that those who have had it rough, working for others, should resign themselves. They'll eat in heaven . . .

HELOISE: And the others?

ABELARD I: The others don't need to believe. They can even subscribe to yo-yo skepticism. Life is an eternal coming and going . . . a yo-yo . . .

HELOISE: And when the yo-yo gets tangled?

ABELARD I: Then we have to appeal to Schopenhauer. And we immediately adopt the philosophy of the bullet in the head . . . It must hurt, no? The world is misery. Like God, it doesn't exist anymore. There's only one remedy. The leap into Nirvana.

HELOISE: That's why you annihilated yourself in me . . .

ABELARD I: Indeed, my life got tangled up in yours, Heloise. At a grave moment, when it's necessary to fight and conquer. Without mercy. In a fascist manner, even. I'm going to make alliances with Spittle and Bensaúde. They're useful.

HELOISE: You told me that couldn't happen here.

ABELARD I: I've studied the matter more carefully. We're part of a whole that's being threatened—the capitalist world. If the imperialist bankers want . . . You know, there comes a moment when the bourgeoisie abandons its old liberal mask. It announces that it's tired of shouldering humanity's ideals of justice, the conquests of civilization, and all the other bullshit! It organizes itself as a class. Like a police force. That moment has already arrived in Italy and it's building little by little in countries where the proletariat is weak or divided . . .

HELOISE: Well then I'm going to go ride some waves with the American.

ABELARD I: Go! He's Our Lord God of the Moolah . . . Play away, my dear.

(*HELOISE exits stage left. Behind her, calling after her, appearing stage right in a turn-of-the-century bathing suit that goes down to her shins, MISS POLOCA.*
Minus HELOISE, plus MISS POLOCA)

MISS POLOCA: Heloise! Heloise!

ABELARD I: (*Blocking her path*) Alone again! You know! I respect you because you're the pure past! That doesn't relax! The core! The coooore!

MISS POLOCA: (*Pleased*) Flatterer!

ABELARD I: (*After a silence*) Tell me, Aunt Thing! Tell me seriously, if you had a million dollars, what would you do?

MISS POLOCA: Well now! Fabulist!

ABELARD I: Tell me. I need to know. I want to know! For example, if I were to blow my brains out and leave everything I own to you . . .

MISS POLOCA: Are you trying to make a fool of me? You won't do it!

ABELARD I: No. I really want to know. Tell me. What is your fantasy? What would you do if you inherited a million?

MISS POLOCA: I'd go to Petrópolis.[23]

ABELARD I: (*Kneeling down*) Allow me to kiss your feet! Little saint! The bathing suit, at least! (*Gets up*) Well, listen, it shall be with me. I'll give you a trip to Petrópolis! We'll take the motorboat, just the two of us. We'll plow the Bay. We'll have dinner in Rio at a grand restaurant. But at night . . . At night . . .

MISS POLOCA: A night of love! At this age!

ABELARD I: The first night! . . . Tell me you accept.

MISS POLOCA: Careful now, I'm not made of steel!

ABELARD I: I'll give orders to prepare the motorboat . . . And some little snacks.

MISS POLOCA: Some pralines! Hussshhh!

ABELARD I: Hush! (*Exiting stage right. Blows a kiss . . . two kisses . . .*) Under the moonlight! Tonight!

CURTAIN

ACT THREE

The same set as Act One, at night. The stage is cluttered with junk repossessed from a health clinic. A stretcher on the floor. A wheelchair. A radio on top of a small table. The evening light enters through the large window. HELOISE wails, clasping ABELARD I's legs.

HELOISE: (*Sitting on the stretcher*) What a disgrace, my darling! What a pity! What a pity!

ABELARD I: I'd rather be frank . . . Heloise. You know why we were getting married . . . It wasn't to form a perfect tableau of domestic bliss, that's for sure . . .

HELOISE: What a pity! My God!

ABELARD I: You'll have to look for another broker . . . You know . . . We were marrying so that you'd be at the American's disposal. But I'm of no use to that imperialist operation anymore. Your body isn't worth anything in the hands of a ruined broker who'll be sent to jail tomorrow . . . Or assassinated by the depositors. This unexpected bankruptcy is going to unmask me . . .

HELOISE: How dreadful! I don't want you to go to jail!

ABELARD I: There's no danger. I won't go. (*Takes a revolver from his pocket, covertly*)

HELOISE: And me, what happens to me? Destitute once again. I don't know how to work, I don't know how to do anything. And my family . . . I'll end up dancing at the Moulin Bleu . . .

ABELARD I: (*Consoling her*) That won't be necessary, my love. You'll marry the thief . . .

HELOISE: (*She continues to whimper and remains weepy and sobbing throughout the entire act.*) Which one? I've already asked!

ABELARD I: The last one, the one who made the final move in this dark game in which I was defeated. . . .

HELOISE: The American doesn't want to marry me . . .

ABELARD I: But the other one will. He's a thief from an old comedy . . . With all the residue of the old theater. Didn't I tell you, we're in a backward country! Look, he stole all the checks made out to cash. He did a magnificent job. But see, he busted the lamp . . . pried open the desk . . . He left his fingerprints all over. Why? If he'd stolen the key to the safe? He's an old-fashioned thief. He'll accept marriage with a ruined noblewoman. For sure!

HELOISE: I know! It's your lion tamer! What a horrid little man, my God! I don't want . . .

ABELARD I: I don't know. Who knows if it isn't Raffles . . . Arsène Lupin, one of those that you like, that you used to love in your adolescence . . . Straight out of Edgar Wallace, eh?[24]

HELOISE: But I like you . . . You can run away . . . Where do you want to go? . . . I'll go too . . . with you . . .

ABELARD I: I'm not going. I'm staying.

HELOISE: (*Spots the revolver and screams*) Put that down, Abelard!

ABELARD I: (*Defending the weapon*) Why, Heloise? The thief who took the money last night left this weapon in its place . . . He gave me a gift . . . The best one he could give . . . He saw that I had no other way out . . .

HELOISE: But my love! (*Gets up and clings to him*) Even if you're ruined. Even if it's true . . . You can still win, and recover . . . You're so intelligent, so active . . .

ABELARD I: So clever! Listen, honey. I was a big pig! Do you know who the bourgeoisie should have built statues to? To bank tellers! Those are the people who are truly colossal! Solid like a rock. Men who resist the temptation of money. Knowing where it goes, what it's used for, where it comes from, the infamy it can cause . . . The ones who resist the call of cold hard cash! In the old days, when the bourgeoisie was still innocent . . . The bourgeoisie was innocent once, it was even revolutionary . . . In the good old days of Romanticism, before cinema invaded the world, people believed in the Call of the Orient, that unfathomable appeal of the mysterious and slow-paced countries, where, at bottom—the cinema later disclosed—there was nothing but palm trees and imperialist exploitation, that's all. In the modern age, for us, the ruling class, there's only one call, my friend—the call of money! I wasn't able to resist the call of money! Being the Candle King, I played at being the Match King. I took possession of everything I could! I gambled all my possibilities on one terrible adventure! I laid my hands on what wasn't mine. I carried my bluff as far as I could! But I was

shamefully defeated by a joker . . . Well then, fine! The Candle King shall not be unworthy of the Match King! . . . (*Brandishes the revolver*)

HELOISE: Abelard. Don't do this crazy thing. Let's start over. We'll run far away from here! Let's . . .

ABELARD I: Begin again . . . a lyrical thatched hut. Like in the days of Romanticism! Solutions outside of life. Solutions inside the theater. Tricks. Never! I have only one solution. I'm a character of my time, ordinary but logical. I'll go on until the end. My end! Death in the Third Act. Schopenhauer! What is life? The philosophy of a desperate, rich class! A diving board over Nirvana! (*Shouts toward the backstage*) Hey! Stage engineer! Close the curtain. For just a minute. It wasn't by chance that I repossessed a health clinic. I ordered everything to be sent here. The stretcher that will carry me away . . . (*He contemplates the spectators in silence.*) Are you there? If you want to witness a stylish agony, just wait! (*Shouts*) I'm going to set my clothes on fire! A national suicide! The Red Light District solution! (*Long hesitation. Finally, he offers the gun to the PROMPTER and addresses him.*) Please, Mr. Cireneu . . . (*Silence. He has been cut loose.*) Take this match away from me . . .

PROMPTER: It's no longer possible!

ABELARD I: What? It's not possible? The author wouldn't care . . . So?

PROMPTER: But the crisis . . . The world situation . . . Imperialism. You can't fool around with foreign capital!

ABELARD I: All right. (*To HELOISE*) You, my funeral flower, give me the final kiss! (*They embrace.*)

(*The curtain closes on the scene. The terrible scream of a woman is heard, followed by a salvo of seven cannon shots. When the curtain rises, HELOISE is lying on the stretcher, sobbing. ABELARD I has fallen into the wheelchair in the middle of the stage. The telephone rings. She sobs. Prolonged silence. The telephone rings insistently.*)

ABELARD I: Don't answer . . . It's the thief. He's calling to see if I'm dead yet. A trick from the cinema. In the theater we don't have any of our own, so he's using this one. He'll come to us. So we can identify him! Look, everyone! (*A noise is heard coming from the right.*) It's him! Shush! Heloise! Stop that crying! (*Absolute silence, the noise increases, persists. Abelard pants and follows it with great interest. Smiles*) The sound of a lock pick! It's him!

(*The door cracks. ABELARD II appears in disguise, with a hood, exaggeratedly dressed as a thief. He has shaved off his lion tamer's moustache. In his hands he carries a flashlight. He is not wearing his monocle. He is almost a gentleman. The same characters, plus ABELARD II.*)

ABELARD I: My alter ego! It was an authentic suicide. Abelard killed Abelard.

ABELARD II: (*Pretending to be taken by surprise, he drops the flashlight, while HELOISE, in the same position, starts again with her interminable sobbing.*) But what happened? What was it? What is all of this? My God. *(Presses the light switch)* A short circuit!

ABELARD I: No. You broke it. Rookie thief! Well done! We'll save on electricity. Last month's bill was too high! Light all the candles! Economic regression. The big corporations are returning to animal-powered carts! We're turning into a humble country. Of wagons and candles! We mortgaged everything to foreign countries, even the landscape! It was the most beautiful country in the world. Now there's not a single cloud that isn't in hock . . . Still, it won't go the route of suicide . . . That's for me to do.

ABELARD II: Why did you do such a crazy thing?

ABELARD I: A man is of no importance . . . Class remains. It resists. The power of spiritualism. Social metempsychosis . . .

ABELARD II: Do you want me to call a doctor?

ABELARD I: What for? To verify that I will live again in you? And that as a result, rich Abelard won't have to pay suicidal Abelard's outstanding bill?

ABELARD II: You can still save yourself. What's going to become of this poor girl . . . Forsaken. *(HELOISE sobs very loudly.)* Do you want a priest? You can still get married . . .

ABELARD I: Why should you marry my widow . . . You're going to have her as a virgin! And all in white . . .

ABELARD II: Virgin! Virgin Heloise! *(HELOISE's sobs diminish.)*

ABELARD I: If the American gives up the right to first dibs . . .

ABELARD II: First dibs?

ABELARD I: Yes, the right to the first night. It's tradition! Relax, you sexual and imaginative petit bourgeois! Don't forget that we're in a semicolonial country. That depends on foreign capital. And that you're taking my place in the national tournament! Tell me, where did you hide the money you made off with?

ABELARD II: What money?

ABELARD I: Our money. The money you withdrew at precisely ten o'clock in the morning. Abelard's money. The money that changes individual hands but always stays in the same class. The money that, through inheritance and robbery, remains in the closed fists of the rich . . . I know you and I identify you, repressed man of Brazil! Product of the climate, of the enslaved economy and the inhuman morality that creates millions of desperate masturbators and pederasts . . . With that sun and those women! . . . Preserving imperialism and the reactionary family. I know you, wild beast on the loose, capable of the worst intentions. Surreptitious fever of the streets of Brazil! Tomorrow, when you come into possession of your fortune, you too will defend the sacred institution of the family, virginity and prudery, so that your money will remain in the line of legitimate sons, in a single class . . .

ABELARD II: I've always defended tradition . . . and morals . . .

ABELARD I: And defend the feudal home too! If you save the plantation from Spittle's militarized claws, preserve the family home. Don't reform a thing! The house was made to hold many servants, a number of maids and old black mammies, recalling the family's roots! And a big cold bedroom for two human beings who detest and betray one another sleeping in the same bed and praying at the same oratory. The old colonial home, a world that endures. Longer than I . . . It was the bullet from the barrel that penetrated deeply, the first one . . . The other bullets encircled the heart! So much pain . . . It's because the heart was left intact . . . The heart, a man's uterus, where we engender our most cherished sons . . . ambition, love, despair, the will to live . . . literature . . . Listen, Abelard! Have you abandoned socialism?

ABELARD II: I'm giving it to you as a gift!

ABELARD I: But I don't accept. Right now I want universal destruction . . . socialism preserves . . .

ABELARD II: You turned Bolshevik! You're all alike . . . When you were the fat-cat millionaire and made loans at fifteen percent a month and I spoke to you of the moderate and humanitarian ideals of socialism, you jeered. You knew everything, read everything, but you laughed . . . And now . . .

ABELARD I: I've always known that only violence is fertile . . . That's why I despised this sham. I even came to prefer Spittle's fascism. But now I want something different . . .

ABELARD II: Communism . . .

ABELARD I: To leave you a poison, at least, mixed in with Heloise and my checks. I leave you both to the American . . . And the American to the communists. How do you like my will?

ABELARD II: You're all alike, you all go over to the other side when you're ruined!

ABELARD I: That's your mistake! If everyone were a cynical opportunist like me, the social revolution would never happen! But fidelity to misery does exist! I'm getting out of the class struggle . . . there's the stretcher where my inert corpse will replace the voluptuous body of Heloise . . . But if I were to recover . . . I'd reenter the arena playing the same position as before. I wouldn't join the cause . . . Maybe I'd change owners . . . I'd go back to working for English imperialism . . .

ABELARD II: Miser!

ABELARD I: . . . Has-been!

ABELARD II: I was your obstacle!

ABELARD I: But your life won't last much beyond the end of this play . . .

ABELARD II: You're killing me?

ABELARD I: What for? Another one would just trump you. We're a barricade of Abelards! One falls, another replaces him, for as long as imperialism and class distinctions exist . . .

ABELARD II: What a guy! Seeing visions at the moment of his death!

ABELARD I: I'm not even a demagogue. This scene is still just one more episode of the same competition. A bourgeois brawl. I want, even after my death, to supplant you in the memory of the woman who will be your wife.

ABELARD II: My wife?

ABELARD I: Just as my brother will be your lawyer! *(Silence)*

ABELARD II: *(Reflecting)* He knows the company system . . .

ABELARD I: We're an avant-garde history. An advanced bourgeoisie . . .

ABELARD II: In a medieval country!

ABELARD I: Cold calculation is our honor. The company system! I won't die as a convert. If I recovered I'd go fight for the money again. I'd be even worse than before. And more cautious. The neurosis of profit! Once you experience it you can never let go. It's the most beautiful position a man can hold on earth! No militancy can compare. No religion. If, in this moment of my death, I look with sympathy upon the masses that will one day emerge from the catacombs of the factories . . . it's because they will take my revenge . . . on you . . . What time is it? Moscow is on the air at this hour. You know! Turn on the radio. Turn it on. Obey! It's the last wish of a dying man of class!

ABELARD II: *(Obeying)* Short wave. Twenty-five, a wave of disrepute. How many times have I heard that . . .

ABELARD I: It's the void beneath our feet, the open abyss . . . catastrophe! *(Silence. The sound of the International is heard.)* The workers' anthem . . .

ABELARD II: The International . . .

(The music ends.)

A VOICE ON THE RADIO: Workers of the world, unite! This is Moscow. Mos . . .

(ABELARD II kicks the radio over and it goes silent.)

ABELARD I: Ah! Ah! Moscow broadcasts into the heart of the oppressed of the whole planet!

ABELARD II: Scum! Demagogue!

ABELARD I: Calm down! You're nothing like Jujuba, except physically. I'm going to tell you the story of Jujuba. He was a simple dog! A stray dog . . . But an idealistic dog! Some soldiers adopted him. He became the battalion's mascot. But Jujuba was a true friend to his street companions! At chow time, he'd show up with two or three other dogs in tow. Before long, the whole filthy, miserable starving pack was filling the barracks yard. One day, the Major put his foot down. But the soldiers opposed the expulsion of its mascot! They took Jujuba up in their arms and shot at the other dogs . . . The pack ran back to the streets. But when the soldiers let Jujuba go, he refused to enjoy the privilege they wanted to grant him. He left to join the others!

ABELARD II: Demagogy!

ABELARD I: No. Jujuba proved that it's not! He never went back to the barracks. He died beaten down and starving like all the others, in the street, in solidarity with his class! In solidarity with his hunger! The soldiers erected a monument to Jujuba in the barracks' yard. They understood his refusal to break faith. They were his brothers. The soldiers and Jujuba belong to the same class. One day they too will leave the barracks in a stampede. There will be a social revolution . . . Those who slumber in doorways will rise up and they will come here, looking for Abelard, the usurer! And they shall find him . . .

ABELARD II: The soldiers are patriots! The soldiers love Brazil. Long live Brazil!

ABELARD I: But Brazil doesn't love its soldiers! How much do they earn a month? To defend those who make twenty contos a week, like the American! And you and I, his lackeys! Before the time of Christ, Tiberius Gracchus used to say of the Roman soldiers: "They call them the lords of the world, but they haven't so much as a rock to lay their heads on!" It's true! I no longer have anything either. I punished myself for betraying my class. I was poor like Jujuba! But I didn't do as Jujuba did . . . I believed that what they call society was a fortress that could only be conquered from within, by someone who penetrates it just as you penetrated my life . . . I did the same thing. I betrayed my hunger . . . *(Silence. The agonizing man's breathing is heard.)*

ABELARD II: Are you feeling better?

ABELARD I: Don't worry. I feel as though I were dreaming about having a brain hemorrhage! . . . A poet once said: "If there is one thing that has exalted mankind, it is the word—freedom!" The struggle for freedom . . . The struggle for money . . . Only money gives you freedom. The freedom to love, kill, lie, rape . . . *(The noise of a car rattling is heard as it passes by.)* Close the window! I don't want to hear those bells! I want to pay everything! On demand!

ABELARD II: What bells?

ABELARD I: I don't want to hear. Close it! I don't want anything for free . . . I won't allow it. The bell comes free . . .

ABELARD II: He's delirious. . . .

(HELOISE sobs again, loudly.)

ABELARD I: I'll pay for everything! The bell is the only thing the church gives away for free! I don't want it! I'll pay for everything! In advance! A mass with my coffin! I don't want bells! Abelard! Open the cage . . .

Whip them! Stop those voices! . . . Open the cage! . . . Open it!

ABELARD II: (Opening the iron door) Right away!

(Silence. Sobbing)

ABELARD I: Stop them from talking. (Listens) What? I'm going to be repossessed? I've turned into an overdue IOU? With no extension? Dogs! Out! Whip them, Abelard!

A VOICE: (Hoarse, terrifying, from the wide-open door that reveals an empty cage) I am the coryphaeus of relapsed debtors! Of delinquent payees! Of those whom capitalist society dishonors! Those whose names have been permanently stained by the red ink of a repossession letter! Those who send someone else to tell the court officials they aren't home! Those who swallow their shame to beg for pennies so they can feed their children! The unemployed who go on hoping without hope! The sick at heart who can't sleep because they're thinking about liens. (Shouts) A-me-ri-ca - is - a - bluff!!! We all moved from one continent to another to get rich. We found nothing but slavery and work! In the claws of imperialism! Today we die of misery and shame! We are poverty's recruits! Millions of transatlantic bankruptcies! For our families, educated in the illusion of A-me-ri-ca, the only choice is between prison and the rendevouz! There is also su-i-cide! Su-i-cide . . .

ABELARD I: It's the revolution . . . Fire! Open fire . . .

(Heavy silence. HELOISE's sobbing increases.)

ABELARD II: His life is ending. My life begins!

ABELARD I: The con . . .

(HELOISE sobs again, loudly.)

ABELARD II: I understand. The common grave . . . There's nothing left. Not even for the funeral or the burial. The company's been doing poorly for quite some time. Poor man! Business with foreigners . . .

He, of all people, after ordering that phantasmagoric mausoleum to be built . . . with nude angels ten feet tall . . .

ABELARD I: The con . . . dle! (Gesticulates impotently)

ABELARD II: What? Do you want something? You want me to press the alarm button? No! It's early still. Keep wishing!

ABELARD I: No . . . (Signals toward something that he wants)

ABELARD II: The telephone? No. A glass of water?

ABELARD I: (With an enormous effort) The candle!

ABELARD II: Ah! You want to die with a candle in your hands? The Candle King. Right! (He opens the showcase and takes out a little tallow candle, the smallest one of them all. Lights it) You don't want to lose your majesty. I'll put it in the gold candlestick!

(Silence. Sobs. The scene emerges from the flickering light of the candle that ABELARD II has placed in the brass candlestick. With a final spasm, the dying man's head falls back and the candle falls to the floor where it remains, upside down.)

HELOISE: (Standing up between heavy sobs) Abelard! Abelard!

ABELARD II: Heloise will always belong to Abelard. It's classic!

(HELOISE hesitates for a moment next to the deceased, then leans against the shoulder of ABELARD II, who holds her tightly in the center of the stage. The chords of the Wedding March are heard and a soft light focuses on the couple. The characters from the Second Act, dressed in formal attire, enter in single file and, paying no attention to the corpse, congratulate the moonlit couple, crossing the stage rhythmically and then moving into position behind them to the sound of the music. The fascist gives a Roman salute. The American is the last one to appear and the only one to speak.)

AMERICAN: Oh! Good business!

THE END

NOTES

All notes to this play are by the translators.

1. The Revolution of 1930 put an end to the First Republic (1889–1930) during which the Brazilian political and economic scene was dominated by the rural oligarchies of Minas Gerais and São Paulo. Power alternated between these two states in what was known as "política do café com leite" (coffee with milk politics) since São Paulo was a large producer of coffee and Minas' economy was based on farm products such as dairy goods. After the international stock market crash of 1929, which dealt a hard blow to the coffee economy, President Washington Luís Pereira de Sousa attempted to protect the interests of the São Paulo oligarchies by breaking with the established pattern and endorsing a candidate from São Paulo in the presidential election of 1930. The defeated candidate of the coalition behind Minas Gerais, Getúlio Vargas, led a military revolt that prevented his rival's inauguration. Vargas was later appointed president by the military junta.

2. Bandeirantes is the name given to members of the Entradas e Bandeiras expeditions organized at the end of the sixteenth century to explore the interior of Brazil. Their objectives were to expand the frontiers, capture and/or exterminate the indigenous, drive out the Spanish Jesuit missions, and look for gold.

3. The Empire of Brazil was established in 1822 when Dom Pedro, the Portuguese prince and the crown's representative in the colony, declared Brazil a

sovereign state and named himself emperor. It ended in 1889, when a crisis provoked in part by the abolition of slavery led to the founding of the First Republic.

4. The reference is to the Lateran Treaties that Pope Pius XI signed with Mussolini's government in 1929. Roman Catholicism was recognized as the official religion of Italy, religious education in schools was reinstated, the Church was given the power to decide laws on marriage and divorce, and the Vatican was financially compensated for the Papal States, which it had lost in 1871 with the unification of Italy.

5. Emil Ludwig (1881–1948), a German, introduced a new style of biographical narrative emphasizing the personality of its subject. In addition to his famous work on the life of Napoleon, published in 1926, he wrote biographies on Goethe, Jesus, Franklin Roosevelt, and Beethoven.

6. João Cândido Felisberto (1880–1969), the "Black Admiral," was the leader of a sailors' revolt known as the Revolta da Chibata (Revolt of the Whip) in Rio de Janeiro in 1910. Following a brutal whipping, and inspired by the examples of the British sailors' movement and the insurrection on the Russian battleship *Potemkin*, Brazilian sailors—mostly poor blacks and mulattoes—took control of four battleships and demanded the end of corporal punishment and compliance with a law that had increased their salaries and reduced their working hours. The government agreed to their demands, but once the sailors surrendered the ships they were arrested. Many died in prison, and others were forcibly exiled in the Amazon. Although João Cândido was later acquitted, he was expelled from the navy and was politically persecuted until his death in 1969.

7. Estácio de Sá (ca. 1520–67), a Portuguese military officer, founded the city of Rio de Janeiro in 1565 and expelled the French from the colony of Brazil in 1567. During the last battle with French forces, he was wounded in the face by a poisoned arrow and died soon after.

8. Paschoal Carlos Magno (1906–1980) was a diplomat, poet, novelist, playwright, and theater critic. In 1938 (after *The Candle King* was written) he founded the Teatro do Estudante do Brasil with university students to stage international classics and works by Brazilian authors. The group, which lasted until the early 1950s, toured the country and was a key factor in the emergence of hundreds of student theater groups.

9. M. Delly was the pen name of the French siblings Frédéric (1870–1949) and Jeanne-Marie Petitjean de la Rosiére (1875–1947), authors of several sentimental novels aimed at female readers. Most revolve around a love story between a rich young man and a beautiful but poor woman and the obstacles they must overcome before marrying and living happily ever after.

10. Yellow, blue, and green are the colors of the Brazilian flag. This is also clearly a reference to the colored shirts worn by fascist groups in various countries (Hitler's brownshirts, Mussolini's blackshirts, the blue shirts in Portugal and Britain, *camisas doradas* or gold shirts in Mexico, etc.).

11. Throughout this scene there are several jokes and puns revolving around Miss Poloca's name. *Polaco* and *polaca* are antiquated Portuguese terms for Polish people. At one time, many prostitutes in Brazil were either French or Polish, and the word *polaca* became a colloquial term for a prostitute.

12. The Academia Brasileira de Letras (Brazilian Academy of Letters) was founded in 1897 and modeled after the Académie Française. It is an elite institution that represents the values of established literary tradition and seeks to defend the Portuguese language against popular speech and foreign words.

13. Jerônimo de Castilho and Lamartine Babo wrote numerous *revistas* (revues) in the 1920s and 1930s. The revue is a genre of musical theater that originated in France in the eighteenth century and was later introduced in Brazil, where it acquired its own characteristics and became extremely popular. Revistas gradually featured increasingly saucy numbers with scantily clad women, and by the first decades of the twentieth century the elite often cited them as one of the causes of the decline of Brazilian theater.

14. *Les Cloches de Corneville* (The Bells of Corneville) is a comic opera in three acts by the French composer Robert Planquette, written in 1877 and staged with great success in Brazil.

15. Princess Imperial Isabel (1846–1921) was the heir to the Brazilian throne during the final decades of the empire. On May 13, 1888, acting as regent while her father, Emperor Dom Pedro II, traveled abroad, she signed the "Golden Law," which abolished slavery.

16. Poloquinha is the diminutive form of Miss Poloca's name, which would normally convey either affection or condescension; Abelard mispronounces it and instead calls her a little whore.

17. This is a reference to the Vargas government's policy of purchasing large amounts of coffee and destroying it in order to maintain artificially high prices after the economic collapse in 1929, which caused worldwide demand for coffee to fall.

18. Itú is a city in the interior of São Paulo. Here it is a reference to the key role of the São Paulo oligarchy in the overthrow of the Second Empire and the proclamation of the Republic of Brazil in 1889. Dissatisfied with the excessive centralization of the imperial government, the oligarchies of São Paulo defended the establishment of a federation, the separation of church and state, and the end of lifelong mandates in the Senate. In 1873, the Partido Republicano Paulista (Republican Party of São Paulo) was founded at a convention in Itú. The support of the party was fundamental to

the Republican movement, which was comprised of a large sector of the military and of liberal professionals from the urban middle class.

19. Dom Pedro II (1825–91), second and last emperor of Brazil, was known for his love of the arts. When the Republic was proclaimed in 1889, he moved to France, where he lived until his death. The reference here is to his poem "A Vida e o Barco" (Life and the Ship), which has to do with the subject of exile.

20. In the original, the American speaks in a mix of English and broken Portuguese.

21. Itatiaia is a mountain range in the Sierra of Mantiqueira between the southeastern region of Rio de Janeiro and the southern region of Minas Gerais. The highest peak is Agulhas Negras at 9,144 feet.

22. The character of Spittle is a reference to the Ação Integralista Brasileira (Brazilian Integralist Ac-

tion), a fascist organization in Brazil that claimed thousands of members. The organization was founded in 1932 by Plínio Salgado, a poet and journalist who had participated with Oswald de Andrade and other modernistas in the 1922 Week of Modern Art.

23. Petrópolis is a mountain resort town near Rio de Janeiro. Known as the Imperial City, it was founded in 1843 by Emperor Pedro II, who established his summer residence there.

24. Raffles, one of literature's most famous thieves, was the creation of E. W. Hornung (1866–1921). Arsène Lupin, "the gentleman thief," first appeared in a story by Maurice Leblanc (1864–1941) in 1907. Edgar Wallace (1875–1932) was a British playwright, novelist, and journalist known for his Victorian sensibility. His suspense and detective stories were the most popular of his time.

CUBA

Electra Garrigó (Virgilio Piñera)

Sophocles's *Electra,* the most famous version of the ancient Greek myth, begins with a long-awaited homecoming. Having been ordered by the gods to avenge his father's death, the hero, Orestes, arrives at his family's ancestral palace and uses a ruse to enter unrecognized. Meanwhile, his sister Electra obsessively relives her personal tragedy in the presence of the Chorus, which already knows the story by heart: her father, King Agamemnon, was brutally murdered by his wife Clytemnestra and her lover Aegisthus. Aegisthus stole the throne, and the treacherous queen ordered her young son Orestes to be killed, though Electra saved the boy and sent him far away under the protection of an old servant. For years, she has been waiting for her brother to return and free her from her confinement so that they can kill their father's murderers. At the end of the play, of course, this is more or less what happens. Electra gains her independence, the throne is assumed by its rightful heir, and the gods' will is fulfilled.

Actors Roberto Gacio (Agamemnon Garrigó) and Gilda Bello (Electra Garrigó) in *Electra Garrigó,* directed by Raúl Martín, Teatro de la Luna, Havana, 2001. (Photo by Pepe Murrieta, courtesy of Vivian Martínez Tabares.)

Virgilio Piñera's *Electra Garrigó* begins quite differently, with the nuclear family still intact and all under one roof. Agamemnon Garrigó is a strapping sixty year old in short sleeves, and his wife Clytemnestra Pla is a ravishing younger woman with a lover, Aegisthus Don, who parades around like Don Juan. Clytemnestra hasn't tried to kill her son or locked her daughter away; on the contrary, she smothers Orestes Garrigó with maternal affection and tries to marry off Electra in order to get her out from underfoot. The faithful servant of Sophocles's drama is now a Tutor, no normal man but a centaur who teaches his apt pupil Electra and the dimwitted Orestes that in the human world, as in the animal kingdom, there are only "events" and the only higher power is the law of necessity. This is modern-day Havana and the gods are dead, so Electra must direct her soliloquies to the non-gods, those "absolute negations of all divinity, of all mythology, of all reverence."

Electra Garrigó is the brazen but baffling first play by Virgilio Piñera (1912–1979), a notoriously quixotic character also renowned for his poetry and prose.[1] In an article called "¿¿¿Teatro???" published in 1947, Piñera argued that despite the many experimental theater groups that had been founded in the previous decade, Cuba had yet to develop what he called a "national theater of our own." While admitting that innovations had been made in stagecraft, he insisted that the rare attempts at homegrown dramaturgy had all suffered from a "profound dissociation between the merely formal part and the content" because what had motivated them was nothing more than a desire for technical modernization.[2] It was a bold challenge from an unproven playwright, and Piñera's first play of his own had a tall order to live up to. Its now legendary debut took place on October 23, 1948, under the direction of Francisco Morín, a young Cuban who had recently returned from studying in New York with the German director Erwin Piscator. Morín, who would go on to become a towering figure in Cuban theater, professed a desire to create a "conceptual theater," one that "reduced the staging to a minimum of elements" in order to find "the essential theater."[3] The young actors who took on the roles of the Garrigós were part of the newly formed collective Prometeo, so called after the Greek hero who defied Zeus and stole fire from Olympus for the benefit of humankind. The name proved fitting, since Piñera's bizarre amalgamation of high culture and insouciant, lowbrow humor provoked outrage among the reigning gods of Cuban theater. According to *Electra* lore, one esteemed director walked out in the middle of the performance and denounced it as "a spitball thrown at Olympus."[4]

Years later the critic Rine Leal called *Electra*'s opening "our battle of Hernani," a reference to Victor Hugo's famous play whose debut in 1830 was the scene of fisticuffs between Romantics and defenders of the classical tradition. An irreverent take on a two-thousand-year-old myth, *Electra Garrigó* is now widely regarded as marking the beginning of modern theater in Cuba. What makes the play distinctly modern, most critics imply, has as much to do with autonomy as it does with time, with the fact that it is neither a servile copy of European cultural forms disconnected from Cuban reality nor a modest representation of the merely local and vernacular. Raquel Carrió calls it a "Cubanization" of Greek tragedy, that supposed fount of Western civilization, and claims that it achieves a "synthesis" or "integration" of the national and the universal.[5] Greek columns are replaced by neo-classical colonial architecture; members of the Chorus wear the simple clothing of Cuban peasants; and the drunken patriarch dresses up in bedsheets that stand in for his missing toga and wanders around lamenting, "I wanted to lead a vaguely heroic life, but I'm only well fed and middle class."

In the prologue to the 1960 edition of his *Teatro completo,* Piñera claimed that the central issue at stake in *Electra Garrigó* was "the sentimental education that our parents have given us." His inscrutable Electra, far from mourning the absence of a long-dead father, takes charge of destiny and carefully orchestrates his downfall. It is she who prompts the clueless Clytemnestra when it is time to murder the "old rooster" Agamemnon, as it is she who instructs Orestes to kill their mother by serving her a poisoned papaya. Electra alone is conscious of what Piñera called "that terrible limitation that blind respect imposed upon us," and her purpose is to free Orestes from the "tyranny" of their mother's affections so that he can cross beyond the columns of the veranda where their drama unfolds and explore the wider world.[6]

As in the Greek *Electra,* however, the family's private saga is a symptom of the public polity. Electra invokes a strange and mysterious "light" so that she can "take measure of the monster who offends the city," despite the Tutor's suggestion that perhaps she should stop making speeches and "make a revolution" instead. If Piñera's play is a spoof on Greek tragedy, Cuba itself was a parody of Athenian democracy at the time of its debut. Although the country had won its independence from Spain in 1898, the First Republic was what the historian Richard Gott describes as a period of "endless violence, dramatic corruption, military revolts, gangsterism and sporadic military intervention by the United States" accompanied by "spectacular economic growth and prosperity for a small section of society."[7] A series of dictators and puppet presidents in the pocket of U.S. interests left the populace so disillusioned that there was only muted opposition in 1952 when former president Fulgencio Batista staged a coup. But by the time *Electra Garrigó* was performed again in 1958 many were certain they knew what the protagonist saw in the blinding light that flooded the stage: the authoritarian, corrupt dictator who ruled their island.

The real revolution came the following year, and Piñera's retrospective interpretation of his play is clearly influenced by the political imperatives of post-1959 Cuba.[8] Yet, despite several stagings in the years after the Revolution that celebrated it as a prophetic precursor, *Electra Garrigó* is hardly a straightforward drama of liberation.[9] The protagonist tells her father that "liberty isn't a domestic principle," but she isn't seeking to escape from the home. In the end, it is her hapless brother Orestes who leaves while she enters "the door of non-departure," an option that "doesn't open any paths, but it doesn't close any, either." What, then, is the meaning of her struggle against tyranny and tradition? Why is it that Orestes can only become "free" by submitting to his sister's implacable will? Does Electra liberate herself, or does she condemn herself to a solitary prison of her own making?

It is easy to fall under the sway of the protagonist's existential ramblings about being and nothingness, to look for answers in the enigmatic riddle about whether destiny is the fish or the hook, and to lose oneself in speculations about the significance of Electra's dispassionate demand for "hygiene." Yet one of the most profound aspects of Piñera's parody is its insight into the ways in which the abstract struggle between power and autonomy is mediated through metaphors and symbolic systems. *Electra Garrigó* may be a theater of ideas, but its philosophical meaning is to be found not simply in its cerebral dialogue but in the encounters it stages between different modes of performance and technologies of representation.

The dissolute sovereign Agamemnon is caught within the conventions of Greek tragic drama. Seemingly unaware that he's been relocated to the tropics, the King of Mycenae and Argos wanders around crying, "What is my tragedy? Because I must have a tragedy like all human beings, a tragedy to fulfill, but it escapes me!" Identification and catharsis, key concepts in the Aristotelian theory of tragedy, underlie the strange pantomime scenes in which black servants silently act out the deaths of Clytemnestra and Agamemnon as the queen and king narrate. Inspired by the nonspeaking slaves in Sophocles's play, they underscore the role of Western theater in establishing a cultural hierarchy whose terms are set by the white elite. Clytemnestra and Agamemnon seek to purge their fears and control reality by representing it, so they order their servants to "die" in their place. When Electra applauds the pretend death of her mother's double, the queen boasts, "While that Clytemnestra doesn't move, look at this one who moves and circulates like a menacing draft of air." Yet the two monarchs are ultimately the victims of their own tragic framework. The black actresses who enact Clytemnestra's death at the beginning of the play turn out to be the agents of her demise in their second and final appearance onstage when they place before her the deadly fruit.

If the Greek sovereigns have a fatal flaw, it is that they ignore the predictions of their onstage audience. Before the action begins, the Chorus foretells the deaths of the *pater* and *mater familias* to the tune of "Guantanamera," trapping them within a dramatic paradigm that is no less fatalistic than the one they themselves attempt to manipulate. As the representative of the Cuban people, the Chorus recites its prophecy in *décimas,* a ballad form composed of ten-line, octosyllabic stanzas that is popular throughout Spanish-speaking countries. In Cuba, décimas telling tales of passionate romance and true crimes were common fare on the radio during the era when *Electra Garrigó* was first performed. Within the structure of the play, then, the Chorus works as a framing device that brings classical drama—the pinnacle of high culture—down to the ground, showing up the limitations of the so-called universal by taking it out of its element and recasting it in a vernacular, though mass-mediated, mode.

There is no doubt that Electra is the real star of the colorful cast. Yet she is less a character than a vague but implacable force of negation that verges on complete nihilism. This "viscous" and amorphous "chaos of Electra-material," as Aegisthus and Clytemnestra refer to her, defies the very possibility of representation. She is pure performance, as her mother tells Aegisthus with disdain when she says that Electra "lives to act. I'm sure she feels nothing. What she shows us is a plaster mask." Electra is the ideal existentialist hero because she is defined solely by her acts; there is no higher meaning to what she does.[10]

Electra Garrigó, however, is not entirely captive to its protagonist's philosophical and performative persuasions. Like all the characters, Electra is at the mercy of the play's relentless humor. When the Chorus describes her as "a gentle flower on a stem \ that grows the sharpest thorns," both the speaker and its subject seem absurd—the Chorus because its quaint, colloquial language is so clearly misapplied to the prickly protagonist and Electra herself because this trite description takes the pomp out of her metaphysical musings. Likewise, Clytemnestra zealously plays the part of the overprotective mother by torturing herself with the thought of "Orestes exposed to the wind, Orestes at the mercy of the waves, Orestes lashed by a hurricane"; yet her melodramatic movie scene suddenly falls flat when she ends this litany of horrors with one final, ridiculous image: "Orestes bitten by mosquitoes."

In "Piñera teatral," Piñera explains that the characters of his tragedy "oscillate perpetually between a high-flown language and a humor and banality, which, among other reasons, has been used to balance and limit both the painful and the pleasurable, according to that salutary principle that nothing exists that is truly painful or absolutely pleasurable."[11] He tells us that this is a reflection of the fact that Cubans as a nation are defined by "the systematic rupture with seriousness." Like *Electra Garrigó,* he suggests, "we are tragic and comic at the same time."[12]

The playwright's diagnosis of his compatriots' character calls to mind the *choteo,* a form of mocking humor that has long been considered a peculiarly Cuban virtue and/or vice. In a now classic lecture given in 1928, the writer Jorge Mañach defined *choteo* as a "habit of disrespect" motivated by a "psychological fact: the repugnance of all authority."[13] Most of Mañach's examples have to do with deriding or "deflating" a performance that holds some sort of prestige or takes itself too seriously: a spectator at the theater, for instance, cracks a joke during an emotional high point or young boys make fun of a girl singing a sentimental romance. It is a kind of performative skepticism that betrays a distinct ambivalence since "many times the *choteador* admires, deep down, the very virtue that he makes fun of."[14] Like Piñera, Mañach sees the choteo as a reflexive habit that developed in response to the country's long history of oppression; it is a form of subterfuge and disorder, a "negation of hierarchy" motivated by "the leveling tendency" that he considers characteristic of Cubans.

This idea of "leveling" is key to understanding what goes on in Piñera's play. Unlike its protagonist, *Electra Garrigó* lays no claim to absolute autonomy, nor does it set out to destroy the classical tradition it so ruthlessly mocks. Rather, it suggests that, just as nothing is all pain or all pleasure, nor are Cuba and the culture of its colonizers two self-contained, discrete entities; each is inexorably implicated in the other. The play is too intentionally disjointed, however, to qualify as a "synthesis" or assimilation of the national and the cosmopolitan under the banner of modernity. Agamemnon Garrigó and his bourgeois clan are not "authentically" Cuban characters who happen to be playing out a drama that is as eternal and universal as lust and revenge. They are still partly Greek, and if they are confused it is because they are not entirely in their element and they are enacting the underside of a master narrative that is and is not their own. The play stubbornly refuses to resolve the contradiction between its opposing selves because this opposition is part of its own constitution. Like the centaur who is both man and beast, it knows that the contradictions don't lie without, but within.

This philosophy poses a tough challenge to the rhetoric of revolutionary triumph because it suggests that every liberatory impulse is bound to the oppressive power it resists. Perhaps this is another reason, in addition to his open homosexuality, why Piñera soon fell out of favor with the postrevolutionary Cuban government. After Fidel Castro famously declared, "Within the Revolution, everything; outside the Revolution, nothing," it was hard to know what to make of a writer like Piñera, whose work is a disquieting reminder that what is on the inside secretly needs an outside in order to exist.[15] In 1968, his play *Dos viejos pánicos* won the prestigious Casa de las Américas Prize, but by the 1970s he had become a marginal figure in Cuban letters; most of his work from this time on went unpublished, and his plays were no longer staged. After his death, however, his writings were discovered by a wider public and began to generate such an intense interest that some have dubbed it"Piñera fever." In 1984, the director Flora Lauten's *Electra,* a loose adaptation in which the Garrigó family became a troupe of circus performers, was credited with helping to revitalize the languishing Cuban theater scene. It has been followed by numerous productions of previously unknown works, as well as periodic reinterpretations of *Electra Garrigó*—including a version that turned Piñera's send-up of high culture into a classical ballet and several others that foregrounded elements of Afro-Cuban culture.[16]

Electra Garrigó is indeed a modern Cuban drama, one that finds its reason for being in all of the paradoxes this implies. It is a foundational drama that exposes the fundamental fault lines of modernity, a negation of all reverence that is also a backhanded homage, and an unconventional act of emancipation that acknowledges the ties of history.

—Sarah J. Townsend

NOTES

1. Piñera had previously written a play called *Clamor en el penal,* but it was never published or staged. His other plays prior to the Revolution include *Jesús, Falsa alarma, El Flaco y el Gordo,* and *Aire frío.* His poetry includes *Isla en peso* and his prose *Cuentos fríos (Cold Tales)* and *La carne de René (René's Flesh).* His one-act play *Una caja de zapatos vacía* was translated as *An Empty Shoe Box* and published in *Three Masterpieces of Cuban Drama,* ed. Luis F. González-Cruz and Ann Waggoner Aken (Los Angeles: Green Integer, 2000).

2. Virgilio Piñera, "¿¿¿Teatro???" *Prometeo: Revista mensual de divulgación teatral* 1 (April–May 1948): 1.

3. Francisco Morín, *Por amor al arte: Memorias de un teatrista cubano, 1940–1970* (Miami: Ediciones Universal, 1998), 83.

4. After a vituperative debate between Piñera and a well-known critic, the Association of Theatre and Cinematographic Redactors ordered *Electra Garrigó* to be stricken from its index of works.

5. See Raquel Carrió, "Una brillante entrada en la modernidad," in *Teatro contemporáneo cubano,* ed. Carlos Espinosa Domínguez, 131–37 (Madrid: Sociedad Estatal Quinto Centenario, 1992).

6. Virgilio Piñera, "Piñera teatral," in *Teatro completo* (Havana: Ediciones R, 1960), 11.

7. Richard Gott, *Cuba: A New History* (New Haven: Yale University Press, 2004), 113.

8. In "Piñera teatral," Piñera claims to have written *Electra Garrigó* in 1941 during Batista's first period in power. However, in other writings he cites other dates, including 1942 and 1943.

9. *Electra Garrigó* was restaged several times in 1960 and 1961 to great acclaim. In 1964, it was selected by the Union of Writers and Artists to commemorate World Theatre Day.

10. Many critics assert that *Electra Garrigó* is the first existentialist drama. If Piñera's claim that he wrote it in 1941 is true, then it predates the 1943 debut of Sartre's *The Flies,* which is usually accorded that honor. *The Flies* also deals with the Orestes-Electra myth, although it depicts Orestes as the hero. Sartre saw the 1960 production of *Electra Garrigó* during a trip to Cuba. In "Piñera teatral," Piñera states, "I am not entirely existentialist or entirely absurd . . . I am absurd and existentialist, but in Cuban style" (15).

11. Ibid., 9.

12. Ibid., 10.

13. Jorge Mañach, *Indagación del choteo* (Miami: Mnemosyne, 1969), 19.

14. Ibid., 36. Mañach's attitude toward the choteo is itself ambivalent. He warns that in its pernicious form it is an exaggerated individualism that can lead to the "negation of all values" (48).

15. In October 1961, Piñera was arrested and briefly imprisoned for engaging in homosexual activities.

16. For an analysis of Lauten's production, see Raquel Carrió, "De *La emboscada* a *Electra:* Una clave metafórica." *Tablas* 2 (1985): 2–8. The version for classical ballet was directed by Gustavo Herrero. Other stagings include one directed by Armando Suárez del Villar in 1986 and a version by Raúl Martín and Teatro de la Luna first performed in 1997 and on numerous occasions since.

SELECTED REFERENCES

Anderson, Thomas F. *Everything in Its Place: The Life and Works of Virgilio Piñera.* Lewisburg, Pa.: Bucknell University Press, 2006.

Barreda, Pedro. "La tragedia griega y su historización en Cuba: *Electra Garrigó* de Virgilio Piñera." *Escritura:*

Revista de teoría y crítica literarias 10 (January–December 1985): 117–26.

Carrió, Raquel. "Una brillante entrada en la modernidad." In *Teatro contemporáneo cubano,* ed. Carlos Espinosa Domínguez, 131–37. Madrid: Sociedad Estatal Quinto Centenario, 1992.

García Chíchester, Ana. "Virgilio Piñera and the Formulation of a National Literature." *CR: The New Centennial Review* 2 (summer 2002): 231–51.

Leal, Rine. "Piñera todo teatral." In Virgilio Piñera, *Teatro completo,* ed. Rine Leal, v–xxxiii. Havana: Letras Cubanas, 2002.

Mañach, Jorge. *Indagación del choteo.* Miami: Mnemosyne, 1969.

Matas, Julio. "Vuelta a *Electra Garrigó* de Virgilio Piñera." *Latin American Theatre Review* 22 (spring 1989): 73–79.

Morín, Francisco. *Por amor al arte: Memorias de un teatrista cubano, 1940–1970.* Miami: Ediciones Universal, 1998.

Piñera, Virgilio. "Piñera teatral." In *Teatro completo,* 7–30. Havana: Ediciones R, 1960.

Piñera, Virgilio. "¿¿¿Teatro???" *Prometeo: Revista mensual de divulgación teatral* 1 (April–May 1948): 1, 27–28.

Quiroga, José. "Fleshing Out Virgilio Piñera from the Cuban Closet." In *¿Entiendes? Queer Readings, Hispanic Writings,* ed. Emilie L. Bergmann and Paul Julian Smith, 168–80. Durham: Duke University Press, 1995.

Electra Garrigó (Virgilio Piñera)

Translated by Margaret Carson

CHARACTERS:

CHORUS
ELECTRA GARRIGÓ
TUTOR
AEGISTHUS DON
AGAMEMNON GARRIGÓ
CLYTEMNESTRA PLA
ORESTES GARRIGÓ
MIMES

ACT ONE

CHORUS:

In the city of Havana,
Cuba's shining pearl,
disgrace descended on
the brave and beautiful
Electra Garrigó—
day by day at home she stayed
until fate came her way
with troubles as big
as the world.

Electra was intelligent
and sensitive and chaste,
a bright bud
from her elders' garden,
a woman of many honors,
she had the finest taste.
But like a sun's implosion
fate went one-on-one—
with strength beyond the human realm
two tombs were opened in her home.

Electra strode into the ring
hardened as a diamond
to tell Orestes whom she loved—
her brother in this sordid storm—
to halt a useless sacrifice
to appease a wicked mother.
Electra, now in mournful tones,
tells this house's tale of woe.

A porch with six columns in the style of old colonial homes in Havana. A floor made of black and white flagstones. There is no furniture. The CHORUS makes its appearances downstage while the music to "Guantanamera" plays in the background. *A harsh yellow light. The action takes place at night. When the CHORUS finishes, ELECTRA appears, dressed in black.*

ELECTRA: *(She enters from between the two central columns. She stops and leans her hands on one of the columns.)* What fury chases me, what invisible animal enters my dreams and tries to drag me to a region of light where my eyes no longer serve their purpose! *(She moves towards center stage.)* Oh, light! Are you this strange animal? *(Pauses)* But . . . how can a twenty year old stand up to the light? Yesterday I read that young girls who meditated too much on light went blind. *(Pauses)* But I've walked countless times in the countryside only a few feet from the sun.

(The TUTOR enters dressed as a centaur and stands behind ELECTRA. He wears a frock coat, a horse's tail, and has hooves.)

TUTOR: Are you making speeches?

ELECTRA: *(Without moving)* Yes.

TUTOR: You're following tradition, and I don't approve. Haven't I told you, you have to make a revolution? *(Pauses)* Why don't you make any demands?

ELECTRA: I will. *(Pauses)* They say the city is full of weird women. Do you know them?

TUTOR: Yes, they're the wise women. I live in fear of them. They follow me with their debates, they ask me to have an open discussion . . . *(Scornfully)* And Electra, I have nothing to say to them.

ELECTRA: Won't they agree to be your lovers, one after another?

TUTOR: They're too frightened of men and horses.

ELECTRA: Then they must be gotten rid of. They're of no importance.

TUTOR: You're frightened too easily, Electra. They're nothing more than one of those plagues that afflict

Virgilio Piñera, Cuba, 1948. Translated from Spanish by Margaret Carson.

every city from time to time. (*Pauses*) Evil isn't something that's here today, gone tomorrow. Any city has its perpetual monster.

ELECTRA: That's why I invoked the light. We need more light so that our eyes can consider and take measure of the monster who offends the city.

(*AEGISTHUS enters carrying a tray in his right hand with an enormous papaya. Forty years old, very handsome and strong, he's dressed in white, like a Cuban pimp.*)

AEGISTHUS: (*To ELECTRA*) I'm looking for Clytemnestra. Have you seen her?

ELECTRA: (*Without looking at him*) No.

TUTOR: The light bothers her.

AEGISTHUS: It's true, there's a lot of light here. (*He looks at his clothes.*) I can barely see my clothes. You'll need to put up screens before long.

ELECTRA: (*Without looking at him*) I prefer the light.

AEGISTHUS: Whatever suits you. (*He walks towards the columns on the left.*) As for me, I'll go to your mother's room. I won't know when daylight comes. The curtains will be closed. (*Exits*)

TUTOR: The monsters meet . . . (*To ELECTRA*) Isn't your father in the city, Electra?

ELECTRA: Yes. (*Pauses*) One of his servants told me that Agamemnon wants to meet me, here, on the porch.

TUTOR: I'll leave, then. (*He turns around in such a way that his tail falls into ELECTRA's hands.*) Dear Electra, can you smooth out my tail a bit? (*He takes a giant comb out of his coat and gives it to ELECTRA.*)

ELECTRA: (*She begins to comb the hair on his tail. Suddenly she stops with her hand raised.*) Tutor, if I comb out your tail it's only an event; if I kill you with this dagger (*she wields the comb as if it were a dagger*) it's nothing more than another event. (*Pauses*) Have I understood correctly, Tutor?

TUTOR: (*While walking off the stage in the way one imagines a centaur walks*) Yes, Electra, you've understood completely.

(*AGAMEMNON enters. He is sixty years old but in robust health, tall and majestic. He wears short sleeves.*)

AGAMEMNON: (*He looks at the columns to the right through which the TUTOR has disappeared.*) The Tutor, still here?

ELECTRA: You hired him to be my teacher. Besides, he pleases me.

AGAMEMNON: All right. Let's forget about the Tutor. (*Pauses*) Do you have any idea why I called you?

ELECTRA: Yes. There are rumors that the Pretender has threatened to carry me off.

AGAMEMNON: Exactly, and I don't want him to carry you off; I don't want him to marry you.

ELECTRA: If you don't want me to marry, if you don't want anyone to carry me off, then what do you wish for me?

AGAMEMNON: I want you to be happy, Electra Garrigó.

ELECTRA: No, Agamemnon Garrigó, it's security you want. (*Pauses*) It would be so amusing if they carried me off. (*Laughs*)

AGAMEMNON: I love you too much to lose you, Electra Garrigó.

ELECTRA: I love myself too much to be lost. You disapprove: I have to leave you, Agamemnon Garrigó. It's that simple.

AGAMEMNON: That's blasphemy, Electra Garrigó. (*Pauses*) All right. But you owe me your obedience.

ELECTRA: I don't owe you a thing. The principle of liberty isn't a domestic issue.

AGAMEMNON: And what about the family? If this city has withstood our enemies for thousands of years, it's because of family unity—of many families forming one big family.

ELECTRA: That's just rhetoric! Besides, what you call family is your own self multiplied over and over. We're part of your mechanism, we have to function according to your movements.

AGAMEMNON: And when your own blood calls?

ELECTRA: Words, just words. In the end my blood must stand up to your blood. My blood is my own business.

AGAMEMNON: Electra Garrigó: I repeat, that's blasphemy. You came from my blood and to my blood you must return.

ELECTRA: I'm determined.

AGAMEMNON: It's useless. We gave you a Christian education. And besides, you love your father more than your theories.

ELECTRA: Don't be so sure. Things change. Sometimes I feel my blood runs stronger than yours. In which case . . .

AGAMEMNON: (*Persuasively*) I trust your affection.

ELECTRA: (*Agitated*) But I can rebel.

AGAMEMNON: You won't do it. (*Pauses*) All right: marry your Pretender, leave home! But you won't do it, you love me too much.

ELECTRA: (*Turns towards the audience*) O, Cruelty!

AGAMEMNON: (*Turns towards the columns*) O, Necessity!

(*CLYTEMNESTRA PLA enters from the right. She's forty years old, tall and beautiful. She wears a purple robe.*)

CLYTEMNESTRA: (*Very agitated*) Have you seen Orestes?

ELECTRA: No. (*Pauses*) Have you seen Aegisthus?

AGAMEMNON: You're upset, Clytemnestra Pla.

CLYTEMNESTRA: I just saw the murder of a young man outside my window.

AGAMEMNON: How did it happen?

CLYTEMNESTRA: A soldier shot him in the neck. The boy jumped in the air as if he were looking for something and then without a sound landed on his back. (*Pauses and sighs*) He was very handsome.

ELECTRA: (*Sarcastically*) I don't understand your horror.

You were always a brave woman. Didn't you educate me in the cult of blood?

CLYTEMNESTRA: I was thinking of Orestes. Ah, Orestes!

AGAMEMNON: You imagined Orestes was shot in his neck?

CLYTEMNESTRA: (*She covers her mouth.*) Be quiet! How could you think such a thing. . .

AGAMEMNON: You'd already thought of it, Clytemnestra Pla.

CLYTEMNESTRA: It's true. But my love makes me imagine even worse possibilities: Orestes exposed to the wind, Orestes at the mercy of the waves, Orestes lashed by a hurricane, Orestes bitten by mosquitoes . . .

ELECTRA: (*Sarcastically*) I imagine a steel blade against Orestes's neck . . .

CLYTEMNESTRA: You're monstrous.

ELECTRA: (*Ambiguous*) I'm trying to save Orestes, that's all.

CLYTEMNESTRA: (*Confused*) What are you saying. . . ! Save Orestes? From what? From whom?

ELECTRA: (*Enigmatically*) That's my secret.

CLYTEMNESTRA: (*Furious, she charges at ELECTRA.*) You're lying! You don't have any secret! Orestes is safe. (*She pauses, doubtful.*) Yes . . . I ask myself: what could happen to him? What. . . ? (*Pauses*) Ah, Orestes!

AGAMEMNON: Nothing, Clytemnestra Pla, nothing can happen to him. Electra is only talking about something unpredictable, accidents . . . For example, a car that comes along as Orestes crosses the street.

CLYTEMNESTRA: (*Wrings her hands hysterically*) Ah, Orestes, don't cross the street. . . !

ELECTRA: Orestes will kill you in the end.

CLYTEMNESTRA: It's your father who'll die first.

AGAMEMNON: Do you know my fate?

CLYTEMNESTRA: No, but I know your daughter. She'll kill you over some disagreement, Agamemnon Garrigó.

AGAMEMNON: (*To ELECTRA, with anxiety*) You'd make me suffer to the point of killing me, Electra Garrigó?

ELECTRA: (*Evasive*) I'd never get in the way of a car.

CLYTEMNESTRA: But you'd marry a man whom your father detests.

ELECTRA: (*To AGAMEMNON, scornfully*) Would that kill you?

AGAMEMNON: (*Innocently*) Yes, that would kill me.

CLYTEMNESTRA: (*To ELECTRA*) Did you hear that, Electra Garrigó? If you don't want to cause your father's death, you must stay under this roof for the rest of your life.

(*ORESTES enters. He's twenty-five years old, very handsome.*)

ORESTES: (*Half-hidden between the columns in the center*) And I'll leave for the rest of mine!

CLYTEMNESTRA: (*Turns around quickly*) Orestes! (*Breathless, she hugs him.*) But what strange word did you just say? Who's talking about leaving?

ELECTRA: Orestes Garrigó, your son, my brother. He must leave.

CLYTEMNESTRA: But I, his mother, haven't demanded it.

ELECTRA: His destiny demands it.

AGAMEMNON: Clytemnestra Pla, what do you think destiny is, the fish or the hook?

CLYTEMNESTRA: (*Pensive*) I think it's the hook.

AGAMEMNON: You're wrong. It's the fish.

ELECTRA: A man throws out his hook and catches a fish: the fish is his destiny.

AGAMEMNON: Snapper or shark . . .

ELECTRA: Good luck or misfortune.

CLYTEMNESTRA: (*Nervously, to ORESTES*) Whatever your destiny is, don't leave.

ORESTES: (*Fearfully*) What about my future?

CLYTEMNESTRA: What about your mother?

AGAMEMNON: (*To CLYTEMNESTRA*) Nothing can stop the course of his destiny.

ELECTRA: When the fish emerges from the water, you'll either be devoured by it or you'll see it served at your table.

CLYTEMNESTRA: (*With a ridiculous affectation*) A good son would never want a harmless snapper to turn into a violent shark for his mother.

ELECTRA: Clytemnestra Pla, are you ignoring the fact that he has no choice but to go after his fish blindly?

CLYTEMNESTRA: No more symbols! You're overwhelming me with these forebodings. (*To ORESTES*) Don't leave, Orestes.

AGAMEMNON: A man must always travel.

CLYTEMNESTRA: And a woman stay at home, is that it? It seems that the question of destiny only affects me. You believe you're rejecting your destiny by forcing Electra to stay in this house. (*Pause*) But if I'm subject to destiny, then you are too.

AGAMEMNON: Electra Garrigó will never abandon her father.

CLYTEMNESTRA: Electra Garrigó will marry the Pretender.

AGAMEMNON: (*Ironically*) Is it so important to you that she leave home?

ELECTRA: Clytemnestra Pla wants me to have what she's had: a husband.

AGAMEMNON: And I want Orestes to have what I had in my youth: a journey to distant lands.

CLYTEMNESTRA: Be quiet, you bird of ill omen, be quiet! Orestes is my son, mine and mine alone. (*Pauses*) Oh, my God! What will happen if one morning I wake up to the news of Orestes's departure?

ELECTRA: You'll stab yourself with a dagger.

ORESTES: In that case, I won't leave. I don't want to torment Clytemnestra Pla.

AGAMEMNON: (*Mockingly*) Do you hear that, Electra Garrigó? Do you hear your brother? He's passing up a brilliant future for the sake of his mother's peace of mind.

CLYTEMNESTRA: Listen, Agamemnon Garrigó: you can see the speck in someone else's eye, but not the beam in your own . . . You blame me for fearing Orestes's departure—but what about you? Could you stand it if Electra married the Pretender?

AGAMEMNON: No, I couldn't. That Pretender isn't worthy of Electra's hand.

CLYTEMNESTRA: Oh, please . . . the Pretender is only a rhetorical device, Agamemnon Garrigó. What's certain is that you fear Electra's departure as much as I fear Orestes's leaving.

ELECTRA: Don't forget to add, Clytemnestra Pla, how much you want me to marry so that you can be queen of this house.

ORESTES: And your fervent wish, Agamemnon Garrigó, is that I leave so that you can be king of this house.

CLYTEMNESTRA: Oh no. . . ! A horrible consort!

AGAMEMNON: Never! This queen will pluck my eyes out!

ORESTES: Then who should be king?

CLYTEMNESTRA: You, beloved Orestes, you, the king of my life!

ELECTRA: (*Sarcastically*) No one but Orestes?

CLYTEMNESTRA: (*Approaches ELECTRA with a ferocious look on her face*) Yes, Electra Garrigó, no one but Orestes.

AGAMEMNON: (*To ELECTRA*) My daughter, don't think that I . . . I was king once.

ELECTRA: What does it matter . . . Look at Clytemnestra, who insists on being queen.

AGAMEMNON: At her age? Is it possible? . . .

CLYTEMNESTRA: I'm not an old woman, Agamemnon Garrigó. A forty-year-old woman is still young. I married you when I was fifteen. If you were forty then, who cares.

AGAMEMNON: It's true, I feel tired.

CLYTEMNESTRA: (*In a somber tone*) You should go to bed if you feel tired.

ELECTRA: Clytemnestra is excited by the glow of queenship.

ORESTES: (*Opens his shirt*) Isn't the heat suffocating?

ELECTRA: I call that avoiding the subject. I don't recognize you, Orestes. Where are you, how can we find you?

CLYTEMNESTRA: Yes, my dear Orestes, the heat is suffocating. Can I get you a lemonade?

ORESTES: I don't want one now. (*Pauses*) But tell me: is it true you couldn't stand it if I were gone?

CLYTEMNESTRA: I would die of sadness, dear Orestes. (*Pauses*) My frenzy would be so strong, that I'd search desperately in the neighborhood for movies about a mother who dies because her child has left!

ELECTRA: But you have two children, Clytemnestra Pla. If your son is gone, you still have your daughter.

CLYTEMNESTRA: I meant to say, because her only son leaves. (*Pauses. Brutally*) Anyway, I wouldn't kill myself if you left.

ELECTRA: And you re-create those movies at night in your dreams, don't you?

CLYTEMNESTRA: (*Vehemently*) Yes, I re-create everything, and much more besides! Anything is possible to a mother who faces the threat of losing her only son. (*Crying and ridiculous*) Yes, who faces the threat of losing you, Orestes, oh, Orestes. . . !

ELECTRA: I, on the other hand, dreamed last night that a mare killed her stallion by giving him some Chinese perfume to smell . . .

ORESTES: Oh, imagine all the whinnying. . . ! I always wanted to be a stud horse. Why can't we ask to be turned into a herd of horses?

ELECTRA: You're right. I'd like to be a mare and sit in my opera box, cooling myself with an enormous feather fan.

ORESTES: While I'd gallop onstage and trample the jeweled head of the prima donna.

CLYTEMNESTRA: Enough of this madness! We're humans, and we can't, no, we mustn't strip ourselves of words and names.

(*At this moment the names of ELECTRA and ORESTES can be heard from a loudspeaker located offstage. On hearing their names, they slowly exit the stage. As they exit, four black actresses enter through the central columns in the following order: the first two are carrying a luxuriously decorated bed. These are the ladies-in-waiting. Following immediately behind is the actress playing a news announcer; and finally, the actress who will play the part of CLYTEMNESTRA. The first three are dressed as servants; the fourth wears a copy of CLYTEMNESTRA's dress.*

The action on stage is as follows: the ladies-in-waiting stand to the left of AGAMEMNON. The news announcer stands between the two above-mentioned columns. The actress playing CLYTEMNESTRA places herself next to the bed. When the four black actresses have finished their entrance, ELECTRA and ORESTES appear again: ELECTRA enters by the column on the extreme right; ORESTES, by the column on the extreme left. They stand with their backs to the audience. CLYTEMNESTRA stands in the middle of the stage, very close to the footlights. AGAMEMNON does the same. There is a long pause. CLYTEMNESTRA claps her hands twice. Another pause. CLYTEMNESTRA and AGAMEMNON also turn their backs to the audience.

In the short farce that follows, CLYTEMNESTRA provides the voices for the four black actresses, who carry out a pantomime.)

CLYTEMNESTRA: (*Completely rigid*) Why have I stopped? Why don't I walk forward? Why do I walk forward? Why do I open my mouth so wide? Oh, my legs tremble. . . ! I'm becoming weak! Oh, my bed. . . ! *(Pauses)* What are you doing, why aren't you taking me to my bed? Oh, my bed! *(Pauses)* I, the unhappy Clytemnestra Pla, wife of Agamemnon Garrigó, mother of Electra and Orestes . . . *(A piercing scream)* Oh, Oresteees, Oreeestes! Call Orestes! Hurry, call him!

(The ladies-in-waiting begin to walk in circles around the bed, as if playing blindman's buff. The news announcer starts making gestures that mime the unexpected arrival of a messenger. She stops next to the bed and takes out a piece of paper from her pocket. She pretends to read it:)

CLYTEMNESTRA: Yesterday morning, at daybreak, Orestes Garrigó, the able engineer of the Australian Iron Company, was torn apart by wild beasts and killed! *(Long pause)* It's a lie! This telegram is a fraud! Orestes couldn't have been killed by wild animals. He himself was a lion, a tiger, a panther . . . I say so, I declare so, I, his mother, Clytemnestra Pla. *(Long pause)* In that case, I'll die as well. *(CLYTEMNESTRA's double lies down on the bed. To the ladies-in-waiting)* I'm going to cover myself with this shawl. Count to ten out loud, then lift off the shawl, and you'll see me dead.

(The ladies-in-waiting make gestures while CLYTEMNESTRA counts emphatically to ten. The ladies-in-waiting take off the shawl, and CLYTEMNESTRA's double appears, recumbent.)

ELECTRA: *(Turning towards the audience, applauding)* Bravo, bravo! Clytemnestra Pla has just died!

CLYTEMNESTRA: *(She turns towards the audience as well. Pause. She stands next to ELECTRA.)* Yes, by means of a double. While that Clytemnestra doesn't move, look at this one who moves and circulates like a menacing draft of air.

ELECTRA: I clap my hands for the one who died onstage. The other will die at an opportune moment.

ORESTES: *(Turns towards the audience. To ELECTRA)* Dear Electra, will I be ripped apart by wild beasts and die?

ELECTRA: You would have to leave for Australia first.

CLYTEMNESTRA: Your predictions are a dead letter. You will be the one to abandon this house and city soon.

AGAMEMNON: It will be Orestes, not Electra.

(The name of ELECTRA is heard over the loudspeaker.)

ELECTRA: Orestes.

ORESTES: Electra.

(The brother and sister exit. Four black actors appear in the following order: the first three—the messengers of ELECTRA's death—place themselves next to the columns on the right. They are followed by the actor who will play the part of AGAMEMNON. The messengers are dressed as servants. The actor who represents AGAMEMNON is dressed like him. The messengers carry long scrolls. AGAMEMNON provides the four voices. The black actors engage in pantomime. At the moment the black actors take their places, ELECTRA and ORESTES appear again: ELECTRA, by the column on the extreme right, and ORESTES, by the column on the extreme left. They stand with their backs to the audience. AGAMEMNON claps his hands twice. CLYTEMNESTRA turns her back again to the audience.)

AGAMEMNON: *(Supplying the voice of the first messenger)* The news just came over the radio about the murder of the beautiful Electra Garrigó at the hands of the Pretender!

AGAMEMNON: *(Supplying the voice of the second messenger)* Because her father refused to allow her to become engaged to the Pretender, the beautiful Electra Garrigó died in a fit of passion.

AGAMEMNON: *(Supplying the voice of the third messenger)* Because the Pretender abandoned her, the beautiful Electra Garrigó killed herself today!

AGAMEMNON: *(Supplying the voice of his double, whose hand is held up to his forehead)* Three versions of the death of Electra . . . *(Pauses)* I'll let chance decide. *(AGAMEMNON's double points his finger at the messengers as AGAMEMNON speaks.)* Eeny meeny miney mo! *(AGAMEMNON's double steps forward and puts his forefinger on the chest of the second messenger.)* Ah, your version has triumphed! Electra has died in a fit of passion. *(Long pause)* And what shall I do now in this world, miserable mortal, deprived of my beloved Electra! Let me die instantly! Oh, cruel life, I call upon death to remedy all my misfortunes! *(Pauses)* Yes: a fit of passion will kill me. *(AGAMEMNON's double lies down on the floor with exaggerated gestures.)* Now he's ready! A father about to die. *(AGAMEMNON's double points to the messengers.)* Count to five. I want to show Clytemnestra that by counting to five, and not ten, a father can die with dignity.

(AGAMEMNON's voice counts each number slowly. The messengers mime the actions. AGAMEMNON's double places the shawl over his head and adopts a reclining pose.)

CLYTEMNESTRA: *(Walking towards center stage. Possessed by fury)* Destiny! Always destiny! Who's going to win? Who's going to lose? Destiny will tell, horrifying destiny!

ORESTES: *(Approaching CLYTEMNESTRA)* What does destiny want with you, Clytemnestra Pla?

ELECTRA: *(Approaching CLYTEMNESTRA)* Destiny claims its part, but I refuse to believe that it will be horrifying. Destiny is only destiny.

AGAMEMNON: *(He walks towards CLYTEMNESTRA and stands back to back with her.)* Who among us is destiny?

(From this moment until the end of the act, the four actors remain completely still, with their hands held down and their fists closed.)

CLYTEMNESTRA: I am.

ELECTRA: That's a lie!

AGAMEMNON: Who among us is destiny?

ORESTES: Is Electra destiny?

CLYTEMNESTRA: Get back, you bitch!

ELECTRA: Bitch, come forward!

AGAMEMNON: Destiny, oh destiny!

ORESTES: It's like glue.

CLYTEMNESTRA: And so inevitable!

ELECTRA: Yes, it's approaching!

AGAMEMNON: Destiny, oh destiny!

ORESTES: Towards whom, Clytemnestra?

CLYTEMNESTRA: Towards Electra Garrigó.

ELECTRA: Bearer of justice.

AGAMEMNON: Destiny, oh destiny!

ORESTES: Why provoke destiny?

CLYTEMNESTRA: Your destiny is the Pretender.

ELECTRA: Your destiny is the departure of Orestes.

AGAMEMNON: Destiny, oh destiny!

ORESTES: Let's kill destiny!

CLYTEMNESTRA: That would kill the Pretender.

ELECTRA: The Pretender isn't destiny.

AGAMEMNON: Destiny, oh destiny!

ORESTES: Perhaps I'm destiny?

CLYTEMNESTRA: No, no, no, you're not!

ELECTRA: Yes, yes, yes, you are!

AGAMEMNON: Destiny, oh destiny!

ORESTES: Who will make me leave?

CLYTEMNESTRA: No one! Destiny doesn't want it.

ELECTRA: Then you will die, Clytemnestra Pla.

AGAMEMNON: Destiny, oh destiny!

ORESTES: Will Clytemnestra Pla die?

CLYTEMNESTRA: Will Agamemnon Garrigó die?

ELECTRA: Will Agamemnon Garrigó die?

AGAMEMNON: Destiny, oh destiny!

ORESTES: Will Agamemnon Garrigó die?

CLYTEMNESTRA: Will Agamemnon Garrigó die?

ELECTRA: Agamemnon Garrigó will die.

AGAMEMNON: Destiny, oh destiny!

(The CHORUS begins to sing. The four characters remain still. The light goes down gradually. Slow curtain.)

CHORUS:
In the waves of the sea,
in the waters of the stream
in the jagged rocks
in the leaves of the palm trees,
in the suffering pines
in the canary's song
in reckless yearnings—
mad passion is revealed.
It spreads from mouth to mouth
with undertones of mourning.

Electra, as you lie in wait
keep your spirits high.
You're the purest rose of May,
a cup of fragrant air,
a gentle flower on a stem

that grows the sharpest thorns.
Break free of your prison
and tell the world your troubles:
tell us what you fear,
Electra of the storms.

ACT TWO

CHORUS:
A city sees an example made:
the temple where a tyrant ruled
will soon be laid to waste and
Electra will be crowned.
The iron will of a young girl
is the rock on which
a demented mind crashes.

(The same set as in Act One. ELECTRA appears dressed in red. A very dim light.)

ELECTRA: *(Enters slowly between the columns on the extreme left. She stops.)* Where are you, non-gods? Where are you, I repeat, you absolute negations of all divinity, all mythology, all reverence, dead forever? I want to see at least one of you. I ask a non-god to appear, here in the middle of this desert. *(Pauses)* Yes, I challenge you, non-existent creatures, shapes who haven't been recorded in any book or painted on an artist's canvas. Electra challenges you, non-gods, who will never be born and will never be divine. This bosom, which treats you with great apathy, is untroubled by the burden of solitude, and never visits sanctuaries nor lies prostrate. *(Pauses)* No, you shall not have any temples or sacrifices. Which of you will humans kneel to? They don't realize that once the gods have died, the new pantheon of non-gods will grant neither rewards nor punishment! *(Moves center stage)* You won't punish Electra. You won't reward her, either. Your apathy is so immense that Electra could take a life and not fear your reproach. You'd treat it like the mute sound of a falling fruit—you who are fruit whirling around and exploding into the violet dilation of oblivion. *(Long pause)* Are you part of a tropical forest, or are you filling it with shapes that are swollen with unpunished or unrewarded acts? *(She gestures as if she is holding onto something.)* Are you merely this arm, this breast, this hair? *(Pauses)* A path leads me to the place of apathy, to the center of indifference, where enormous leaves are engulfed by water reflecting images of breasts colliding, of claws and beaks passing through thorns until they fall at the side of a woman forgotten on a table. *(Pauses)* No tribunal, no judge can be convened. Will anyone demand a final judgment that can never be made? *(Long pause)* Ah, Electra. . . ! Ascend, always ascend. You should step towards the mansion of light in order to get the weapons you need. (*The lights onstage become brighter.*) Electra! Electra is turning! Lying in wait! Electra is lying in wait! (*Pauses*) I'm not moving forward, I'm spinning, in the direction of the light. Shapes of light, show me the path and find the crown I must destroy. Beautiful animals riding on the vertiginous wavelength of your apex; lines that will not cross lest the eye be overcome with horror. (*Pauses*) Forward, Electra! Surround your body with more and more light. Its teeth have pierced your flesh, but you won't be torn apart, you'll be exalted. (*Long pause*) No rewards and no punishments, Electra. A violent undulation prevents these shapes from becoming objects of veneration. Oh shapes, you are surrounded by non-divinity! I can annihilate this body, and light will soon return it to its place. (*The light becomes blinding.*) Here is the dividing line! I'll block it, so that the center of apathy recovers its domain. (*Pauses*) Get back, phantoms of the old gods. Gods of nothing with eyes of nothing! You will fall into the center of this light and orbit for all eternity as part of a whole that never feels self-pity. Come here, leaves and tree trunks, heads, feathers, swinging vines, roots of light! The blood to be spilled will make a cold sound as it collides with the final resistance of pity. (*Pauses*) Electra will get rid of the dividing line. Done! No need to open your eyes; the shapes have turned into millions of eyes watching each other. Does light have any need to see itself? Does light see anything, or anyone? Its effects, like useless Furies, will flow over Clytemnestra Pla and Agamemnon Garrigó. (*Long pause*) Oh at last, I know my name is Electra! I'm the one who knows the exact quantity of names. I'm the one who coldly presides over events. What could penetrate me? What could penetrate or pass through me? A hand that entered my right side would find itself on my left side. Touch me not—or you'll be fooled: I won't leave the smallest print, the most poetic trace, for I compose neither elegies nor see lovers pass by. (*Pauses*) It is to you, non-gods, that I say: I am the non-divinity, let me through! (*When Electra finishes her monologue, a gust of wind ripples her dress. She stands still.*)

AEGISTHUS: (*Enters followed by CLYTEMNESTRA*) Let her through, yes, let the divine Electra through! (*He takes ELECTRA's hand and kisses it.*) Have you finished yet, Electra? Is it with that phrase—Let me through!—that you say everything? (*Pauses*) Again. . .! Next time it'll sound better. (*To CLYTEMNESTRA*) She'd be a great actress.

CLYTEMNESTRA: (*Taking ELECTRA's chin in her hand*) She's already a great actress. She lives to act. I'm sure she feels nothing. What she shows us is a plaster mask. (*Pauses*) As for me, I prefer life itself! I've got everything at the tip of my breasts! Aren't I Clytemnestra Pla, the woman with the prophetic breasts?

AEGISTHUS: Dearest friend, are your oracular breasts going to reveal something?

CLYTEMNESTRA: (*With affectation*) Not at the moment, my dear Aegisthus, loyal friend of this house. No, I haven't come to make any revelation. I've simply come to tell Electra what the entire city already knows.

ELECTRA: (*Without any curiosity*) What does the entire city already know?

CLYTEMNESTRA: (*Feigning indifference*) The Pretender killed himself at three o'clock this afternoon. The night edition is out and the paperboys are announcing it on the street. Haven't you heard?

ELECTRA: (*To herself*) He's the first to go. (*To CLYTEMNESTRA*) I don't need a paperboy to know the ultimate fate of the Pretender. Besides, his death isn't important to me. He's the first, and others will follow.

CLYTEMNESTRA: Your father is celebrating this death by making a mess. The patio is covered with broken bottles.

ELECTRA: Is Agamemnon drunk?

AEGISTHUS: He's had two cases of beer. As you know, he has a generous throat.

ELECTRA: (*Pensive*) This way he'll suffer less . . .

CLYTEMNESTRA: (*Grabbing her by the arms*) What do you mean?

ELECTRA: Nothing.

AEGISTHUS: And now what will you do, poor Electra? Wasn't the Pretender your supreme hope?

ELECTRA: There's never a supreme hope. I'll stay here for the rest of my life.

CLYTEMNESTRA: (*Looking at AEGISTHUS*) That won't suit you. You're very young and other men will court you. The world is full of handsome men.

ELECTRA: None of them interests me.

AEGISTHUS: What is your father plotting? The Pretender killed himself because your father refused to give him your hand. Does Agamemnon want you to be with him for the rest of his life? (*To CLYTEMNESTRA*) Don't you agree, Clytemnestra Pla?

ELECTRA: As I said, I'm destined to stay here. You've heard the cliché about the captain who goes down with his ship . . . well, I'll go down with this house. I'm staying, and that's final.

AEGISTHUS: (*To CLYTEMNESTRA*) Are you happy with the idea of a vestal virgin under your roof, Clytemnestra Pla?

CLYTEMNESTRA: To be honest, no. (*To ELECTRA*) I won't give up until I've found another Pretender for you.

(*AGAMEMNON enters, wearing bedsheets and a washbasin to imitate the garments and helmet of a Greek leader. He's drunk, but behaves with dignity.*)

AGAMEMNON: (*Walking towards the three characters*) The cruelty of a god is infinite. If I please Mercury with libations, I offend Jupiter with my horses. Mercury has rewarded me with happy news: the Pretender has died. *(To ELECTRA)* Have you heard, dear Electra, that your Pretender departed for Avernus?

CLYTEMNESTRA: And what did Jupiter offer you, Agamemnon Garrigó?

AGAMEMNON: *(Slapping himself on the forehead)* His horns! You've cuckolded me, Clytemnestra Pla.

AEGISTHUS: *(Terrified, but pretending not to be)* And who has Clytemnestra left you for, brave Agamemnon?

AGAMEMNON: *(Poking his forefinger into AEGISTHUS's chest)* You, Aegisthus! I know you're sleeping with Clytemnestra, my wife, daughter of Tyndareos and Leda, wife of Agamemnon, mother of Electra and Orestes, Iphegenia and Chrysothemis.

CLYTEMNESTRA: Don't offend us, Agamemnon Garrigó. But we forgive you because you're drunk. I am the forever chaste Clytemnestra Pla.

AGAMEMNON: You have a terrible sense of humor, Clytemnestra Pla. Will you never see me as Agamemnon, King of Mycenae and Argos, from the House of Atreus, brother of Menelaus, leader of the Greeks, who sacrificed Iphigenia? *(Long pause. He looks upwards.)* I wanted to lead a vaguely heroic life, but I'm only well fed and middle class. *(Pleading)* Tell me, I beg you, tell me. What is my tragedy? Because I must have a tragedy like all human beings, a tragedy to fulfill, but it escapes me!

AEGISTHUS: *(Sarcastic)* Beer has given him epic dimensions. *(To AGAMEMNON)* You don't have any tragedy to fulfill. You're a happy father who amuses himself by improvising pleasant comedies, a father who is so merry that he dresses up in sheets and washbasins. . . *(Slapping him on the back)* Go on, Agamemnon of Cuba! Go on, have some more beer! Maybe that will help you decipher the secret of your life.

AGAMEMNON: *(Backing away majestically)* A tragedy! I'm living through a tragedy and I don't know what it is. *(He stops. To ELECTRA)* Farewell, dear Electra, I'm going to drown myself in sleep. *(He reaches the columns.)* I'm living through a tragedy; would anyone care to tell me what it is? *(He disappears.)*

AEGISTHUS: *(To CLYTEMNESTRA, cynically)* Chaste Clytemnestra, I need to know: are we having an illicit affair, an adulterous passion?

CLYTEMNESTRA: That's exactly what I was going to ask you, noble Aegisthus, loyal friend to husbands, loyal companion to wives: are we having an illicit affair?

ELECTRA: *(Circling around CLYTEMNESTRA)* I don't see any sin, Clytemnestra Pla. You like Aegisthus Don, you sleep with Aegisthus Don. It's that simple.

CLYTEMNESTRA: How dare you. . .? Are you drunk like your father?

ELECTRA: I know everything. Why the charade? It's useless. You know I'm not afraid.

AEGISTHUS: You're insulting us by presuming . . .

ELECTRA: Dear Aegisthus: I don't blame you. You're my mother's lover, you're trying to get rid of my father, you're after his riches, and Clytemnestra is backing you. What are you waiting for?

CLYTEMNESTRA: Which oracle have you consulted, Electra?

ELECTRA: My father's fate is sealed. Your hands are free to act.

(The voice of the TUTOR can be heard offstage growing nearer. He enters followed by ORESTES.)

TUTOR: *(To the three characters)* . . . He doesn't want to understand that in the animal kingdom there are only events, nothing but events.

ELECTRA: In the human kingdom as well, Tutor, events, only events.

TUTOR: Agreed, you're more advanced than your brother. I'm trying to make him understand that in the animal kingdom . . .

ELECTRA: *(To ORESTES)* Nothing but events, Orestes.

TUTOR: If something is destined in the animal kingdom, no judge, no divine or human power, can stop it.

ELECTRA: *(Claps her hands)* The law of necessity!

AEGISTHUS: Bravo, Electra, bravo! Long live necessity!

CLYTEMNESTRA: *(Clapping)* Yes! *(Pauses)* But tell me: which of us is necessity?

ELECTRA: You, Clytemnestra Pla. Right now, you are necessity. Don't miss the chance.

CLYTEMNESTRA: *(Leaning on AEGISTHUS, with her hand on her forehead)* Am I necessity? Oh, Orestes, my beloved son! Am I necessity?

ORESTES: How can I know, Clytemnestra, if I have no idea what necessity you're talking about. *(To the TUTOR)* Do you mean that the law of necessity will cause, for example, my mother's old rooster to be killed today, pecked to death by the hens?

TUTOR: I heard your mother order it a moment ago. She commanded the head servant, "Do away with that rooster immediately. He's full of pox. My hens will finish him off." *(To CLYTEMNESTRA)* Isn't that so, divine Clytemnestra?

CLYTEMNESTRA: *(Absorbed)* Yes, Tutor, I gave that order.

ORESTES: *(Takes the TUTOR by the arm)* So, Tutor, a sacrifice is merely an event. *(They begin to walk towards the columns.)*

AEGISTHUS: *(He catches up to them.)* I'm going with you. I'm crazy about cockfights. Although in this case the hens will be the killers. In any case, if they don't do away with him quickly, I'll strangle him myself. *(He shows them his hands. They exit.)*

CLYTEMNESTRA: *(To ELECTRA, in a solemn voice)* Did you hear that, Electra? The death of my old rooster . . . Do you know which I'm referring to? The one your father gave me as a gift two years ago.

ELECTRA: I know perfectly well which rooster you're referring to. He must die today.

CLYTEMNESTRA: But . . . must he really die today?

ELECTRA: Yes, Clytemnestra, today. His open sores threaten us with an epidemic. Besides, he's ugly. He must die today.

CLYTEMNESTRA: Don't fool yourself, Electra. He's not that sick. He could last for a long time . . .

ELECTRA: He must die today.

CLYTEMNESTRA: (Looking at ELECTRA insistently) Cover me with your shawl, Electra.

ELECTRA: (She removes her shawl and places it on CLYTEMNESTRA's head.) Go, Clytemnestra!

CLYTEMNESTRA: (She walks in circles with her hands outstretched, as if playing blindman's buff. The light dims slowly.) No doubt about it! The old rooster must die today! A firm hand must strangle him; he has a strong neck. I'm afraid my hens won't be able to peck him to death. Was I a sibyl when I named my rooster Agamemnon? (Pauses) Agamemnon, old rooster, today you must die, or you'll discover that I'm having an affair with Aegisthus Don. (She roars with laughter.) What the hell do I mean? How could a rooster know about an affair between humans? And why would it care? (She laughs again.) But he's so jealous . . . of mother and daughter. (Pauses. She begins to raise her voice.) I understand: for years, you've been king of the henhouse, and now you realize you've been pushed aside by a magnificent rooster. (Pauses) Is this magnificent rooster the executioner my hens need? I proclaim him a rooster of noble bearing! When he kisses me, I grow weak with delight. (She laughs convulsively.) What nonsense. How can a beak kiss my lips? Besides, compared to me, a rooster is tiny . . . And how could its feathers stick to my flesh? (Pauses. She becomes very serious.) I'm completely justified. I'm referring to the old rooster, of course. He's intolerant and abusive and he's made me suffer. On the other hand, because of his cursed plan to keep his daughter fenced inside this coop forever, he's spoiling my affair with Aegisthus. (Pauses) Yes, with Aegisthus: there's no reason to hide it. (Raises her voice louder) What we need is to cleanse our blood! This old rooster must die today. I'm an unhappy woman who can't enjoy her lover because of an old, crippled, stooped-over, pockmarked, filthy, stinking rooster. (She turns around two more times.) It's so invigorating to spin around! Everything looks red. It makes me stronger. Strength, come to me! A poor woman only asks that a horrible old rooster be taken away from her lovely sight. (In a thunderous voice) Young rooster, virile rooster: come to the aid of a beautiful woman! (To ELECTRA) What should I do, Electra, what should I do?

ELECTRA: Do something.

CLYTEMNESTRA: (Turning around) Yes, do something, do something quickly. (Shouting) Aegisthus, Aegisthus! (A gigantic shadow of a rooster appears between two of the central columns.) Beautiful white rooster, handsome virile rooster: come! This is the day of blood! (The shadow moves in a grotesque way. CLYTEMNESTRA takes off the shawl. She runs towards the shadow.) Aegisthus, go to the old rooster, the black rooster! Today he must die! Yes, Aegisthus, finish him off with your spurs! (She beats the shadow.) Old rooster, black rooster! (The shadow disappears. CLYTEMNESTRA exits through the columns, shouting.) Old rooster, black rooster!

CHORUS:
Death shoots its lightning
at Agamemnon:
Clytemnestra and her
deadly lover strike.
The whisper of sheets
round the neck of the king—
a snake drops
in the midst of horror.

Hear, O Clytemnestra,
the orchestra of doom.
Your wanton love
foretells a certain death.
Traitorous mother,
you'll see your fortune
turn for the worse
and become a mortal feast.

CLYTEMNESTRA: (Enters between the columns. She is absorbed in thought.) A sacred rooster is within the marital chamber now. He's no longer an ignoble old rooster. Death has given him nobility. And we are alive: Orestes, Aegisthus and I. (Pauses) And Electra will leave us soon; she'll take her madness to the desolate cliffs of a forgotten coast, and hurl herself against the rocks. (Pauses) My beloved Orestes will have whatever he wants, he need only ask. Except for one thing: he's to be eternally celibate! He belongs to me. I don't want him to leave, I don't want any woman to enjoy him. I'll be the one he adores, the one to whom he offers sacrifices—bloody or not! He'll be king of a city built by my crimes! (Pauses) But Electra is still under this roof. She doesn't reveal her dreams or her visions. A minute ago she recited a speech, but they weren't her words, she was simply reciting. I must be careful. (To ELECTRA) You're still here, Electra?

ELECTRA: I don't know how long I was dreaming. Unfortunately my dream was unclear, as dreams are.

CLYTEMNESTRA: Wake up! You think you're still dreaming. Tell me: was a crime committed in your dream?

ELECTRA: No, Clytemnestra Pla, the crime was committed as I was dreaming. Go now, try to sleep. I'll wipe out all traces of the crime; I'll turn that corpse into a mound of ashes.

CLYTEMNESTRA: But now he's a sacred rooster.

ELECTRA: No, Clytemnestra, not at all! He's just a dead rooster to be disposed of!

CLYTEMNESTRA: You're right. The law is so annoying.

ELECTRA: The law? What I care about is hygiene.

CLYTEMNESTRA: Well, if you don't care about the law, why don't you arrange the royal funeral?

ELECTRA: I don't want to waste my time on empty ceremonies. Agamemnon Garrigó is dead, isn't he? Why deceive the city with hypocritical praise?

CLYTEMNESTRA: (*Turning towards AEGISTHUS who has entered*) Here's Aegisthus. (*To AEGISTHUS*) Electra insists that we go to sleep, darling Aegisthus.

AEGISTHUS: An excellent idea. After the disturbance we've had, we deserve a rest. (*He walks away with CLYTEMNESTRA. To ELECTRA, from the columns*) Electra, wake up! We're going to sleep. What will you do now?

ELECTRA: I'm going to incinerate the old rooster. (*She moves towards center stage.*) It's a question of hygiene, a simple question of hygiene.

(*CLYTEMNESTRA and AEGISTHUS move away, laughing loudly.*)

ELECTRA: (*Pensive*) I've taken care of Agamemnon! Now: Clytemnestra! That's it: a question of hygiene, a simple question of hygiene. (*She stands without moving.*)

CHORUS:
Suddenly a death
and an example is set:
a father mustn't stand
in his daughter's path.
A shocking destiny is met
as the king, asleep at night,
finds death between his sheets.

Unfaithful Clytemnestra
hear our fateful song.
Crafty woman,
selfish mother,
you'll share the fate that struck the father
of your cold unyielding daughter.

ACT THREE

CHORUS:
O city, now you've seen
the solemn wing of death
that stalks a sinful father
with its somber shadow.
A matter of hygiene, and
a brother and sister are saved:
quick-moving fingers
have liberated a city.

But death has not
ended its toll,
death wants radiance,
flashes, bolts of lightning,
and to see Clytemnestra
in agony in her bed.

(*The set is the same. The only changes: the door on the left is closed. There is a door on the right. An intense yellow light. The action occurs at night. ORESTES and the TUTOR enter.*)

ORESTES: (*Laughing*) Excuse me for saying it again, but the late-night death of the old rooster has put me in a marvelous position.

TUTOR: I'm not blaming you at all, Orestes. I'm pleased that you're satisfied. Besides, I see that something, at least, has amazed you. It's a good sign.

ORESTES: (*As if talking to himself*) What a hard life that old rooster had!

TUTOR: I myself was surprised. I always thought that he would collapse from terror. But that's not what happened. (*Pauses*) By the way, did you notice what skillful fingers Aegisthus has, perfect for strangling?

ORESTES: I agree. He broke the bird's neck with only two fingers. Of course, a bird's neck doesn't offer the same resistance as a human one.

TUTOR: (*Raising a hand*) In this case, Orestes, I'm not talking about a superior force that opposes an equally strong resistance. I'm not talking about what makes the resistance strong. I'm referring, specifically, to the skill of Aegisthus's fingers. He'd have needed no more strength to strangle a man—for example, your father, who has the neck of a bull.

ORESTES: I confess, Tutor, that I was fascinated when Aegisthus broke the bird's neck so delicately.

TUTOR: And what's to be said about the elegant movement of the handkerchief over the bird's head! He used it to avoid a long, agonizing death, and the bird was snuffed out immediately. (*Pauses*) I'm certain the poor rooster was grateful.

ORESTES: I've heard Clytemnestra say that Aegisthus traveled to India as a youth.

TUTOR: No, no, no, Orestes! Drop any idea of investigating, forget about playing Scotland Yard! Aegisthus is a consummate strangler. That's all.

ORESTES: That's why I'm telling you! I'd like to learn this art. Maybe Clytemnestra would let me leave, if she knew I was attracted to India and its stranglers.

TUTOR: Really? Does Clytemnestra Pla know the art of strangulation? Has she also traveled to India?

ORESTES: No, not at all! But she admires Aegisthus so much . . . to her, Aegisthus is the sum of all knowledge.

TUTOR: And all tricks. Maybe that's why I've never been able to figure out what he's thinking. He's the consummate sophist of the drawing room.

ORESTES: That's my impression, too. It's not what he

says, it's how he says it. He's the best "decorator" in the city.

TUTOR: And Clytemnestra Pla is so decorative!

ORESTES: Of course! I don't know how to get permission from my mother for my trip. I'm sure that if Aegisthus showed me his tricks, Clytemnestra would agree to it.

TUTOR: He'll never show them to you. A conjurer never reveals the secret of his illusions. Even I'd be more likely to teach you the art of strangulation.

ORESTES: That's something you haven't taught me, and you never will. (Pauses) In our city, the gymnasts and the chatterboxes form the highest caste. That's not counting people with weapons up their sleeves. Despite your teaching, I couldn't even strangle myself.

TUTOR: Let virtue flow, not blood, just as water, not wine, flows from a fountain, though the Aegisthuses of the world would say otherwise. (Pauses) This noble city has two enormous lice on its head: the dominance of its women and the machismo of its men.

ORESTES: But when your human part is offended, you at least can hide under your horse part . . .

TUTOR: Then they'd beat my horse part. (Pauses) No, there's no escape.

ORESTES: There's always sophistry . . .

TUTOR: It's true. In a city as vain as this, full of exploits that never happened, monuments never built, virtues that no one practices, sophistry is the weapon par excellence. If one of the wise women tells you that she's a prolific author of tragedies, don't contradict her; if a man declares that he's a consummate critic, second his falsehood. Don't forget—we're talking about a city where everyone wants to be fooled.

ORESTES: So the idea is to leave. But how? (Pauses. He looks at his watch.) It's eleven o'clock. I'm going to bed. I'm due at the gymnasium at six.

TUTOR: The gymnasium . . . . . Orestes?

ORESTES: (From the columns) That's right, Tutor, habit is the fiercest of gods. Will I leave these hostile columns one day, to find the ocean?

(As ORESTES begins to leave, he is stopped by CLYTEMNESTRA, who enters accompanied by AEGISTHUS. She wears a black robe with silver adornments around her waist and in her hair. On her chest there is a large red hibiscus. AEGISTHUS is dressed in white.)

CLYTEMNESTRA: (Approaches the TUTOR) He tired you out, didn't he, with that same old song about leaving? (To ORESTES) You're a bad boy. (Pauses) Have you forgotten that life begins on this side of the columns? What lies beyond those columns is death and decomposition.

TUTOR: (To ORESTES, intentionally) Your mother is telling the truth, Orestes. Beyond those columns is the sea, and right now, it's as unpredictable as the sea

that cast Odysseus on the beaches of the divine Calypso. (He turns to AEGISTHUS, and raises a hand as if greeting him.) Health to you, strangler of roosters! I don't think you know much about Aesculapius, because the rooster you sacrificed to him was sick.

CLYTEMNESTRA: (Laughs loudly) Old, lame, hoarse, and smelly! A simple question of hygiene, as Electra said. (Laughs even harder) A question of hygiene! Now we're happy. . . ! (Walks across the stage) Let this palace be filled with happiness and red flowers, like the one emblazoned on my chest. This house has been possessed of good health, and all that's ugly, all that's strange, must disappear. (She stops next to ORESTES.) Did you know that Agamemnon left last night?

ORESTES: Through these columns, headed towards the sea. . . ?

CLYTEMNESTRA: Headed towards the sea . . . No mortal can say if he'll return or not.

ORESTES: I think my father made an excellent decision. Isn't the most important part of that equation the first part, that is, his leaving?

CLYTEMNESTRA: But that means death. (Pauses) You will not leave.

ORESTES: (Pretending) No one's talking about leaving, Clytemnestra Pla. And if someone did, the destination would only be India . . .

CLYTEMNESTRA: I don't see how going to India will spare you the dangers of Australia.

ORESTES: It won't, but I'll learn how to strangle. (To AEGISTHUS) Aegisthus, didn't you learn the art of strangulation in India?

AEGISTHUS: That's absolutely right. Years ago, unfavorable winds blew my ships towards Calcutta. One month was enough to learn how to strangle elegantly, using the ten fingers of my hands.

TUTOR: Yes, in an ascending order. Two fingers for poultry, for example, roosters; five fingers for a rabbit or a snake; ten fingers for a human being.

ORESTES: Wait! I don't think that ten fingers are required for the delicate neck of a woman.

AEGISTHUS: Orestes is right. I saw a young woman being strangled in Marseilles with only two fingers. It's true, the girl's jugular wasn't any bigger than the jugular of a mother hen.

ORESTES: (Pointing to CLYTEMNESTRA) Here she is: here's the mother hen! (He puts his thumb and forefinger around CLYTEMNESTRA's neck.) Couldn't I strangle you, Clytemnestra Pla, with only these two fingers?

CLYTEMNESTRA: (Filled with terror, she removes his fingers from her neck.) Let me go! I won't be strangled to death! No, I won't be strangled!

TUTOR: Who was talking about death, madam?

CLYTEMNESTRA: (Seeking refuge in the arms of AEGISTHUS) Orestes, my son, do you plan to strangle me?

ORESTES: No, Clytemnestra, I still haven't traveled to India . . . *(Pauses)* In any case, Aegisthus would be . . . *(Pauses)* Haven't you noticed his arm around your neck?

CLYTEMNESTRA: *(She removes AEGISTHUS's arm violently; at the same time she uses both of her hands to protect her neck. She stares at AEGISTHUS, who stands with his hand upraised forming a circle with his thumb and forefinger.)* You, too, Aegisthus? I'm not that girl in Marseilles, I'm not an old hen . . . I'm your . . . *(Pauses)* Excuse me, I'm absolutely hysterical. Why do you talk about such things? *(She approaches the TUTOR.)* Tell them I'll die in my own bed.

TUTOR: I'm not an oracle, Clytemnestra Pla. *(He shows her his tail.)* This tail declares very clearly that I'm a centaur. My job is to teach, not make predictions. You pay me, and I fill your children's heads with my science.

CLYTEMNESTRA: So then, who will tell me my fate?

CHORUS:
Don't ask, Clytemnestra,
about your life or death.
Your neck shows no wounds
from the cockpit.
Don't ask, Clytemnestra,
what destiny holds for you:
your life is headed
towards a shocking end.
Lady, your rose is black:
it suits your nature.

TUTOR: Divine Clytemnestra, I wash my hands, as always . . . *(He makes a gesture of washing his hands.)*

CLYTEMNESTRA: As long as you don't put them around my neck . . . *(She covers her neck again with her hands.)*

AEGISTHUS: *(He removes CLYTEMNESTRA's hands from around her neck.)* Careful, divine Clytemnestra! You could strangle yourself with your own hands!

ORESTES: *(As if making a prophecy)* Clytemnestra Pla will not be strangled.

CLYTEMNESTRA: *(Embraces ORESTES)* Orestes, my son, the passion of my life! A mother full of troubles thanks you for your declaration. *(Pauses. To everyone)* Did you hear that? My beloved Orestes has guaranteed that I won't be strangled to death.

ORESTES: Don't rejoice too much, Clytemnestra Pla. So many deaths remain . . .

CLYTEMNESTRA: *(Furious)* Listen, everyone: I want to live forever, I want to be immortal! I won't accept any death, tragic or not. *(Pauses)* In the end, of course, I'll accept death, but only when I'm very old, in my own bed. *(To AEGISTHUS)* Let's go, Aegisthus! My seer will tell me what none of you can predict. *(She starts to leave. At the columns, she stops. To ORESTES)* Orestes, don't cross . . . don't cross . . . *(AEGISTHUS and CLYTEMNESTRA exit.)*

ORESTES: *(Absorbed in his thoughts. Addresses the TUTOR)* What did she say?

TUTOR: That you shouldn't cross . . .

ORESTES: I shouldn't cross. . . ? What?

TUTOR: She meant beyond the columns . . . *(He walks towards the columns.)* I, for my part, am going to cross over. Electra is waiting for my lesson on apathy. *(He is at the columns.)* Will you join us? Electra is searching desperately for you. *(Exits)*

(As the TUTOR speaks, ORESTES becomes absorbed in thought. He suddenly runs impulsively towards the first column on the right. From there he calls ELECTRA in anguish. He repeats his call from the rest of the columns. He leans against the final column with his hands behind him. The light becomes very tenuous. A long pause)

ORESTES: Electra won't come. That's the problem: Electra won't come. *(Pauses)* But let's analyze this a piece at a time. Electra won't come, I can't leave, the Pretender has died, Agamemnon has died, Clytemnestra is afraid of dying. *(Pauses)* Now, put it together. *(He moves away from the column and takes two or three steps across the stage.)* But the whole picture escapes me . . . *(Pauses)* What links Agamemnon's death and Clytemnestra's fear? And what does Clytemnestra have to do with Agamemnon's death? This question leads to the next: why did Clytemnestra, who has an indescribable fear of Electra, cause Agamemnon's death—allowing Electra to be master of her own will? *(Pauses)* And what, then, does Electra have to do with the death of Agamemnon? Did it have something to do with the Pretender? No, Electra wouldn't scheme so arduously for the sake of any Pretender . . . *(Pauses)* Let's look at other possibilities: Electra's excessive hate as a result of Agamemnon's excessive love? Electra's excessive love as a result of Agamemnon's excessive hate? *(Pauses)* Either way, excessive love provides deadly weapons to the excessive love or hate that it has provoked. *(Pauses)* But did Electra love or hate Agamemnon Garrigó? What if Electra neither loved nor hated Agamemnon Garrigó? *(Pauses)* Why then did she take part in our father's death? To give aid to Clytemnestra Pla? That leads to the next question: if Agamemnon Garrigó was the perfect husband for Clytemnestra Pla, what was her motive in bringing about my father's death? Did she think it would make Electra's soul grieve? Or did she think that Agamemnon's death would hasten Electra's departure from this house? *(Pauses)* But Clytemnestra would never want her to leave for her own good. She truly hates Electra. Why does she hate her? Not because of beauty—Clytemnestra believes she's the most beautiful of all. Not because of worldliness—Clytemnestra believes she's the worldliest of women. Not because of wisdom—Clytemnestra believes she's the wisest of all. No, that's not why! Clytemnestra would never hate anyone without a reason. There must be something specific. (Pauses) Because I love Electra more than her? No, in that case Clytemnestra would have killed Electra. Clytemnestra can't conceive of my loving anyone but her. She is so certain of my love! (Long pause) To recapitulate: Clytemnestra clearly wanted to get rid of Electra and Agamemnon . . . why? (Pauses) Let's look at Clytemnestra's preferences: I'm in first place. (Pauses) Then . . . (The lights come up suddenly.) Aegisthus! The palace favorite, Clytemnestra's paramour, Clytemnestra's confessor, Clytemnestra's servant, Clytemnestra's echo, Clytemnestra's lover! (Long pause) Agamemnon's fate was sealed. Three people had an interest in his death. But I could have cared less. If Agamemnon couldn't work things out by himself, that was his problem. Between Agamemnon and me there was no bond to speak of. What's important was that there were three people with a strong interest in his death. (Pauses) But Agamemnon . . . did he really want to die? No, not at all. He was overpowered by something stronger. (Pauses) And on the other hand—I want to leave, but there's a force opposed to it. What is that force? Clytemnestra Pla! Another force, of equal strength, wants me to leave. Electra! (Pauses) But there's something contradictory about Electra: according to the Tutor, she desperately wants to see me. I shout out her name, I stand by the columns and call her, and she doesn't come. I've realized that these columns are barriers. (Pauses) The columns are excuses! Excuses! Weak soul, won't you ever understand? (Pauses) Here's what it boils down to: me, Clytemnestra, the columns, my departure . . . I have to destroy that part of myself that resists, and once I've done that, have to achieve the other goal, that is, eliminate Clytemnestra Pla. And then immediately tear down the columns, and then, and then only, leave.

(ORESTES remains standing with his back to the columns. A long pause. ELECTRA enters through the opening between the central columns. The light is very weak.)

ELECTRA: (Stops at the columns) The time has come. Here is the foreigner. Certain signs tell me that he is my beloved brother Orestes. The Tutor told me that he put his fingers around Clytemnestra's neck, but is that enough to identify him as my brother? It's also significant that he dared to tell Clytemnestra that many other violent deaths will happen. What if I question him and determine that he isn't Orestes, that he's simply a foreigner? I'd have to kill him. Electra cannot let a foreigner know that she can't find her brother. (Pauses) But I must question him. I must hear from his own lips whether or not he is Orestes. Only if he is Orestes can he kill Clytemnestra and leave. (Pauses) It's decided! I will question him. (She approaches ORESTES and taps him on the shoulder.) Foreigner: What is your name?

ORESTES: (He turns around reluctantly.) Orestes.

ELECTRA. Excuse the questions of an inquisitive woman. I had a brother with that name, but I lost him at a young age because of the romantic intrigues of our parents. Orestes and I were very young when we were separated. My father took me, and my mother took Orestes. Over the years I've tried to recognize my brother in the many other Orestes that have arrived at this palace. None of them was the real Orestes.

ORESTES: How did you know?

ELECTRA: I subjected them to a test that never fails.

ORESTES: What is the test?

ELECTRA: Like the sphinx, I posed a question to the would-be Orestes. A correct answer would prove he was the real Orestes; an incorrect answer would send the impostor to his death.

ORESTES: A truly harsh test. (Pauses) And they risked it?

ELECTRA: Yes. Curiosity is stronger than death. And truthfully, didn't they feel deep down that something from the real Orestes touched them? Something that, with a strange persistence, was present without revealing itself?

ORESTES: (Anxiously) And none of those foreigners could resist taking the test?

ELECTRA: Oh, no, not one! And in the end none of them was the real Orestes.

ORESTES: (Crosses his hands over his chest and stands at attention in front of ELECTRA) If you think I'm the Orestes you're looking for, why do you hesitate to give me the test?

ELECTRA: (Doubtful) If you fail, it would mean your death. And I've already killed so many Orestes . . . And you're so handsome.

ORESTES: Not one more word. I insist on taking the test.

ELECTRA: As you like. Here's the question: What would the real Orestes do?

ORESTES: (Speaks slowly) The real Orestes would kill his mother, and then leave.

(The light becomes intense.)

ELECTRA: Oh, you are Orestes! (Pauses) I'll give you the weapon you need.

ORESTES: I'll wait for you eagerly.

ELECTRA: We must be careful. Clytemnestra sees enemies all over. Her neck is covered with a sheet of solid silver. She's afraid of being strangled.

ORESTES: (Anxiously) Must I strangle Clytemnestra, Electra?

ELECTRA: No, you'd be copying Aegisthus. Clytemnestra will be poisoned with her favorite fruit.

ORESTES: The papaya!

ELECTRA: Exactly: at the right moment you'll offer her a slice. She'll eat it without hesitation. She trusts you blindly.

ORESTES: Let's not lose a minute, then. Clytemnestra likes to take the air at this hour.

ELECTRA: *(Taking ORESTES by the arms and pointing to the columns)* We're going to cross to the other side of those columns, because death and decomposition will soon be on this side. *(They exit.)*

CHORUS:
Now brother and sister meet,
long separated by a wall
their sullied parents built
to hide appalling guilt.
The powerful hand
of immutable fate
brings down its weight
on a wicked mother.
Orestes will declare
Clytemnestra guilty.

(CLYTEMNESTRA enters. She is wearing a silver collar around her neck. She seems defeated, terrorized. She stands center stage and surveys her surroundings.)

CLYTEMNESTRA: I see Electras all over. Electras who assault me like the flakes of a cruel snowstorm I've never seen. If I see a chair, it's Electra. If I see a comb—Electra; a mirror, the sun as it sets, these flagstones, those columns, Electra. *(Pauses)* Everything is Electra. It's dreadful. That woman is chasing me. *(She looks cautiously around her again.)* She wants me to die. And what's more, she casts horrible spells . . . Once she's looked at an object in this palace, I can no longer look at it. Electra is what looks at me; what I look at is Electra; whatever feels me looking at it, turns into Electra. I myself will turn into Electra in the end! *(Pauses)* But no—before that, death. That viscous woman, that woman-object, that woman who's only a character in a tragedy. *(Pauses)* Can a character in a tragedy be killed? Can a shadow be poisoned? She's all that . . . *(Pauses)* She's made me desperate—I can't enjoy my crime in peace. She looks at me, and with those bovine eyes of hers she says "I won't burden you with guilt, you'll die like the one whose death you caused." *(She touches her neck.)* That's the reason for this silver collar. Actually, it's not that bad—it makes my neck more flexible. But Orestes guaranteed that I wouldn't be strangled. *(Pauses)* Oh, I bite into this lovely morsel: Orestes, Orestes is the antidote against Electra! Why didn't I realize it before? Of course, it's very simple! I'll let Orestes leave under one condition: what? Electra's death. But, did I say that Orestes will leave? Over my dead body. I'd rather see Electra everywhere. *(She stares in the direction of the columns.)*

(CLYTEMNESTRA's servants enter from the central columns. AGAMEMNON's servants follow, and after them, the TUTOR. AEGISTHUS is at the end of the procession. The first black actress carries a hand mirror; the second, a plastic comb; the third, a small table; the fourth, a silver tray with a slice of papaya.)*

CLYTEMNESTRA: What does this procession mean?

(The first black actress gives the mirror to CLYTEMNESTRA; the second, the comb; the third places the table on the floor; the fourth places the tray on the table.)

CLYTEMNESTRA: What does all this mean? *(She sees AGAMEMNON's servants.)* Are they still under this roof? What is the majordomo doing? Not one more minute in this house!

(The female servants begin to walk in a circle around CLYTEMNESTRA.)

CLYTEMNESTRA: Are you abandoning me as well?

(The female servants nod their heads mockingly three times. They exit through the central columns, followed by the black male servants who make an exaggerated bow.)

TUTOR: *(Approaches CLYTEMNESTRA)* Divine Clytemnestra: I've finished my mission. Your children can stand on their own two feet. I'm leaving.

CLYTEMNESTRA: Tutor, wait. I'm not throwing you out of my house. This is a house of happiness. What could be better for a philosopher than happiness?

TUTOR: If happiness is called Electra, I agree. *(Pauses)* Agamemnon has left . . . His servants are going, your servants are going, Orestes will leave; Aegisthus is waiting to say farewell; finally, you too will leave.

CLYTEMNESTRA: *(In distress)* Should I leave, Tutor?

TUTOR: Yes, because this palace is going to be filled with a new fluid called Electra. Everything here will become Electra. Would you like to be part of that infinite multiplication of Electras?

CLYTEMNESTRA: *(Absorbed in thought)* An infinite multiplication of Electras . . . That's it: an infinite multiplication of Electras . . . *(Pauses)* Here everything is Electra. The color is Electra, the sound, Electra, hate, Electra, the day, Electra, the night, Electra, revenge, Electra. *(Shouts between sobs)* Electra, Electra, Electra, Electra, Electra!

TUTOR: *(Moves away)* Soon you'll have a rest from Electra.

CLYTEMNESTRA: *(Breathing rapidly)* What did you just say?

TUTOR: *(From the columns)* That you'll have a rest very soon . . . *(Exits)*

AEGISTHUS: *(Approaches CLYTEMNESTRA)* Clytemnestra Pla . . .

CLYTEMNESTRA: You, too, Aegisthus?

AEGISTHUS: *(Sarcastically)* Me, too, divine Clytemnestra. Your house doesn't agree with me, and neither does your money; your house is Electra, your money, Electra. This house is creaking, it's threatening to become a chaos of Electra-material. Clytemnestra, I don't want to be crushed to death under so dark a substance. You know how much I adore white clothes.

CLYTEMNESTRA: But with your strangler's hands, you

could free me from this dark weight. *(Pauses)* If you put an end to the father, you could do the same to the daughter. Then you'd be the absolute master of my house.

AEGISTHUS: *(Laughs)* Do you think it's possible to strangle a fluid? Didn't you hear the Tutor? I'd rather leave. Aren't you going, too?

CLYTEMNESTRA: *(Furious)* Everyone tells me to go, but I haven't planned any trip.

AEGISTHUS: Because you'd be traveling against your will?

CLYTEMNESTRA: Everything I do is according to my will. I don't want to take that trip. *(Pauses)* But I do want you to get rid of Electra.

AEGISTHUS: Electra can't be eliminated. Get that into your lovely head.

CLYTEMNESTRA: *(Turns her back to him)* Very well. Leave. Orestes will stay with me.

AEGISTHUS: *(Starts to leave)* I wouldn't count on Orestes. *(He stops.)* Clytemnestra Pla: I'm a narcissist, I'm a killer, but I don't want you to die. Watch out for Orestes.

CLYTEMNESTRA: *(Furious)* Get out of here! You miserable slanderer, get out of this house! Orestes is part of me, he's my heart, these eyes, these hands. If I die, Orestes will die.

AEGISTHUS: If that's what you think . . . *(Exits)*

CLYTEMNESTRA: *(Looks attentively at the comb)* What a nightmare! An Electra-comb. *(Pauses. She looks in the mirror.)* An Electra-mirror.

(ORESTES enters cautiously. He approaches CLYTEMNESTRA from behind and puts his hands over her eyes.)

CLYTEMNESTRA: *(Shouts)* Electra!

ORESTES: *(Takes away his hands)* No, Orestes.

CLYTEMNESTRA: No, you're not Orestes, you're Electra. I'm not Clytemnestra, I'm Electra. Are you forgetting that everything here is Electra?

ORESTES: You're too nervous, Clytemnestra. You should rest.

CLYTEMNESTRA: *(Stares at ORESTES)* I'm starting to think that you're in on the game.

ORESTES: What game, Clytemnestra?

CLYTEMNESTRA: The one that says I should rest . . . *(Looks into the mirror)* Maybe they're right. I look a little tired. *(Puts the mirror on the table)* Tomorrow I'll be radiant again. *(Puts the comb on the table)* Oh, Orestes, these objects. . . ! Don't fight against them. When objects put up resistance to humans, they're more ferocious than humans.

ORESTES: Do the objects hate you, Clytemnestra Pla?

CLYTEMNESTRA: Electra has ordered them to hate me. *(Pauses)* Maybe she's also ordered them to make me abandon my own house?

ORESTES: Abandon your house. . . ?

CLYTEMNESTRA: They say that, too, they say I should leave . . .

ORESTES: Did you know I'm in charge of making you leave?

CLYTEMNESTRA: You?

ORESTES: Yes, but we still have time.

CLYTEMNESTRA: *(Horrified)* You? You, Orestes?

ORESTES: Yes, me. *(Pauses)* Eat your favorite fruit. *(He points to the papaya.)* In this case the Court's finding is correct, and you'll be leaving for the unknown.

CLYTEMNESTRA: *(Laughing)* Oh, thank you, my son, thank you for amusing your afflicted mother with your delightful sense of humor! *(Pauses)* I'm so distracted! I looked at the table and I didn't see the fruit. Who put that magnificent slice there? Was it you, Orestes?

ORESTES: One of your servants put it there. I bought it on the street. It weighs ten pounds. Doesn't it have a dazzling color?

CLYTEMNESTRA: Yes, it's glorious. *(She picks up the papaya and looks at it.)* It's so absolutely pure—nothing bad could be inside its delicate pulp. *(She begins to eat it.)* How arrogant! *(Sobbing)* I'm very annoyed with Electra. *(Pauses)* What an exquisite taste . . . Thank you, Orestes, for this excellent gift. *(Pauses, sobs)* Electra, you know, is responsible for all the misfortunes in this house . . . *(Laughs)* You said it weighs ten pounds? *(Pauses, sobs again)* I didn't want to tell you, but I've been threatened with death again. *(Pauses)* What magnificent fruit, Orestes! *(Pauses)* I had your father killed, yes, I had your father killed. *(Pauses, hysterical)* And now, Orestes, try to kill me! *(She lets the papaya drop and falls into ORESTES's arms.)*

ORESTES: *(He pushes her away gently.)* Don't be afraid, Clytemnestra Pla; before Electra can carry out her somber plans, you'll be out of her reach.

CLYTEMNESTRA: How, my son?

ORESTES: I'll keep you out of danger. Aren't I the one in charge of making you leave?

CLYTEMNESTRA: If you kill your sister I'll consent to the journey you've desired for so long.

ORESTES: You mean, your journey, Clytemnestra?

CLYTEMNESTRA: No, yours. The one you've been asking for all this time.

ORESTES: Your permission is no longer necessary. I'm leaving after you go on your trip.

CLYTEMNESTRA: *(Laughing)* Orestes, don't you ever tire of making jokes? *(Becomes serious)* But Electra is even more tireless with her schemes. You know . . . *(She interrupts herself, puts her hands on her forehead.)* Everything is spinning . . . I'm light-headed . . . It must be the heat . . . Yes, it's very hot, even here in the doorway. *(Pauses)* I was saying that Electra is tireless, she's chasing me. *(Pauses. Speaks with effort)* How strange! My ears are ringing . . . *(She clutches her stomach.)* Now my stomach . . . I was saying, Orestes . . . *(She interrupts herself, choking.)* You could easily strangle her. She's like that girl from Marseilles . . . *(Pauses)* Oh, it's in my stomach! I can't go on . . . I'm going to bed . . . *(Walks away)* Tomorrow we'll discuss this again . . . *(Pauses)* Don't look at me like that, I'm your mother . . . I feel like I'm dying . . . *(Pauses)* I was saying . . . *(Pauses. She reaches the columns at the center.)* I was saying that Electra plans to get rid of me . . . *(She suddenly encounters ELECTRA who is leaning against one of the columns at the center. CLYTEMNESTRA falls at her feet. ELECTRA throws a red shawl over her head.)*

ELECTRA: *(Fiercely)* Now we're rid of you, Clytemnestra Pla!

CLYTEMNESTRA: *(Lets out a muffled scream)* Electra! *(She drags herself across the floor until she is behind the columns. Only her head covered by the shawl can be seen.)*

ELECTRA: *(Moves close to ORESTES who remains still)* It's a question of hygiene! A question of hygiene!

ORESTES: What should I do, Electra?

ELECTRA: Leave! *(She points to the door that is closed.)* Here is the door of your departure. *(Takes ORESTES to the door)* It's always good to leave . . . *(Opens the door and a bright light enters)* Go ahead! *(With tragic joy)* Leave, Orestes, leave! *(ORESTES exits, and ELECTRA closes the door again. She faces the other door.)* Here's my door, the door of non-departure. The Electra-door! *(Moves center stage. Gazes upward attentively)* And the Furies? I don't see them, they haven't come. Come, now! *(Laughs)* No, there are no Furies, there's no remorse. I was expecting the flutter of wings . . . There are no wings because there are no Furies. *(Pauses)* There is this door, the Electra-door. It doesn't open any paths, but it doesn't close any, either. Non-existent Furies, consider the powerful reality of this door! Don't rejoice, non-existent Furies: you're not the murmur that I alone can perceive. The Electra-murmur, the Electra-noise, the Electra-thunder, the Electra-thunder . . . *(Exits through the door and closes it slowly)*

Night of the Assassins, directed by Diana Taylor, Dartmouth College, 1987. (Photo courtesy of Diana Taylor.)

Night of the Assassins
(José Triana)

Since *Night of the Assassins* (*La noche de los asesinos*) was published in Cuba 1965, it has inspired avid, even extreme, interpretations both inside and outside postrevolutionary Cuba. Set in the 1950s in a dingy, claustrophobic attic or basement, the play focuses on three adult children who obsessively enact the murder of their parents. The two-act play takes place in a sealed room, and all three characters take turns acting the many roles. Lalo, the brother, insists that killing his parents is the only way out of their deadening situation: "I want my life. Every day of it, every hour, every minute. I want to do what I want and feel what I want. But my hands are tied. My feet are tied. My eyes are blinkered. This house is my world. And this house is getting old and dirty and smelly. Mum and Dad are to blame." Cuca, one of the two sisters, wants to impose order by cleaning and straightening up the room. Instead of Lalo's radical upheaval, she proposes reorganization. Beba usually goes along with whatever is happening, and both of her siblings count on her to support them in their efforts. Yet when at the end of the play she announces, "Now it's my turn," it's hard to know what direction, exactly, the drama will take. While there are absurdist qualities to this play that upset the given order of things ("In this house the ashtray belongs on the chair and the vase on the floor"), commentators have had a hard time deciding what, if anything, actually happens. Is it a game? A ritual? A rehearsal for revolution? Or a condemnation of the revolution Cuba had recently experienced?

Although an international jury awarded *Assassins* Cuba's prestigious Casa de las Américas Prize in 1965, José Triana's work was met with suspicion inside Cuba. The Cuban Revolution, which had succeeded in displacing the military dictator Fulgencio Batista in 1959, wanted a clear ideological message. And, while Triana was an active participant in the revolutionary efforts, the circularity and ambiguity of the play's plot did not promote any straightforward position. Members of Unión de Escritores y Artistas de Cuba (UNEAC, the Union of Cuban Writers and Artists, of which Triana was a founding member) considered ambiguity itself antirevolutionary, arguing that "the problems of our times are not abstract; they have names and are concretely localizable. We must define that against which we fight as well as the name in which we fight."[1] Some commentators spoke of Triana's inability to develop aesthetic resources capable of representing the revolutionary reality.

While they admired his dramatic techniques in prerevolutionary plays such as *The Major General Will Speak of Theogony* (1957) and *Medea in the Mirror* (1960), which was inspired by Virgilio Piñera's *Electra Garrigó* (translated in this volume),[2] noting that "he maintained a critical attitude toward the national past," they lamented that "the critical vision of the prerevolutionary past maintained by Triana was static; it did not permit him to evolve; hence it was impossible for him to reflect the new social reality transformed by the new system."[3] Román V. de la Campa adds that "from that moment onward, instead of bringing him fame, as had happened in the United States, and situating him in the vanguard of Cuban dramatists, his works stopped being produced in Cuba and became only a remnant of a period that had been overcome."[4] Other critics tried to reconcile their support for the Revolution with their recognition of Triana's work by claiming, as Hernán Vidal does, that *Night of the Assassins* was in fact a reflection on the degradation of Cuba's prerevolutionary period.[5] Set in the 1950s, during Batista's dictatorship, the play "is a concrete judgment against Cuba's prerevolutionary society and history." Triana himself actively promoted this view, repeatedly stressing that he began writing *Night of the Assassins* as early as 1957–58. As a person who had left Cuba as a persona non grata in 1955 under Batista, he considered himself profoundly revolutionary and wanted to deflect all political critiques of the play as antirevolutionary.

Outside of Cuba, *Night of the Assassins* received the widest international reception and reached the largest audience of any Latin American play written between 1965 and 1970. It was staged at Stratford-upon-Avon by the Royal Shakespeare Company in 1967 (as *The Criminals*) and published in *The Drama Review* (TDR) in 1970. Foreign critics generally praised it enthusiastically as a "universal" play, as an example of the Artaudian theater of cruelty, as theater of the absurd, as Genetian ritual, and as *danse macabre*. While Triana had seen *The Maids* by Genet, Beckett's *Waiting for Godot,* and Ionesco's *The Bald Soprano* when in Madrid from 1955 to 1959, he playfully or strategically, perhaps, converted these First World artistic products into vehicles for the expression of his own specific cultural and historical concerns. Nonetheless, commentators ignored how the play addressed the dramatic political situation in Cuba and the impact it had on local audiences. Instead, they tended to situate the work in a European dramatic tradition or, more universal still, in "a planet-wide culture, whose common denominator, in the western world, seems to be the individual's show of alienation."[6]

Yet, as I argue at length in *Theatre of Crisis,*[7] Triana does have something important to say about the Cuban Revolution, "revolutionary theater," and theater in periods of revolution. Triana's *Assassins* is particularly interesting in that it is one of the first works to raise the most urgent questions about the nature and meaning of revolution from within the very frame of the revolutionary movement. It is important to stress that Triana's work was not politically reactionary or antirevolutionary as its critics at the time suggested. He was not "outside," removed from, or against the movement. On the contrary, when he describes that period, he always speaks of himself as "dentro de la revolución" (in the Revolution),[8] echoing Fidel Castro's famous axiom: "Within the Revolution, everything; outside the Revolution, nothing." Triana participated actively in restructuring Cuba after the Revolution as a member of UNEAC. His critical inquiry into the nature of revolutionary roles and discourse does not necessarily indicate that he was experiencing personal disillusionment or crisis. But the reception of *Assassins,* written at the height of his influence in the fidelista movement, precipitated an estrangement that culminated in the playwright's exile to France in 1980.

The "problems of our times" as represented by Triana's *Assassins,* including the nature and character of revolution, are anything but namable and localizable. We, as the audience, look on while three adult children (Lalo, Cuca, and Beba) lock themselves in a filthy basement or attic and reenact or rehearse Lalo's murder of their parents. Judging by the nonchalant attitude of the sisters, and by their words, Lalo's "representation" takes place time and time again. Cuca and Beba assume supporting roles in Lalo's drama, alternately playing along with and antagonizing him. Although everything takes place in a closed space, and no one ever passes through the door that connects this peripheral room to the house proper, the three characters take turns playing out several of the key figures in their lives: parents and neighbors. The end of Act One coincides with the end of the siblings' representation, the climactic moment when Lalo goes to murder his mother and father. In Act Two, Cuca and Beba, as policemen, supposedly find the butchered bodies and arrest Lalo. As prosecutors, they keep after him to confess his crimes. His confession again calls for role-playing: the siblings "become" the parents and represent scenes of familial anger and unhappiness leading to the crime. Lalo's participation in the conflict ends with a whimper of defeat and despair: "If only love could do it . . . If only love . . . Because in spite of everything, I love them." Beba now resumes the onslaught: "Tear this house down." Lalo precipitates the first act (the murder); Cuca takes control of the second act (the trial). Lalo, Beba, and Cuca act out a crime and punishment cycle in which they take turns purging their environment alternately by means of anarchy and order. Lalo, in Act One, attacks the foundation of the social structure. By "killing" his parents he avenges the sacrifice of the individual in a dehumanized family setting. In Act Two, Cuca reinforces the social edifice with concepts of institutionalized justice and collective well-being. When at the end of the play Beba announces, "Now it's my turn," we, as the audience, can only guess what the future holds. The play gives us nothing to hold on to. We never know where, when, or what—if anything—actually happens. Have they killed their parents? Are they acting? Playing? We lack both the perspective (like Triana's foreign commentators) and the critical distance (like his Cuban colleagues) to discern what is taking place. Audience and characters are trapped in a totalizing, closed world that refuses to let us see beyond the limiting discursive and perceptual frames. We can speculate, but we cannot know. By situating us in the middle of a closed world and depriving us of all knowable links to the outside, *Assassins* calls attention to the unlocalizable nature of this space, to the simultaneous and paradoxical centrality and marginality of the onstage world. All markers orienting us have disappeared. Like Lalo, we cannot find our bearings in this womblike world: "We float with our feet in the air and our heads hanging down." Like the fetus in the uterus, these characters are central to the larger body, within yet not in the world. Is this an island (Cuba) paradoxically in the middle of nowhere? The disorienting inclusion works also as a form of exclusion, prefiguring Triana's ostracism and exile with all its political, existential, archetypal, psychological, and sexual overtones.

Since moving to France, José Triana has continued to write for the theater: *War Ceremonial* (1968–73) and *Worlds Apart* (1979–86, known as *Palabras Comunes* in Spanish). In the autobiographical *War Ceremonial,* he depicts a wounded soldier who has been abandoned by his fellow revolutionaries and left to die. By 1979, when he began writing *Worlds Apart,* Triana had made his peace by accepting exile and his decision to live his separate life. *Worlds Apart* was staged by the Royal Shakespeare Company in 1986. Yet international recognition, he knew, would not augment his impact in his beloved Cuba. In leaving Cuba, he said, "I've left no footprint in the sand."

—Diana Taylor

NOTES

1. "Declaración de la UNEAC," in Antón Arrufat, *Los siete contra Tebas* (Havana: UNEAC, 1968).

2. Besides the ones mentioned in this introduction Triana's plays include *El parque de la fraternidad* (1961), *La muerte del Ñeque* (1964–96), *Una pelea cubana contra los demonios* (with Tomás Gutierrez Alea, 1969–70), *Revolico en el Parque de Marte* (1971–95), *Cruzando el puente* (1991), *La fiesta* (1992), and *Ahí están los Tarahumaras* (1993). Triana also writes poetry and short stories.

3. Román V. de la Campa, *José Triana: Ritualización de la sociedad cubana* (Minneapolis: Institute for the Study of Ideologies and Literature, 1979), 14.

4. Ibid.

5. Hernan Vidal, prologue to ibid., 12.

6. Anne G. Murch, "Genet-Triana-Kopit: Ritual as Danse Macabre." *Modern Drama* 15 (March 1973): 369.

7. Parts of this essay are drawn from my *Theatre of Crisis: Drama and Politics in Latin America* (Lexington: University Press of Kentucky, 1991). For an in-depth discussion of some of the points raised here, refer to chapter 2, "Theatre and Revolution: José Triana."

8. José Triana, interview by Diana Taylor, in *En busca de una imagen: Ensayos críticos sobre Griselda Gambaro y José Triana,* ed. Diana Taylor (Ottawa: Girol, 1989), 116.

SELECTED REFERENCES

Albuquerque, Severino João. *Violent Acts: A Study of Contemporary Latin American Theatre.* Detroit: Wayne State University Press, 1991.

Alvarez-Borland, Isabel. "La noche de los asesinos: Text, Staging, and Audience." Trans. David George. *Latin American Theatre Review* 20 (fall 1986): 37–48.

Campa, Ramón V. de la. *José Triana: Ritualización de la sociedad cubana.* Minneapolis: Institute for the Study of Ideologies and Literature, 1979.

Hoeg, Jerry. "Coding, Context, and Punctuation in Triana's *La noche de los asesinos.*" *Gestos: Teoría y Práctica del Teatro Hispánico* 8 (April 1993): 83–98.

Lima, Robert. "José Triana and the Tragic Mode: Three Plays." *Neophilologus* 88 (October 2004): 559–68.

Pratt, Dale J. "Audience Authority in *La Noche de los Asesinos.*" *Gestos: Teoría y Práctica del Teatro Hispánico* 9 (November 1994): 81–91.

Stevens, Camilla. "Tearing Down the House: The End of an Epoch in Cuba." Chapter 2 in *Family and Identity in Contemporary Cuban and Puerto Rican Drama.* Gainesville: University Press of Florida, 2004.

Taylor, Diana. "Framing the Revolution: Triana's *La Noche de los Asesinos* and *Ceremonial de Guerra.*" *Latin American Theatre Review* 24 (fall 1990): 81–92.

Taylor, Diana. "Theatre and Revolution: José Triana." Chapter 2 in *Theatre of Crisis: Drama and Politics in Latin America.* Lexington: University Press of Kentucky, 1991.

Night of the Assassins (José Triana)

Translated by Sebastian Doggart

Oh so much! Oh so little! Oh the others!
—Cesar Vallejo

. . . we are all dream monsters to ourselves.
—André Malraux

*. . . this human world penetrates us, participates in the
dance of the gods, without looking back, on pain of being
turned into our selves: into pillars of salt.*
—Antonin Artaud

*Can we only love
Something created by our own imagination?
Are we all in fact unloving and unlovable?
Then one is alone, and if one is alone
Then lover and beloved are equally unreal
And the dreamer is no more real than his dreams.*
—T. S. Eliot

CHARACTERS:

LALO
CUCA
BEBA

SETTING

The 1950s. A basement or an attic. A table, three chairs, rolled-up carpets, dirty curtains
with large floral-patterned patches on them, vases, a judge's gavel, a knife and various
objects discarded in the corner next to a broom and a duster.

ACTING NOTE

While these characters play other characters, they must do so with the utmost simplicity
and spontaneity. They must not use characterizing devices. They are capable of representing the world without any artifice. Bear this in mind for the production's staging and set.
These characters are adults, but exhibit a fading adolescent grace. They are figures in a
ruined museum.

ACT ONE

LALO: Shut the door. *(Beats his chest. Exalted, wide-
eyed)* An assassin. An assassin. *(Falls to his knees)*

CUCA: *(To BEBA)* What's all this?
BEBA: *(Indifferently, watching LALO)* The performance
has begun.
CUCA: Again?

BEBA: (*Annoyed*) Of course! It's not the first time.

CUCA: Please don't get upset.

BEBA: Grow up.

CUCA: Mum and Dad haven't gone out yet.

BEBA: So?

LALO: I killed them. (*Laughs. Stretches his arms solemnly out to the audience*) Can't you see the two coffins? Look: candles, flowers . . . We've filled the room with gladioli. Mum's favorite. (*Pause*) They can't complain. Now they're dead we've made them happy. I myself dressed their stiff, sticky bodies . . . And with these hands I dug a deep, deep hole. Earth, more earth. (*Gets up quickly*) They still haven't discovered the crime. (*Smiles. To CUCA*) What are you thinking about? (*Caressing her chin as if she were a child*) I understand: you're scared. (*She moves away.*) Oh, you're impossible.

CUCA: (*Dusting the furniture*) I can't stand all this nonsense.

LALO: Nonsense? You think a crime is nonsense? How cold you are, little sister! Nonsense? Do you really think that?

CUCA: (*Firmly*) Yes.

LALO: Then what *is* important to you?

CUCA: I want you to help me. We have to tidy up this house. This room is a pit. Cockroaches, rats, moths, caterpillars . . . the whole bloody lot. (*Takes an ashtray from the chair and puts it on the table*)

LALO: How far do you think you're going to get with that duster?

CUCA: It's a start.

LALO: (*Authoritatively*) Put the ashtray back in its place.

CUCA: The ashtray belongs on the table, not on the chair.

LALO: Do what I tell you.

CUCA: Don't start, Lalo.

LALO: (*Picks up the ashtray and puts it back on the chair*) I know what I'm doing. (*Picks up the vase and puts it on the floor*) In this house the ashtray belongs on the chair and the vase on the floor.

CUCA: And the chairs?

LALO: On the table.

CUCA: And what about us?

LALO: We float with our feet in the air and our heads hanging down.

CUCA: (*Annoyed*) Fantastic! Why don't we try it? What would people say if they heard you now? (*In a harder tone of voice*) Look, Lalo, if you keep being pushy, we're going to have problems. Leave me alone. I'll do what I can.

LALO: (*Purposefully*) Don't you want me to help you?

CUCA: Don't mess things up.

LALO: Then don't mess with my things. I want the ashtray there. The vase there. Leave them where they are. It's you who's being pushy, not me.

CUCA: Oh right! Now it's me who's being pushy? Darling, that is priceless! Now it's me. . . ? Look, Lalo, please shut up. Order is order.

LALO: There is none so deaf as she that won't hear.

CUCA: What?

LALO: You heard.

CUCA: Well, darling, I don't understand. That's the honest truth. I don't know what you're on about. It all sounds crazy. It gets me into an utter state. I can't say or do anything. And if it's what I think it is, then it's sick.

LALO: Scared again? Get something into your tiny little head. If you want to live in this world you have to do many things, and one of them is to forget fear.

CUCA: Doesn't that sound easy!

LALO: Well, do it then.

CUCA: Stop hassling me. And don't preach, it doesn't suit you. (*Dusting a chair*) Look at this chair, Lalo. How long since it was last cleaned? There are cobwebs even. Ugh!

LALO: Shocking! (*Approaching cautiously, purposefully*) The other day I said to myself: 'We must clean up'; but then we got sidetracked into some nonsense and . . . Look, look at it. (*Pause. Purposefully*) Why don't you help?

CUCA: (*Almost on her knees next to the chair, cleaning it*) Leave me out of it.

LALO: Go on.

CUCA: Don't push.

LALO: Just for a bit.

CUCA: I'm no use.

(*BEBA, who has been upstage cleaning some old furniture and pots and pans with a rag, moves downstage. She smiles. Her movements are slightly reminiscent of LALO's.*)

BEBA: Those corpses are unreal. Spectacular! They give me goose pimples. I don't want to think any more. I've never felt so happy. Look at them. They're flying, they're breaking up.

LALO: (*Grandly*) Have the guests arrived?

BEBA: I heard them coming up the stairs.

LALO: Who?

BEBA: Margaret and old Pantaleón.

(*CUCA doesn't stop her work, although occasionally she pauses to look at them.*)

LALO: (*Contemptuously*) I don't like those two. (*In another tone of voice. Violently*) Who told them?

BEBA: I don't know! No, don't look at me like that. I swear it wasn't me.

LALO: Then it was her. (*Points to CUCA*) Her.

CUCA: (*Still cleaning the furniture*) Me?

LALO: Yes, you. As if butter wouldn't melt in your mouth.

BEBA: Perhaps no one told them. Perhaps they decided to come themselves.

LALO: (*To BEBA*) Don't try and cover for her. (*To CUCA, who gets up and mops her brow with her right arm*) You! You are always spying on us. (*Starts walking around* CUCA) You watch our every step, every word we say, everything we think. You hide behind curtains, doors, windows . . . (*With a sly smile*) Ha! The spoilt brat plays detective. (*Roars with laughter*) Two and two make four. Elementary, my dear Watson. (*Suddenly*) Ugh! (*Softly, like a cat watching its prey*) You're never satisfied. What do you want to know?

CUCA: (*Fearful, not knowing what to do*) Nothing, Lalo, nothing . . . honestly . . . (*Sharply*) Don't get at me.

LALO: Then, why do you watch us? And why do you mix with such dreadful people?

CUCA: (*Her eyes filling with tears*) I didn't mean to . . .

LALO: *That's what I can't forgive.*

CUCA: They're my friends.

LALO: (*With furious contempt*) Your friends. You're pathetic. (*With a triumphant smile*) Don't think you can fool me. You're being ridiculous. You resist, but you really want to run away . . . little Miss Muffet. I already know you haven't got the guts to call things by their real names. (*Pause*) If you're against us, show us your teeth. Bite! Rebel!

CUCA: Stop it.

LALO: Come on!

CUCA: You're getting on my nerves.

LALO: You can do it.

CUCA: (*Choking*) I'm sorry, I'm really sorry.

LALO: Come on, get up.

BEBA: (*To* LALO) Don't torment her.

LALO: (*To* CUCA) Look at me.

CUCA: My head hurts.

LALO: Look at me.

CUCA: I can't.

BEBA: (*To* LALO) Give her a few moments.

CUCA: (*Sobbing*) It's not my fault. It's just how I am. I can't change. I wish I could.

LALO: (*Irritated*) What a dunce you are.

BEBA: (*To* CUCA) Come on then. (*Takes her aside and walks her over to a chair*) Dry your tears. Aren't you embarrassed? He is right you know. You're being difficult. (*Pause. She strokes her hair.*) There, there. (*In an affectionate tone of voice*) Don't look so sad. Give us a smile. (*In a maternal tone of voice*) You shouldn't have done it; but if you've started, you might as well finish. (*Joking*) Your nose has gone all red, just like a baby tomato. (*Tapping her nose with the index finger of her right hand*) What a silly-billy you are! (*Smiles*)

CUCA: (*Staying close to* BEBA) I don't want to see him.

BEBA: Calm down.

CUCA: I don't want to hear him.

BEBA: He won't eat you.

CUCA: My heart . . . Listen to it, it sounds like it's going to explode.

BEBA: Don't be a crybaby.

CUCA: I swear, I swear.

BEBA: Well, get used to it.

CUCA: I want to run away.

BEBA: It will pass.

CUCA: I can't stand it.

BEBA: It gets easier.

CUCA: I feel terrible.

LALO: (*Holding a cauldron in his hand, making an invocation*) Oh, Aphrodite, illuminate this night of infamy.

CUCA: (*To* BEBA, *distressed*) He's starting again.

BEBA: (*To* CUCA, *soothingly*) Sshh. Don't pay any attention to him.

CUCA: I want to spit on him.

BEBA: Don't go near him. He bites.

LALO: (*As Roman emperor*) Come to my aid; I'm dying of boredom.

(CUCA, *incapable of putting herself on the same level as* LALO, *reproaches him in a mocking tone of voice.*)

CUCA: What a performance! He's just like your uncle Chicho, don't you think, Sis? (*In disgust*) You're a monster.

LALO: (*As important gentleman*) When the gods are silent, the people shout. (*He throws the cauldron downstage.*)

CUCA: (*As mother. Sarcastically*) That's right, smash the place up, you don't have to pay for it.

LALO: (*Smiling, facing the door*) What a delightful surprise!

BEBA: (*To* CUCA) Are you feeling better? (CUCA *nods.*)

LALO: (*Greeting imaginary people*) Do come in . . . (*As if he were shaking their hands*) Oh, how *are* you? Hello!

BEBA: (*To* CUCA) Sure? (CUCA *nods.*)

LALO: (*To* BEBA) They've arrived.

BEBA: (*To* LALO) Keep them at a distance so they will go away.

LALO: (*To* BEBA) They've come to get us.

CUCA: (*To the imaginary people*) Good evening, Margaret.

LALO: (*To* CUCA) They've come to sniff out the blood.

BEBA: (*To the imaginary people*) How *are* you both?

CUCA: (*To* LALO) You and your suspicious mind.

BEBA: (*To* CUCA, *as mother*) Don't make things worse. (*To the imaginary people*) Asthma is such a pyrotechnic illness. It must still be wreaking havoc among the masses.

LALO: (*To* CUCA) I won't forgive you for this.

CUCA: (*As if she were paying attention to what the imaginary people are saying. With a wicked smile to* LALO. *Between her teeth*) An eye for an eye . . .

BEBA: (*As mother. To* LALO, *between her teeth*) Pretend you didn't hear, son.

LALO: (*To* BEBA) How rude. (*In another tone of voice. With a hypocritical smile at the imaginary people*) And how *are* you, Pantaleón? It's been so long since I last saw you. Have you been lost?

BEBA: (*Pestering the imaginary people*) How's your urine? They told me the other day . . .

CUCA: (*Pestering the imaginary people*) Is your bladder working OK?

BEBA: (*Amazed*) What? They *still* haven't operated on your sphincter?

CUCA: (*Scandalized*) Really? And what about the old hernia?

LALO: (*With a hypocritical smile*) Margaret, you're looking terrific. Is that cancerous growth of yours still growing? (*To BEBA*) You deal with them.

BEBA: (*To LALO*) I've run out of things to say.

LALO: (*Aside. Pushing her*) Say anything. It doesn't matter.

(*Goes upstage*)

BEBA: (*Looks at LALO, distressed. Pause. Immediately afterwards she throws herself into the fun of make-believing.*) How *lovely* you are . . . It must be spring which gives you . . . I don't know . . . a special aura, a power . . . Oh, I don't know . . . Oh, isn't it hot? I'm sweating absolute *buckets*. (*She laughs.*) Ohhh, Pantaleón! Panties Pantaleón! You are a one! An absolute cad. Oh yes, you are. You can't play the fool with me. And that wart really has increased your pulling power.

LALO: (*As Pantaleón*) Oh stop it, I don't believe a word of it. The years, my child, the passing years wither a man away and turn him into an old dishcloth. (*He laughs mischievously.*) But if you'd seen me in my prime, in the good old days . . . Oh, if only I could have them again . . . But what's the point? That's asking for the impossible. (*In a special tone of voice*) Today I have a little pain right here. (*Points to his abdomen*) It's like a pinprick . . . (*Sighs*) I'm old, a rusting wreck of a man. And it gets worse every day. Our children don't respect us, and they don't forgive us either.

BEBA: (*As Margaret, annoyed*) Don't say that. It's not fair. (*Aside*) There's a time and a place for everything. (*Smiling*) What will these kind, lovely children think? (*To CUCA*) Come here, pumpkin. Why are you hiding? Who are you afraid of? Who's the bogeyman? (*CUCA doesn't move.*) Come on, what's the matter, am I an ugly old woman? Come here, don't be silly, my sweet. Tell me something: how are your mummy and daddy? Where's your mummy?

LALO: (*Leaping up from his chair. Violently, to the audience*) You see? What did I tell you. That's what they came for. I know them. I'm right. (*To CUCA. Accusingly*) They're *your* friends. Get them out of here. They're trying to find out . . . (*Shouting*) Tell them to go to hell. Do you hear me? It's all over.

(*CUCA doesn't know what to do. She moves, gesticulates, tries to say something but is neither able nor dares to do so.*)

BEBA: (*As Margaret. To CUCA*) I don't want to leave just yet. We've come round for our regular visit. We've been meaning to come for weeks. And anyway, I'm feeling a bit woozy. Your mother should have some herbal tea.

LALO: (*Frantically*) Tell them to go, Cuca. Tell them to fuck off. (*As if he were holding a whip and were threatening them*) Out. Get out of here. Into the street.

CUCA: (*To LALO*) Don't be so rude.

BEBA: (*As Margaret. Crying in outrage*) I can't believe it. They're just throwing us out. It's outrageous. What beastly children.

CUCA: (*To LALO. In control of the situation*) You have a terrible temper.

BEBA: (*To the imaginary visitors*) I beg you to forgive him.

CUCA: (*To LALO*) They haven't done anything to you.

BEBA: (*To the imaginary people*) He has a terrible temper.

CUCA: (*To LALO*) You just don't *think*.

BEBA: (*To the imaginary people*) The doctor says he needs plenty of rest.

CUCA: (*To LALO*) So tactless, so ill-mannered, so . . .

BEBA: (*To the imaginary people*) Such an uncalled for attack.

CUCA: (*To LALO, who is laughing slyly*) God will never forgive you for this.

BEBA: (*To the imaginary people*) Good-bye Margaret. Goodnight Pantaleón. Don't forget, Mum and Dad went away to the country and we're not sure when . . . Oh, they'll be back pretty soon, I expect. Bye! Bye-bye! (*Blows them a kiss with feigned tenderness. Pause. To LALO*) You made that really hard for me! (*She sits down upstage and starts to polish some shoes.*)

CUCA: (*Subtly threatening*) When Mum finds out . . .

LALO: (*Angrily*) Go on, then, tell her. (*Calling*) Mum, Dad. (*Laughs*) Mum, Dad. (*Defiantly*) Don't wait. Go on. Run along and tell them. I'm sure they'll be grateful. Come on. Run, run. (*Takes CUCA by the arm and leads her to the door. He returns downstage center.*) You're a disaster. You can never make up your mind. You want to and you don't want to. You are and you aren't. Do you think that is enough? If you really want to live, you always have to take risks. It doesn't matter if you win or lose. (*Sarcastically*) But you want safety. The easy way out. (*Pause*) That's where the danger lies. Because that's where you hang around, dithering, not knowing what to do, not knowing what you are and, worst of all, not knowing what you want.

CUCA: (*Sure of herself*) Don't puff yourself up too far.

LALO: You'll never save yourself, however hard you try.

CUCA: Nor will you.

LALO: It won't be you who stops me.

CUCA: Every day you will grow older . . . Here, here, here, shut up with the cobwebs and the dust. I know it, I can see it, I can breathe it. (*She smiles wickedly.*)

LALO: So?

CUCA: You're going down, down.

LALO: That's what you'd like to see.

CUCA: Don't make me laugh.

LALO: It's the truth.

CUCA: I'll do what I like.

LALO: At last you're using your claws.

CUCA: I'm just speaking my mind.

LALO: You don't realize that what I am proposing is simply the only solution we have. *(Takes the chair and moves it about in the air)* I want this chair to be here. *(He suddenly puts the chair down in a particular place.)* And not there. *(He suddenly moves the same chair to another particular place.)* Because here . . . *(Quickly returning it to the first place)* . . . it's more useful to me. I can sit down more comfortably and more quickly. And here . . . *(Places the chair in the second position)* . . . It's useless, just a silly whim . . . *(Puts the chair back to the first position)* Dad and Mum don't allow such things. They think that what I think and what I want to do are completely illogical. They want everything to stay where it is. Nothing must move from its proper place. And that's impossible. Because you and I and Beba . . . *(With a scream)* It's intolerable. And they think I'm just doing these things to contradict them, to fight them, to upset them . . .

CUCA: In a house, the furniture . . .

LALO: *(Rapidly, energetically)* That's just an excuse. Who cares about this house, who cares about this furniture if we ourselves are nothing, if we simply pass through the house and between the furniture, just like an ashtray, a vase, or a floating knife? *(To CUCA)* You could be a vase. Would you like to discover one day that's all you are? Or that you've been treated like a vase for most of your life? I could be a knife, couldn't I? And Beba, are you happy being an ashtray? No, no. That's stupid. *(In a mechanical rhythm)* Come over here. Go over there. Do this. Do that. Do the other. *(In another tone of voice)* I want my life. Every day of it, every hour, every minute. I want to do what I want and feel what I want. But my hands are tied. My feet are tied. My eyes are blinkered. This house is my world. And this house is getting old and dirty and smelly. Mum and Dad are to blame. I'm sorry but that's how it is. And the worst thing is that they don't stop a moment to consider whether things shouldn't be different. Nor do you. And Beba's even worse. If Beba plays our game, it's only because she has nothing else to do.

CUCA: Why do you blame Mum and Dad for everything?

LALO: Because they made me into a useless thing.

CUCA: That's not true.

LALO: Why should I lie?

CUCA: You're trying to cover yourself.

LALO: I'm trying to be as sincere as possible.

CUCA: That doesn't give you the right to demand so much. You're terrible as well. Do you remember the games you made up? You destroyed all our dolls. You invented crazy games. You wanted us to live in your shadow—or worse, you wanted us to be just like you.

LALO: That was the only way to free myself from the burden they placed on me.

CUCA: You can't deny they've always taken care of you, that they've always loved you.

LALO: I don't want them to love me like that. I've been everything to them, except a human being.

(From upstage, still polishing the shoes, BEBA imitates her father.)

BEBA: *(As father)* Lalo, from now on you will scrub the floors. You will mend my clothes and you will do so with great care. Your mother is not well and somebody has to do these things. *(She continues polishing the shoes.)*

CUCA: Mum and Dad have given you everything . . .

LALO: *(To CUCA)* At what cost . . . ?

CUCA: But what did you expect? Remember, Lalo, what Dad earned. Next to nothing. What more could he have given you?

LALO: Why have they always told me: 'Don't walk to school with so-and-so'; 'don't go out with what's-her-name'; 'so-and-so is a bad influence.' Why did they make me believe I was better than anyone else? Mum and Dad think that if we have a room, a bed and food, that's enough, that we should be grateful. They told us a thousand times that very few parents did as much, that only rich children enjoyed the kind of life we had.

CUCA: Try and understand them. That's the way they are . . . But sooner or later you were bound to try to get rid of them.

LALO: I couldn't. I believed in them too much. *(Pause)* And what happened to my desires? My dreams?

CUCA: Since you were a kid, you always wanted your own way.

LALO: Since I was a kid, since I was that tall, they've been telling me: 'Do this.' And if I did it badly: 'You're useless.' And then came the beatings and the punishment.

CUCA: That's what all parents do. It doesn't mean you have to turn the whole house upside down.

LALO: I want things to have a real meaning, so that you, Beba, and I can say: 'We'll do this,' and we'll do it. And if it doesn't work, we can say: 'Too bad. Let's try again.' And if it does work, we can say: 'Great! Let's move on to the next thing.' Haven't you ever thought what it means to be able to think, to decide and to do things on your own?

CUCA: You know we can't just . . .

LALO: *(Violently)* We can't. We can't.

CUCA: Mum and Dad are right.

LALO: I'm right, too. Just as right as they are.

CUCA: Are you rebelling?

LALO: Yes.

CUCA: Against them?

LALO: Against everything.

(At this moment BEBA repeats the imitation of her father.)

BEBA: *(As father)* Lalo, you will wash and iron. Your mother and I have agreed on this. There are the sheets, the curtains, the tablecloths and my office trousers . . . You will clean the toilets. You will eat in a corner in the kitchen. You will learn. I swear you will learn. Do you hear me? *(She goes upstage.)*

CUCA: Why don't you leave home then?

LALO: Where the hell would I go?

CUCA: Try.

LALO: I already have. Don't you remember? I always come home with my tail between my legs.

CUCA: Try again.

LALO: No . . . I know I can't live on the streets. I get confused . . . lost. I don't know what's wrong with me. I seem to fade away. They didn't teach me. No, they just mixed me up.

CUCA: How can you be a leader if you yourself admit . . . ?

LALO: This house is what I know. I'm resigned to it.

CUCA: Are you ready to start again then?

LALO: As many times as it takes.

CUCA: And see it right through?

LALO: It's my only escape.

CUCA: But don't you think the police will find out?

LALO: I don't know. Maybe . . .

CUCA: How can you win?

LALO: Wait and see.

CUCA: Well, I won't help you. Understand? I'll defend them tooth and nail if I have to. I'm not interested in any of this. I accept what Mum and Dad say. They don't interfere with me. They give me everything I need . . . You're the pigheaded one, not me. Dad's right when he says you're like a cat: you close your eyes so you can't see the food they're giving you. *(Steps forward)* Go away. I won't play your game. *(To BEBA)* Don't you count on me either. *(In another tone of voice.)* Oh, God, get me out of this mess. *(Pause)* They're older than us. They know more about life. They've struggled, made sacrifices. They deserve our respect at the very least. If something goes wrong in this house, it's because it was bound to . . . No, no, I won't fight them.

LALO: *(Amused. Clapping)* Bravo. A fine performance.

BEBA: *(Amused. Clapping)* You deserve an award.

LALO: We'll have to invent one.

BEBA: She's one to watch.

LALO: She's an imbecile.

BEBA: She's sensational.

LALO: She's an idiot.

BEBA: She's a saint. *(They applaud furiously and mockingly.)*

CUCA: Go on, laugh. My time will come. And then I'll show no mercy.

LALO: What do you mean?

CUCA: I'll do what I feel like.

LALO: You just try.

CUCA: You can't order me about. *(She walks back a few steps, moving away from them.)*

LALO: *(Sarcastically)* You're getting scared. *(Laughs)*

CUCA: *(Furiously)* I've got hands, nails, teeth.

LALO: *(Aggressively, defiantly)* I'm in charge now.

CUCA: Don't come near me.

LALO: You'll do what I tell you. *(Seizes her arm and they begin to fight)*

CUCA: *(Furiously)* Let go.

LALO: Will you obey me?

CUCA: Bully.

LALO: You'll do anything I tell you.

CUCA: You're hurting me.

LALO: Yes or no?

CUCA: It's not fair . . . *(Totally defeated)* All right, I'll do anything you tell me.

LALO: Quick. Get up.

CUCA: *(To BEBA)* Help me.

(BEBA walks towards CUCA. LALO stops her with one movement. CUCA pretends that she cannot get up.)

LALO: Let her get up on her own.

BEBA: *(To LALO)* Forgive her.

LALO: *(Shouting)* Keep out of this.

BEBA: *(Desperately)* Oh, you're always shouting! I can't stand it. I came here to help you or to have fun. Because I don't know what else to do . . . Round and round we go . . . We get shouted at for anything: for a glass of water, a bar of soap on the floor, a dirty towel, a broken ashtray . . . Aren't there more important things to live for? I wonder sometimes what the clouds, the trees, the rain, and the animals are all for. Shouldn't we stop and think about these things? And I run to the window and stick my head out . . . But Mum and Dad start shouting again: 'What are you thinking of, child? Look at the dust and soot on the window. Get inside, or you'll catch a cold.' If I go to the living room and turn on the radio, they say: 'You're wasting electricity. Last month and the month before that we used so much and we can't go on like this. Turn it off. That noise is driving me crazy.' Or if I start singing that song you made up recently, 'The living room's not the living room,' the whole house explodes like an upturned ants' nest, and they start shouting again: Mum and Dad shout at Lalo, Lalo shouts at Mum, Mum shouts at Lalo, Lalo shouts at Dad, Dad shouts at Lalo, and I'm left in the middle. In the end I come and hide here . . . But you don't even notice and carry on arguing, as if this house's problems could be solved with words. And now you two end up rowing as well. Oh, I can't bear it anymore. *(Determined)* I'm getting out. *(LALO grabs her arm.)* Let me go. I don't want to hear any more about it. Deaf, blind. Dead, dead.

LALO: (*Tenderly but firmly*) Don't say that.

BEBA: That's what I want.

LALO: If you helped me, perhaps we can save ourselves.

BEBA: (*Looking up at him suddenly amazed*) What do you mean? (*She holds on to his arms.*) All right, we can do it. Today.

(*LALO quickly picks up two knives. He examines their edges and starts scraping them against each other.*)

BEBA: (*To LALO*) Are you going to tell the story again?

CUCA: (*To BEBA*) Quiet, please.

(*BEBA moves about the stage. Each character takes up a distinctive position.*)

BEBA: (*As gossiping neighbor*) Shall I tell you something, Cacha? It was in all the papers. Yes, dear, yes. But you know old Margaret who lives at the corner, and Pantaleón, who's only got one eye? Well, they saw everything, and I mean everything. And they told me all about it.

LALO: (*Scraping the two knives quite firmly*) Ric-rac, ric-rac, ric-rac, ric-rac, ric-rac, ric-rac.

BEBA: (*As drunk shopkeeper*) Old Pantaleón and Margaret know everything . . . Bloody hell! Some mothers do 'ave em, I tell you. What is the world coming to. . . ? Have you seen the photo on the front page?

LALO: (*Scraping the two knives violently*) Ric-rac, ric-rac, ric-rac, ric-rac, ric-rac, ric-rac, ric-rac.

BEBA: (*As Margaret speaking to her friends*) We dropped round there about half past nine . . . The usual time. Well dear, the moment I walked in I said to myself: 'Goodness gracious me. Something's funny here.' You know me, I have a nose for these things, and sure enough. What a sight, dearie! (*Horrified*) Blood all over the place. It was frightful. Look at my hair, it's still standing on end. Oh, it makes me shiver all over. I can't describe it properly, you should have seen the . . . Ugh! It's horrible even thinking about it. A stream, incredible . . . I think there were some syringes. Isn't that right, Pantaleón? And pills and ampoules . . . Those children are wicked, and it's in their family. Oh, Consolación, ask Angelita what she saw a few days ago . . . Awful! And such sweet parents, and so self-sacrificing. It's that Lalo, he's the ringleader. No doubt about it. It was him, him and no one else . . . Ah! you should have seen his knife . . . Dear Lord, what a butcher's knife!

LALO: (*In his own world*) Ric-rac, ric-rac, ric-rac, ric-rac, ric-rac, ric-rac, ric-rac, ric-rac, ric-rac, ric-rac.

BEBA: (*As Pantaleón*) I said to Maggie: 'Hold your horses, woman.' But she immediately started blathering on about the youth of today, and how awful they all are . . . You know what a blabber she is. They . . . No, I tell a lie. *He*, Lalo . . . Although at times I can't help thinking that . . . Well, goodness knows who did it . . . But I could almost swear on it. Because the girls . . . I can't see it. If you had seen Lalo's face . . . It was incredible. He looked possessed . . . Yes, yes, the

devil in person. He almost tried to beat us up . . . And me with my arthritis . . . I won't stand for it. I don't care what he does; that's his problem. But insulting us . . . Well, God may forgive him, but I won't! He's a nasty piece of work, a right bastard . . . Ah, if you had seen that bloodbath . . . And smelt the stench . . . It's all so weird, isn't it! (*With an hysterical giggle*) You're lucky you didn't see it . . . It was grisly . . . Grisly, yes . . . Grisly is the word . . . We must do something. (*Grandiosely*) We would like to make a formal complaint against this inhuman child. (*In another tone of voice*) What do you think?

LALO: (*Still playing his bizarre game*) Ric-rac, ric-rac, ric-rac, ric-rac, ric-rac, ric-rac, ric-rac, ric-rac, ric-rac, ric-rac.

(*LALO continues scraping the knives together. This simple action, combined with the sounds that he makes, builds up to a delirious climax. CUCA becomes a newspaper boy, BEBA goes upstage.*)

CUCA: (*Yelling*) Morning news! Latest news! Murder on Church Street! Buy a copy, lady. Don't miss it, sweetheart. Thirty-year-old son butchers his parents! See how the blood ran . . . Full-colour supplement. (*In a sing-song voice*) Forty times he stabbed his wrinklies! Forty times! Photos of the innocent parents! Buy it! It'll really shock you, sir! Frightening, folks! Morning news! (*To back. Drifting off*) Latest news.

LALO: (*Continuing to play his game*) Ric-rac, ric-rac, ric-rac, ric-rac, ric-rac, ric-rac, ric-rac, ric-rac, ric-rac, ric-rac, ric-rac, ric-rac, ric-rac, ric-rac.

(*Pause. BEBA walks downstage center.*)

BEBA: (*As father*) Lalo, what have you been up to? What are you staring at? Take that look off your face. Who have you been with? Tell me. Knives? What do you think you're doing with those knives? Answer me. Have you lost your tongue? Why are you home so late?

LALO: (*As teenager*) I bumped into some friends, Dad . . .

BEBA: (*As father*) Give those to me. (*Taking the knives away violently*) Always messing about. (*Checking the sharpness of a knife*) That is sharp. Are you planning to kill someone? Tell me, I want an answer. Don't just stand there, you idiot. Who do you think you are? Why didn't you ask my permission? If I've told you once, I've told you a thousand times: this is no time to come home. (*She slaps him around.*) When will you learn some respect? How do you think your mother feels? Eh? You're breaking her heart! Is that what you want? Do you want us both to die of broken hearts? You just don't think! And take that look off your face. (*She pushes him towards the chair.*) Sit down. Do you want me to ground you again? (*LALO makes a gesture.*) Don't answer back. Such insolence. I've given you everything. You brat, you wicked, ungrateful brat. It's me who makes all the sacrifices . . .

Yes, your mother gets at me for going out with my friends and the girls from the office. Well, more than one business deal has fallen through because of you and the rest of my family. Can't you see the sacrifices I've made? Thirty years . . . Thirty years behind a desk getting ulcers from being pushed around by my bosses, doing without . . . I don't even have a proper suit or a decent pair of shoes. And this is how you pay me back! Thirty years is no joke. Thirty years working for my son, and today he turns out to be a good-for-nothing, a slob who doesn't want to work or study . . . Well, tell me, what do you want? And what have you been up to?

LALO: (*Trembling*) We were reading . . .

BEBA: (*As father*) Reading? Reading what? What do you mean, reading. . . ?

LALO: (*Thoughtfully*) An adventure magazine, Dad.

(*CUCA walks downstage center confidently, with mischievous intent. BEBA goes upstage.*)

CUCA: (*As mother*) Magazines. Magazines. Magazines. That's a lie. Tell us another. Tell us the truth. (*BEBA, as father, approaches LALO aggressively.*) No, Albert, don't hit him. (*To LALO*) Where is the money I hid in the sideboard? Did you take it? Have you spent it? Have you lost it? (*With hatred*) Thief. You little swine. You bastard. (*Tears welling in her eyes*) I'll tell your father. No, don't say anything. You're a disgrace. He'll kill you if he finds out. Holy Mary, mother of God, what have I done to deserve this? (*Furiously, to LALO*) Come on, give me back the money. Give it back or I'll call the police . . . (*Rifles through LALO's pockets. He submits completely. She screams.*) Thief. You bloody thief. I *will* tell your father. I ought to beat you. Whip you. Put you in reform school. (*LALO has his back to the audience.*)

BEBA: (*From upstage, like a little child*) Mum, mum, is this an elephant?

LALO: (*As father*) Beba, come here. Show me your hands. (*BEBA walks downstage center. Shows him her hands*) Those nails must be cut. They make you look like a . . . (*To CUCA*) Give me some scissors, woman. (*CUCA goes up to LALO and whispers in his ear.*) What? What's that? Really? And Lalo? Where's he gone? (*CUCA and LALO look at BEBA with evil intent.*) Is it true what your mother says? Come on, own up. Own up, or I'll . . . So you lifted your skirt and showed your knickers off to a bunch of perverts? Can this be true? (*BEBA gesticulates silently.*) You filthy creature. (*CUCA, as mother, smiles.*) I'm going to . . . (*LALO and CUCA corner BEBA.*) Do you want to become a whore, is that it? Huh? (*Shaking BEBA by the shoulders*) Well, not while I'm alive, do you hear? If I catch you doing anything sluttish, I'll kill you. Is that clear? (*Pause*) Where is your brother? (*Calling*) Lalo, Lalo! (*To CUCA*) You say he's stolen some money from you?

BEBA: (*Coming out of part*) I can't. My head's exploding.

LALO: (*Ordering*) Go on, you can't stop.

CUCA: (*Sarcastically*) Do what your master says.

BEBA: (*Agonized*) Air, I need some air.

LALO: (*To BEBA*) The doorbell's ringing.

(*BEBA collapses onto a chair.*)

CUCA: (*As mother*) Have you heard, Albert?

BEBA: (*Desperately*) Please, I think I'm going to be sick.

LALO: (*Annoyed*) She ruins everything, she does.

CUCA: (*As mother*) Sshh! Wait a second, children. There goes the doorbell again.

BEBA: (*As father. Greeting an imaginary person who comes through the door*) Come in, Angelita. How lovely to see you.

CUCA: (*As mother. To BEBA*) Tell me, poppet. Go on, you can tell me. What's wrong? (*Feigning self-denial and concern*)

LALO: (*As father. To the imaginary person*) Don't stand on ceremony, Angelita. (*His tone of voice is convincingly cordial and spontaneous.*) Make yourself at home. Please sit down.

CUCA: (*As mother. To BEBA*) Make yourself comfortable, honey. Do you want a cushion? (*Her words are heavy with sincerity.*) Why don't you just lean back and relax?

LALO: (*As father*) And Lalo? Where's he hiding? Oh, Angelita, you have no idea what those kids are like. Only three of them, but it's still like living in a war zone.

CUCA: (*As mother. To LALO*) Albert, I think . . . (*To the imaginary person*) I'm so sorry, Angelita, I'm not looking after you very well, but I think my little girl might be sick; she's got a tummy ache . . .

LALO: (*As father*) Have you taken her temperature? (*CUCA nods.*)

CUCA: (*As mother*) How very embarrassing.

LALO: (*As father, to the imaginary person*) You see what I mean? They're little devils. But I don't let them get away with anything. I rule them with a rod of iron, although not literally of course.

CUCA: (*As mother. Anxious. To LALO*) What can we do?

LALO: (*As father*) Does she have a temperature? (*CUCA shakes her head.*) Have you given her some chamomile tea?

CUCA: (*As mother*) She doesn't want anything.

LALO: (*As father*) Well, make her then.

CUCA: (*As mother*) She'll be sick.

LALO: (*As father*) Give her some normal tea then.

CUCA: (*As mother*) Oh, Angelita, you can't imagine the suffering, the grief . . . Why did we ever have children?

LALO: (*As father. Forcing her to drink from a teacup*) Drink. (*BEBA rejects it.*) Do what I say. Drink it all up.

BEBA: (*Screams, out of part*) Just leave me alone. (*Gets up furiously. Center stage*) You're monsters. You're both the same. (*Shouting upstage*) I want to go. Let me go. *(CUCA and LALO try to stop her, but she gets to the door. Screaming)* Mum, Dad, get me out of here. *(Falls beside the door, crying)* Get me out of here.

LALO: *(As father)* What's going on?

CUCA: Nice performance. *(Going up to BEBA)* You, it had to be you . . . You always push me into it: 'Go on, don't be wet. It'll be a laugh.' I can't believe it. Come on, up you get. *(Helps her to get up. As mother)* Remember we've got a visitor. *(To the imaginary visitor)* They're so spoiled, it's exhausting . . . *(To BEBA. Taking her back to the chair where she had been sitting)* That's a girl, aren't you a good girl, well done . . .

BEBA: *(As little girl)* I want to go.

CUCA: *(As mother)* Where do you want to go, pet?

LALO: *(Out of part, violently)* This isn't right. There's no point.

CUCA: *(As mother)* Don't lose your temper, Albert.

LALO: *(Out of part)* I feel like strangling her.

CUCA: *(As mother)* Patience.

BEBA: *(Crying)* I'm scared.

LALO: *(Out of part)* Scared of what? Why is she crying?

CUCA: *(As mother)* Ignore it. That's the best way, Albert.

LALO: *(As father. Awkwardly)* It's just that sometimes . . . *(Slapping his right knee)* You don't understand, woman.

CUCA: *(As mother)* What do you mean I don't understand? *(Sighs)* Oh, Albert, what a baby you are. Isn't he, Angelita?

BEBA: *(Furiously. Gets up)* I want to do something. I'm going to crack up. I want to go. I can't stand being shut up. I'm suffocating. I'm going to die and I don't want to be crushed, buried in this room. Anything but that. I don't want any more of this. Please, please, please, let me go.

(CUCA goes up to BEBA and puts her arm around her. She feigns great tenderness with her expression and gestures.)

CUCA: *(As mother)* Go if you must, my darling. You are a little worked up. *(BEBA stays in the dark, upstage. CUCA returns with a smile that gives way to laughter.)* Have you ever seen anything like it? It was as if we were torturing her. What imaginations these children have. . . ! *(Sits down and arranges her hair)* Look at me. I must look like a dog's dinner. I haven't had time to catch my breath all day. What an ordeal, Angelita, what an ordeal! I'm so sorry I've not been looking after you better . . . *(Listens to the imaginary person)* But you're like one of the family. *(Smiles hypocritically)* All the same, I do like to do things properly. Don't I, Albert? Don't lose your cool so easily, dear. We must stay perfectly calm and collected. *(LALO gets up.)* Where are you going? Think carefully before you do anything. *(LALO looks at her pointedly.)* Ah yes, I understand. *(LALO walks to the dark side of the stage.)* He's gone to keep an eye on what those little terrors are up to. You need eyes in the back of your head, or rather everywhere . . . You have to keep your ear to the ground. You always have to be on the watch, on the lookout, because they can be very, very naughty.

(At this moment LALO enters with an old and dirty bridal veil. LALO imitates his mother in her youth, on her wedding day in church. In the background, BEBA hums the wedding march. LALO's movements should not be exaggerated. A certain ambiguity prevails on this occasion.)

LALO: *(As mother)* Oh, Albert, I'm scared. The smell of the flowers, the music . . . So many people have come, haven't they? Your sister Rose didn't come, nor did your cousin Lola . . . They don't like me! I know they don't, Albert! I know it! They've been saying horrible things about me, and about my mother too. Oh, I don't know! Do you really love me, Albert? Do I look pretty? Ah, my tummy hurts. Smile. There's that creep Dr. Nuñez and his wife . . . Do you think people are counting the months? If they find out, I'll die of embarrassment. Look, Espinosa's daughters are smiling at you, those sluts, whoops, did I say that word. . . ? Ah, Albert, I feel dizzy, my tummy hurts, hold me, don't tread on my train or I'll fall over . . . Oh, honey, I want to get rid of this baby . . . I know you're determined to have it, but I don't want it . . . Oh, I'm going to faint . . . Albert, Albert, this is ridiculous . . . We didn't have to get married today, another day would have been better . . . Oh, that music and the smell of those flowers, ugh! And there's your mother, that bitch, whoops, did I say that word. . . ? Ah, I don't know . . . Albert, I can't breathe . . . This damned brat! I'd like to rip it out myself . . .

CUCA: *(As mother. Hatefully, biting the words)* You make me sick. *(Wrenching the veil off him)* I don't know how I gave birth to such an abortion. I'm ashamed of you, ashamed of your whole life. And now you want to save yourself? No way; forget about salvation . . . Drown yourself. Die. Do you think I'm going to let you, you of all people, criticize me, in front of visitors? Don't you see what you are? You're a cretin! *(To the imaginary person)* I'm so sorry, Angelita. Please don't go. *(In her previous harsh and firm tone of voice)* I've been asking you to help me for ages. There are loads of things to clean in this house: the dishes, the fridge, the dust, and those marks on the mirrors. So much to be done: mending, darning, sewing. *(LALO goes up to CUCA.)* Get out. You want to turn this house upside down and I won't allow it. Not over my dead body. The ashtray goes on the table. *(Puts the ashtray on the table)* The vase goes on the table. *(Puts the vase on the table)* Who do you think you are? I'll tell your father right now . . . *(With disgust and rancor)* You wretch, what would you do without us? What have you got to moan about? Do you think we are stupid? Yes? Well, I'll tell you, we're no better or worse than anyone else. But if you think we'll let you order us around, you're very wrong. Do you know what I've sacrificed to keep this house running smoothly? Do you think we'll just give it up like that? If you want to go, go. I'll pack your bags myself. There's the door.

(CUCA stands with her back to the audience. LALO approaches the table and contemplates the knife with indifference. He picks it up and caresses it. He stabs it into the center of the table.)

LALO: How much longer? How much longer?

BEBA: Don't get impatient.

LALO: If only we could do it today.

BEBA: You're being stupid.

LALO: Right now.

(LALO grabs the knife from the table. He looks at his two sisters and rushes upstage.)

BEBA: Don't do it.

CUCA: You'll be sorry.

BEBA: Be careful.

CUCA: *(Sings weakly)* The living room is not the living room.

(The two sisters are in position, BEBA stage right, CUCA stage left. They have their backs to the audience. Simultaneously, they utter a frightful, shattering scream. LALO enters. The two sisters fall to their knees.)

LALO: *(Holding the knife)* Silence.

BEBA and CUCA: *(Start singing quietly)* The living room is not the living room, the living room is the kitchen. The bedroom is not the bedroom, the bedroom is the bathroom.

LALO: Now I feel calm. I'd like to sleep, sleep, sleep forever . . . But I'll do that tomorrow. Today I have a lot to do. *(The knife slips from his hands and falls to the ground.)* How easy it all is . . . ! You just walk into the room. Slowly, on tiptoes. The slightest noise would mean disaster. And you move forward, hanging in mid-air. The knife doesn't tremble. Nor does your hand. You know what you're doing. The wardrobes, the bed, the curtains, the vases, the carpets, the ashtrays, the chairs: they all push you towards the naked, wheezing, sweating bodies. *(Pause. Determined)* And now we must clean up the blood. Wash them. Dress them. And fill the house with flowers. Later on, we'll dig a deep, deep hole and wait until morning . . . *(Pensively)* So easy . . . so terrible.

(The two sisters have stopped singing. CUCA picks up the knife and starts cleaning it on her apron. Long pause)

CUCA: *(To BEBA)* How do you feel?

BEBA: *(To CUCA)* All right.

CUCA: *(To BEBA)* It's tiring.

BEBA: *(To CUCA)* The worst thing is, you get used to it.

CUCA: *(To BEBA)* But someday . . .

BEBA: *(To CUCA)* It's like everything.

LALO: Open the door. *(Beats his chest. Exalted, wide-eyed)* An assassin. An assassin. *(Falls to his knees)*

CUCA: *(To BEBA)* What's all this?

BEBA: The first part has ended.

(Blackout)

ACT TWO

(As the curtain rises, LALO is on his knees, his back to the audience, his head hanging low. CUCA is standing up, looking at him and laughing. BEBA impassively takes the knife, which is lying on the table.)

CUCA: *(To BEBA)* Look at him. *(To LALO)* That's how I like to see you. *(Laughing)* Now it's my turn. *(Laughs long and hard)*

LALO: *(Imperiously)* Shut the door.

CUCA: *(To LALO, closing the door)* I can't stand you!

BEBA: *(To CUCA, looking at LALO disdainfully)* You're pathetic.

CUCA: *(To LALO)* What's wrong with you? Listen, little one: we've got to carry on. We're not going to do things by half this time. I'm fed up with leaving the job unfinished.

LALO: *(Crestfallen)* We always have to begin again.

CUCA: Fine. I agree. But I still say that today . . .

LALO: *(Annoyed)* Yes, yes . . . Whatever you say.

CUCA: Whatever I say, no. Whatever must be. Or am I now the inventor of all this? That's a good one!

BEBA: *(Annoyed. To CUCA)* But you love . . .

CUCA: *(Offended)* And what do *you* want me to do, little girl?

BEBA: Anything but that.

CUCA: No, my sweet, the time has come and I have to see it through to the end.

BEBA: You know I'm right.

CUCA: I don't care.

BEBA: Then I'm going.

CUCA: You're staying.

BEBA: You're trying my patience.

CUCA: Don't threaten me.

BEBA: I can scratch and kick.

LALO: That's enough arguing.

CUCA: *(To BEBA)* That's right: pipe down.

BEBA: Hah! I don't believe it. I am not going to let myself rot away behind these walls. I hate this place. You two like all this rubbish. But I'm young, and one of these days I'm going to get out of here and not come back and then I'll be able to do what I like. What do you think of that? *(Pause)* You didn't want to do it at the beginning, did you? But now you're capable of killing to get what you want. It's as if the salvation of your souls were at stake . . . Yes, your salvation . . . Don't look at me like that. Salvation from what? Maybe you just want to save your own skin? *(Deliberately)* That's why you called the police. That's why you're about to start the investigation and the interrogation. Did you do this? No, no. You didn't do it?

Hey, officer, how could I have done it? But we've found a clue. There are the fingerprints. One of you committed the crime. Do you think you can fuck with us, eh? Do you think you can take us for a ride? I don't want to get involved in that.

CUCA: You have to see it through to the end.

BEBA: It never ends.

CUCA: Don't give up.

BEBA: I'm tired. It's always the same. Do this. Do that. Why do we go round and round like this . . . ? (More intimate) Anyway, I don't want to get mixed up . . . (Changes her tone of voice) It's no fun.

CUCA: Everything you're saying is complete crap. (Like her mother) A right little gem you've turned out to be! Do you think I'm just going to sit back and watch after what he has done? I will defend Mum and Dad's memory. I will defend them against anything.

BEBA: Don't touch me.

CUCA: (As mother, with authority) Put that knife back where you found it. (BEBA obeys and drops the knife on the floor.) Not like that.

BEBA: (Furiously) You do it then.

CUCA: (Slyly, with a smirk) Control yourself. Come on, let's have everything back in its proper place. (Changes her tone of voice) The best is yet to come. (BEBA replaces the knife in a satisfactory way.) We must be very careful.

BEBA: (Furiously) Count me out.

CUCA: (Mentally arranging the room) The lamps, the curtains . . . It's a mathematical question.

BEBA: (Furiously) Go and find someone else. Or do it all yourself.

CUCA: You've been in on it from the start. You can't pull out now.

BEBA: We'll see about that.

CUCA: (Authoritarian, as mother) Nobody can foul up.

BEBA: Let's hope the unexpected happens.

CUCA: I'm depending on that as well. (To LALO) Get up. (LALO doesn't reply.)

BEBA: (Furiously) Leave him alone. Can't you see he's suffering?

CUCA: Keep out of this.

BEBA: You should have waited. Maybe . . . Just a moment.

CUCA: I know what I'm doing.

BEBA: (With subtle sarcasm) It's all right by me. But remember I'm on my guard. Ready, at any moment . . .

CUCA: (Rapidly, furiously) To do what?

BEBA: To break out.

CUCA: Really? So you are against it. . . ? Well, listen very carefully to what I'm going to say: don't even think I'm going to let you interfere. You're just a tool, a cog, a screw . . . You should be happy about that. (Pause) Don't make that face. (In a threatening tone of voice) All right, but you'll have to take the consequences. In this house, everything is part of the

game. (She moves around, trying to arrange things, and listing them.) Vase, knife, curtains, glasses . . . water, pills. The police will be here in a minute . . . Syringe, ampoules . . . All we have to do is disappear . . . vanish. (BEBA makes as if to leave. CUCA stops her.) No, my sweet. Don't be silly. You understand? (CUCA's sarcastic tone of voice makes BEBA flinch.) What? You don't like what we're doing? Do you want to throw a spanner in the works. . . ? We'll be invisible. Do you have anything to add? We are innocent. Do you want to take sides? (To LALO) Get up. It's late. (To BEBA) Are you going to defend the indefensible? Perhaps he's not an assassin? (To LALO) Tidy yourself up a bit. You look like a corpse. (LALO gets up clumsily. BEBA puts a pack of cards on the table and then spreads them out. To BEBA) That would never have crossed my mind.

LALO: (His back still to the audience. To BEBA) Bring me some water.

CUCA: (Imperiously) No, that's not allowed. (Approaching LALO, straightening out his clothes. Quite tenderly) You have to wait. (As mother) That collar is a scandal . . . You look like a tramp.

LALO: My throat is dry.

BEBA: (As mother, quite tenderly) Did you not sleep well?

LALO: I need to go outside for a while.

CUCA: (Violently) You're not going anywhere.

LALO: Just for a minute.

CUCA: Absolutely not. Everything is ready. What are you trying to. . . ? Are you playing with me? Well, I won't let you.

(CUCA tries to stop LALO, who moves to escape. She grabs him by his shirt collar. They struggle violently. For a moment, BEBA just watches them in amazement. Then she becomes morbidly interested in the fight and starts to walk around CUCA and LALO.)

LALO: Let go of me.

CUCA: No way.

LALO: Who do you think you are?

CUCA: Who do you think you are?

LALO: You're scratching me.

CUCA: All part of the game. This is life or death. And you can't escape. I'll do anything to see you put away.

(BEBA runs to the dark side of the stage where the door is.)

BEBA: (Screaming) The police, the police.

(The two siblings stop fighting. LALO falls into a chair, beaten. BEBA stands beside the closed door. CUCA stands on the other side of the door, also upstage.)

CUCA: (In her previous tone of voice, furiously) I'll never forgive you. It's your fault. All your fault. If you want to die, go ahead and die.

BEBA: Sshh! Be quiet.

(Long pause. BEBA and CUCA start to move slowly, almost in slow motion. They are now the two policemen who discover the crime.)

CUCA: (*As policeman 1*) Very dark in here.

BEBA: (*As policeman 2*) Smells horrible.

CUCA: (*As policeman 1*) Bloodstains everywhere.

BEBA: (*As policeman 2*) Looks like they've killed a couple of pigs.

CUCA: (*As policeman 1*) It was pigs what did it.

BEBA: (*As policeman 2*) Swine.

(*The two sisters walk as if in a darkened gallery. LALO remains in the chair. The sisters stop in front of him and pretend to shine a torch on him.*)

BEBA: (*As policeman 2*) Got him.

CUCA: (*As policeman 1*) What a fight he put up. (*To LALO, violently*) Get up. Come on, move it, move it. (*LALO tries to shield himself from the torch's glare.*)

BEBA: (*As policeman 2*) Hey, boy . . . One move and I'll blow your head off.

CUCA: (*As policeman 1*) Come on, get up.

BEBA: (*As policeman 2*) It's curtains for you, boy. (*LALO gets up and puts his hands up.*) We'd better be quick.

CUCA: (*As policeman 1*) Frisk 'im.

BEBA: (*As policeman 2*) This guy is dangerous. (*Frisks LALO's clothes and body*) Where are your papers? What's your name? (*LALO makes no reply.*) Can't you see you're under arrest? If an officer of the law asks you a question, you answer him. Now who screamed?

CUCA: (*As policeman 1*) Have you killed someone?

BEBA: (*As policeman 2*) Where's all the blood from?

CUCA: (*As policeman 1*) Do you live with your parents?

BEBA: (*As policeman 2*) Do you have any sisters and brothers? Answer.

CUCA: (*As policeman 1*) You did 'em in, didn't you? Answer. It's in your own interest.

LALO: (*Very vaguely*) Don't know.

BEBA: (*As policeman 2*) What do you mean, 'don't know'? Do you live on your own?

CUCA: (*As policeman 1*) And all these clothes. . . ? Let him be. (*Smiles*) He'll talk in the end.

BEBA: (*As policeman 2*) Nobody can save him now, mate. (*Smiles. Crudely*) He's a hard bastard. He probably started by robbing them. But that wasn't enough, so he decided to kill them. (*To LALO*) Your own parents? I can hardly believe it. Did you poison them? (*Holds up the box of pills and puts it back on the table*) How many pills. . . ? (*LALO doesn't reply. He occasionally smiles.*) Come on, out with it . . . If you talk, it'll be easier for you. (*To CUCA, showing her the syringe*) Look. He probably . . .

CUCA: (*As policeman 1*) It looks like this crime's a real whopper. (*To LALO*) Where are the bodies? (*To BEBA*) No sign of them.

BEBA: (*As policeman 2*) Where did you hide them? Did you bury them?

CUCA: (*As policeman 1*) We'll have to search the house from top to bottom. Comb it, every inch of it.

BEBA: (*As policeman 2*) Why did you kill them? Answer. Did they abuse you?

LALO: (*Dryly*) No.

CUCA: (*As policeman 1*) Time's up, sonny. Why did you kill them?

LALO: (*Confidently*) I didn't do it.

CUCA: (*As policeman 1*) You've got a nerve!

BEBA: (*As policeman 2*) Were they asleep?

CUCA: (*As policeman 1*) Don't play tough guy with me. So you didn't kill anyone? Not your parents? Not your brothers? None of your relations? (*LALO shrugs his shoulders.*) Then what have you done?

BEBA: (*As policeman 2*) Did you smother them with their pillows?

CUCA: (*As policeman 1*) How many times did you stab them?

BEBA: (*As policeman 2*) Five? Ten? Fifteen?

CUCA: (*As policeman 1*) You're not going to tell me this is all a game. There's blood all over the shop. Look, you're covered in it yourself. How can you deny it? I've never seen such a crime. (*Suddenly*) Where are your parents? Stuffed in a trunk? (*Pause. Reconstructing the scene*) You walked slowly, on tiptoes, so as not to make a noise . . . Your parents were snoring. You were holding your breath and the knife in your hand didn't even tremble . . .

LALO: (*Proudly*) Wrong. You're lying.

CUCA: (*As policeman 1*) Then what did happen? (*Exhausted*) Ah, this house is a labyrinth.

BEBA: (*As policeman 2. He has been examining the room.*) Here's the proof. (*Points to the knife*) We're getting there. (*Stoops to pick it up*)

CUCA: (*As policeman 1, shouting*) Don't touch it.

BEBA: (*As policeman 2*) We have to check it for fingerprints. (*Picks the knife up with a handkerchief and puts it on the table*)

CUCA: (*As policeman 1*) If he continues refusing to . . .

BEBA: (*As policeman 2*) I'll sort him out in a moment. (*To LALO*) Come here. You better talk or else I'll . . . Look. I don't want to have to resort to violence. But who do you think we are? We're not just here for decoration. (*In a tone of voice which is both threatening and persuasive*) Talk, it's in your own interest. You've had plenty of time to think. (*In a friendlier tone of voice*) Talk, come on, it's for your own good. (*Looking at CUCA*) It'll all be taken into account, don't worry. (*CUCA goes to the side of the stage, searching for clues.*) You'll feel much better once you've told us all about it. It's very easy, very, very easy. (*In an almost familiar tone of voice*) How did you do it? Why did you do it? Did they abuse you verbally or. . . ? Was there some kind of robbery? What really happened? Perhaps you've forgotten? Try and remember . . . Let's see, take your time.

LALO: (*Very haughtily*) None of you could understand.

BEBA: (*As policeman 2, persuasively, smiling*) Why do you say that? (*More intimately*) Come on, boy, own up.

CUCA: (*As policeman 1, offstage*) Don't worry. I've found

it. (*Comes on stage, rubbing his hands together*) Just take a look! It's a disgusting sight! Horrible! It'd make anyone's hair stand on end. (*Reconstructing the scene*) There's a pick and a shovel. He's dug this massive hole. I don't know how he did it on his own . . . And there, at the bottom are two bodies with a little earth on them. (*Going up to LALO and slapping him on the back*) So this young gentleman did nothing, did he? (*BEBA goes over to the place from where CUCA has come.*) Yes, yes, I understand. (*With a smile of satisfaction*) The young gentleman is innocent. Well, well, well . . . (*Stares at him disdainfully*) This young gentleman's days are numbered. (*In a vulgar tone of voice*) You've signed your own death warrant, Sonny-Jim.

BEBA: (*Coming on set, no longer as policeman 2*) It's awful.

CUCA: (*As policeman 1, in a vulgar tone of voice*) Don't get melodramatic.

BEBA: It made me go weak at the knees.

CUCA: (*As policeman 1*) This kid is quite something.

BEBA: It was bloodcurdling.

CUCA: (*As policeman 1*) Come on, pull yourself together. (*To LALO, disdainfully*) You're a . . . You make me want to . . . (*To BEBA*) Let's draw up the charges.

BEBA: What? But he hasn't confessed yet.

CUCA: (*As policeman 1*) It's not necessary.

BEBA: I think it will be.

CUCA: (*As policeman 1*) We've got enough evidence.

BEBA: We should at least try . . . (*Going up to LALO*) Lalo, you must tell us. You must talk. Why? Why, Lalo?

CUCA: (*As policeman 1*) Don't let up on him now.

BEBA: (*To LALO, almost begging*) Don't you understand, it's a formality. We need a confession. Say whatever you like, whatever comes into your head, even if it's illogical or absurd. Please say something. (*LALO remains impenetrable.*)

CUCA: (*As policeman 1*) Let's get back to the station. The charges. The report.

(*BEBA walks gravely over to the table and sits down. From this moment on, the stage should take on a new dimension, an eerie strangeness. The elements used are vocal sounds, beating on the table, and rhythmic foot tapping, first by BEBA and then by both BEBA and CUCA.*)

CUCA: (*Dictating, automatically*) In the neighborhood of this police station, and being the fifth day . . .

BEBA: (*Moving her hands over the table, automatically*) Tac-tac-tac-tac. Tac-tac-tac-tac. Tac-tac-tac-tac.

CUCA: . . . in the presence of the duty officer, we the undersigned, Officer 421 Cuco and Officer 842 Bebo, brought in for questioning an individual claiming to be called . . .

BEBA: Tac-tac-tac-tac. Tac-tac-tac-tac. Tac-tac-tac-tac. (*CUCA moves her lips as if she were still dictating.*)

CUCA: . . . The officers affirm that finding themselves in the area corresponding to their assigned patrol . . .

BEBA: (*Beating her hands on the table with great sense of rhythm*) Tac-tac-tac-tac. Tac-tac-tac-tac. Tac-tac-tac-tac.

CUCA: . . . heard raised voices and a public disturbance . . .

BEBA: Tac-tac-tac-tac. Tac-tac-tac-tac.

CUCA: . . . arguing and fighting . . .

BEBA: Tac-tac-tac-tac. Tac-tac-tac-tac.

CUCA: . . . and having heard a cry for help . . .

BEBA: (*Beating her hands on the table and tapping her feet rhythmically and automatically*) Tac-tac-tac-tac. Tac-tac-tac-tac. Tac-tac-tac-tac.

CUCA: . . . and upon entering the aforementioned house . . .

BEBA: Tac-tac-tac-tac. Tac-tac-tac-tac.

CUCA: . . . discovered two bodies . . .

BEBA: Tac-tac-tac-tac.

CUCA: . . . with contusions and first-degree injuries . . .

BEBA: Tac-tac-tac-tac. Tac-tac-tac-tac.

(*CUCA starts to beat on the table and to tap her feet like BEBA. The scene reaches a delirious climax which lasts a moment. Pause. BEBA and CUCA seem to return to normality. CUCA shows a piece of paper to LALO.*)

CUCA: (*Authoritatively*) Sign here.

(*Pause. LALO looks at the piece of paper. Looks at CUCA. Takes the paper with contempt and studies it closely*)

LALO: (*Furiously, firmly, defiantly*) I don't accept. Do you understand? This is all rubbish. It's disgraceful. (*Pause. Almost mockingly*) I think it's splendid, terrific, that you should try and interrogate me using these appalling techniques. It's so logical. Almost . . . normal, natural. But what do you want? Do you think I'm going to sign this shitty piece of paper? You call this the law? You call this justice? (*Shouting. Tears up the piece of paper*) Crap, crap, crap. This is the dignified thing to do. This is the exemplary thing to do. This is the respectable thing to do. (*Angrily stamps on the torn-up paper. Pause. Smiling bitterly, almost crying*) How nice, how dignified, how exemplary it would be if you were just to say: guilty. And be done with it. Next case, please. But to do what you're doing now . . . (*To CUCA*) Are you not satisfied with what has happened? Why are you trying to feed me with a pile of fictions? Do you think I'm a moron? (*Mockingly*) Or do you think I'm trembling with fear. Well, let me say it loud and clear: no. I am not afraid. (*BEBA hits the table with the gavel.*) I'm guilty. Yes, guilty. So judge me. Do what you like. I'm entirely in your hands. (*BEBA bangs the gavel again. LALO's tone of voice becomes less violent, although he still acts arrogantly.*) If your Honor will allow me . . .

BEBA: (*As judge*) The public will remain silent, or the court will be cleared and this hearing will proceed *in camera*. (*To CUCA*) Prosecution may proceed.

CUCA: (*To BEBA*) Thank you very much, your Honor. (*To LALO*) The accused is aware of the difficulties we have encountered in our attempts to clarify the circumstances surrounding the events which took place on that ill-fated morning . . . of . . . *(BEBA bangs the gavel.)*

BEBA: *(As judge)* I must ask the prosecution to be more specific and clear in the formulation of his questions.

CUCA: *(As public prosecutor)* Excuse me, your Honor, but . . .

BEBA: *(Moving her gavel)* I must ask the prosecution to attend exclusively to his cross-examination.

CUCA: *(As public prosecutor. To BEBA)* Your Honor, throughout all previous questioning, the accused has been exceptionally evasive, which has made it impossible to reach any . . .

BEBA: *(As judge. To CUCA. Bangs the table hard)* Keep to the point.

CUCA: *(As public prosecutor. Solemnly)* Your Honor, let me repeat that the accused has systematically obstructed all attempts to arrive at the truth. For this reason, I submit for the consideration of the court the following questions: is he permitted to make fun of the Law? Should he make fun of the Law? Is not the Law, the Law? If we are *permitted* to make fun of the Law, does the Law stop being the Law? If we *should* make fun of the Law, is the Law something other than the Law? In short, ladies and gentlemen of the jury, do we all have to become mind readers?

BEBA: *(As judge. Implacable, hammering the table)* I insist that the prosecution does not stray beyond its remit.

CUCA: *(As public prosecutor, showing off her theatrical abilities)* Ah, ladies and gentlemen, the accused, like every guilty man, fears the weight of Justice . . .

LALO: *(Furiously, but containing himself)* You're trying to trap me. I can see you coming. You're trying to destroy me, I won't let you.

CUCA: *(As public prosecutor. Solemnly and furiously. To BEBA)* Your Honor, the accused is behaving in contempt of court. In the name of the Law, I request that correct procedure be followed. What is the accused trying to do? Is he trying to disrupt proceedings? If that is his objective, we have to rule him publicly out of court. The processes of Law and Justice must remain logical. Nobody can complain about their methods. They were made to suit mankind. But it appears that the accused either does not understand, or does not want to understand, or perhaps he suffers from mental disorder . . . Or maybe he prefers to hide himself, to take cover behind a smokescreen of stupidity and aggression. I must ask every single member of this jury and the court in general to examine his attitude carefully and, at the appropriate time, to deliver a verdict which is both balanced and implacable. Ladies and gentlemen, on the one hand, the accused openly declares his guilt, that is, he admits that he has killed. This regrettable deed lies beyond the limits of normal behavior and represents an intolerable threat to everyone who walks the streets of this city. On the other hand, the accused denies everything, in an indirect way of course, and seeks to muddle up the chain of events through a cunning combination of sophistries, contradictions, banalities, and absurdities. Phrases like: 'I don't know'; 'possibly'; 'maybe'; 'yes' and 'no'. Are these answers? Note also the frequent resort to: 'if I had a clear memory of events' . . . Ladies and gentlemen of the jury, this is all inadmissible. *(Comes forward until he is center stage, with great theatrical effect)* The Law cannot stand idly by in the face of such a case, where degradation, malice, and cruelty are combined so horrifically. Standing before you, ladies and gentleman, you see the most repulsive assassin in all of history. Look at him. Could anyone fail to feel revulsion at this scum, this nauseating rat, this pool of phlegm? Doesn't he make you want to be sick, to curse him? Can the Law just stand by and watch? Ladies and gentlemen of the jury, ladies and gentlemen of the court, can we allow such an individual to share our hopes and ideals at a time when humanity, or rather our society, is marching on the resplendent path of progress, heading towards a golden dawn? *(LALO tries to say something, but the torrent of CUCA's oratory blocks any act, gesture or word from him.)* Look at him. Indifferent. Relaxed. Immune to any feeling of tenderness, understanding, or pity. Look at that face. *(Loudly)* The cool face of a killer. An assassin. The accused denies committing the murder for money, either in order to steal or to inherit his parents' meager pension. Why did he kill then? We cannot be certain about any of his motives. May we conclude that he did it out of hatred? Revenge? Or was it simple sadism? *(Pause. LALO moves impatiently in his chair. CUCA continues in a measured tone of voice.)* Can the Law allow a son to kill his parents?

LALO: *(To BEBA)* Your Honor . . . I want . . . I should like . . .

CUCA: *(As public prosecutor)* No, ladies and gentlemen of the jury. No, ladies and gentlemen of the court. A thousand times no. The Law cannot accept such contempt. The Law has created order. The Law is eternally vigilant. The Law demands good manners. The Law protects man from primitive and corrupt instincts. Can we have pity on a creature who violates the principles of natural law? I ask the ladies and gentlemen of the jury, I ask the ladies and gentlemen of the court: can we allow ourselves the indulgence of pity? *(Pause)* Our entire city rises up in anger. A city of proud and silent men comes forward determined to claim for Justice the body of this monster . . . demanding that he be exposed to the fury of true human beings whose only desires are for peace and harmony. *(Grandly)* And so, I demand that the accused help us establish the true course of events. *(To LALO)* Why did you kill your parents?

LALO: I wanted a life.

CUCA: *(As public prosecutor, violently)* That's not an answer. *(Rapidly)* How did you do it? Did you give them some concoction, some poison? Or did you smother them with their pillows as they lay helplessly in bed? Where do the syringes and pills come in? Or are they just red herrings? Explain, prisoner at the bar. *(Pause)* Did you kill them in cold blood? Was it planned step by step? Or was it a crime of passion? You tell us. Did you only use this knife? *(Exhausted)* And finally, prisoner at the bar, why did you kill them?

LALO: I felt they were persecuting me, harassing me.

CUCA: *(As public prosecutor)* Persecuting you? How? Harassing you? How?

LALO: They never let me alone.

CUCA: *(As public prosecutor)* But the witnesses testify that . . .

LALO: The witnesses are lying . . .

CUCA: *(As public prosecutor)* Are you contesting the statements made by the witnesses?

LALO: *(Firmly)* There was nobody there that night.

BEBA: *(As judge. To LALO)* The accused must be more precise in his answers. This is absolutely necessary. Are you sure you mean what you've just said? The Court demands both truth and precision. The Court expects the accused to observe, without prejudice, these articles of procedure . . . The prosecution may proceed.

CUCA: *(As public prosecutor)* Let us now turn to your close relatives. Your grandmother, for example, your aunts and uncles, all your nearest and dearest. Did you see each other often? What kind of relationship did you have with them?

LALO: None.

CUCA: *(As public prosecutor)* Why?

LALO: Mum hated Dad's family and Dad didn't get along with Mum's family.

CUCA: *(As public prosecutor)* Aren't you exaggerating?

LALO: None of our relations visited us . . . Mum didn't want them to come round. She said they were jealous and hypocritical. Dad said the same thing about Mum's relations. And they wouldn't let us visit them either . . .

CUCA: *(As public prosecutor)* This doesn't seem to have much basis in fact to me. Why. . . ?

LALO: They kept on telling us that we were better people, that they were all common, that they had no class . . .

CUCA: *(As public prosecutor)* And you never tried to make contact with them?

LALO: I tried once, but it didn't work.

CUCA: *(As public prosecutor)* Do you know the witness Mrs. Angelita. . . ? *(To the audience)* Her surname, please. Thank you. The witness Angela Martínez.

LALO: Yes.

CUCA: *(As public prosecutor)* Did she go to your house, either before or after the incident in question?

LALO: She did. Before. *(Pause)* At around 6 pm.

CUCA: *(As public prosecutor)* In her statement, she insists that you were all playing a strange game. What was the game that you played at home? *(Pause)* Wasn't it a bit . . . unhealthy? *(Pause)* Answer. Wasn't it a deviant game?

LALO: *(Firmly)* I don't know.

CUCA: *(As public prosecutor)* Your parents, according to my understanding, complained about you.

LALO: All my life, as long as I can remember, I've been hearing the same complaints, the same sermons, the same nagging.

CUCA: *(As public prosecutor)* They must have had some reason for complaining.

LALO: Sometimes they did, sometimes they didn't . . . When a reason is hammered home over and over again, it stops being reasonable.

CUCA: *(As public prosecutor)* Were your parents really so demanding?

LALO: I don't understand.

CUCA: *(As public prosecutor)* The question is this: what kind of relationship did you have with your parents?

LALO: I'm sure I've told you already. They questioned me. They made demands on me. They spied on me.

CUCA: *(As public prosecutor)* What questions did they ask? What demands did they make? Why were they spying?

LALO: *(Desperate)* I don't know. I don't know. *(Repeating in a mechanical voice)* Wash the dishes, wash the tablecloths, wash the shirts. Clean the vase, clean the bathroom, clean the floors. Don't sleep, don't dream, don't read. You're useless.

CUCA: *(As public prosecutor)* Ladies and gentlemen of the jury, ladies and gentlemen of the court, do you believe these are motives strong enough to drive an individual to commit a murder?

LALO: *(Stammering)* I wanted . . .

CUCA: *(As public prosecutor)* What did you want? *(Pause)* Answer.

LALO: *(Sincerely)* A life.

CUCA: *(As public prosecutor. Sarcastically)* And did your parents take your life away from you? *(To the audience)* Objection, M'lord, the accused is evading the question.

LALO: *(Passionately)* I wanted, I longed, I desperately longed to do things for myself.

CUCA: *(As public prosecutor)* And did your parents stop you?

LALO: *(Confidently)* Yes.

CUCA: *(As public prosecutor)* How?

LALO: They said I was a fool, a slob, a no-hoper.

CUCA: *(As public prosecutor. With great patience)* And

what were the things you wanted to do? Would the accused care to elaborate?

LALO: *(Tormented, making a great effort, a little confused)* It's very hard . . . I don't know. Things. You know? Things. How can I put it? I know they exist, that they're out there . . . I just can't at the moment. *(CUCA smiles maliciously.)* Look . . . I know it's something else, it's just that . . . *(Confidently)* I tried every way I could to please them . . . I caught pneumonia once and I . . . No, I can't tell you about that . . . I just . . . Things always went wrong for me. I didn't want it to be that way but I couldn't do anything else; and then . . .

CUCA: *(As public prosecutor)* Then what?

LALO: They shouted at me, they hit me, they punished me, endless hours locked in my room. They told me a thousand and one times I was better off dead, that they wanted to see me leave home to see how I coped and whether I would die of starvation.

CUCA: *(With a cynical smile)* Are you sure about what you're saying?

LALO: Yes.

CUCA: *(As public prosecutor)* Go on, go on.

LALO: I was very unhappy.

CUCA: *(As public prosecutor)* Why?

LALO: It felt like the house was caving in on me.

CUCA: *(As public prosecutor)* I don't understand. Exactly what do you mean?

LALO: The walls, the carpets, the curtains, the lamps, the sofa where Dad took his siesta, and the bed, and the wardrobes, and the sheets . . . the whole lot, I hated them, I wanted them to go away.

CUCA: *(As public prosecutor)* You hated the whole lot. And your parents? You hated your parents as well, didn't you?

LALO: *(Distracted)* Maybe I should have just run away. Gone anywhere: to hell or Timbuktu.

CUCA: *(As public prosecutor)* Ladies and gentlemen of the jury, ladies and gentlemen of the court . . .

LALO: *(Continuing, as if hypnotized)* One day, when I was playing with my sisters, I suddenly discovered . . . *(Pause)*

CUCA: *(As public prosecutor)* What did you discover?

LALO: *(In the same tone of voice as before)* We were in the living room; no, I lie . . . We were in the back room. We were playing . . . Or rather, we were acting . . . *(Smiles foolishly)* You might think it silly but . . . I was the father. No, that's not true. I think at that moment I was the mother. It was just a game . . . But there, right at that moment, I had this idea . . . *(Smiles foolishly again)*

CUCA: *(As public prosecutor)* What idea?

LALO: *(Smiling as before)* It's very simple, but it gets complicated. You never know whether you're saying what you feel. I . . . *(Moves his hands as if he were trying to explain things with this movement.)* I knew what

my folks were offering me wasn't life, and could never be life. So I said to myself: 'If you want to live you have to . . .' *(Stops and makes a stabbing gesture or clenches his fists as if tearing something apart)*

CUCA: *(As public prosecutor)* What did you feel at that moment?

LALO: I don't know. You tell me.

CUCA: *(As public prosecutor)* Were you afraid?

LALO: I think I was, just for a second.

CUCA: *(As public prosecutor)* And then?

LALO: Then I wasn't.

CUCA: *(As public prosecutor)* You got used to the idea?

LALO: I got used to it.

CUCA: *(As public prosecutor)* What? *(Banging the table)* Ladies and gentlemen, this is unprecedented.

LALO: It's true. I got used to it. *(As LALO progresses through the monologue, he becomes transformed.)* It sounds terrible, but . . . It's not how I wanted it, but the idea kept on buzzing around in my head. At first, I wanted it to go away. Do you know what I mean? But it kept on telling me: 'Kill your parents. Kill your parents.' I thought I was going crazy, I swear. I jumped into bed. I started getting the shivers . . . I had a temperature. I thought I would pop like a balloon. I thought the devil was beckoning to me. I lay trembling under the blankets . . . You should have seen me . . . I couldn't sleep. Not a wink night after night. It was dreadful. I saw death creeping up on me from behind the bed, from between the curtains, from inside the wardrobe. It became my shadow and whispered to me from inside the pillows: 'Assassin.' And then, as if by magic, it disappeared. And I sat in front of the mirror and saw my mother lying dead in her coffin and my father hanging by his neck laughing and shouting at me. And at night I felt my mother's hands in the pillows, scratching my face. *(Pause)* Every morning I woke up in pain. It was as if I were rising from the dead, clasped by two corpses which had been chasing me in my dreams. There were moments when I was tempted . . . but no . . . no . . . Leave home? No way! I knew what I was up against . . . I would always come back and then I would promise never to do it again. By then I was determined never again to embark on that crazy adventure. Anything but that! Then I had the idea of arranging the house in my own way, of running things myself . . . The living room is not the living room, I said to myself. The living room is the kitchen. The bedroom is not the bedroom. The bedroom is the bathroom. *(Short pause)* What else could I do? If I didn't do that, I would end up destroying everything. Everything. Because everything was complicit, everything was plotting against me; everything knew my every thought. If I sat down in a chair, the chair wasn't the chair but my father's corpse. If I picked up a glass of water, I felt that what

I had in my hands was my dead mother's damp neck. If I played with a vase, an enormous knife would suddenly fall out of it. If I cleaned the carpets, I could never finish the job because they turned into an enormous clot of blood. *(Pause)* Haven't you ever felt like that? I was suffocating, suffocating. I didn't know where I was or what it was all about. And who could I talk to? Was there anyone I could trust? I was stuck in a deep hole and there was no way out . . . *(Pause)* But I had a strange idea that I could save myself . . . I don't know what from . . . Anyway, it's just an expression . . . You try to explain the whole thing and you almost . . . usually you can't . . . Perhaps I wanted to save myself from the suffocating, from being shut in . . . Soon after, without knowing why, things began to change. I heard a voice one day, but I didn't know where it was coming from . . . And then I heard my sisters laughing and joking all round the house. And mixed in with their laughter I heard thousands of voices repeating in unison: 'Kill them. Kill them.' No, I'm not just making it up. I swear it's true. *(As if inspired)* From then on I knew what I had to do. Gradually I realized that everything, the carpets, the bed, the wardrobes, the mirror, the vases, the glasses, the spoons and my own shadow, they were all murmuring, telling me: 'Kill your parents.' *(He says it in an almost musical ecstasy.)* 'Kill your parents.' The whole house, everything, everything was pushing me towards this heroic act. *(Pause)*

CUCA: *(Violently)* I'm leaving. You're cheating.

LALO: We've got to see it through to the end.

CUCA: I can't let you . . .

LALO: You've tried to make it go your way as well.

CUCA: I can't believe you're doing this. We each have a part; we agreed.

LALO: Is that so? All right then . . .

BEBA: *(As judge, banging her gavel)* Order! Silence in court!

CUCA: *(As mother. To BEBA)* Officer, forgive my interruption; but I must ask for a thorough investigation of this case, right from the beginning. I demand a retrial. That's why I'm here. I want to make a statement. My son is making himself out to be a victim, but that's the complete opposite of the truth. I demand that justice be done. *(BEBA starts to repeat the tac-tac of the typewriter. Exaggerating)* If you knew what this beast has done to our lives. It's so dreadful, so . . .

BEBA: *(As officer. To CUCA)* Go on . . .

LALO: *(Almost out of part)* But Mum, I . . . *(LALO feels cornered.)* I . . . I swear . . .

CUCA: *(As mother)* Don't you swear at me. You want to come across as a fool, but I know your tricks, your games. I know them because I gave birth to you. Nine months of dizziness, vomiting, aches, and pains. And they were just the warnings of your arrival. Are you trying to confuse me? Why are you swearing these things to me? Do you think you've won over your audience? Do you think you can save yourself? Well tell me, save yourself from what? *(Roars with laughter)* What planet are you living on, sonny? *(Mockingly)* Oh, my little angel, I'm so sorry for you. You really are, well, I won't say what you are . . . *(To BEBA)* Do you know something, officer? One day he got it into his head that we should rearrange the whole house the way he wanted it . . . As soon as I heard this ridiculous idea, I refused to listen to another word on the subject. His father hit the roof. You can't imagine what it looked like . . . The ashtray on the chair. The vase lying on the floor. Awful! And then he started singing at the top of his voice, running all round the house: 'The living room is not the living room. The living room is the kitchen.' When that happened I pretended not to hear, as if I were listening to the rain. *(To LALO)* You've only told the bits which interest you. Why don't you tell the rest of the story? *(Mockingly)* You've told them about your martyrdom, now tell them about ours, your father's and mine. Let me refresh your memory. *(To BEBA, transformed)* Your Honor, if you knew the tears I have shed, the humiliation I have suffered, the hours of anguish, the sacrifices . . . Just look at these hands . . . It makes me sick to look at them. *(On the verge of tears)* My hands . . . If you had seen them before I got married . . . Now I've lost everything: my youth, my happiness, all my little pleasures. I've sacrificed everything for this animal. *(To LALO)* Aren't you ashamed? Do you still think you've done something heroic? *(Disgusted)* You wretch. I don't know how I could have carried you for so long in my belly. I don't know why I didn't drown you at birth. *(BEBA bangs her gavel.)*

LALO: Mum, I . . .

CUCA: *(As mother)* Shut up. Just shut up. You're not worth the bread we put on your plate. You're not worth one of the contractions I had giving birth to you. Because you, you are the guilty one. And no one else.

LALO: *(Violently)* Leave me alone. Just leave me alone.

CUCA: *(As mother. Violently)* I'm getting old. Think about that and make some sacrifices. Do you think I don't have a right to live? Do you think I'm going to spend my whole life in perpetual agony? Your father doesn't care about me and neither do you. Where will I end up? Yes, I know you're waiting for me to die, but I won't give you that satisfaction. I'll shout to the neighbours, to everyone in the street. You'll see. That will be my revenge. *(Shouting)* Help! Help! They're killing me. *(Bursts into tears)* I'm a poor old woman dying of loneliness. *(BEBA bangs her gavel.)* Yes, your Honor, I'm imprisoned by these four dirty walls. I never see the light of day. My children don't care. I'm withered, wilting . . . (*As if she were looking at herself in a mirror. Starts stroking her face and ends up slapping it*) Look at this skin. Look at these wrinkles. (*Pointing to her wrinkles with rancor and disgust. To LALO*) You'll get them one day. All I want is for you to go through the same as I have. (*Haughtily*) Your Honor, I have always been an honest woman.

LALO: (*Slightly mockingly*) Are you sure? Think carefully, Mum.

CUCA: (*As mother*) What do you mean? What are you suggesting?

LALO: (*Sarcastically*) I mean, I know you're lying. I mean, you once accused me of . . .

CUCA (*As mother. Indignantly, interrupting him with a cry*) Lalo! (*Pause. Gently*) Lalo, are you trying to say. . . ? (*Pause. Takes a few steps. She looks annoyed again.*) This is just the limit! Your Honor . . . (*Almost sobbing*) Oh, Lalo . . . (*Wiping her tears away*) You say I. . . ? (*With obvious doubt*) Is that possible? (*With a faint smile*) Oh, I'm sorry, your Honor . . . I could have done it . . . But it was just a silly mistake. (*Laughs crudely*) I got completely hooked on this red taffeta dress I saw in the window of the New Bazaar. It was so divine. My husband was earning a pittance. You can't imagine . . . I had to perform miracles every month just to make ends meet. So, as I was saying, your Honor, I was mad about that dress. I had to have it. I had dreams about it. I even saw it in my soup. At last, one day I decided to buy the dress with the housekeeping money. So I made up a story.

BEBA: (*As judge*) What kind of story?

CUCA: (*As mother. With great self-confidence*) When Albert got home, drunk as usual, I said to him: look, dear, will you have a word with your son . . . (*Goes up to BEBA to whisper in her ear*) Because I think he's stolen some money from us.

BEBA: (*As judge*) Why did you do it?

CUCA: (*As mother. Vulgarly*) I don't know . . . It was easier that way . . . (*She finishes the story with a flourish.*) So Albert took off his belt and beat poor little Lalo . . . Oh, I hate to think how many times he beat him . . . In fact, he was completely innocent, but . . . I wanted that red dress so much! (*Going up to LALO*) Do you forgive me, my son?

LALO: (*Hard*) There's nothing to forgive.

CUCA: (*As mother. Slightly hysterical*) Have some respect, Lalo. (*In a dramatic tone of voice*) I've changed. I'm fat and ugly now . . . Ah, this body!

LALO: Don't think about it.

CUCA: (*As mother. With authority*) Show some respect, I said.

LALO: I was only playing around.

CUCA: (*As mother. Hard and imperious*) Well, don't play with me. Your father is an old fool who's chasing something which doesn't exist. So are you. Let him be a lesson to you . . . He thinks he's Superman, but actually he's a nobody. He's always been a failure. He's always been all talk, and he thinks he can carry on like that. Sometimes I wish he'd lie down and die. Why did I have to get hitched to a man who couldn't offer me a better life than this? (*Pause*) Come on. (*Pause*) If it wasn't for me, your Honor, this house wouldn't even be standing . . . It was all me . . .

LALO: (*As father. In an assured, almost frightening voice*) She's lying, your Honor.

CUCA: (*As mother. To LALO*) How dare you?

LALO: (*As father. To BEBA*) It's true. She's trying to paint everything black. She sees only the motes in the eyes of others, not the beam in her own. I have been at fault at times as a parent. And so has she. (*In a more assured tone of voice*) Like all parents we've done some things which have been unfair and other things which have been unforgivable.

CUCA: (*As mother*) You used to come home with lipstick on your collar.

LALO: (*As father*) Shut up. You don't want me to tell the truth.

CUCA: (*As mother*) Your Honor, he was always drinking, he used to bring his friends over at all hours of the night . . .

LALO: (*As father*) Who wears the trousers in our house?

CUCA: (*As mother*) I'm in charge of the house.

LALO: (*As father*) There. 'I'm in charge of the house.' Yes, you, you're in charge all right. That's all your life comes down to. You've made fun of me. You've humiliated me. That's the truth. Domination. (*Short pause*) I've been an idiot, a complete asshole, if you'll excuse my French.

CUCA: (*As mother*) Well done. At least you admit it.

LALO: (*As father*) What's the point of denying it? (*Pause. Ordering his thoughts*) I went into marriage with few illusions. If I said I was pinning all my hopes on marriage, I'd be both exaggerating and lying. I went into it like most people, thinking that it would sort out a few problems: clothes, food, stability . . . some company and . . . well . . . a few little liberties. (*Kicking himself inside*) Idiot! You idiot! (*Pause*) I never thought it would turn out like it did.

CUCA: (*As mother*) You never thought, full stop. 'You take the low road and I'll take the high road.' That's what a lot of people think. But I was different.

LALO: (*As father*) She's right there. She certainly was very different. The problems started a few days before the wedding: the church wasn't smart enough, the train on your dress wasn't long enough. And your sisters said this, and your mother said that, and your cousin said the other, and your aunt said something else, and your friends didn't agree at all, and your granny thought we should have invited the so-and-sos, and that the cake should have been ten rather than nine tiers high, and that your friends should come from better backgrounds . . .

CUCA: (As mother) Go on, go on. Spit it all out, get it all out of your system. At last I can see that you hate me.

LALO: (As father) Yes, I do. And I don't know why. But I know I do. When we were just going out you went to bed with me because you knew that was the only way you could catch me. And that's the truth.

CUCA: (As mother) Carry on, carry on. Don't stop.

LALO: (As father) You didn't want kids. You hated them. But no way could you stay single. No way. You had to catch a husband. It didn't matter who. Having one was all that mattered.

CUCA: (As mother. Going up to him furiously) I hate you, I hate you, I hate you.

LALO: (As father) A husband made you feel secure. A husband made you respectable. (Ironically) Respectable . . . (Pause) I can't quite explain . . . Anyway, life is like that, so if you want to . . .

CUCA: (As mother) Lies, lies, lies.

LALO: (As father) Will you let me finish?

CUCA: (Out of part) You're cheating again.

LALO: (As father) You don't want people to know the truth.

CUCA: (Out of part) I'm talking about something else.

LALO: (As father) You're scared of seeing it through to the end.

CUCA: (Out of part) You're trying to crush me.

LALO: (As father) And you? What have you been doing? Tell me. What have you done to me? And to them? (Mocking) 'I'm growing ugly, Albert. I'm in the family way. We can't bring them up on your salary.' (Pause) And I didn't know the reasons, the real reasons. And today, I say to you: 'Put your hand on your heart and answer this question: Did you ever love me?' (Pause) Oh well, don't say anything. I can see clearly now. It's taken years to sink in. 'Albert, those children . . . I can't handle them. You take care of them.' As time passed, your demands grew greater, and your selfishness grew with them. (Pause) And me, in the office, with my figures, and the gossip and the friends who came up to me and said: 'How long are you going to put up with this, mate?'

(CUCA starts singing: 'The living room is not the living room, the living room is the kitchen. The bedroom is not the bedroom, the bedroom is the bathroom.' CUCA's singing and LALO's words should proceed in counterpoint. BEBA starts singing, first as a growl and then gradually becoming a sweet, simple, almost naive song.)

LALO: (Continues, mockingly) And you? 'Your sister called today. She's so nosey. Oh, these children. Look at my hands: the washing up did this. I'm losing my mind, Albert, I wish I were dead.' And then came your tears and the children started screaming and I thought I was going mad and everything started spinning . . . I used to escape from the house, sometimes at midnight, and go for a few drinks, and I felt like I was drowning, drowning. (Pause. Without taking a breath) And other women were there and I didn't dare think about them . . . And I felt a terrible urge to leave, to fly away, to break with everything. (Pause) But I was afraid, and fear paralyzed me and I couldn't make up my mind and I got stuck between two stools. I thought one thing and I did another. It's terrible to have to admit it. And only to realize at the end. (Pause) I couldn't do it. (To the audience) Lalo, if you want to do it, you can. (Pause) Now I ask myself why I didn't live out all my thoughts, all my desires. And I have to reply: because I was afraid, afraid, afraid.

CUCA: (As mother. Sarcastically) Well, honey, you can't blame me for that. (Pause, defiantly) And what did you want me to do? Those children were a nightmare. They turned my house into a pigsty. Lalo ripped the curtains and smashed the crockery. Beba wasn't content with tearing apart the pillows . . . And you expected to come home and find everything tickety-boo. Do you remember when Lalo peed all over the living room? You threw a fit and said, 'That never happened in my home.' Was that my fault as well? Eh? I used to put a chair here. (Moves a chair) And I would find it over here. (Moves the chair to another place) What was I supposed to do?

LALO: (As father. Beaten) The house had to be cleaned. (BEBA stops singing.) Yes . . . The furniture had to be changed . . . (Pause. With great melancholy) We really should have found a new house. (Pause. Slowly) But we're old now and we can't. We are dead. (Long pause. Violently) You always thought you were better than me.

CUCA: (As mother) I've wasted my life away on you.

LALO: (As father. Vengefully) You can't escape, love. Carry on. Carry on. Carry on.

CUCA: (As mother. Sobbing) You pathetic pen pusher. I wish you were dead.

BEBA: (As LALO. Shouting and moving in circles around the stage) Throw out the carpets. Pull down the curtains. The living room is not the living room. The living room is the kitchen. The bedroom is not the bedroom. The bedroom is the bathroom. (BEBA and LALO are at opposite ends of the stage with their backs to the audience. LALO doubles up slowly with a piercing scream.) Ayyyyyy! (Sobbing) I can see my dead mother. I can see my father with his throat cut. Tear this house down.

(Long pause)

LALO: Open the door.

(LALO falls to his knees. CUCA slowly gets up, walks over to the door upstage and opens it. Pause. Goes over to the table and picks up the knife)

BEBA: (In a normal tone of voice) How do you feel?

CUCA: (In a normal tone of voice) Stronger.

BEBA: Satisfied?

CUCA: Yes.

BEBA: Really?

CUCA: Really.

BEBA: Are you ready to do it again?

CUCA: You know the answer to that.

BEBA: One day we'll do it for real.

CUCA: *(Interrupting)* Without anything going wrong.

BEBA: Were you surprised you managed to do it?

CUCA: Everything's surprising.

LALO: *(Sobbing)* Oh, Beba, Cuca, if only love could do it . . . If only love . . . Because in spite of everything, I love them.

CUCA: *(Playing with the knife)* That's ridiculous.

BEBA: *(To CUCA)* Poor little thing, let him be.

CUCA: *(To BEBA. Laughing mockingly)* Look at him. *(To LALO)* That's how I like to see you.

BEBA: *(Serious again)* All right. Now it's my turn.

CURTAIN

ARGENTINA

The Camp, directed by Mara Sabinson, Dartmouth College, 1992. (Photo by John Sheldon.)

The Camp (Griselda Gambaro)

The 1960s and 1970s were a particularly turbulent period throughout Latin America. In various countries, the armed forces responded with a wave of brutal dictatorships to what they claimed was the threat of communism stemming from the Cuban Revolution of 1959. Brazil experienced a coup in 1964, Augusto Pinochet took power in Chile in 1973, and the coup by the Argentine military in 1976 ushered in the "Dirty War," a seven-year period in which thirty thousand civilians were "disappeared"—tortured and killed. Griselda Gambaro (born in 1928), one of Latin America's most important playwrights, has always been among the first to recognize changes in the political climate of her country. In the dozens of plays she has written during the past forty years, she scrutinizes the role of theater and theatricality in Argentina's criminalized society from the 1960s until the end of the dictatorship in 1983, and she continues to explore the challenges that persist into the present as Argentines coexist with their ex-torturers and endure violent political upheavals.[1]

As early as 1963, Gambaro's plays were already depicting the abductions and concentration camps, the victims and victimizers, and the escalation of political violence that would become the grim reality of the Dirty War in the 1970s. *The Camp* (*El Campo,* 1967) illustrates Argentina's growing militarism and fascination with fascism. This play followed the particularly repressive coup of 1966, the fifth the country had suffered since 1930.[2] By then, as historians Thomas E. Skidmore and Peter H. Smith note, the "deadly toxin" of violence had corroded the "Argentine body politic," undermining distinctions between social, family, and personal space.[3] Each sphere was invaded and terrorized. In *The Camp,* violence at first seems to be a game of dress-up and sound systems. Franco, whose name conjures up the late Spanish dictator Francisco Franco, says he wears a Nazi uniform only because it gives him pleasure ("I'm not hurting anyone."). Only gradually does Martin, the new accountant, realize that behind all the apparent bureaucratic scaffolding he is in fact in a concentration camp. At the end, Martin and Emma, an inmate, believe that they have been released. In fact, however, the home Emma and Martin run to at the end of the play is as unfamiliar, and as lethal, as the concentration camp they thought they had left behind. The very idea of release seems hopelessly nostalgic in a world in which the home has become indistinguishable from torture chambers and death camps. The home in the final scene foreshadows Gambaro's use of a house as a terrifying theater space in her *Information for Foreigners* (1972), an extraordinary play that is widely available in English.[4] As state-sponsored terrorist attacks, abductions, and violations decimate individuals and families, the home itself becomes the site of official terror. Human bodies are literally inscribed with political insignia. Thugs from the concentration camp enter Martin's desecrated home and brand a number on him. The spectators enter the *univers concentrationnaire* associated with the Holocaust and the literature of atrocity.[5]

The similarities between Gambaro's work and European depictions of fascism and nazism are not accidental. The ties between Argentine and European fascism are old and strong. Not only was the modern Argentine army trained by German officers at the beginning of the twentieth century, but immigrants from Germany, Italy, and Spain in the 1920s and 1930s often espoused fascist ideals. During World War II, Argentina remained officially neutral, though President Juan Perón favored the Axis coalition and was a frequent guest of the Spanish dictator Francisco Franco after the war. As *The Camp* illustrates, even after they subsided in Europe, fascism, "Franco," and concentration camps lived on in Argentina, where fascist World War II war criminals and their ideologies found a receptive home in some quarters. *The Camp* accentuates the links between the two by setting the action in a modern Argentine neo-Nazi concentration camp. The noise of machine guns, the smell of burning flesh, the allusions to showers, the prisoners forced to sing as they're marched off to the fields, and references to "Work will make you free" and schoolchildren "walking . . . as if they were moving from their house" leave no doubt that this camp is modeled after its German original. However, it is fundamental to recognize that *The Camp* is not about the Holocaust. Although it deals with the historical fact of Argentine fascism and criminal politics, it has no historical documentary intent. Unlike the theater of the Holocaust, it is not a testimonial; it need not face the challenge of depicting "a sense of what it must have been like in the ghettos and the camps."[6]

Rather, there is an *as if* quality to *The Camp*: Franco dresses up *as if* he were a Nazi; Emma looks *as if* she were a victim from Auschwitz forced to perform for a captive audience. Nonetheless, Gambaro seems to warn us not to dismiss the *as if* as pretending. Martin tries to understand the strange theatricality and insularity of the room in which he is to work. Everything that he hears or sees seems regulated by the intercom device situated on Franco's desk. Martin thinks he hears field workers singing, but when he looks out the window he sees nothing. The window, as in theatrical sets, only suggests the existence of an external, visible reality. When Martin pushes the button on the intercom, the singing stops. The sounds of children screaming, of people running in the halls, of ferocious dogs "barking at a close range, as if . . . attacking someone" suddenly break in through the white noise, the "bland, insipid music." Against the clean and orderly setting, the groans, harsh reprimands, and screams seem "at times like an auditory hallucination." Nothing is as it appears. Franco's face seems "almost kind" in spite of his "dazzling SS uniform" and whip, and his erratic manner and constant change of topic add to the perplexity: "The Americans are good writers. . . . You're a coward, aren't you?" Emma acts as if she were an adored celebrity in spite of the fact that she is shaved, branded, and dressed in rags. Martin is thrown into a state of confusion; he cannot interpret what he sees with his own eyes or hears with his own ears. As in many of Gambaro's early plays, the victim has stumbled onto the wrong stage. The theatricality of the scene lulls the victim into believing that the deadly situation is not "real" and hides no actual danger.

In *The Camp*, Gambaro focuses particularly on the sexualization of brutality as a means of disarming the victims and spectators. The act of torture can be transformed to look like an erotic fantasy. Franco informs Martin that he has invited a woman ("Venus, a touch of frivolity") to spend the evening with them ("I've invited her over for you. . . . Be nice to her") and then he leaves to change back into his Nazi outfit. What has been set up supposedly as a sexual encounter, whether a blind date or act of prostitution, is actually something quite different. Emma is shoved into the room. Her body itches terribly; she is emaciated, and she wears a prisoner's smock; her right palm is marked by a black and blue mark; she is barefoot. She scratches herself uncontrollably until she bleeds. Her body, in fact, has been converted into a surface of living pain, which the script equates with the concentration camp itself: "I don't have lice," she explains to Martin. "Absolutely not. They've been eradicated in this zone." Which zone? Body or camp? However, this woman, whose body has become a source of torment, is obviously expected to seduce Martin as if she were a movie actress: "She stands up straight and smiles, making a visible effort to do so, as if she were beginning to perform." Confronted with Martin's astonished reaction, she asks, with the look "of a frustrated coquette. . . Don't you like me?" She "keeps talking with a pretense of social gaiety" of her admirers, her secretary, her impossible social schedule. The scenario is a cruel parody of the sex symbol that must please her fans; without her admirers she is nothing. It also painfully reflects the gender-specific condition of woman as desired object. If Martin does not like her or find her attractive, she is nothing. Her body has been transformed into the source of her pain; her femininity used as one more instrument of torture against her.

The purpose of this playacting, however, is to ensure that Martin will not leave the camp, as he has already threatened to do. Emma is the bait, live bait. While Emma has been victimized, Martin is the intended victim of this scene. Franco strikes at Martin (the innocent bystander, the spectator) through her. Martin is horrified by her: "I feel sorry for you. It reminds me of . . ." He cannot speak the unspeakable. Like many others faced with atrocity, he resists thinking and speaking about violence. The live bait "catches" him but not through the grotesque sexuality: "MARTIN: *(He covers her legs.)* What are you doing? Calm down. You're showing me your legs and you seem like an escaped . . . *(He stops, surprised, as if it was only then that he realized she looks like a prisoner who escaped from a concentration camp.).*" He feels compassion for her. Not once in the course of the play does Gambaro eroticize or romanticize their relationship. Martin sides with Emma as a fellow human being, and he feels rage at her tormentors. He has seen and understood the nature of her suffering. He is engaged, no longer free to leave. He, too, becomes a victim of Franco's regime.

Handwritten margin notes:

sense of blindness and unbelieving

Martin is almost symbolic of the Argentinians who either ignore and/or are indifferent to the suffering of the rest of the country. The rich, white Argentinians are not targeted and rarely affected.

As Elie Weisel said about the Holocaust indifference is the worst.

Are their really innocent bystanders? Isn't the point of the message to not stand idly by? Erotic vouyerism of being just a spectator

But what is the audience's role in the spectacle of torture? The play challenges the notion that individuals and publics protect themselves by pretending that they do not see or understand what is going on. The only way Martin could conceivably extricate himself from the situation would be by not caring. He could ignore Emma's plea ("I beg you, don't leave me here") and abandon her to her fate. He could justify this by seeming to believe in the pathetic drama being enacted before his eyes ("My hair is short. It's because of my wigs"). But turning one's back on the victim is hardly a viable solution to victimization, and *The Camp* does not really offer Martin the possibility of walking away. He enjoys only the illusion that he is free to go. As in most situations in which people feel that it is dangerous to sympathize or side with the victim, or dangerous to see and acknowledge what is happening, it is already too late. People become participants, and at times complicitous, in the acts of violence they pretend not to see. As Gambaro makes clear in her early plays, going along with the fiction is actually more dangerous than saying "no," enough.

In 1967, Gambaro's *The Camp,* set against the backdrop of the Holocaust, was a warning of things to come for the Argentine population. The replay suggests, as the saying goes, that those who do not learn from history are condemned to relive it. Unfortunately, in 1967 the Argentine population was still to endure one of the most horrific periods of its history. The violence lay ahead not behind. Griselda Gambaro would be forced into exile, the Dirty War would pit the armed forces against the population, the Mothers of Plaza de Mayo would take to the Plaza de Mayo to protest the disappearance of their children, and investigators would turn up the 320 clandestine centers in which the Argentine military tortured and killed its citizens. How Argentines are to live with that history has become the subject of Gambaro's most recent plays.

—Diana Taylor

NOTES

1. Gambaro's many plays include *Los siameses* (1965), *Decir sí* (1981), *Antígona furiosa* (1986), *Atando cabos* (1991), and *Es necesario entender un poco* (1995). Her 1974 play *El despojamiento* was translated by Marguerite Feitlowitz as *Strip* and published in *Holy Terrors: Latin American Women Perform,* ed. Diana Taylor and Roselyn Costantino (Durham: Duke University Press, 2003).

2. For a discussion of the historical background, see *The Argentina Reader: History, Culture, Politics* (Durham: Duke University Press, 2002); Thomas E. Skidmore and Peter H. Smith, *Modern Latin America* (New York: Oxford University Press, 1984); Nicholas Shumway, *The Invention of Argentina* (Berkeley: University of California Press, 1991); and Diana Taylor, *Disappearing Acts: Spectacles of Gender and Nationalism in Argentina's "Dirty War"* (Durham: Duke University Press, 1997).

3. Skidmore and Smith, *Modern Latin America,* 103.

4. See Griselda Gambaro, *Information for Foreigners: Three Plays by Griselda Gambaro,* ed. and trans. Marguerite Feitlowitz (Evanston: Northwestern University Press, 1992). This volume includes *The Walls, Information for Foreigners,* and *Antígona Furiosa.*

5. Sections of this introduction are from my *Theatre of Crisis: Drama and Politics in Latin America* (Lexington: University Press of Kentucky, 1991). For an in-depth study of this play and other early works by Griselda Gambaro, see "Theatre and Terror: Griselda Gambaro," chapter 3 in *Theatre of Crisis.*

6. Saul Friedländer, *Reflections of Nazism: An Essay on Kitsch and Death,* trans. Thomas Weyr (New York: Harper and Row, 1984), 99.

SELECTED REFERENCES

Boling, Becky. "Reenacting Politics: The Theater of Griselda Gambaro." In *Latin American Women Dramatists: Theater, Texts, and Theories,* ed. Catherine Larson and Margarita Vargas, 3–22. Bloomington and Indianapolis: Indiana University Press, 1998.

Bulman, Gail A. "Moving On: Memory and History in Griselda Gambaro's Recent Theater." *Studies in Twentieth and Twenty First Century Literature* 28 (summer 2004): 379–95.

Contreras, Marta. *Griselda Gambaro: Teatro de la descomposición.* Concepción: Ediciones Universidad de Concepción, 1994.

Cypess, Sandra Messinger. "The Plays of Griselda Gambaro." In *Dramatists in Revolt: The New Latin American Theater,* ed. Leon F. Lyday and George W. Woodyard, 95–109. Austin: University of Texas Press, 1976.

Feitlowitz, Marguerite. "Crisis, Terror, Disappearance: The Theater of Griselda Gambaro." *Theater* 21 (summer–fall 1990): 34–38.

Franco, Jean. "Self-Destructing Heroines." *Minnesota Review: A Journal of Committed Writing* 22 (1984): 105–15.

Giordano, Enrique L. "Ambigüedad y alteridad del sujeto dramático en *El campo* de Griselda Gambaro." *Alba de América: Revista Literaria* 7 (July 1989): 47–59.

Molinaro, Nina L. "Discipline and Drama: Panoptic Theatre and Griselda Gambaro's *El campo.*" *Latin American Theatre Review* 29 (spring 1996): 29–41.

Taylor, Diana. *Disappearing Acts: Spectacles of Gender and Nationalism in Argentina's "Dirty War."* Durham: Duke University Press, 1997.

Taylor, Diana. "Theatre and Terror: Griselda Gambaro." Chapter 3 in *Theatre of Crisis: Drama and Politics in Latin America.* Lexington: University Press of Kentucky, 1991.

Ure, A., ed. *Poder, deseo y marginación: Aproximaciones a la obra de Griselda Gambaro.* Buenos Aires: Puntosur Editores, 1989.

- Moral Relativism - any action can be justified.
- Recontextualize
  vs.
- Staring evil in the face?

    Power of the Regime - even if you don't believe it, it's enough that you say it.

- Blinding oneself - self-editing - internally convincing oneself

Revisit what world this play is representing.

The Camp (Griselda Gambaro)

Translated by Margaret Carson

CHARACTERS:

MARTIN
FRANCO
EMMA
SERVANT
The PIANO TUNER
A BUREAUCRAT
GROUP of SS OFFICERS
NURSES
GROUP of PRISONERS
MALE NURSES

FIRST ACT

SCENE 1

An interior with gleaming white walls. Towards the left of the stage, as the only furniture, a desk, an armchair, and a chair. A wastepaper basket. Two doors, one on the right leading to another room, and the other on the left leading outside. A window in back.

After a moment, the door on the left opens and a polite voice is heard saying:

SERVANT: Come in, leave your suitcases here. The master will see you at once.

(MARTIN enters. He is wearing a coat, gloves, and a scarf. He takes off his gloves and scarf and puts them on the desk. He sits in the armchair. His gestures are slow, relaxed. He takes a piece of gum out of his pocket and puts it in his mouth. All of a sudden, children's shouts and cries can be heard, strangely mixed with dry, authoritarian orders, of which only a confused "One! Two!" can be understood. Beneath it all, an undercurrent of moaning that seems at times like an auditory hallucination. MARTIN gets up and listens while chewing his gum. He looks at the clean surface of the desk, which is bare except for an intercom. He presses one of the buttons on the intercom and a bland, insipid music is heard, like elevator music. He smiles and presses the button again. The noise from outside also stops. He sits down. Someone is running in the hallway and a voice between furious and amused shouts, "Run! No, not that way! Not that way!" Ferocious barking at a close range, as if the dogs were attacking someone. The door opens for a moment and then slams shut again. The noise stops. MARTIN walks to the door and opens it. He looks out. He doesn't see anything and

closes the door with a shrug of his shoulders. He picks up his scarf and gloves from the desk and puts them in the pocket of his overcoat. As he begins to take off his overcoat, the door to the right opens and FRANCO enters. He is dressed in a dazzling SS uniform and a whip is tied to his wrist. Despite this, he doesn't seem threatening at all: he's a young man with a face that seems almost kind. He walks in, busy at work. He's carrying so many papers and old file folders in his hands and under his arms that they begin to fall as he crosses the room.)

FRANCO: *(Complains good-naturedly while picking up the papers)* Those kids! They're so lively! *(He places the papers and folders on the desk. He removes the whip in a smooth motion and pushes it with his foot under the desk. He stretches his hand out to MARTIN.)* Here I am at last. How are you? Were you waiting long?

MARTIN: *(Looks at him, surprised)* No.

FRANCO: *(He picks up other papers from the floor.)* Take off your coat. *(MARTIN bends over to help him.)* No, don't bother. I'm used to things falling. I'm so clumsy! *(He unbuttons his jacket a little.)* Ugh, it's so hot!

MARTIN: *(Bending under the desk to pick up a sheet of paper)* There's another one here.

FRANCO: *(Separates it with his foot so that it doesn't touch the whip)* No, leave it.

MARTIN: *(Annoyed)* Excuse me, what's this?

FRANCO: *(Pointing to the papers, indignant)* This place is a goddamn mess! *(He sits down in the armchair. Shows him the chair on the other side of the desk. Friendly)* Sit down! How are you? Take off your coat.

MARTIN: *(Sits down)* I'm fine.

FRANCO: *(Without listening)* We have good heat. Sometimes it's a little cold, sometimes it's a little hot,

El campo, Griselda Gambaro, Argentina, 1967. Translated from Spanish by Margaret Carson.

but otherwise it's ideal. (*Once again, the same children's shouts and cries can be heard along with orders and a muffled wailing. FRANCO pushes a button on the intercom. With a slow but authoritarian, threatening voice*) I want the children to be quiet. (*The shouts and cries cease. He smiles, and puts his hands on a disorganized pile of papers on the desk.*) Here's everything. Well, just a part—the books are in the office. (*Looks at MARTIN, who has been observing him, half amused, half annoyed. Friendly*) What surprises you?

MARTIN: Nothing.

FRANCO: No, say it!

MARTIN: The uniform.

FRANCO: (*Astonished*) Everyone says the same thing! What shitty times we live in!

MARTIN: But why that uniform?

FRANCO: What uniform should I wear?

MARTIN: Why that one?

FRANCO: I like it. You have to indulge yourself a little. I'm not hurting anyone. I'm not armed. (*Suddenly*) Jewish?

MARTIN: (*Smiles*) No.

FRANCO: Communist?

MARTIN: No. (*He chews his gum. A pause. He leans towards FRANCO.*) Tell me, why does it matter?

FRANCO: (*Astonished*) What are you doing? Chewing gum? (*To himself, unpleasantly surprised*) What a disgusting habit!

MARTIN: (*Unperturbed*) I smoke less.

FRANCO: I chewed on licorice. (*He opens a box on the desk.*) Do you want some?

MARTIN: No, no. I can't stand licorice.

FRANCO: I can't stand chewing gum.

MARTIN: (*Calm*) Really? Is it that bad? (*He points to the papers.*) Should we have a look?

FRANCO: (*Courteous*) You've just arrived! I'm not a slave driver. (*He brushes off his jacket.*) This might give you the wrong impression, but I'm not a slave driver!

MARTIN: (*Smiles*) I know. You brought the papers, and I'd like to look them over.

FRANCO: (*Timidly*) You're not saying that only because it's your job?

MARTIN: No. I wasn't tired by the trip.

FRANCO: That's good! (*Dryly*) But I don't think we can work if you're chewing gum. Really, I don't think so. (*MARTIN spits his gum into the wastepaper basket in an almost rude way.*) Thank you, thank you! (*Children's voices and laughter are heard now, without any orders or moans in the background. FRANCO pays attention and smiles.*) Listen to those kids. They're not obedient. They're playing in the patio. (*With a strange smile*) One kid even wanted to come inside. (*He laughs. Suddenly*) What do you think about Vietnam? Excuse me for asking. What do I care?

MARTIN: Nothing. (*He's fed up.*) Are we going to look at these papers?

FRANCO: Right now. It's a thorny issue for me. (*He leans back in the armchair.*) Is it right, is it wrong? The Americans are so strong, it's a great nation. I don't know anything about the other side. Do you?

MARTIN: (*Dryly*) No. (*He takes out a piece of gum and puts it in his mouth.*)

FRANCO: (*While looking at him with more and more disgust*) No one knows about them, so it's hard to have a fair idea. Everyone knows about the Jews. About Communists, not as much, but at least we can get a handle on them. It's not that difficult. We've read Russian Communists, Gorky, I've read him. "Mother." What a book! And . . . (*He can't remember, he doesn't know, or he's fixated on MARTIN, who's chewing gum.*) . . . so many others. (*His voice weakening, he begins to plead.*) Stop it. (*MARTIN stops chewing for a moment. FRANCO, with renewed energy*) I'm thinking about Vietnamese writers. Look, I make no distinction— South Vietnamese, North Vietnamese, they're the same to me. Who knows them, who reads them? What language do they speak? The question can't be resolved. (*Softly*) Can't you stop chewing gum?

MARTIN: It amuses me.

FRANCO: (*Humble*) You're not amused by my conversation?

MARTIN: Yes, very amused.

FRANCO: So then?

MARTIN: I'd like to get to the point. (*A pause*) Excuse me, I don't want to be rude.

FRANCO: No, you're not being rude. (*He bangs his fist on the desk.*) I like people who are blunt!

MARTIN: (*Points to the papers*) What's this? Why aren't these numbered?

FRANCO: (*Amused*) What do you mean, numbered? They're all screwed up!

MARTIN: Okay, but we have to start somewhere. (*He gets up in order to lean over the papers.*)

FRANCO: (*Gestures at him to stop*) Don't move! I'll give them to you. That's an order! Sit down. (*MARTIN sits down, chewing his gum. FRANCO rummages through the papers without purpose.*) It's so hot! I'm suffocating. (*He unbuttons his jacket almost completely.*) Here's the payroll. The personnel working for the company since . . . (*He reaches over to give a page to MARTIN, but stops. Dryly*) Okay, out with the gum.

MARTIN: (*Extends his hand*) Let me look.

FRANCO: The accounting is a real mess. You're going to have a big job.

MARTIN: That's why I was hired.

FRANCO: (*With envy, opening his eyes wide*) And at what a salary! (*He fans himself with a sheet of paper.*) You must think I'm stupid.

MARTIN: (*Fed up*) No. Generous.

FRANCO: (*Sweetly*) How nice! (*He places the piece of paper on top of the pile again. Slowly and dryly*) Come on, take it out.

MARTIN: What?

FRANCO: (*He points to his mouth. Irritated and authoritarian*) Take it out! (*Furious, MARTIN spits out the gum. FRANCO, suddenly*) Did you say Yankees?

MARTIN: No.

FRANCO: The Americans are good writers. I've read a lot of them. The Beats, Ferlinghetti, people with real guts, fearless. How many of us could be like that? You're a coward, aren't you?

MARTIN: (*Fed up*) No.

FRANCO: That's good! But aren't you warm-blooded? Take off your coat.

MARTIN: I'm fine as I am.

FRANCO: (*Satisfied*) You're no wimp!

MARTIN: (*As if by dare, he stands up, takes off his coat, folds it in half and places it on an empty side of the desk.*)

FRANCO: (*Without standing up, he stretches his body and with a sweeping arm gesture, gently pushes the coat to the floor.*)

MARTIN: What are you doing?

(*He puts his jacket back on the desk, but as soon as he turns away FRANCO pushes it to the floor again. A field song is heard, but it isn't a traditional song. Rather, it is a crude imitation, perhaps something like the chorus in the Spanish zarzuela "La rosa del azafrán": "Ay! ay! ay!, qué trabajo nos manda el Señor, The work the Lord sends us," etc.*)

FRANCO: Can you hear? We still have old-fashioned field workers.

MARTIN: Can I take a look?

FRANCO: (*Suspicious, dryly*) Why?

MARTIN: Out of curiosity.

FRANCO: (*Relaxes*) Sure, have a look. If that's the case, no objection! (*MARTIN walks to the window and looks out. FRANCO, as if he knew the answer*) What do you see?

MARTIN: Nothing.

FRANCO: What? I can tell from the song that they must be under the window. There's a path below, and when they begin to sing . . . (*He sings the refrain.*) . . . they're always under the window.

MARTIN: (*Opens the window. The same refrain sung by FRANCO can be heard. He leans out.*) They're not here. (*He hides his disappointment, like a painful memory he can't exactly remember. He walks to the desk again. He points to the papers.*) Should we look through them?

FRANCO: Of course! (*He presses a button on the intercom and the singing suddenly ends. He stands up and pushes MARTIN behind the desk. Coldly*) This is your place. Stay in your seat. (*Very courteously*) I was rude.

MARTIN: (*Dryly*) No.

FRANCO: (*Gives him a sheet of paper, begins speaking with a businesslike voice*) These are the taxes we paid in . . . (*He doesn't remember or doesn't know.*) It's so hot! The air is burning. (*Accusatory*) You left the window open!

MARTIN: (*Stands up halfway*) I'll close it.

FRANCO: No, no! Do your job. The field workers will return. (*Looks at his watch*) They'll return in five minutes.

MARTIN: Enough already!

FRANCO: What do you want? With today's machines, work is a snap. (*Makes a gesture*) Puff! and it's ready. They go to the fields for the sake of tradition, to sing. I can't stand it anymore! (*He takes off his jacket and puts it on the desk. Only afterwards does he ask sweetly*) Do you mind?

MARTIN: No. What did you give me? This is a stack of children's math problems.

FRANCO: (*Very surprised*) Children's math? (*He raises his hand to his mouth.*) They switched files on me! (*He leans over the desk and almost ferociously snatches the papers away from him.*) Give them to me! (*He shuffles the papers on the desk. He laughs.*) My God, what a mess they've made! How did this get here? Children's homework, drawings. (*To himself, with a vague smile*) Do they bring the kids with their homework? (*To MARTIN*) Look at this. (*He shows him a drawing.*) Lovely. (*Surprised*) Don't you like it?

MARTIN: Yes. But what is it doing here?

FRANCO: You're asking me?

MARTIN: (*Slowly*) I saw some photographs once . . . Children going to . . .

FRANCO: You weren't there?

MARTIN: (*Astonished*) Me? I saw photographs. Children walking . . . as if they were moving from their house, carrying their schoolbags . . .

FRANCO: (*Interrupts him, furious. He throws his jacket to the floor.*) This dirty rag reminds you of that! This piece of garbage! (*He stomps on it. With remorse*) I can't even give myself a little pleasure, everyone starts making associations. (*He fixes his shirt. Dryly*) Now I look different. Let's keep going. Let's find a way out of this mess. (*Reacts to MARTIN's gesture*) You, stay there. (*He mixes the papers, protesting.*) No! No! Homework, drawings! (*To MARTIN, in a friendly voice*) A little patience. (*He looks at a paper.*) This one must be a little slow. It's so hot! Ah! Here are numbers, names. Do you mind if I take off my boots?

MARTIN: Do whatever you like.

FRANCO: (*Offended*) Isn't that a little rude?

MARTIN: It's my tone. Do whatever you like.

FRANCO: Oh, no! Absolutely not! I'll do what you like. If it bothers you, okay, forget it. I'll let my feet broil inside these damned boots.

MARTIN: No! It doesn't bother me. Take them off.

FRANCO: Good! Let's get to work! (*He begins to force his boots off.*) Discipline comes from within; we can be more relaxed about outward appearances. Except for long hair: that means you're short on intelligence.

MARTIN: I agree. Is this establishment yours? Or does it belong to someone else?

FRANCO: You'd love it if there were other owners, right?

MARTIN: (He shrugs his shoulders.) No. Why?

FRANCO: I don't know . . . Maybe I haven't made such a good impression?

MARTIN: No, I just wanted to know.

FRANCO: Professional curiosity. Very well—here's my answer: it's a corporation. (He struggles with his boots.) I can't get these off. I'm calling for help. (His hand is poised over the intercom.) No. These damned boots! Oh, don't think they let me do whatever I want. I was always crazy about uniforms. I don't have a gun, I'm not hurting anyone. That's it, that's enough. (He finally gets his boots off.) Ah, my feet are free! Get some air, my darlings. (He puts his feet on the desk and moves them around, almost under MARTIN's nose. MARTIN pushes his chair back a little.) Stay where you are! (He touches his socks, which are made of white wool.) So hot! (He holds out a stack of papers to MARTIN.) Take these, have a look. Don't think I haven't noticed.

MARTIN: (Takes the papers) Haven't noticed what?

FRANCO: The uniform. Nobody likes it. It's harmless.

MARTIN: (Looks through the papers) Why didn't you choose another one?

FRANCO: Another one? Why? They're all the same. But this one has a history.

MARTIN: (Unperturbed, without raising his head) Of sons of bitches.

FRANCO: (Offended) Oh no! You're using that language, too?

MARTIN: (Looks at him) Only when it's necessary.

FRANCO: (Looks at him as well. A pause. Suddenly, satisfied) Quick answer: I like it this way. I'm taking off my socks. (He takes them off.) That doesn't bother you, does it?

MARTIN: (Amazed and impatient) What are you doing? Are you going to strip naked?

FRANCO: No. Only my socks. My feet are clean. I won't stick them under your nose, if that's what you're afraid of.

MARTIN: I came to work, not to discuss your feet.

FRANCO: (Pleased) Good answer. Bravo! (Singing is heard.) That song! They're returning! Yes! Look.

MARTIN: (Irritated) I don't feel like it. (He looks through the papers.)

FRANCO: (Walks to the window) What a sight! They're carrying hoes and shovels. Tradition. Tradition never dies. Come here!

MARTIN: (Leaves the papers on the chair and walks to the window)

FRANCO: They're gone. (The singing, however, can still be clearly heard.)

MARTIN: (Smells something)

FRANCO: What do you smell? Food?

MARTIN: A strange odor. What is it?

FRANCO: Oh! It's a garbage dump. Sometimes it catches on fire. The children set bonfires with the garbage. I can't explain it. They're so careless!

MARTIN: It's a disgusting smell. Why don't they prevent it? It smells like burning flesh.

FRANCO: There could be a dead dog in the garbage. A dead cat. Children can be cruel. Sometimes they're not completely dead. (He closes the window. The singing ends. Impatient) Let's get to work.

MARTIN: (Walks towards the desk, points to all the papers) This doesn't tell me anything. It's a mess.

FRANCO: (Very happy) Yes, yes, I told you so! So, how did you travel here?

MARTIN: By train.

FRANCO: Why didn't you come by car? Then you could take long drives. The surrounding area is marvelous. You go a little way and you're in another world, you can bury yourself in bucolic nature, in the backwoods . . .

(Dogs are heard barking ferociously. FRANCO stops talking and listens with great interest. Suddenly an intense and growing sound can be heard of a detonator or wire that has ignited and is burning, as if there had been a short circuit. FRANCO rushes towards the door on the left. He opens it, looks out, and closes it again, preventing MARTIN, who has followed him, from seeing what is happening outside. He laughs.) Those kids! What screams! They're hanging upside down from the wires. Their screams!

MARTIN: (Extends his arm, serious) Let me see.

FRANCO: Later. (A pause. He leans against the door, smiling.) Later . . .

SCENE 2

The desk with the armchair and chair. The papers and file folders have disappeared. At the other side of the stage, a round table covered with a white tablecloth, where FRANCO and MARTIN are seated opposite each other. They have finished eating. FRANCO's feet are still bare and his jacket is still off. His clothes are where he left them in the previous scene, on the floor, along with MARTIN's coat.

FRANCO: As I was saying, if we don't eat, we die. What are you going to do now?

MARTIN: I'm going to take a walk.

FRANCO: Around here! What are you going to see? You can't reach town by foot.

MARTIN: (Stands up) It doesn't matter. I'm going to stretch my legs.

FRANCO: You'll be up to your neck in garbage. (He leans towards MARTIN.) Sit down. I've got another plan.

MARTIN: (Reticent) What?

FRANCO: You don't like me, dammit!

MARTIN: I don't understand you.

FRANCO: That's okay! Take your time. You worked

hard today. What a mess! As long as we were making money, what did we care about paperwork? (*Laughs*)

MARTIN: The employees don't know how to do anything. Not a thing. One of them doesn't even know how to write. His hand shook and he made crosses. He could only make crosses!

FRANCO: (*With admiration*) Tell me about it! You see their incompetence? Assholes. Let's not talk about work now! One question. (*He hesitates.*) Are you married?

MARTIN: No.

FRANCO: There are some pretty boys around here. (*Laughs*) No, I didn't mean that . . . There are some pretty women. (*A pause*) They don't come near me.

MARTIN: Why?

FRANCO: I guess it's the uniform. But you . . . you have a real presence. (*MARTIN laughs. FRANCO, perturbed*) I'm not hitting on you, okay?

MARTIN: Yes, I know.

FRANCO: People think the worst. I work hard to be nice and I don't get anywhere. We're having a visitor.

MARTIN: Today? Tonight?

FRANCO: Yes, what are you surprised about? I'm going to get changed. (*He picks up his boots, his socks and his jacket from the floor. Then with his free hand, he lifts MARTIN's coat.*) I'll take your coat. (*He drags it on the floor.*)

MARTIN: Don't drag it on the floor!

FRANCO: My, aren't you careful! How charming! (*He stops and then, as if playing, drags it a little more and even steps on it, as if polishing the floor.*)

MARTIN: (*Moves towards him*) Pick it up!

FRANCO: (*Stops immediately and picks up the coat*) Don't be angry! Let me shake it out. (*He shakes it and tries to fold it with his free hand, but all he does is wrinkle it and turn it into a ball.*) I'm so clumsy!

MARTIN: (*Grabs it from him*) Leave it alone! I'm going for a walk.

FRANCO: No, no walks. I don't want you to get lost. Later I'll have no choice but to get the dogs and look for you. Be here to meet the lady. I've invited her over for you. We can't stand her up.

MARTIN: Who is it? Why won't you let me do what I want?

FRANCO: I just wanted to be nice! I was thinking of you: a day of work, a group of strangers, far from home, a woman, Venus, a touch of frivolity . . .

MARTIN: (*Folds his coat, puts it on the chair, tired*) Cut it out.

FRANCO: (*Very courteously*) Of course! Right away. (*Pleads*) Be nice to her. It'll only take me a minute to get changed.

MARTIN: Who is it?

FRANCO: My only friend. A childhood friend, don't think otherwise. Be friends with her. (*In a complicit voice*) Good luck!

(*He leaves through the door on the right. On his way out, as if by accident, he throws the coat on the floor again. MARTIN, furious, picks it up and puts it on the chair. Almost immediately, the door on the left opens and EMMA is pushed violently onto the scene, almost thrown into the room. She stands beside the door, motionless, with an expression between surprised and defensive. She is a young woman with a shaved head wearing a tunic made from rough grey fabric. There is a black and blue mark on the palm of her right hand. She is barefoot. MARTIN turns and looks at her. She stands up straight and smiles, making a visible effort to do so, as if she were beginning to perform. She approaches him with a welcoming gesture. Her actions do not agree at all with her appearance. These are the gestures and attitudes of a woman wearing a party dress. Her voice is sophisticated, almost pretentious, except when it reveals itself and matches her anguished, forlorn appearance.*)

EMMA: Sit down! Were you having dinner? Don't go to any trouble for me. Franco told me you were the new administrator. I wanted to meet you. How do you do? (*She extends her hand. MARTIN, astonished, doesn't shake it. EMMA keeps her hand out.*) Why don't you greet me? (*Briskly*) Shake my hand! (*Amazed, he offers his hand. EMMA, subdued*) Don't squeeze. (*She shakes his hand and doesn't release it. She looks at it.*) What beautiful fingers! I'm a pianist, that's why I always look at fingers. (*She has the look of a frustrated coquette.*) Don't you like me? (*She laughs and releases his hand.*) Sit down. (*She sits down, crossing her legs with an air of conventional elegance. An embarrassing silence. MARTIN observes her. She remains still, then suddenly becomes tense, as if something had begun to torment her. She rubs her hands, at first as a distraction, and then, with growing urgency, scratches her hands, her arms, her entire body. At the same time, she smiles and keeps talking with a pretense of social gaiety, highly mannered.*) I don't have lice. Absolutely not. They've been eradicated in this zone. (*Pause*) I have . . . a burning itch . . . all over my body. I was lying on the grass, maybe that's why, the grass is full of insects. . . all kinds of them, little bugs, fireflies. Fireflies don't bite. They have a light inside their bodies, have you seen them? (*With a sad, vulnerable voice*) The light goes on and off as if they were calling for help. What help? No one understands. The night stays dark and silent and we look on.

MARTIN: (*Leans towards her and speaks haltingly, in confidence.*) What help?

EMMA: (*Assumes her social voice, but still scratches herself*) This is so annoying. You see? (*She stretches out her arm.*) I don't have any lice. How annoying. Just imagine. I'm playing the piano in a concert and I can't scratch myself. (*With a trembling smile*) Maybe I play better this way. The tension grows, I achieve better things. Do you want me to play something for you? (*She scratches herself with an increasing frenzy.*) Why don't you talk to me? I'm not disgusting.

MARTIN: You . . . you're the friend of . . .

EMMA: (*Quickly*) Franco! Did he talk to you about me? (*Smiles*) What a darling! What did he say?

MARTIN: (*As if he were chewing his words*) A childhood friend. That's what he said.

EMMA: Exactly!

MARTIN: Who are you?

EMMA: (*Making a big effort to reply, she tries to remember but can't, then pulls herself together, quickly.*) Don't you have a little mirror? I forgot my purse, my comb, everything. I can't touch up my makeup—do I need to?

MARTIN: No.

EMMA: A handkerchief, do you have a handkerchief? (*She looks at her wounded hand.*)

MARTIN: (*He takes one out and hands it to her.*) Yes, take it.

EMMA: Thanks. (*She keeps her hand raised.*) Is it clean? (*Martin nods his head yes. She takes it and brings it nearer to her hand, but stops halfway. Not knowing what to do, she rubs her face, then leaves the handkerchief on the table while she keeps scratching herself.*)

MARTIN: (*Leans over and picks up the handkerchief.*) What's wrong?

EMMA: (*Doesn't listen. She raises her skirt a little and looks at her leg. She bends her head forward so far that it seems as if she's hiding her face. She stays like that for a moment. MARTIN approaches her and is about to touch her in compassion, but she suddenly raises her head, smiling like a satisfied flirt.*) What do you think you're doing?

MARTIN: (*Steps back*) Nothing.

EMMA: (*Smiles*) They all say the same thing. But as soon as you let down your guard, they descend on you. (*She looks at her leg again.*) They chase after me in the streets. Yes, here I have a scab. (*She pulls it off.*) At least that's a sign. Otherwise you look at your skin and see nothing, it's firm and white, so where does the itching come from? From below? (*She laughs. Silence. She keeps scratching herself, and wears a public smile, frozen, a stereotype that betrays her anguish. MARTIN, tense, observes her. EMMA straightens up, raises her head, and walks like a movie star.*) Why don't you talk and keep me amused? They said you wanted to see me. For this? Or I wanted to see you. I thought I'd have a good time: a fervent admirer, my secretary told me. The new administrator is a fervent admirer of yours, he said. Do you admire me?

MARTIN: Yes.

EMMA: I only give a few interviews, I'm terribly busy. (*She stops, becomes withdrawn.*) Terribly. (*Silence*)

MARTIN: (*Approaches her, gently*) What's going on with you? I didn't see a secretary, I didn't talk to anyone. (*She starts scratching herself.*) Don't scratch yourself.

EMMA: I'm not scratching myself. (*She keeps scratching. A public smile, stereotypical*) That's a rude comment to make. Who could think of such a thing? (*She strokes her shaved head as if she were caressing a great mane of hair.*) You seem so polite! (*She raises her skirt.*) Beautiful legs.

MARTIN: (*He covers her legs.*) What are you doing? Calm down. You're showing me your legs and you seem like an escaped . . . (*He stops, surprised, as if it was only then that he realized she looks like a prisoner who escaped from a concentration camp.*)

EMMA: (*With a smile*) Escaped? (*Tough*) From what? Don't say stupid things. (*Laughs*) I've escaped from a dance. I'm wearing my dress. (*She smooths it.*) I came back last night, at dawn. We danced . . . (*She thinks.*) on the lawn. And I've got the proof here—the itching, the insects. I lost my purse. (*She scratches herself.*) Oh, it's bleeding!

MARTIN: (*He holds out his handkerchief.*) Take this. Stop scratching yourself. You'll hurt yourself.

EMMA: No. I have long fingernails. That's what it is. (*She wipes away the blood and is about to wrap the handkerchief around her wound, but she can't make up her mind or doesn't dare to, and she returns the handkerchief to MARTIN.*) I'm giving this back to you.

MARTIN: Keep it.

EMMA: No, no. Gifts from men are never without strings.

MARTIN: (*Takes her outstretched arm and turns it so that he can see the other side*)

EMMA: (*Laughs*) Oh, you saw how strange it is?

MARTIN: You're branded.

EMMA: My father. He was afraid I'd get lost. I always liked to follow umbrellas. I'd see someone using an umbrella and I'd follow behind. It was terrible on rainy days. They would shout out my name in the streets while searching for me, they were afraid for me, a little girl, a girl who had to grow, a hand that would grow, an intelligence that would grow. With so much to hope for, how could they not be afraid?

MARTIN: (*He strokes her arm with sadness.*) You're branded.

EMMA: I'm telling you, no! It's for good luck: four sevens, a three. Touch me, if you want. (*She holds out her arm, but he doesn't take it. Surprised*) Don't you want to?

MARTIN: No.

EMMA: It was my father. An eccentric man. It wasn't really necessary.

MARTIN: Did it hurt?

EMMA: (*Dryly*) Not at all! I was very young. (*Almost with anger*) It's not branded on my skin! It's ink. Indelible ink.

MARTIN: Do they beat you? Does he beat you, that son of a . . . He's crazy about uniforms!

EMMA: (*Tense*) Be quiet! (*Effusive*) My public adores

me. My last concert was a triumph. People went wild asking for my autograph. They ripped apart my shawl, they all wanted a souvenir. *(Solemn and pensive)* They almost destroyed me. *(She looks straight at him.)* Completely.

MARTIN: Yes, you're destroyed. But why? Who shaved your head? *(As if she didn't understand him)* Answer me!

EMMA: *(Sharp)* My hair is short. It's because of my wigs. I need to change my hairstyle for each concert. It's more practical. I put on a wig and that's that.

MARTIN: And what about this? *(He touches her clothes.)* And your shoes? And your teeth?

EMMA: *(She covers her mouth. Overdramatic)* You pig!

MARTIN: No, I feel sorry for you. It reminds me of . . .

EMMA: *(Singing softly)* From sorrow to love, there's only one step. Do you like me? *(She sidles up to him, insinuating, with a coquettish smile.)* I'd be so pleased. *(She presses herself against his body.)*

MARTIN: *(With involuntary disgust)* Get off me!

EMMA: *(Upset)* Why? Don't you like me? My short hair, my itching? You'll get used to it. And I try not to scratch myself when Franco is around. But right now this itching is driving me crazy. Maybe it's because my blood is running faster. I want you to like me . . . they told me your name. *(She tries to remember.)* I'll call you . . . *(She searches for a name, any name, but can't come up with one.)* Anyway, who cares?

MARTIN: *(Gently)* My name is Martin.

EMMA: *(Her face lights up.)* Yes, a name! *(Excuses herself with a shy smile)* I only remember a few names. Franco and . . . what was your name?

MARTIN: Martin.

EMMA: Oh!

MARTIN: *(Takes her by the arm, almost tenderly.)* Who branded you? How long ago?

EMMA: *(Is about to touch his face, but stops)* Don't worry about that. *(Suddenly suspicious)* What did you ask me?

MARTIN: Who branded you by fire?

EMMA: No. They didn't use fire.

MARTIN: *(Almost shouting)* Who?

EMMA: *(Startled)* Don't shout. I'll say any name, okay? It was . . . *(She searches in vain. She forces a smile.)* Calm down, my dear. I'm the lady of the house. You're overwhelmed! Let me autograph a photo for you.

MARTIN: *(As if testing her)* What are you like in your photo?

EMMA: *(Laughs)* I look fabulous. Just a bit retouched.

MARTIN: Give me one.

EMMA: When Franco comes—he keeps them. He's my guardian. No. My . . . *(She forgets. Becomes reflective)* Maybe the dog gave me eczema. Or the grass. *(To MARTIN)* There's no mud, you can't see the ground, it's all grass, a manicured lawn. No doubt you thought there'd be mud, you thought you'd get splattered with it. We live in the countryside, but times have changed.

MARTIN: *(Almost with surprise, he looks at his well-shined shoes.)* You . . . collected buckets of shit *(She overreacts, raising her hand to her mouth)* and fertilized the fields. You did this all day long, buried in mud, in the snow.

EMMA: Snow? We don't have snow.

MARTIN: I can't deal with this. That idiot and . . . you. There's no mud, there's no snow. I can leave! I'm packing my bags and I'm leaving. Right now.

EMMA: What's going on with you? What are you saying? You're the new administrator. We pay well. You never dreamed of being paid so much.

MARTIN: *(Wavering)* Yes.

EMMA: So what's bothering you, dear. . . ? *(Can't remember his name)* You haven't started yet.

(FRANCO enters, once again wearing an impeccable SS uniform. He approaches EMMA and kisses her hand. The scene becomes highly mannered.)

FRANCO: My lady!

EMMA: My dear Franco! How are you?

FRANCO: Very well. And you? Always so impeccable.

EMMA: Do you know my friend . . . ? *(Tries to recall his name)*

FRANCO: Yes, we work together. *(He extends his hand to MARTIN. In a low voice, referring to EMMA)* What do you think of her?

MARTIN: Why are you asking me?

FRANCO: Why not?

EMMA: *(She walks towards FRANCO and speaks in a servile tone, quickly getting her words out, as if MARTIN weren't present.)* He wants to leave. I didn't offend him, I swear it. He's got a bad temper. We were having a pleasant conversation and . . . and suddenly he came out with that! I . . . I tried to be friendly, but he's very strange . . . *(She tries to convince him, ingenuous.)* Franco, he's very strange . . .

FRANCO: *(Smiles)* It can't be true! He's leaving!

EMMA: *(In the same servile tone)* Yes, yes, that's what he told me.

FRANCO: *(Cold)* Persuade him not to.

MARTIN: May I . . . *(FRANCO makes a signal for him to be quiet and points at him to EMMA.)*

EMMA: *(Scratches herself. Silence. It's obvious that FRANCO's words have reached her a few seconds late. She puts on a fake smile. To MARTIN)* Tomorrow I'm giving a concert. Some friends are going to attend, a very select group. You have to stay. *(She manages to get his attention by tugging on the sleeve of his jacket and pulling him towards her in a peculiar way. At the same time, she addresses him with an exaggerated friendliness.)* Stay, my dear friend . . . *(She can't remember his name. With a vacillating smile and as if reciting from memory)* The language of music . . . is . . . the language . . . of the soul!

FRANCO: Exactly. (*To MARTIN*) Aren't you happy here?

MARTIN: No.

FRANCO: (*Complaining*) To hell with him! I paid him in advance. (*Hits himself on the head*) I'm so stupid! (*He walks back and forth, hitting himself on the head.*)

MARTIN: (*Surprised*) No, no, it was only an impulse.

FRANCO: (*Immediately stops, smiles*) You mean, leaving?

MARTIN: Yes.

FRANCO: (*Jumps in the air*) Hurray! (*Stops. To MARTIN*) All the same, you would have given back the money, I'm not that stupid.

MARTIN: I know. (*Very nervously, as FRANCO moves his head with each sentence, nodding like a puppet*) But I warn you: everything has to be put in order. I need the facts. Without them nothing can be done—I won't know where to start. Why did I come here? (*Almost shouting*) Work is the only thing I care about!

FRANCO: (*Without conviction*) We'll begin tomorrow. Tomorrow.

EMMA: (*Like a model student*) And you won't be bothered by any distractions.

FRANCO: That's what I said.

EMMA: (*Same tone*) Work will make you free . . .

FRANCO: That's enough.

EMMA: Franco, can he have the afternoon off? (*To MARTIN*) I'll play for you. And for a select public. They're absolutely charming. (*She puts her hand under her neckline and scratches.*)

FRANCO: (*Without listening to her*) Why are you moving around so much?

EMMA: (*When she hears the question, she freezes.*) Me?

FRANCO: Yes, you, what's wrong with you?

EMMA: With me? (*She looks at FRANCO with ever-growing apprehension. In a fake voice*) Nothing's wrong with me. I'm in good health.

FRANCO: What's that on your hand, a wound?

EMMA: (*She hides her hand.*) No.

FRANCO: I saw blood. Show it to me.

EMMA: (*Standing stiffly, looks straight at him and holds out her left hand*) There's no wound, it's fine.

FRANCO: (*Cold*) The other one.

EMMA: (*After a moment, holds out her other hand. FRANCO, at a distance, leans towards her and looks at her hand in silence, without touching it. EMMA, as if standing at attention, startled*) There's no wound, it's fine. I'm in good health. (*Her voice begins to quiver.*) He . . . can tell you that. I'm qualified for all kinds of work. Carrying rocks, buckets, cleaning . . . toilets, digging . . .

FRANCO: (*He keeps looking for a moment, then straightens up and breaks the tension.*) What are you saying, my darling . . . (*Pauses, amused*) my queen? What kind of work could your hands do, your precious hands, besides what they do now? (*He takes her hands and kisses them. But this warmhearted gesture slowly turns menacing, as if he were subjugating her. He stares at her.*) What's making you itch?

EMMA: Nothing. (*She suddenly frees her hands and crosses them over her chest, in desperation.*) This damned itch! What did they give me?

FRANCO: Who?

EMMA: The . . . (*She stops, lets out a loud laugh.*) The dog! (*She deliberately shouts at FRANCO.*) That mangy dog! (*To MARTIN*) And you, my poor dear, why are you so quiet? (*With a hysterical laugh*) Why don't you scratch me? Let's sit down. (*She pushes him into one of the chairs and sits down on his lap, hugging him.*)

MARTIN: Leave me alone. (*He pushes her aside and stands up. To FRANCO*) What is this? I came to work. What does she think? She's a raving lunatic. Where did you find her? (*To EMMA*) Don't bother me! I want to work, that's all.

FRANCO: (*As if he didn't understand*) Not now! What impatience!

EMMA: (*To FRANCO, in a fearful outburst*) Don't listen to him! Don't listen to him! (*To MARTIN. Her hands move hesitantly, then she covers his mouth with the healthy one. MARTIN pushes her hand away.*) Don't say anything. Tomorrow you'll think differently, you'll feel at home. I feel very much at home.

FRANCO: (*Sweetly*) What harm did this lady do to you? Where were you brought up? You've offended her.

EMMA: (*Sad*) It's true.

MARTIN: Forgive me.

EMMA: (*With a false smile again*) You're forgiven. (*She hangs on his arm.*) Do you like me?

MARTIN: (*Pushes her away gently*) No.

EMMA: (*Confused*) What do you mean? You said I was very . . . seductive. Why are you pushing me away? You shouldn't keep secrets from Franco.

MARTIN: I'm not hiding anything! I'm going to take a walk.

FRANCO: Take it easy.

EMMA: Franco, tell him.

FRANCO: About what?

EMMA: You didn't tell him? (*She interrogates him anxiously with her eyes, then, to MARTIN*) I shouldn't sit by myself. Come, sit here. I won't bother you. (*She asks him sweetly, pointing to the chair.*) Here. Please, sit here. (*MARTIN sits down. EMMA stands behind the chair, hesitates over which hand to use, and then begins to caress him with the healthy one.*) My dear, you're so charming . . .

FRANCO: (*Interrupts, annoyed, like a stage director*) Not that way! It's so clumsy!

EMMA: (*Humble*) I'll do it better. (*Begins again*) When the music plays . . .

FRANCO: I throw up.

(*MARTIN stands up and heads for the door.*)

FRANCO: (*Stands in the way, authoritarian*) Stay here.

(They look at each other and MARTIN decides to move away in the direction of the table. With a sweep of his arm, he clears the glasses and dishes away. He sits down, puts his elbows on the table and rests his head in his hands.)

EMMA: *(Looks at him, then at FRANCO)* Franco, tell him. It's very difficult.

FRANCO: Ah! You're so clever! You want me to do it. Don't stop! *(EMMA doesn't move. FRANCO)* Your hand?

EMMA: *(On hearing the question, she approaches MARTIN again, tries to touch him, hesitates, caresses the back of the chair.)*

FRANCO: *(Shouts)* Not the chair! *(Forcefully)* Lower! *(MARTIN raises his head, bewildered. Silence)*

EMMA: *(In anguish, to MARTIN)* Don't go. I beg you, don't leave me here.

FRANCO: Stop begging. The most desirable woman. Why are you resorting to such methods?

EMMA: *(Stands up and with effort, raises her head. To MARTIN, overacting as if in a silent movie)* Kiss me.

FRANCO: *(In a low voice)* Disgusting. *(His tone changes.)* You're having a breakdown. *(As if he didn't know)* Your concert?

EMMA: It's tomorrow. I rehearsed all afternoon. A select public.

FRANCO: *(Tenderly)* That hand . . . will it be ready? Let me see it again.

EMMA: *(She closes her fist.)* There's nothing on my hand! *(FRANCO tries to open her fist, but she hides it, pressing herself against MARTIN's back.)*

FRANCO: *(He finally manages to open her fist. He looks at it, almost cheerfully.)* You have lice.

MARTIN: Leave her alone.

FRANCO: *(Solicitously)* Oh! I don't want to bother the two of you. Darling, do you want me to leave?

EMMA: No. *(She presses herself firmly against MARTIN. She lowers herself against him until she is sitting in his lap.)*

MARTIN: *(Tense)* Please, leave me alone.

EMMA: No, no, don't leave me here. I have to make you happy. Do you want to. . . with me?

FRANCO: *(Who has taken a few steps away)* As long as it's well before the concert, my dear.

EMMA: Do you want to?

MARTIN: No.

FRANCO: *(On all fours, searches under the desk)* Where is it?

EMMA: I have good teeth. *(She covers her mouth.)* No, no. I have . . . *(She thinks.)* . . . good . . . *(She makes a vague attempt to reveal her cleavage.)*

FRANCO: *(Still searching)* Keep him amused, my dear. I'm happy when others are happy, how strange. *(He shouts with joy.)* I found you! *(He gets up with the whip in hand, but his manner isn't threatening.)*

EMMA: *(Very low, pleading humbly)* Say yes . . . It's just a

moment . . . I'm healthy . . . My hand . . . *(She tries to hide it.)* They look and . . . *(Smiles)* they . . .

MARTIN: *(Holds her face firmly. Shouts)* Who?

EMMA: That's it, hold me tighter, don't be afraid . . . that's it . . .

FRANCO: *(Satisfied)* Can I tell everyone? *(Shouts)* It's started!

EMMA: No, dear FRANCO, wait . . . not yet, wait . . . *(To MARTIN)* Hold me tighter, you're hurting me.

(MARTIN releases her face. FRANCO, who has been playing with the whip, raises it and lashes the floor on the other side of the stage. EMMA cries out as if she received the blow. On hearing her, MARTIN suddenly gets up, throwing her to the floor.)

MARTIN: *(Leans over her, worried)* Did I hurt you? Sorry, did I hurt you? *(He tries to help her stand. EMMA clings to him and hides her face against his body.)*

FRANCO: Darling, what was it? Did I frighten you?

EMMA: *(After a moment, she reveals her face. She struggles to put on a conventional, everyday smile.)* No, dear Franco, I know your little quirks.

FRANCO: I like the sound. Can I. . . ? You'll have time for that later. Can I?

EMMA: Yes.

MARTIN: What?

FRANCO: I asked her. You won't be frightened by the sound. Has the itching stopped?

EMMA: Yes.

FRANCO: *(Walks towards her, touches her face and traces its outline with his finger)* A longing on every square inch of your skin. You were scared, but it passed. I'm not bothering you, am I? I like the sound, but I don't want to terrify you.

EMMA: No.

FRANCO: I've never hit anyone. Not even in self-defense. You know that already, my dear. *(He walks back to pick up the whip. He tightens his fist around it and waits.)* And?

EMMA: *(As if reciting a lesson while FRANCO lashes the floor rhythmically and forcefully)* You've never hit anyone. I already know that. We're childhood friends. *(Silent)*

FRANCO: *(Pleads)* A little more!

EMMA: *(Same tone)* You've never hit anyone. The boys ran after me, he defended me. One against four, one against five, one . . . *(FRANCO cracks the whip against the floor. EMMA, shaking, growing weaker)* I can't take it any longer!

MARTIN: So, is it true?

FRANCO: *(Cracking the whip loudly)* What doubts do you have?

MARTIN: *(To EMMA, shouting)* Is it true?

EMMA: What? *(She's waiting for the sound of the whip against the floor and isn't paying attention.)*

MARTIN: That you're locked up, that they've beaten

you? (*EMMA tries to laugh, but her face remains frozen. She covers her ears.*)

FRANCO: (*He stops cracking the whip, looks at them and lets out a loud laugh.*) Answer him, my dear! Answer him!

(*Laughs while EMMA slowly removes her hands from her ears and pulls her fingers across her face with her eyes closed. She opens her eyes again and stares ahead, while MARTIN, standing still, looks at her. FRANCO slowly stops laughing. They remain motionless. A brief silence*)

SCENE 3

A few long benches, like those in a church or a school auditorium. In front of these, a piano on a raised platform. MARTIN is on one of the benches, sitting up straight, his hands on his legs. FRANCO is at his side, standing, with a bouquet of flowers in his hands. A PIANO TUNER is working lethargically on the piano. Suddenly, FRANCO slaps himself on the forehead.

FRANCO: (*Upset*) The programs! I knew I would forget something! (*To MARTIN*) Should we cancel it?

MARTIN: What difference does it make?

FRANCO: You think so? (*Smiles*) Well, I don't know what she's going to play. (*Joking*) "Variations on an Itch."

MARTIN: Why doesn't a doctor see her?

FRANCO: (*Childishly threatening*) Oh, no, no! Mind your own business. (*Serious*) Don't you think I take care of her? That she's being seen by doctors? She's been vaccinated! Vaccinated against all contagious diseases!

MARTIN: Her hand . . .

FRANCO: (*Interrupts, innocently*) Is healthy! She says so. (*To the PIANO TUNER*) Are you finished yet?

PIANO TUNER: (*Without moving*) In a minute. (*He listlessly strikes a key.*)

(*EMMA enters. She is wearing a ridiculous wig on her shaved head. A silk train drags behind her that has been crudely sewn onto her grey tunic. She rubs her hands, exaggerating a performer's excitement before a concert.*)

EMMA: (*Smiles*) I'm so nervous! It's stage fright! I couldn't sleep!

FRANCO: (*Steps towards her and gives her the bouquet of flowers. Sincere*) Good luck.

EMMA: Thank you, dear Franco. How nice of you! You shouldn't have. (*She takes the flowers, but keeps them at a distance, unaffected.*)

FRANCO: Smell them.

EMMA: (*As if she had forgotten*) Ah, yes! (*She smells them.*) What a delicious fragrance!

FRANCO: There's no fragrance. They're artificial.

EMMA: Oh, I didn't know. They're perfect!

FRANCO: Is the piano in the right place? Is everything set?

EMMA: (*Looks*) Yes, thanks for your concern. (*She looks at the floor, amazed.*) The floor's been swept so clean!

FRANCO: (*Very courteously*) Not a bit of trash. It's the least I can do. I'm happy to contribute to your success.

(*A group of SS OFFICERS file in, impeccably dressed with well-shined boots. Behind them, a GROUP OF PRISONERS, filthy, inmates from a real concentration camp. They wear the characteristic uniform with big black shoes that are falling apart. The SS OFFICERS sit on the benches in the first two rows, and the PRISONERS sit in the last row.*)

FRANCO: (*Suave*) People are arriving. Don't be nervous. Just remember that I'm here, that I only want to hear you play. (*He points to MARTIN.*) The administrator also wants to hear you. (*To MARTIN*) Didn't you greet her?

MARTIN: (*Tense*) You told me not to move.

FRANCO: But not to that extreme! Greet her. (*MARTIN gets up and walks towards EMMA, who waits for him with her stereotypical smile. They look at each other silently. Little by little EMMA's smile disappears from her face and is replaced by an enormous sadness. MARTIN gets closer to EMMA and finally kisses her on her cheek. FRANCO, with approval*) Excellent, such good manners, so delicate and elegant! (*Dry, to MARTIN*) You did what I asked. Sit down. (*MARTIN obeys. FRANCO, to EMMA, friendly*) People are arriving. Don't be nervous. Aren't you . . . completely drained?

EMMA: (*Immediately straightens up*) Oh no, it's my nerves! (*She walks from side to side, with a smile of feigned excitement.*) The . . . the . . . imminent performance of my art, of . . . being judged, of . . . handing over my heart.

FRANCO: (*Speaks naturally and, without her knowing it, steps on the train attached to her tunic. EMMA walks and the train comes off.*) Yes, it disturbs you. (*With a hint of irony*) Your . . . itching?

EMMA: (*Discovers the train on the floor, picks it up, doesn't know what to do with it. FRANCO takes it out of her hands, rolls it into a ball and throws it into a corner of the room while she speaks.*) Oh, it disappeared! It must have been the insects on the lawn. My skin is so sensitive! It completely . . . went away. Although . . . (*Hesitates*) when I'm about to play, I always feel like . . . I start tingling and then . . . (*She looks at her hands and is about to scratch herself, but represses the urge.*) I . . . (*She squeezes her face savagely, in an unstoppable impulse. A brief laugh*) Excuse me.

FRANCO: Too much tension. The hall is full. The crème de la crème. Aren't you happy?

EMMA: Clap loudly for me.

FRANCO: With pleasure. (*He bends towards her and politely kisses her hands. He looks at the palm of her injured hand. Almost tenderly*) How is that doing!

EMMA: Better. It's dry. It's healing. (*The apathetic notes being played by the PIANO TUNER can be heard.*) Why hasn't he finished yet? This is intolerable! Couldn't he have come earlier? (*Almost shouting*) How? How did this happen?

FRANCO: Organizational details. I'm to blame. I sent the invitations, I took care of the flowers, I had the hall cleaned, but I forgot the most important thing.

EMMA: (*Very nervous*) I know, I know! You don't want to make them wait! There are so many important people!

FRANCO: No, no. Today you're the most important person. Don't forget. (*To the PIANO TUNER, roughly*) Come on, finish already! I'm sick of that noise. (*To EMMA, friendly*) Once again, I wish you success.

(*He walks away and sits on an empty bench in one of the middle rows. The PIANO TUNER, as impassive as ever, picks up his tools and leaves. EMMA makes an exaggerated stage entrance, and waves at the audience with the bouquet of flowers in her hands. The SS OFFICERS stand up and greet her with a slight nod of the head and a dry click of their heels. They sit down again. The PRISONERS don't move. One of the SS OFFICERS in the first row turns around and gives them a harsh look as a warning. Suddenly, the PRISONERS seem to wake up and one begins to stomp his feet. Silence. EMMA leaves the flowers on the piano and sits on the piano bench. The PRISONER begins to stomp his feet again, and the others join him one by one, at shorter and shorter intervals, as the tension grows.*)

MARTIN: (*Stands up, shouts*) Shut up!

(*Two SS OFFICERS silently get up, stand at his side, put their arms around his shoulders, as in a friendly gesture. MARTIN attempts to break free but cannot. They put a hand over his mouth and make him sit down. The intensity of the stomping feet grows louder. When it reaches a crescendo, it abruptly stops. Only then does the SS officer in the first row stand up and turn to the PRISONERS.*)

SS OFFICER: Silence, you idiots!

(*At the same time the two SS OFFICERS stop holding MARTIN down. They smile at him in a friendly way. They don't leave the bench.*)

MARTIN: (*Stands up, furious*) I'm going to break your heads!

(*The SS OFFICERS laugh good-naturedly. Whistles, demands for silence. MARTIN takes out a handkerchief and dries his mouth. When EMMA speaks, he goes to the front and sits on another bench in an empty row. The SS OFFICERS begin to run, in a covert, surreptitious way, like someone in a crowded audience who is moving around stealthily during a show. They surround him again. Two more officers join them.*)

EMMA: (*Wrings her hands, very nervous; suppresses an obvious urge to scratch herself. Announces*) I will play . . .

FRANCO: (*Warns her, smiling*) No, no announcements!

EMMA: (*Smiles apologetically, sits down at the piano, makes herself comfortable, but then she can no longer resist and begins to scratch herself furiously.*)

ONE OF THE PRISONERS: (*Joking*) Is it over?

(*A loud burst of laughter from the PRISONERS. The SS OFFICERS turn around and whistle weakly. FRANCO stands up and takes out from under one of the benches a bottle with a dark liquid and a ball of cotton lying on the floor. He approaches EMMA and as he passes by MARTIN, protests under his breath.*)

FRANCO: I don't take care of her! He says I don't take care of her! What nerve!

(*He reaches EMMA, wets the ball of cotton with the liquid and rubs it on her skin. She remains seated on the bench but tries to avoid being touched.*)

EMMA: Nothing is wrong with me! Please.

FRANCO: Be still! This will help. I always take care of you and this idiot says I don't. Did you tell him stories?

EMMA: (*Surprised*) No! What did he say? He's a liar.

FRANCO: That's better. Act with dignity. I organized this concert. Make sure it turns out well.

EMMA: I'll play magnificently. For you, Franco. I'm a great concert pianist.

(*Her exasperation at the itching seems to grow. The PRISONERS imitate her, becoming grotesquely agitated in their seats. They scratch each other. One PRISONER takes off another one's shoes and scratches him on the soles of his feet. This PRISONER doesn't try to stop him; rather, he holds onto the bench and endures it, laughing hysterically. The SS OFFICERS walk towards MARTIN and one of them scratches MARTIN's cheek with his finger. MARTIN knocks his hand away but the other three officers surround him. The fourth one closes in on MARTIN and with both hands outstretched, scratches MARTIN's face with his fingernails. When the officer draws back his hands, MARTIN's face is bloody. All this has been done in an almost tender way, without any violence.*)

FRANCO: (*He closes the bottle, crushes the cotton ball.*) I'll keep this. Cotton is so hard to come by.

(*He deposits everything on the floor, then takes EMMA's hands and puts them on the keyboard. The PRISONERS immediately stop scratching themselves and put their hands on their thighs. Only an intermittent hiccup from the PRISONER who was laughing can be heard. FRANCO*) Start playing. The audience is getting impatient. They paid admission. They're getting impatient, aren't they? (*Only then is the humming of the PRISONERS heard. FRANCO returns to his seat, signaling them to be quiet. The humming stops immediately. The SS OFFICERS surrounding MARTIN, who is cleaning his face with a handkerchief, put their hands on his shoulders and make him sit down. An expectant silence. EMMA is still making herself comfortable on the piano bench, scratching herself, adjusting her clothes. Coughing, throats being cleared, and then silence once again.*)

EMMA: (*Puts her hands on the keyboard and plays. Two or three notes are heard, but when she plays the other keys, no sound comes out, except for once or twice when the hollow sound of a broken toy piano can be heard.*)

A PRISONER: *(Joking.)* Let her play her ass!

THE OTHER PRISONERS: *(In a chorus)* Let her play her. . . !

SS OFFICER: *(Stands up, shouts ferociously)* Silence! *(For a moment, an absolute silence. Then the PRISONERS begin to stomp their feet on the floor. SS OFFICER)* Why don't you obey? *(With a distorted smile that turns into a irrepressible laugh)* How dare you refuse to obey?

FRANCO: *(Approaches EMMA)* Play.

EMMA: *(Places her hands over the keyboard, plays some keys, nervously shakes her head, raises her hands and interrogates FRANCO with her whole face)* It doesn't . . . make any sound!

FRANCO: What do you mean, it doesn't make any sound? We just had it tuned. Use your mouth. Pretend. How embarrassing! I'll make you pay for this! And stop scratching yourself!

EMMA: I can't . . . What did you put on me?

FRANCO: Water—is it burning you?

EMMA: I can't stand it any longer!

FRANCO: That's too bad! Play! How can you let our administrator go without hearing a concert? He's never heard you play before. Martin, have you ever heard this lady play before? *(Looks around for MARTIN)* Where is he? *(The SS OFFICERS who surround MARTIN force him to stand up. One of them raises MARTIN's arm. FRANCO)* There you are! Have you heard her before?

MARTIN: *(Doesn't answer. An SS OFFICER moves MARTIN's head to indicate "no." MARTIN, to the SS OFFICER)* Leave me alone! *(They all laugh and nod their heads yes. They stand aside. MARTIN, to FRANCO)* What is this?

FRANCO: *(To MARTIN)* Sit down. *(Repeats, very authoritarian)* Sit down! *(MARTIN sits down. FRANCO, to the rest, as if warning a group of students)* Anyone who makes trouble must leave the room. *(He points to the group of SS OFFICERS around MARTIN.)* Officers! Don't make this gentleman feel uncomfortable. Have some respect. Martin, do you want to hear this lady play?

MARTIN: *(Takes a step forward, explodes)* Don't bother her! Damn you! *(The SS OFFICERS surround him at once and forcibly return him to his place.)*

FRANCO: *(As if he hadn't seen or understood)* No, I mean do you want to hear her.

SS OFFICER: *(To MARTIN, gently)* Calm down.

MARTIN: Don't put your hands on me again! *(The SS OFFICERS raise their hands and hold them apart.)*

SS OFFICER: *(Apologizing)* Excuse us! *(But the four officers immediately lunge at MARTIN, grab him and make him sit down again. At the same time, the PRISONERS hold their hands to their mouths like a megaphone and yell.)*

PRISONERS: We want to hear her! We want to hear her!

FRANCO: *(To EMMA)* You see? A logical reaction. They paid their admission. Don't upset the audience. Then nothing will satisfy them, they'll become too demanding. Don't upset them.

PRISONERS: *(In chorus)* Play, play, don't scratch yourself!

FRANCO: I won't say it again. *(Smiles at her)* Come on! It's your art!

(EMMA sits again at the piano. She strikes the keys. No sound. She stretches her arms and plays all of the keys until reaching the last, which only produces a hollow sound. Obscene noises from the PRISONERS. Everything has an unreal air, like a student prank.)

FRANCO: *(Claps his hands until there is silence)* The distinguished pianist here today will entertain us now with a piece from her repertory. *(To EMMA, in secret)* Which one? Okay, whatever you want. *(EMMA stands up and tries to walk. FRANCO makes her sit down, pats her on the head in a friendly way and as he does so, knocks her wig off. He holds it for a moment, amused, and then places it on the piano.)*

PRISONERS: *(In a chorus, like children)* Baldy, baldy!

MARTIN: *(Frees himself from the SS, takes a few steps, shouts)* Leave her alone!

EMMA: Why is this man making a scene? He should leave. Liar!

SS OFFICER: *(With the others, grabs MARTIN, drags him to his seat, this time with brute force. Reproaches him with an offended sensibility)* You'll be removed from the concert hall. Where do you think you are? *(They hold him down and cover his mouth.)*

FRANCO: Be quiet! *(To EMMA)* Play. An unexpected situation like this shouldn't intimidate you. I taught you that. *(He steps down from the platform and returns to the bench. EMMA places her hands above the piano keys and begins to imitate a piano with her voice, producing sounds that seem like random notes with no intonation. At the same time, her itching becomes unbearable and she scratches herself secretly, violently.)*

PRISONERS: Phony, phony!

(The SS OFFICER in the first row turns towards the PRISONERS and looks at them without standing up.)

SS OFFICER: *(Shouts)* Be quiet! *(Stands up suddenly, ferocious)* Be quiet, you dogs! *(The PRISONERS become upset. They look at each other, frightened. The SS OFFICER, good-naturedly)* That's how I like it.

FRANCO: *(Rises, shrugging his shoulders)* It's a shame! *(He approaches EMMA, whispers some words into her ear. She looks at him, alarmed, and he smiles and returns to his seat. EMMA pretends to play the piano with grandiose arm movements while humming Chopin's Grand Polonaise.)*

FRANCO: *(Stands up, applauding)* Bravo!

PRISONERS: Encore! Encore!

EMMA: *(Takes a hesitant bow and looks at FRANCO, searching for instructions.)*

FRANCO: *(Matter-of-factly)* Play another!

(*EMMA sits down again at the piano and begins to play again with the same sweeping arm motion. At a certain point, the SS officer in the first row gives a sign to the PRISONERS and they begin to sing, with their mouths closed and softly at first, but the volume grows louder and louder with the clear purpose of covering EMMA's voice. She raises her voice as well, but despite her efforts, which become increasingly desperate, the chorus of PRISONERS' voices manages to bury her own. When another sign is given by the SS officer, the PRISONERS suddenly stop singing. EMMA keeps pretending to play, but when she opens her mouth, only a low croak can be heard. FRANCO starts applauding.*)

PRISONERS: (*Mechanically*) Encore! Encore!

FRANCO: No, that's enough! Let that be all! (*He approaches EMMA, changes his tone of voice.*) That was charming, my dear! A fine performance! You outdid yourself. I congratulate you. (*He kisses her hand. In confidence*) Darling, take a bow.

PRISONERS: Flowers! Throw us flowers!

FRANCO: Why not? (*He puts the bouquet of flowers in her hand.*)

(*She takes the bouquet and throws some flowers, but the PRISONERS don't react, as if they had already fulfilled an assigned role. When the SS OFFICER gives a sign, they stand up in an orderly way and file out, shuffling their feet. The SS OFFICERS, including the four who held MARTIN down, follow behind and guard the PRISONERS as they leave.*)

FRANCO: (*To MARTIN*) Haven't you complimented our concert pianist? She'll be very pleased. Come here. (*MARTIN rises and approaches the platform. FRANCO*) Congratulate her. Tell her she was fabulous. (*To EMMA*) And you, hold out your hand. (*To MARTIN*) Or do you prefer her cheek? (*Smiles*) It's more intimate. (*Dry*) Not as much risk of contamination . . . I guess. (*EMMA and MARTIN don't move.*) Come on! Didn't you like her performance? It was so demanding. (*To EMMA*) And you, stop scratching yourself, my dear! (*Laughs*) Do you want me to apply a little more water?

EMMA: (*Terrified*) No! I'm not scratching myself. It's gone. Totally. It's nerves. (*Hesitating, she holds her hand out to MARTIN.*)

FRANCO: (*Brutally*) Not that rotten hand, no! (*EMMA closes her fist and draws her hand back. She holds out her healthy hand. FRANCO, to MARTIN, authoritarian*) Congratulate her.

MARTIN: I . . . I . . . (*He tries to talk but can't.*)

FRANCO: What happened? Did you lose your tongue? (*He grabs MARTIN's face and shoves him back until MARTIN frees himself with a punch. Gently*) Careful, what are you doing? Why so rude? Do you want to lose your job? (*He sniffs. As if it were pleasurable*) What a smell! That smell has returned! They've started burning again! (*MARTIN raises his hand to his mouth to stifle a scream and falls to the floor. FRANCO*)

What's wrong? Do you feel sick? Is it the smell? Get up! (*He tries to lift him off the floor.*) The children are burning dogs again, dead dogs. What bad timing! (*In a low, gentle voice*) Savages . . .

(*MARTIN covers his mouth to stifle a moan, tries to hug EMMA's legs.*)

EMMA: (*Terrified, pushes him away*) Why are you crying? (*To FRANCO*) Get him off me!

FRANCO: (*As if from a distance, removed*) He wanted to have a good time. (*With a threatening sadness*) We planned everything to keep him happy. Why have we failed?

EMMA: We haven't failed! He's stupid. (*She leans towards MARTIN, searches his face. Anxiously*) Say that you had a good time! It was a joke for your benefit. Nothing is itching me. I shaved my head. I like being bald. Because of my wigs. Say you had a good time! I enjoyed the joke so much! If it wasn't for this . . . this damned itch! . . . (*She scratches herself wildly.*)

FRANCO: (*With naive hope*) Yes? You both had a good time?

EMMA: (*Shouting*) Yes! Say yes! Oh! I can't, I can't . . . stand it!

(*She twists her body while scratching herself. Finally she can no longer endure the unbearable itching and she throws herself on the floor, rolling around and scratching herself. MARTIN raises his head and looks at her. EMMA sits in a corner, overwhelmed, crying like a little child, choking back her sobs.*)

FRANCO: (*Leans towards MARTIN and puts a hand on his shoulder.*) Did you have a good time?

(*Silence*)

MARTIN: (*On his knees, looks at EMMA, who is sobbing.*) I had a very . . . very . . . good time . . .

SECOND ACT

SCENE 4

Onstage, as the only furniture, a standing embroidery frame and a stool, except that the stool, which is painted black, is too high and doesn't seem to go with the frame; it seems more like an artist's stool.

MARTIN and EMMA. MARTIN is sitting on the floor, surrounded by mountains of papers and files, and is writing on a flat surface supported by his knees. EMMA is sitting up straight and embroidering. Her arm motion starts off elegantly but turns clumsy: she's holding the needle in her left hand. Her right hand is covered by a filthy bandage. She scratches herself, but with less frequency. Bland music can be heard. Silence.

EMMA: I'm so clumsy with my left hand!

MARTIN: How's the other one doing?

EMMA: It's better. Franco put some ointment on it. Real ointment.

MARTIN: And that's what made it better?

EMMA: Yes! It's a little swollen, but . . .there's no . . . there's nothing wrong with it! Do you want me to show it to you?

MARTIN: No. Who injured it?

EMMA: (Suspiciously) What are you suggesting? Or do you think I would cut my own hand with a knife?

MARTIN: I thought they wounded it.

EMMA: (Sour) Do you think I'm stupid? (In an affected voice) With all the care I devote to my hands! (Caresses them) My fingers are . . . golden. (Brusquely) Franco told me to be wary.

MARTIN: Of whom?

EMMA: You told him stories. Franco, who's always there for me, who treats me like his little girl. (Sad) Why did you do that?

MARTIN: (Docile) I didn't do anything.

EMMA: Yes, you did. Apologize. Right in the middle of the concert, in front of the audience. Such elegant people! (As if she were sleeping) A sweet kindness that tempers all cruelty . . .

MARTIN: They scratched me.

EMMA: (Upset) Where?

MARTIN: On my face. They covered my mouth.

EMMA: You must have done something. You shouted. I heard you.

MARTIN: The piano didn't make any sound.

EMMA: So what? It was an accident. I don't blame anyone.

MARTIN: (Puts the writing board on the floor) How did you wind up here?

EMMA: (Alarmed) Keep working!

MARTIN: I want to know . . .

EMMA: I won't answer any questions! (In anguish) They brought you here to work! If you keep it up, I'll close my mouth. Or else they'll accuse me of distracting . . . (doesn't know what to say) everyone.

MARTIN: (Picks up the writing board and his pencil) Well, what now?

EMMA: I was working in the garden. I cut myself with the scissors we use for the roses. It wounded me. But Franco took it well. He didn't ask me any questions. He's so understanding, a real darling! I'm hardly scratching myself now, did you notice?

MARTIN: Yes.

EMMA: I took cold showers, like . . . (Forgets. Suddenly, terrified) No. Not showers! They go to the showers and . . . (Smiles. Confused) they forget about . . . (Ends with a vague gesture)

(Suddenly ferocious barks are heard, machine-gun fire.)

MARTIN: What's that?

EMMA: (In a hurry) A foxhunt, didn't they invite you? I never used to miss any, but now . . . with this itching . . . and this useless hand. Not useless, but I can't work. I love hunting. Don't you?

MARTIN: (Stops working, addresses her in anguish) No.

EMMA: (Urgently) No, no. Don't stop working. You have to follow orders. Don't let them accuse me of anything! I'm embroidering. A little goat. Come and look. (Reconsiders) No, stay there.

MARTIN: (Lets his pencil fall) What's happening?

EMMA: (Approaches him, puts the pencil in his hand, pushes the papers towards him) Don't tremble. Here, take it.

MARTIN: I'm not trembling. Who are they chasing?

EMMA: Get to work! Nothing's happening. Franco told me about a movie once. The horses, the riders, the riding jackets, the polished boots . . .

MARTIN: Who are they chasing?

EMMA: The crack of the whip . . .

MARTIN: That's machine-gun fire. The doors were left open . . . They thought they were free. It couldn't be true, but it was: the doors were open, smiling faces invited them to leave . . .

EMMA: Of course, they love hunting . . . Start writing. And I have to finish this embroidery. Don't drop your pencil!

MARTIN: They went out and the others stalked them, the spotlights were turned on, the target was abundant, perfect.

EMMA: No, no. That's how rabbits are hunted. I'm telling you, this is a foxhunt. It's more refined.

MARTIN: Foxes? (An anguished laugh)

EMMA: Finally, you understand! Just think, during the hunt the fox is never out of sight. It loses its breath, its lungs burst, poor thing. (Sad) How does a fox feel? There's no way to know. (Ferocious barking is heard, brutal orders.) There's the pack of dogs, can you hear them? It's so loud! They get excited. It's a passionate sport. (Nervous) And Franco is such an accomplished athlete, he does everything, swimming, rowing, big game hunting, boar hunting in the south. . . (MARTIN lets the writing board and pencil fall to the floor. She places the board on his knees, tries to make him hold the pencil. He is tense because of the noises. He's shaking and the pencil drops again from his fingers. EMMA insists, tries to guide his hand. At the same time she keeps talking with an artificial superficiality.) He's a talented guy. A real champion. You've never been to one?

MARTIN: No.

EMMA: (Keeps playing the same game) The hounds prick up their ears and follow the scent, and the fox runs, it does nothing but run. As soon as one moves out of line, the dogs attack, and the fox is hauling stones and can't go on. It falls down, it's all over. What a thrill, it's so exciting!

MARTIN: They eat them . . .

EMMA: Of course, or why else would they go hunting?

MARTIN: They're beaten back with clubs because they eat the rotten meat of the cadavers. . .

EMMA: Who? The children? Yes, they're mischievous

here as well, but it's delicious . . . the meat . . . (*With an exasperated smile*) Oh, they shout so much! They're in the forest . . . it's too much . . . What a way to have fun! They lose control.

MARTIN: I can't stand it any longer. I'm taking a look.

EMMA: Don't be foolish. Keep working. It's dark outside. The hunt is at night, what lunatics! Afterwards they burn them.

MARTIN: (*Embraces her*) Be quiet . . . !

EMMA: Oh, you're hugging me? What if Franco saw us? He's not my boyfriend, he's a childhood friend . . . but we should tell him. (*Laughs*) He'll be so pleased!

MARTIN: Don't say such things!

(*The sound of the machine-gun fire grows more distant, then stops.*)

EMMA: Don't go away! We were so comfortable!

(*FRANCO enters, wearing the same uniform, but the SS jacket has been replaced by a hunter's jacket. He carries a rifle under his arm.*)

FRANCO: (*Laughs*) Aha! I leave you alone, and look how you pass the time! (*Joking, to MARTIN*) You, there! (*He points to the pile of papers on the floor.*) When are you going to put this in order? (*He looks around.*) Isn't there a chair? I can't stand up. I'm exhausted. All that running! (*He sits on the stool. He's obviously not tired. A pause*) And? No questions? You didn't hear anything?

EMMA: (*Tries to speak but cannot. Recovers her voice*) You were hun . . .hunting?

FRANCO: Yes. (*Pause. Brusque*) Go outside and look.

EMMA: (*Looks at MARTIN, points to him indecisively*) Him?

FRANCO: (*Emphatic*) No. You.

EMMA: No thanks, Franco. Those poor animals bleed . . . they're white, they turn white immediately . . . I can't bear it. (*She starts to scratch herself.*)

FRANCO: Oh, no! We agreed you were cured!

EMMA: (*Takes her hands away from her body*) I am. This friend . . . (*shouts*) what's his name?

MARTIN: Martin.

EMMA: He can tell you. We were talking and I never . . . (*Her hand is about to touch her body.*)

FRANCO: (*Smiles*) You're dying to scratch yourself. It's not very feminine, but . . . Scratch yourself, my dear, don't hold back for my sake.

EMMA: (*Panting*) Really?

FRANCO: Give yourself some pleasure. Go ahead. (*EMMA scratches herself ferociously for a moment. FRANCO, cold*) Now—leave.

EMMA: No. Later. I have to finish the . . . (*She points to the embroidery frame.*)

FRANCO: (*Without animosity*) You've been talking. You should have thought of that earlier. (*Joking*) I'll finish it myself.

EMMA: (*Laughs*) You! The stitch is almost invisible, you need to have a steady hand . . . (*Walks to the embroidery frame. When she passes by FRANCO, he sticks out

his arm, not letting her finish her sentence, and makes her turn halfway towards the door.*)

FRANCO: Didn't you understand? Go outside and look.

EMMA: Why?

FRANCO: There's a pile of animals outside the door. If you like any, you can have them. We use everything: hair, nails, skin, hide, everything. Go ahead!

EMMA: No, no. Stop it, Franco . . . I honestly don't need anything.

FRANCO: (*Ferocious*) Go outside!

MARTIN: (*Takes EMMA's hand*) Come on . . . I'll go with you.

FRANCO: Not you.

EMMA: (*Desolate*) No, wait . . . I'll go by myself . . . He said only me . . . each person goes alone.

FRANCO: (*Laughs*) No, my dear, what are you thinking of? Martin has a lot of work, he's falling behind. Tomorrow morning he'll have time. There's enough for everyone. Ugh! There's plenty! Tomorrow, Martin can also choose a piece, and eat it, if that's what he wants. We'll leave everything out all night in the dew, au naturel. (*Laughs. Opens the door, good-naturedly*) My dear, if you like . . .

EMMA: (*Without moving*) Yes, I'm going.

FRANCO: (*As if playing, he points the rifle at her, joking.*) Come on.

EMMA: (*To MARTIN*) Good . . . bye

MARTIN: Where are you going?

FRANCO: My dear, we're not condemning you to death! How somber! I thought you'd like to see . . . it's not that we had any luck today. Small game, lots of it, but small game. Dark hides, dull, short, half-eaten by mange . . . But good bones, strong ones. Some teeth can be recovered . . . My dear, the cold is coming in . . . (*A pause. EMMA leaves. FRANCO rubs his hands, laughs, complicit.*) Have you two become friends? That took a lot of effort on my part. You're stubborn, proud. She's a pretty girl. Did you lose your tongue?

MARTIN: No.

FRANCO: (*Pointing to the paper on the floor*) Come on, show me, how's the work going?

MARTIN: How should it be going?

FRANCO: How blasé! You seemed so competent! Show me what you've done.

MARTIN: Are you joking?

FRANCO: (*Sincere*) I'll be damned if . . . ! You must have organized something.

MARTIN: What? These are old documents, loose pages, things from different companies, what do you want me to do with them? You know very well it's impossible to organize this! (*Desperate*) And what for?

FRANCO: What do you mean, what for? We need order. Or do you think I'm paying you just to throw money away? (*Looks through the papers without any *interest, throws them into the air any which way. Indifferent)* I think you're totally lost.

MARTIN: Yes. *(Shouts)* What was going on outside?

FRANCO: Of course! It was to be expected! No one can handle this. Do you want us to cancel your contract? What was going on, you asked? A hunt. Every now and then, we go hunting.

MARTIN: For . . . ?

FRANCO: They let us. I'm not talking about the staff—they can live with chaos. But the people on top—no. It's too disorganized. *(Reflects)* What about the children's drawings?

MARTIN: I saved them.

FRANCO: Why?

MARTIN: *(Sad)* For myself.

FRANCO: Oh, how sentimental! How exquisite! I'm terminating your contract. That's it, I decided.

MARTIN: What does that mean?

FRANCO: When do you want to leave?

MARTIN: *(Stupefied)* Today.

FRANCO: What a shame! I was beginning to like you. You gave up chewing gum. That disgusting habit. *(Pats MARTIN's back)* Yes, I began to like you. And you, me—right? This shitty uniform! I'll pay you in full.

MARTIN: *(Suspicious)* You don't owe me anything.

FRANCO: Yes, yes, I do. You performed well. You were efficient. It's not your fault if you failed. We let things slide, and it turned into a goddamn mess. *(Hands MARTIN an envelope)* This is for you. *(MARTIN, after some hesitation, takes the envelope, but doesn't open it. He feels the envelope nervously. FRANCO)* Open it!

MARTIN: *(Opens the envelope and looks at its contents. Suspicious)* It's a lot of money. I don't want it.

FRANCO: Don't worry. We've got plenty of money. *(Brusquely)* But take her with you!

MARTIN: Who?

FRANCO: *(Rude)* Her! You got real lovey-dovey with each other, eh? And then? *(His tone changes.)* I can't stand her any longer. Someone else can take care of her. She came for a day and . . . *(Scratches himself)* she wouldn't leave. I'm afraid she'll contaminate the children. You can drop her off en route, in a hotel. Set her up in a nice hotel, not just any one. Do you have any money?

MARTIN: Yes.

FRANCO: I can't stand her! Always scratching herself! Acting like a prima donna! Who does she think she is? And every time I see her, she wants me to kiss her rotten hands! She makes me feel rotten—me! I'm fed up with her!

MARTIN: *(Confused)* You?

FRANCO: Yes. I'll bet you're surprised. I'll bet you are. It seemed the other way around. Oh, no. I'm the victim.

MARTIN: She . . . she can leave?

FRANCO: I told you, I want to be free of her! Don't you

see? *(Scratches himself)* I talk about her and the fleas start biting. She's filthy! *(Recovers)* No, maybe filthy is too strong. I don't know what it is, she's always scratching herself. But . . . besides that . . . she's a good girl, very helpful. I'm asking you, do me this favor.

MARTIN: *(With a vacillating smile, somewhat hopeful)* Yes, I'll take her with me . . . You said we can leave . . . okay! I'll take her . . .

FRANCO: *(In a burst of emotion)* Thank you! *(Takes MARTIN's hands and kisses them)*

MARTIN: *(Pushes FRANCO away)* What are you doing?

FRANCO: *(Very content)* No more fleas! There's a type of soap . . . *(Tries to remember, snapping his fingers)* Get some lye soap! Afterwards, when you've gained her trust, ask her to play the piano. She's really bad, but she's entertaining.

(The door opens and EMMA is pushed inside the room. She's wearing a long, dark, old-fashioned coat over her tunic. She is still barefoot. She has a small black suitcase in her hand.)

FRANCO: Darling! Are you ready? You're in such a hurry to leave us. *(Goes up to her and kisses her hands. He closes his eyes.)* I'll miss your music so much! We've had such good times together. Tell me something, anything to console me. *(Humble)* Show me that you care. . .

EMMA: *(Holds out her hand fearfully, with a kind of undisguised repugnance, towards FRANCO's head, which remains bowed. She extends her hand, and then draws it back slowly, without having touched him.)*

FRANCO: *(As if she had caressed him)* Thank you. *(Smiles, natural)* Did you see what we caught? What did you think?

EMMA: You mean, if . . . if I saw them? *(She steps back slowly and starts laughing as if unexpectedly amused by the question; her laughter becomes hysterical, unending.)*

SCENE 5

The interior of MARTIN's house. It is decorated simply, with a table and a few chairs, one of which has fallen over. On top of the table there are some cups and on one side, several notebooks and school materials. Two doors, one leading to the outside and the other leading to the kitchen and beyond. A window.

MARTIN and EMMA enter from the street. MARTIN, who has no coat, gloves, or scarf, places his two suitcases on the floor. EMMA is holding her small black suitcase and is wearing MARTIN's shoes, which are far too big.

MARTIN: No one's home? Wait, I'll go and see. *(Disappears through the interior door)*

EMMA: *(Sits down without letting go of her suitcase. Muses)* Those pigs! They could have given me some shoes. *(She takes off MARTIN's shoes. Reflects)* They have mountains of shoes, of hair . . . (*She touches her head, and abruptly stands up.*)

MARTIN: (*Returns*) They aren't home. (*He touches one of the cups on the table. Slowly*) The cup is still warm.

EMMA: (*Terrified*) Did they disappear?

MARTIN: (*Laughs*) No! They must have left for a moment. (*He puts the chair upright. He reaches to pick up EMMA's black suitcase.*) Let me have it.

EMMA: (*Clutches it tighter*) No, no. To each his own. Here are your shoes. (*She pushes them towards MARTIN.*) I'll take care of my suitcase.

MARTIN: Whatever you prefer. Have a seat. (*He offers her a chair. EMMA sits down.*) Do you feel better?

EMMA: Yes. I can play the piano. A little more study, some rehearsal, and . . . once again! (*She raises her hand over the table, as if she was going to play the piano, but this gesture saddens her in a vague way. She keeps her hand motionless in the air. Then she scratches her cheek, softly, slowly.*)

MARTIN: (*Implores*) No, don't start that again.

EMMA: (*Realizes that this time it is true*) Strange—it's not itching. (*She mechanically scratches herself with one hand while holding the suitcase to her chest with the other, bandaged hand.*)

MARTIN: I'm going to look for some ointment.

EMMA: Don't leave. I'm all right. (*With difficulty, she stops scratching herself. The same children's shouts and cries as were heard at the beginning return, but without any orders or moaning.*)

MARTIN: (*Approaches the window, looks outside*) Nobody's there. (*Pause*) Ah, yes, children! My brothers aren't here. (*He turns to EMMA.*) I have lots of them, all younger than me, like this. (*With his hand he draws the outline of a staircase. Moves over to the table*) They left their homework half-finished . . . (*As if by accident, he pushes the papers to the floor and doesn't pick them up.*) They slipped out to play. The cup is still warm. What's your name?

EMMA: Me?

MARTIN: Yes.

EMMA: You're Franco, aren't you?

MARTIN: No. I'm Martin!

EMMA: Yes, yes! (*She crosses her legs, looks around her with a critical air.*) This is a modest home.

MARTIN: Sorry.

EMMA: (*To herself*) That's what they say.

MARTIN: Later on, you can leave.

EMMA: Yes, when I start touring again. . . ! Then you won't see me any more. (*She touches her head.*) Will my hair grow back soon?

MARTIN: Yes.

EMMA: (*Uneasy*) The children are playing so loud! (*Pause*) Can't you make them be quiet?

MARTIN: Why?

EMMA: Never mind. I was saying. It's hard for me . . . to adapt.

MARTIN: Do you want to eat and then rest?

EMMA: Yes! But not eat. (*As if she were asking for something impossible*) I'd like . . . a cup of tea. (*She points to the teacups.*) It's a . . . craving.

MARTIN: I'll make one for you.

EMMA: Wait! First I should unpack. Help me. (*In a theatrical voice*) No, I'll manage by myself. You're not my maid. My secretary took care of my suitcases. It's been some time since I've had to carry one myself. (*She caresses her hand.*) Maybe . . . he mixed everything up, the coats and . . . the bottles of perfume and . . . the musical scores . . . and . . . (*Barking is heard from the street. EMMA, frightened*) Dogs! Franco, there are dogs here too!

MARTIN: Those are strays. Martin, call me Martin.

EMMA: (*Without hearing him, in anguish*) I thought I wouldn't see any more dogs, anywhere, on any street, not even in a cemetery . . .

MARTIN: (*With a kind of rage, exasperated*) Those dogs don't bite, they're stupid, they don't know how to obey. They don't obey, they play all day long. When they're puppies they destroy things, eat socks, rip apart mattresses, bury a miserable little bone in a flower pot and then stupidly dig it up and rip up the plants! (*Shouts*) They're stupid!

EMMA: No, no!

MARTIN: (*Controls himself*) Yes, look. (*Goes to the window, looks out*) It's an old dog, just skin and bones.

EMMA: (*Tense*) What do you mean, skin and bones?

MARTIN: Nothing. It's any old dog. (*Suddenly, from the midst of the children's shouting, something like a scream of pain can be heard. The shouting slowly dies down. MARTIN*) Did you hear that?

EMMA: (*Firmly*) No. Your family, what are they doing? Didn't you tell them you were coming?

MARTIN: Yes. I don't know why they left the house empty, but children often run out . . .

EMMA: (*Incredulous, low*) Is it possible?

MARTIN: (*With sadness*) Run out into the street, to a park . . . to run after a ball. (*Smiles*) I've gone after them many times, I've brought them back by their ears . . .

EMMA: (*Sour*) And now? Why don't you go now? What a welcome! I couldn't think of living here alone with you. Gossip spreads quickly. This house is too modest, I'm not used to that. Find me a room in a hotel.

MARTIN: First you should rest.

EMMA: (*Nervous*) Yes, but what have I been doing all this time if not resting?

MARTIN: I'll get other clothes for you.

EMMA: (*Bangs on her suitcase*) I've got clothes here.

MARTIN: (*Walks into the kitchen*) I'll bring you some tea.

EMMA: Don't bother. I didn't mean to offend you. (*Fearfully*) Franco, I didn't mean to offend you.

MARTIN: (*Appears in the doorway.*) Don't call me Franco. My name is Martin. (*Sweetly*) Martin.

EMMA: (*Humble*) Yes. I always forget names. Don't let it bother you.

MARTIN: (*Returns to the kitchen*) I won't.

EMMA: (*Nervous and as if amused*) Once there were so many dogs running after me, I thought I'd die. I got off the train and everything was dark, there were so many people, some hungry, others thirsty, or needing to . . . and children, children squeezed together like sardines . . . I got off and fell on my face! (*Laughs*) I couldn't see them, I was like someone born blind who suddenly sees the light. An enormous dog jumped on me and bit me, guess where. I was lucky, but . . . there wasn't much flesh and it hurt. . . Such an essential part! (*She laughs hysterically.*)

MARTIN: (*Enters with a cup of tea*) Drink the tea. (*He puts it on the table and stands at EMMA's side. With a gesture of gentle compassion, he puts his hand on her shoulder.*)

EMMA: (*Stops laughing*) That's very kind of you. (*She eyes the hand resting on her shoulder suspiciously.*) What's that?

MARTIN: (*Takes his hand away*) Drink the tea.

EMMA: (*Drinks*) It's delicious. Hot and delicious. I'd forgotten how it tastes. (*With disgust*) But it's not English tea.

MARTIN: No.

EMMA: That's the only kind I can drink. (*Miserable*) Why would I have drunk that?

MARTIN: (*Looks out the window again*) All the children have gone. All of them. (*Somewhat relieved*) But people have come out. Finally . . . A couple, and men who are going off to work . . . (*He sees something that makes him laugh.*) A fat man slipped and everybody is laughing. Come and hear the laughter. We should put it in a safe and keep it. (*He rubs his eyes.*) No, what am I saying? (*He moves away from the window. A brief pause*) Do you want more tea?

EMMA: (*She is moved by his words. With a timid spontaneity she has never shown before*) No. Thank you. (*MARTIN looks at her, smiles. EMMA does the same.*) You threw the notebooks on the floor. (*She leans over and picks one up. MARTIN leans over and picks up all of them. He returns them to the table. EMMA*) You spilled some ink on the cover. The teacher will scold you . . . (*They exchange a brief, sad smile. EMMA*) What's your name?

MARTIN: Martin.

EMMA: (*Caresses MARTIN's hand, which rests on the table. With sadness*) I don't know anyone, that's why I can't remember any names, it's hard for me . . .

MARTIN: Tell me my name.

EMMA: (*Makes an effort*) Mar . . .

MARTIN: (*Helps her*) Martin.

EMMA: Yes, I've got it now. (*She doesn't say his name.*) Will my hair grow back soon?

MARTIN: (*Smiles*) In a month.

EMMA: That's so long!

MARTIN: Fifteen days, a week.

EMMA: That's too much time!

MARTIN: Tomorrow.

EMMA: Tomorrow?

MARTIN: Now. It's growing now.

EMMA: (*Touches her head, smiles weakly*) No, it's not. I'm not that stupid. That's a silly joke. Nothing good happens.

MARTIN: Yes, it does. That other thing is over.

EMMA: For everyone?

MARTIN: I don't know.

EMMA: (*Sadly*) And if you don't know. . . ?

MARTIN: (*He squeezes her shoulder.*) It's over, I'm telling you.

EMMA: Good. I'm going to open my suitcase. I want to change my clothes. Is there a room I can use? This house is quiet. One could almost believe everything was . . . okay.

MARTIN: (*Points*) There's a bedroom over there.

EMMA: I want to change . . . to take this off. Always the same dress . . . I need to change colors . . . to put shoes on. I . . . I had a red dress. (*Puts the suitcase on the table, opens it, puts her hand inside and then takes it out. Her face changes.*)

MARTIN: (*Moves towards her*) What is it?

EMMA: (*She slams the suitcase closed. With an affected voice*) Didn't I tell you? Who packed this suitcase? Don't you know? My secretary or my maid? No, my secretary, there's nothing like a man for that. (*MARTIN steps closer and opens the suitcase. EMMA pushes him away.*) Leave it alone! Only one dress, and for a party! What do they think? That I don't have a private life? That I don't need nightgowns, negligees, dresses, another pair of shoes? This is pretty! Look! (*She takes out a tunic that is exactly the same as the one she's wearing and spreads it out.*)

MARTIN: It's a stupid joke.

EMMA: What joke? I'm to blame, I'm the one who's always willing to give concerts, to offer up my art . . . to welcome. . . ! (*As she speaks, the door to the exterior opens, silently, and an individual with the face of a happy pig appears in the doorway. He whistles to attract their attention and rubs his hands, wearing an almost abject smile that apologizes and expresses satisfaction at the same time. EMMA keeps talking, exasperated.*) Rehearsals, trips from one place to another, without ever stopping, tours, interviews, the hustle and bustle! And I'm to blame! (*As if she had noticed the person at the door and chose to ignore him.*) They think I don't have a personal life, that . . . that. . . I can't fall in love . . . have secrets, be private like everyone else . . . There are a lot of people outside. That's what you said, Fran . . . (*Tries to remember MARTIN's name, but fails*) Children, and . . . a fat man fell down! You were laughing. . . !

MARTIN: (*Who immediately noticed the intruder's entrance*) Be quiet . . . (*Tense*) What do you want?

BUREAUCRAT: Excuse me. The door was open . . .

MARTIN: (*Louder*) What do you want?

BUREAUCRAT: (*Apologetic*) Nothing.

MARTIN: If you don't want anything, leave.

BUREAUCRAT: Why did you leave the door open? If it had been closed, I wouldn't have come in. I said to myself, who knows. . . ?

MARTIN: Who are you? What do you want?

BUREAUCRAT: (*Submissive*) Nothing. I'm not trying to sell anything. Look. (*Opens the palms of his hands and shows them. Then starts rubbing them again*) It feels good in here, nice and warm.

EMMA: (*With a semihysterical laugh*) Franco ordered him here! With that face, it was Franco!

BUREAUCRAT: (*Categorically and sincerely*) No, no, I don't know him. You two just arrived and . . . I saw you pass by. (*To MARTIN*) I know you by sight, and you know me, don't you?

MARTIN: No. And I don't want to know you!

BUREAUCRAT: (*Apologetic, unctuous*) But I'm . . . what choice do you have?

MARTIN: Get out! You're in my house!

BUREAUCRAT: (*Apologetic. At the same time noises can be heard as if a table or a gurney with iron wheels were being pulled down the hallway.*) Yes, I'm in your house. It's lovely. If you had closed the door completely . . .

MARTIN: (*Takes two steps forward and then stops, as if he were tied. Furious*) Get out! I'm locking the door!

BUREAUCRAT: (*Smiles, gentle*) It's useless. I want to make you happy. (*Looks at the room*) Lovely. As you can see, I'm not leaving, but I'm not entering, either. (*With desire*) Were you drinking tea?

EMMA: Offer him a cup of tea and then he'll leave!

BUREAUCRAT: (*Very servile*) Yes, we'll leave whenever you'd like. Some tea . . . I'd like that . .

EMMA: (*Laughs maniacally*) He wants a cup of tea!

BUREAUCRAT: Yes, but afterwards.

MARTIN: What do you want?

BUREAUCRAT: A formality. Believe me, I'm a such a . . . such a good person, I don't want to bother anyone, I want everyone to be like me and . . . (*rolls his head from side to side, never moving from the doorway*) and . . . in truth, for everyone to be happy. (*The noise comes closer. He looks briefly behind him.*) Soon. (*As if apologizing*) Here are . . . my boys. . . (*To MARTIN*) Your brothers? How big they've grown. They were this high yesterday. (*Gestures with his hand*) And today . . . they're sprouting moustaches. (*Laughs. With a friendly interest*) Jewish?

MARTIN: No!

BUREAUCRAT: (*Same tone*) Communist?

MARTIN: No! I told Franco no!

BUREAUCRAT: (*As if to console him*) All right, then you must be something else . . . We're all something, it's difficult to choose . . .

(*He laughs while three strong men who appear to be nurses enter. They're pulling a portable table with various instruments that cannot be seen and a burner that is turned on. EMMA gets up from the chair, dragging her open suitcase and the tunic and slowly walking backwards until she curls up into a ball in a corner of the room. She scratches her cheeks and then weakly folds the tunic, awkwardly trying to fit it into the suitcase. One of the men, with utmost naturalness, puts a branding iron on the flame of the burner. The others slowly move towards MARTIN who is clumsily arranging the cups on the table. A cup falls and breaks, and he stands still, looking at the floor dumbfounded. The men stop. EMMA begins to laugh softly. It gradually turns into a low, interrupted moan.*)

BUREAUCRAT: (*Referring to the cup*) What a shame! I could have waited for the tea. (*Softly*) Are you vaccinated?

MARTIN: (*Raises his head confidently, but terrified*) Because of that? Yes! I'm vaccinated! Vaccinated against all diseases!

BUREAUCRAT: (*Same tone*) Except for one. (*Pause*) Just a second and you'll be ready. We won't bother you anymore.

MARTIN: (*With the same mixture of confidence and terror*) You're leaving!

BUREAUCRAT: That's what they say . . . but . . . it's hard for us to leave. It's so nice and warm here . . .

(*At his signal, the two men start walking slowly towards MARTIN again.*)

EMMA: (*Without watching the scene, absorbed by the task of folding and packing the tunic inside the suitcase*) I would get lost . . . I used to follow umbrellas . . . and then . . . I needed some kind of mark . . . I couldn't go out in the world, escaping like a smile that disappears from a mouth . . . I couldn't be left unbranded . . . (*Laughs*) To know who we are, a small mark . . . (*In a desperate cry*) Martin!

(*The BUREAUCRAT signals his approval, never losing his smile. Meanwhile, one of the men has prepared an injection on the portable table. The needle falls on the floor and the man picks it up and puts it back into the syringe. He whistles softly, rocking back and forth. MARTIN doesn't move; only the sound of his breathing can be heard, like that of an animal about to be trapped. The other two nurses step towards him and with an almost feminine concern remove his jacket and roll up his sleeves.*)

NURSE: (*Natural*) His undershirt as well . . . You're dressed very warmly . . .

(He smiles at MARTIN in a friendly way. There are frequent smiles, completely at odds with what is taking place. MARTIN suddenly begins to struggle with a savage, desperate energy that stops when he is injected. He shouts. Then he becomes listless, overcome. The NURSES hold him in an almost kindly way. One takes a handkerchief out of his pocket and wipes the sweat from MARTIN's face. When the iron is red-hot, the BUREAUCRAT moves from the doorway, takes the iron, and walks towards MARTIN. Only EMMA's moans can be heard as she closes her suitcase.)

CURTAIN

It seems as if the whole world is a prison and their escape from the "concentration camp" is not conducive of gaining freedom. Gambaro references the similarities to the Holocaust the Argentine dictatorship and "dirty wars"

COLOMBIA

Documents from Hell
(Enrique Buenaventura)

Documents from Hell (*Los papeles del infierno*) is a cycle of one-act plays by one of Latin America's most important, and most recognized, theater practitioners, Enrique Buenaventura (1925–2003). The founder and director of the Teatro Experimental de Cali (TEC), Buenaventura and his company were leaders of the collective theater movement that sprang up throughout the Americas during the 1960s and 1970s.[1] All of the group's theater pieces explore a society in crisis, the result of Colombia's protracted civil conflict (*la violencia*) that claimed three hundred

The Schoolteacher, directed by Enrique Buenaventura, Irvine, California, 1990. (Photo courtesy of Diana Taylor.)

thousand lives from 1948 to 1965 alone. The current violence in Colombia suggests that the crisis has not been resolved, and the country continues to be held hostage in the ongoing struggle between the military and armed drug lords. Buenaventura and TEC created work that spoke to the urgent issues in their society; they worked together using improvisational techniques and engaged in ensemble-type rehearsals in which all actors took turns with all the roles. Final role assignments were often made just before the performance in order to break with the naturalist acting tradition and star system. The artistic goals of the movement mirrored its political goals. Inspired by Bertolt Brecht and Erwin Piscator, theater practitioners in the Americas found that the Marxist-inspired "collective" could create theater directed to large "popular" audiences rather than the small cultural elites that dominated the national cultural arena. Artists surrounded by extreme social inequity and brutal political violence could not justify an "art for art's sake" mentality or co-optation into state-sponsored agendas favoring programming developed for other countries, other audiences, other realities.

Latin American theater artists, as opposed to the famous Latin American novelists of the same period, had few possibilities for working if they separated themselves from the intense struggles affecting their societies. Enrique Buenaventura aptly summed up this predicament in a 1968 article, "Theatre and Culture": "Many Latin Americans who belong to the international republic of arts and letters resolve [the] contradiction by making a radical separation between arts and politics. . . . The best way to do this is to live in Europe and support Cuba. . . . A director-actor-playwright . . . does his job with his whole organism, and transmits experience through a form that is direct, alive—and ephemeral. He cannot pack up his way of life and memories and go off to set them down in some tranquil place without soldiers, without

245

guerrillas, without starving proletarian masses, without students. I confess that I regret very much that I am unable to escape, that every day I have to make an almost mystical effort not to run away."[2] Buenaventura, TEC, and similar collective theater groups throughout Latin America chose to stay in their war-torn countries and produce the best theater they knew how to produce—aesthetically important work that addressed the urgent realities of their countries in a complex, antidogmatic way.

Documents from Hell illuminates aspects of colonialism that have deformed Colombia's citizens into grotesque figures scrounging for a living, accepting the crumbs from the elites, and tearing each other up out of hunger, greed, and desperation. Buenaventura chose to avoid both commercialism and agitprop. Instead of "kick[ing] and scream[ing] against the system," Buenaventura clung to the goal of "true artistic subversion, undermining the system in its essentials: the consciences and conduct of its victims."[3] Rather than a good/bad, innocent/guilty approach to social dis-ease, Buenaventura challenged audience members to recognize how they participated in the corrupt and corrupting system, internalizing its greed, violence, and self-deception.

Buenaventura's *Documents from Hell* reflects the ruptures and violent discontinuities of his sociopolitical environment. The short vignettes are shards, bits and pieces of a mosaic. Some, like *The Schoolteacher* and *The Twisted State,* included here, are short—running about ten minutes. The longer one-act plays, such as *The Orgy* (also included), run about forty-five minutes in performance. No one agrees on which, or how many, plays make up the cycle or in what order the plays should appear. To complicate matters further, there are several (sometimes as many as four) versions of the same play—the result of changes incorporated at the suggestion of actors or the audience during rehearsal or production.[4]

The fragmentation of the cycle, though a source of frustration for commentators, underlines its thematic concern with Colombia's ongoing history of crisis, rupture, and fragmentation.[5] These documents are about torture, violent landgrabs, victimization, and a society's ongoing history of colonization. As the word *documents* (*papeles,* papers) suggests, the work is about History (with a capital *H*) in general and a reflection on Colombia's predicament in particular. A series of disconnected pieces of information without beginning or closure, the cycle forces us, as readers and theater practitioners, to take the place traditionally reserved for historians. It presents us with "documents" and asks us to interpret them on the basis of questionable facts and nondefinitive texts. But, whereas legal or official documents purport to present raw material as a basis for further interpretation or action, these vignettes, however simple and straightforward they appear, are highly elaborate stage pieces. Legal documents aspire to disinterested objectivity by recording facts; these plays are personal, interested representations of those facts. Rather than discrediting the validity of the cycle, the dubious objectivity of the documents makes us question the veracity of documents in general. No documents, however legal and official, are innocent; they just seem so. They are created to serve a specific function and further specific interests. They are the bricks out of which History is constructed. Hence, the cycle raises questions about documents, especially in a society that has long been dominated by colonization and criminal politics. How do we select between the various versions or agree on their order? How do we decide which plays to include, which to exclude? Evidence that might give us a "definitive" grasp eludes us. We must chart our own course and bring our own direction to this extremely complex, interwoven material. Given the elusiveness of the facts, we need to rely heavily on interpretation. These works, then, are anything but doctrinaire and prescriptive.

Regardless of the order or even the number of plays we include in the "documents," Buenaventura clearly focuses on several interrelated roles and themes: victims and victimizers make up the harsh and desolate landscape of a society undone by corruption. In the short plays, *The Schoolteacher* and *The Twisted State,* these figures may seem to exist in isolation, each in her or his own play, but their personal tragedies clearly tie into the country's misfortune. In *The Schoolteacher,* the soldier who kills the father and rapes the teacher insists that he, personally, is not to blame. He is following the orders of those who want to remove the "big chiefs and fat cats of the last government."[6] One of the torturers in *The Twisted State* also claims that being a torturer is just a job like any other. "Have you ever seen an honest doctor or butcher? Are they eaten up with scruples?" When the main character's wife complains about his occupation, he accuses her of hypocrisy because she benefits from what he does: every nail he rips from a victim's finger buys her a new pair of stockings and a new dress.

What the structural fragmentation underlines, however, is that violence exceeds all social boundaries devised to contain it. The pieces can never be kept separate; victim, victimizer, and collaborator all make up the larger picture. The interconnections belie the notion that violence is an isolated affair or "a marginal phenomenon in the political realm."[7] Violence, within this context, is central to every action and interaction. And, although criminal societies may try to keep violence separate (the torture chamber) and compartmentalized (the legal system), it threatens to undermine all distinctions between private and public, innocent and guilt, justice and atrocity. The soldiers target those they consider pillars of the old society, but that essentially means everyone in the society. The teacher describes how death struck indiscriminately like lightning from the sky. The torturer, unable to break his victim, turns on his wife. Her eyes remind him of the prisoner's eyes; he tears them out as he kills her.

The Orgy is a longer one-act play with a large cast and wonderfully theatrical and metatheatrical staging. In a visually intense and, at times, humorous fashion, the play presents victims participating in the drama of their own humiliation and destruction. The Old Woman, ugly, degenerate, impoverished, wants to relive a glorious moment in her past when the Prince of Wales, on his first and only visit to South America, kissed her hand. She hires beggars at a miserable wage to dress in the fine though threadbare garments of her late lovers—a colonel, an ambassador, a bishop—and pay homage to her. She steals money from her son, the Mute, who scrounges a living by shining shoes. The beggars—hungry, worked up by their roles, and fed up with the Old Woman's miserliness—kill her, eat the food, and steal the Mute's money. The Mute, arriving just as the beggars have left, turns to the audience and signs "Why?"

As this overview indicates, more and more plays could be added to the cycle without disrupting its basic composition. More documents and papeles can be added to the archive without altering this history of misery. All we have is an intensification of the same, a spiral encompassing more and more violence and desolation. The fragmentary vignettes need not gloss over the lacunae, the ruptures and contradictions incompatible with totalizing and coherent narratives. Buenaventura focuses his inquiry precisely on the breaks, the dead spaces, the meaningless voids—"meaningless" insofar as they have not been officially inscribed. By inscribing, performing, and documenting that which otherwise would disappear without a trace, without evidence, Buenaventura's cycle calls attention to the limitations inherent in Colombia's major narrative. History, then, is redefined; its validity is tested as much by what it leaves out as by what it records. *Documents from Hell* challenges the possession of History by those in power; their emplotment of events grants them a place at the center of things. The fragmented cycle allows for no center; it decenters the narrative and opens the material to other interpretations. Now others can make claims to history. Decolonization, the cycle suggests, requires a struggle for history, for culture, for telling one's own stories in one's own voice. The fight to produce and control the "record" is as vital as armed warfare.

What the "documents" inscribe is not just the history of erasure or even history as erasure. The void, the crisis, the collapse of moral, judicial, and ideological frameworks show erasure as the history of Colombia. Behind the fictions, the cycle shows a world undone by violence. *Documents from Hell* addresses the problem of social crisis in the very mode of crisis—fragmentation, ambiguity, spatial and temporal suspension. The cycle has no agenda, no "solution." In fact, it challenges all myths of liberation, including the revolutionary. The road that the beggars embark on is long, difficult, and relatively unexplored. Who has the answers? Where will the crisis end? These vignettes promise no closure. The *spirale du pire* continues its infernal trajectory, on and on, worse and worse.

—Diana Taylor

NOTES

1. Some examples of collective theater in the United States would include Bread and Puppet Theatre, Teatro Campesino, and the San Francisco Mime Troupe. For more information on collective theater in Latin America, see the introduction to this reader.

2. Enrique Buenaventura, "Theatre and Culture," trans. Joanne Pottlitzer, *TDR: The Drama Review* 14 (winter 1970): 151–56.

3. Ibid., 153.

4. For more information about the other plays in the cycle, see chapter 5, "Destroying the Evidence: Enrique Buenaventura," in Diana Taylor, *Theatre of Crisis: Drama and Politics in Latin America* (Lexington: University Press of Kentucky, 1991). This introduction is drawn, in part, from that chapter.

5. Buenaventura and TEC adapted the fragmented structure of Bertolt Brecht's *Fear and Misery of the Third Reich* to describe the political violence in their countries.

6. For a description of the two performances of *The Schoolteacher* directed by Jorge Huerta and Enrique Buenaventura at the Humanities Research Institute at the University of California, Irvine, in 1990, see Diana Taylor, "The Representation of Otherness in Chicano and Latin American Theatre and Film," *Theatre Journal* 43 (October 1991): 377–79.

7. Hannah Arendt, *On Revolution* (Harmondsworth: Penguin, 1963), 19.

SELECTED REFERENCES

Bravo Realpe, Nubia. "La violencia en la dramaturgia de Enrique Buenaventura." *Estudios de Literatura Colombiana* 7 (July–December 2000): 49–59.

Buenaventura, Enrique. "Brecht y el nuevo teatro colombiano." *Primer Acto: Cuadernos de Investigación Teatral* 235 (September–October 1990): 23–27.

Buenaventura, Enrique. "Theatre and Culture." Trans. Joanne Pottlitzer. *TDR: The Drama Review* 14 (winter 1970): 151–56. In Spanish: "Teatro y cultura." *Teatro: Revista de la Escuela de Teatro* (1970): 20–33.

Campa, Román de la. "The New Latin American Stage: An Interview with Enrique Buenaventura." *Theater* 12 (1980): 19–21.

Costa, Elena M. de. "Historical Discourse as Collective Remembrance in Enrique Buenaventura's *Los papeles del infierno:* The Socio-Historical Role of Artist." *Cincinnati Romance Review* 16 (1997): 144–50.

Kronik, John. "Enrique Buenaventura in the Context of Spanish American Theater." In *Studies in Honor of Myron Lichtblau,* ed. Myron Lichtblau and Fernando Burgos, 185–94. Newark: Juan de la Cuesta, 2000.

Rizk, Beatriz J. *Buenaventura: La dramaturgia de la creación colectiva.* Mexico: Grupo Editorial Gaceta, 1991.

Taylor, Diana. "Brecht and Latin America's 'Theatre of Revolution.'" In *The Brecht Sourcebook,* ed. Carol Martin and Henry Bial, 172–84. New York: Routledge, 2000.

Taylor, Diana. "Destroying the Evidence: Enrique Buenaventura." Chapter 5 in *Theatre of Crisis: Drama and Politics in Latin America.* Lexington: University Press of Kentucky, 1991.

Weiss, Judith A. with Leslie Damasceno, Donald Frischmann, Claudia Kaiser-Lenoir, Marina Pianca, and Beatriz Rizk. *Latin American Popular Theatre.* Albuquerque: University of New Mexico Press, 1993.

The Schoolteacher

(Enrique Buenaventura)

Translated by Gerardo Luzuriaga and Robert S. Rudder

CHARACTERS:

THE TEACHER
JUANA PASAMBÚ
PEDRO PASAMBÚ
SQUINT-EYED TOBIAS
OLD ASUNCIÓN
SERGEANT
OLD MAN
PEREGRINO PASAMBÚ

A young woman is seated on a bench, downstage. Behind her, or to her side, certain scenes will take place. There should be no direct interaction between her and the characters in those scenes. She doesn't see them, and they don't see her.

THE TEACHER: I am dead. I was born here, in this town. In the little house made of red clay, with a straw roof. By the road, across from the school. The road is a slow-moving river of red clay in winter, and a whirlwind of red dust in summer. When the rains come you lose your sandals in the mud, the mules and horses get their bellies smeared with mud, the saddles and even the faces of the horsemen are spattered with mud. In the months when the sun hangs high and long in the sky, the entire town is covered with red dirt. The sandals go up the road, filled with red dirt, and the hooves and legs of the horses, and the snorting nostrils of the mules and horses, and the manes, and saddles, and the sweaty faces, and hats, all become filled with red dirt. I was born from that mud, and from that red dirt, and now I have returned to it. Here, in the small cemetery that watches over the town below, surrounded by daisies, geraniums, lilies, and thick grass. The acrid smell of red mud mingles with the sweet odor of *yaraguá* grass, and in the afternoon even the smell of the woods drifts overhead, and rushes down upon the town. (*A pause*) They brought me here in the evening. (*A funeral procession, upstage, with a coffin*) Juana Pasambú, my aunt, came.

JUANA PASAMBÚ: Why didn't you eat?

THE TEACHER: I wouldn't eat. Why eat? Food had no meaning anymore. You eat to live, and I didn't want to live. Life no longer had meaning. Pedro Pasambú, my uncle, came.

PEDRO PASAMBÚ: You liked bananas and corn on the cob with salt and butter.

THE TEACHER: I liked bananas and corn on the cob, but I wouldn't eat them. I kept my mouth tightly closed. (*A pause*) Squint-eyed Tobias is here: he was the mayor years ago.

SQUINT-EYED TOBIAS: I brought you water from the spring where you drank when you were a little girl; I brought it in a cup made of leaves, and you wouldn't drink it.

THE TEACHER: I didn't want to drink. I kept my lips pressed together. God forgive me, I began to wish the spring would dry up. Why did water continue to gush out of the spring? I wondered. For what reason? (*A pause*) Old Asunción was here. The midwife who brought me into the world.

OLD ASUNCIÓN: Oh, woman! Oh, my child! I brought you into this world. Oh, my baby! Why wouldn't you take anything from my hands? Why did you spit out the soup I gave you? My hands that have healed so many, why couldn't they heal your torn flesh? And while the murderers were here . . . (*The people in the funeral procession look around with terror. The old woman continues her mute wailing while the TEACHER speaks.*)

THE TEACHER: They are afraid. Some time ago fear

La maestra, Enrique Buenaventura, Colombia, 1968. Translated from Spanish by Gerardo Luzuriaga and Robert S. Rudder. Originally published in *The Orgy: Modern One-Act Plays from Latin America* (Los Angeles: UCLA Latin American Center, University of California, 1974). Copyright © 1974 University of California.

came to this town and hung suspended over it like a great storm cloud. The air reeks of fear, voices dissolve in the bitter spittle of fear, and the people swallow it. Yesterday the cloud ripped open, and the thunderbolt fell upon us.

(The funeral procession disappears. A violent roll of drums is heard in the darkness. When the light comes on again, where the procession was there is now an old farmer, on his knees, his hands tied behind his back. In front of him stands a police SERGEANT.)

SERGEANT: *(Looking at a list)* Your name's Peregrino Pasambú, right? *(The old man nods.)* Then you're the big chief here. *(The old man shakes his head.)*

THE TEACHER: Father had been named mayor twice by the government. But he understood so little about politics that he didn't realize the government had changed.

SERGEANT: You got this land because of politics, isn't that right?

THE TEACHER: That wasn't true. My father was one of the founders of the town. And because he was one of the founders he had this house next to the road, with some land. He gave the town its name. He called it "Hope."

SERGEANT: Aren't you gonna talk? Aren't you gonna say anything?

THE TEACHER: My father didn't talk much.

SERGEANT: This land ain't divided right. We're gonna divide it all over again. It's gonna have real owners, with deeds and everything.

THE TEACHER: When my father came here, it was all a jungle.

SERGEANT: The jobs haven't been given out too well, neither. Your daughter's the schoolteacher, ain't she?

THE TEACHER: It wasn't really a job. They seldom paid me my salary. But I liked to be the schoolteacher. My mother was the first teacher the school ever had. She taught me, and when she died I became the teacher.

SERGEANT: Who knows what that dame teaches.

THE TEACHER: I taught reading and writing, and I taught catechism, and love for our country and our flag. When I refused to eat and drink, I thought about the children. It was true that there weren't very many of them, but who was going to teach them? And then I thought: why should they learn the catechism? Why should they learn to love their country and their flag? Country and flag don't mean anything anymore. Maybe it wasn't right, but that's what I thought.

SERGEANT: Why don't you talk? This isn't my doing. I'm not to blame. I'm just following orders. *(He shouts.)* You see this list? All the big chiefs and fat cats of the last government are on it. We got orders to get rid of them all so we can set up the elections. *(The SERGEANT and the old man disappear.)*

THE TEACHER: So that's the way it was. They put him against the mud wall behind the house. The sergeant gave the order, and the soldiers shot. Then the sergeant and the soldiers came into my room and one after the other they raped me. Then I wouldn't eat or drink again, and so I died, little by little. Little by little. Now it will rain soon, and the red dirt will turn to mud. The road will be a slow-moving river of red mud and the sandals will come up the road again, and the mud-covered feet, and the horses and mules with their bellies full of mud, and even the faces and the hats will go up the road, splattered with mud.

THE END

The Twisted State

(Enrique Buenaventura)

Translated by José Barba Martín and Louis E. Roberts

CHARACTERS:

TORTURER
HIS WIFE
FIRST DETECTIVE
SECOND DETECTIVE
THIRD DETECTIVE
ATTENDANTS

Bedroom-dining room combination with doorway up center.

TORTURER: (*Eating, seated at the table*) How many pairs of stockings do you go through in a day?

HIS WIFE: (*While putting on a pair of stockings*) Why do you come out with that now? For Christ's sake, sometimes a pair lasts me a week.

TORTURER: Tell me precisely how many pairs of stockings you go through in a day. No evasions.

WIFE: I use what any woman uses. If you want, I'll go without stockings. They'll talk about you, not about me.

TORTURER: Don't try to worm out of it. Confess!

WIFE: If you like, I will prepare a list of everything I put on, with prices. Maybe I can try to get back the money you spend on other women?

TORTURER: I'm not talking about that. I know your tricks! I know you people!

WIFE: Who? (*Pause*) Who?

TORTURER: The meat is tough. The knife won't even cut into it. It's a piece of shoe leather.

WIFE: If you weren't so stupid and asked more for that lousy job you do, I could get you good meat. Top round. (*Long pause*) Don't I have pretty legs? If I had thin legs or crooked legs you'd maybe have a right to object. None of your buddies' women have legs like mine. The other day I made a comparison, and I left them with their mouths open. Your own boss . . .

TORTURER: Shut up!

WIFE: You're tired.

TORTURER: I have a tough job.

(*Pause*)

WIFE: You worry too much.

TORTURER: If I worked in an office, if I were a god-damned bureaucrat, I wouldn't have to worry. But they bring me some guy to make him talk, and I have to make him talk!

WIFE: If we went out a little bit, once in a while . . .

TORTURER: To make him talk. Do you know what that is?

WIFE: We could have a second honeymoon. You know, the fact is we haven't gotten on so well since we've been married.

TORTURER: I have to make him talk. That's all I know. That I have to make him talk.

WIFE: I'm still pretty, aren't I?

TORTURER: If he talks fast, I go crazy. I don't know what to do. He talks and talks, and I yell at him to talk, and he talks and I yell at him to talk, and he talks and talks, and I yell at him to talk. Sonofabitch! The knife won't cut! Instead of going around primping yourself, you ought to cook some meat that the knife'll go through. Who're you showing off for anyway? For the boss? You're a married woman.

WIFE: What the hell's gotten into you today?

(*Pause*)

TORTURER: Oh, I got a tough one. I got one tougher than a rail. (*He picks up the meat.*) This is a piece of leather.

WIFE: If it's a matter of being jealous, it ought to be me, not you. I've heard about your affairs. Both those before and those now.

TORTURER: He didn't open his mouth. You got this in a shoe store.

WIFE: (*Laughing*) They've filled you with stories. That old slob . . .

TORTURER: Why don't you confess? You must've cooked this in acid. What do they want? We've got

La tortura, Enrique Buenaventura, Colombia, 1968. Translated from Spanish by José Barba-Martin and Louis E. Roberts. Originally published in *TDR: The Drama Review* 14 (winter 1970). Copyright © 1970 TDR: The Drama Review.

them surrounded. We know who they are. For Christ's sake, don't they understand?

WIFE: That old fool can be your boss as much as he likes, but for me, I don't like him.

TORTURER: We gave him the fingernail treatment, and all he did was look at us. He looked at us with the eyes of a cow with her throat cut. All eyes!

WIFE: Don't make that noise with your knife. It sets my teeth on edge.

TORTURER: All eyes! The eyes filled the room!

WIFE: Even if he says he's going to give you a raise, I don't like it either.

TORTURER: We burned the soles of his feet.

WIFE: I'm sorry I can't help you in this, but I don't like it either.

TORTURER: Finally he started to shake. After a real fit of the shakes they always talk. But nothing!

WIFE: I don't like it.

TORTURER: Not a word. Not one damned word.

WIFE: I don't want to hear it. I don't like you to talk about these horrible things!

TORTURER: Ahhh. You don't like it?

WIFE: No. I don't want to know anything about your damned job. Aren't you able to do anything else? There are lots of jobs in the world. Why did you have to pick the most disgusting? When we got married you told me you worked with the police. But you didn't tell me what you did.

TORTURER: Then you don't like my job.

WIFE: No. It makes me sick. I'm ashamed. I can't . . .

TORTURER: Come on. Confess. Spit everything out.

WIFE: I can't have any girlfriends.

TORTURER: But boyfriends you can . . . I'm well informed. Go on. Get it all out.

WIFE: I can't look anybody in the face. It's as if I had a sickness.

TORTURER: You want to call it a sickness. I call it a job. Whoring.

WIFE: I want to explain to people that I don't have anything to do . . . that I don't like what you do. I don't like it. These things you do are repulsive to me.

TORTURER: But you like the repulsive things you do. (*He knocks the table over violently.*) And you like the food that's paid for with my repulsive work. You like your dresses bought with my dirty work! (*He goes to the dresser and begins to throw out and rip up dresses, stockings, etc.*) All this comes out of my filthy job. A nail torn out by the roots was changed into these shoes, and these stockings came from flesh torn with pincers. (*He tears off his WIFE's dress.*) Get out! Go on to the boss—naked. You whore, you shitty whore!

WIFE: Juan, you're crazy.

TORTURER: You have eyes like his.

WIFE: Juan, it's me.

TORTURER: Your eyes are like his. Just like his. The whole room is filled with eyes. (*He picks up a knife from the floor where it had fallen when he overturned the table.*) So the nails aren't enough, huh? Why don't you confess? Just confess. Why don't you tell me about all the men you have? They come here? Do you do it in that bed?

WIFE: Juan . . .

TORTURER: Why isn't it enough with the nails? Why isn't it enough to burn your feet?

(*WIFE exits through door up center. The TORTURER follows her. Stage darkens. When lights come up, three DETECTIVES are onstage.*)

FIRST DETECTIVE: Apparently they fought every day these last few months.

SECOND DETECTIVE: They say she had her own little affairs.

THIRD DETECTIVE: The chief used to drool over her.

FIRST DETECTIVE: And Juan's promotion was ready. They were going to appoint him bodyguard to someone important (*short pause*) who travels a good deal.

SECOND DETECTIVE: Yeh, but . . . to cut out her eyes.

THIRD DETECTIVE: We've had some tough times, but they're gonna pass. Some day we'll be through with them.

FIRST DETECTIVE: I hope God hears you.

SECOND DETECTIVE: But to take out her eyes.

FIRST DETECTIVE: It's a crappy job. You remember Pepe? One day he just started to throw up everything he ate. Finally he vomited blood. He had an ulcer this big.

SECOND DETECTIVE: But Juan seemed to be used to it. He was like the Squint-Eye. The Squint-Eye always said: It's a job, like medicine or butchering. Have you ever seen an honest doctor or butcher? Are they eaten up with scruples? Juan used to go through four or five sessions and come out as fresh as he started. He'd come out telling jokes.

(*Two detectives enter, cross the stage and leave with the TORTURER in handcuffs.*)

FIRST DETECTIVE: Who'll handle the defense?

SECOND DETECTIVE: Colonel Perez. He'll get him off. He'll make a formidable discourse on feminine infidelity.

(*Sound of a crowd outside and voices crying "Move on! Move on!" Then a police wagon is heard leaving.*)

THIRD DETECTIVE: And that sonofabitch never confessed to anything.

FIRST DETECTIVE: Nothing. He died the third time around without so much as a word. It was enough to crack the nerves of anybody.

THIRD DETECTIVE: Not Juan. With him it was jealousy.

SECOND DETECTIVE: Yeh, but to pull out her eyes.

(*Two attendants come in with a stretcher.*)

FIRST DETECTIVE: Come on! I can't stand looking at bodies.

The Orgy (Enrique Buenaventura)

Translated by Gerardo Luzuriaga and Robert S. Rudder

CHARACTERS:

The OLD WOMAN
The MUTE
FIRST BEGGAR
SECOND BEGGAR
THIRD BEGGAR
The DWARF

Sitting in a very old easy chair in front of a mirror, the OLD WOMAN primps. On both sides of the chair are two piles of clothing that had once been lovely and elegant.

OLD WOMAN: How could I possibly know where you hid it! You always hide it in the strangest places, and then you accuse me of stealing it. It's always the same thing! God, our heavenly Father, who is on high and can see everything we do, knows I don't steal your money! Who knows where you stuck it, you greedy little pig! Your greed is eating you up.

(A pause. She starts to primp again. Her son, a MUTE, grunts furiously. He looks everywhere. Then he turns to the audience and makes motions, accusing his mother of stealing the money he earns from shining shoes.)

Besides, even if I spend a few cents, I'm not stealing them. I have the right to spend them, because I gave birth to you, and I raised and supported every inch of you. I'm your mother.

(The MUTE turns to her and asks again for the money.)

What's wrong with you is that you're jealous. You're jealous! Jealous . . . jealous; jealousy is going to eat you up. How long has it been? Oh, forget about that money! Listen to me! Oh, how could he hear, anyway? He's as deaf as a post! This is my punishment from God! How long has it been? Thirty . . . forty years. Forty-five? Forty-seven, maybe . . . You looked exactly the same then as you do now; you were born that way.

(The MUTE makes indications that she has stolen thirty-five dollars from him.)

Thirty-five! That's not true. I took twenty miserable dollars for the Orgy of the Thirtieth. Twenty miserable dollars. You liar! Now he's going to say that he's the one who supports me! If it wasn't for the generosity of those people, that's right, of those people you hate, those people who make you so jealous, I would die all alone in this hovel.

(A pause. She begins to primp again. The MUTE grunts in an impotent rage. He makes signs that he would like to kill her, that he would like to wring her neck.)

You would, too. You would. *(A pause. She continues to primp; she ostentatiously combs her gray hair.)*

How long has it been? Fifty years? Has it been fifty already? I didn't steal thirty-five dollars from you. I took twenty for the Orgy of the Thirtieth. Today is orgy day. And don't you say one word to me. You talk too much. *(A pause)* How could he talk? He's as dumb as a doorknob. *(A pause)* Look at your father there. *(The MUTE smiles beatifically. He feels a great veneration for his father. He looks at the picture. His rage melts away.)*

He was the gabbiest man in the world. How his moustache used to move . . . In fact, I sometimes get the feeling it's still moving. *(The MUTE grunts.)* You're even jealous of him. How long has it been? Let's say it was exactly forty years ago. *(She starts to do an actual striptease as she talks. She takes off clothes that are so old they're about to fall apart.)*

The prince who was to be king kissed my hand on the train in Argentina. Come on, come on, help me. Do it for your father! He loved this story!

(She caresses him. That calms him down, and he begins to help her.) You're there. We're on the train. *(The MUTE smiles. He likes the train. He imitates it.)*

We can see the Pampa through the window. The whole Pampa! This is the prince's first trip to South America. He's in my compartment. Straighten up!

La orgía, Enrique Buenaventura, Colombia, 1968. Translated from Spanish by Gerardo Luzuriaga and Robert S. Rudder. Originally published in *The Orgy: Modern One-Act Plays from Latin America* (Los Angeles: UCLA Latin American Center, University of California, 1974). Copyright © 1974 University of California.

The prince looks like he's swallowed an umbrella! Come to attention! The prince looks like he has a pea stuck up his ass. *(She pulls back her hand that the MUTE is clumsily trying to kiss. The MUTE clutches desperately at the hand, struggling to kiss it.)* Stop it! Stop it, you imbecile! Now you're just trying to flatter me! You greedy thing! *(The MUTE becomes furious. He grabs hold of a pot that's on the table, backstage.)* Our food. Leave the food for the orgy there: I bought it with my money. With my money. Mine! Oh, my God! God, why did you give me this punishment! I'm paying for my sins with him, Lord! Mea culpa! Mea culpa! Mea fucking culpa! *(The MUTE lets go of the pot and goes to her. He kneels down beside her. He crosses himself amid tender grunts. He lays his head in her lap. He pushes against her, as though wanting to return to the womb. She caresses him. She smiles.)* You'd like to get back in there, wouldn't you? You'd like to curl back up inside here again. *(She touches her stomach.)* And when you were there, you used to kick, trying to get out. That's just like a man! They spend nine months, struggling to get out, and all their lives fighting to get back in. *(She laughs so hard that tears come to her eyes.)* All right, all right, calm down. Don't hug me so tight that you wake up the devil in me. Instead of being so loving you should be more generous. Get up. Don't grunt. You have to go to Jacob's and to Peter's and . . . Stop your growling and grunting. Let's have no jealousy here. There's nothing here any longer, my dear. I don't get aroused now. My poor flame has burned itself out. It doesn't even smolder anymore. And their flames have all gone cold too. Peter's, John's, Jacob's, Anthony's, and the ones who are dead too, may they rest in peace. What you used to watch through the cracks doesn't exist anymore. Oh, you little rascal. You used to like to look at your mother. You liked to see these things, didn't you? I know that you hate these men, but you have to go to them and pry money out of them. Since you're such a greedy fellow, I have to beg them to help. I'm a beggar too! Like my own beggars! Like my beggars from the Orgy of the Thirtieth. The ones you hate. *(The MUTE makes signs that she's wasting money on these disgusting people. He spits on them, actually spitting toward the audience.)* It's my money; I earned it. I earned it when I was myself, and I still earn it for old times' sake.

(He makes signs, indicating that that isn't true, that she steals it all from him. He turns his pockets inside out to indicate what she does to him.) You're a greedy pig, a goddam greedy little pig. Yes, I spend money on those beggars—I have fun with the beggars. I have a right to enjoy myself. Go on, get out and make some money. Go shine the shoes of the whole world. You despicable thing, get out! *(She threatens him with a broom. The MUTE runs off, laughing and playing with her. The OLD WOMAN sits down on her decrepit old chair, exhausted. A pause)* Jacob, is that you? The prince who was to be King of England took his first trip to South America back at the time of the first war. And his last trip too. How could you want him to come back to this horrible South America we have now? We were on the same train. I had a whole compartment all to myself . . . You could see the Pampa through the windows . . . the train . . . Little money, not much money, little money, not much money.

(She goes faster and faster until she ends in convulsions.) But that cost . . . *(She begins quickly, and gradually slows down to a complete stop.)* Lots of money, loads of money, lots of money, loads of money . . . Shshshshshshshshsh . . . *(As though the engine were letting off steam)*

(FIRST BEGGAR enters.)

FIRST BEGGAR: Lord be praised.

OLD WOMAN: Did you get here all right? Where were you, you scabby son of a bitch?

FIRST BEGGAR: I don't feel so good . . . my chest . . . *(He coughs. He spits into a bloody rag.)*

OLD WOMAN: Don't act so pompous. You don't have any right to get such a delicate illness. In my time that was a very distinguished illness. Now everybody's uncle has it.

FIRST BEGGAR: If I could get something to eat at these Orgies of the Thirtieth, I'd feel a lot better. At least, once a month!

OLD WOMAN: Well, this is a spiritual observance. A memorial. I won't allow it to be dirtied by the materialism of these days.

FIRST BEGGAR: Today I'm charging a dollar thirty.

OLD WOMAN: Why?

FIRST BEGGAR: I live further away. I have to take a bus.

OLD WOMAN: Jacob used to ride in a carriage. A big horse-drawn carriage.

FIRST BEGGAR: Who?

OLD WOMAN: Get dressed.

(The BEGGAR, who is nearly skin and bones, takes off his clothes. He shivers. He pulls an old, fancily decorated shirt from one of the piles of clothes, and puts it on. He coughs.) Don't you go and get Jacob's clothes dirty.

(The BEGGAR puts on a moth-eaten jacket. Pants. Everything is too big for him. He puts on the top hat, but he can't get the gloves on. His fingers are all bent and twisted from arthritis.) Jacob, you've grown smaller . . . Oh, my dear, bring me a chair. Pull that curtain open; I can't see very well. Hand me the binoculars. My God, you old scab! Stick your gloves up your ass, but don't keep twisting them around, trying to put them on . . . You're going to make me dizzy!

FIRST BEGGAR: They don't fit.

OLD WOMAN: Don't talk.

FIRST BEGGAR: (Enraged) But I can't get them on.

OLD WOMAN: Shut up.

FIRST BEGGAR: Don't shout at me. (He throws down the gloves.)

OLD WOMAN: (She shouts.) Do you want to leave here without the orgy? Do you want to lose your alms?

FIRST BEGGAR: (Humiliated) No. No, Ma'am.

OLD WOMAN: Pick up your gloves! (The BEGGAR picks up his gloves, and goes into a fit of coughing.) Don't cough! (The BEGGAR struggles to stop coughing.)

FIRST BEGGAR: What . . . (He starts coughing again; he holds it back.) I've got to cough!

OLD WOMAN: Hold it back.

FIRST BEGGAR: (With a great effort) I've got tu-ber-cu-lo-sis.

OLD WOMAN: Don't talk about that. (A short pause) Start in. I'm anxious to get started. (A pause) While we wait for the others to get here.

FIRST BEGGAR: You want me to start?

OLD WOMAN: Go ahead.

FIRST BEGGAR: (He takes a deep bow.) How beautiful you are, Maria Cristina. (He has a fit of coughing in order to cover up his laughter.)

OLD WOMAN: Don't cough.

FIRST BEGGAR: Listen to the way my chest sounds. (His chest rumbles.)

OLD WOMAN: Dear Jacob, pull up that chair for me. And draw back that curtain; I can't see very well. Hand me the binoculars. (She looks at the audience through the pair of rickety binoculars that the BEGGAR hands her.) Look. There they are. And every one of them with his little private life all under lock and key . . . They've come here not to see. They don't want to see. That's why they come. If they could see they'd be frightened. Do you think they're dead? No. That one over there just moved. Old what's-his-name. What's-her-name supports him and she's so-and-so's mistress. Look at that one. (She whispers animatedly in his ear. They both laugh.) Look at her, over there. (She hands him the binoculars. He looks. He gives the binoculars back to her and whispers at great length into her ear. He talks so long that he chokes and starts coughing.) You goddam pig, turn your head away when you cough! (She looks through the binoculars.) And that one, that one there!—Oh, that one over there!

(She whispers into the BEGGAR's ear. The two start laughing louder and louder. The BEGGAR points to someone in the audience, and they burst into shrieks of laughter. Suddenly the OLD WOMAN's laughter breaks off, and she pulls the BEGGAR's arm down.) Don't point. They're starting to notice. (She motions the BEGGAR to stoop down so she can tell him a secret. He bends over. She whispers the secret to him. He nods his head. He looks through the binoculars and whispers into her ear. The game begins to move faster. They pass the binoculars back and forth very quickly and say things in a jumble. SECOND BEGGAR comes in.)

SECOND BEGGAR: 'Evening.

OLD WOMAN: Don't interrupt. We're at the theater. (SECOND BEGGAR pretends to become interested. He looks at the audience.)

SECOND BEGGAR: What are they performing?

OLD WOMAN: Their own lives. (She points at the audience.)

SECOND BEGGAR: How is it?

OLD WOMAN: Boring. Get dressed. It's your turn to play Peter today.

SECOND BEGGAR: From now on I'm going to charge a dollar fifty for the Orgies of the Thirtieth.

OLD WOMAN: (To FIRST BEGGAR) What an interesting play. The best one I've seen. Look. (They start the game again, but more slowly this time.) Oh, Jacob, gossip excites me so. (FIRST BEGGAR whispers at length into her ear. In the meantime the SECOND BEGGAR undresses. Under his ragged clothing he has on an old prisoner's uniform. He puts on a large silk coat over it, and a ragged top hat. The FIRST BEGGAR is still whispering in the OLD WOMAN's ear.) That one? (She points. The FIRST BEGGAR moves her hand.) Oh, that one? (He moves her hand. The OLD WOMAN gets up.) Oh, oh, that one, that one. (He moves her hand. They both move forward, toward the audience.) Oh, that one? (He moves her hand. They move even closer.) This one, then? (He moves her hand. They reach the edge of the stage.) This one. (The OLD WOMAN pulls back her hand, as though her finger had been burned.) We're pointing. Do you think they've noticed? No? (She looks out tenderly at the audience.) They haven't noticed. They're so innocent . . .

SECOND BEGGAR: I said that from now on I'm going to charge a dollar fifty for each Orgy of the Thirtieth.

OLD WOMAN: (To FIRST BEGGAR) Wash out your mouth once in a while, you scabby old thing. It's nothing but a sewer. (To SECOND BEGGAR) The others aren't here yet.

SECOND BEGGAR: If you aren't going to pay, then I'm going to take off these clothes. (He makes a motion as though he's going to undress.)

FIRST BEGGAR: That's a lot of money, Ma'am. He's taking advantage of you.

SECOND BEGGAR: You suck-ass!

OLD WOMAN: That lazy bunch of good-for-nothings. Those scabby old bums. I always have to wait for them.

SECOND BEGGAR: Then I'm getting out of these clothes. (He takes off his coat.)

OLD WOMAN: You goddam ungrateful bastard. Who got you out of jail? Who do you owe your freedom to? How much is your freedom worth?

SECOND BEGGAR: I live a long way from here. I get here all out of breath . . . and then . . .

OLD WOMAN: Then what?

SECOND BEGGAR: Then the food gets worse at every orgy . . .

OLD WOMAN: Can't you people think about anything besides eating? Is food the only thing you live for? Don't spiritual things mean anything to you? That's why this country is in the shape it's in. Because the only thing anybody thinks about is eating.

FIRST BEGGAR: That's true, Ma'am. (*To SECOND BEGGAR*) All you think about is eating.

SECOND BEGGAR: It's because my stomach always hurts.

FIRST BEGGAR: He's so materialistic, Ma'am. (*To SECOND BEGGAR*) I'm asking for a dollar thirty, and I have to take the bus.

SECOND BEGGAR: (*Going up to him*) You poor thing. Do you want me to tell some other things about you?

FIRST BEGGAR: Ma'am, we're at the theater. (*He looks at the audience through the binoculars.*)

SECOND BEGGAR: You Jesuit.

OLD WOMAN: All right, let's cut out the squabbling. I'll raise the alms of the Orgy of the Thirtieth to a dollar twenty, but not one cent more.

FIRST BEGGAR: The bus costs thirty cents, and it's going to go up to forty.

OLD WOMAN: A dollar twenty, and no more.

SECOND BEGGAR: That's exploitation.

FIRST BEGGAR: (*To SECOND BEGGAR*) You lost it all. I already had my dollar thirty.

OLD WOMAN: If you don't like it, I'll get some other beggars. They're like this. (*She opens and closes the fingers of her right hand to indicate how many there are.*) We're swarming with them.

SECOND BEGGAR: Pure exploitation.

OLD WOMAN: And the others still aren't here.

SECOND BEGGAR: If we can all agree on this . . .

OLD WOMAN: Everyone knows that it's on the thirtieth of every month. The thirtieth. Every month has thirty . . .

FIRST BEGGAR: We should have agreed on it before. The only one that doesn't have thirty is August, and it has thirty-one.

SECOND BEGGAR: And every time she gives us less food. What does she do with the leftovers? Why doesn't she put out all the food?

OLD WOMAN: Nobody can forget the thirtieth.

FIRST BEGGAR: She gets crazier every time we get together.

OLD WOMAN: Thirty miserable beggars.

SECOND BEGGAR: Thirty thirsty thieves . . .

FIRST BEGGAR: Thrashing through the thorny thicket. (*They laugh.*)

OLD WOMAN: On every thirtieth of the month.

FIRST BEGGAR: (*Keeping up the joke*) Today is the twenty-ninth. There's only twenty-nine days in the month.

OLD WOMAN: And what happens to the thirtieth? (*The BEGGARS shrug.*) In other countries I've been to—even Argentina—all the months have thirty days. But since this country is full of thieves, they steal the thirtieth from some months.

SECOND BEGGAR: They stole the thirtieth today.

FIRST BEGGAR: And this is the twenty-ninth.

OLD WOMAN: Then not everybody will come.

SECOND BEGGAR: All the better. There'll be more for us to eat.

FIRST BEGGAR: We could take the lid off the pot.

OLD WOMAN: Jacob, remember that you have a very small appetite.

FIRST BEGGAR: Who?

OLD WOMAN: You.

FIRST BEGGAR: Me?

OLD WOMAN: Yes.

FIRST BEGGAR: I didn't know that.

OLD WOMAN: You're Jacob today, and Jacob never ate very much. He was a gentleman.

FIRST BEGGAR: A gentleman with no appetite . . . What a goddam waste.

OLD WOMAN: Set the table. (*The BEGGARS jump to get the pot.*) I said the table; I didn't say to bring the pot. Put it back.

FIRST BEGGAR: But, Ma'am . . .

SECOND BEGGAR: I haven't had a bite to eat since yesterday.

OLD WOMAN: I said the table.

FIRST BEGGAR: Please.

SECOND BEGGAR: Come down to earth, damn it.

FIRST BEGGAR: A crumb for a poor, starving old man. (*He takes the lid off the pot.*)

OLD WOMAN: Put the lid back on the pot.

SECOND BEGGAR: (*He puts in his hand and pulls something out, quickly putting it in his mouth.*)

OLD WOMAN: You goddam pig.

SECOND BEGGAR: (*With his mouth full*) Mmm. Mmm . . . mmmmm. (*He indicates that he is hungry.*)

OLD WOMAN: You thief. You thief. (*She runs after him with a stick. Meanwhile the FIRST BEGGAR puts his hand into the pot and starts stuffing his mouth. The OLD WOMAN throws down the stick and goes over to the table. She picks up a knife and stands next to the pot.*) If either one of you comes one step closer I'll send his soul packing.

FIRST BEGGAR: My soul is very weak, Ma'am.

SECOND BEGGAR: I ate mine quite a while back.

FIRST BEGGAR: Don't make such a big thing out of it, Ma'am. Remember, I'm Jacob. (*He straightens his clothing.*)

SECOND BEGGAR: And I'm Peter. (*He does the same.*) How were Peter's grinders, Ma'am?

OLD WOMAN: (*Going along with the game*) He was toothless.

SECOND BEGGAR: Like me. But I have gums as hard as a rock.

OLD WOMAN: (*With the knife in her belt*) Put the flowers on the table. (*They bring out a jug with old, decrepit artificial flowers. The OLD WOMAN starts playing the game again.*) Colonel Gray sent them to me this morning. Aren't they beautiful? Smell them.

SECOND BEGGAR: (*Going along with the joke*) What an aroma.

OLD WOMAN: (*To the SECOND BEGGAR*) You smell them, sir.

SECOND BEGGAR: They're roses.

OLD WOMAN: They're fuchsias.

SECOND BEGGAR: I mean fuchsias.

OLD WOMAN: (*Remembering, caught up*) Colonel Gray always used to send me fuchsias. (*THIRD BEGGAR enters.*) Colonel! (*Her hand is trembling. The BEGGAR hesitates for a second. The other two BEGGARS are dying with laughter. The THIRD BEGGAR kisses her hand. She turns away in disgust.*) What made you so late? You goddam pig. Hurry up and get dressed. Put on the uniform. Today you're Colonel Gray. The full-dress uniform. (*The THIRD BEGGAR begins to rummage through the pile of clothes.*) Law and order are here. If you don't keep order and discipline, you'll lose your alms and the orgies of the thirtieth each month.

FIRST BEGGAR: But every time we meet we get less to eat.

SECOND BEGGAR: Last month there was a lot left over.

OLD WOMAN: There always have to be leftovers.

FIRST BEGGAR: Why?

OLD WOMAN: Because there's a lot of food.

SECOND BEGGAR: And what do you do with the leftovers?

OLD WOMAN: I throw them, I fling them away, I pitch them out . . . like this.

FIRST BEGGAR: Where do you throw them?

OLD WOMAN: Jacob!

FIRST BEGGAR: Damn Jacob to hell! I want the leftovers!

OLD WOMAN: Shut up, you mangy old animal. If you start in again, it's all over for you, and you'll never get back in here again. Colonel, I have a lot of complaints for you about these two.

THIRD BEGGAR: You ought to throw him out, Ma'am. He's nothing but a lousy bastard.

SECOND BEGGAR: Or not let him into the orgies of the thirtieth. The members of the orgies ought to be chosen very carefully.

FIRST BEGGAR: You sons of bitches! (*He throws down his gloves.*)

OLD WOMAN: Shut up. Pick up your gloves, Jacob. Are you ready, Colonel?

THIRD BEGGAR: Yes, Ma'am, but I wanted to tell you . . .

OLD WOMAN: No, no, no. Don't tell us again.

THIRD BEGGAR: . . . that the orgies . . .

OLD WOMAN: Don't tell us again.

THIRD BEGGAR: . . . are really cheap. I mean, Ma'am . . . I mean, a dollar isn't much for an orgy . . . I was thinking . . .

OLD WOMAN: We don't want to know how you lost your leg in the Thousand Days' War . . . There are so many versions. But it's the ten thousandth time you've told it, Colonel . . . How did it happen?

THIRD BEGGAR: I don't want to make out that I'm a big shot, but I've got something that's really good for orgies, Ma'am. I'm missing a leg. That's something not everybody can say.

OLD WOMAN: Your leg. Your precious leg that's on the country's altar. Lying there. Along with the other ideals. (*A brief pause*) Rotten, stinking, full of worms. It's disgusting.

THIRD BEGGAR: (*Shouting*) No, Ma'am. It's something . . . something special. If you won't pay me two dollars for the orgy, my leg won't work. (*A pause. An awkward silence*)

FIRST BEGGAR: It went up to one twenty. She won't give a penny more.

SECOND BEGGAR: Either we all get more money, or none of us gets any.

THIRD BEGGAR: You two have both your legs.

OLD WOMAN: All right, it's over. You can all get out of here. This is an orgy of art and memories, it's not something commercial. Do whatever you want to. I can get other beggars. I have a lot of them who want to join. Right out there. (*She repeats the gesture with her fingers.*) They're just swarming all over the place. (*The BEGGARS huddle into a conference. A pause*)

THIRD BEGGAR: (*Coming to attention*) Ma'am! I'm ready.

OLD WOMAN: Your leg, your tired old leg . . . How did it get up and start to walk away all by itself?

THIRD BEGGAR: I was marching along at the head of the liberal forces. I was carrying the red flag, and it was waving and waving in the breeze.

OLD WOMAN: Fluttering, you say fluttering.

THIRD BEGGAR: Fluttering. And there, up in front of us, were the damn conservatives.

SECOND BEGGAR: Don't you start saying bad things about the conservatives. I won't allow it, Ma'am. He's always using the orgies of the thirtieth for political purposes.

THIRD BEGGAR: The fuckin' conservatives, those goddam, almighty conservatives . . .

SECOND BEGGAR: I won't allow it, Ma'am. I won't put up with it. Do you want to lose another leg? (*The*

FIRST BEGGAR *is shaking with laughter.)* Do you want to lose another leg? *(He pulls out a knife, presses the button, and the blade flies open.)* Do you want another wooden stick full of termites on the other side? *(The THIRD BEGGAR pulls a dagger from his crutches.)*

OLD WOMAN: I just adore political battles. *(To the FIRST BEGGAR)* Jacob, what are you?

FIRST BEGGAR: *(Breaking off his laughter, and crossing himself)* A Christian. *(The female DWARF enters.)*

DWARF: Ooh hoo hooo: Here I am! *(A pause. Silence. The DWARF looks at everyone.)* Did the orgy begin yet? *(The two BEGGARS slowly put away their weapons. The DWARF turns to the OLD WOMAN.)* I got here late because today's not the thirtieth; it's the twenty-ninth. But I asked this morning at church, and they told me it was the end of the month. But it's not the thirtieth, I said. It's leap year, they told me. Then I came.

OLD WOMAN: And now, my story.

SECOND BEGGAR: It's already been told ten jillion times.

FIRST BEGGAR: You were on the train.

OLD WOMAN: *(Carried away)* Yes.

SECOND BEGGAR: You could see the Pampa out the window.

OLD WOMAN: Yes. *(A pause)* There it is.

FIRST BEGGAR: Out there in the Pampa *(he points to the audience)* the sun hasn't come up yet. It's still dark.

DWARF: Should I get dressed?

OLD WOMAN: Yes.

DWARF: What should I dress as?

OLD WOMAN: Anything. The Bishop, if you want.

DWARF: Oh, yes! The Bishop! *(She begins to get dressed.)*

THIRD BEGGAR: The prince who was to be King of England . . .

FIRST BEGGAR: . . . was taking his first and last trip through South America.

SECOND BEGGAR: He was on the train . . .

OLD WOMAN: Little money, not much money, little money, not much money . . .

THIRD BEGGAR: You had an entire compartment all to yourself.

OLD WOMAN: *(Speeding up)* Little money, not much money, little money, not much money . . .

FIRST BEGGAR: *(Raising his voice)* And then the prince who was to be king . . .

OLD WOMAN: *(Like background music)* Little money, not much money, little money, not much money, little money, not much money, little money, not much money . . .

SECOND BEGGAR: He came to your compartment and . . .

THIRD BEGGAR: He kissed your hand! *(He kisses her hand.)*

OLD WOMAN: Ohhh.

(This cry is the signal for the orgy to begin. The FIRST BEGGAR grabs an untuned guitar and begins to play. They all dance. The OLD WOMAN passes around the bottle and everyone takes a drink. The DWARF puts the pot on the table and everyone rushes over to eat.) Just a minute. Another drink and another dance. *(They pass around the bottle. They take enormous swigs, and they dance. The DWARF and the OLD WOMAN raise their skirts and the BEGGARS fondle them. The women affect prudishness. The OLD WOMAN pushes away the SECOND BEGGAR as he puts his hand around her waist.)*

SECOND BEGGAR: That's enough: let's eat.

FIRST BEGGAR: Let's eat.

THIRD BEGGAR: It's time to eat.

DWARF: I'll serve. *(She says the blessing.)* In nomine Patris, et Filium . . .

OLD WOMAN: All right, that's enough. Pass the bottle, you filthy little midget. Let's drink freely and eat moderately, like ladies and gentlemen. This is a decent orgy.

FIRST BEGGAR: It's getting harder and harder to eat at these friggin' orgies.

OLD WOMAN: Come here, Jacob. You're the Governor. You here, Mr. Mayor. You tell me how the Government is doing. *(The FIRST BEGGAR gives a very complicated pantomime of how the Government is doing.)* I don't understand a bit of it, and I'm laughing. *(She laughs very theatrically.)*

DWARF: I'm at the Government's side. Dominus, Dominus . . .

OLD WOMAN: Jacob, give your speech.

DWARF: Dominus, Dominus, Dominus. *(She goes on as background music.)*

OLD WOMAN: Speak, Mr. Governor, we're waiting.

FIRST BEGGAR: *(Standing on the chair, with the pathetic tone and gestures of a very serious political leader)* I would like something to eat.

BEGGARS: Hooray!

OLD WOMAN: He's always such a demagogue! *(The other BEGGARS applaud.)*

FIRST BEGGAR: We ought to be able to eat all we want at these damn orgies of the thirtieth. I ask you, ladies and gentlemen: Why can't we eat? Why do we have to go hungry when the meal is sitting here? What is the answer to this riddle, ladies and gentlemen? Who can solve it? My stomach is stuck against my spine, we're starving like dogs, the meal is sitting here, and we can't even move our little fingers! Let's have something to eat at these orgies of the thirtieth! *(He has a coughing fit.)*

OLD WOMAN: One of the best speeches from one of the best governors at one of the best orgies.

SECOND BEGGAR: It's not right for there to be leftovers.

THIRD BEGGAR and DWARF: No! It's not right!

OLD WOMAN: Even the masses are getting stirred up!

DWARF: Christ gave out the loaves of bread and the fish and the frijoles and the tortillas.

FIRST BEGGAR: We want the leftovers.

SECOND BEGGAR: We want the leftovers.

DWARF: We want the leftovers.

THIRD BEGGAR: We want the leftovers.

ALL THE BEGGARS: We want the leftovers! We want it all!

FIRST BEGGAR: (*Taking the lid off the pot*) All!

OLD WOMAN: Let's stop this right now! I'll give out the food when I get good and ready! (*She grabs hold of the pot.*)

SECOND BEGGAR: Let go of that pot!

THIRD BEGGAR: You stingy old bitch!

OLD WOMAN: (*Struggling*) You animals! You filthy drunks! You're all full of shit. Get back. (*For a second the BEGGARS move back. The DWARF, still standing behind her, tries to reach the pot with her cane. The OLD WOMAN picks up a knife. The DWARF moves back.*) You're nothing but a pile of crap. You aren't my gentlemen. You just take advantage of a helpless old lady who has only a mute son.

SECOND BEGGAR: (*Advancing toward her*) The play is over! The play is over!

THIRD BEGGAR: You crazy old lady! You crazy old lady!

OLD WOMAN: (*Throwing the knife*) Get back, you stinking pile of shit.

FIRST BEGGAR: You old murderer. You stabbed me. You stabbed me.

SECOND BEGGAR: You old murderer.

DWARF: Ooh hoo hee! Let's have the orgy.

(*She hits the OLD WOMAN over the head with her cane.*

The OLD WOMAN falls back onto the table. The BEGGARS fall on her, beat and stab her. She lies sprawled out on the table. Her hand hangs down and her gray hair touches the floor. Silently, the BEGGARS devour the meal. The FIRST BEGGAR starts to leave.)

SECOND BEGGAR: Where are you going?

FIRST BEGGAR: To piss.

SECOND BEGGAR: You're lying.

THIRD BEGGAR: You're going out to look for the Mute's money.

DWARF: (*To the corpse of the OLD WOMAN*) Ego te absolvo in nomini Patris, et Filium, et Spiritu Sancti . . .

SECOND BEGGAR: Let's get out of these clothes and we'll all go looking for it. (*They take off their costumes and put on their ragged old clothes again.*)

FIRST BEGGAR: She was crazy as a loon.

SECOND BEGGAR: They say the Mute has a lot of money hidden somewhere. He's been hoarding it for thirty years.

THIRD BEGGAR: That's not true. She stole it all from him.

FIRST BEGGAR: Someone stand guard while we look for the money.

DWARF: Requiet canti in pace. Amen.

SECOND BEGGAR: Let the Dwarf stand guard. (*They lift her up to the table and she pretends to be looking through a window.*)

DWARF: Here comes the Mute. (*The BEGGARS run out, followed by the DWARF. The MUTE enters, counting his money. He sees the OLD WOMAN, runs over to her and lifts up her head. Then he goes to the front of the stage and asks the audience why, why did all this happen . . . Why?*)

BLACKOUT

ARGENTINA

Personal Belongings
(Diana Raznovich)

Diana Raznovich is one of Argentina's most audacious and humorous feminist playwrights and cartoonists. Since she began writing in 1967, she has decried the criminal politics, misogyny, and homophobia of Argentina's militarized system. As a Jewish, bisexual woman coming of age during the time of the Dirty War (1976–83), the challenges have been considerable. Her career as a playwright stalled when repeated threats on her life by the armed forces pressured her into exile in 1975, shortly before the military coup that initiated the Dirty War. She did not realize at the time that her first husband was actively involved in the armed, anti-military resistance movement and had stored an armory of weapons in their apartment. He had gone underground, and she found out later, from her exile in Spain, that he had been assassinated in 1978. Whether his own group killed him, or the armed forces posing as his collaborators, she does not know.

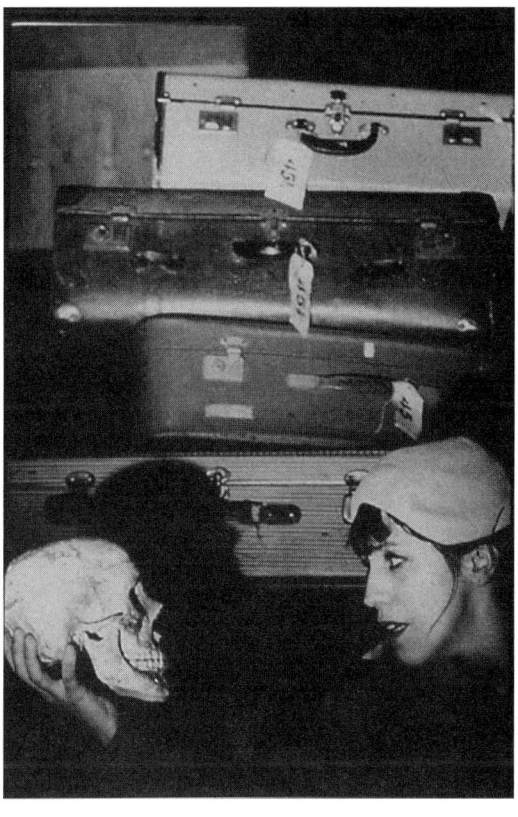

Dasha Blahova as Casalia Belprop, aka the Diva, in *Personal Belongings,* directed by Ros Horin, Sydney, Australia, 1984. (Photo by Deborah Georg, courtesy of Diana Raznovich.)

The one-woman, one-act play included here, *Personal Belongings* (*Efectos personales*), dates from this period. Raznovich sat down to write it in 1975, her bags packed and apartment emptied, as she waited to set out, alone, for a place she did not know. Nothing prepares one for exile. Casalia Belprop, her character, searches for her personal belongings among unclaimed luggage in some unknown location: "When you go on a long trip without knowing whether you'll return, you take along so much ridiculous stuff. The things you really need you leave behind." Elegant and filled with self-importance ("My admirers call me Diva"), Casalia initially seems merely put off by the inconvenience of displacement. Did she bring her red crocodile luggage or the red, white, or mauve set? Where is the attendant? Before long the growing sense of exile disorients her; she loses her sense of place, color, self. Casalia does not know if she is coming or going. Has she arrived? Is she still in transit? Where? "Day or night? Before or after?"

Trapped in the luggage room, with no visible exit, she experiences the pull between perpetual mobility and utter immobility. The room may be stuffed with abandoned luggage, designed for travel and destined for somewhere, but the suitcases (like her, the audience assumes) will never leave that room. The exiled person, by definition, is trapped in constant motion, caught in the very act of banishment. But the motion leads nowhere. If the person were to resettle, put down roots, the exile would be over. "So much mobility," Diana Raznovich stated in a recent interview, "becomes a kind of prison."[1]

Personal Belongings marks the arena in which one's personal story intersects with history and politics writ large. As Casalia frantically holds up the baggage claim tag, number 46, and scrounges around for her lost luggage, she stumbles on entire histories bursting out of forgotten bags. Human bones spill out of boxes marked 46, signaling other histories of lost loves and disappearances. The original *Mona Lisa* pops out of a trunk marked 46, evidence of the sacralization of art goods that sustains notions of national belonging and identity: "All Europe rests in this painting. At night they sleep in peace because the wife of Zenobio del Giocondo guarantees them an enduring past." All these horrors and glories are hers (they all bear her number) and not hers. Her frenetic monologue illustrates the way she tries to explain herself to her imaginary interlocutor. She confesses to crimes (stealing the painting, bomb smuggling) in an effort to lure the attendant into dialogue. She defends herself from her own accusations: "What's the point of stealing the Mona Lisa if my house has been occupied by the Army? And Victor's famous tarsus, won't it be used as evidence against me?" The exiled person is simultaneously invisible and an object of suspicion—not only in the eyes of those who forced her out, but in the eyes of all who consider taking her in. Denied all services, she internalizes the suspicion directed at her, becoming suspicious in her own eyes: "My umbrella is wet. The water proves I've been somewhere else. A rainy place. With threatening clouds. I had to leave in a hurry. They got me out in time." Personal and political history become entangled. Casalia's story of exile, told through her personal search for her individual belongings, becomes the story of a country in "a so-called war" in which presidents can order their citizens killed by firing squads and in which people "disappear" permanently. "It's not the person that moves," says Raznovich, "it's the whole history of the continent, all the stories lodged within those bags."

Personal Belongings was prohibited in Argentina and has never been performed there, even though the ban has long since been lifted. Since it was first staged in 1984 as part of the International Theatre Festival in Sydney, Australia, it has undergone several rewrites and multiple variations in terms of staging. As *Stages of Conflict* has made clear, the practice of rewriting and updating texts is not unusual for Latin American dramatists whose lives are deeply entwined with their sociopolitical environment.[2] After her political exile in 1975, Raznovich experienced two more "exiles" to Spain—an economic one in 1989 (a period of crippling hyperinflation) and another in 2001, this time for personal reasons—"an *exilio sentimental*," she calls it, "like those of the tangos." Sometimes, the text of *Personal Belongings* changes to reflect these different experiences of exile. Directors have also chosen to highlight different facets of the work—the humorous, the poetic, the existential, as well as the political—and accentuate the oppressiveness of Casalia's entrapment by adding loudspeakers, surveillance cameras, and other distancing effects. Audiences have seen the entire performance on video monitors, as if they were in charge of surveilling the room. Raznovich finds the distancing appropriate and forceful and thinks the work is most effective when Casalia is viewed from afar, in a box, alone and fearful. The proximity of the audience diminishes the sense of abandonment that Raznovich feels is essential to the piece, though in this version she refrained from adding stage directions so that directors can interpret the predicament as best they see fit.

Raznovich's life and career have been profoundly affected by exile. Like many dramatists from Latin America who went into exile (Griselda Gambaro, Augusto Boal, and Ariel Dorfman to name only a few), she found it difficult to continue writing for the stage while away from her native country. Audiences abroad are different; the issues, humor, even linguistic expressions are different. While novelists thrived abroad, dramatists often felt a particular urgency to return to their countries and their audiences. Even when foreign audiences react positively to a production, as with the successful run of Dorfman's *Death and the Maiden* in London and New York, they often miss the point. The Dorfman play, written as the Truth Commission in Chile was trying to deal with the aftermath of the torture and disappearance of civilians at the hands of Augusto Pinochet's armed forces, poses vital questions for societies that have suffered criminal politics. How can members of society continue to coexist with the very people who tormented them? But works that may have been written as an indictment of criminal politics can play like a whodunit for audiences that lack the background necessary to understand the sociopolitical situation and the intended critique.[3]

Raznovich returned to Argentina in 1981 to participate in the Teatro Abierto (Open Theatre) festival. Teatro Abierto was one of the world's most important theater events because it showed the power of theater in times of brutal repression. This "open" festival brought together 150 blacklisted dramatists, directors, actors, and technicians to stage a cycle of twenty-one one-act plays that would be performed every week—three a night for seven nights. The cycle demonstrated that Argentina's artists had not succumbed to the dictatorship's silencing tactics. The long lines of people waiting to see the performances night after night, month after month, showed that the public was also ready to defy the culture of fear and silence. The military reacted violently, burning down the Picadero Theatre on the night that Raznovich's play *Disconcerted* was presented. Teatro Abierto moved to another locale and continued to stage its productions in the face of growing governmental opposition and growing popular support.

Teatro Abierto showed that much had changed in Argentina in the fifteen years since Gambaro wrote *The Camp*, which is included in this volume. Gambaro's prescient depiction of concentration camps and disappearances had come to pass. Raznovich's one-woman *Disconcerted* features a pianist who no longer knows how to coax music from the piano, recalling Emma's attempts to give a concert in *The Camp*. For Raznovich, the problem now had less to do with the fascistic violence of the armed forces, which by 1981 was brutally clear, than with the social effects of years of silencing and playing along with criminal politics. Gambaro's contribution to Teatro Abierto in

1981, *Saying Yes,* focused on much the same theme. When, both dramatists wondered, would people learn to say "no!" Teatro Abierto, as an event, proclaimed a resounding "No!"

Since the fall of the dictatorship in 1983, Raznovich's work both as a cartoonist and in the theater has been marked by fierce humor and her love of disruption. The military dictatorship might be gone, but many of the oppressive systems remain in place—especially with regard to issues of gender and sexuality. Plays such as *Inner Gardens* (*Jardin de otoño,* 1983), *MaTrix, Inc.* (*Casa Matriz,* 1991), *Rear Entry* (*De atrás para adelante,* 1995), *From the Waist Down* (*De la cintura para abajo,* 1999), and *Manifesto 2000 of Feminine Humor* (2003) use humor to explore the violence of social expectations and norms.[4] *Inner Gardens* explores the intimate relationship of two middle-aged women who live together as roommates, their love for each other channeled into their love of a soap opera star, whom they decide to kidnap. In *MaTrix, Inc.,* the thirty-year-old Gloria hires a Substitute Mother, a professional who performs a spectrum of different mothers—from the ever popular "suffering mother" to the coldhearted businesswoman who jets around the world and ignores her daughter. Each mother provokes profound reactions in Gloria, eliciting a different "daughter." In a society in which everything can be bought and sold, Raznovich shows the social production of emotions and desires with all the performative strings showing. In *Rear Entry,* a transsexual son banished from his homophobic father's home comes back as a beautiful and successful daughter to cure him on his deathbed. *From the Waist Down* suggests that yesterday's torturers are today's sex therapists and entrepreneurs. The sexologist a couple hires to activate their sexually dormant marriage transforms their bedroom into a temple of sadomasochism. They instantly become a national and international phenomenon, hounded by foreign journalists titillated by Argentina's torturous past and domestic journalists defending their national patrimony. The illusion of sex mediated through porn magazines becomes more satisfying—financially if not emotionally—than an intimate relationship could hope to be. There are different kinds of violence, Raznovich reminds us, different kinds of repression. Throughout her career, she has turned to humor to challenge normative and repressive systems of behavior. "I wish people understood how subversive humor really is," Raznovich says. Even though for her, as for many Argentines, life has been no laughing matter, she maintains that "you can say a lot more with laughter than with tragedy."

—Diana Taylor

NOTES

1. This quotation and all other statements by Diana Raznovich cited in this essay are from a personal interview with Diana Taylor conducted in Buenos Aires in July 2006.

2. See the essay on Enrique Buenaventura's *Documents from Hell* in this book for another example of a playwright who has continually rewritten texts to reflect changing circumstances and staging practices. Another salient example is the Mexican playwright Sabina Berman, whose work has been translated in *The Theatre of Sabina Berman: The Agony of Ecstasy and Other Plays,* trans. Adam Versényi (Carbondale: Southern Illinois University Press, 2003).

3. *Death and the Maiden* deals with a woman who was imprisoned several years earlier under the dictatorship. When her husband's car breaks down on the highway and a Good Samaritan gives her husband a ride home, she recognizes the stranger's voice as that of

the doctor who tortured and raped her while in prison, and she traps him in the house and interrogates him. Most reviewers of the Broadway staging, which starred Gene Hackman as the doctor and Glenn Close as the victim, saw the doctor as an innocent man unjustly accused, the implication being that Glenn Close's character was a hysterical, traumatized woman. The political context of the play was lost as its personal, "universal" elements were highlighted. See also Roman Polanski's 1994 film version starring Sigourney Weaver.

4. *Disconcerted, Inner Gardens, MaTrix, Inc.*, and *Rear Entry* were published (in Spanish and English translation) in Diana Raznovich, *Defiant Acts: Four Plays by Diana Raznovich / Actos desafiantes: Cuatro obras de Diana Raznovich,* ed. Diana Taylor and Victoria Martínez (Lewisburg, Pa.: Bucknell University Press, 2002). *From the Waist Down* and *Manifesto 2000* appear in *Holy Terrors: Latin American Women Perform,* ed. Diana Taylor and Roselyn Costantino (Durham: Duke University Press, 2003).

SELECTED REFERENCES

Arancibia, Juana A., and Zulema Mirkin. "Introducción." In *Teatro argentino durante el proceso (1976–1983),* 181–95. Buenos Aires: Instituto Literario y Cultural Hispánico, 1992.

Giella, Miguel Angel. *Teatro Abierto, 1981: Teatro argentino bajo vigilancia.* Buenos Aires: Corregidor, 1991.

Graham-Jones, Jean. *Exorcising History: Argentine Theater under Dictatorship.* Lewisburg, Pa.: Bucknell University Press, 2000.

Larson, Catherine. *Games and Play in the Theater of Spanish American Women.* Lewisburg, Pa.: Bucknell University Press, 2004.

Milleret, Margo. *Latin American Women on/in Stages.* Albany: State University of New York Press, 2004.

Raznovich, Diana. *Defiant Acts: Four Plays by Diana Raznovich / Actos desafiantes: Cuatro obras de Diana Raznovich.* Ed. Diana Taylor and Victoria Martínez. Lewisburg, Pa.: Bucknell University Press, 2002.

Taylor, Diana. *Disappearing Acts: Spectacles of Gender and Nationalism in Argentina's "Dirty War."* Durham: Duke University Press, 1997.

Taylor, Diana. "Fighting Fire with Frivolity: Diana Raznovich's *Defiant Acts.*" In *Performance, pathos y política de los sexos: Teatro postcolonial de autoras latinoamericanas,* ed. Heidrun Adler and Kati Röttger, 69–81. Frankfurt: Vervuert, 1992.

Taylor, Diana. "What Is Diana Raznovich Laughing At?" In *Holy Terrors: Latin American Women Perform,* ed. Diana Taylor and Roselyn Costantino, 73–92. Durham: Duke University Press, 2003.

Personal Belongings (Diana Raznovich)

Translated by Margaret Carson

The Set. *The stage is crowded with suitcases, trunks, packages, backpacks and all sorts of boxes and cartons. It appears to be a baggage check, judging from the quantity of suitcases that have been deposited there, each with a numbered tag. These numbers are oversized and extremely visible, in all different shapes and colors. If this is indeed a baggage check, there is nothing to confirm it, nor is there anything identifying its location on the planet. Some of the suitcases are ancient and falling apart with an ashlike dust covering them. Others gleam as if they were just purchased; their design is quite modern. Arranged in orderly stacks, these suitcases are the only scenic element onstage. As there are no doors or windows, the lighting is carefully artificial, at times cold, and at other times, warm. This space is a space of its own, which no one can enter or leave.*

CHARACTER:

CASALIA BELPROP, *also called* DIVA *or* THE ACTRESS. *A woman of an uncertain middle age. Exotic. Beautiful, extravagant.*

ONE ACT

At first, an absolutely unreal light that allows the audience to gradually distinguish the suitcases, to intuit them en masse, to become aware of a world that's been packed up, along with its shadows. CASALIA BELPROP, tall and elegant (even taller in high heels), is dressed in a stylish silver-grey raincoat with matching gloves and a shiny umbrella. She wanders around looking for her luggage with claim ticket number 46 in hand. She's trying to find the suitcases she checked in, with no success. Her search intensifies. The light slowly increases.

CASALIA: *(She seems agitated. To calm herself, she repeatedly checks the number of her ticket against the numbers hanging from the suitcases. She does this over and over, at an ever-increasing speed.)* 3 . . . 15 . . . 794 . . . 1011 . . . 50826. How can I keep track? Where does it start? Who am I counting for? Does it count? This is too much! *(She kicks a suitcase in anger. It's like a stone. Her foot bounces back. She lets out a scream and grabs her ankle. Howling with pain, she hops on one foot.)* I could have broken my foot. Casalia, you're so stupid, so impulsive . . . I hurt my fibula, or is it my tibia? *(She sits on an enormous trunk and takes off her shoe to check the damage.)* My heel is burning, that kick . . . my knee was hurt on the rebound. What's inside these suitcases? I've got to pull myself together. That's all. I'd better keep moving. Up, down, forward, backward. *(She stands up, limping.)* Oww. I need a doctor, someone who can help me. *(She looks around, hopping on one foot.)* Apparently, they're not interested in giving me the attention I deserve. This won't do. I'm a fairly well-known person. My name is in the newspapers every week. I can talk and I'll tell all. Don't fool around with me. I have connections. This will be reported. There are stories about me all the time. I have a lot of influence. If my foot is broken . . . or sprained . . . *(She pauses, then begins counting suitcases again.)* They'll have to pay for the operation. I can sue them, I'm not afraid of going to court. They're getting into big trouble with me. I'm Casalia Belprop. Does that ring a bell? I'm also called Diva . . . so now you know who you're dealing with. I've told you. I'm the one on all the covers. *(Counting)* 40 . . . 41 . . . 42 . . . 43 . . . 44 . . . 45 . . . 45 1/2 . . . 45 3/4 . . . 46! Casalia! 46. 46. *(She waves her ticket.)* Here's my number. *(She holds it out, waiting for someone to take it. Impatient. In a shrill voice)* What's wrong? Are you on strike? Who's in charge of this rotten checkroom? Tell me—who's the boss here? *(She looks conspicuously at her watch.)* These are business hours. *(To herself)* People have been waiting a long time for me. I can't let them down because of this. I'm never late to an important appointment. *(Once again, in a loud voice)* Hey. Come on. I need my luggage! Now! *(She writes something in a small notebook.)* There must be a written record. I have number 46. That's clear. And here are suitcases with number

Efectos personales, Diana Raznovich, Argentina, 1975. Translated from Spanish by Margaret Carson.

46. Of course mine were green. Or were they mauve? Have I lost my sense of color? Is this induced color blindness? What did they give me to drink? My vision is blurry. What color were my suitcases? Let's start at the beginning. I've always been absent-minded, from the start. What suitcases did I check in? The other ones? *(She sits on a luggage cart.)* When you go on a long trip without knowing whether you'll return, you take along so much ridiculous stuff. The things you really need you leave behind. You can't make up your mind. They can tear apart a home with one hand and erase a history with the other, put panic in your heart, such silly things, so uninteresting. The doorbell rings. Ding-dong. Every minute is a minute of life. *(She laughs.)* Well, from the way I'm dressed, I must have taken the white ones. It's natural. Or at least it makes sense. Forty-six matches 46. And I have number 46. I'm sure I checked my white suitcases, but I don't see them. And don't ask me why I don't see them. *(She puts on her glasses.)* Now I see less than before. *(She takes out a pair of high-powered binoculars.)* I have my ways of seeing and not seeing. But there are a lot of us here. More than we seem. Countless people affected by this political mess. And each of us, each one of us, thinks we're alone. *(Looks for someone who will assume responsibility)* Where's the Manager? *(With an expression of disgust, to herself)* I haven't changed my clothes in such a long time. *(Clapping her hands as she walks, she pulls a handkerchief from her pocket and waves it to attract attention. As she walks around, she steps on the suitcases, fairly out of her wits.)* They don't have the right to keep travelers in suspense, not knowing whether we've arrived or whether we're still in transit. *(To herself)* At least if I knew, I could adopt another stance. Someone who's about to meet a lover. Or the classic farewell scene. *(She puts the handkerchief away. She starts to check her ticket obsessively against the suitcases tagged with number 46. Somewhat anxiously, she asks:)* Is this a national holiday? Is the staff on break? Maybe it's Independence Day? *(Nervous, as though she were at fault)* If that's true, they should have told me in advance. I would have worn my plaid outfit and pinned a big ribbon on my chest in the colors of the country in question. That way, at least I would have known what country they'd sent me to. What's more: I'd enthusiastically wave the flag of that country. What's the big deal if I show some solidarity with the country I hope will take me into its bosom? *(She moves a whole stack of suitcases from right to left. Behind this stack is a kind of tricycle with a little motor and a set of metallic suitcases. It's a broken-down, dilapidated vehicle that no longer has any use. She tries the ignition. The motor doesn't start, but it makes strange noises. She gets behind the steering wheel and goes around while the vehicle sputters, then stops dead.)* It's out of gasoline, of course! *(She checks the silent motor and gets grease all over her.)* This is a junkyard. Useless vehicles. Unidentified people. Motors on their deathbed. Absent supervisors. Take notes. Keep taking notes. No doubt they changed the contents, the circumstances, during the long, hard journey. I can't remember but I'm almost sure my suitcases were red crocodile. I recognize their shape, their size, and even the pleasure I felt when I stroked them. *(She goes underneath the absurd vehicle to search.)* Crocodile is such a distinctive lizard. I got mine just hatched, right out of the egg. The mother lay forty-six little eggs. Mine was destined to become a suitcase and it will always accompany me under that guise. Maybe I'm not telling the whole truth. Maybe I've never known a thing about crocodiles. That's how it is. Maybe no one is aware. Not even me. When you've lost your trust, it's better not to leave behind any traces. Maybe we're not a family with crocodile luggage. It's far from certain. It's only probable. *(She emerges from under the vehicle, very dirty, with two cardboard suitcases that were underneath.)* These are painted cardboard, but they're number 46. Now you can see. *(She puts the cardboard suitcases down to the side.)* Now things are clearer. It was an "intentional accident." They replaced crocodile with painted cardboard. As long as I can follow the thread of this discussion, they won't defeat me. It's not about thinking, it's about being reasonable. *(CASALIA stands on the top of the car with suitcases. She screams at the top of her lungs.)* Is this how this country receives Casalia Belprop? My admirers call me Diva. Where are my hosts? *(She poses in various positions with the suitcases as if she were at a photo shoot.)* Did they forget that they promised to take pictures? *(She takes out some cream and cleans herself as best she can, then combs her hair with objects she removes from a pocketbook she's found. She turns on a hair dryer. She changes her hairstyle with gel, applies makeup, and puts on a pair of outlandish sunglasses. She sprays perfume on herself and then sprays the entire space. She walks like a runway model.)* What world do we live in, darling? How organized can we expect others to be if there's not even a decent baggage check? Hmm? *(Long pause)* If they put me in jail because I've taken someone else's personal belongings, who will be the judge and who will be the accused? That's too many questions at once. Let's proceed. Let's investigate. Let's see what goes and what doesn't go. *(Since there's no response, she pulls out some suitcases and decides to open them. She tries different keys until she opens a very flamboyant suitcase with the number 46.)* I'm opening this suitcase, Mr. Manager, just because it has number 46. *(When the suitcase opens a great quantity of human bones falls out. She recognizes the bones and lets out a scream.)* Pedro. Catalina. Francis. Isabel. Alex.

Guillermo. *(She goes through the bones, turning them over, extremely moved.)* My dear Herminia. That idiot Humberto. *(Each person she names corresponds to a bone.)* Rita's jawbone! Grandma Gertrude's coccyx! *(She's visibly moved.)* Victor's infamous tarsus! *(Crying)* Victor, what a beautiful tarsus! Oh, what times we had at the border! Our love, our hope, our sorrow hasn't died. Fallen angel with wings of moonlight. So incredibly young, so irreverent. I didn't know how to say it at the time, Victor, but I waited for you like a little girl behind a wall that was suddenly washed away by the rain . . . Victor, you'll never be alone again. Your familiar and unmistakable tarsus makes me understand what my voice is saying. *(With Victor's tarsus and another bone she talks to an imaginary Police Commissioner.)* I guarantee, Mr. Commissioner, I'm not going to move all these bones from the other side of the planet! The numbers match, but I assure you that claiming Sonia's palatal is quite different from holding hands with her and running on the endless beaches of Santa Teresita. This is your claim ticket, Diva, be very careful. The proof is incontrovertible. Victor's tarsus. You weren't expecting this ingenious move. It was carried out to perfection. No doubt a powerful organization is backing them. You checked people in and you got bony substances back. *(She's somewhat lost on the stage. She kicks suitcases and they fall over. With a small bone in her hand, Casalia addresses an invisible Manager.)* Look, Mr. Checkroom Manager, this isn't the coccyx, this isn't the coccyx, this isn't the coccyx of my darling Horacio. I would know, because when we last met he was extremely thin. *(She picks up a skull.)* Ivan. Ivan. Exposed to all the elements. Betting on the needs of others. Your desperate messages. Laughing, Ivan, laughing to erase the traces in the mirror. And today you're waiting in this prank of destiny. Ivan, when I see you I can't help but think of the madness of Hamlet. *(She looks at the skull as she talks, evoking Hamlet.)*

"And therefore as a stranger give it welcome,
There are more things in heaven and earth, Horatio,
Than are dreamt of in your philosophy."

I may be playing the fool, but I'm perfectly sane, and my madness is a ruse to defend myself . . . *(She carefully puts the skull away and hides the suitcase. The atmosphere becomes suddenly intimate. She takes her raincoat off and places it ceremoniously on a suitcase. She's wearing an identical raincoat underneath. She fishes around in its pockets and takes out a piece of colored paper. Amused)* Forty-six, Casalia. You're in luck!! *(She takes off this raincoat as well. There's another one underneath. She rummages around in its pockets.)* Everything shows that circumstances are pointing in your favor. Forty-six once again, but in blue. The other was yellow! *(She jumps for joy. Her excitement is exaggerated.)* I have forty-sixes in such cute colors! Who wants them? *(She laughs.)* Whoever gave them to me is a real comedian. He deserves a promotion. Congratulations. *(Pauses. Defiantly)* I thought that Europe was better organized. Who's in charge of the Old World? *(Defiantly)* A continent that keeps the *Mona Lisa* in a tiny gallery, that doesn't have uniformed guards at its front door? What if I'd come to steal the *Mona Lisa*? Answer me! And what if I'd stolen it? *(She becomes decisive. With great energy, she pulls out a trunk and places it in the middle of the stage. The rest of the stage becomes dark. A bright light illuminates the trunk. Without a key and like a magician who pulls a rabbit out of a hat, CASALIA opens the trunk. Leonardo da Vinci's Mona Lisa is inside. No one should doubt that it's the original.)* That's what happened. I stole the *Mona Lisa*. I carried off the famous Neapolitan lady, the wife of Zenobio del Giocondo. You tell me, Mr. Commissioner, how could I have pulled off this spectacular theft while the entire world looked on? How could I have taken her from the Louvre in broad daylight and crossed Paris carrying the most famous painting in the world, without anyone stopping to ask: "What are you doing with the *Mona Lisa*? Where are you taking her?" Well, Mr. Commissioner, I was so conspicuous that everyone thought it was a silly joke. I'm very sorry. Now the joke is hanging in the Louvre and the real *Mona Lisa* is with me. I always wanted to have the *Mona Lisa* in my home. *(Amused)* It goes well with my best furniture. *(Shouts)* The person in charge still hasn't appeared. Will no one confront this suspicious woman who's making a confession? Are there any lawyers around? *(She waves the Mona Lisa like a flag. She displays it ostentatiously to the audience. Shouting)* Europe: Pay attention! What will be left on this continent if you let me run off with the *Mona Lisa*? All Europe rests in this painting. At night they sleep in peace because the wife of Zenobio del Giocondo guarantees them an enduring past, and lets them step confidently into the future. *(She smiles like the Mona Lisa.)* That enigmatic smile, so thoroughly studied, protects Europe from an incurable depression. *(Very defiantly)* And now, what will you do without her? I say that out of guilt, a moral condition that undermines my impeccable crime. I'll bring it to the attention of the Queen of England, but she'll say, "At last, the French have lost a battle!" Then I'll address the King of Spain, "Your Majesty, I've left Europe without its *Mona Lisa*." "My dear, the French left Spain out of Europe for years and now that we're back, why should we care what happens to the *Mona Lisa*? If you'd stolen *Las Meninas,* there'd be an uproar, since Velázquez's light can only be compared to the divine. Anyway, the *Mona Lisa* was painted in Italy: go speak to the Pope." *(CASALIA claps her hands energetically.)* Europe: is the fake *Mona Lisa* the same to you as the precious original I stole? Europe is silent. The U.S. takes control. *(Suddenly alarmed)* Could it be I'm in South America? Where is South America? Could I be smuggling the *Mona Lisa* into Paraguay? Maybe this is Brazil. Did you bring your Carnival costume? Do they still celebrate Carnival on these white beaches? And what if I'm in Argentina? *(Very worried)* Mr. Manager of this continent or of this country . . . or, more modestly, Mr. Manager of this checkroom: I need my things. Personal belongings. *(Pauses)* If I've arrived in South America. If I've arrived in Argentina, or if I'm being thrown out of Argentina, I must have done something. Maybe there's a new dictator and he's writing his inaugural speech before assuming the Presidency. A coup d'é-tat! They get rid of the thinking class, Casalia. *(Pauses)* I told them I was an influential person. I'm famous all over. *(Pauses)* Make a complaint? What kind of complaint can I make? Make a claim? What's there to claim? I have a ticket but my things haven't turned up! *(She walks in between the suitcases. Grandiloquent)* What's the point of stealing the *Mona Lisa* if my house has been occupied by the Army? And Victor's famous tarsus, won't it be used as evidence against me? If this so-called country were in a so-called war and tomorrow we had a President who could have you killed by firing squad or, more likely, already had you killed, what difference would it make if you found your documents, my dear? *(She takes off two identical grey raincoats, not before digging through their pockets and turning them inside out in search of her documents. In each raincoat she finds number 46 in a variety of colors. She's left wearing a raincoat identical to the ones she took off.)* How tiresome. Orders and counterorders. Keep your head up. Sing the triumphant songs they taught us in school. *(Worried)* What triumph? Who triumphed? By what means did they triumph? The Director who will lead the Homeland to victory hasn't even appeared. To arrive in Argentina on the day of the coup d'état, unable to prove who I am! *(She takes an enormous umbrella out of a suitcase. It's dripping wet.)* And everything is incriminating. My umbrella is wet. *(She opens it and there's a shower of water.)* The water proves that I've been somewhere else. A rainy place. With threatening clouds. I had to leave in a hurry. They got me out in time. *(Disoriented, but in a great rush, she searches among the suitcases and kicks them. She crawls on all fours over several of them. She rearranges others. She picks up a heavy suitcase but can't hold onto it. She lets it go. It falls on her and she's crushed underneath. Only her hands and her feet can be seen, wriggling as if she were an animal caught in a trap.)* General: Tell them to take this weight off me. I don't know anything, I assure you. I'm going to count to ten and I want them to get this suitcase off me. One, two, three, four. *(Threatens)* Or else I'll contact the International Press. Every country will ask about me. Every human being on the planet will clamor for Casalia Belprop . . . five, six, seven, eight, nine, ten, eleven, twelve, thirteen fourteen, fifteen, sixteen. I'm a bird calling through the fog to a deaf man who's buried in the dark. *(She makes an enormous effort. The suitcase is extremely heavy. Finally she manages to lift it and free herself.)* I won the first battle. But this could have been just a pretext. Don't forget about the future. Don't lose your sense of wonder. As long as you have that, you'll never get old. *(She picks up a small suitcase.)* This troublesome suitcase contains a little June cloud and a little September cloud. I'm sure of it. *(She opens it. At the same time, smoke begins to billow out of the suitcase that crushed her. The smoke spreads throughout the space.)* When the clouds collide, it will rain. And that rain will have the same chemical composition as the water that keeps falling from my umbrella. I'm totally implicated. *(The smoke covers her.)* Okay: it's time they told me where this place is. What seas surround it? What animals start prowling at bedtime? What plants undulate in the golden forest? *(She falls on her knees with the open umbrella.)* Will my butterflies survive? Is Pedro's white cat breathing? Are the palm trees growing in my greenhouse? Is there still a street where there's dancing? Is someone falling hopelessly in love and singing in a state of grace throughout the immense night? *(Pauses)* When the clouds collide the Great Flood will come. Everything implicates me. Even if I had a garden full of suitcases that were safe. *(She closes the suitcase which is still spreading smoke.)* They're even suspicious of water. It's polluted. We drink invisible radioactivity. *(She lets go of the smoking suitcase.)* Everything indicates that they're deliberately not revealing where I am. *(She finds a whistle in her pocket. She blows on it.)* What if I were in China? It would be a big event if I were in China. My name is Casalia Belprop, but friends call me Diva. Diva, what a problem! Unrestrained individualism. Addicted to Marlboros. Drinks plenty of Coca-Cola. And then, to top it off, my sophisticated clothes. I'm a fashion victim. But it's common knowledge that everything I say is a lie. I'll change my name! How do you say "red" in Chinese? Communists are crazy about that color. And bulls. *(With great effort, she manages to open a suitcase full of grey raincoats, all identical to the ones she's been wearing. She throws them gleefully into the air.)* God is on my side. God is everywhere. God. Can God be spoken about in this Paradise? My individualism is over. My name is no longer Diva. I use the same name as everyone. The same name? What name? I don't want to be noticed. I want to think the same as everyone.

Do the same things. *(Discouraged)* Oh, what a disaster. I'll always call attention to myself. They'll always be aware I exist. It will always rain. They'll always suspect me. *(She finds a suitcase full of sardine cans.)* But they won't let me die of hunger. *(She tries to open a can.)* I'm hungry. What time is it? Day or night? Before or after? *(Walks impatiently with the can in her hand. Throws it at the suitcases. It explodes like a hand grenade. She's frightened. She covers her ears. She protects herself by using her pocketbook as a shield.)* I want to make a complaint. I'm involved in an international scandal. Bomb smuggling. A pile of bones. *(Pauses. She throws more cans, which explode. Finally she chooses a suitcase that seems designed to contain her. She opens it. She sees if she fits. She places herself inside and closes it. The lights fade and only the suitcase in which she's enclosed herself remains lit. Her voice can be heard.)* If only they would tell me whether I'm on my way or whether I've arrived yet. If only they would tell me whether this is the beginning or the end. If only they would tell me something. *(Silence. She is one more suitcase.)*

LIGHTS OUT

U.S. involvement
always in support/ facilitating
the overthrow

Salvador Yende — overthrown
Socialist leader in Chile
1970s.
U.S. Funded coup
- Ideology
- business ventures

Civilians murdered / disappeared

CHILE

Isabel Banished in Isabel
(Juan Radrigán)

Valerie Cihylik (*left*) and Berioska Ipinza sharing the title role in *Isabel Banished in Isabel,* directed by Martín Balmaceda, LaMicro Theater, New York, 2003. (Photo courtesy of LaMicro Theater.)

"He said that people are born when they meet, that the rest don't matter at all."

This is one of the many memories that the protagonist of Juan Radrigán's play *Isabel Banished in Isabel* (*Isabel desterrada en Isabel*) has of her partner who disappeared, dragged away by the cops for the crime of killing birds. Now that he's gone, she wanders the barren streets on the edge of town and rarely meets anyone—when she speaks to passersby, they don't respond. Her need for dialogue is so pressing that she turns an old oil drum into an interlocutor. But she's not truly crazy; on the contrary, she's all too aware that her personal drama is nothing but a lonely monologue. Although her final words are directed toward the unresponsive drum, they are meant for those sitting in the audience: "Please, talk to me, talk to me, talk to me . . ."

Isabel's sense of isolation is partly existential in nature. But it is also a historical condition, a reflection of Chilean society under the dictatorship of Augusto Pinochet. After September 11, 1973, when the military bombed the presidential palace and overthrew the democratically elected president, Salvador Allende, Chile became a testing ground for neoliberal policies designed by economists at the University of Chicago. Industries that had been nationalized or collectivized under Allende's Popular Unity government were opened up to foreign investment, the social security system was privatized, and workers were stripped of bargaining rights. Although the restructuring was lauded as progress by those who benefited, it led to skyrocketing unemployment and a poverty rate that had nearly doubled by the end of Pinochet's seventeen years in power. The *poblaciones callampas* (shantytowns) on the outskirts of Santiago and other major cities mushroomed as the income gap between Chile's haves and have-nots grew to become one of the widest in Latin America.[1] In its drive to eradicate obstacles to the economic reorganization, the government tortured more than twenty-eight thousand "subversives" (students, union activists, even petty thieves), while thousands more were disappeared, their bodies buried in unmarked graves or thrown into the sea.[2]

After the coup, many actors, directors, and playwrights went into exile, and those who stayed worked under the threat of blacklists and imprisonment. University theaters that had fostered the development of internationally renowned playwrights such as Isidora Aguirre and Egon Wolff in the 1950s

271

and 1960s were either shut down or reorganized in accordance with the new conservative ideology. Yet by 1977 there was a resurgence of theater collectives and several new playwrights had begun to emerge. Surprisingly, in the midst of a repressive environment, the theater became a space of relative freedom. Whereas the press and other mass media venues were strictly censored, independent theater groups managed to stage plays that were overtly critical of the devastation wrought by the government's "reforms."[3] In her study of Chilean theater under the Pinochet regime, Catherine Boyle suggests several reasons for this show of leniency: first, the number of theatergoers was so small that opposition in this sphere was considered a containable threat; second, the regime needed to be able to point to some evidence of artistic freedom to refute its critics; and, third, repression was deemed counterproductive because independent theater was the province of the politically important urban middle class.[4]

Juan Radrigán, one of Chile's most highly renowned playwrights, is unusual among his peers in that he comes from a working-class background. Born in 1937 in the far northern town of Antofagasta, he worked for many years in a textile factory and did not begin writing drama until several years after the coup. In early works such as *Hechos consumados* (When All Is Said and Done, 1981) and *El toro por las astas* (The Bull by the Horns, 1982), he brought society's most marginalized figures to center stage and dramatized the spiritual and material costs of Pinochet's so-called economic miracle.[5] His characters include prostitutes, unemployed factory workers, people who get by doing odd jobs, and others who don't manage to get by. These are not the working-class heroes of many dramas of the 1960s, when there were more reasons to be optimistic that their battles were about to be won. In Radrigán's plays, people have been pushed so far beyond the pale where power resides that they are unable to envision a political solution and can only express a profound sense of anguish and defeat.

Radrigán is not unique in his concern with society's outcasts; indeed, many have pointed to marginality as the defining paradigm of Chilean theater from the late 1970s through the 1980s. Yet his plays are distinct from other notable dramas of the time period such as Sergio Vodanovic and ICTUS's *La mar estaba serena* (The Sea Was Calm, 1981) or *Tres Marías y una Rosa* (Three Marías and a Rose, 1979), developed by David Benavente in conjunction with the Taller de Investigación Teatral. For one, he does not subscribe to the collective approach to writing. Although he worked closely with members of the Teatro Popular el Telón, the group he helped found in 1981, he stated that he disliked collaborative works because they are "aimed at being the story of everyone and in the end they are nobody's story."[6] This insistence on the importance of the individual subject can be read as an implicit critique of populist social movements that make political claims in the name of a vaguely identified "people." But it is also an attempt to counteract the dehumanizing effects of material deprivation and the government's modernization project. The characters in Radrigán's plays are dispossessed, but they have their own stories to tell.

This emphasis on the idea of *telling* rather than simply *representing* is important because it distinguishes his concern for the individual from a retreat into individualism and it links his concept of subjectivity to the social. The protagonist of *Isabel* is banished not just by poverty but also by the police state's decimation of the public sphere. When people go missing and talking can get you in trouble, you learn to keep to yourself. And if we really are born when we meet, then isolation and silence are themselves a form of social and subjective death. As Isabel asks, "What's going on with everyone? What's going on that they don't talk? . . . What's wrong with them that it seems like they're dead?" She isn't physically attractive, and her rough, colloquial language at times seems maudlin, but the audience isn't being asked to see itself in her. What she is looking for is not empathy but something much more difficult: solidarity.

This conception of theater is reflected in Radrigán's approach toward the process of production and interpretation, as well as in the diverse audiences he seeks out. The stark set design and simple costumes that characterize his works make it possible for them to be staged in circumstances not unlike the ones they portray, and the Teatro Popular el Telón got its start performing in workers' halls, shantytowns, and schools, where the playwright and cast members often stayed to discuss the show with the audience. As a result, his plays achieved a popularity that few other playwrights can claim; even before being published, photocopies of his scripts circulated throughout the country, passed from hand to hand and publicized by word of mouth. However, when *Isabel's* official debut took place in 1981, it was not in the marginalized zones of the *callampas*, but at the Teatro Bulnes, not far from the presidential palace in the very heart of Santiago.[7] Radrigán never loses sight of the distance that separates his characters from their middle-class audiences, which explains the almost antitheatrical quality of his plays—he resists the tendency to make a spectacle out of poverty and despair. The critic Hernán Vidal, writing while Pinochet was still in power, suggested that Radrigán's decision to put marginalized characters onstage before a relatively privileged audience represented "an attempt to maintain a dialogue between classes amidst social circumstances in which that is very difficult to do."[8] He saw this as evidence that theater had become a substitute for other public arenas that had been closed off, leaving different sectors of the population isolated and unable to find a common cause.

The issue of communication and the obstacles it faces were of a different nature when a small theater company called LaMicro staged *Isabel* in New York City in June 2003. It was over twenty years after the work had first been performed; Pinochet had left power in 1990, and most people in the United States knew little about Chilean society. Language was also an issue since the play is written in a Chilean dialect that can pose difficulties even for other Spanish speakers. The members of LaMicro chose to literalize the experience of inner exile evoked in the title by dividing the role of Isabel between two actresses: one who portrayed Isabel as she appears in the original play; and another who performed the roles of the people she recalls, including her younger self. Past and present were put into dialogue with one another, as were English and Spanish—while the "older" Isabel spoke in English, her alter ego delivered most of her lines in Spanish, modified so as to be comprehensible to non-Chileans.

Isabel's hemispheric journey was timely because she has plenty to tell audiences in this country about a reality that is not so distant. Although Pinochet no longer rules Chile, much of his economic and social program remains intact, and after exporting its ideology the United States is now trying to bring it all back home. George W. Bush has referred to Chile's privatized pension plan as a "great example," even though all evidence indicates that it has enriched corporations but left countless retirees in poverty.[9] Here, too, there are those who would like to redefine social security as a problem for individuals to tackle alone while using national security as a dogma to justify disappearing suspected "subversives" into jail cells under extralegal measures. *Isabel's* stage directions state that her monologue can take place "on any street of anywhere," and it is a poignant testament to what theater alone *cannot* do that now, more than twenty years after the play was written, those words ring true.

—Sarah J. Townsend

NOTES

1. In 1989, at the end of the military regime and after several years of a supposed economic boom, 44 percent of the Chilean population was at or below the poverty line. See James Petras and Fernando Ignacio Leiva, *Democracy and Poverty in Chile: The Limits to Electoral Politics* (Boulder: Westview, 1994).

2. The figure on torture victims comes from the "National Commission on Political Imprisonment and Torture Report" released on November 29, 2004. The number of people killed or disappeared is generally placed between three and four thousand.

3. This is not to say that the theater was free of constraints. Posters and other materials that contained sensitive material were not allowed, and those who distributed it were subject to arrest. There were also high taxes on revenues; Chilean productions were supposedly exempt, but Radrigán has stated that this was applied selectively and his plays were never exempted.

4. Catherine M. Boyle, *Chilean Theater, 1973–1985: Marginality, Power, Selfhood* (Rutherford, N.J.: Fairleigh Dickinson University Press, 1992). Boyle estimates that during the 1970s only 1 percent of Santiago's population attended independent theater productions on a regular basis. However, most critics suggest that this number grew substantially during the late 1970s and 1980s precisely because the theater was afforded more artistic and political freedom and became an alternative source of information for many.

5. Radrigán's works have been performed throughout Latin America, the United States, and Europe. His later plays include *La contienda humana* (1987) and *Los fantasmas borrachos* (1997). He continues to write about marginalized figures and the transformation of Chilean society under Pinochet. *Piedra de escándalo* (1990) deals with the response to AIDS victims while one of his latest plays, *Carta abierta* (2004), is about the discrimination faced by Peruvian immigrants to Chile. Translations of several of his plays were recently published in Juan Radrigán, *Finished from the Start and Other Plays*, trans. Ana Elena Puga and Mónica Nuñez-Parra (Evanston: Northwestern University Press, 2008). Radrigán's numerous awards include the National Prize awarded by the Academia de Bellas Artes de Chile in 2002.

6. Juan Radrigán, "Shanty Town Theatre," trans. John Lyons, *Index on Censorship* 14 (February 1985): 10. In this article, Radrigán is interviewed by Tito Valenzuela.

7. According to Radrigán, El Telón gave discounted tickets to people of limited economic means and drew large numbers from the shantytowns to the downtown theaters. His plays were so successful that at one point during *Isabel's* year-long run he had three other plays being performed at theaters in Santiago and Valparaíso, Chile's second-largest city.

8. Hernán Vidal, "Juan Radrigán: Los límites de la imaginación dialéctica," in Juan Radrigán, *Teatro de Juan Radrigán,* ed. María de la Luz Hurtado et al. (Minneapolis: CENECA, University of Minnesota, 1984), 40.

9. Larry Rohter, "Chile's Retirees Find Shortfall in Private Plan," *New York Times,* January 27, 2005, A1.

SELECTED REFERENCES

Boyle, Catherine M. *Chilean Theater, 1973–1985: Marginality, Power, Selfhood.* Rutherford, N.J.: Fairleigh Dickinson University Press, 1992.

Boyle, Catherine. "Text, Time, Process, and History in Contemporary Chilean Theatre." *Theatre Research International* 26 (July 2001): 181–89.

Bravo Elizondo, Pedro. "Juan Radrigán, la dictadura y su teatro." In *Resistencia y poder: Teatro en Chile,* ed. Heidrun Adler and George Woodyard, 99–111. Madrid: Iberoamericana, 2000.

Cozzi, Enzo. "Political Theatre in Present-Day Chile: A Duality of Approaches." *New Theatre Quarterly* 6 (May 1990): 119–27.

Hurtado, María de la Luz and Juan Andrés Piña. "Los niveles de la marginalidad en Radrigán." In Juan Radrigán, *Teatro de Juan Radrigán,* ed. María de la Luz Hurtado et al., 5–37. Minneapolis: CENECA, University of Minnesota, 1984.

Puga, Ana Elena. "The Missing Witness." In Juan Radrigán, *Finished from the Start and Other Plays,* trans. Ana Elena Puga and Mónica Nuñez-Parra, xxvii–lxiv. Evanston: Northwestern University Press, 2008.

Radrigán, Juan. "Shanty Town Theatre." Trans. John Lyons. *Index on Censorship* 14 (February 1985): 9–10. Interview with Tito Valenzuela.

Thomas, Eduardo. "Representación y trascendencia de lo absurdo en el teatro chileno contemporáneo." *Revista chilena de literatura* 54 (April 1999): 5–30.

Vidal, Hernán. "Juan Radrigán: Los límites de la imaginación dialéctica." In Juan Radrigán, *Teatro de Juan Radrigán,* ed. María de la Luz Hurtado et al., 39–61. Minneapolis: CENECA, University of Minnesota, 1984.

Zegers Nachbauer, María Teresa. *25 años de teatro en Chile (1970–1995).* Santiago: Ministerio de Educación, Departamento de Programas Culturales, División de Cultura, 1999.

Isabel Banished in Isabel (Juan Radrigán)

Translated by Ana Elena Puga[1]

CHARACTER: ISABEL

The action takes place on any street of anywhere. The set is limited to a garbage can, half of an oil drum. A white, sad light illuminates the scene.

(The woman (ISABEL), shabby, any age over 40, enters limping. From one of her hands hangs, half-dragging, a flour sack that constant use has turned an indefinite color. In it she keeps some of her belongings. She quickly looks around. She returns to the drum, leaves the sack on the ground, and sits on the curb.)

ISABEL: *(Taking off a shoe)* Damn, a flat, just what I needed. *(She examines it.)* Oh well, it's just a nail. *(Searching with her glance)* There ain't even a rock. Sheesh, we're messed up Isabel. *(To the can)* You got somethin you can borrow me to hammer with? I'll give it back right away. *(She stands, looks, takes out a piece of metal.)* Here it is. Thanks man, you're the only good guy I've met today. All the others take off when I get close; they take off like I had the plague. *(She shrugs.)* Well, whaddya gonna do? That's life. OK, ready Isabel, with this metal we're all set. One tiny tap in case dust comes up when we hit it, and we get down to work. *(To the can)* Yeah, ya gotta take good care of your throat: doncha know that smog makes ya hoarse? *(She sits down again, rummages in the jacket, takes out a bottle and drinks. She closes it, puts it away. She picks up the shoe and begins to bang it. Examines the result)* Know what else, Isabel?

If you keep smashing it, it's gonna break in two, better fix it right at home. *(To the can)* Yeah, I got a home. *(Pause)* But it's not like me to be cooped up; I like to be in the middle of life: see houses, people, dogs, trees, birds, all those things that let you know you're not dead, though your heart has fallen in a hole where there ain't no light. It's true, I'm alone every day, but Sunday it's like I'm twice-abandoned. Dunno why that happens to me, dunno why on days off the loneliness hurts me deeper inside. That's why I go out to walk. *(She pays attention to a passerby who is not visible. As he goes past)* Hey, gotta smoke you can give me? It's been so many days . . . *(The passerby seems to go on without stopping. ISABEL shrugs. To the*

can) What was we saying? Ah, the house. Of course, I do got one. I'm not going to tell you that it's a terrific house, no, not gonna tell you no story. It's just a good little one that Aliro and I put up at the end of Santa Rosa . . . You know, we was doin real good, but suddenly they decided to build one of them pretty buildings where the people with the big bucks live, and they came and they took all of us off to other places. They dint even give Aliro and me the time of day cuz we wasn't married at all and dint have no kids. I loved him and he loved me, but they asked us for a signed paper where it said that. *(To the audience)* Listen, I said to the man that was writing, that paper could only be signed by God. And where we gonna find him? And I started to ask. *(Gesturing)* Do you know where he's at? Do you know where he's at? Do you know where he's at? *(To the can)* Folks would shrug, they'd look away, or they'd start laughing, like I'd asked about someone who'd died a long time ago. But he hasn't died, right? Cuz if he'd died, life would have died too . . . Well, the thing was that they took em all, and they left us throwed out until the machines came to knock everything down. It's the same as living in a cemetery: that's where the pure elements live, the day, and the night, and the moon and the wind. All things that don't answer when you talk to em and I like to talk, ya know, that's why I go out . . . I've been walking since my mother died, go figure how long that's been . . . No, better not think about nothin. Cakehead was right. He always use to say to me: "Don't think Chabela, cuz thinking is the same as if they was to slash hope's throat right in front of your eyes." *(To the can)* Cakehead was a guy who always wanted to take me home with him but I never believed it, cuz the poor guy was crazy. When he didn't have enough to drink, or when he fell in love with some girl who didn't pay him no mind, he'd go and stick his head in some oven to kill him-

Isabel desterrada en Isabel, Juan Radrigán, Chile, 1981. Translated from Spanish by Ana Elena Puga. Originally published in Juan Radrigán, *Finished from the Start and Other Plays,* trans. and ed. Ana Elena Puga and Mónica Nuñez-Parra (Evanston: Northwestern University Press, 2008). Copyright © 2008 Northwestern University Press.

self: that's why they called him that . . . One time Death got fed up that she had to come for nothing, and she didn't let him shut off the gas . . . I think he should have fallen in love with life and not with people. Whadda you think? (*She bangs the can happily.*) Damn, I wish I could be with Aliro, now that I found you to talk to. Course he's a little jealous, yeah? But since you talk so little . . . Still, there's gonna be plenty of chances for him to get jealous, right? . . . We used to go all over together, he was even gonna take me to Lota one time, so's I'd get to know his family: my mother-in-law and my brothers- and sisters-in-law.[2] We couldn't go cuz the sale of bones and papers got bad and he wanted me to go real sharp. "Cuz since they ain't in love with you, they're only going to look at your clothes," he'd tell me . . . Now who knows when we'll be able to go cuz he's doin time. He's been inside a long while . . . What's he thinking? Does he remember me? He wasn't mad at all, he was laughing as he left. He stared at me and said, "Nice, the way you show you like me, good thing I didn't kill no horse." And he laughed and laughed. (*Pause*) Maybe that's why I talk so much. Loneliness sucks, huh? It's like a dog after you; it follows you wherever you go. But the hardest thing is the night. That's when the troubles suddenly hit you all at once. Memories is the worse executioners there is, cuz they scream on the inside and you can't make em shut up with nothing. I don't know why things you done before have to bother you so much. Damn, I'd be OK with it if bad things hurt, but it turns out that what bugs you the most are the good things! So, what really gets to you is the days when you was young and pretty, the time when a guy grabbed you and kissed you down at the park on Independence Day; the time when you had a mother and father and everybody talked to you: that's what makes you wanna cry when you find yourself thrown out. (*Pause*) They say that you can go crazy thinking, that you don't even notice when you start talking to yourself: that's the scariest . . . But I say: How can you go crazy just from loneliness when there are so many people all around? It can't be. That's how I stand it. Jeez, imagine if I went crazy, who'd wait for Aliro? (*Nostalgically*) Good ole Aliro . . . (*Cheered up*) One day, I'm gonna introduce him to you, ya know? He's really great . . . Do you know how I met him? I was eating this real good thing that a lady had given me, it was over by a plaza that's down by San Diego. I was bent over like this, eating, when suddenly, I hear someone singing . . . I'm going to remember it as long as I live, that song that goes: (*she sings a bit of one of those weepy boleros by Lucho Barrios or Ramón Aguilera*) Pretty, huh? It was him ya know, it was him that was singing down the middle of the plaza, drunk up to his eyeballs. When he got to where I was, he stopped and stared:

"Hey honey," he said. "Where am I?"

"Right there," I said. "Can't you see yourself?"

It was one of those cloudy and humid days, one of those days when it seems like they're crying on top of you. But when I told him that, he busted out laughing and it was like the sun had suddenly come out all over. He said he'd come the other day from Lota, and he'd hit the bottle cuz he dint even have one friend. "So when you finish lunching, I'll treat you to a *digestif*," he says to me and busted out laughing again. He didn't want to talk no more bout himself, and he didn't want me to tell him stuff about me, cuz he said that people are born when they meet, that the rest don't matter at all. And me, that had never loved nobody, and that nobody had ever loved, began to feel like I wanted to thank life for things, like I wanted to hug it . . . That's how we got to know each other and we started to . . . (*She falls silent, looks around, listens.*) Could be this guy has a smoke, the night is so long . . . (*She smooths her dress, fixes her hair, smiles. When the man, who is not seen, passes by her*) Sir, might you have a cigarette that you could give me? (*She stops, follows him a few steps with her shoe in her hand.*) It's been about a week since . . . Damn, how can he not have . . . (*She turns, discouraged.*) With that fancy getup and he's not gonna have cigarettes . . . (*She sits again. To the can*) No, I do got some, it's just that I've only got two left, and I'm so scared of the night . . . Damn, I'm just like a blind woman that can't get away from biting dogs. I'm so calm and all of a sudden I get a big bite from out of nowhere . . . In fact, this morning I got up real happy. (*To the can*) I dunno, I dunno why. (*She shrugs.*) The summer, the sky, the people in short sleeves, I don't know. The thing is I found out there was a party in a house over by San Paulo and I went to look for the leftovers. I told the housekeeper there I could help her clean and she went to ask the boss and then she told me OK. Damn, there was stuff there! Chicken, potatoes, sandwiches, everything. (*Gestures as if drinking*) And this stuff, what can I say, anything you'd want. Course I don't do none of those strange labels. I'm not gonna put you on. Aliro would. Aliro goes crazy when he sees them colored bottles. Not me, cuz I take a swig and fall flat on my face. Can't you see I'm not used to it? Rotgut is safer. Well, the thing was that the sly girl had me bustin my butt for her all morning, she even had me mop the bathrooms for her and when she was making up the bag lunch for me, in comes the old man, the boss that is, and he tells her: "No, no. These people aren't used to eating. Give her a bottle of wine and she'll appreciate it a lot more. But give her the bad one, because that's what these people drink." And he came and gave me this bottle. (*She shows it.*) That was when I felt a jerking inside cuz I remembered one time when we went with my dad to ask a neighbor to borrow us a few bucks and he said he didn't have it . . . My dad begged him, cuz hunger was making us see everything black. Then the neighbor invited us to drink a bottle of wine, and we went with him, hoping he'd borrow us some cash, but he had us drinking all afternoon and then the neighbor got mad: "Snotty bastard," he said to him. "Even after I give ya enough to get ya shit faced, you still want me to borrow you money." When we got home, my dad started to cry. (To the can) Have you seen a man cry? They don't say nothing, they don't whine, they don't yell; they stare off like into the distance, and suddenly you see the tears start running down their face, and when you catch them, they try to smile, and then it's like they was crying twice . . . I was about six, but I remember real good . . . That's why I started to cry when the old man passed me the bottle; he laughed and told the girl: "Didn't I tell you that these people will go so far as to cry with happiness when they see a bottle of wine? Don't I know them." What was I gonna say to him? I came back, got to walking . . . We was always hungry, hungry for food, for clothes, for happiness and for everything, and that hunger we had since we was born got even bigger when my mom had a fight with my daddy cuz he couldn't find work and she told him to hit the road. "And the kids?" he said. "They stay with me, I'm gonna work to feed em," she told him. (To the can) I don't know much, but if one person forgets another all of a sudden, it's cuz they've got something new in their heart, right? Why does your mom stay with you always? I got to know hopelessness looking at my daddy's eyes, looking at his eyes you got to a dark courtyard, a courtyard where everything was dead; my mother had sorrow in her face, but my father had sorrow in his heart, he had sorrow there where it don't come out no more, where the stain stays forever . . . Why does your mother stay with you your whole life? (Takes out the bottle) That's when things got worse for us, cuz after all he'd get some job here or there, but my mom hardly ever got work. (Pause) Hunger, my friend, is long and black, like a hole that you never stop falling into. But you don't fall down the middle, free like this, no, you fall hitting yourself against the sides, tearing off bigger and bigger pieces of yourself. That's life for us, to fall and hit yourself inside and out, but especially inside. In the afternoon I went to look for banged-up fruit at the market; at about six the garbage trucks arrive, and then they begin to take the cans from the stalls. Before, that was a real good scoop, but now lots of people get there and they crowd in behind the dump trucks. Old people, young people, children, everybody, even pregnant women and women with babies come to feed . . . They get like wild animals: they scream,

they shove, they fight; and since they all get in up to their elbows looking for the least rotten, right away the fruit gets crushed, it ends up a mush the color of earth, and they start eating it right there or they put it in a nylon bag to divvy up at home . . . I couldn't grab nothing. Actually, I had caught an apple, caught it in the air, just as it was falling from the can into the truck. But this kid turns up, about eight years old, she hadn't been able to get into the dump truck and she started to look at me: she was long and skinny, her bones stuck out all over the place . . . But the worst thing was the eyes she had, the eyes of an animal that's been run over, the eyes of a sick kid. She just stared at me; didn't say nothing to me. And what did she need to talk for, cuz her eyes was screaming everything that was happening to her . . . When I gave her the apple, she took it with both hands, and she bit it so eager that I got to wanting to cry . . . She didn't even realize she was eating the rotten part, that soft part, coffee colored, that turns to mud inside your mouth; I knew she was gonna start to throw up, so I left . . . Poor kid. How much longer will she last? (Pause) Damn, if I was God's wife, I'd say: "Listen up, Old Man, you're so into the miracle thing, open the eyes of the dopes down there. They're making a mess of the life you gave them. They dished out the laughter and bucks to a few, and to the others they gave silence and kicks in the ass. I know you don't want to get involved in nothing, that you want them to learn on their own, but they don't learn man, and you can't just stand there with your hands in your pockets. How do you expect them to warm up to you when they eat in garbage dumps and sleep thrown out on the streets? That's a lot to ask, ya know. And it's also a lot to ask the other ones to remember you because they're very busy having fun and dining out, it's a serious problem man: if you don't send a little miracle soon we're going to end up more alone than loneliness; and what's more, they killed the son. Wake up, wake up old man, we're dying down there." (She laughs.) The Wife of God, the things that pop into your head when you don't have no one to talk to . . . (She takes out the bottle, drinks, sad . . .) Yeah, well, the only one who talked to me was Aliro; but now he's in prison . . . Want me to tell you the truth? I put him in prison; I didn't know that without him this was gonna happen to me . . . Know why I put him in prison? Cuz he squeezed the birds. See, we sold birds. When they stopped buying bones and papers at San Camilo's, Aliro got the idea of selling birds, it went good for us. See, it didn't cost us nothing, ya know? But I hadn't never got it that when he handed em to the people, he'd give em a little squeeze. Then they'd die in two or three weeks, they'd be dying little by little. He'd say that that's how the business had to be so's the sales wouldn't stop; but I couldn't stand that, it made me very sad, cuz it's like killing children. Now no one talks, no one laughs, no one says hello; the birds are the only ones that sing. If they're quiet, all of life will be quiet, and us that don't have nothin, we's gonna die crushed by the silence . . . I begged him, I cried, but there was no way: "That's how life is, Isabel," he said to me. "If we don't kill the birds, you're going to die of hunger. I do it so you don't die." He said a lot of things, but I couldn't stand it, and I went and turned him in. Fair is fair . . . What else could I do? How much time do they give you for killing birds? He must have been in there more than a year by now and I haven't been able to see him, cuz first they took him one place, then another. I've asked, but no one knows. *(To the audience)* Where could he be? Where could he be? Where could he be? *(Discouraged)* No one knows where God is or where the people are . . . *(To the can)* What's going on with everyone? What's going on that they don't talk? What's wrong with them that they don't kiss, that they don't laugh? What's wrong with them that it seems like they're dead? *(As if someone were going by)* Hey, listen, don't you have a . . . *(Discouraged)* Damn, I missed him cuz I was talking. *(She looks all around.)* Wonder what time is it? Must be real late . . . But there's no one in the room, what's the point of going? Where I live, there's not much traffic, so you don't even get to hear the hustle of the buses. Shit, it's a crime what they're doing with me; they're killing me, and I ain't done nothin to nobody, just be poor, go round like this. But that's not a crime, ain't no reason to leave me alone, no reason not to talk to me . . . *(She picks up the bottle, drinks. She rummages through the jacket, takes out a pack of Liberty, shows it to the can.)* Can't you see, I got some. But it's just two and the night don't never end when you live missing someone, cuz it's not just him that's gone. See, with Aliro we'd have tea, we'd make a tomato salad, and we'd get to chatting: that disappeared too. When he was drunk, he'd sing, he'd laugh at everything and chase me round the room . . . And he was so funny when he talked; see, I'm the queen of shut-eye, so every night I'd bundle up good and cuddle up by his side and tell God, "Dear God, make it so that the night will last forever, so that it don't never end." And then he'd come and tell me, "Get with it, girl, one day he's gonna pay attention to you and it's gonna be your fault that we kick the bucket." He always talked to me like that, with some smart remark . . . But there ain't nothin like that nowhere now; there ain't nothin but silence, nothin but darkness. No, I can't be in the bedroom: what with all his eyes saw, all his hands touched, it throws me into sadness. Sometimes I look at a chair and I feel like I've been stabbed from head to toe: that's why I go out. *(She drinks.)* But that don't

get me nothin neither cuz when its daytime and there's lots of people in the street nobody even looks at me cuz they're scared I might ask em for somethin. What can I do then? I'm not gonna start talkin to myself cuz that's what scares me, goin crazy . . . Damn, if Aliro don't get out soon, my daddy could at least turn up around here. *(To the can)* Don't laugh. You think cuz I'm old I've never had a father? I remember when I was little and I went out with him, he always used to say to me: "If you ever get lost, just sit and wait for me right there. Don't get to walking round, cuz that's worse. You sit and wait for me." I don't know where I lost him, don't remember; but sometimes when I go out to walk, I sit an hour or two out there in case he comes to look for me . . . But he hasn't never turned up. And how's he gonna turn up, since he's lost too . . . *(To the can, after a pause)* Are you tired of talking to me? Well don't get tired. Can't you see that I don't wanna go yet? After all, there's a nice breeze here and we're comfy. Ain't it true that we're comfy? Sure, see, we're fine; it's not like you're just OK when you've got bucks, no: you're fine when you've got somebody to listen, to pay attention, just like you. Cuz if you're not gonna talk to nobody, you're better off dead, see; no point in goin through the motions. *(Thoughtful)* But people are real strange, huh? Like yesterday I was sittin in a park, fixin this piece of crap *(showing the shoe)*. When some guy comes and sits next to me. Made me happy, ya know. "Now you're gonna talk and talk, Isabel," I tole myself. But I didn't even look at the guy, cuz you can't be so bold neither. Don't you know that right away they think something else? And just cuz you're poor it's not like you don't have no dignity, ya know. So I kept fixin the shoe like nothin was goin on. And suddenly I hear him talk. But since he talked on this side *(gestures to her left)* and I'm kinda deaf in that ear, I didn't understand nothin. Then I turns around and I says with all due respect: "Excuse me sir, but I didn't understand nothing you said to me." The guy kept blabbering without paying me no mind, so I told him again to forgive me, but that I couldn't hear nothin on that side cuz once I'd been smacked there with a bat in a fuss we had with some neighbors who wanted to hit Aliro over there in a bar in San Rafael. Listen, and when I finished explaining the matter good, the guy turns round to me madder than if I had cussed him out, he looked at me with these crazy-man eyes and said to me, "So get it through your head, busybody bitch, I'm not talkin to you, I'm talking to myself!" And he got up and he went off swearing at me. *(To the can)* What do you make of that? *(Wondering)* By himself. Talking to himself . . . Damn, that's gotta be sad. Don't I tell you that people is goin crazy little by little? Listen, the worst is that nobody gets it, like in everything, when it's too late we are just going to stare *(she looks at the audience)* and we're gonna say: "How could we let this happen? How could we let it happen?" *(She is quiet. She keeps thinking. She turns her head slowly toward the can and looks at it fixedly.)* Listen, well, damn, I've been talking to myself for a while now, ya know. So ain't you my friend? Didn't you lend me a piece of metal? Didn't you listen to me for about an hour? *(Aggressive)* Or you think you're hot shit too? *(She hits the can.)* Talk then. Ain't I a person? *(Anguished)* Ain't I a person? *(She shakes the can.)* Talk, talk, talk! *(Weepy)* There ain't nobody in the room. There ain't nobody nowhere . . . *(ISABEL shakes the can desperately.)* Please, talk to me, talk to me, talk to me . . .

NOTES

All notes to this play are by the translator.

1. I would like to acknowledge the assistance of Mónica Núñez-Parra in deciphering Chilean slang. Without her help the translation would not have been possible.

2. Lota is a mining town in southern Chile.

BRAZIL

Denise Stoklos in Mary Stuart
(Denise Stoklos)

Denise Stoklos in *Denise Stoklos in Mary Stuart,* Hemispheric Institute of Performance and Politics Encuentro in Lima, Peru, 2002. (Photo by Dawn Peterson.)

Denise Stoklos, one of Latin America's most brilliant solo performers, started writing and acting as a child in the southern state of Paraná, Brazil and became a professional artist in 1968, four years after the military coup of 1964. After working with several theater companies and collectives in Rio de Janeiro and São Paulo, she left for England in the late 1970s to escape the tyranny of Brazil's military dictatorship. Abroad she trained in mime, solo performance, and other corporeal techniques with various European and U.S. based performance practitioners and composed her first solo piece. Abroad, too, she developed her theory of "essential theater," which strips the stage of everything except the body of the actor—a practice that, as she describes it, involves minimum gestures producing maximum dramatic possibilities: "I want the stage naked . . . I want no decoration . . . I want it dry . . . Throw away the brooch. Put the chest onstage."[1]

As a performer, author, theorist, and producer, Stoklos began her work alone in voluntary exile, writing her own material, and producing her own shows. A solo artist on an empty stage, her expressive body communicated different spaces and registers of possibility. In several ways, then, she is the quintessential "solo" performer. In other important ways, however, the solo signals not political isolation or a retreat into aestheticism but a firm commitment to civil disobedience (the title of one of her works) in the tradition of Thoreau. "The only obligation which I have the right to assume," Stoklos says in that work, quoting from Thoreau's *Civil Disobedience,* "is to do at any time what I think is right."[2] For Thoreau, as for Stoklos, politics is a solo act. What makes Stoklos's trajectory as a Latin American artist so unusual is that she created politically committed and progressive solo work starting in the 1970s, an age characterized by progressive collective work such as Enrique Buenaventura's collaborations with TEC and Grupo Cultural Yuyachkani, both of which are also represented in this volume.

Stoklos has created and performed work all over the world, seeking always to find verbal and corporeal expression that can carry meaning across different linguistic and cultural borders. She found that English offered her a "lightness" that freed her from the "vision and vicinity of torture and dictatorship" of the Brazilian military regime. "The expression of 'feeling in Portuguese' and 'communicating in English' reveals the denial of the emotional flow that occurs spontaneously when one uses one's native language. I perceived that this divergence dramatized the encounter between signs . . . between the sound and the meaning of the word." This insight became part of her signature as an artist, brilliantly displayed in *Denise Stoklos in Mary Stuart* when she starts speaking in Portuguese only to interrupt herself: "I am sorry. I should be trying to speak in English. . . . Communication problem. Problem. Communication. No problem. I'll start the whole thing over again." On a superficial level, her appreciation of the liberating possibilities of working in a foreign language— unthinkable for many performers—enables her to perform her works not only in Portuguese and English but also in Spanish, French, Ukrainian, Russian, and German. On a deeper level, however, this gap between sound and meaning allows her to radically (and often humorously) separate sound from meaning. The multiple sounds she can generate for a single word often crash up against its meaning. She growls, whispers, declaims, and sputters out syllables, sometimes in sounds that are recognizable as words, sometimes as effects of far more visceral forms of expression that signal that communication is, in fact, a profound problem—far deeper than a mere linguistic divide.

The power and originality of Stoklos's work lie in the humor and intensity with which she transforms the most disparate artistic and political traditions into a forceful and highly personal performance project. In her forty years as an artist, she has explored the bizarre mix of Brazilian militarism and postmodern alienation (*Casa*, 1990),[3] responded to the ongoing effects of colonialism (*500 years—a Fax from Denise Stoklos to Christopher Columbus*, 1992), reflected on the torturous abuse of power and its effects on women as political leaders and as mothers (*Denise Stoklos in Mary Stuart* and *Des-Medéia*, 1995), and examined the political options that citizens face at the end of the twentieth century (*Civil Disobedience*, 1998). *Calendar of Stone* (2001), inspired by Gertrude Stein, turns unremarkable acts of everyday life such as buying the newspaper or taking a nap into a riveting performance. In each of these solo works the performer draws from the repertoire of artistic traditions—mime, vaudeville, Brechtian epic theater, juggling—to convey a message that is uncompromisingly her own. For example, Stoklos always includes a short mime sequence to cite the training she received even as she rejects its political neutrality. Mime, then, furthers her own project, which is politically positioned and committed. Denise Stoklos's address to Columbus, as the title indicates, is absolutely personal, direct, and contemporary. She explores the role of the artist, the intellectual, the theater, and the audience in the tragic history of her country. "Read it," she says, "it's all in the books." Later, once the audience fully comprehends the magnitude of her critique, she has the house lights turned up: "The doors of the theater are open for those who want to abandon this ship in flames."[4]

Denise Stoklos in Mary Stuart, which debuted in 1987 at La Mama Experimental Theatre in New York, put the solo performer on the international map. The piece enacts the struggle between Elizabeth I of England and her cousin, Mary Queen of Scots. While the topic was not new, Stoklos's approach to it was powerful, humorous, and stunningly original. The text, included here, has Stoklos as the Narrator recounting the situation in the third person even as she performs the two queens. At times Stoklos keeps her distance, as when she answers a ringing phone: "Hello? A phone call from 400 years ago? International? Mary Stuart!" Yet her powerful enactments pull us into the very bodies of the warring women. Elizabeth, though the most powerful of the two, comes across as scattered, vain, self-satisfied, bored, and frantic to a degree bordering on derangement. Stoklos performs Mary as the more powerful in other ways: she is centered, focused, fighting intensely for her life. Stoklos describes Elizabeth even as she plays her in a completely different register. As a queen, she tells us, Elizabeth was "subject to fits of melancholy" alternating between "flamboyant merriment and . . . convulsive rage!! *(She runs her hands through her hair and changes her facial expressions into different 'masks' by using her tongue.)* Oh yes, Elizabeth was terrible." Stoklos's humorous and wild enactment critiques the character even as it brings Elizabeth's quirkiness to life. The extreme physicality of the performance brings audience members into close and intimate contact with the queen, who bites her fingernails, yanks at her toenails, pulls at her hair, and prances around the stage in a tunic that, through a magical gesture of the hands, turns into a bustle and gown.

Immediately, however, the intimacy is broken, interrupted by the Narrator, who pulls us back to the *now* of the twenty-first century: "Every day it gets harder to do Latin American theater!" she complains, after getting stuck, literally, on a line: "The delicate issue of the Queen's marriage began to cast its shadow across the political scene, and in her attitude, in her attitude, in her attitude, in her attitude *(phrase and physical movement are repeated like a skipping record).*" Even in live performance, Stoklos suggests, technologies of communication cast shadows over one another as many modes of transmission jumble together in a cacophony of themes and images drawn from different cultural repertoires. How can we understand each other when everything pulls us apart—from sound to meaning to body language to linguistic and technological systems of communication and transmission? We are bound to get stuck, she suggests, as she juggles the past to tell a story about the here and now.

The here and now dimension of the story is also about unequal power relations and the abuse suffered by Latin America due to its colonial status. Elizabeth represents the dominant and deranged powers; Mary Stuart enacts all the futile attempts at dialogue and communication that characterize the weak. *Mary Stuart,* Stoklos says, is "about the potentiality of Mary Stuart's power, condemned by her sentimentalism and passion, confronted by a Queen Elizabeth [who is] objective, and has tremendous physical strength. [Mere] potentiality of power is always destructive. It's a metaphor for the Latin American situation: our future, part free, part imprisoned by political motives. We are violated, fecundated by the First World, seduced."[5]

In Brazil, her audiences recognize Stoklos's fierce engagement with national and international politics. A production of hers is an event that receives national attention.[6] In the United States, the issues, the stakes, and the viable spaces of contestation are profoundly different. While clearly one of Latin America's most imaginative and talented performers, she has not found the audience she deserves in the United States.[7] Hopefully the text included here will give readers some sense of the work of this very powerful artist.

—Diana Taylor

NOTES

1. Denise Stoklos, "Selections from Writings on Essential Theatre," trans. Diana Taylor, in *Holy Terrors: Latin American Women Perform*, ed. Diana Taylor and Roselyn Costantino (Durham: Duke University Press, 2003), 137–39.

2. Henry David Thoreau, *Walden and Civil Disobedience* (New York: Penguin Classics, 1986), 387.

3. *Casa*, translated by Denise Stoklos and Diana Taylor, appears in Taylor and Costantino *Holy Terrors*, 140–51.

4. Denise Stoklos, *500 Anos—Um Fax de Denise Stoklos para Cristóvão Colombo* (São Paulo: Denise Stoklos Produções Artísticas, 1992), 9.

5. Denise Stoklos, interview with María Teresa Alvarado, 1991, trans. Leslie Damasceno.

6. Denise Stoklos has won the Best Actress award nine times in Brazil; she has been the recipient of a Guggenheim award and a Fulbright fellowship, and her work has been translated and staged in thirty-one countries.

7. The reasons behind this are discussed at greater length in "Denise Stoklos: The Politics of Decipherability," in Diana Taylor, *The Archive and the Repertoire* (Durham: Duke University Press, 2003).

SELECTED REFERENCES

Bruckner, D. J. R. "The Stage: Mary Stuart." *New York Times,* late ed., February 24, 1987, C17.

Damasceno, Leslie. "The Gestural Art of Reclaiming Utopia: Denise Stoklos at Play with the Hysterical-Historical." In *Holy Terrors: Latin American Women Perform,* ed. Diana Taylor and Roselyn Costantino, 152–78. Durham: Duke University Press, 2003.

George, David. *Flash and Crash Days: Brazilian Theater in the Post-dictatorship Period.* New York: Garland, 2000.

Ramírez-Cancio, Marlène. "The Personal Is Not Political." http://homepage.mac.com/cancio/stoklos/

Stoklos, Denise. Personal Web site. http://denisestoklos.uol.com.br/

Stoklos, Denise. "Selections from Writings on Essential Theatre." Trans. Diana Taylor. In *Holy Terrors: Latin American Women Perform,* ed. Diana Taylor and Roselyn Costantino, 137–39. Durham: Duke University Press, 2003.

Stoklos, Denise. *Teatro Essencial.* São Paulo: Denise Stoklos Produções Artísticas, 1993.

Taylor, Diana. "Denise Stoklos: The Politics of Decipherability." In *The Archive and the Repertoire,* 212–36. Durham: Duke University Press, 2003.

Denise Stoklos in Mary Stuart (Denise Stoklos)

Translated by Denise Stoklos and Marlène Ramírez-Cancio

The stage is bare, except for a simple wooden chair stage right. Stoklos, dressed in black leggings and a beige top, walks center stage, barefoot.

NARRATOR: Elizabeth, having no experience in State affairs, was twenty-five years old when she succeeded her half sister on November 17, 1558. England was very fortunate to be ruled by a new Queen whose blood and upbringing made her a remarkable woman. There was no doubting who her father was. Her commanding stance, auburn hair, eloquence of speech, and natural dignity marked her as King Henry's daughter. Other, other, other . . . *(Narrator's voice switches to a higher pitch, she looks at her nails.)* Many other similarities *(bites her nails and spits them out)* were soon observed: *(strong, declamatory voice)* extreme courage in moments of crisis, an imperious resolution when defied, and an inexhaustible fund of physical energy. She enjoyed many of the same pastimes as the King—she had a passion for hunting, was skilled in archery and hawking, and was accomplished in dance and music. She could speak six languages, and was well read in Latin and Greek. *(Narrator's hand begins to shake violently in front of her face.)* The times demanded a politician: a head of State with a calculating, devious spirit, and *this,* Elizabeth possessed. She also had an incredible gift for choosing the most able men to help her get the job done.

(She runs from one side of the stage to the other.)

The Queen's quickness of mind was surpassed by few of her contemporaries, and many envoys to her Court had good reason to admire her wit. She was subject to fits of melancholy, which alternated between flamboyant merriment and . . . convulsive rage!! *(She runs her hands through her hair and changes her facial expressions into different "masks" by using her tongue.)* Oh yes, Elizabeth was terrible! She was often brazen and even crass in manners and expression. When she got angry, she would smack her Treasurer's ears or throw a slipper in her Secretary's face. *(Narrator runs upstage left. With her back to the audience, she undulates and shakes her hips.)* She was very free in her more intimate relations. *(Turns around toward the audience, runs downstage)* In a sense, her relationship with her subjects was one long flirtation. She gave her country the love she never surrendered to any one man, and her people responded with a loyalty that almost amounted to worship. There's a reason why she was known as Good Queen Bessie.

(As if balancing on a tightrope) The delicate issue of the Queen's marriage began to cast its shadow across the political scene, and in her attitude, in her attitude, in her attitude, in her attitude *(phrase and physical movement are repeated like a skipping record)* one could see the, one could see the, one could see the . . . *(She stops, adds as an aside:)* Every day it gets harder and harder to do Latin American theater! *(Finishing her phrase)* One could see the strength of Elizabeth's character.

If she married an Englishman, her authority might be weakened, and there would be fighting among her suitors. Those perils dawned on her as she watched her Court's reactions to her long and deep affection for Robert Dudley, Northumberland's son, whom she named Earl of Leicester. Marrying into one of Europe's ruling families would mean entangling herself in its European politics and facing the hostility of her husband's rivals. *(Goes over to a chair stage right and sits down)*

Meanwhile there was Mary Stuart, Queen of Sssssssssssssssssssscots. Quem, aos olhos da Europa católica possuia mais direitos ao trono inglês que sua prima Elizabeth. *(Gets up and jumps around. In Portuguese, she speaks in a frantic "gossipy" tone as she plays with her hair.)* Seu jovem marido morreu logo depois de subir ao trono da França e em dezembro de 1560 ela retorna ao seu país, a Escócia. Bem a Mary era assim mais simpleszinha que a Elizabeth, ainda em que elas se achassem em posição similar: Maria também descendia do rei da Inglaterra Henrique VI e assim como Elizabeth estava sem marido . . . *(Catches herself. Regains composure)* I am sorry. I should be trying to speak in English. I am really sorry. *(She paces in a circle around the stage.)* It's just that when I go deep into my feelings, out comes this Portuguese, which is such an isolated language. Communication problem. Problem. Communication. No problem, I will start the whole thing over again:

Denise Stoklos, Brazil, 1987. Translated from Portuguese and other languages by Denise Stoklos and Marlène Ramírez-Cancio.

(She walks offstage, and comes back in. She walks in circles around the stage as she speaks.)

Mary Stuart, Queen of Scots, was born in 1542. She was Catholic, and was persecuted for being heiress to the throne of England, a newly Protestant country. She inherited a wealth of misfortunes and lost many battles in her private and political life. At the age of 22, she was imprisoned by her cousin, Queen Elizabeth of England. One day, after Mary had been in jail for twenty-two years, Elizabeth received a visit from Walsingham, one of her counselors. *(She moves the chair downstage left, and sits.)* He said: "I think that you should kill Mary Stuart." Elizabeth didn't want to. She said: "Nooooooooooo, noooooooooo, Mary is a distinguished lady! She has her own crown, why would she want mine? No I won't kill her, I won't kill her, I won't kill her." Back in those days, you know, it wasn't like today, where governments just go around killing people. Nooooooo, back in those days there were trials and stuff. But Walsingham insisted: "Kill her, kill her. She's a Catholic and you're a Protestant," and things like that. *(Moves chair to downstage right, sits)* And Elizabeth would say: "Nooo . . ." *(Picking at her toenails)* "I would feel horrible if I were guilty of a colleague's death, a sovereign colleague! No, I won't kill her, I won't kill her." But then, Walsingham got a hold of some of Mary Stuart's letters . . . Because Mary Stuart wrote many letters. My God, how many letters she wrote! She wrote so many letters that I had to write a whole scene where I write and send letters. I write and send letters. You will see it in a few moments. I had to write the scene because there were too many letters in this story. So, the letters proved that Mary Stuart really did want Elizabeth's crown. And so Elizabeth finally signed her death sentence. Twenty-four hours later she regretted it and tried to stop the execution—but it was too late. *(Pause. She moves the chair offstage. Walks center stage)*

Mary Stuart's death was a terrible blow to History's imagination. When the news arrived in London, shouts of celebration were heard in the streets. That entire day, Elizabeth stayed alone in her bedroom. *(Runs downstage and addresses the audience)*

In this play, which is starting now, I'd like to perform for you just a few images of these two women whose power made them enemies: Queen Elizabeth of England *(puts both hands near her waist and splays her fingers, indicating a wide skirt, smiles)*, and me *(voice changes to a tired, low whisper, as she mimes the surface of a wall with her hands)* Mary Stuart, Queen of Scotland, in this prison where I am condemned to feed myself with my own thoughts.

A cold and premeditated rape forced me to marry him. I denounced him to the State Council: I proclaimed, the Earl of Bothwell took possession of me,

the Queen, forcing me into the State Council, where he raped me. "It is in the name of love that I rape you, my love. God Save the Queen!" My destiny is to provoke furious, naive, lacerating love. My loyal secretary. I remember this. It is more real than this present moment. I was in a place that looked like this one here, and then I saw him. It was strange because he was crawling. He clung to my skirt crying: "My lady, save me, save me!" He was stabbed fifty times in front of me! I rode on horseback fifty miles, almost delivering the child in my womb. What if I had aborted the future king of Scotland? Where was the father of my baby? Where was my mother? *(Screaming, increasingly dramatic)* Mother, mother, mom, mummy. . . ! *(Aside)* This is only theater. Ce n'est que du théâtre. É soltanto teatro. É teatro, nada mais que teatro . . . *(As Mary Stuart again)* Who says I can share this difficult delivery? The child came out shoulders first, ripping me apart. Let me feed him. "Your milk is defective." I want to forget. I want to forget everything I lived through before I ended up in this prison. I just want to remember when I won the battles. How audacious the Queen looked, astride her horse, no armor, inciting and inspiring her Army. Uselessly. To fall prisoner, at the age of 22. Prisoner of my cousin, Queen Elizabeth of England.

(Lights fade to black. When they come back up, Stoklos is the cheerful Queen Elizabeth, prancing around the stage with her hands splayed out, indicating the Queen's skirt. She stops. Speaks more seriously)

QUEEN ELIZABETH: Yesterday, out in the courtyard, I saw a young man with bright eyes. "Bring him here." I understand the French Ambassador is waiting to see me. Let him wait! First, bring me that young man. *(She turns around and mimes going through a closet full of clothes.)* I, Queen Elizabeth of England, have three thousand dresses, but none of them suits me well. Boots made of deerskin, dog skin, brocade, taffeta. Some parts of my body I never see. *(She puts her hands on her genitals. She is quiet, slows down.)* It is said we are born naked. When I bathe I have four strong women around me who cover me in bright oils, vapors and foam. I am growing old without becoming aware of my own body. *(She bites her nail and spits it out, whining softly.)* *(Beat. She laughs and runs to a corner, where a spotlight shines down on her. Her back is to the audience, her hands in the "skirt" position.)* Oh there's the young man! Come closer, do not be afraid, my boy. What is your name? Hum, hum, hm? What's your name, hm?! Did you lose your tongue? Hum, hum?! It doesn't matter. Your silence and your strong legs say more about you than your name ever could. Now, take off your clothes. Yes, take them off. I only want to look at you. You are so young, beautiful, white. Now, naked like that, come here in front of me, get down on your knees and kiss my feet! *(She shrieks with pleasure.)* Now, dress yourself, and go back to the courtyard. *(Lights back up. She turns around, smiling, and shouts out an order.)* Give this young man two gold coins, right now! Yes, let the French Ambassador in. AH!

(Blackout. When lights come back up, Queen Elizabeth is sitting on a chair, center stage.)

QUEEN ELIZABETH: I proclaim the Parliament open. I've been crit— . . . I've been critici—I've been c–cockle doodle doo! *(Tries to regain composure. Enunciates carefully)* I. Have. Been. Criticized. *(She is pleased her words finally came out right.)* Oh. I have been criticized today for having summoned both Chambers: the House of Lords, and the House of Commons. One does not like democracy *(looks over to the Lords and smiles),* and the other loves democracy *(looks over to the Commons and gives them the finger).* I am not ashamed for having summoned the Commons, who have been absent and speechless for so long. These people here are the merchants, the peasants, the common people, the workers, the people who are fucked. Our Lords are frequently intolerant for no reason. If they only understood how much their silence and their political passivity have helped me rule this country doing whatever I want! Then our Lords would be less, I mean much, much, much less intolerant. These people have helped us pay off our debts by getting loans at minimum, minimum, interest rates. They have proven to be wise, considerate and concerned, manifesting a new kind of intelligence, the kind that can keep this country united. Thus, thus, I proclaim that from this day forth, these people will be able to vote in Parliament just like the Lords. Don't even bother complaining, being offended, crying out in despair. I see you, Lord Hamilton. You look furious, horrified. Your face is bright red like the wattle of an enraged turkey. Bring him a bit of water and some vinegar. Brace yourself, Lord Hamilton, because there's more change to come: From this moment on, those who earn more will pay higher taxes than those who earn less . . . *(YAWNS repeatedly, stretching her body, scratching herself)* This topic always makes me sleepy. Those who earn more will be taxed more, and those who earn less will be taxed less. I have heard this before. Anyway! Changing the subject, moving on to something that is constantly on your minds, keeping you from considering much more essential matters, let's address the eternal issue of: my wedding. To those of you who think it's impossible for an unmarried woman to rule a country, I would like to say that my husband is my country and all my subjects are my children. *(She gets dreamy, childlike, and breast-feeds an imagined child in her arms. She is sad, weeps, has a hard time speaking.)* However, however, however, in the meantime, to demonstrate my goodwill, I will consider all suitors

who wish to court me. I must always consider the interests of England as paramount. Maybe I will never choose to marry any of them. In such an event, I wish to have this written on my tombstone: "Here lies a Queen who lived and died a virgin!" The session is closed. AH!

(Blackout. Opera music. A rectangle of light up on Stoklos, who moves silently along with the music: She writes, signs, folds, and sends letters in a repeated cycle of movement.)

MARY STUART: Dear cousin Elizabeth. I write you so many letters from my prison. And you never answer any of them. Maybe you want to prove to me that when we live in times like these, where there is no respect for justice or dignity, then any attempt at communication is useless. Should I stop? Should I stop? Does anything I am trying to do here make any sense to you, or should I stop? I don't know. *(Addressing the audience)* But I think that for you, who left your families at home and came to the theater so you could reflect about freedom—and for me—if the only way I can express my desire for freedom is by writing a letter, then I will certainly write you another letter: Dear cousin Elizabeth!! *(She steps out of the rectangle of light, and walks to a new circular spotlight. Throughout this next letter, she begins by walking in circles, and by the end, she is dragging herself in circles on the floor.)* Some time ago, people used to say: if one of us had been a man, we would have been the most sensible couple in History. I would have married you with pleasure. If that could have happened, we would be happy right now. We would see England and Scotland united in a lovely and harmonious bond. Am I getting sentimental? Am I getting old and sentimental? If Scotland wanted to remain Catholic, this marriage would be its ruin. I always worshipped you. I would give my life to see you. The enamel ring with your initials still embraces my finger. I wrote you many letters. I came to you as a supplicant, and you, trampling on the laws of hospitality, have held me between these walls. Had you recognized me as the heir that I am, you would now have the comfort and support of a loyal and devoted relative. Europe is watching you, my Queen. Act with justice. From the one who loves you most and you love least: Mary Stuart.

(Blackout. When the spotlight comes back on, Mary Stuart is standing behind a chair.)

MARY STUART: Dear cousin Elizabeth: I write you another letter from my prison. But you never answer any of them. Maybe you want to prove to me that when we live in times like these, where there is no respect for human values, for justice, for equality, then any attempt at communication is useless. Should I stop? Am I making sense? Should I go work in soap operas? I think that for you, who left your families at home and came to the theater so you could reflect about freedom—and for me, right now at this very moment, if the only way we can express our desire for freedom is by writing a letter, oh, then I will certainly write you another letter. Dear cousin Elizabeth! Maybe you don't answer me because you don't understand my bad English? But Portuguese is such an isolated language. Communication problem. No problem, I will try over and over again. Dear cousin Elizabeth. One thought alone dominates my mind, holding it in joy and sorrow, so that I hear the voices of hope and fear as I lie awake at night. And if my heart chooses this missive as messenger, and announces my desire to see you, then, dear sister, a new fear seizes me, because it lacks the power to prove its sincerity. I see the boat in the harbor, almost hidden and held back by the storm and the force of the waves, and the serene face of heaven darkened by night. So I too am beset by my own fears and worries. Not fear of you, my sister, not fear of you, but fear of the establishment that hurls down the sail in which we put our hopes for social change.

(A phone rings. Blackout. It keeps ringing in the dark. Pause. When the lights come back up, Stoklos is sitting in a chair center stage, her back to the audience. We hear a chorus sing: "One, two, three, four, five, six, seven, eight . . . " Stoklos stands up and moves around the stage, performing repeated actions like touching the wall, brushing her teeth, punching the air, touching her face, running in place . . . Music stops. Blackout.

The phone rings. Lights up on Stoklos, who is lying on the floor in front of the chair with her eyes closed. Startled by the ringing of the phone, she wakes up and answers, grabbing a phone from under the chair.)

STOKLOS: Hello? A phone call from 400 years ago? International? Mary Stuart! You are in prison too!? AH!

QUEEN ELIZABETH: *(Lying on the ground, sucking her thumb)* I remember my mother coming to my bedroom before I fell asleep. I would lie there waiting for her. Then I would hear her steps on the wooden floor, and she would enter in a rush of velvet, her lilac perfume mingling with her sweat. Beautiful Anne Boleyn seldom walked. She ran. Her neck extended ahead of her. That long and delicate neck was cut by an axe. Whack! That beautiful mother's head dropped into the basket. *(She writhes in pain.)* You know? I don't like to read the newspaper. I always think I'll see headlines about the lack of protection from my Father State and my Mother Society. I don't like to open baskets: I always think that when the lid comes off, I will be looking at my mother's head.

(Opera music. Fade to black)

QUEEN ELIZABETH: *(Sitting on a chair, laughing)* I've been thinking about the political situation in Latin America! . . . *(She laughs hysterically)* . . . The laws! It cannot be serious, no! The leaders! Ha! The so-called free elections!! Ha ha ha!!

(Beat. She grows serious.)

STOKLOS: There is a fascism that doesn't belong only to the fascists.

There is an oppression that isn't just enforced by the police.

There is a resistance that isn't only about weapons in our hands.

And so many times in a day, in a year, we let our lives go, feeding superficialities, feeding lies, emptiness. But there is a human flag, there is an honor in refusing disgrace, refusing passive acceptance of misery—social and emotional misery—and this is what I'm talking about here: about this struggle, the struggle for honor.

(Blackout. When the lights come back up, Queen Elizabeth is skipping around the stage, calling her servants in a frivolous tone.)

QUEEN ELIZABETH: Hanna! Caroline! Come here, girls. Come and help this old Queen Elizabeth take off her boots—careful with the heel! Careful with the heel!—and take off my dress. I want to be naked! Today in the Parliament I declared that everyone will vote. Lord Hamilton was as red as the wattle of an enraged turkey. What? What? What did you say? What? Speak up, girl! What? I'm always the last person to find out what's going on . . . Captain Hawkins wants my financial help to bring some black people from Africa and sell them as slaves in, ah, in that new country, what is it called again? That country without any kind of future besides soccer? Ah, yes: Brazil! Brazil. Well let me see: I give him the money, he goes, grabs the slaves, comes back, sells them, and then we share the profits. Sounds like a good deal! Who knows, maybe one of those slaves will have a grandson called Pelé. Hmm. Okay, okay. But tell Captain Hawkins that if he gets caught, I have nothing to do with this. Tell him to teach that political strategy to that new country. They will love it. They will copy it. Yes, this business of giving an order and then, if necessary, pretend like you know nothing, nothing, nothing.

What? What? Speak up, girl! What? A young writer named William Shakespeare wants my help to build a theater? Oh, yes, give him some stones, I love to support the arts. Give him some stones, and tell him to build the first wooden theater in the world. But, there's just one thing: the style must be Elizabethan!

What? What? Speak up, girl. Another letter from Mary Stuart? No! No, I don't want read it. All she does is write letters. Besides: paper, envelopes, stamps, those are too many props for Essential Theater.

What? Mary Stuart, Queen of Scotland gave birth to a son?

—What about you, my Queen?

(The Queen lets out a long shriek, as the stage lights dim and only a spotlight remains on her.)

QUEEN ELIZABETH: (*Speaking softly*) All of your worries echo through my barren womb. My royal bed is a desert. My entrails are dry! A son for the throne, a son for the country, a son for the crown? And what about me? I have teeth, I have hands, I have a liver! When, you ask, will you announce the sovereign nuptials? If I were one of those white pigs we raise in our meadows. If one of those pigs is sterile, they say: it must be decapitated. I, who have given birth to my own mind. This mind that is England. I lived in books and notebooks. I learned Latin, Greek, Italian, Spanish, French. My memory has become like the wings of a great bird soaring over the globe. I have learned Mathematics, Physics, I even learned how to observe the stars. One hundred masters shoved their wisdom into my brain. The fortune you spent on my education, oh inconsiderate people! The treasures of a kingdom collected to create a Queen. Now you are willing to toss it into the sea for the tiny head of a king! So small it could not even carry the weight of a few jewels on the crown of England.

(*Beat. As an observer*)

OBSERVER: So what? There are so many people dying of starvation and the Queen is talking about the jewels on the crown!

(*Quick blackout, then lights very dim. Stoklos stands upstage. Speaks loudly*)

POLITICAL PRISONER: My name? My name is Ulrike Meinhoff. My name is Nelson Mandela. My name is the name of any political prisoner. I am here. Locked up for four years in a modern jail of a modern State. Offense? Attacking private property and the laws that defend private property and the owners' rights to extend their property beyond all limits of everything, everything. The property of our thoughts, our gestures, our words, our love, and even the property of our lives. I hear a little noise. The door opens. A guard comes in. She looks at me like I don't exist, like I'm transparent. In her hand she carries a lunch tray. She puts it on the table. She goes out and locks the door. Again, silence. All is white here. The walls are white, the bed is white, the neon light is always burning, day and night. I never know when it's nighttime, I never know when it's daytime. That is my torture. Sensorial deprivation. And when the right moment comes they will give me more than a hand. (*She puts her hand to her neck.*) A clean little job. Just as clean as the whole society that is preparing to kill me. I can see them already at the door. No, it's forbidden to take photographs, it's forbidden to ask for a second examination, it's forbidden to write about it, to talk is forbidden, everything is forbidden!

(*Lights up. Beat*)

MARY STUART: What a nightmare! Shit!

(*Blackout. Lights fade back up immediately.*)

QUEEN ELIZABETH: Mary! Mary!

MARY STUART: Elizabeth! I have been waiting for you so many years. I am glad you came, to get me out of this prison. I am glad you came, Elizabeth.

QUEEN ELIZABETH: But I didn't come. This is only a theatrical scene: We never met in real life.

MARY STUART: Please free me, Elizabeth.

QUEEN ELIZABETH: Please do free me, Mary.

MARY STUART: Help me.

QUEEN ELIZABETH: Help me.

MARY STUART: So, give it up.

QUEEN ELIZABETH: Could we give up power?

MARY STUART: Could we?

QUEEN ELIZABETH: Could we eat a piece of bread and leave it at that?

(*In the dark*)

MARY STUART: Could we write a poem, and nothing else?

(*Opera music plays. Then a small light shines only on Stoklos's feet. We hear the sound of thunder as she speaks.*)

QUEEN ELIZABETH: It is the whole system of power that has to be changed, the whole system of power.

Sniveling slavery to reign . . . Stupid, sordid, suffocating slavery! Can we call a man a King, a woman a Queen, who cares only about pleasing the world? No, I cannot kill Mary Stuart. To cut off the head of a monarch? It is too dangerous a precedent. It would make it much easier for an uncontrollable mob to demand my own head tomorrow. No, the monarchs and the governments are and must remain untouchable. They must be protected under Divine Law. Our desire for corruption is a kind of tradition. It is like an itch. I remember when I was little, the public executions in the square, people eating fried fish and sausage. They wouldn't stop eating, except to watch those bodies that suddenly got covered in blood. So beautiful. Today is no different: So many people around the world are condemned daily by social injustices, lack of love, power struggles, violence, violence. Rwanda, Sarajevo. Then just for a moment, people stop eating fried fish and sausage, applaud whoever is in power and then they all go back to eating fried fish and sausage, passively watching TV.

It is intolerable that, still alive, I weave my own funeral shroud. Mary Stuart, our two, two religions are mortal, mortal enemies. History, history demands a choice. Either you or me. It is not the Queen but the Lords of England who choose. Is there no one to free me from my executioner's duty?

Warden, I have entrusted you with the precious life of Mary Stuart, and you have guarded it well. But the words of a reigning monarch must not be taken too literally. If you listened with your heart, your own misgivings might lift the weight of such a terrible decision from this woman's shoulders. Uh? Venom. Poison might work more quietly than a public execution. The Lords are screaming for Mary Stuart's head but I cannot condemn her without risking my own head.

MARY STUART: Here I am before you, Lords of Justice. They did not allow me a chair. It doesn't matter, I will stand. They did not allow me a lawyer. It doesn't matter. I will defend myself. First of all, as a foreign sovereign, I declare that you do not have the right to prosecute me for treachery. As a foreign sovereign—yes, because my internal lands are ruled by different laws—I cannot submit to your laws without bringing an insult to myself, to my king, and to my people. I declare that, as a foreign sovereign, I did seek the help of my relatives, the sovereigns of France and the sovereigns of Spain, to remove me from the indignity of this captivity.

STOKLOS: Then, in the interview, they asked me what I thought. Then I said what I think and they said no, this is not possible, then I said no then they said yes . . . Do you understand what is going on here? There is no meaning at all. No, because many things in our civilization have no meaning, so there is this moment in the play where there is no meaning also. Yes, because children dying of starvation have no meaning, social, racial and sexual discrimination, have no meaning so, we . . .

MARY STUART: To remove me from the indignity of this captivity. But I swear I never took part in any conspiracy against the life, life of my cousin Elizabeth. All I wanted was my right of succession. The succession of values. But Elizabeth, overwrought with religious concerns, refused to concede it to me. Yes, I fought justly and well for my rights, but all efforts to change, change values seem like walking backwards. Any innocent prisoner wants to escape by any means, and wants to rebuild a damaged reputation. And, being a Queen, I ask to be treated properly by you.

STOKLOS: Then they asked me in the interview—just tell me if this is a question to be asked—what did I think about AIDS? I think that I think that I think, think . . . Think!

MARY STUART: Any innocent prisoner wants to escape by any means, and wants to rebuild a damaged reputation. And being a Queen, and we all are Queens and Kings in our human rights, we have to be treated properly. Life is too short.

STOKLOS: Then they asked me in the interview what is my favorite kind of man. If I prefer the romantic type, you know, the one who opens the car door for you, the one that sends you flowers. Or if I prefer the macho man, hairy chest, the one who uses only lemon perfume, the ones that make noise with their key chains. Then they wanted to know what my favorite kind of food was.

MARY STUART: For days I have not touched, metaphorically, my food, metaphorically. I am afraid, metaphorically, of dying by venom, metaphorically. I do not ask for grace, only for a dignified death.

STOKLOS: Now Maria Stuart enters the room where she will die. Around the scaffold, a hundred Lords sit, waiting, not changing this destiny. Maria Stuart's torture begins. It is just another torture in the memory of mankind. It is just another crime unpunished, the tragedy of power in human history, and it keeps repeating, repeating every day. Can you believe it?

Today, February 8th, 1587, at 10 o'clock in the morning, Maria Stuart, Queen, Queen of herself and Scotland, ceases to exist. The burning star that bore her name is extinguished. The chain was loosened to free the prisoner. Now she paces in the silence of her own undying dream. Mankind forgets that what one lives is not mortal.

Where I come from, one of the most popular names is Maria.

Is the torture session really over?

THE END

Author's Note: This play was written by Denise Stoklos, but 10 percent of the text is from Dacia Maraini's "Mary Stuart" (example: the scene of "the meeting with the boy," the talk with Captain Hawkins, some words in the Parliament, and various sentences throughout the play; this could be checked in the book *Clytemnestra and Other Stories* where Maraini's "Mary Stuart" was published). There is a poem by Romain Gary as well—the one about fascism when the actress is sitting in the chair.

PERU

Adiós Ayacucho (Novella by Julio Ortega, adapted for the theater by Miguel Rubio Zapata for Grupo Cultural Yuyachkani)

Augusto Casafranca in Grupo Cultural Yuyachkani's performance of *Adiós Ayacucho,* Hemispheric Institute of Performance and Politics Encuentro in Monterrey, Mexico, 2001. (Photo by Lorie Novak.)

In 1990, the year that Yuyachkani (or Grupo Cultural Yuyachkani, as the performance group is officially known) staged *Adiós Ayacucho,* Peru was at the height of its *guerra interna* or Dirty War. Adapting a 1986 novella by Julio Ortega, a noted Peruvian novelist and scholar, for the stage, Yuyachkani created the work to make visible the disappearances that were taking place around them. Since Grupo Cultural Yuyachkani formed in 1971, this internationally acclaimed collective theater group has been staging Peru's history of struggle and trauma, and its aftermath in the present. When Yuyachkani began, Teresa Ralli (a founding member and a lead actor) tells, "the first thing we had was the name."[1] "In Quechua, the expressions 'I am thinking,' 'I am remembering,' 'I am your thought' are translated by just one word: Yuyachkani," the noted Peruvian commentator Hugo Salazar del Alcazar wrote in one of his many pieces on the Yuyachkani theater group.[2] The name posits thought and memory as interchangeable, and it also underlines the deep connection between the "I"—as the subject who is thinking—and the "I" who is a product of another's thought. These "I"s are deeply interrelated, suggesting the profound connectivity that members of Yuyachkani feel with and for their country. Actors Teresa Ralli, Rebeca Ralli, Ana Correa, Débora Correa, Augusto Casafranca, Julián Vargas, Amiel Cayo, the director Miguel Rubio, and the technical director Fidel Melquíades now have their own 200-seat theater and work space, Casa Yuyachkani, and have worked together for thirty-six years, a momentous achievement given the severe economic and political hardships they have faced. As Rebeca Ralli puts it, their work represents the Peruvian people's struggle for survival even as it represents their own struggle to survive both as individuals and as a group. "We put up with so much just to be able to live, just to be able to create."[3]

One of the defining features of Yuyachkani's work has been the context of criminal violence in which they have worked and to which they have born witness. During the 1980s and 1990s, the Armed Forces and paramilitary death squads waged war against the Maoist guerrilla group called *Sendero Luminoso,* or the Shining Path. The state and anti-state terrorists ravaged the country, disappearing and killing at least 75,000 people in their struggle for dominance and displacing another million. During this period, Yuyachkani

291

developed several pieces as a way of thinking through the civil violence and the apparent impossibility of respectful coexistence in a country torn apart by injustice and rage. Disappearances and mass murder had become common political practice. How, Yuyachkani asked itself, can theater elucidate the theatricality of political violence? Miguel Rubio sums up the challenge: "Nothing that you create on stage can compare with what is happening in this country."[4] Furthermore, the heightened spectacularity of political terrorism forced potential witnesses to look away. It blinded the very spectators that theater calls on "to see." What role do artists have when, as Adorno asks, genocide is part of our cultural heritage?

In the most lyrical of forms, Yuyachkani's plays of this period (*Contraelviento, Antígona, Rosa Cuchillo*) pose the most urgent of questions. How can indigenous and mestizo communities address genocidal policies and practices that are often not acknowledged by the national or international community? Through performance—the music, masked figures, and ritual incantations—the plays suggests, atrocity can be "remembered" and "thought" even when there are no external witnesses, no photos, and no recourse to archival documentation. *Adiós Ayacucho* takes the question of witnessing further: the dismembered victim of torture and disappearance is forced to act as sole witness to his own victimization.

Adiós Ayacucho tells the story of a peasant, Alfonso Cánepa, who has been tortured, murdered and disappeared by the military. Suspected of being a "terrorist," he was blown up with a grenade, his body parts dispersed along the side of the road. As the play begins, the members of the audience see a ramp displaying a suit of clothing and candles laid out in a funerary ritual—the symbolic trace of Cánepa's body. The play opens as an indigenous masked dancer from Andean traditional fiestas arrives to see the clothes of the dead man laid out for mourning. With no body to mourn, and no witnesses to the violence, the clothes are all that attest to the existence of this life, now disappeared. The dancer, Q'olla, decides to take the shoes, arguing that he needs them more than the dead man. As he puts on the shoes, the spirit of Alfonso Cánepa comes back, speaking in and through him to tell his story. With touching simplicity and humor, he relates his ordeal and outlines his demand: he wants his body parts back together; he wants a decent burial; he wants the President of Peru to know about the violence visited on him, an innocent peasant. He writes a letter that he himself will hand deliver to the President. And, in a final act of personal reconstitution, he raids the tomb of the conqueror Pizarro, housed in Lima's cathedral. He helps himself to the bones he needs and buries himself in the shrine—why should this fetish of the national body be glorified when the individual and social body has been torn apart? Without an external witness, and with no survivors, no one but he himself can demand that justice be served.

The play poses several important questions for people in theater and performance studies. Some have to do with acting as a form of embodiment and even trance—how does the Q'olla figure channel Alfonso Cánepa? Theater and performance always require the live actor to lend physical embodiment to an absent character. We, as audience, gradually come to see Cánepa in and through the dancer. As Cánepa recomposes himself and regains his sense of identity, he starts to shed the clothes, manner, and voice of Q'olla. Yuyachkani takes this acting process further by asking theater to make visible not just the characters but the conflicts and problems that have been disappeared through violent politics. The funny and nervous dancing figure that steals shoes gives way to Cánepa's moving and dignified struggle to reclaim not only his body but to claim the "truth" of his ordeal—he takes back his limbs, his identity, and his voice on both the personal and national levels. All of a sudden, theatergoers become witnesses to an atrocity that the military tried to render invisible. Everyone in Peru knew what was going on; they just did not know how to respond, or how to restore peace. The play offers one path towards communal regeneration and coexistence by asking everyone to accept the "truth" of what they are seeing and accompany Cánepa on his journey toward social justice. Yes, the play acknowledges, the journey is dangerous and full of pit holes, but there is no other way to reach the closure and peace that Cánepa experiences without facing those dangers.

The haunting image of the burial suit in the set of *Adiós Ayacucho* suggests the ways in which Yuyachkani layers its approach to representing violence. The clothes laid out in memory of the dead re-present the missing body of the victim of disappearance, even as it echoes an ancient burial practice. These practices are alive; other bodies will perform them just as Cánepa fits himself back into the waiting clothes. Andean performance practices, this play shows, are not dead things. Rather, ritual practices are constantly reactivated to give form to current crises. Ritual, theater, and performance are all intermingled in this play, which is part text, part ritual, part theater representation, and part performance intervention in a dangerous political environment.

These performance practices, whether drawn from age-old repertoires or marginalized traditions, allow for immediate responses to current political problems. Every response to political violence carries with it a history of responses, conjured up from a vast range of embodied and archival memories. For Yuyachkani, performance is not about going back, but about keeping alive. Its mode of transmission is the repeat, the reiteration, the yet again-ness of "performance." The violence of the past has not disappeared.

Yuyachkani's performances make visible a history of cumulative trauma, an unmarked and unacknowledged history of violent conflict. As in *Adiós Ayacucho,* the attempts at communicating an event that no one cares to acknowledge need to be repeated again and again. For members of traumatized communities, such as the Andean ones Yuyachkani engages, past violence blends into the current crisis. As in *Adiós Ayacucho,* trauma becomes transmittable, understandable, through performance—through the re-experienced shudder, the retelling, the repeat. The fact that there is no "over" in situations of social violence attests to the continuing effects of trauma, but it also offers survivors the opportunity to reassert their capacity for intervention, no matter how overdue. Performance can help them cope with the violence by enabling them to reconstruct their own stories and give testimony. Understanding this power of performance, Yuyachkani began collaborating with Peru's Truth Commission to work with victims and survivors in rural areas. In

1999, Grupo Cultural Yuyachkani won Peru's highest honor for work in human rights.

Looking at performance as a retainer of social memory engages history without necessarily being a "symptom of history"—that is, the performances enter into dialogue with a history of trauma without themselves being traumatic. *Adiós Ayacucho,* like Yuyachkani's other plays, are carefully crafted works that create a critical distance for "claiming" experience and enabling, as opposed to "collapsing," witnessing. This performance event has an "outside," which is what, according to Dori Laub, allows for witnessing.[5] Yuyachkani, as its name indicates, hinges on the notion of interconnectedness—the "I" who thinks/remembers is inextricable from the "you" whose thought "I" am. The I/you of Yuyachkani promises to be a witness, a guarantor of the link between the I and the you, the "inside" and the "outside." The "I" is never alone—as Ana Correa's presence onstage through *Adiós Ayacucho* reminds us. Yuyachkani becomes the witnesses to the ongoing, unacknowledged drama of atrocity, and asks their audience to do the same. The group's practice points to a radically different conclusion than the one Adorno arrived at in "Commitment." Representation, for Yuyachkani, does not further contribute to the desecration of the victims, turning their pain into our viewing pleasure. Rather, without representation, viewers would not recognize their role in the ongoing history of oppression which, directly or indirectly, implicates them. Who, *Adiós Ayachuco* asks, will take on the responsibility of witnessing? The hope offered by Yuyachkani's play, *Antígona,* is that the spectator, like Ismene, will say "I." These performances teach communities not to look away. The witness, like Boal's "spect-actor," accepts the dangers and responsibilities of seeing and of acting on what one has seen. And witnessing is transferable—the theater, like the testimony, like the photograph, film or report, can make witnesses of others. So, rather than think of performance primarily as the ephemeral, as that which disappears, Yuyachkani insists on creating a community of witnesses by and through performance. The group counters the performance-as-disappearance model of colonialism that pushes autochthonous practices into the oblivion of the ephemeral, the unscripted, the understudied, the uncontrollable. For many of these communities, on the contrary, when performance ends, so does the shared understanding of social life and collective memory. Performances such as *Adiós Ayacucho* warn us not to dismiss the "I" who remembers, who thinks, who is a product of collective thought. As the name Yuyachkani suggests, attention to the interconnectedness between thinking subjects and subjects of thought would allow for a broader understanding of historical trauma, communal memory, and collective subjectivity.

—Diana Taylor

NOTES

1. Personal interview, Paucartambo, Peru, July 1999.

2. Hugo Salazar del Alcazar, "Los músicos ambulantes," *La escena latinoamericana* 2 (August 1989): 23.

3. Interview, Rebeca Ralli, Casa Yuyachkani, June 1996.

4. Quoted in Brenda Luz Cotto-Escalera, "Grupo Cultural Yuyachkani: Group Work and Collective Creation in Contemporary Latin American Theater." PhD diss., University of Texas, Austin, 1995, 156.

5. Dori Laub, "Truth and Testimony: The Process and the Struggle," in Cathy Caruth, ed., *Trauma: Explorations in Memory* (Baltimore: Johns Hopkins University Press, 1995), 66.

SELECTED REFERENCES

A'Ness, Francine. "Resisting Amnesia: Yuyachkani, Performance, and the Postwar Reconstruction of Peru." *Theatre Journal* 56 (October 2004): 395–414.

Bell, John. "Rediscovering Mask Performance in Peru: Gustavo Boada, Maskmaker with Yuyachkani." *TDR: The Drama Review* 43 (fall 1999): 169–81.

Cárdenas, Gisela. "Grupo Cultural Yuyachkani: Performance and Politics in Peru." Hemispheric Institute of Performance and Politics. http://www.hemi.nyu.edu/cuaderno/yuyachkani/

Cotto-Escalera, Brenda Luz. "Grupo Cultural Yuyachkani: Group Work and Collective Creation in Contemporary Latin American Theatre." PhD diss., University of Texas, Austin, 1995.

Lockert, Lucia. "El teatro popular 'Yuyachkani': Objetivos dinámicos de su integración." *Alba de América: Revista literaria* 7 (July 1989): 373–79.

Moser, Annalise. "Acts of Resistance: The Performance of Women's Grassroots Protest in Peru." *Social Policy International* 2 (October 2003): 177–90.

Murguercia, Magaly. "Cuerpo y política en la dramaturgia de Yuyachkani." In *Indagaciones sobre el fin de siglo (Teatro iberoamericano y argentino),* ed. Osvaldo Pellettieri, 43–61. Buenos Aires: Galerna, Fundación Roberto Arlt, 2000.

Rubio Zapata, Miguel. *Notas sobre el teatro.* Ed. Luis Ramos-García. Lima and Minneapolis: Grupo Cultural Yuyachkani and the University of Minnesota Press, 2001.

Taylor, Diana. "Yuyachkani: Remembering Community." In *Performing Democracy: International Perspectives on Urban Community-Based Performance,* ed. Susan C. Haedicke and Tobin Nellhaus, 310–25. Ann Arbor: University of Michigan Press, 2001.

Taylor, Diana. "Staging Traumatic Memory: Yuyachkani." In *The Archive and the Repertoire: Performing Cultural Memory in the Americas,* 190–211. Durham: Duke University Press, 2003.

Adiós Ayacucho

(Novella by Julio Ortega, adapted for the theater
by Miguel Rubio Zapata for Grupo Cultural Yuyachkani)

Adapted from Edith Grossman's translation of the novella

CHARACTERS:

ALFONSO CÁNEPA, Campesino Organizer (disappeared)
Q'OLLA, Dancer from the Qapaq Q'olla de Cusco Ensemble

On the stage is a ramp on which the jacket, pants, and shoes of a man who was disappeared are displayed for mourners. Flowers and candles have been placed at the foot of the ramp. At the extreme left of the stage, on a blanket filled with musical instruments, a woman plays music.

Note: All of the lines are delivered by a single actor, who speaks in two different voices to distinguish between the masked Q'olla dancer and the disappeared man, Alfonso Cánepa.

Q'OLLA: *(He appears out of a large black bag holding a small white flag in his hand. He sees the funeral bier and approaches it.)* Who was this man? What a shame! He's dead, my little dove. Why? All over the town many men and women are being killed, they're being disappeared. Oh, my brother, look at this! *(He looks at the dead man's shoes.)* You don't need these anymore and I need them . . . Excuse me . . . *(He steps into the shoes and his body begins to tremble.)*

ALFONSO CÁNEPA: I came to Lima . . .

Q'OLLA: . . . to take back my corpse.

ALFONSO CÁNEPA: That's how I'd begin my speech . . .

Q'OLLA: . . . when I got to that city.

This isn't my voice. Who are you? Where are you?

ALFONSO CÁNEPA: That's what I thought while I climbed out of the pit where they'd thrown me after burning and mutilating my body. I was missing half my bones because they'd been taken away to Lima.

Last week, in this month of July when there's no rain, I decided to go in person to the police station in Quinua. The sergeant stood up when he saw me walk in.

"Don't play the fool. You're dangerous—you're a terrorist."

I knew they'd accuse me of being a terrorist, but they knew I wasn't one. So what did they want me to confess to?

Q'OLLA: What a mess you got yourself in . . .

ALFONSO CÁNEPA: First they cut off the first joint of my little finger, and I didn't even know it. I yelled a lot. That's when I must have realized they wouldn't stop, and then my body wouldn't stop trembling. Afterward they took me just outside town, near the high hill, and without stopping the jeep they threw me into the ravine. I rolled down, yelling, looking for a stone, a gully where I could hide.

Q'OLLA: And?

ALFONSO CÁNEPA: But they tossed in a grenade that exploded right beside me and I could see, as if it belonged to someone else, that my right arm blew off and waved good-bye to me as it sailed through the air. And I fell, knowing that I was dying.

Q'OLLA: You could have hidden yourself anywhere, brother.

ALFONSO CÁNEPA: Another phosphorous grenade exploded behind me, emptying my head and ripping open my stomach as if it were a rag.

While I did somersaults in the air I could see the guards scrambling down the sides of the ravine and howling like wolves. Then I realized that my left leg

Novella by Julio Ortega, adapted for the theater by Miguel Rubio Zapata for Grupo Cultural Yuyachkani, Peru, 1990. *Adiós Ayacucho,* in the form in which it appears in this reader, reflects Grupo Cultural Yuyachkani and Miguel Rubio Zapata's theatrical adaptation of the novella *Adiós Ayacucho,* written by Julio Ortega and translated by Edith Grossman as *Ayacucho, Goodbye* (Pittsburgh: Latin American Literary Review Press, 1994). This version consists of excerpts from Edith Grossman's translation of the novella assembled by the editors of this volume, with stage directions added based on Miguel Rubio's script in Spanish. This version of *Adiós Ayacucho* has been compiled and included here with permission from Julio Ortega, Miguel Rubio Zapata, and Latin American Literary Review Press.

was missing. They dragged me toward the bottom of the hill, where the rocks are bigger and the grass is thinner, but they were so rough that a few more of my bones were left behind. I told myself I would have to keep strict account of my lost parts so I could get them back later and have myself buried.

But when they finally threw me into a broad, shallow hole and began to cover me with stones and straw, I thought I saw one of the police poking around with a plastic bag in his hands, and I suddenly knew that this son of a bitch would pick up my pieces and make off with half my body.

This same cop, before we came to the hole that would be my grave, stuffed my belly with dry straw, laughing at me as if I were a doll that had been put together only to be pulled apart again.

I was a long time dying, though I must have been dead already when they covered me with rocks and straw, and I did some thinking about my short life as a naive Peruvian.

Q'OLLA: Of course, only a fool would go to the police station knowing that they were searching for him.

ALFONSO CÁNEPA: There I was, remembering and getting madder and madder. This time my anger was directed against myself. Everybody knew they were committing murder everywhere, that after a month some prisoners with tortured bodies turned up in common graves. But I had been hacked to pieces. With an arm and a leg missing, I couldn't go very far.

I began to move the stones away, and little by little, precisely because I had only half a body, I was able to slip and slide, roll a little, and pull myself up beside a burned tree on the path. I climbed the incline slowly, and when I reached the top I could see the dark, red town far below, and I felt a long, tranquil sorrow. I yelled and what came out was shrill and unpleasant like the screech of a wet cat. I yelled again, "Give me back my body. Where have you taken my bones?"

Whatever happens, I'm going to Lima to recover what's mine.

Q'OLLA: Listen, I've got to go. I have things to do, too. I've got to get going, brother. I wish you the best of luck. I hope everything goes well. Until we meet again.

ALFONSO CÁNEPA: Dawn was breaking by the time I reached the highway, and I sat down to wait for Don Luciano to pass by in his wagon. He's the old man who delivers milk to the town early in the morning. As soon as I saw him I climbed onto the back, the way little kids do, but without him seeing me. The wagon entered the town at the first cobbled street and stopped as always in front of the first house, the Robles' house. The door opened immediately and Rosa Robles came out and greeted us. I greeted her

back, but if she heard it she must have thought it was another of the decrepit mule's quirks.

"Don Luciano, have you heard anything about Alfonsito?"

"How could I not hear something? They say he was killed."

"They're coming here from Lima and they're killing all over."

"There's nothing we can do. When the government kills, everything gets erased."

The wagon turned onto the first unpaved street. I wanted to stand and see for the last time the streets where I grew up, but I controlled myself.

"They've killed my boy. His soul won't be able to rest. We have to find him and give him a Christian burial," my mother said.

"If you hear anything," my father said, "let us know, Don Luciano."

My father's voice sounded fainter than my mother's. Or does half of me only hear half of them? Maybe I've lost the part of my body that comes from my father and that's why I can't hear him well.

"Papá, mamá, so much death! So much suffering!"

"Outta here, dog, beat it," Don Luciano shouted.

On the Ayacucho road it was a four-day trip to Lima. So far nobody had spotted me, and with luck no one would until I got to Lima. Maybe I would have to show myself when I got to Lima. The people there were used to seeing corpses on television. As soon as I told them my story, there'd be no problem finding volunteers to bury me. "Wait for me, Mr. President, I want to see you!" I yelled suddenly. But the dogs barked like crazy. The milk in the jugs had splashed my face, and the straw from the wagon had stuck all over my body. I probably looked more like one of those dolls from the highlands that can stand the cold and the snow.

At a crowded stop I managed to find a truck: "The Little Peruvian," even though the name made me apprehensive.

Q'OLLA: That's understandable. What if it drove off the road into the ravine—you'd be killed twice over for being Peruvian.

ALFONSO CÁNEPA: But it was the best truck for me. It was full of boxes of fruit, sacks of potatoes. So I dragged myself through the cargo and settled into a sheltered corner close to the cabin. The driver and his assistant were having a couple of early drinks of pisco[1] to fight off the cold. Finally, without wanting to, they started the motor and turned on the radio.

We were moving slowly, when I heard someone whistling near me. I couldn't help jumping. I poked my head out and beside me I saw the face of the man who was whistling. He looked at me as if nothing was wrong. Suddenly the truck left the road down a narrow curve. It went down a tree-lined path and stopped in front of a small cemetery. An uncontrollable fear entered me. The truck stopped. The driver came back and moved some sacks and uncovered my face.

Q'OLLA: He couldn't recognize you, of course.

ALFONSO CÁNEPA: I'm still not sure, because he suddenly pulled out a plastic bag.

Q'OLLA: Which must have been left over from some funeral.

ALFONSO CÁNEPA: Meanwhile his assistant had returned after leaving some flowers at a grave. Then we returned to the main road. It was a bad road for sure. With hundreds of potholes and thousands of curves. The truck rattled so much my bones were pulverized.

Q'OLLA: The few you had left.

ALFONSO CÁNEPA: It must have been after we left Abancay, more or less, that I began to look at the people who crossed the road at regular intervals. Some traveled on enormous rocks. I suspected they were like me, disappeared, and I was overcome with emotion. Wasn't I the only one who was going to Lima to recover my bones? Out of the quiet a military patrol appeared.

"What branch are they from?" someone said.

"Is it a jeep or a truck?"

"A truck," said another. "And it might be a sinchi truck."[2]

"Around here the sinchis only use helicopters. But it's an Army truck."

"What's going on? Why did you stop?" a pale, young lieutenant asked.

"Nothing, Lieutenant," the driver answered. "It's the battery, that's all, but we're going now."

"What about that?" asked the lieutenant, pointing at me. I didn't move a muscle. My arm went in one direction and my leg in the other. False alarm. They didn't recognize me. They went away, and I composed myself as best I could.

We were about to continue on our way when a strange noise stopped us. Suddenly, coming from the opposite direction, a patrol of Marines appeared in their truck, which was a real fortress.

We saw that they had taken about ten boys as prisoners. They were singing a dark litany in Ayacuchan Quechua. I saw their round faces, their simple eyes, their cheeks burned by frost, their shaggy hair. There was no mystery about them. They were as much flesh and blood as anyone else, even a little more so because they knew they were going to be killed. And that knowledge filled them with the madness of the final days. So much death, and nothing. The truck stopped next to ours. The Marines stared without changing expression. The boys raised their fists in silence.

"Good-bye, and careful on this road," the captain said, and they continued on their way. We started on ours, too.

Soon we'd be in Huanta, one of the centers of the military counterinsurgency. Not long ago enormous common graves, secret tombs, were discovered there. The unrecognizable corpses were still lying in the square. While mothers wept in chorus as they looked for their dead, I listened to the cracking of bones, heard the intermittent weeping. So much killing! So much desperation! And nothing.

At the entrance to town we were stopped by a completely hysterical mob crowding around a half-naked preacher who was announcing the end of the world. As soon as we crossed into the square we saw that a funeral procession was on its way to the largest church, where the authorities were waiting in the atrium. Some local boss was sentenced to death, I thought. A funeral trumpet imposed silence but when it stopped playing explosions of dynamite made the ground shake. The square filled up with soldiers. We were moving by sheer horn power, braking and accelerating. As we were leaving the town, this time through the elegant district, we passed a group of well-dressed people who were listening to a speaker of their own who promised peace at the end of the world.

Q'OLLA: This is the first letter that I thought of:

Dear Mr. President:

By means of this letter the undersigned, Alfonso Cánepa, a Peruvian citizen residing in Quinua, occupation campesino, wishes to inform you, as the highest political authority in the Republic, of the following:

On the 15th of July I was arrested by the civil guard in my town, held incommunicado, tortured, burned and mutilated. I was dead, but was declared disappeared. You no doubt have seen the national protest that has ensued, to which I now add my own, requesting you to return to me the portion of my bones that were taken away to Lima. As you well know, all the laws of the nation, all international treaties, as well as all charters of human rights proclaim not only the inalienable human right to life but also the right to one's own death and burial with a complete body. The basic duty to respect human life supposes another even more basic duty that forms part of the code of military honor: the dead, Sir, are not mutilated. The corpse is, so to speak, the minimum unit of death, and dividing it, as is done today in Peru, means breaking the natural and social law. Your anthropologists and intellectuals have determined that the violence originates in the system and in the State that you represent. One of your victims, who has nothing more to lose, tells you this from his own experience. I want my bones, I want my literal, complete body, even if it is entirely dead. Finally, I seriously doubt that you will ever read this letter. An ancestor of mine, much more candid than I, wrote a two-thousand-page letter to the King of Spain that took two hundred years to be read. However, Valverde's discourse and Uchuraccay's discourse will be read in the schools of this country as the two pillars of the State.[3] In conclusion, I am certain that you will do everything possible to expedite my burial.

Thank you, brother. I think that came out well, and I'll need it for this journey.

ALFONSO CÁNEPA: The truck climbed up a chain of mountains, passing deep ravines. Slowly. Suddenly, when we had crossed a narrow bridge, an explosion about twenty meters away from us raised a wind full of dust and debris. A group of armed boys surrounded us.

"Nobody move!" somebody ordered while pointing a gun at us. They immediately began to unload some of the cargo, which they carried to a small, broken-down truck that drove away in a cloud of dust. The driver decided he wanted a receipt to prove that his load had been expropriated, but this caused a violent argument with the head of the operation, who turned out to be a woman. She threatened to shoot him on the spot. (There was no reason to doubt her intentions.) When she passed by me she said:

"You see? That's what you get for being a reformer. You're not dead, and you're not alive. Do you want to come with us?"

"No thanks."

"Everything is illusion except power. Make out a receipt for the driver."

She signed and handed the paper to the driver, who was still in a sweat. Then they sped away in another cloud of dust. We were tired and remained silent. The driver shared the coffee from his thermos, and a loaf of cornbread was passed around.

When we arrived at the entrance to the great city, we found a crowd engaged in the business of waiting: there were little food stands, shyster lawyers, bribe negotiators, photographers, police. The relatives of the disappeared showed each other photographs of their dead. It looked like a Peruvian game of cards with the fate of their children as their stakes. The avenue was filled with cars. When the red light stopped the traffic, a crowd of beggars, peddlers and children appeared, circulating among the cars and crying piteously. When I walked out onto the street I smelled a strong, familiar odor. Lima smelled impartially of urine.

When I was lost in the throng of buyers and sellers, I was horrified to see a third crowd composed of all kinds of madmen and lunatics who came and went in a hurry. They talked to themselves, dressed in rags, or naked and painted. At last I had a practical idea: I'd pretend to be crazy and then nobody would notice me anymore. I couldn't believe it: a peddler woman offered me an orange, another gave me a comforting pat. Others looked at me with a kindness that frightened me at first.

The cathedral was almost empty at that hour. From the top of the bell tower I could see the vast Plaza de Armas, the Government Palace, and all the corners occupied by assault troops. Little by little, all kinds of beggars, some one-armed, some crippled, some ill, entered the Plaza. I decided to go down. I'd easily pass for a beggar.

"Does anyone know why we're here?"

"The President is giving a little speech about the need for Christian charity."

What luck! I could give him my letter in person. Voices giving orders were heard at the doors of the Palace. At last, the President in person, his arm raised, moved to the center of his escort and walked forward, stopping right in front of me. I couldn't believe it. Here was the man responsible for my death, but I was sure he didn't even know my name and had more than one explanation to prove his personal innocence. Clearly, he was a politician. But if laws mean anything he was directly responsible, even if he had not given his formal sanction to the multiplication of death in this country. Now that his government was coming to an end, he at least should feel with his eyes the gaze of one of his victims. His voice sounded pleasant but remote. I don't know who he was talking to, certainly not to us. We would remember him, however, not for the number of votes but for the number of deaths. I got as close to him as I could and held out my letter and I saw him put it in the pocket of his blue jacket.

A kick in the ass lifted me off the ground and I flew through the air before I fell, tumbling at his feet. His guards searched me from head to toe. I couldn't believe it.

A boy rescued me with astounding courage.

"Stop, stop, he's my father!"

And the taciturn guards released me at once.

I was trying to recover with the boy's help, when I saw my letter, crumpled and unopened, on the dark pavement. Again I felt alone and didn't know what to do. I looked at the closed balconies of the Government Palace, where the conquistador Francisco Pizarro had been assassinated. I looked at the Plaza de Armas, now almost empty.

"Let's go, I'll hide you in the caves along the Rimac River," the boy said.

We were about to turn the corner at the Palace when the sight of the cathedral made me stop, full of doubts . . .

"Come with me."

The darkness under the great domes of the cathedral had deepened. As I passed by the sarcophagus of Francisco Pizarro, I hesitated. The case was made of glass and marble, with a golden lion of Spain on top, and inside you could see the remains of the savage founder of Lima: a ruined skull and a few scattered bones.

"Help me, we have to raise the lid. Here, take the true skull of Pizarro. You can sell it. And these bones, too."

The boy stared at me and said:

"Everyone will think you're Pizarro. That's all right, we'll bring you flowers. But I swear, when I'm President of Peru, I'll look for your bones." He was pale when he made his vow.

Inside the wide coffin my voice sounded like someone else's. I heard myself in the echoes, and I realized my time was near. Before long I would rise up from this earth like a column of stone and fire.

NOTES

All notes to this play are by the editors of this volume.

1. *Pisco* is a popular alcoholic drink in Peru.

2. *Sinchi* refers to the state security forces.

3. The letter in question is Guaman Poma's *Nueva Corónica y Buen Gobierno* (ca. 1615), which was addressed to King Philip III of Spain and was fiercely critical of Spanish colonial rule. Vicente de Valverde was the Dominican missionary who accompanied the Spanish conquistador Francisco Pizarro during his first encounter with the Inca emperor Atau Wallpa in 1532. Valverde gave Atau Wallpa a Bible, telling him that the word of God spoke in it, and Atau Wallpa, hearing nothing, threw it to the ground. The Spanish soldiers took this action as a sign to attack and captured him. Uchuraccay is a rural area in Peru where eight journalists investigating the Dirty War were killed in 1983. A presidential commission investigating the crime concluded that the journalists had been killed by *campesinos* who mistook them for Sendero Luminoso (Shining Path) guerrillas. The role of the military in inciting the campesinos was never investigated.

Manteca (Alberto Pedro Torriente)

Manteca, one of the most critically acclaimed Cuban plays of the 1990s, has almost no entrances or exits. There are no set changes, and the three characters—two brothers and a sister—spend the entire play in the cramped, cluttered living room of their apartment with the windows tightly shut. But if the atmosphere seems stifling and their actions, the small rituals of everyday existence, appear to be leading them nowhere, their words cover plenty of ground. Their conversation wanders from Cuban iguanas, German tanks, Russian meat, and Indian cows all the way to the North Pole. And all the while they ask themselves: "Should we do it?"

Actors Celia García (Dulce), Jorge Cao (Celestino), and Michaelis Cué (Pucho) in *Manteca,* directed by Miriam Lezcano, Teatro Mío, Havana, 1993. (Photo courtesy of Vivian Martínez Tabares.)

Alberto Pedro Torriente's comedy takes place during the "special period" that began in 1989 when the Soviet bloc began to dissolve and Cuba was left standing as one of the world's few remaining communist countries. After the fallout between the postrevolutionary government and the United States in 1961, the Cuban economy had been fueled mainly by trade with the Soviet Union. As the Cold War era ended, however, this avenue of support ceased to exist and the United States strengthened its long-standing embargo, isolating the country and creating the conditions for a crisis. For several years, as foreign capitalists waited with baited breath for Fidel to fall, and as he rolled with the punches by reorienting the economy toward international tourism, Cuba experienced severe shortages of basic goods such as food and medicine; even those with money had to buy food on the black market or devise ways of growing it themselves because stores had nothing to sell.[1]

The issue of food in its most elementary sense is reflected in the title, *Manteca,* which means "lard." It is also the name of the song that is heard throughout the play, a Latin jazz classic written by the Cuban composer Chano Pozo and Dizzy Gillespie.[2] The song's title was originally an allusion to marijuana, adding to the impression that whatever is going on in this apartment in the hours leading up to the New Year must be illicit. What is the violent act these three comic siblings must commit and who is their intended victim? What exactly are they arguing about?

A lot of things, it seems. Pucho is a gay intellectual, a writer and self-proclaimed existentialist who was fired from his position as a university professor for his dissident views and, most likely, his sexual preferences. Celestino is a macho communist who studied engineering in the Soviet Union and chalks every problem up to a "lack of balls." Their sister Dulce, the champion of domesticity, is the most sentimental member of the trio, but her earthy wisdom is tainted by some provincial prejudices. They evoke well-known "types" in Cuban society, much like nineteenth- and early-twentieth-century *costumbrista* plays that reflected local customs and created "representative" portraits of Latin America's fledgling nations. But the legacy of *costumbrismo* carries some heavy baggage in Cuba, where it took the form of a genre known as *teatro bufo* whose humor revolved around the parodic effect of white actors wearing blackface. Beginning in the second half of the nineteenth century and continuing into the 1950s, three stock characters dominated the Cuban stage: the lusty mulatta, the *gallego* (a white, lower-class Spanish immigrant), and the *negrito* (little black man). As a depiction of "Cuban" identity, teatro bufo was a vehicle for anticolonial sentiment, yet, like minstrel theater in the United States, it tended to reify racial categories through its acts of racial impersonation.[3]

Although many of Alberto Pedro's plays deal explicitly with race and feature black characters (the playwright himself was black), *Manteca* poses a more indirect challenge to costumbrismo's racialized representations, as well as to more recent manifestations of "realism": the Soviet-style socialist realism that the Cuban government endorsed in the 1970s and 1980s, and magical realism, the literary style that Gabriel García Márquez—the butt of several jokes in the play—turned into one of Latin America's most successful exports. Pucho, Dulce, and Celestino are distinguished from one another by their different beliefs and modes of social belonging—things that aren't immediately visible to the naked eye—and they are more complex and contradictory than the parts they have chosen to play. They argue about whether the odor that pervades the house is a "stench-stench" or merely a "subjective stench," in which case Celestino says it doesn't count. Pucho, however, slyly insinuates that perhaps his beefcake brother isn't as straight as he pretends. Dulce insists that "As long as the family's united let the wind blow where it may," yet she gets caught up in elaborating an entire theory of geopolitics that revolves around the distribution of dinosaurs. Celestino informs Pucho that life isn't a novel, and there is a disagreement over whether Pucho's statements are metaphors or, as Dulce insists, "utter nonsense."

But they also have things in common. Celestino berates himself because he couldn't stop his wife from taking their kids with her when she moved back to Russia. Dulce's children are also halfway across the globe, and her husband found another woman when he was sent abroad in the service of the Revolution. Pucho devotes all his energy to writing a novel that he knows will never be published. Above all, they share a sense of apprehension. They can't stay in this stuffy apartment forever; Cuba can't survive as an island, and their own immobility is all the evidence they need to know that there's no longer anything revolutionary about what's taking place. The "outside" world that is quickly closing in, however, isn't exactly cause for celebration. Rather than the material bounty that global capitalism claims to offer, what their words reflect are neo-Nazis in Germany, ethnic cleansing in Bosnia, and Hawaiians who have to turn themselves into "natives" so they can be tourist attractions for the rich. This fractious family might spend its time arguing about what went wrong and why, but the main question on everyone's mind is what to do "when the moment comes."

When it premiered in 1993, *Manteca* wasn't a look back at a time of hardship and uncertainty; the play was written, rehearsed, and staged in the midst of the circumstances it represents. Part of Alberto Pedro's motivation in writing the piece was to provide work for three particular actors who belonged to Teatro Mío, the company he founded in 1987 with his wife, the director Miriam Lezcano.[4] Some of the performances were held in the lobby of a theater during the daytime because blackouts (like the one that occurs in the play) were so frequent that it was deemed wise to take advantage of the natural light. The minimalist set included details that were at once naturalistic and symbolic, including props from previous productions such as a globe and an old bust of Lenin. Live music contributed to the sense of immediacy and presence, though it also added a jarring note to the intimate atmosphere. As the script indicates, the music is not meant to be "decorative" but rather "annoying." The characters' unusual costumes, too, helped turn the appearance of everyday reality into something out of the ordinary, as did the mystery surrounding the unnamed character who never appears onstage, though he is the pivot on which the characters' conversation turns.[5]

According to Alberto Pedro, who recently died at the age of fifty, what "saves" theater in the face of increasing competition from television is "its drive to desacralize, to transgress ethical, political, and, especially, aesthetic values." It doesn't have to be an expensive endeavor because what makes it effective is the opportunity for dialogue—it is a "conspiracy" between the actors and the audience that can only come into being through the "thrusting of people together in a cavern or grotto." Like many contemporary playwrights, Pedro emphasized the ritualistic nature of theater, but he added an important caveat. "Good theater," he said, "is like a ritual, like a religion rejected by its own participants: the reign of doubt is what enchants me."[6]

Given that they dwell in a cavern of their own, one can also glimpse an argument for a certain kind of embodied performance amid the existential allegory of Pucho's novel, Celestino's hands-on pragmatism, and Dulce's quixotic affectivity. *Manteca* is a comedy, albeit one with something serious to say, and much of its humor and pathos results precisely from this juxtaposition of the abstract, the material, and the emotive. The symbolic stench that truly smells, the bloody ending that is also about blood ties, the *manteca* at the center of it all—their meanings arise out of the interplay and overlay of all these elements. Pucho is dressed as a clown, and although he tends to have his head in the clouds, the play does what a lot of slapstick humor does: it takes metaphors and makes them literal and uses the mundane world of the material to poke fun at our tendency to think that the truth is always abstract. But it also elevates the concrete and corporeal by showing that what seems to be most immediate and self-evident can also gesture toward something that lies beyond its own bounds. If costumbrismo and other ossified forms of realism claim to provide portraits of the people, *Manteca* insists that what comes out in the flesh is not simply what has been bred in the bone.

Theater can foreclose possibilities and reinforce stifling certainties. It can convince us that what we've got is as real as it gets, or that everything is appearance and the desire for a true alternative is just another illusion. But the stage is also a place where impalpable ideas are acted out by people and where bodies and objects, the tangible reality of the here and now, are capable of becoming something other than what they are. It can be a place where the material bumps up against the ideal, where what we see before us and what it seeks to represent play off one another in a way that gives rise to a laugh or a wince that is also the germ of a heretical doubt.

As the audience discovers in the second half of the play, *Manteca* really is about lard and what many Cubans had to do during the special period in order to eat. At the same time, it speaks to the problem of how to fill a different kind of lack, one that has been experienced by people all the way from the southern tip of Africa to the North Pole. The lost page of Pucho's novel describes a mythical time when "pigs and bread, eggs and their chickens, multiplied" and "the world turned into a delirium of meats within everyone's reach." But it wasn't enough, and so some of the people began to slaughter the others, locking the survivors away in museums as artifacts of an imperial imagination. Why? "Because eating wasn't the problem; rather, it was the loss of the possibility of something different. That which was once called a more just society, a better world, something which nobody could remember, because the cannibal hour had struck."

—Sarah J. Townsend

NOTES

1. For more information on the special period, see "Cuba Stands Alone, 1985–2003," chapter 8 in Richard Gott, *Cuba: A New History* (New Haven: Yale University Press, 2004).

2. Luciano "Chano" Pozo González, born in Havana in 1915, helped create Latin jazz, which mixed bebop and Cuban rhythms. His music was influenced by his involvement with Afro-Cuban religious traditions. In 1946 he was introduced to Dizzy Gillespie and became a featured soloist in his group. "Manteca," composed by Pozo in collaboration with Gillespie, was recorded in 1947, as were other hits, including "Cubana Be," "Cubana Bop," and "Tin Tin Deo."

3. For more information on the history of teatro bufo and its relationship to other, literary expressions of costumbrismo, see Jill Lane's *Blackface Cuba, 1840–1895* (Philadelphia: University of Pennsylvania Press, 2005). Lane details the prominent role that teatro bufo played in the debates surrounding Cuban independence from Spain. She also makes the argument that teatro bufo was a form of popular ethnography that shaped the scientific discipline of ethnography, which emerged in the late nineteenth and early twentieth centuries. Interestingly, teatro bufo enjoyed something of a resurgence in the 1990s, sparking debates about

whether this vernacular tradition could be reappropriated and used critically, or whether it should be relegated to the past. See Elizabeth Ruf-Maldonado, "Cubanidad and the Performance of Blackness in the Theater of Cuba's 'Special Period.'" (PhD diss., Columbia, 2006).

4. Alberto Pedro's other plays include *Weekend en Bahía* (1986), *Delirio Habanero* (1994), *Mar Nuestro* (1997), and *Esperando a Odiseo* (2001). He also wrote for and acted in television productions.

5. *Manteca* has already acquired the status of a classic. In 2000, Teatro Mío restaged the play at the Teatro Nacional de Cuba; it continues to be performed periodically in Cuba. Its English-language premiere took place in October 1997 at the Theatre Centre in Toronto, where it was staged under the direction of Sue Miner. In 1997, the Miami-based Grupo Cultural La Má Teodora staged a Spanish-language production under the direction of Alberto Serraín; the company restaged it in 2002. During its 2003–4 season, the Teatro de la Luna company in Washington, D.C., staged the play in Spanish with simultaneous English translation. It has also been performed in France and Spain.

6. Vivian Martínez Tabares, "Theater as Conspiracy," trans. Nancy Westrate, *South Atlantic Quarterly* 96 (winter 1997): 55.

SELECTED REFERENCES

Boudet, Rosa Ileana. "New Playwrights, New Challenges: Current Cuban Theater." Trans. Nancy Westrate. *South Atlantic Quarterly* 96 (winter 1997): 31–51.

Lane, Jill. *Blackface Cuba, 1840–1895.* Philadelphia: University of Pennsylvania Press, 2005.

Martínez Tabares, Vivian. "'Manteca': Catharsis and Absurdity." Trans. Christopher Winks. *TDR: The Drama Review* 40 (spring 1996): 44–48.

Martínez Tabares, Vivian. "Theater as Conspiracy: An Interview with Alberto Pedro." Trans. Nancy Westrate. *South Atlantic Quarterly* 96 (winter 1997): 53–63.

Monleón, Rafael. "Alberto Pedro Torriente." *Primer acto* 255 (September–October 1994): 97–100.

Muguercia, Magaly. "The Gift of Precariousness: Alberto Pedro Torriente's 'Manteca.'" Trans. Christopher Winks. *TDR: The Drama Review* 40 (spring 1996): 49–60.

Muguercia, Magaly. *Teatro y utopía.* Havana: Ediciones Unión, 1997.

Stevens, Camilla. *Family and Identity in Contemporary Cuban and Puerto Rican Drama.* Gainesville: University Press of Florida, 2004.

Manteca (Alberto Pedro Torriente)

Translated by Christopher Winks

CHARACTERS:

PUCHO
CELESTINO
DULCE

The action takes place in the living room of the three siblings, which, due to their present situation, they have had to convert into a type of warehouse. Rusty cans of preserves, sacks, boxes of every type are scattered around the scene. CELESTINO is fiddling around with a few empty oil-cans and a bicycle wheel, using his tools in the repair or fabrication of God knows what kind of strange artifact. PUCHO is searching among the pages of his novel for something fundamental that he can't find. DULCE is ceremoniously sorting rice. The light rises and falls monotonously, giving the impression that time has come to a standstill. The background music of the play is always the same: Chano Pozo's "Manteca" (Lard), at all imaginable levels. CELESTINO is memorizing verses in English without for one moment interrupting his activity. PUCHO breaks the monotony when the director deems that the public has sufficiently grasped this sensation of stasis. The light comes and goes intermittently throughout the play, as the director pleases, but the characters do not interrupt their activity. PUCHO is dressed like a clown, DULCE is wearing high heels with a sequined lamé dress that is no longer in style, CELESTINO is wearing tweed overalls and high boots. The music is annoying; it stands out. It's not decorative.

PUCHO: We gotta do it.

DULCE: Do it!?

CELESTINO: Do it?

PUCHO: Yeah. Do it.

DULCE: No way.

CELESTINO: Drink, drank, drunk . . .

PUCHO: This situation's unbearable.

CELESTINO: So get out then.

PUCHO: Why? I was born here. I got more rights than even he does, 'cause I'm from Havana. And he's from the country.

DULCE: *(Laughs)* Aah Pucho, the things you think of! For sure, brother, you're a born writer! The day they publish that novel of yours you're gonna be more famous than that García Márquez guy . . . So you're from the city and he's from the country. Aah Pucho, you're nuts!

PUCHO: You're the ones who're the nuts around here! If we don't do it fast, it'll be all up with us.

CELESTINO: And who's gonna do it? There's somebody I know who faints when he hears the word "blood." So who's gonna do it then?

PUCHO: I hate violent acts. I'm a pacifist. I'm just trying to use words to convince the tough guys—the guys with balls, the real macho types who're ready for action.

DULCE: Don't let's get started again!

CELESTINO: *(While PUCHO stomps on the floor upstage, saying "Cockroaches, cockroaches!")* Let's suppose it gets done. What about afterwards? Happiness for fifteen or twenty days as always, conga, going on a bender the way we Cubans like to do. And afterwards, what? Put up with hunger, hunger! Living day by day is something only fit for animals. That's the great discovery of the rich.

PUCHO: "I love the moment because in it palpitates the voice of the eternal," as the poet said. I'm a pacifist, but besides that I'm an existentialist.

CELESTINO: The day the writers stop eating is when I start believing the fairy tale that they nourish themselves on the spirit.

DULCE: Good writers always go through hunger; that's what the forewords to their books say. They all go through hunger and want, from Cervantes to that García Márquez guy who was from a country village and who's much worse than Pucho is and got himself a Nobel Prize. You just keep right on going, brother, right on with your papers like you were doing just

Alberto Pedro Torriente, Cuba, 1993. Translated from Spanish by Christopher Winks. Originally published in *TDR: The Drama Review* 40 (spring 1996). Copyright © 1996 MIT Press Journals.

now, and the minute they publish your first line you'll remember me.

CELESTINO: When they publish him!

DULCE: When they publish him.

CELESTINO: Put, put, put. Teach, taught, taught . . .

DULCE: For sure this García Márquez guy is from Colombia and the lights are going out there too.

PUCHO: I'm going to write about you in my novel, Celestino, and you're going to be the only character with his real name, Celestino. I'll write about you, names, nicknames, and all, Celestino. A whole chapter only about you, where the world will hear about what a coward you are, Celestino. This cowardice of yours is the worst of all because you aren't even brave enough to admit that you're scared, Celestino. Because I know you're afraid, Celestino.

CELESTINO: We gotta give it a lot of thought. You can't make a hasty decision.

DULCE: It's still not the time.

PUCHO: Waiting, waiting. It isn't fair. We've turned ourselves into a bunch of slaves.

CELESTINO: Hunt, hunt, hunt. Kept, kept, kept. Know, knew, known.

PUCHO: We've got a life, *a* life, only one. Who knows if all of a sudden one of us won't get sick to his stomach and go merrily off to the grave?

DULCE: Pucho, come on, my God, these last few days my chest has been hurting like it does every New Year's Eve!

PUCHO: And where in the world does this happen? In what minimally civilized city?

DULCE: Pucho, the neighbors!

PUCHO: We have to get this over and done with and open the windows, open them wide so the air will come in!

DULCE: Pucho, the neighbors!

PUCHO: We can't go on kidding ourselves. We gotta get out of this damned cloister and all this morbidity.

CELESTINO: Lead, led, led. Understand, understood, understood. *(To PUCHO)* Mary Astor is an actress. *(Silence. Chano Pozo's "Manteca" is heard.)*

DULCE: We never had dinosaurs, that's the problem. That's the way nature is. This thing about the Americans lifting this embargo thing, like they're saying, and then everything will be settled, that's just people's ignorance. The real problem isn't with the Americans but because we never had any dinosaurs. See, without dinosaurs there's no petroleum. Jarahueca's another story.[1] You can't do it without dinosaurs. How many dinosaurs does it take to fill up a barrel of petroleum? Those seven countries that are always busy having meetings over there in Europe must have gotten hold of all the dinosaurs for themselves. And don't even mention Arabia! That's how nature is; it just so happened that we were born in the part of the world that didn't have dinosaurs. Though who

knows if what happened here was because the Spaniards got involved, because if Father Las Casas couldn't stop them from killing the Indians, how could he stop them from eating the iguanas?[2] And didn't the iguanas look more like dinosaurs than any other animal? But here they didn't let them grow, evolve. Not the iguanas we have now, but the ones in the beginning who, if all went well, would have turned themselves into dinosaurs. Though to tell you the truth, I don't know if it was the Spaniards who brought this hatred for the iguana or if it was around during the Indians. It was always like that because nature wanted it that way. The world's divided into countries who had dinosaurs and countries who didn't have them. And the countries who had dinosaurs always did what they wanted to do with the others, like those seven countries that are always busy having meetings over there in Europe. *(Silence)*

CELESTINO: *(Referring to DULCE's work with the rice)* Potatoes are much more nutritious. The moment will come when rice will no longer be the basis of our diet.

PUCHO: It'll be potatoes.

(DULCE sets aside a small bag of rice and interrupts: "Monday.")

CELESTINO: Potatoes, yes, potatoes! In the Soviet Union we ate potatoes, lots and lots of potatoes, and nobody died of them.

(DULCE interrupts with "Tuesday," placing another paper bag next to the first.)

PUCHO: Taters, you mean. In Russia they call them taters.

CELESTINO: That story about potatoes causing stomach acid is a fairy tale. Over there, the kids eat potatoes and they grow up much stronger than the ones here.

(DULCE says "Wednesday" and sets aside a third paper bag.)

PUCHO: In Russia?

CELESTINO: It'll always be the Soviet Union for me.

(DULCE repeats the action, saying "Thursday.")

PUCHO: Not for the Russians.

CELESTINO: They were better off when they were Soviets.

(DULCE repeats the action and says "Friday.")

PUCHO: Eating taters.

CELESTINO: Yes, eating potatoes. I ate them for seven years and I got my engineering degree and I was a lot more on the ball than I am now.

(DULCE says "Saturday" and repeats the action.)

PUCHO: Thanks to the taters.

CELESTINO: At least back then there weren't any beggars, and not so many drug addicts or muggers. Nobody panhandled and everybody ate.

(DULCE interrupts with "Sunday," setting aside the last paper bag with the rice for the week.)

PUCHO: Taters, they ate taters.

CELESTINO: I wish my kids could eat taters! Even if that was all, taters, only taters. (*Silence. Chano Pozo's music is heard.*)

PUCHO: I'm gonna put this in my novel.

DULCE: What?

PUCHO: That bit about the dinosaurs. Mind you, your theory's got a contradiction. There're countries that had dinosaurs which aren't among the seven countries that are always getting together. And on the other hand, other countries that never had any are living like they always had them.

DULCE: It's being smartasses that hurts us the most. Just check it out: what do they live on in Hawaii? On the innocence of the natives. Those girls with all the flowers in their hair and those necklaces, also made of flowers, dancing all innocent-like. You can tell they're genuine natives. But we can't do that here, because anyone can tell right away that these mulattas and these black women aren't natives at all through sheer smartassedness, and millionaires aren't dummies. Being smartasses is a lot worse than not having any dinosaurs.

CELESTINO: Maybe that's the right answer. Who knows if deep down, that isn't the solution. In short, what the fuck, let the sun rise when and where it has to.

DULCE: Aaah, Celestino!

CELESTINO: (*To PUCHO*) You're right, I'm a coward.

PUCHO: I was just kidding about putting you in my novel.

CELESTINO: I didn't have the balls for the important stuff, I just didn't have the balls.

DULCE: The children are okay, that's what the letters say.

CELESTINO: Reality's something else. All you have to do is read the papers, watch television.

PUCHO: Television! Papers!

CELESTINO: I didn't have the balls to stop her from taking the kids with her. No balls! No balls! No balls at all! (*Silence*)

DULCE: You did what had to be done. The children belong to the mother, that's the way it's always been. If she wanted to take them to the place where she was born, she's got that right. They couldn't have wished for a better father than you. But every people's got their customs. Including her, who's from, what's that place again?

PUCHO: Kirghizia.

DULCE: Right, they aren't Chinese or anything, but then again they don't stop being what they are. But they feel the same way all mothers do.

CELESTINO: I dreamed about them. Take notes, writer. It was night, but it looked like day, the way it does in the Leningrad nights. It was cold, really cold, but I didn't feel it. I was going around in short sleeves like I was here in Havana. The children asked me why I wasn't cold. What was I doing there? I don't know. Suddenly they fell asleep. Their mother served me a cup of tea. "They're cold," I said. And do you want to know what she answered? "I got this far and I'm not going back. I'd rather they froze. Do you hear me, Celestino? Let them freeze!"

DULCE: Those are very fine sentiments. She didn't like the heat because it was very humid and she got dehydrated, and she didn't like the cold because there was too much air. What did Mama want? Did you think she wouldn't protest? What could she do, the poor thing?

CELESTINO: Hey you, writer, how is it possible for a mother to prefer that her children freeze?

PUCHO: It's only a dream.

CELESTINO: She wants it that way. I know she wants it that way. How is it possible for her to prefer that her children freeze? I was there before the disaster and there was no shortage of cheese, every kind of cheese, nor meat, nor wine, nor vodka, nor bread, every kind of bread—black bread, white bread, brown bread, baguettes, twists, buttered bread, bread sticks. How could things have reached that point? Who could have told me it would end up like this? With the kids over there and me over here, so far away, and unable to do anything about it?

DULCE: I don't know why people screwed around with the Russians. It had to be because of what they did with the movies—swapping those lovely films with Dolores del Rio[3] and her hair all loose for the ones with Russian women dressed up like soldiers, with their hair tied back, and all desperate for a German tank like the ones in Hitler's time to run them over. I don't know what it was, because that Russian meat—the stuff they sent us at the beginning of the American blockade along with the circus and the missiles which they came back later to take away and the people were shouting, "Nikita you prick, we'll dance on your grave, you went and took back what you gave"; that meat with the cow painted on the wrapper, that people said was a bear, and that the meat was bear meat; that meat that saved us, because no country wanted to send us anything—I really liked that meat, and that canned meat too. Although there were people who also said that it was human meat from the prisoners in Siberia in the concentration camps, like that Chinese guy said who ran the restaurant on the avenue where the empty store's located now and who came from Canton. He said he came here fleeing Mao Tse-Tung, but communism got him again here and people said he really flipped out. To tell you the truth, I never paid attention to any of that. The one I couldn't stand from the start, not because he was Russian, but because . . . I never could stand him from the start . . . was that guy Mikoyan.[4]

Because that whole business about leaving his wife's funeral and coming over here . . . but old Nikita always struck me as a very decent person. That whole story about him taking off his shoe at the UN and pounding it on the table, I never believed it. Sure, I'd like my niece and nephew to be here, because no matter what, they aren't Russians, and the poor kids must be suffering.

CELESTINO: Especially the girl.

DULCE: Poor little thing! Because the boy's an angel, but that niece of mine was born too clever for her own good. Just think, her mother tried to teach her Russian and got absolutely nowhere. Not to mention that soup she always made for her. That kid would hide it, flush it down the toilet, and then she'd go and eat her plate of black beans all nice and creamy. And then she'd go to her mama with some cooked-up story about how she'd eaten all her soup, what's it called?

CELESTINO: What?

DULCE: The soup. What's the name of that soup?

PUCHO: Borscht.

DULCE: Borscht. It was all Mama's fault. Look at how everybody was telling her, "Don't get involved, you're not the kid's mother," but Mama always kept on with her: "My granddaughter's not Russian, my granddaughter's not Russian." Jeez, Mama! What that poor woman had to put up with! The thing is, Cubans have always believed that foreigners aren't aware of how tricky we are. And because of that, now look, the Russians got tired of it. Especially the Russian women. 'Cause you guys are capable of putting up with anything, anything at all, except monogamy. You live and die dreaming about your harem. And you're not even Lebanese or anything!

CELESTINO: I didn't have the balls, I didn't have the balls!

DULCE: Ohmigod, Celestino, for the love of God, it's been days now that my chest has been hurting the way it does every New Year's!

CELESTINO: One of these days I'm going to ride out on my bicycle and throw myself in front of a truck and then it'll all be over. (*The Chano Pozo tune is heard.*)

DULCE: In front of a truck!?

PUCHO: A truck? (*PUCHO hides a knife that is being used as a bookmark from CELESTINO.*)

DULCE: That's two accidents now you've had with that bicycle, and every time you run into a truck.

PUCHO: The same truck.

CELESTINO: How did you find out?

DULCE: I found out.

CELESTINO: And here I warned them not to tell you! Anyway, nothing happened.

PUCHO: It still could.

DULCE: You almost got yourself killed. They pulled you out from under the rear wheel.

PUCHO: Everyone thought you were done for.

DULCE: The driver was as white as a sheet.

PUCHO: It was the same driver as before.

DULCE: Why do you always run into the same truck at the same time of day?

PUCHO: And the same driver, too.

CELESTINO: Hold, hold, hold. Hunt, hunt, hunt.

DULCE: Why do you always run into the same truck, Celestino?

CELESTINO: Because I always take my bicycle out into the same street at the same time of day and the guy always drives his truck past the same corner!

PUCHO: Where there's a traffic signal that says YIELD. You'd think you'd have remembered that by now after getting hit the first time.

CELESTINO: Well, I don't remember that sign. I don't know why, but I never see it.

PUCHO: You never see it.

CELESTINO: You've got to be there first thing in the morning on odd-numbered days, with your containers. Let's see if we can pull ourselves together. It isn't much, but it helps. Everything is hard. We don't even have vaccines, not a single one! If a virus comes, an epidemic will break out. Because we aren't alone. How many people are in this same situation? Surviving!

DULCE: Why do you always, at the same time of day, run into the same truck with the same driver? Why don't you see the YIELD signal, Celestino?

PUCHO: Do you want me to read a little bit of my novel? (*PUCHO collects his papers and reads.*) "Night descended upon the accursed city and the smell of the sea was the only hope of its blinded residents who now no longer slept, nor did they wake. And it was then that that enormous Negro, the terror and delight of that place's old white repressed vaginas, climbed up to the highest roof and without so much as an 'I have returned,' took out his oversized member and pissed copiously, and the people thought it was rain from the sea, or the salty sea itself which was falling upon their heads. And there was light . . ." (*The light goes out.*) Fucking son-of-a . . . (*In darkness*) "And there was light, light once again and forever upon the city forgotten even by silence."

CELESTINO: Let's see if that Negro of yours comes back to piss. (*They all light candles.*)

DULCE: That was very nice, I've heard worse from that García Márquez guy. (*Silence. In the darkness, they all continue with their usual tasks.*) Oh, God forgive me, I just thought I saw Mama!

PUCHO: What about that noise?

CELESTINO: What noise?

PUCHO: I don't know, a strange noise.

DULCE: Could they have heard us? It's just like I've been telling you. These discussions are inappropriate. Just do what you have to do, period. (*Raising her* voice *so they can hear her outside)* And anyway, what are all these countries sending us? To get to this point after spilling so much blood! And the Bosnians, bombs here and bombs there, blood flowing every which way. And don't even talk about Africa. And with all those cows running loose in India. And now in Germany: no blacks, no Turks. So they were able to knock down that statue? Let's see now, there're Vietnamese, Chinese, and Koreans over there . . . If oil doesn't show up in Jarahueca . . . because it's in Varadero.[5] Where is that country anyway? Where did these people come from? Because they aren't white, but they sure aren't blacks either, or mulattoes. So what's that ship going to bring us? *(The lights come back on. They all blow out their candles and applaud. They run offstage momentarily, leaving the stage empty. Then all three come back in smiling.)*

DULCE: *(Timidly)* Do you all smell it?

CELESTINO: What?

DULCE: Oh, nothing, nothing. *(Pause)* You really don't smell it?

CELESTINO: What, Dulce?

DULCE: Nothing, nothing, nothing. It's all in my head. *(Pause)* You really don't smell anything? Nothing at all, at all?

CELESTINO: What's the problem, lady?

PUCHO: The stench! It stinks, doesn't it?

DULCE: Something awful.

CELESTINO: It doesn't stink something awful. It's a normal stench.

PUCHO: It's a horrible stench.

DULCE: Is it coming from here?

CELESTINO: It's coming from the street.

PUCHO: Everything's closed. It has to be coming from here.

CELESTINO: Well, it isn't from here. That stench isn't from here.

DULCE: It's true! The stench from here is a different kind of stench.

PUCHO: It's still a stench.

DULCE: No, Pucho. The stench you can't avoid is one thing, but you know that people make an effort and disinfect themselves with alcohol or whatever, and the stench-stench, the flat-out stench, which is a stench because it's a stench, is another thing entirely.

CELESTINO: There's no stench here, there's a strong smell, nothing more. But a stench, what they call a stench, isn't here because the two of us don't smell it, and a stench perceived by a single person is a subjective stench, so your stench is worthless. *(Silence. "Manteca" is heard.)*

PUCHO: Where will this all end? What is it all coming to?

CELESTINO: Where it's going. The main thing is to have balls.

PUCHO: Nature, like society, has laws which have

nothing to do with balls. This is sterile, stupid, and cheap voluntarism.

DULCE: They say that García Márquez guy writes with a machine.

PUCHO: I've got to do it with my balls, simply because I want to. I've got to think like that with my balls, it has to start raining thanks to my balls, you have to be happy thanks to my balls and it's gotta stop raining thanks to my balls, and start up raining again thanks to my balls.

DULCE: But if it's the machine that's writing the novels, that García Márquez guy can't be as good a writer as they claim.

PUCHO: It's because of that that we're the way we are.

CELESTINO: Due to a lack of balls.

PUCHO: Due to an excess of balls, as you would put it.

DULCE: And I'm almost sure that this machine isn't even from Colombia, because the Japanese are the ones who know the most about those kinds of things. *(She cuts up a piece of bread and shares it among the three of them.)*

CELESTINO: Due to a lack of balls.

PUCHO: *(Eating his piece of bread)* "He found himself in the neighborhood of the Asteroids 325, 326, 327, 328, 329, 330. He began therefore by visiting them in order to add to his knowledge. The first of them was inhabited by a king. Clad in royal purple and ermine, he was seated upon a throne, which was at the same time both simple and majestic. 'Ah! Here is a subject,' exclaimed the king when he saw the little prince coming. And the little prince asked himself, 'How could he recognize me when he had never seen me before?' He did not know how the world is simplified for kings. To them, all men are subjects."

DULCE: *(Eating her bread)* Good heavens!

PUCHO: "Since he was tired, he yawned. 'It is contrary to etiquette to yawn in the presence of a king,' the monarch said to him. 'I forbid you to do so.' 'I can't help it,' replied the little prince, thoroughly embarrassed. 'I have come on a long journey, and I have had no sleep.' 'Ah then,' the king said, 'I order you to yawn.' He was an absolute monarch. But because he was a very good man, he made his orders reasonable. 'If I ordered a general,' he would say, by way of example, 'if I ordered a general to change himself into a seabird, and if the general did not obey me, that would not be the fault of the general. It would be my fault.'"

DULCE: *(Eating)* Of course!

PUCHO: *(Throwing away his bread)* "One must require from each one the duty which each one can perform. Authority rests first of all on reason. Never ask more of men than they are capable of doing. If you order your people to go and throw themselves into the sea, they will rise up in revolution."

CELESTINO: So now it's Saint-Exupéry!

PUCHO: *(To CELESTINO)* Do you still remember? Will you ever go back to the way you were, or is it all just a part of the past, of those times we went to the library together; you always invited me along, do you remember? You weren't such a big old tough guy then. You liked classical music and the ballet.

CELESTINO: *(To DULCE)* Is tomorrow an odd or even day?

PUCHO: My friend asked after you.

CELESTINO: Which friend?

PUCHO: Our friend.

CELESTINO: My friends aren't your friends.

PUCHO: My friend the painter asked after you.

CELESTINO: What painter?

PUCHO: *The* painter! He said he bumped into you the other day by chance and you didn't say hello.

CELESTINO: I must not have seen him.

PUCHO: He said you did.

CELESTINO: I must not have recognized him. Time's passed, he'll have put on some weight.

PUCHO: He's in good shape.

CELESTINO: Then he's gotten older.

PUCHO: No, he doesn't look any older.

CELESTINO: I didn't feel like saying hello to him!

DULCE: Why did you do that, Celestino? Wasn't he the one from the exhibition? Such a nice person. Why did you do that?

CELESTINO: I don't have to say hello to everybody I see, and this guy in particular I don't care for.

PUCHO: You didn't think like that before.

CELESTINO: That was then.

PUCHO: And how long since you changed your opinion?

CELESTINO: And who ever told you I felt differently? *(Silence. They go back to listening to the music of "Manteca.")*

DULCE: What a shame, such a decent and elegant young man, in spite of his color. Sure, when I saw him for the first time, I thought he was an athlete—one of those basketball players—and the minute he opened his mouth I felt so ashamed because he was an artist. An artist in spite of his size and his color! You learn something new every day. And what happened with him? Did he keep on painting? They say that he was real good at it. But to tell the truth, I didn't understand his paintings.

CELESTINO: He didn't either.

DULCE: Those blots looked like cockroach legs, and the colors just kind of fell on top of you. I didn't know what to say to him the time he invited me to the exhibition. All those paintings terrified me. I got chills and he laughed. Poor guy. What became of him?

PUCHO: Nothing. Now he's painting landscapes for tourists and decorations for the hotels. He's going to marry a foreigner. *(To CELESTINO)* And he asked after you, you, you!

CELESTINO: Tomorrow's an odd-numbered day.

DULCE: If he's going to marry a foreigner, he can leave and come back.

CELESTINO: Especially leave.

PUCHO: And come back again.

CELESTINO: And leave again. Everybody wants to come back and leave again.

PUCHO: Not you.

CELESTINO: I had a job, I had children, I was married, and I came back. I didn't have any problems. I could have stayed, and I returned. If you were in my shoes, you wouldn't have done it because you don't have the balls for it.

PUCHO: He wanted to paint you in the nude. Do you remember? With a laurel wreath on your head, and the hammer and sickle in your hand.

DULCE: In the nude?

PUCHO: Did you reach an agreement in the end, or didn't you?

CELESTINO: An agreement about what?

PUCHO: You were going to go to his studio.

CELESTINO: What studio?

PUCHO: His studio. The one he had in his house.

CELESTINO: I never arranged with anybody to go to any studio.

PUCHO: He told me you had reached an agreement.

CELESTINO: Because that's what he wanted.

PUCHO: He got you on the phone, and you agreed to pose in the nude for him with the laurel wreath on your head and the hammer and sickle in your hand.

DULCE: And what does that mean? All artistic works have one of those—what do you call them?

PUCHO: They've got a message.

DULCE: And what's the message of Celestino in his birthday suit with a laurel wreath on his head and the hammer and sickle in his hand?

PUCHO: Ask him.

CELESTINO: What is it you want, Pucho?

PUCHO: For you to take off that disguise.

CELESTINO: What disguise?

PUCHO: The disguise of a macho tough guy!

CELESTINO: I don't get mixed up in your business, so stay out of mine.

PUCHO: Your business affects us all.

CELESTINO: And yours doesn't?

PUCHO: *(Weeping)* It was your idea; that's why we're living like this, if you can call this living! It isn't easy living with a brother like you!

CELESTINO: Oh right, because it's very easy to live with a brother who acts the way you do!

DULCE: Celestino!

CELESTINO: What, Dulce? I'm fed up with his double meanings, his little insinuations. Always pick, pick, picking on me!

PUCHO: I don't live here because I want to.

DULCE: Pucho!

PUCHO: I'm putting up with it because there's nothing else I can do.

DULCE: Everything's normal, Pucho, everything's normal for us. Normal, normal, Pucho, normal!

PUCHO: No it's not, Dulce, no it's not!

DULCE: But it's as if it was!

PUCHO: As if!

DULCE: It's not important, Pucho, it's not important at all!

PUCHO: It is for him. Why do you think he spends his life rubbing his balls in my face? Basically, machismo just conceals other weaknesses.

CELESTINO: What did you say?

PUCHO: Such a big song-and-dance and you were going to get yourself painted.

CELESTINO: Goddammit, show me some respect!

PUCHO: Respect yourself first!

CELESTINO: What happened to me could happen to any man.

PUCHO: I'm not talking about your wife; I'm talking about our friends.

CELESTINO: Your friends, your friends!

DULCE: Who were your friends too.

CELESTINO: They were never my friends.

DULCE: And you all got along very well.

CELESTINO: It was just out of politeness.

DULCE: Politeness is saying hello and leaving it at that. You didn't go to the movies or the exhibitions with them just out of politeness.

CELESTINO: I had to do it out of necessity.

DULCE: Necessity? *(Silence)*

CELESTINO: Out of necessity. When I came back from Moscow I found Mama completely torn apart because he had told her the truth.

DULCE: You did that? You did that, Pucho? Look me in the eye. Did you do that? *(PUCHO nods.)* Oh, my God! *(Silence. The music is heard.)*

CELESTINO: I didn't want to get in a confrontation with him because he was being very aggressive—they had just expelled him from the University. I tried to get him out of that environment, and because of that I got involved with him, I got to know his friends. I tried to save him but I couldn't.

PUCHO: You tried to save me.

CELESTINO: To save you, yes! It would have been different in other countries, but here people have their own way of thinking.

PUCHO: If it bothers you so much you can stop your treatment, there's still time.

CELESTINO: Listen to me, goddammit, you're my brother! I don't give a fuck about what the world thinks. And I'll beat the shit outa anybody who tells me otherwise! Could you believe that? *(Pause)* Tomorrow's an odd-numbered day and you're coming with me with your container. You won't stop being a writer just because of that.

PUCHO: I'm leaving this city for good. I'm going to get in permanent touch with the sea. That's what I am. A son of the waves. A sad puppet of the tides. A sailor on land.

DULCE: This place belongs to the three of us. Our parents left it to us.

CELESTINO: Don't go playing the victim. Nobody said anybody had to go anywhere. This guy's capable of living underneath a bridge just as long as he doesn't have to get up early. Don't go looking for any more excuses. Tomorrow I'm rousting you out of bed before sunrise and we're going together. I can't handle these containers by myself.

DULCE: How could you have told Mama?

PUCHO: You and me with these cans?

CELESTINO: Yes, with these cans.

PUCHO: If we do what you tell us, we'll keep going as we are, Celestino. It's true I don't like to get up early, but that's not what we're talking about. We have to make a decision. We can't go on this way—killing cockroaches, shooing flies, speaking softly, getting in each other's faces over the slightest thing—just because we can't finish doing what we have to do.

DULCE: How could you have told Mama?

PUCHO: It's New Year's Eve! Let's put up with each other until the year ends!

DULCE: How could you have told Mama? *(Silence. "Manteca" is heard. DULCE goes over to PUCHO's table and hurls his ballpoint pens to the floor in an obvious act of aggression. Tearfully, PUCHO picks them up.)*

CELESTINO: The water was the last straw. Before the water it was something different. And then the fish. Although we've also got to see in the New Year. Besides, no matter how shut in we are, we've got to open the door, we've got to come in and go out somehow. We're all fishes out of water here! You may disagree, but we're flat out of water. And all the time that's passed since I saw a light airplane! These are the tropics, it's not just our fault. Not a single light airplane! *(They all start killing mosquitoes.)* We never had mosquitoes here, but they're already making themselves felt. Just look at that, I go out on the roof and not one airplane! And the harbor—now it's a harbor in name only.

DULCE: How could you have told Mama? *(Silence. "Manteca" is heard from farther away.)*

DULCE: Maybe that's what writers are like. Weirdos.

PUCHO: The kind who are capable of killing their own mothers in order to write. That's not my line, don't be scared. I read it somewhere.

DULCE: But that's horrible.

PUCHO: It's a metaphor.

DULCE: It's utter nonsense. And to think there are countries ruled by writers!

PUCHO: Who knows if things are working out there?

DULCE: There, where?

CELESTINO: Life isn't a novel. Some matters can't be solved through literature because you risk making impractical decisions. Don't panic, the world will never be ruled by writers.

PUCHO: What I'm asking for is more than practical. It's New Year's Eve. That was the agreement . . .

CELESTINO: All right, end of discussion. You're absolutely right. We'll do what you say. But you're responsible for what happens—afterwards. Shall we do it now?

DULCE: Now?! We've got to make preparations for that, we can't just go off and do it. We've got to plan it out, make preparations, thorough preparations and not mess things up or else it'll make a huge racket and then for sure everything will be found out. It's the first time. You've never done anything like this. Think it over, Celestino!

CELESTINO: *(To PUCHO)* When?

PUCHO: How should I know? So now the problem's all mine.

DULCE: In spite of everything I'm fond of him. I don't know if it's the custom, but . . . you get in a fight, you cuss the guy out, but when the moment of truth comes you forget about all the trouble he's put you through and you don't want that moment to happen.

CELESTINO: It's real tough, people grow attached . . .

DULCE: If we hadn't had to see him every day, every minute and every hour, it would be different, but you have to see him all the time, see him like that, every minute of the day. He's become part of the family.

CELESTINO: Yes, it's like he was one of the family. Like your father or your son.

DULCE: It's going to have to be that way, but you feel like—I don't know—a murderer!

PUCHO: But he's an animal, an animal!

DULCE: *(Shushing him)* Pucho, for your own good, be quiet!

PUCHO: A goddamned animal who's got us all neurotic and hidden away!

DULCE: *(Shushing him)* For your own good, Pucho!

PUCHO: Let the whole building hear this—the neighbors, the foreign press. We're clandestinely raising a pig, a pig! And we can't take it any more because there're three of us and the apartment's too small and we're living like prisoners so the stench doesn't escape. We're raising a pig that's not letting us live, breathe, or receive visitors! A pig, a pig, a pig! We're raising a pig on the threshold of the year 2000, secretly, in an apartment building, defying the sanitary laws that have made it possible for the cities of the planet to flourish, because we need protein, protein, and lard, lard above all, lots and lots of lard, tons of lard! Because what is happiness if not the greasily eternal prolongation of lard? And with this pig we will be able to succeed in living peacefully for the rest of our days, eating pork rinds and never worry-

ing about lard; satisfying mankind's ever-increasing needs, eating pork rinds, pork rinds, pork rinds in the paradise of lard, because we'll have lots of lard and for eternity we'll be able to fry plantains, eggs, potatoes, and we'll keep on frying up whatever we feel like without any fear, forever and ever, everything that can be humanly fried, because we're not going to know what to do with all that lard, lard, lard. Ma-an-te-e-e-e-ca-a-a! *(Pause)* You go do what you like; it's all the same to me if you kill him now or the day after tomorrow, or this time next year if we're still alive. I don't have anything to decide. I don't like to decide on anyone's behalf. You decide!

CELESTINO: No, you decide.

DULCE: Will the two of you come to an agreement already? 'Cause with all that shouting all of Havana must have heard. What are you going to do?

PUCHO: He'll know.

CELESTINO: I'll know. It's always the same. You don't have the balls to make any decision.

DULCE: What are you going to do?

CELESTINO: Pucho?

PUCHO: You're eaten up by doubt too. Although you won't admit it, you've spent your whole life doubting. Doubting whether you acted well or badly in going off with your Russian woman. You don't know if you would have been better off staying there or coming back with her again. Doubts are eating you up and the only thing you know how to do is study English and Russian and go around shouting "Balls, balls, balls!"

(Silence. Suddenly PUCHO takes out the knife he had hidden earlier and runs around the stage shouting aggressively. The others protect themselves. Then PUCHO puts it inside the pot. CELESTINO grabs it and dashes offstage.)

DULCE: *(Shouting)* Celestinoooo! *(A long silence. The volume of "Manteca" goes up, diminishing in intensity as PUCHO picks up his novel)*

PUCHO: "But night was not night until the sharp-edged blade of that cry cut through the shadows and unleashed the hemorrhage of stars that it drank near the bridge, that same bridge which joined the two opposing shores forever: the shore of life and the shore of death."

(CELESTINO has returned with the bloody knife in his hand. He is the living image of Mark Antony as played by Marlon Brando in his speech to the people after the death of Caesar.)

CELESTINO: What happened to me could happen to any man! Any man! Any man! She wanted to leave, okay, she left, terrific, terrific! Yeah, terrific! Terrific! She had the right. She took the kids against my will? Okay! So what? It's my business, my pain, mine, because I'm the only one who's hurting. That one week after her arrival there, she met a Russian man? So what? So what? We got to know each other on a

Friday and by Monday we were living together. Over there they think differently. It's not like here where women have to know you before they open their legs. Over there they open them up and then they get to know the guy. Europe's something else, and the Russians, whether they like it or not, are Europeans too. The fact that she fell in love with me doesn't mean she was in love with me before she left. She left because she's from over there and she didn't understand this country, and there was no reason she had to anyway, and if she understood it she wasn't obligated to live here. I can't blame her because I did the same thing she did—I went back to where I came from. It's natural, she's from over there, and we're from over here. She's over there, I'm over here. That's why I had to bad-mouth the people from here who were over there, because they weren't aware that they were from over here and that we have to think the way we do over here. Although there are a lot of people who've never left here, but who happen to think the way they do over there, or the way they themselves think they do over there. We're from over here and I keep thinking that way, although lots of people over here don't think the way I thought they thought when I was over there. What happened to me could happen to any man. If she was in love since the time she was here, if she didn't care for me any more, I don't give a fuck, I'm from here. She's over there with her worlds and her problems. I'm from here! A communist over here, yes, a communist, every day I'm more of a communist, more of a communist from here! I was a communist, I am a communist, and I'm going to keep on being a communist, a communist from here! I'm a fucking communist, a communist! I like being a communist, a communist from here. (*Shouts louder*) Communist, communist! I'm a communist! (*Silence*)

PUCHO: And what about the change? (*Silence*) What about the change? (*Silence*) What about the change?

DULCE: Tomorrow's an odd-numbered day.

CELESTINO: What can you expect from people who want us to eat each other alive?!

DULCE: Tomorrow's an odd-numbered day.

CELESTINO: A lot of people think, "Communism's finished, let's go shopping," but what they don't know is that what's coming, if it isn't fascism, it sure looks a lot like it.

DULCE: Our great-grandmother was Jewish and those people went through it all. What are we going to do?

CELESTINO: What we're doing now.

DULCE: Why are they skinning their heads?

PUCHO: Shaving. (*To CELESTINO*) Until when?

DULCE: Why are they shaving their heads?

CELESTINO: (*To PUCHO*) Until whenever.

DULCE: I'm panicking over them. Luckily they won't get here by sea, but now that air travel's become fashionable, they could show up at any moment, and watch out if you've got a Pole in your family.

PUCHO: I at least will continue to be a member of my party.

DULCE: What party?

PUCHO: My own.

DULCE: Which party, Pucho?

PUCHO: A group that has nothing to do with politics.

DULCE: Then it's not a party. (*DULCE prepares sugar water.*)

CELESTINO: Fortunately water isn't a problem today.

PUCHO: (*To DULCE*) We all know it's a party, but nobody mentions the word.

DULCE: Sugar water all 'round! (*She pours and serves.*) And what do you all do?

PUCHO: Nothing. We read texts, hold masquerade balls.

DULCE: Masquerade balls! A party that holds masquerade balls!

PUCHO: We get together to talk about our business.

DULCE: What kind of business?

PUCHO: Our business. We're the weak link in the chain: blacks, women, queers, and AIDS patients.

DULCE: Jeez, Pucho!

PUCHO: When the moment comes, we'll have to be together. Each one in his group. It's the only way to confront xenophobia.

CELESTINO: Water!

DULCE: What counts is the family.

PUCHO: Racism and xenophobia. That's what I always say, racism, xenophobia, and fundamentalism.

DULCE: We have to stick together, everyone with his own religion, but always together.

CELESTINO: Now midnight's struck and the animal's in there.

DULCE: As long as the family's united let the wind blow where it may.

PUCHO: Integrationism is exclusivist.

DULCE: (*Toasting*) Happy New Year! (*They all raise their glasses of sugar water and toast. DULCE dances.*) In the end the only people you can count on are your parents, your children, your brothers, your blood. (*They all drink.*)

PUCHO: (*After a pause*) Now what?

CELESTINO: Whaddaya mean, "what"?

PUCHO: What do we do with that?

CELESTINO: Whaddaya mean, "that"?

DULCE: What's left to us is to stick together.

PUCHO: (*To CELESTINO*) What about that? What do we do with that?

CELESTINO: Boil the water.

DULCE: What for?

CELESTINO: To skin him.

DULCE: Skin him?!

CELESTINO: We can't eat him with the skin on.

DULCE: I can't think of trying it! I can't think of trying it! What happens afterwards?

CELESTINO: Afterwards?

DULCE: Afterwards.

CELESTINO: We gut him.

DULCE: Gut him?

CELESTINO: Take out his guts.

DULCE: Slit open his belly.

CELESTINO: Slit open his belly.

DULCE: *(To CELESTINO)* And you're brave enough to do that? You're brave enough to cold-bloodedly slit open the belly of a little animal who came here as a baby, in a hat, all bristly, like a fuzzy little bear?

PUCHO: "But to follow him thither with modesty enough, and likelihood to lead it; as thus: Alexander died, Alexander was buried, Alexander returneth to dust; the dust is earth; of earth we make loam; and why of that loam whereto he was converted might they not stop a beer barrel?"

CELESTINO: William Shakespeare. *(Silence. Music)*

DULCE: I had to give him milk in a bottle, like you do with little babies. He was exhausted from being weaned, they separated him from his mother too early. I don't know why he didn't die on us.

PUCHO: I looked for the milk, the bottle, and the nipple.

CELESTINO: No, I looked for the nipple.

PUCHO: I gave him the milk in the beginning. Every three hours, because you were both sleeping.

DULCE: The first time he ate on his own I almost fell over. What a feeling! I was lying back taking a siesta and I heard a noise. I got up scared, thinking something had happened to him and when I saw him, eating on his own, I felt something in my breast. Does it have to be with hot water?

CELESTINO: Boiling. Pigskin's real tough.

DULCE: Boiling yet! And afterwards?

PUCHO: We hang him up somewhere so that the blood will drain out well.

DULCE: String him up like a pig. And afterwards?

CELESTINO: Cut him into pieces, make it through the crisis, put him in the freezer, and then we're gonna eat him up bit by bit.

DULCE: And afterwards?

CELESTINO: Afterwards?

DULCE: Afterwards. *(Long silence. "Manteca" is heard.)*

DULCE: At least fattening him up was a pleasurable illusion of sorts. Without this little animal, what's going to become of this house from now on?

CELESTINO: Shit, Dulce!

DULCE: What's going to become of us? We can't live without illusions and we have no more illusions. What other illusion do we have? Come on, tell me!

PUCHO: None. It's the loss of utopia.

CELESTINO: Utopia.

DULCE: This little animal kept the family together and the family is the main thing. Look at yourself in the mirror, Celestino! Don't even mention me, a son in Africa and another at the North Pole. And I can't blame them because the first one to get started was my husband. That's why our marriage ended, because he spent more time in the place they sent him to than in his own home, and of course he met another woman and ended up staying there. And what was I to do? Go with him? What do I have to do with those machines, or with rocks, or with dynamite? When that missile crisis, as they call it, happened, we were much better off. When daybreak came we could have been wiped off the face of the earth, as they say, but all of us were together right here: Mama, Papa, the three of us, my children, the whole family. When that all finished, the craziness started. Even I myself don't know how it happened, some went this way, others went that way, because they were needed and they were soldiers in the production of those things that have no family other than machinery, rocks, and dynamite. The real democracy that they all talk about so much is in this house where everyone is the way they are, but blood is respected. That's why I was at the party for no more than five minutes and right away I went home. What kind of New Year's Eve party is it where most of the people boogying around deep down hate each other? Forget about politics, work, religion. The main thing is the family, and that little animal kept what was left of the family together.

PUCHO: It's the diaspora, the diaspora.

CELESTINO: Diaspora or the loss of utopia?

PUCHO: Diaspora, but above all the loss of utopia. That's how I explained it to my university students.

CELESTINO: That's why they kicked you out.

PUCHO: You too need a utopia.

CELESTINO: What I need is to finish preparing the animal. You didn't want to kill him? Well if the pig was our utopia, as you say, you killed him, so shut up.

PUCHO: You killed him.

CELESTINO: You kept insisting. Or were you speaking in metaphors again?

PUCHO: Maybe. The metaphor of someone who pleads and shouts for an inevitable end that he doesn't want to reach.

DULCE: What a metaphor!

PUCHO: I hadn't been working on the novel for almost a year before the pig came. They say that the most favorable condition for creation is suffering. It must be true.

DULCE: What a New Year's Eve!

(PUCHO cannot find the page of the novel he needs. CELESTINO removes the paper from one of his pockets, unfolds it, and reads out loud.)

CELESTINO: "And pigs and bread, eggs and their chickens, multiplied. And the world turned into a delirium of meats within everyone's reach: magnificent cows lowing at the moon like stray cats. And the people no longer wished to eat or drink that alcohol which did them no harm and was as good as water, because they needed something else, something else, something else. And so it was that the Filipinos began to disappear, because blacks and gypsies were out of fashion. And the last Bosnian who had survived the great cataclysm was installed under heavy guard in New York's Metropolitan Museum, because eating wasn't the problem; rather, it was the loss of the possibility of something different. That which was once called a more just society, a better world, something which nobody could remember, because the cannibal hour had struck, predicted by that prophet to whom nobody listened." *(He holds the paper out to PUCHO.)* It blew away the other day when you opened the window without permission. What are we waiting for?

DULCE: I don't want to see it.

CELESTINO: I'm not asking you to see it.

DULCE: I don't want to see it.

CELESTINO: I'm asking you to heat up the water.

DULCE: I don't want to see it.

CELESTINO: We'll do the work ourselves.

PUCHO: Don't count on me. I'm not a butcher.

CELESTINO: Well, I can't do it myself and besides I don't want to.

DULCE: How does he look?

CELESTINO: He?

DULCE: The little animal, Celestino. Are his eyes open or shut? And his little feet? What I liked best were his feet. He wiggled them like this when he asked for food. Poor little thing. I can't do it.

CELESTINO: All right, we'll exchange him for one just like him, same weight, same size, and we'll eat him too.

DULCE: I'll never eat pork again, because it'll just remind me of him. I'm banning pigs from my diet.

CELESTINO: So what do you want, sister? To embalm him?

PUCHO: Why don't we sell him and buy peanuts with the money we make?

CELESTINO: Peanuts?

DULCE: Peanuts!

PUCHO: Peanuts! Let's go find some sugar, make some peanut brittle, and we'll dedicate ourselves to something else.

DULCE: We'll sell peanut brittle!

PUCHO: There are more and more kids in Havana these days.

DULCE: I'm not going to go all over Havana selling peanut brittle.

PUCHO: We can go straight to the door of the children's hospitals.

DULCE: I'm not going to sell peanut brittle in front of the children's hospitals.

PUCHO: It's a utopia like any other. The only thing is

it's better than a pig because it doesn't create bonds of affection.

DULCE: El Cucalambé, Pucho, El Cucalambé, El Cucalambé already said it.[6] We have to look for some land. This is the best climate in the world. You plant a seed like they say and by noon you're eating mangos, avocados, cherimoyas, mammees, soursops.

PUCHO: With the money from the peanut brittle we could buy ourselves a farm.

CELESTINO: A farm, no, but certainly a piece of land . . . a plot.

PUCHO: You've got to start somewhere.

CELESTINO: Earth and pots, Celestino. Lots of earth and lots of pots, and Dulce will take care of the flowerpots. You'll see, we'll have no shortage of garlic, chilis, onions, or cilantro because I'll grow them right here.

PUCHO: What about the water?

CELESTINO: I know where to get that from. In Roman times there wasn't any gasoline either, and they still made aqueducts.

DULCE: We've got the right altitude. We can even harvest coffee. We're on the fifth floor.

PUCHO: Somebody was able to grow grapes. I've eaten them. Cuban grapes. Of course they weren't as sweet as the ones from the cold countries.

CELESTINO: But they're still grapes.

DULCE: We could even keep our own beehive here, in the family. Our own honey. Not a whole lot of it, one or two small bottles. In any case, we don't want it for export purposes. We could set aside one or two flowerpots for medicinal herbs, so that if anything serious happened, we wouldn't have to go down and see the doctor.

CELESTINO: We'll have to look for more containers, what we've got isn't enough.

DULCE: The graveyard! Do you remember those Bulgarian roses we once saw in the graveyard? How lovely they were! I always dreamed of having a garden. I think I'm going to grow a few pots of roses. You can't think just about eating. Decoration's very important too. That's why I like gourds, because they fulfill both functions at once—the nutritional and the ornamental. And they grow on their own. Creepers from the gourd and flowers. I think I'm also going to grow squash.

PUCHO: What about that? *(Points at the floor. Silence. They watch a trail of blood flowing across the floor.)*

CELESTINO: Blood!

PUCHO: Blood!

DULCE: Blood!

("Manteca" is heard.)

DULCE: This music, that blood. That blood, this music. Show a little consideration for these citizens. That music! *(The music stops.)*

PUCHO: It's always the same, from music to blood and from blood to music.

CELESTINO: Moaning and groaning, moaning and groaning. What do I get out of moaning and groaning? What do we get out of moaning and groaning? Do you think I like all this? I'm a professional, not a pig breeder or a bicycle repairman. But what do I get out of moaning and groaning? What do we get out of moaning and groaning? What is it you want, what can we do? Well, what can we do, what can we do? *(Silence)*

DULCE: Aaah, Celestino, are you thinking what I'm thinking? Are you thinking what I'm thinking? *(To PUCHO)* Are you?

CELESTINO: We gotta do it.

DULCE: We gotta do it.

PUCHO: We gotta do it.

CELESTINO: We have to do it.

ALL: We have to do it.

CELESTINO: We gotta buy another one.

DULCE: Another one!

PUCHO: Another one!

DULCE: And don't let it be very big.

CELESTINO: Or very small.

DULCE: Another one just like the other one.

CELESTINO: The same.

DULCE: Like the other one!

CELESTINO: They say that around the Mabuya area they sell fully grown miniature ones.

DULCE: Little black ones!

CELESTINO: Little red ones!

DULCE: And the feet!

PUCHO: The color's the least of it.

CELESTINO: What counts is the breed.

DULCE: And the feetsies!

CELESTINO: And the food.

PUCHO: And its appetite.

DULCE: And the feetsies.

CELESTINO: We have to look for one that looks good.

PUCHO: That *is* good.

DULCE: Like the other one.

CELESTINO: Pigs are surprising.

DULCE: None could be better than the other one.

CELESTINO: Pigs are like children.

PUCHO: The last one didn't grow.

CELESTINO: You could wind up with either good or bad ones.

DULCE: It was by accident.

PUCHO: We have to think about the lard.

DULCE: And the feet.

PUCHO: For lard, you need a pig from Vuelta Abajo.

CELESTINO: Such regionalism!

DULCE: The last one was from Vuelta Arriba.

CELESTINO: The stupidity of some people! *(The lights have gone out. They speak in darkness.)*

PUCHO: Some of my friends went to Vuelta Abajo.

CELESTINO: That one was from Vuelta Arriba.

DULCE: It can come from anywhere, but don't forget the feet.

PUCHO: And the lard.

CELESTINO: From Vuelta Arriba.

DULCE: The feetsies.

PUCHO: From Vuelta Abajo.

CELESTINO: Not too expensive.

PUCHO: From Vuelta Abajo.

DULCE: The feet.

CELESTINO: But not too cheap either.

DULCE: The feetsies, the feetsies, the feetsies!

(Chimes and shouts ushering in the New Year)

THE END

NOTES

All notes to this play have been added by the editors.

1. Jarahueca is a small village in central Cuba that has light oil deposits.

2. Bartolomé de las Casas (1484–1566) was a Spanish priest who became a famous advocate for the indigenous population in the Americas after witnessing their near total genocide in the Caribbean.

3. Dolores del Río (1905–1983) was a legendary star of Mexican cinema and the prototype of the classic Latin beauty.

4. During a visit to Cuba in February 1960, the Soviet statesman Anastas Mikoyan signed an agreement with the Cuban government under which Cuba would sell its sugar to the Soviet Union in exchange for oil and other goods. He was also a key player in the Cuban Missile Crisis of October 1962. Along with Nikita Kruschev, he was important in establishing the close ties between Cuba and the Soviet Union.

5. Varadero, east of Havana, is now Cuba's main tourist resort. Like Jarahueca, it has oil deposits, although they are not sufficient to meet the national demand.

6. El Cucalambé was the pseudonym of Juan Cristóbal Nápoles Fajardo (1829–62?). Nápoles Fajardo was one of the most famous cultivators of the *décima guajira,* a ten-line, octosyllabic poem that typically exalted the Cuban countryside and the rural peasant lifestyle. Related to both *costumbrismo* and the indigenist school of *siboneyismo,* his poetry continues to be popular and often serves as the basis for song lyrics. His pseudonym, El Cucalambé, may have come from the name of an African dance, although he was the son of a wealthy slave-owning plantation owner in eastern Cuba. Nápoles Fajardo mysteriously disappeared in 1862.

Petrona de la Cruz Cruz (*left*) and Isabel Juárez Espinosa in *The Demon's Nun,* San Cristóbal de las Casas, Mexico, 2003. (Photo courtesy of Doris Difarnecio.)

The Demon's Nun (Petrona de la Cruz Cruz and Isabel Juárez Espinosa)

Petrona de la Cruz Cruz and Isabel Juárez Espinosa, who founded and run a Mayan women's center in San Cristóbal de las Casas, Chiapas, are "firsts" in several respects. They are considered the first indigenous playwrights in Mexico and the first also to publish their work. Isabel Juárez Espinosa is the author of *Cuentos y teatro tzeltales* (1994), and Petrona de la Cruz Cruz published her 1991 play *Una mujer desesperada* (*A Desperate Woman*) in both Spanish and English.[1] Cruz Cruz was the first indigenous artist to win the prestigious Rosario Castellanos Prize in 1992 for that same play. Their women's collective, Fortaleza de la Mujer Maya (Empowerment of Mayan Women or FOMMA), which focuses on native women and children in Chiapas, received a national award from the Mexican Institute of Research on the Family and Population in 1999. They are also, no doubt, among the first native women playwrights to have inspired a fair amount of scholarship.

Cruz Cruz, a Tzotzil speaker from Zinacantán, and Juárez, a Tzeltal speaker from Ahuacatenango, have worked together since their early days in the Sna Jtz'ibajom, a Mayan theater collective in San Cristóbal founded in 1988. How they began participating in that group, why they finally left, and how they founded their own theater and cultural collective are examples not only of their strength and tenacity but of the harsh gender and race realities of Mexico, particularly within native communities.

Both Cruz Cruz and Juárez came from small communities outside of San Cristóbal in which native girls cannot expect an education. Rather they are routinely married off very young and, at times, even sold or given to men who have raped them. Both women shared a history of violence and social marginalization. Petrona was kidnapped and raped when she was seventeen and raised the son who was born of that violence. Isabel's husband was murdered while she was pregnant (the topic of FOMMA's 2005 play *Soledad y esperanza*) and she, too, was forced to raise her child as a single mother. Both women were ostracized from their communities, and both went to San Cristóbal to work as domestic servants. There they learned Spanish and received eight or nine years of education. Isabel Juárez was the first woman to join a Mayan theater group, Sna, which at the time worked mostly with oral traditions, compiling stories from the surrounding indigenous communities and staging them using puppets. Juárez worked as a puppeteer, but when the group started using actors instead of puppets it needed more women. Petrona and a few others were invited to join.[2]

In 1992, after four or five years of working with Sna, the two women left the group—Isabel in June, Petrona in December. One was forced to leave after becoming pregnant by one of the male actors; the other was pushed out after winning the important Premio Chiapas, a prize granted by the state government for best artist. As Cynthia Steele notes, it was the women's "ambiguous status as single mothers from fractured primary families that made it possible for them to become actors and playwrights," but it was this same ambiguous status that made the men of Sna critical of their independence and jealous of their success.[3]

In 1994, after a few attempts to organize a woman's performance group, Cruz Cruz and Juárez founded FOMMA. They struggled to find a small house in which to work. In addition to performances in Spanish and their native languages, they offered workshops: reading and writing in their native languages, cooking, sewing, accounting, and, of course, theater. As Juárez puts it, one thing led to another: "We saw that many women came with babies and small children, saying, 'Well, I do want to learn, but I don't have anybody to take care of my child.' So we opted for starting a day-care center for the children while the women attend the workshops. That's how FOMMA started to grow."[4] They eventually bought a larger building with rooms for workshops and a large outside patio for performances. Since founding FOMMA, the women have worked together with a shifting population of six to eight other members who come and go depending on family and financial situations. They have developed a dozen new performances and continue to tour throughout the Americas. They are currently expanding their house to include a large covered performance and workshop space, a gallery, and better workshop spaces. Since 1999, FOMMA has worked closely with the Colombian theater director Doris Difarnecio, who has helped it develop five works (*Crecí solo con el amor de mi madre, La voz y la fuerza de la mujer, Soledad y esperanza, La bruja monja,* and *Viva la vida*). In 2007, they entered into a collaborative relationship with the Hemispheric Institute of Performance and Politics to form the first "Centro Hemisférico" in Latin America.

The Demon's Nun (2003) offers a very humorous view of very serious issues in Chiapas, and Mexico as a whole—violence against women, alcoholism, limited educational opportunities for women, and the role of religion in native communities.[5] Domitila, the principal character, is married to Elias, a drinker and lecher. According to him, he and his wife have never had sex. We overhear her asking God to let her feel love for her husband, but her emotional energies seem directed at the *santitos,* small statues of saints, that she keeps in her modest home. Her erotic longings fixate on the angel in her dreams: "He touched my ears, my shoulders, my stomach . . . He made me feel ticklish all over my body . . . He has big eyes . . . *(She talks as if in love)* and a soft face . . . a tender mouth that made me want to kiss him, Father!" Elias first turns in despair to the Catholic Church, which offers him no comfort. Like many others recently in native communities throughout Mexico and Latin America, he finds a more receptive home with the Evangelicals, who promise him "love" and induce him to give up drinking. While there are several reasons why a reformed Elias decides to leave Domitila—her sexual unavailability and her unkempt appearance—he also critiques her Catholicism: "Why is it that you spend all your time talking talk to these saints as if they were your children . . . the neighbors are spreading the word that you're a witch." Father Benjamin, who gives Domitila reading lessons using the Bible as a text, allows her refuge in the convent. There, however, he tries to rape her and then warns her against telling anyone. Domitila is back on the street. The rest we know only by hearsay, offered by two masked characters that make their appearance toward the end of the play. They are Domitila's sons. She has become an alcoholic, married the barkeeper, and borne twins. At the end, Domitila fulfills the role of wife and mother that had been assigned to her all along but ruins her life and her aspirations in the process. She has been betrayed not only by her husband but by the Catholic Church. She has no place to turn. Alcoholism and family—announced almost in the same breath—are the afterthought, the postscript to a life gone wrong. While their audiences laugh at the characters and enjoy the acting, especially the constant cross-dressing, the play points to a dearth of options for native women.

This story, like all the ones that FOMMA stages, speaks to the tensions that many experience in native communities. There are few options for the poor: Domitila cannot turn to the legal system, the Catholic priests betray her, and she has no money or way to earn a living. While life is hard for almost all native peoples in Mexico, women have an especially hard time. Although some Mayan groups have staged acts of resistance, including the armed wing of the Zapatistas, women continue to experience double marginalization both within the Zapatista movement and in their own communities.[6] So how can native women perform these stories without alienating their audiences? *Feminism* is a bad word and a dangerous concept. Antichurch and clerical comments stir disapproval. FOMMA has successfully negotiated conflicting forces by using humor, exploiting popular genres such as the soap opera and telling stories drawn from their own communities. Their audiences can enjoy what they see onstage even as they recognize that these are "real" stories told by the women who have lived through the experiences. The Mayan women and children who make up the majority of the audiences see themselves and their stories reflected artistically, often for the first time. But, as Petrona de la Cruz Cruz and Isabel Juárez Espinosa say, even men often enjoy the performances and the representations of themselves, humorously distanced through the cross-dressing.[7] Theater, for FOMMA, allows the women to do the undoable: speak their minds and call the shots.

—Diana Taylor

NOTES

1. *A Desperate Woman,* translated by Shanna Lorenz, was published in *Holy Terrors: Latin American Women Perform,* ed. Diana Taylor and Roselyn Costantino (Durham: Duke University Press, 2003).

2. See Harley Erdman, "Gendering Chiapas: Petrona de la Cruz Cruz and Isabel J. F. Juárez Espinosa of La FOMMA (Fortaleza de la Mujer Maya/Strength of the Mayan Woman)," in *The Color of Theater: Race, Ethnicity, and Contemporary Performance,* ed. Roberta Uno with Lucy Mae San Pablo Burns (London: Continuum, 2002).

3. Cynthia Steele, "'A Woman Fell into the River': Negotiating Female Subjects in Contemporary Mayan

Theatre," in *Negotiating Performance: Gender, Sexuality, and Theatricality in Latin/o America,* ed. Diana Taylor and Juan Villegas (Durham: Duke University Press, 1994), 251.

4. Quoted in Erdman, "Gendering Chiapas," 164.

5. See clips of this performance on the Hemispheric Institute Web site, http://hemi.nyu.edu/eng/seminar/usa/text/moreevents.shtml#

6. See Teresa Marrero's "Eso sí pasa aquí: Indigenous Women Performing Revolutions in Mayan Chiapas," in Taylor and Costantino, *Holy Terrors;* and Coatlicue Theatre's play *Caracol: Heart of the Earth—Flower of Hope,* which focuses on Mayan women within the Zapatista movement. See video clips of the performance on the Hemispheric Institute's Web site, http://hemi.nyu.edu/eng/seminar/brazil2005/bio_coatlicue.html.

7. Personal interview with Diana Taylor, October 2004.

SELECTED REFERENCES

Erdman, Harley. "Gendering Chiapas: Petrona Cruz Cruz and Isabel J. F. Juarez Espinosa of FOMMA." In *The Color of Theater: Race, Ethnicity, and Contemporary Performance,* ed. Roberta Uno with Lucy Mae San Pablo Burns, 159–70. London: Continuum, 2002.

Frischmann, Donald H. "Active Ethnicity: Nativism, Otherness, and Indian Theatre in Mexico." *Gestos: Teoría y Práctica del Teatro Hispánico* 6 (April 1991): 113–26.

Frischmann, Donald H. "New Mayan Theatre in Chiapas: Anthropology, Literacy, and Social Drama." In *Negotiating Performance: Gender, Sexuality, and Theatricality in Latin/o America,* ed. Diana Taylor and Juan Villegas, 213–38. Durham: Duke University Press, 1994.

Frischmann, Donald H. "El nuevo teatro maya de Yucatán y Chiapas: Grupos Sac Nicte y Sna Jtz'ibajom." *Tramoya* 33 (October–December 1992): 53–78.

Marrero, Teresa. "Eso sí pasa aquí: Indigenous Women Performing Revolutions in Mayan Chiapas." In *Holy Terrors: Latin American Women Perform,* ed. Diana Taylor and Roselyn Costantino, 311–30. Durham: Duke University Press, 2003.

Steele, Cynthia. "'A Woman Fell into the River': Negotiating Female Subjects in Contemporary Mayan Theatre." In *Negotiating Performance: Gender, Sexuality, and Theatricality in Latin/o America,* ed. Diana Taylor and Juan Villegas, 239–56. Durham: Duke University Press, 1994.

Underiner, Tamara L. *Contemporary Theatre in Mayan Mexico: Death-Defying Acts.* Austin: University of Texas Press, 2004.

The Demon's Nun (Petrona de la Cruz Cruz and Isabel Juárez Espinosa)

Translated by Margaret Carson

CHARACTERS:

DOMITILA
ELIAS
FATHER BENJAMIN
FATHER FACUNDO
PEDRITO and PEPITO, twin brothers

This play is based, more than anything else, on the improvisational work of the two actors. We don't see any objects onstage; they are created in the audience's imagination by the way the actors move their bodies. To perform this play, two plain wooden chairs are needed that suggest a simple, modest home. The actors create the different characters by changing their voice, expression, and clothes.

SCENE ONE

(DOMITILA enters. We see her returning from the henhouse talking happily to herself. She's drying her hands.)

DOMITILA: The cocks are fighting over the hens! *(She turns to her saint, Saint Tiburcio, and talks to him.)* I've neglected you, Saint Tiburcio! Your face—it's so dirty! *(She cleans it with her saliva.)* A rat went by and peed on you. I think it's been there for days—it's so dry, I can't get it off. *(With improvised motions, she lights a candle.)* Keep me safe tonight, Saint Tiburcio. *(She crosses herself in front of him and then walks to an imaginary mirror and looks into it.)* I'm a wreck. *(She combs and braids her hair and keeps looking into the mirror.)* What's wrong with the mirror? Am I fat or thin? *(She stops braiding her hair and looks at her face in the mirror. She unwraps her rebozo and shakes it out, then wraps herself again. She moves towards the bed, which is a chair with a Bible on it, and covers herself with an imaginary blanket.)* Sleeping Child, may I sleep in peace tonight. *(The position she takes suggests that she is asleep.)*

(ELIAS enters.

He strolls in with his hands in his pockets. He walks towards the table where he keeps his liquor. As he walks he looks at the sleeping DOMITILA. He pours two glasses. Then he takes out his cigarettes and smokes. He goes to the window and the second time he looks out he sees Rosita who is passing by.)

ELIAS: Pssst! psssssst! Come here! Come on! *(Speaking slowly and quietly so his wife won't hear him)* What time do you buy bread? Good. I'll wait for you. Don't stand me up! *(ELIAS begins to sing while he undresses, inspired by Rosita's bottom.)*

SONG: "RUMBO AL SUR"

(DOMITILA opens her eyes, alarmed by ELIAS's singing, and picks up the Bible. She begins to pray in a low voice, pretending to be busy at prayers in order to avoid her husband's drunken advances.

ELIAS goes to the bed and sings in a lower voice while he tries to seduce DOMITILA.)

DOMITILA: Saint Tiburcio, help me care for him, love him . . . since I'm already living with him.

ELIAS: Put away the Bible, okay?

(ELIAS begins to embrace his wife, first around her shoulders and then around her knees. It's clear he wants to have sex with his wife but she resists.)

DOMITILA: I don't want to!!

(ELIAS, rejected and furious, picks up his clothes and leaves.)

SCENE TWO

(The actor who plays ELIAS is transformed; he becomes the priest FATHER BENJAMIN. Meanwhile, DOMITILA dreams of an angel.

We see DOMITILA alone on the stage. She's dreaming and

La bruja convertida en monja, Petrona de la Cruz Cruz and Isabel Juárez Espinosa, Mexico, 2003. Translated from Spanish by Margaret Carson.

laughing as if this imaginary angel were tickling her. It is a sensual, amusing moment. She laughs so hard that she wakes up from her dream, alarmed. Then she realizes that it's late and remembers that FATHER BENJAMIN is coming to give her a Bible class, during which she's also learning how to read.)

DOMITILA: It's late, the priest will be here soon.

(She takes a broom and sweeps contentedly while recalling her dream about the angel. She laughs. She dances and twirls around with the broom as if it were the angel. She is joyful, she laughs, she dances. As she dances around the room the priest enters and surprises her in midstep. Embarrassed, she lets go of the broom.)

FATHER BENJAMIN: Good morning, my child.

DOMITILA: Good morning, Father. *(She quickly kisses the priest's hand.)* Come in, sit down. I'll get you some coffee. *(By means of improvisation, she serves him coffee. She laughs when thinking about her dream but tries to control herself to avoid offending the priest.)* Here's your coffee, Father. *(Laughing, she stands behind his chair. The priest takes a sip.)* Do you like it?

FATHER BENJAMIN: Yes, it's delicious . . .

DOMITILA: Sorry I didn't make any tortillas. I couldn't wake up. *(She laughs, and continues laughing. The priest looks at her strangely.)*

FATHER BENJAMIN: Don't worry, my child, it's all right. Why are you so happy? Come, sit down and tell me.

DOMITILA: *(Nervous, not sure whether she should describe her dream, she hesitates as she speaks.)* Look, Father . . . *(She looks at him and begins to smile.)* Last night I dreamed I was playing with the angel . . . He touched my ears, my shoulders, my stomach . . . *(FATHER BENJAMIN crosses himself, surprised.)* He made me feel ticklish all over. He's tall . . . like the orange tree in the patio *(She looks at the priest.)* He has big eyes . . . *(She talks as if in love)* and a soft face . . . a tender mouth that made me want to kiss him, Father! He put the palms of his hands on my head. *(DOMITILA stops and then walks to the front of the stage. FATHER BENJAMIN puts the imaginary coffee cup down on the imaginary table and stands up to listen.)* He spread his enormous wings like an eagle, and took me flying above the clouds. We flew and flew. We saw hills full of vegetation, we listened to the sparrows sing, and the fragrance of the colorful flowers was so intense I couldn't pick out any one smell in particular. *(She smiles as if in ecstasy.)* Suddenly I saw a thick black cloud of smoke. The angel approached me . . . I saw that a house was burning. People were running all over, women were carrying their children and shouting for help. They were crying. Surrounded by fire, red as blood, the men extended their arms as if they wanted to fly. The corn was burning. I was afraid. The angel took the feather of a bird out of his garments and with the sign of a

cross gave them a white light. Afterwards there was only silence and peace. *(As if in love and slightly frenzied, she looks at FATHER BENJAMIN.)* I want to be with that angel!

FATHER BENJAMIN: Calm down, my child, it's only a dream. Let's look at the reading.

DOMITILA: You're right, Father. *(They sit down on the chairs and begin the lesson.)*

FATHER BENJAMIN: Let's go to page twenty-five, chapter five.

DOMITILA: Which chapter?

FATHER BENJAMIN: Chapter five. "I stay in the hills."

DOMITILA: *(She repeats incorrectly)* "I say in the hills."

FATHER BENJAMIN: *(Looks up at the sky impatiently but continues)* No. "I st-t-t-ay in the hills."

DOMITILA: *(Repeats correctly)* "I stay in the hills."

FATHER BENJAMIN: "And you are with the sheep."

DOMITILA: "And you are with the ship."

(FATHER BENJAMIN takes away the Bible and holds DOMITILA's hands. Face to face, they repeat:)

FATHER BENJAMIN: "And you are with the sheep . . ."

DOMITILA: "And you are with the ship . . ."

FATHER BENJAMIN: *(Impatiently)* "And you are with the sheep . . ."

DOMITILA: *(In a loud voice)* ". . . with the sh-sh-eeee-p." *(FATHER BENJAMIN imitates DOMITILA's pronunciation repeating it in a low voice.)*

(DOMITILA and FATHER BENJAMIN, with their hands intertwined, both laugh when DOMITILA pronounces the word correctly. DOMITILA laughs loudly and FATHER BENJAMIN is so amused that his shoulders shake. While they are laughing, FATHER BENJAMIN touches DOMITILA's knee. She is surprised and draws back her hand.)

DOMITILA: I think it's getting late, Father . . . you'll be late for Mass.

FATHER BENJAMIN: *(Embarrassed)* Yes, you're right, my child. *(He looks at his watch.)* I'll go now.

(He picks up the Bible and practically runs out.)

DOMITILA: Give me your blessing, Father. *(She bows her head and is surprised that FATHER BENJAMIN only partially blesses her as he's running out.)*

(The actor changes back into the character of ELIAS.)

DOMITILA: What could have happened to Elias? He hasn't been home for three nights. What'll I find when he comes back . . . and if he beats me? . . . and if something happened to him? . . . I better look for him in the cantina he usually goes to. *(DOMITILA leaves.)*

SCENE THREE

In the Church

ELIAS: *(He enters, singing.)* "I'm a drunkard . . ." *(He realizes he's in a sacred place.)* Hey stupid! You're in a church! *(He looks around him and makes the sign of the* cross. *He enters a confessional, turns over a chair, and raps on it to let the priest know he's there.*)

ELIAS: Father!

FATHER FACUNDO: I'm coming!

ELIAS: (*Raps on the chair again, impatiently*) Father!

FATHER FACUNDO: I'm coming, my son. If God was patient . . .why aren't you? (*He sits and opens an imaginary window. He smells alcohol and recoils.*) What is troubling you, my son?

ELIAS: (*Drunk*) Father, please help me.

FATHER FACUNDO: Tell me.

ELIAS: Father, speak to my wife please, I've lived with her for eight years and she's never been my wife. She doesn't even let me give her a little kiss, Father.

FATHER FACUNDO: These are things that happen between a man and a woman. You should talk to your wife . . .

ELIAS: Father, speak to her, she comes to Mass every Sunday.

FATHER FACUNDO: A lot of people come to Mass and I don't know them.

ELIAS: Well, all right, Father, I give up . . . give me a peso, just one peso for a drink.

FATHER FACUNDO: If you're hungry, the nuns will give you some food, over there in the kitchen.

ELIAS: I don't know why I came here. I'd better leave. (*He walks to the front of the stage. He improvises the presence of Saint Bartolo and addresses him.*) Saint Bartolo, I'm going to take a peso for a drink, don't scold me . . . just a peso, nothing more, you see? (*He turns his back to the public.*)

FATHER FACUNDO: My son, you should take the good path, and give up alcohol. (*FATHER FACUNDO exits to become DOMITILA.*)

ELIAS: (*He makes a gesture that shows he's not interested in what the priest says.*) If priests can drink their wine, why can't I drink?! (*He walks and looks towards the audience. He looks at his empty pockets and starts to sing:*) "with or without money, I'll always do as I please . . . I'm still the king . . ." (*He sees a leaflet on the floor and thinks it's a bill.*) I thought it was money . . . but it's not. (*He looks at it closely, without realizing it's an evangelical leaflet. He reads it.*) "Here you will find love." (*He meditates.*) Love . . . I want to be in love. Love. (*He exits.*)

SCENE FOUR

We see DOMITILA, happy, sitting on a chair in the middle of the stage, embroidering a handkerchief. She smiles and begins to talk when ELIAS, sober, reappears. ELIAS stands at a diagonal observing and listening to his wife.

DOMITILA: I'm so happy! It's been days since you stopped drinking. Look, I'm embroidering you a handkerchief to wear on Sunday. Did you hear that the mother pig had fifteen little piglets? When they grow we're going to sell them at the market and with that money we'll buy something for the house, you can buy something for yourself, and I'll buy a little saint.

ELIAS: (*He's heard enough.*) Domitila! We have to talk!

DOMITILA: Yes, tell me. . . !

ELIAS: A few months ago I found some evangelical leaflets. I read them. I analyzed them. I decided to go where they have their meetings. I went there, and I saw men, women, and children come in . . . all of them smiling, inviting me to join them. Suddenly, they all stood up when the music started and they began to move their bodies. No one felt pain or sadness in their hearts. I listened to the music and felt so happy, happy . . . but I wasn't with you, Domitila. (*ELIAS approaches DOMITILA.*) Why is it that you spend all your time talking to these saints as if they were your children . . . the neighbors are spreading the word that you're a witch.

DOMITILA: That's not true!

ELIAS: Look in the mirror. You don't comb your hair, you don't change your clothes, your skirt stinks.

DOMITILA: Elias . . .

ELIAS: (*Sarcastically*) You think you're a nun? The Demon's Nun! (*He approaches her.*) I'm leaving!

(*DOMITILA grabs hold of ELIAS, first around the waist and then around his knees, refusing to let him go.*)

ELIAS: Let me go! Let me go! (*DOMITILA's arms are wrapped around his knees.*) Don't be stupid! Let me go!! (*He frees himself and threatens her.*) I'm leaving and don't follow me, Domitila! (*He exits.*)

(*DOMITILA is alone. She looks sadly at the audience. She's desperate, and doesn't know what to do or where to go.*)

DOMITILA: What did I do wrong? Why did he leave? What was my fault? . . . I'm going to talk to Father Benjamin and see if he'll let me stay in the convent.

(*FATHER BENJAMIN comes in. He walks in a circle and beats his breast.*)

FATHER BENJAMIN: By my fault, by my fault, by my most grievous fault . . . Because I have sinned greatly . . . (*He notices DOMITILA, who is nervously waiting to speak to him. He stretches out his hand so that she can kiss its holy surface.*)

DOMITILA: (*As she kisses his hand*) Good morning, Father!

FATHER BENJAMIN: Good morning, my child.

DOMITILA: Forgive me for interrupting your prayers . . . Elias has left me. (*The priest looks up and continues to walk in a circle while saying prayers.*)

DOMITILA: I came to see if you'd let me stay in the convent.

FATHER BENJAMIN: Yes, my child, you're welcome, you don't need to ask. I know that ever since you were a child you've been close to God. Go to the nuns who will give you clothes to wear.

DOMITILA: Thank you.

(*She leaves and looks for the chair with a nun's habit.*)

FATHER BENJAMIN: (*He finishes his prayer of penance.*) Domitila came here six months ago . . . she cleans the windows in the church . . . dusts the altar . . . she prays in the morning, at noon, and at night and when she prays . . . she smiles . . . of course! At God.

(*While the priest speaks, we watch as DOMITILA puts on a nun's habit with a few gestures. When he finishes, she stops and begins to sing. Her song is like a Gregorian chant. She turns towards the audience and sits down. With her eyes closed, she sings with the voice of an angel. She opens her eyes as if seeking an answer from God. She stands and walks to the front of the stage, kneels, and sings and prays in a low voice. FATHER BENJAMIN approaches and puts his hands on DOMITILA's shoulders.*)

DOMITILA: Is there something you need, Father?

FATHER BENJAMIN: (*He moves his hands away.*) No, my child! Continue. (*DOMITILA keeps singing and FATHER BENJAMIN starts to embrace her and touch her breasts as if he'd lost control. DOMITILA is about to scream, and FATHER BENJAMIN covers her mouth.*)

FATHER BENJAMIN: Let yourself go! I've always liked you. If Adam and Eve sinned, why not you and me? (*He grabs her tightly by the waist. We see DOMITILA struggling to run away, but FATHER BENJAMIN restrains her with his hands around her waist.*)

DOMITILA: No! (*Moving backwards*)

FATHER BENJAMIN: Yes! (*Pulling her towards him*)

(*This exchange is repeated twice. DOMITILA frees herself except for an arm. They repeat "No!" "Yes!" two more times, and with the third "No!" DOMITILA falls to the floor on her rear end.*)

FATHER BENJAMIN: (*He goes to DOMITILA and takes her head in his hands.*) Nothing happened here. If you say anything about this, watch out. When they ask you "Why are you leaving?" tell them it's your decision! (*He exits and takes the chair with him.*)

DOMITILA: (*Alone and in shock, she looks at the audience and asks*) What can I do, what can I do, what . . . My heart is in pain. (*She exits*).

(*PEPITO enters walking very proudly.*)

PEPITO: Good afternoon, I'm Pepito, Domitila's son. My mother went back to her town, but when she arrived she found an empty house. Even the mattress was taken by that scumbag Elias. He left behind only her saints. But then, when she started drinking heavily, she had to pawn her saints to buy alcohol. My mamá was a regular at the cantina run by the man who's my father. When he met her . . . he showed her respect, took care of her, and fell in love with her. They got married.

(*PEDRITO enters.*)

PEDRITO: Sorry I'm late!

PEPITO: You're always late. Well, as I was saying, from that marriage my brother and I were born. When my mamá was pregnant (*showing his stomach*) I was here . . . and my brother was here . . . and when my brother was born . . .

PEDRITO: (*Interrupting*) Sssssshhhhh! (*In a low voice*) Don't say I came out like shit, you moron.

PEDRITO and PEPITO: We're twins.

PEPITO: Our parents taught us to work the land . . .

PEDRITO: . . . to take care of it . . .

PEPITO: . . . and more than anything else, to respect it . . .

PEDRITO: . . . and not gossip . . .

PEPITO: . . . yes, we said that already. Because our parents taught us to work, I'm king of the roads . . .

PEDRITO: . . . he sells eggs.

PEPITO: Shsst! Don't say that! And my brother sells things, too.

PEDRITO: Yes, I sell chiles, pots, lard, and even underwear!

PEPITO AND PEDRITO: And we're always together.

PEDRITO: Hey, stupid! We have to go!

PEPITO: Yes, we have to go because it's time to eat and mamá is waiting for us.

PEDRITO: It's the weekend and she cooked something delicious. Good-bye!

(*They walk away arm in arm. They realize that they haven't introduced themselves by name, and they stop.*)

BOTH: Ah, our names are Pepito, Pedrito Gutiérrez, Ramírez, Jolchitom. At your service. Pleased to meet you, have a good afternoon.

THE END